PHILIP'S

STREET

Hertfordshire

Hemel Hempstead, Luton, St Albans, Stevenage, Watford

www.philips-maps.co.uk
First published in 1993 by Philip's
a division of Octopus Publishing Group Ltd
www.octopusbooks.co.uk
Endeavour House 189 Shaftesbury Avenue
London WC2H 8JY
An Hachette UK Company
www.hachette.co.uk

Fourth colour edition 2008
Second impression 2011
HERDA

ISBN 978-1-84907-179-6 (pocket)

© Philip's 2008

Ordnance Survey®

This product includes mapping data licensed from Ordnance Survey® with the permission of the Controller of Her Majesty's Stationery Office. © Crown copyright 2008. All rights reserved. Licence number 100011710.

Speed camera data provided by **PocketGPSWorld.com Ltd**

Printed in China

Contents

II	Mobile safety cameras
III	**Key to map symbols**
IV	**Key to map pages**
VI	**Route planning**
VIII	Major administrative and Postcode boundaries
1	**Street maps** at 2⅔ inches to 1 mile
177	**Index** of towns, villages, streets, hospitals, industrial estates, railway stations, schools, shopping centres, universities and places of interest

Digital Data

The exceptionally high-quality mapping found in this atlas is available as digital data in TIFF format, which is easily convertible to other bitmapped (raster) image formats.

The index is also available in digital form as a standard database table. It contains all the details found in the printed index together with the National Grid reference for the map square in which each entry is named.

For further information and to discuss your requirements, please contact
philips@mapsinternational.co.uk

Mobile speed cameras

The vast majority of speed cameras used on Britain's roads are operated by safety camera partnerships. These comprise local authorities, the police, Her Majesty's Court Service (HMCS) and the Highways Agency.

This table lists the sites where each safety camera partnership may enforce speed limits through the use of mobile cameras or detectors. These are usually set up on the roadside or a bridge spanning the road and operated by a police or civilian enforcement officer. The speed limit at each site (if available) is shown in red type, followed by the approximate location in black type.

Mike Harrington / Alamy

A119
30 Hertford, North Rd

A409
30 Bushey, Heathbourne Rd

A411
30 Bushey, London Rd
30 Elstree, Barnet Lane
30 Watford, Hempstead Rd

A414
40 Hemel Hempstead, St Albans Rd
40 Hertford, Hertingfordbury Rd

A505
70 Royston Rd between Baldock and Royston near Slip End farm
30 Hitchin, Cambridge Rd

A600
30 Hitchin, Bedford Rd

A602
40 Hitchin, Stevenage Rd
40 Stevenage, Broadhall Way
40 Stevenage, Monkswood Way

A1000
40 Potters Bar, Barnet Rd

A1057
40 Hatfield, St Albans Rd West
30 St Albans, Hatfield Rd

A1170
30 Wormley, High Rd
30 Turnford, High Rd

A4125
40 South Oxhey, Sandy Lane
30 Watford, Eastbury Rd

A4145
30 Watford, Tolpits Lane

A4147
30 Hemel Hempstead, Leverstock Green Rd

A4251
30 Bourne End, London Rd

A5183
30 Elstree, Elstree Hill South
30 St Albans, Frogmore Rd

A6141
60 Letchworth, Letchworth Gate

B156
30 Cheshunt, Goffs Lane

B176
30 Cheshunt, High Street

B197
30 Baldock, London Rd
30 Stevenage, North Rd

B462
30 Bushey, Aldenham Rd

B487
30 Harpenden, Hatching Green, Redbourn Lane
40 Hemel Hempstead, Queensway

B488
40 Tring, Icknield Way

B556
30 Potters Bar, Mutton Lane

B1004
30 Bishops Stortford, Windhill

B1197
30 Hertford, London Rd

B1502
30 Hertford, Stansted Rd

B4505
30 Bovingdon, Chesham Rd

B4630
30 St Albans, Watford Rd

B5378
30 Elstree, Borehamwood, Allum Lane
40 London Colney, Shenleybury

B6426
30 Hatfield, Cavendish Way

UNCLASSIFIED
30 Cheshunt, Hammond St Rd

30 Hemel Hempstead, Bennetts End Rd

30 Hemel Hempstead, High Street Green

30 Hemel Hempstead, Long Chaulden

30 Hoddesdon, Essex Rd

30 Letchworth, Pixmore Way

30 Royston, Old North Rd

30 South Oxhey, Hayling Rd

30 St Albans, Sandpit Lane

30 Stevenage, Clovelly Way

30 Stevenage, Grace Way

40 Stevenage, Gresley Way

40 Stevenage, Monkswood Way

30 Watford, Radlett Rd

30 Welwyn Garden City, Heronswood Rd

30 Welwyn Garden City, Howlands

Symbol	Description
(22a)	**Motorway** with junction number
	Primary route – dual/single carriageway
	A road – dual/single carriageway
	B road – dual/single carriageway
	Minor road – dual/single carriageway
	Other minor road – dual/single carriageway
	Road under construction
	Tunnel, covered road
(30) (30)	**Speed cameras** - single, multiple
	Rural track, private road or narrow road in urban area
	Gate or obstruction to traffic (restrictions may not apply at all times or to all vehicles)
	Path, bridleway, byway open to all traffic, road used as a public path
	Pedestrianised area
DY7	**Postcode boundaries**
	County and unitary authority boundaries
	Railway, tunnel, railway under construction
	Tramway, tramway under construction
	Miniature railway
Walsall	**Railway station**
	Private railway station
	London Underground station
	Tram stop, tram stop under construction
	Bus, coach station

Symbol	Description
◆	**Ambulance station**
◆	**Coastguard station**
◆	**Fire station**
◆	**Police station**
✚	**Accident and Emergency entrance to hospital**
H	**Hospital**
+	**Place of worship**
i	**Information Centre** (open all year)
	Shopping Centre
P	**Parking**
P&R	**Park and Ride**
PO	**Post Office**
Å	**Camping site**
	Caravan site
►	**Golf course**
✕	**Picnic site**
Prim Sch	**Important buildings, schools, colleges, universities and hospitals**
	Built up area
	Woods
River Medway	**Water name**
	River, weir, stream
	Canal, lock, tunnel
	Water
	Tidal water
Church	**Non-Roman antiquity**
ROMAN FORT	**Roman antiquity**
87 / 58	**Adjoining page indicators**

Abbr	Full	Abbr	Full	Abbr	Full
Acad	Academy	Inst	Institute	Recn Gd	Recreation Ground
Allot Gdns	Allotments	Ct	Law Court		
Cemy	Cemetery	L Ctr	Leisure Centre	Resr	Reservoir
C Ctr	Civic Centre	LC	Level Crossing	Ret Pk	Retail Park
CH	Club House	Liby	Library	Sch	School
Coll	College	Mkt	Market	Sh Ctr	Shopping Centre
Crem	Crematorium	Meml	Memorial	TH	Town Hall/House
Ent	Enterprise	Mon	Monument	Trad Est	Trading Estate
Ex H	Exhibition Hall	Mus	Museum	Univ	University
Ind Est	Industrial Estate	Obsy	Observatory	W Twr	Water Tower
IRB Sta	Inshore Rescue Boat Station	Pal	Royal Palace	Wks	Works
		PH	Public House	YH	Youth Hostel

■ The small numbers around the edges of the maps identify the 1 kilometre National Grid lines

■ The dark grey border on the inside edge of some pages indicates that the mapping does not continue onto the adjacent page

The scale of the maps on the pages numbered in blue is 4.2 cm to 1 km • 2⅔ inches to 1 mile • 1: 23810

0 ¼ ½ ¾ 1 mile

0 250 m 500 m 750 m 1 kilometre

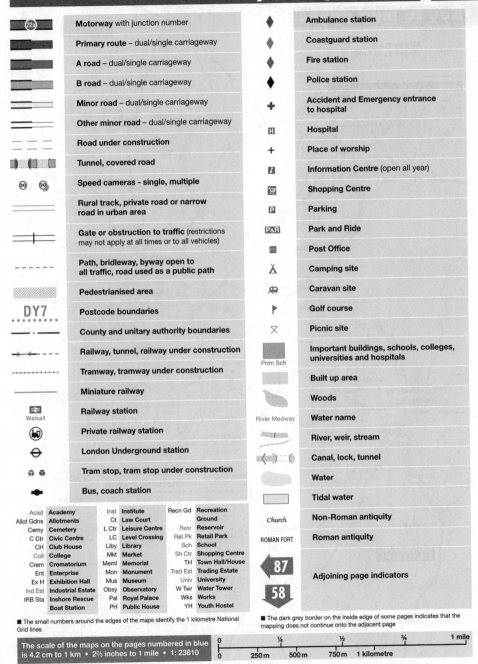

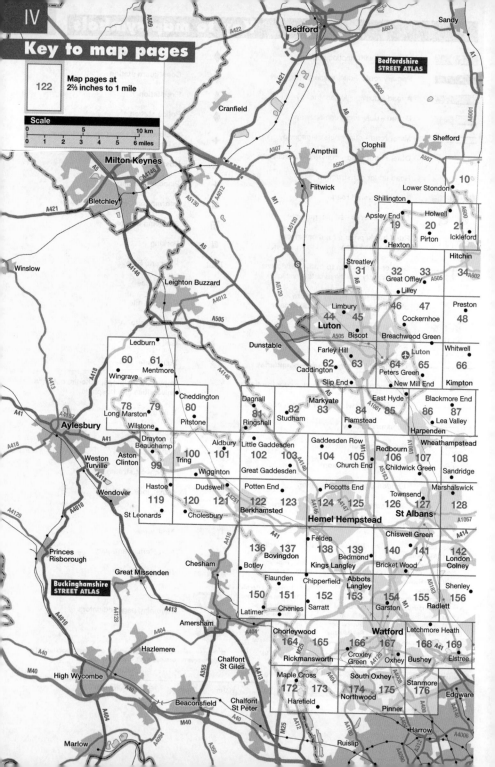

Key to map pages

IV

122 — Map pages at 2⅔ inches to 1 mile

Scale
0 ... 5 ... 10 km
0 1 2 3 4 5 6 miles

Bedfordshire
STREET ATLAS

Buckinghamshire
STREET ATLAS

Bedford · Sandy

Cranfield

Milton Keynes

Bletchley

Winslow

Leighton Buzzard

Aylesbury

Weston Turville
Aston Clinton
Wendover

Princes Risborough

Great Missenden

Chesham

High Wycombe

Hazlemere

Amersham

Chalfont St Giles

Beaconsfield

Chalfont St Peter

Marlow

Ampthill
Clophill
Flitwick
Shefford
Lower Stondon

10

Shillington
Apsley End
19
Holwell
20
Pirton
Hexton
21
Ickleford

Streatley
31
Great Offley
32
33
Lilley
34
Hitchin

Limbury
44 **45**
Luton
Biscot
46 **47**
Cockernhoe
Breachwood Green
Preston
48

Dunstable
Farley Hill
62 **63**
Caddington
Slip End
64
Peters Green
New Mill End
65
Luton
66
Kimpton
Whitwell

Ledburn
60 **61**
Wingrave
Mentmore
Cheddington
80
Pitstone

Dagnall
81
Ringshall
Studham
82
Markyate
83
Flamstead
84
East Hyde
85
Blackmore End
86
Lea Valley
87
Harpenden

Long Marston
78 **79**
Wilstone
Drayton Beauchamp
99
Tring
Aldbury
100 · **101**
Wigginton
Little Gaddesden
102
Great Gaddesden
103
Gaddesden Row
104
Church End
105
Redbourn
106
Childwick Green
107
Wheathampstead
108
Sandridge

Hastoe
119
Dudswell
120 **121**
Cholesbury
St Leonards
Potten End
122 **123**
Berkhamsted
Piccotts End
124 **125**
Hemel Hempstead
Townsend
126 **127**
St Albans
Marshalswick
128

Felden
Bovingdon
136 **137**
Botley
138
Bedmond
Kings Langley
139
Chiswell Green
140 **141**
Bricket Wood
London Colney
142

Flaunden
150 **151**
Latimer
Chenies
Chipperfield
152
Sarratt
Abbots Langley
153
Garston
154 **155**
Radlett
Shenley
156

Chorleywood
164 **165**
Rickmansworth
Watford
Croxley Green
166 **167**
Oxhey
Bushey
Letchmore Heath
168 **169**
Elstree

Maple Cross
172 **173**
Harefield
South Oxhey
174
Northwood
175
Pinner
Stanmore
176
Edgware

Ruislip
Harrow

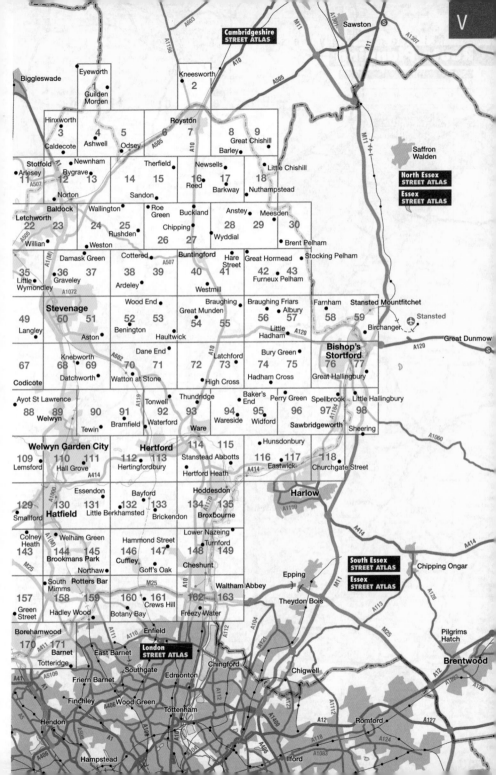

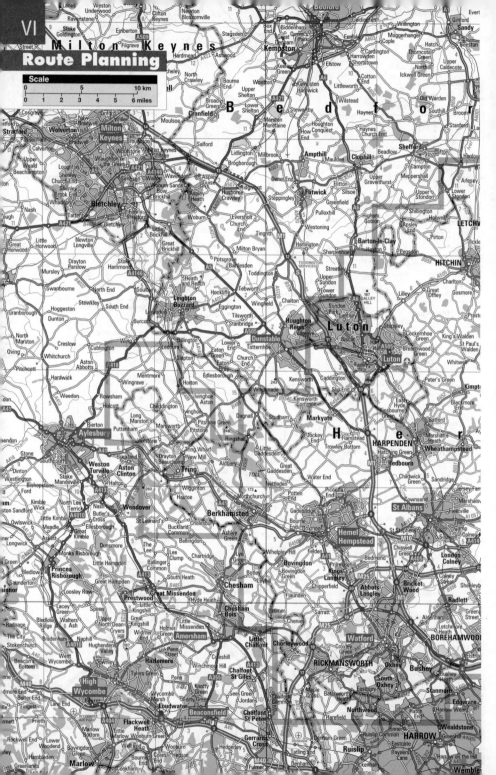

Scale
0   5   10 km
0   1   2   3   4   5   6 miles

Major administrative and Postcode boundaries

County and unitary authority boundaries
District boundaries
Postcode boundaries
Area covered by this atlas

Scale
0   5   10   15 km
0   5   10 miles

Cambridgeshire

Essex

East Hertfordshire

Hertfordshire

North Hertfordshire

Stevenage

Welwyn Hatfield

St Albans

Dacorum

Luton

Bedfordshire

Buckinghamshire

Hertsmere

Watford

Three Rivers

Broxbourne

London

Royston
Barley
Barkway
Anstey
Furneux Pelham
Braughing
Bishop's Stortford
Stansted Mountfitchet
Harlow
Sawbridgeworth
Much Hadham
Ware
Stanstead Abbots
Hoddesdon
Broxbourne
Cheshunt
Goff's Oak
Waltham Abbey
Enfield
Crews Hill
Cuffley
Potters Bar
Welham Green
Barnet
Borehamwood
Bushey
Northwood
Harefield
Rickmansworth
Chorleywood
Sarratt
Watford
Radlett
London Colney
Bedmond
St Albans
Redbourn
Harpenden
Wheathampstead
Sandridge
Kimpton
Peters Green
Markyate
Caddington
Luton
Jockey End
Hemel Hempstead
Kings Langley
Bovingdon
Berkhamstead
Bourne End
Tring
Aldbury
Chollesbury
Marsworth
Long Marston
Wingrave
Mentmore
Dagnall
Hatfield
Welwyn Garden City
Welwyn
Knebworth
Stevenage
Graveley
Hitchin
Letchworth
Baldock
Stotfold
Ashwell
Kelshall
Sandon
Preston
Whitwell
Lilley
Great Offley
Pirton
Cromer
Benington
Walton at Stone
Dane End
Thundridge
Hertford Heath
Hertford
Bayford
Buntingford
Furneux Pelham

SG19 SG18 SG17 SG16 SG15 SG9 SG8 SG7 SG5 SG4 SG2 SG1 SG3 SG6
SG14 SG13 SG12 SG11 SG10
AL6 AL7 AL8 AL9 AL10 AL4 AL5 AL3 AL1 AL2
LU3 LU4 LU6 LU1 LU2 LU7
MK45
HP1 HP2 HP3 HP4 HP5 HP22 HP23
WD3 WD4 WD5 WD6 WD7 WD17 WD18 WD19 WD23 WD24 WD25
HA5 HA6 HA3 HA7 HA8
EN1 EN2 EN3 EN4 EN5 EN6 EN7 EN8 EN9 EN10 EN11
N20 NW7
E4
CM24 CM22 CM23 CM21 CM20 CM17 CM19
UB9
SL9

SP TL
SU TQ

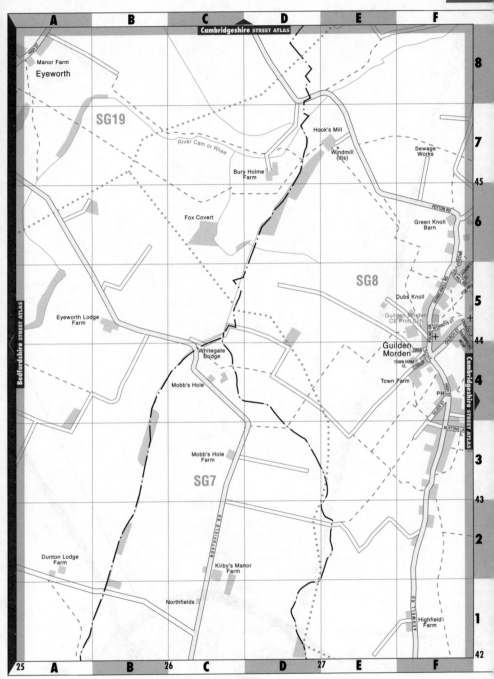

Cambridgeshire STREET ATLAS

Bedfordshire STREET ATLAS

Cambridgeshire STREET ATLAS

Manor Farm
Eyeworth

SG19

River Cam or Rhee

Hook's Mill

Windmill (dis)

Sewage Works

Bury Holme Farm

Fox Covert

POTTON RD

Green Knoll Barn

SG8

Dubs Knoll

LONG KNOLL RD

POTTON RD

FOX HILL

Eyeworth Lodge Farm

Guilden Morden CE Prim Sch

WORBOYS CT

CAMMICS CT

CHEQUERS LA

MANOR RD

CHURCH ST

Whitegate Bridge

Guilden Morden

SWAN LA

TOWN FARM CL

CONDUIT LA

Mobb's Hole

Town Farm

Town Farm

PH

HIGH ST

SILVER ST

BUXTONS LA

Mobb's Hole Farm

SG7

NORTHFIELD RD

Dunton Lodge Farm

Kirby's Manor Farm

Northfields

ASHWELL RD

Highfield Farm

25 A B 26 C D 27 E F 42

8 7 45 6 5 44 4 43 2 1

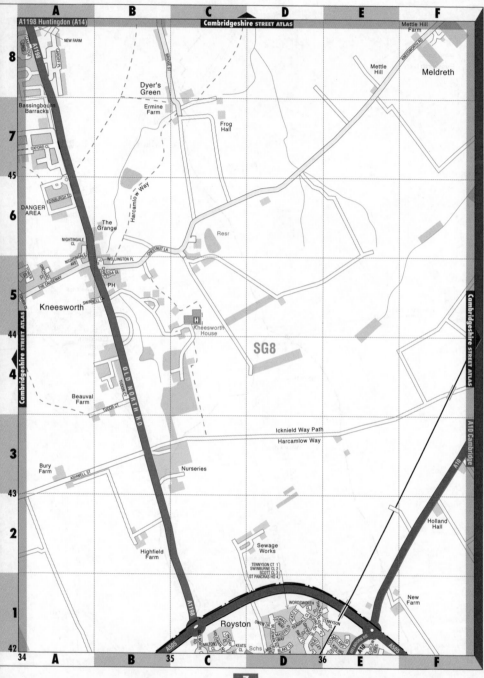

A1198 Huntingdon (A14)

Mettle Hill
Farm

NEW FARM

Dyer's
Green

Mettle
Hill

Meldreth

Ermine
Farm

Bassingbourn
Barracks

OXFORD CL

Frog
Hall

45

DANGER
AREA

Harcamlow Way

EDINBURGH ST

The
Grange

Resr

NIGHTINGALE
CL

CHESTNUT LA

NIGHTINGALE
AVE

WELLINGTON PL

ORCHARD CL

THE CAUSEWAY

LEUDA CL

PH

SWINNELL CL

Kneesworth

H

Kheesworth
House

SG8

44

OLD NORTH RD

Beauval
Farm

TUDOR CT

Icknield Way Path

Harcamlow Way

3

Bury
Farm

ASHWELL ST

Nurseries

A10 Cambridge

43

Holland
Hall

2

A1198

Highfield
Farm

Sewage
Works

TENNYSON CT 1
SWINBURNE CL 2
SCOTT CL 3
ST PANCRAS RD 4

New
Farm

WORDSWORTH

TENNYSON

1

Royston

OWEN DR

MASEFIELD
WAY

Schs

KEATS
CL

MILTON'S RD

A505

A10

A505

42

34   A   B   35   C   D   36   E   F

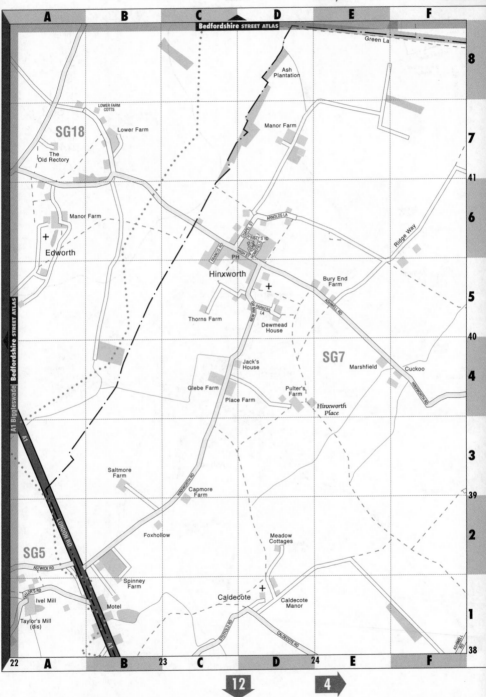

Green La

8

Ash
Plantation

SG18

LOWER FARM
COTTS

Lower Farm

Manor Farm

7

The
Old Rectory

41

Manor Farm

ARNOLDS LA

6

CHRISTY'S YD

Ridge Way

+

Edworth

PH

HIGH ST

Hinxworth

Bury End
Farm

5

Thorns Farm

PARKERS
LA

Dewmead
House

40

ASHWELL RD

SG7

Jack's
House

Marshfield

Cuckoo

4

Glebe Farm

Pulter's
Farm

Place Farm

Hinxworth
Place

3

Saltmore
Farm

Capmore
Farm

39

Foxhollow

Meadow
Cottages

2

SG5

ASTWICK RD

Spinney
Farm

Caldecote

Caldecote
Manor

TAYLOR'S RD

Ivel Mill

Motel

1

Taylor's Mill
(dis)

CALDECOTE RD

38

A B C D E F

8

Green Lane
Ridge Way
Barrowsford Bridge

Cold Harbour

SG8

ASHWELL RD
NORTHFIELD RD

7

41

Sewage Works

COMMON LA

6

Bluegates Farm

River Rhee

Ashwell End

Bluegates Dairy

Elbrook House

SG7

Cemy

Baldwin's Corner

5

40

BUTTWAY

Ashwell Bury

FORDHAM CL

MILL ST

SPRINGHEAD

LUCAS LA

GREEN LA

THE MALTINGS

Icknield Way Path

Love's Farm

LOVE LA

Ashridge Farm

Quarry Hills Farm

WOLVERLEY HO 1
THE OLD GRANARY 2
THE DOVECOTE 3

Ashwell Village Mus

Hotel

WALKER'S LA

STATION RD

4

HINXWORTH RD

Whittington Farm

WOLLYS LA

ALMS LA

LUCKWELL

PO

WOODFORDE CL

PH

HIGH ST

SILVER ST

WEST END

BACK ST

DIXIES CL

MORDENS CL

SWAN ST

MELBOURN ST

CLAYBUSH RD

ASHWELL ST

Ashwell Prim Sch

JOHN BALE CL

GARDINERS LA

3

Ashwell

Newnham Hill

39

NEWNHAM WAY

PARTRIDGE HILL

Arbury Banks

Claybush Hill

Icknield Way Path

2

Ash Hill

ASHWELL RD

1

38

25 A B 26 C D 27 E F

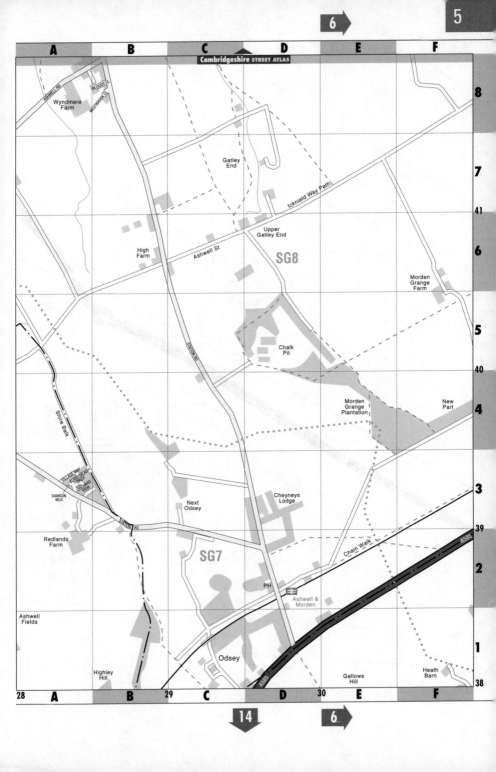

Cambridgeshire STREET ATLAS

A B C D E F

8

Wyndmere
Farm

ASHWELL RD
PLOUGH CL
WESTBROOK CL

Gatley
End

7

Icknield Way Path

41

Upper
Gatley End

High
Farm

Ashwell St

SG8

6

Morden
Grange
Farm

5

Chalk
Pit

40

Morden
Grange
Plantation

New
Part

4

Shire Balk

BALDOCK RD

VILLAGE WAY
SPRING HEAD
OLD
ORCHARD

DAMSON
WLK

BRIDGE RD

Next
Odsey

Cheyneys
Lodge

3

Redlands
Farm

SG7

39

Chain Walk

A505

2

PH

Ashwell &
Morden

Ashwell
Fields

Odsey

A505

Highley
Hill

Gallows
Hill

Heath
Barn

1

38

28 A B 29 C D 30 E F

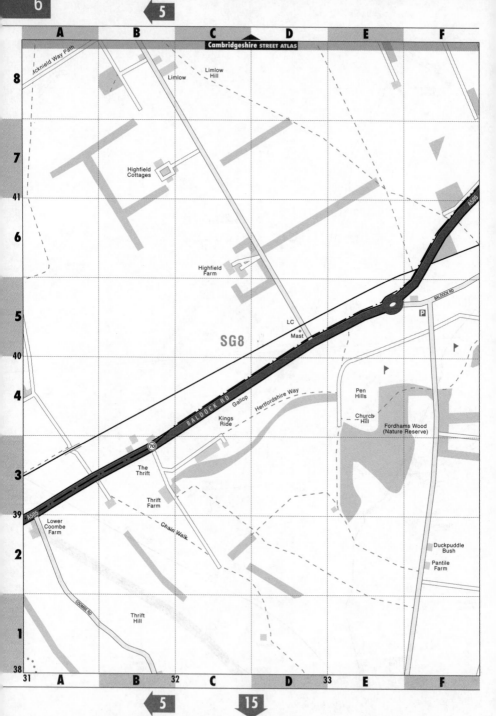

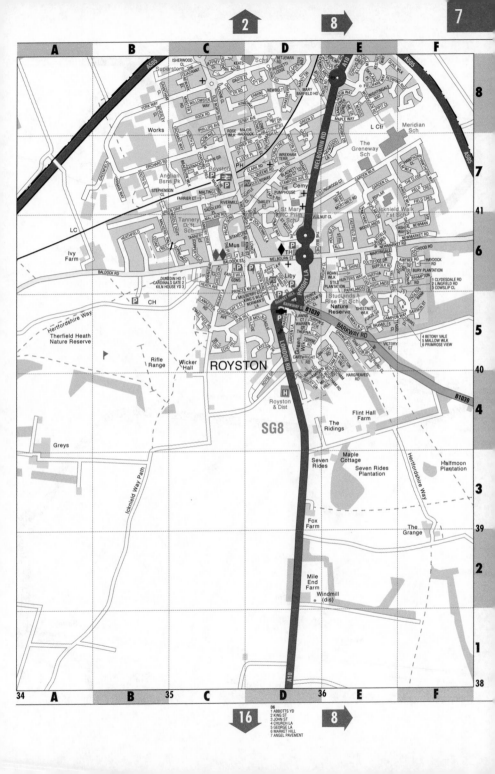

A	B	C	D	E	F

A505 Newmarket (A11)

A505

8

Heath Farm

Hazelmow Way
Icknield Way Path

Cumberton Bottom

Mast

7

A505

Hyde Hill Farm

Hillside Farm

Noon's Folly Farm

41

Icknield Way Path

Mast

NEWMARKET RD

6

Burloes Plantation

Wardington Bottom

Burloes Hall

5

Burloes Farm

40

Lowerfield

SG8

Cow Plantation

Poor's Land

4

B1039

Works

Eagle Tavern

New Stud Farm

Heath Farm

3

Whiteley Hill

B1039

ROYSTON RD

39

BAINES LA

B1368

2

HIGH ST

Newsells Park Stud

HORSESHOE CL 1
TOMLINS CL 2

Barley

HONOUR DR

GREENWAY

CROSS END

CHURCH END

1

Newsells Barn Farm

LONDON RD

THE MOUNT

SMITHS END LA

Horeshoe Farm

Smith End Farm

38

STOCK BANK

Duck's Nest

CAMBRIDGE RD

B1368

A	B	C	D	E	F

37

38

39

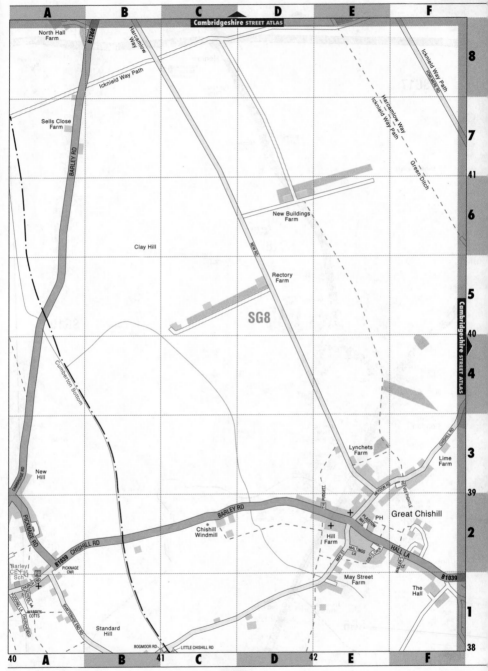

North Hall Farm

Haramlow Way

Icknield Way Path

BARLEY RD

B1368

Sells Close Farm

Clay Hill

Cumberton Bottom

New Buildings Farm

Rectory Farm

SG8

Haramlow Way

Icknield Way Path

Icknield Way Path

PARKER RD

Green Ditch

Cambridgeshire STREET ATLAS

Lynchets Farm

Lime Farm

CHISHILL RD

REEVES PIGHTLE

New Hill

BARLEY RD

THE PIGHTLE

HELION RD

PLAISTOW WAY

PH

Great Chishill

CAMBRIDGE RD

PICKNAGE RD

CHISHILL RD

B1039

PICKNAGE CNR

Chishill Windmill

Hill Farm

MALTINGS LA

HAY ST

COLTS CROFT

MAY ST

HALL LA

LEIT WAY

Barley CE Fst Sch

CHURCH END

SCHOOL LA

WARREN COTTS

CHURCHFIELD

SHAFTENOE END RD

May Street Farm

The Hall

B1039

Standard Hill

BOGMOOR RD

LITTLE CHISHILL RD

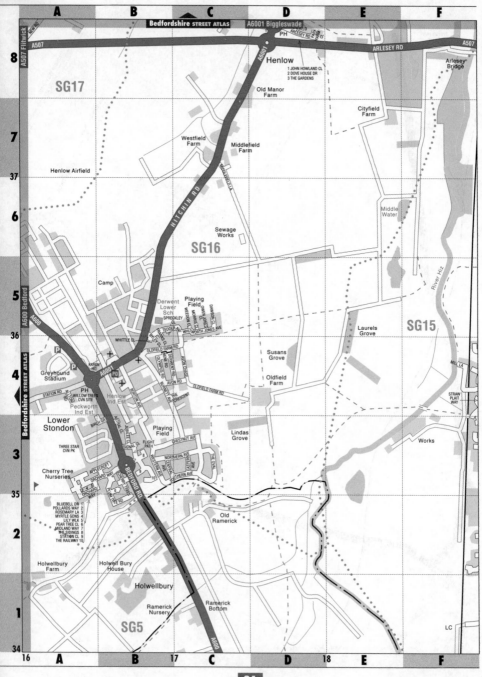

A6001 Biggleswade

A507 Flitwick

A507

ARLESEY RD

A507

Henlow

1 JOHN HOWLAND CL
2 DOVE HOUSE DR
3 THE GARDENS

Old Manor Farm

Arlesey Bridge

Cityfield Farm

SG17

Westfield Farm

Middlefield Farm

Henlow Airfield

HITCHIN RD

Middle Water

Sewage Works

SG16

River Hiz

Camp

Derwent Lower Sch
SPRECKLEY

Playing Field

Laurels Grove

SG15

WHITTLE CL

OLDFIELD FARM RD

Susans Grove

MILL LA

A600 Bedford

A600

Greyhound Stadium

Oldfield Farm

STRAW PLAIT WAY

STATION RD

PH
WILLOW TREES

Henlow Ind Est

OLDFIELD FARM RD

THE CRESCENT

AVON CL

Peckworth Ind Est

Lower Stondon

BIRCH LA

Playing Field

CHESTNUT AVE

Lindas Grove

Works

THREE STAR CVN PK

FLIGHT PATH

NORTHERN AVE

THE OVAL

Cherry Tree Nurseries

APPLECROFT
ORCHARD WAY
ORCHARD CL

EASTERN AVE

SOUTHERN AVE

BEDFORD RD

BLUEBELL DR 1
POLLARDS WAY 2
ROSEMARY LA 3
MYRTLE GDNS 4
LILY WLK 5
PEAR TREE CL 6
MIDLAND WAY 7
THE SIDINGS 8
STATION CL 9
THE RAILWAY 10

Old Ramerick

Holwellbury Farm

Holwell Bury House

Holwellbury

A600

Ramerick Nursery

Ramerick Bottom

SG5

LC

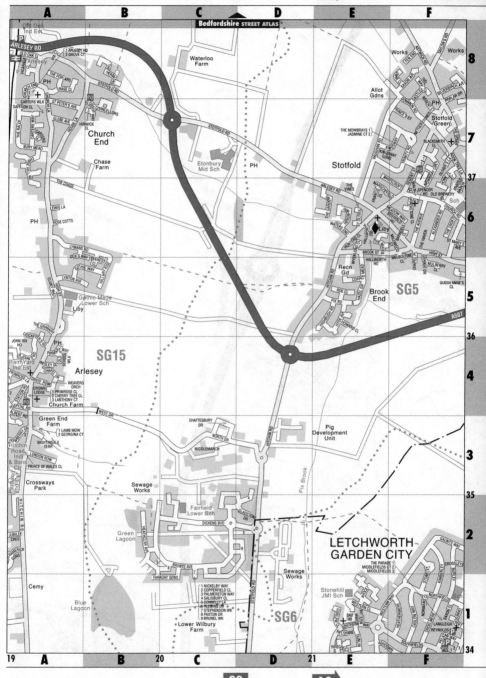

Waterloo Farm

Church End

Chase Farm

Etonbury Mid Sch

Stotfold

Stotfold Green

Blacksmith

The Mowbrays 1
Jasmine Ct 2

Arlesey Rd
The Vines

37

Liby

Brook St
Hallworth Ho

SG5

Recn Gd

Brook End

A507

36

SG15

Arlesey

John Rix Ho

Weavers Orch
1 Primrose Cl
2 Cherry Tree Cl
3 Lanthony Ct

Church Farm

West Dr

Green End Farm
1 Lamb Mdw
2 Georgina Ct

Shaftesbury Dr

North Dr

Pig Development Unit

Middlemarch

Plix Brook

Sewage Works

Fairfield Lower Sch

Dickens Blvd

Gladstone Dr

Green Lagoon

Bronte Ave

Faraday Gdns

LETCHWORTH GARDEN CITY

The Parade 1
Middlefields Ct 2
Middlefields 3

Stonehill JMI Sch

SG6

Crossways Park

Cemy

Blue Lagoon

Lower Wilbury Farm

1 Nickelby Way
2 Copperfield Cl
3 Palmerston Way
4 Salisbury Cl
5 Connell Ct
6 Flemming
7 Stephenson Wk
8 Paxton Dr
9 Brunel Wk

34

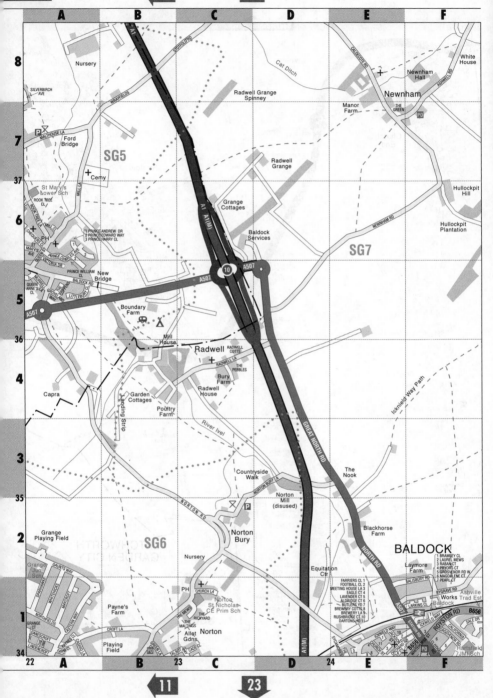

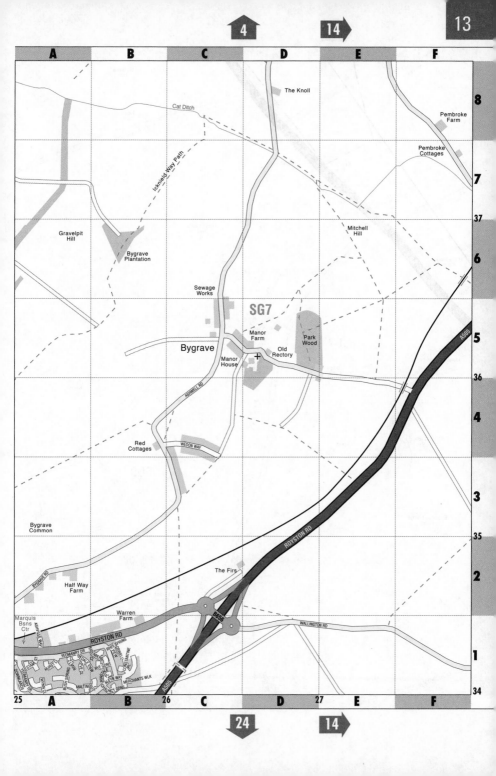

A **B** **C** **D** **E** **F**

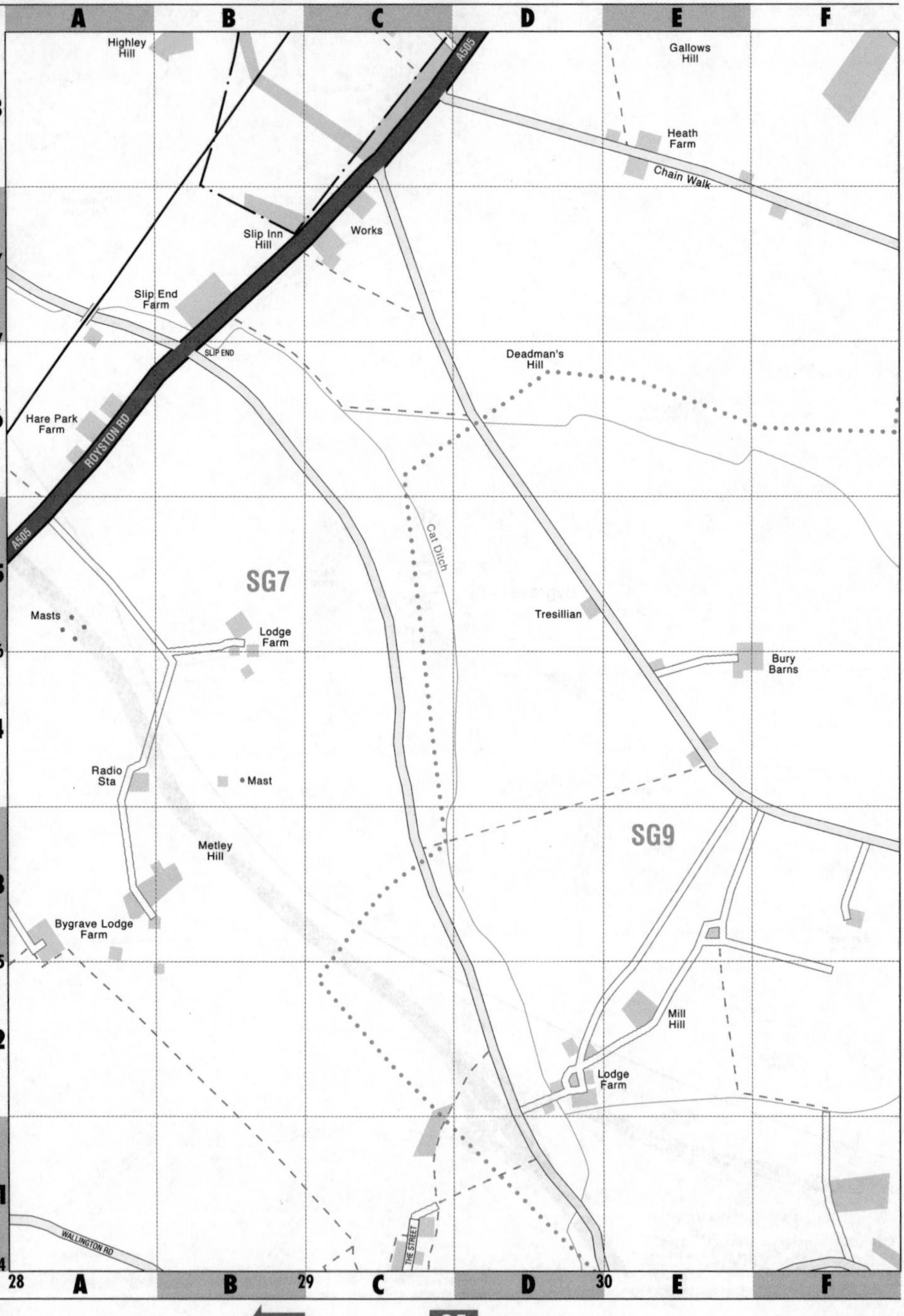

8

Highley
Hill

Gallows
Hill

A505

Heath
Farm

Chain Walk

7

Slip Inn
Hill

Works

Slip End
Farm

37

SLIP END

Deadman's
Hill

6

Hare Park
Farm

ROYSTON RD

A505

Cat Ditch

5

SG7

Masts

Tresillian

36

Lodge
Farm

Bury
Barns

4

Radio
Sta

Mast

SG9

Metley
Hill

3

Bygrave Lodge
Farm

35

Mill
Hill

2

Lodge
Farm

1

34

WALLINGTON RD

THE STREET

28 **A** **B** **29** **C** **D** **30** **E** **F**

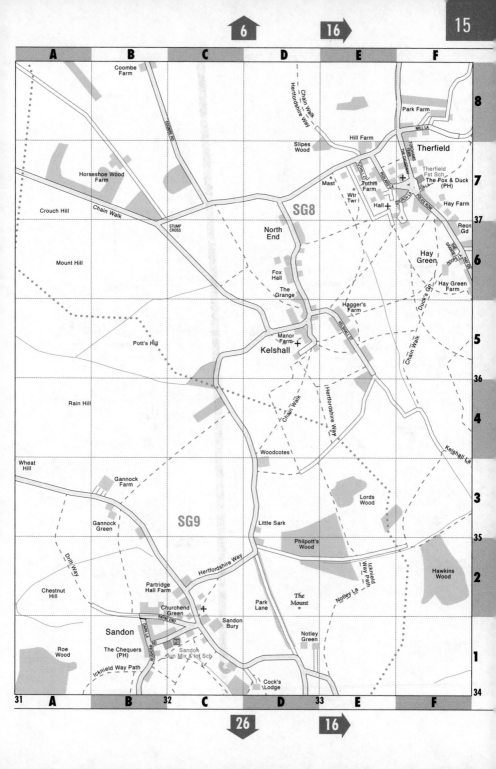

A B C D E F

8

7

37

6

5

36

4

3

35

2

1

34

Icknield Way Path

MEADOW WAY

HAYWOOD LA

Washingditch Green

River Rib

Mardlebury

Reed End

Holborn Farm

ROOKSNEST LA

Dane End

Rooksnest Farm

Kelshall La
Icknield La
Way Path

Chapel Green

River Rib

Sewage Works

DANE END

Slate Hall Farm

SG8

Mast

Southview

Brandish Wood

Hilly Wood

Reed Wood

SG9

A10

Hatchpen

Hertfordshire Way

THE JOINT

BRICKYARD LA

WILLOW CL

BLACKSMITH'S LA

HOBDS HAYES

JACKSON'S LA

Reed Fst Sch

NICROLLS YD

Reed

CHURCH LA

FIRST ST

The Cabinet (PH)

DRIFTWAY

Queenbury

CHURCH CL

Reed Hall

Wisbridge Farm

Gannock Grove

Gannock Green

Southfield Grove

34 A B 35 C D 36 E F

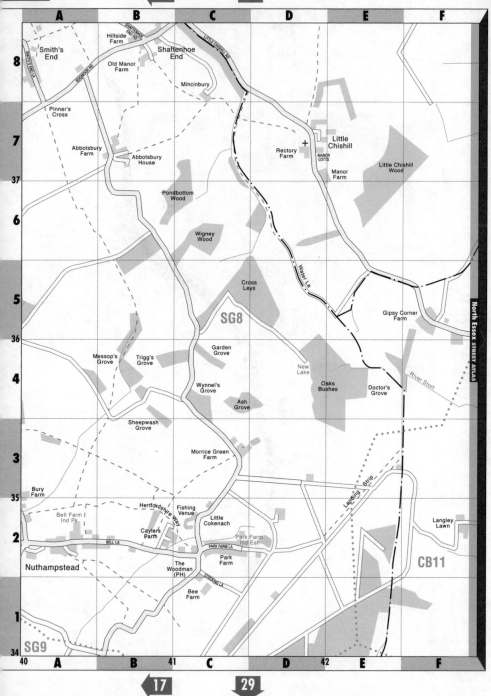

17
9

A   **B**   **C**   **D**   **E**   **F**

8

Smith's
End

Hillside
Farm

Shaftenhoe
End

Old Manor
Farm

Mincinbury

7

Pinner's
Cross

Abbotsbury
Farm

Abbotsbury
House

Rectory
Farm

Little
Chishill

MANOR
COTTS

Manor
Farm

Little Chishill
Wood

37

Pondbottom
Wood

6

Wigney
Wood

Water La

Cross
Leys

5

SG8

Gipsy Corner
Farm

36

Messop's
Grove

Trigg's
Grove

Garden
Grove

New
Lake

River Stort

4

Wynnel's
Grove

Ash
Grove

Oaks
Bushes

Doctor's
Grove

Sheepwash
Grove

Morrice Green
Farm

3

Bury
Farm

Landing Strip

35

Bell Farm
Ind Pk

Hertfordshire Way

Fishing
Venue

Little
Cokenach

Park Farm
Ind Est

Langley
Lawn

Caylers
Farm

2

BELL LA

PARK FARM LA

Park
Farm

CB11

Nuthampstead

The
Woodman
(PH)

STOCKING LA

Bee
Farm

1

SG9

34

40   **A**   **B**   **41**   **C**   **D**   **42**   **E**   **F**

North Essex STREET ATLAS

17
29

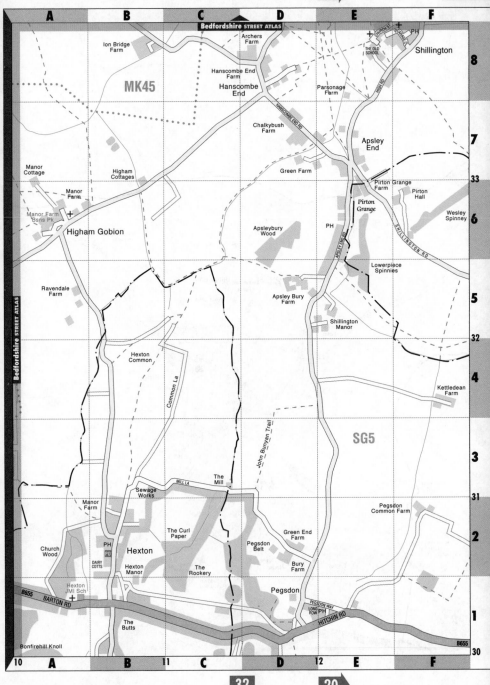

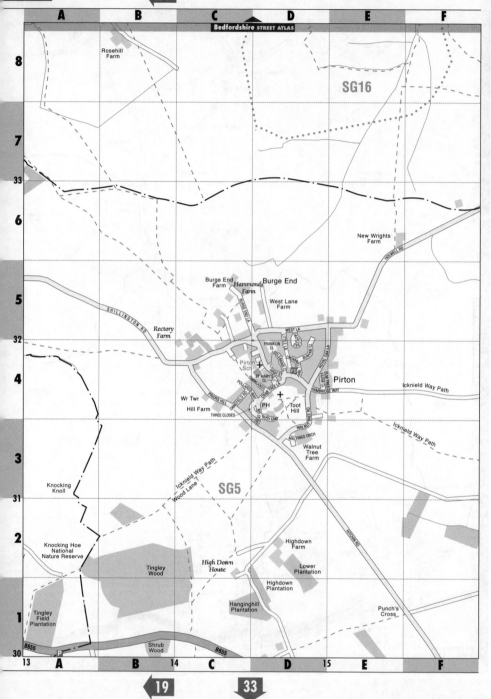

19

Bedfordshire STREET ATLAS

SG16

8

7

33

6

New Wrights Farm

HOLWELL RD

5

SHILLINGTON RD

Burge End Farm
Hammonds Farm
Burge End

West Lane Farm

Rectory Farm

BURGE END LA

WEST LA

LITTLE LA

FRANKLIN CL

CROSSMEAD WALK

BURTON CL

ROYAL OAK LA

32

Pirton Sch

ST MARY'S

HIGH ST

SHAMBROOK RD

ELM TREE LA

4

Wr Twr
Hill Farm

PRIORS HILL

POLLARDS WAY

DANEFIELD RD

CROFT LA

TREE LA

HAMBRIDGE WAY

Pirton

Icknield Way Path

THREE CLOSES

BURY END

PH

Toot Hill

WALNUT TREE RD

Icknield Way Path

MALTINGS ORCH

Walnut Tree Farm

3

Icknield Way Path
Wood Lane

SG5

HITCHIN RD

31

Knocking Knoll

2

Knocking Hoe National Nature Reserve

Highdown Farm

Lower Plantation

Tingley Wood

High Down House

Highdown Plantation

Hanginghill Plantation

Punch's Cross

1

Tingley Field Plantation

B655

30

P

Shrub Wood

B655

13   **A**   **B**   14   **C**   **D**   15   **E**   **F**

19

33

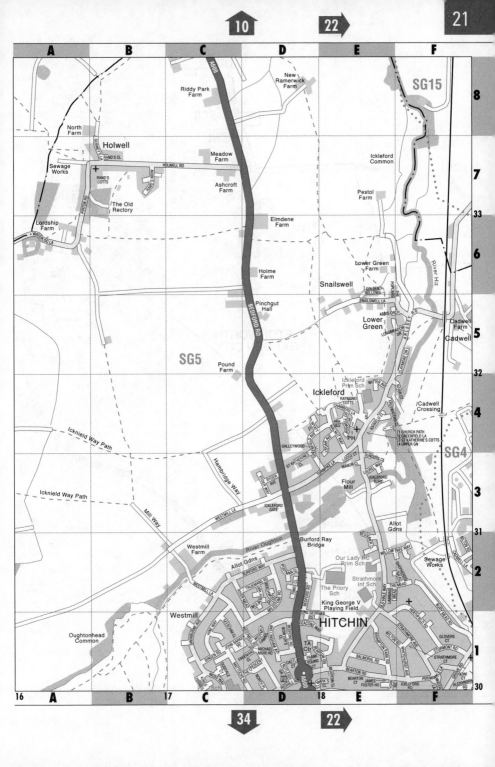

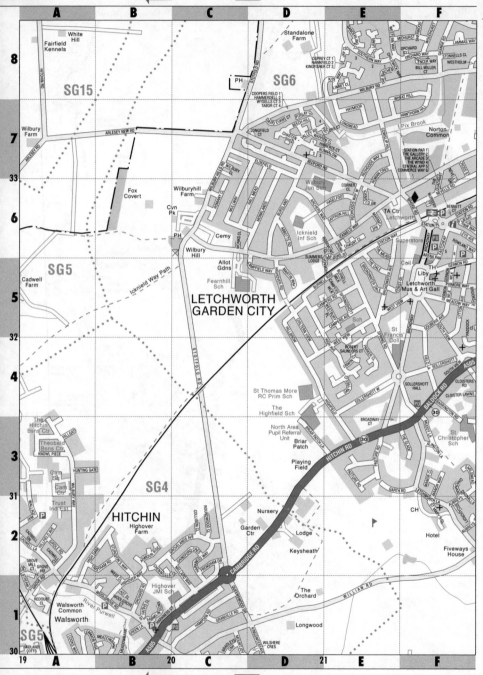

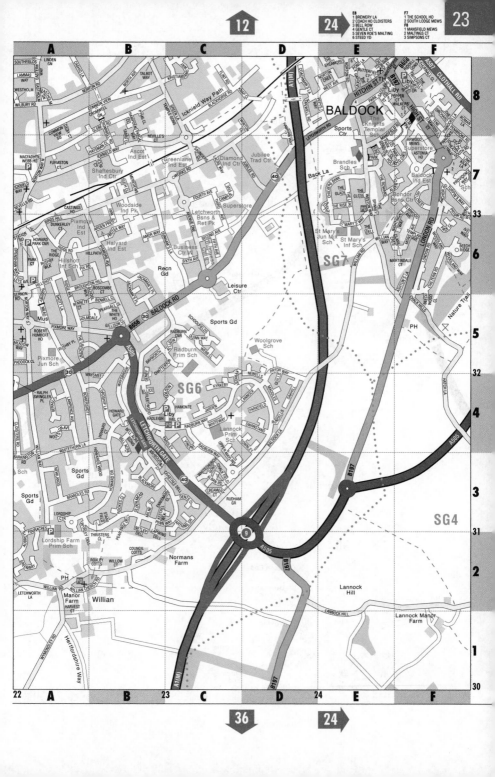

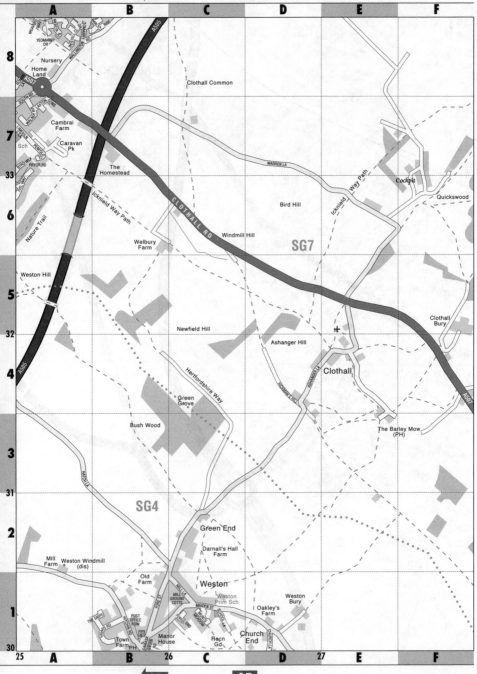

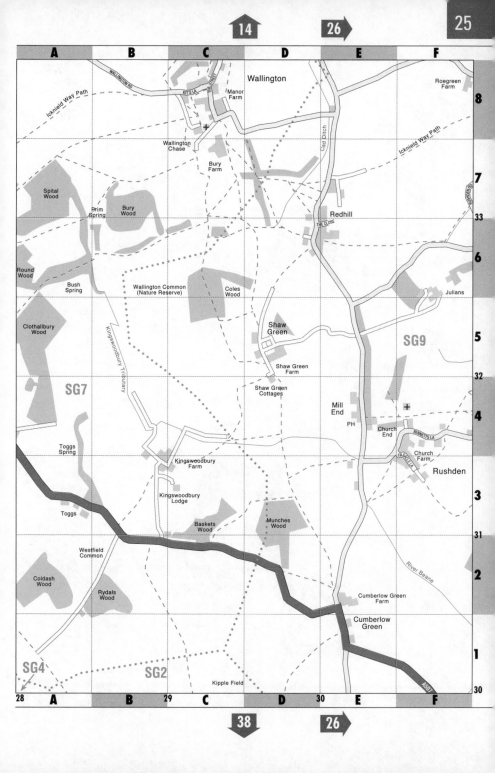

25
15

25
39

A   **B**   **C**   **D**   **E**   **F**

8   7   33   6   5   32   4   3   31   2   1   30

Tichney Wood

Five House Farm

West Wood

SG8

Hertfordshire Way

Icknield Way Path

Killogs Farm

HIDDEN RD

Roe Green

Rockells Jersey Farm

Green End

Green End Farm

BECKFIELD LA

Nursery

Beckfield Farm

River Beane

Doebridge Farm

Friars Grange

Friars La

Friars Wood

Chain Walk

Bird's Nest Farm

Mill End

Offley Green

Chain Walk

Wood Farm

Mill End Farm

Bachelor's Wood

Chain Walk

Lye End Farm

Little Manor Farm

Southern Green Farm

Whitehall

Burgess La

Southern Green

Broadfield Lodge Farm

SG9

Park Wood

Ellen Green

Bush Wood

Steward's Ley

Middle Wood

Great Wood

Chain Walk

Lodge Farm

Chapel Wood

Hall Farm

Needle Spring

Boldero's Wood

Broadfield Hall

Chain Walk

Foxholes Wood

Southfields Farm

Little Wood

Horneywood La

Foxholes

Throcking

Water Tower

COTTERED RD

Throcking Hall

31   **A**   32   **B**   **C**   33   **D**   **E**   **F**

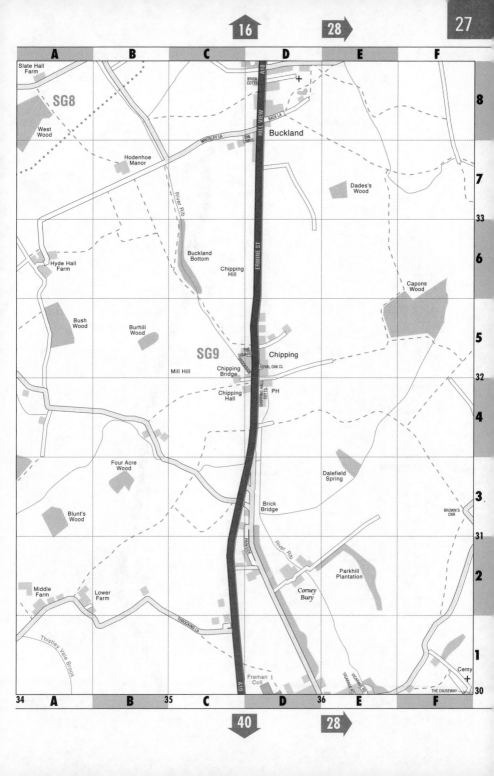

A   B   C   D   E   F

SG8

Slate Hall
Farm

West
Wood

8

BRICK
COTTS

HILL VIEW

BACK LA

Buckland

WHITELEY LA

THE
LIMES

ERMINE ST

A10

Hodenhoe
Manor

River Rib

Dades's
Wood

7

33

Hyde Hall
Farm

Buckland
Bottom

Chipping
Hill

6

Capons
Wood

Bush
Wood

Burhill
Wood

SG9

Chipping

5

Mill Hill

Chipping
Bridge

THE
SQUARE

SPRINGSIDE

ROYAL OAK CL

32

Chipping
Hall

CHIPPING HALL COTTS

PH

4

Four Acre
Wood

Dalefield
Spring

Blunt's
Wood

Brick
Bridge

3

BROWN'S
CNR

31

River Rib

Parkhill
Plantation

2

Middle
Farm

Lower
Farm

THROCKING LA

Corney
Bury

Thistley Vale Brook

RAILWAY

1

Cemy

Freman
Coll

VICARAGE CT

VICARAGE RD

THE CAUSEWAY

30

A10

34   A   35   B   C   D   36   E   F

27
17

A B C D E F

SG8

B1368 LONDON RD

North End Farm

8

7

Biggin Bridge

Biggin Manor

River Quin

BIGGIN HILL

Northey Wood

33

CAVE GATE

6

Cave Bridge

Stapleton Bridge

Lincoln Hill

5

Forty Acre Plantation

Cavehall Plantation

New Barns

32

Cherry Orchard Plantation

SG9

Wyddial Hall

Peartree Field Wood

Bushleys Grove

Fox Hill

4

ROSE COTTS

CHERRY ORCHARD LA

SOUTHSIDE Wyddial

Home Farm

Beauchamps

Flint Cottages

River Quin

3

MOLES LA

Silkmead Farm

31

Moles Farm

Beauchamp's Wood

2

Beauchamp's Plantation

Bradbury Farm

Works

1

B1368

30

37 A B 38 C D 39 E F

A   B   C   D   E   F

CB11

8

Scales Park

SG8

White Hill

7

Bandons

Pain's End

Northey
Wood

Two Acres
Farm

DIMSDALE
COTTS

Cheapside

CASTLE COTTS
The Blind Fiddler
(PH)

BURY
FIELD

33

Anstey
Castle

Anstey

The Hale

Lower
Green

Anstey
Fst Sch

ELM
COTTS

Meesden

6

Snow
End

LINCOLN
HILL

Daw's
End

Coltsfoot
Farm

Manor
Farm

5

SILVER
ST

32

Anstey
Bury

River Ash

4

Hertfordshire Way

Puttock's
End

SG9

Cole
Green

3

Mill
Mound

Brick House
Farm

31

B1038

2

Borley Green
Cottage

Hormead
Hall

Three Acre
Wood

1

HALL LA

HALL
COTTS

Black Ditch

CONDUIT LA

Dane End
House

B1038

30

40   A   B   41   C   D   42   E   F

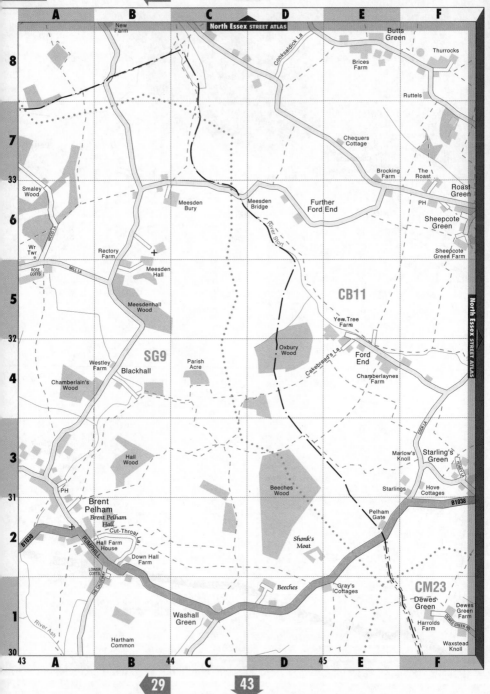

North Essex STREET ATLAS

North Essex STREET ATLAS

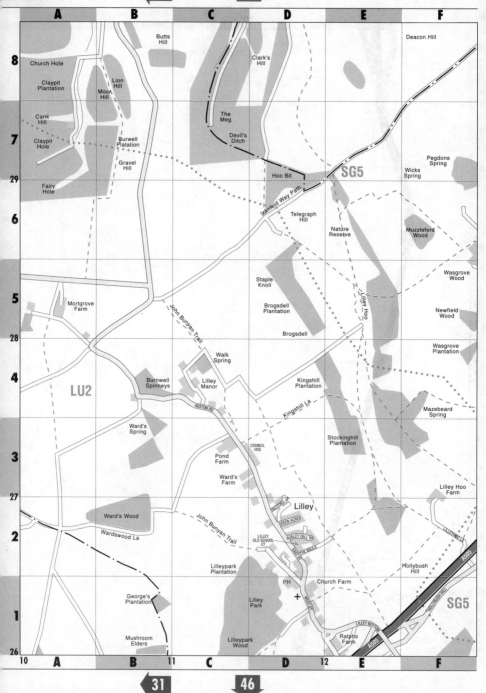

A B C D E F

8
Church Hole
Claypit Plantation
Lion Hill
Moon Hill
Butts Hill
Clark's Hill
Deacon Hill

7
Cank Hill
Claypit Hole
Burwell Platation
Gravel Hill
The Meg
Devil's Ditch

29
Fairy Hole
Hoo Bit
SG5
Wicks Spring
Pegdons Spring

6
Icknield Way Path
Telegraph Hill
Nature Reserve
Muzzleford Wood

5
Mortgrove Farm
John Bunyan Trail
Staple Knoll
Brogsdell Plantation
Lilley Hoo
Wasgrove Wood
Newfield Wood

28
Brogsdell
Wasgrove Plantation

4
LU2
Burnwell Spinneys
Lilley Manor
Walk Spring
Kingshill Plantation
Mazebeard Spring

HEXTON RD
Kingshill La

3
Ward's Spring
COUNCIL HOS
Pond Farm
Ward's Farm
Stockinghill Plantation

27
Lilley Hoo Farm

2
Ward's Wood
Wardswood La
John Bunyan Trail
RECTORY LA
GREEN ACRES
PUTTEY DELL RD
IN THE BAULK
LILLEY OLD SCHOOL CT
Lilley
LILLEYHOO LA
A505
Hollybush Hill

1
George's Plantation
Lilleypark Plantation
PH
Lilley Park
Church Farm
LILLEY BOTTOM
POULTERS HILL
A505
SG5

26
Mushroom Elders
Lilleypark Wood
Ralphs Farm

10 A B 11 C D 12 E F

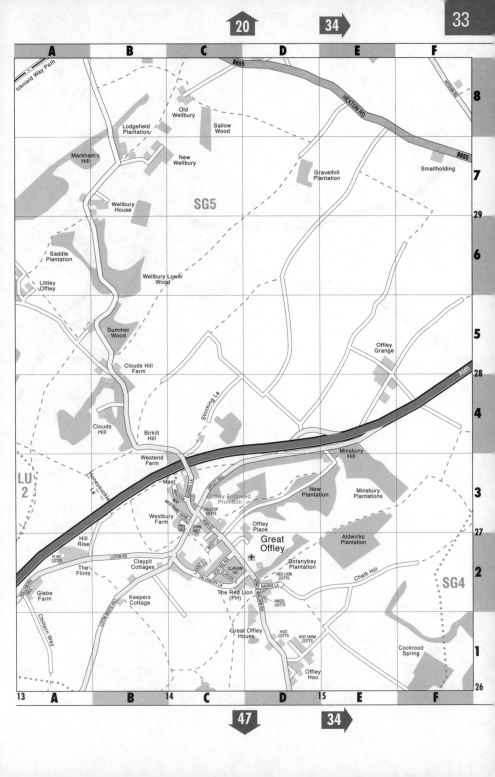

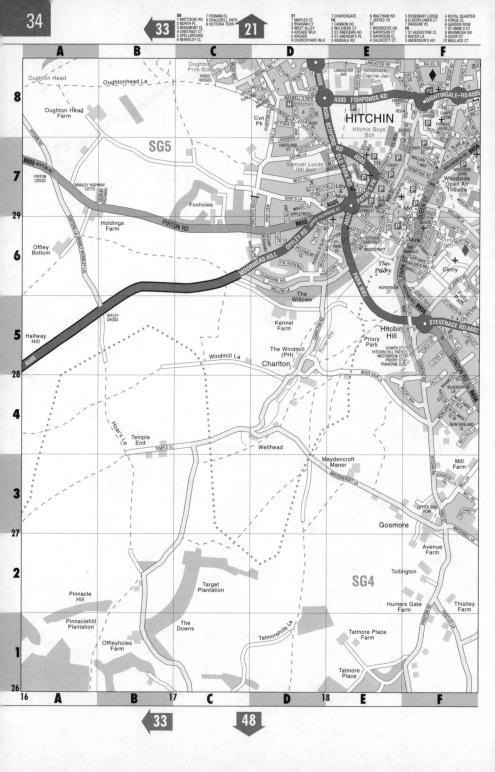

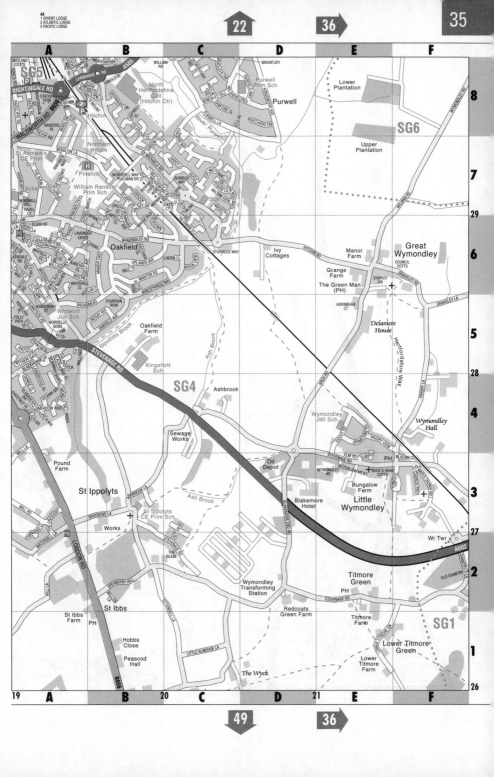

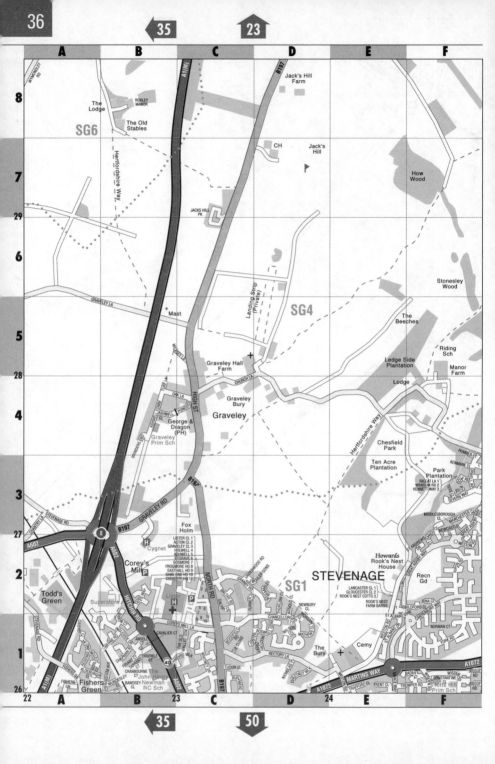

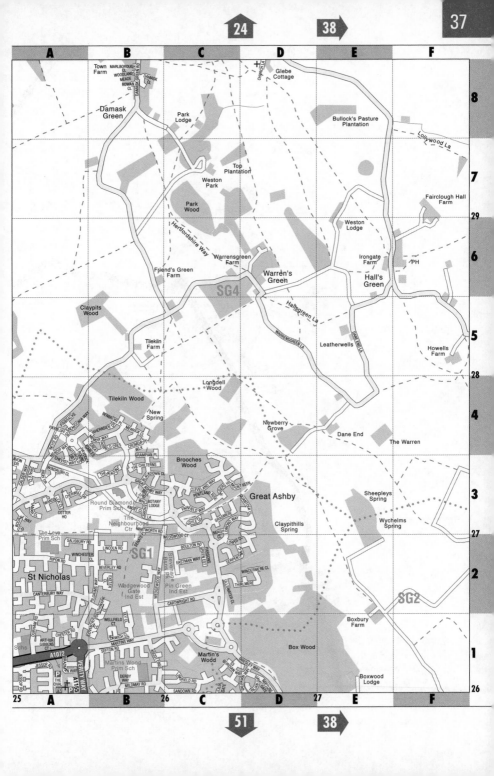

37
25

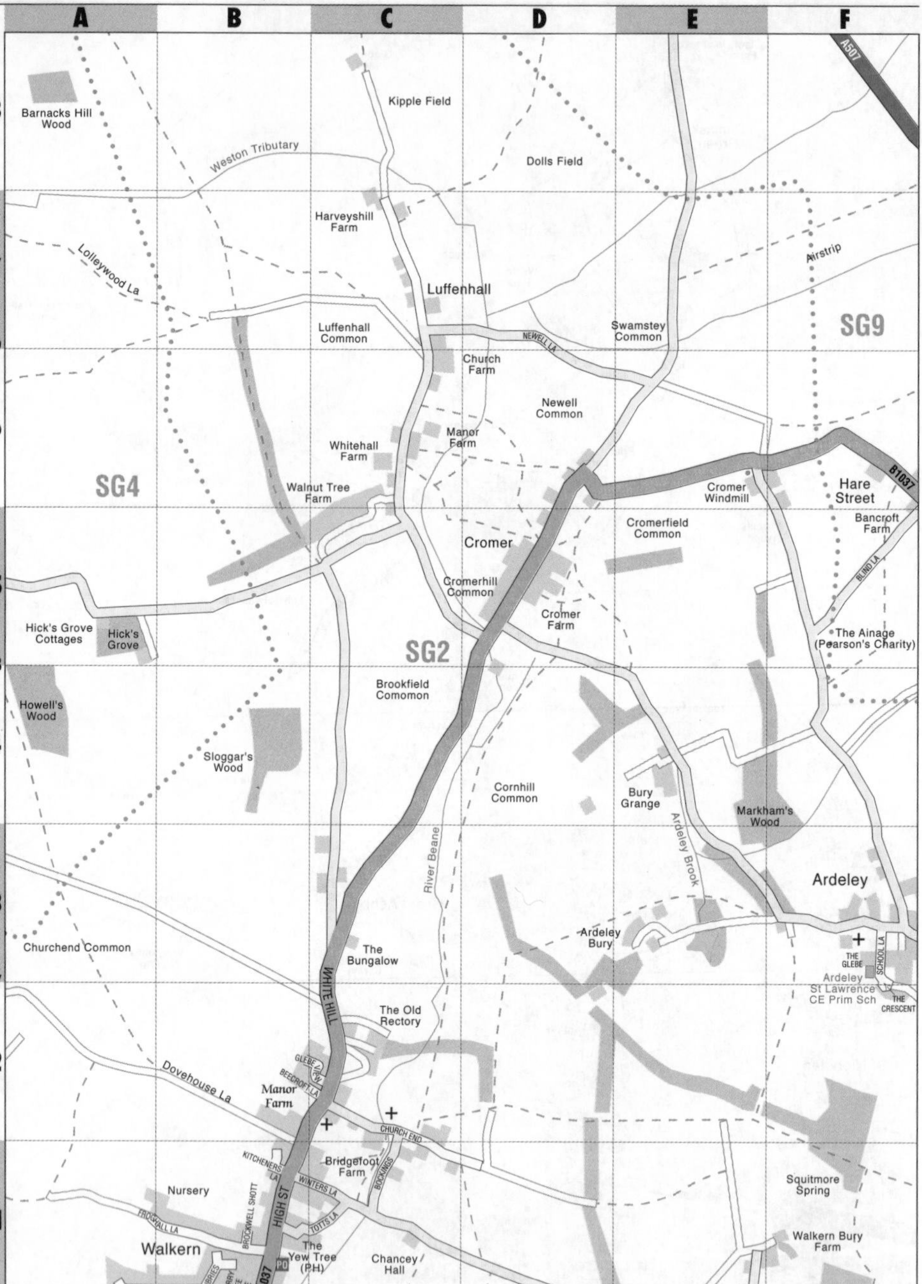
A
B
C
D
E
F
8
7
29
6
5
28
4
3
27
2
1
26
28
29
30
A507
Barnacks Hill Wood
Kipple Field
Weston Tributary
Dolls Field
Harveyshill Farm
Lolleywood La
Airstrip
Luffenhall
Luffenhall Common
Swamstey Common
SG9
NEWELL LA
Church Farm
Newell Common
Manor Farm
Whitehall Farm
B1037
SG4
Walnut Tree Farm
Cromer Windmill
Hare Street
Cromerfield Common
Bancroft Farm
Cromer
BLIND LA
Cromerhill Common
Cromer Farm
Hick's Grove Cottages
Hick's Grove
The Ainage (Pearson's Charity)
SG2
Brookfield Comomon
Howell's Wood
Sloggar's Wood
Cornhill Common
Bury Grange
Markham's Wood
Ardeley Brook
River Beane
Ardeley
Churchend Common
Ardeley Bury
THE GLEBE
SCHOOL LA
The Bungalow
WHITE HILL
Ardeley St Lawrence CE Prim Sch
THE CRESCENT
The Old Rectory
GLEBE VIEW
Dovehouse La
BEECROFT LA
Manor Farm
CHURCH END
KITCHENERS LA
Bridgefoot Farm
BOCKINGS
WINTERS LA
Nursery
Squitmore Spring
BROCKWELL SHOTT
HIGH ST
TOTTS LA
FROGHALL LA
Walkern Bury Farm
The Yew Tree (PH)
Walkern
Chancey Hall
PO
AUBRIES
CHERRY TREE RISE
MOORS LEY
B1037

37
52

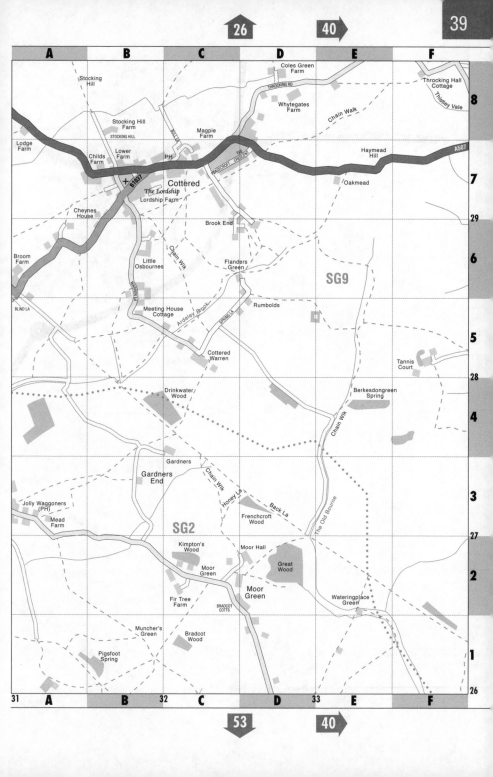

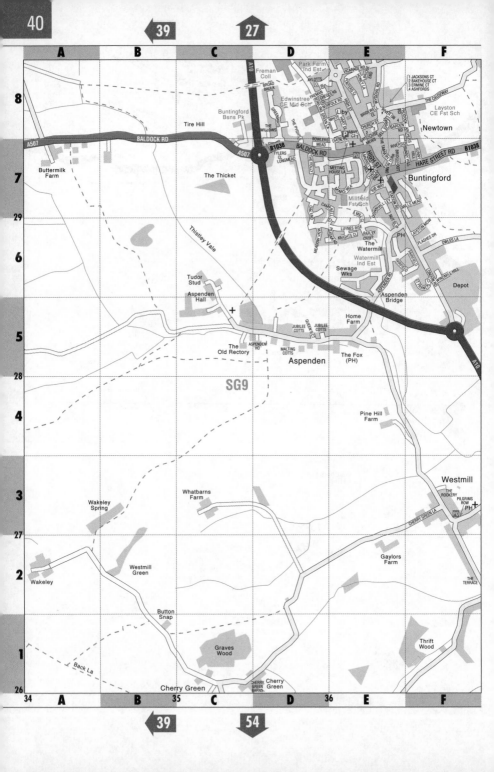

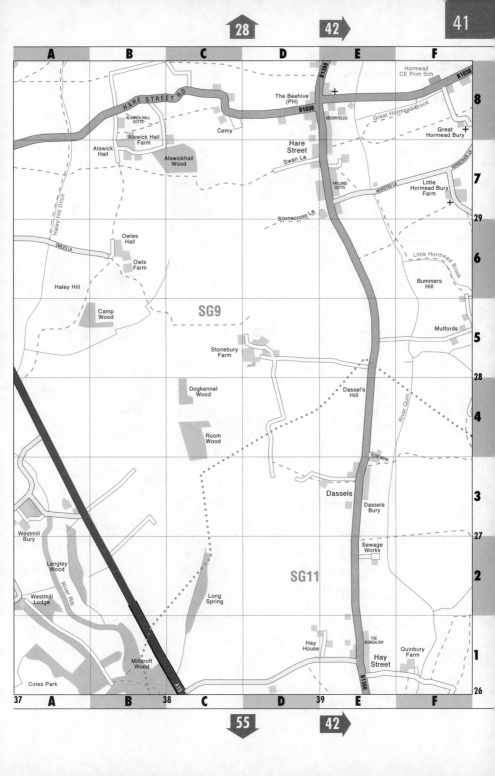

41
29

A B C D E F

8

B1038
Three Tuns (PH)
Great Hormead
HORSESHOE HILL
JUBILEE COTTS
WILTON CL.
St Patrick's Wood
Church End Cottage
Hertfordshire Way
Sparksfield

7

The Thrift
Great Hormead Park

29

PARK VIEW
Glebe House
Little Hormead Brook
SG9

6

Balons Farm
Little Hormead
Bulls Farm
Fair Lady Wood
The Willows
Lady Wood

5

Mutfords
Mutton Hall
Duck Street Cottage

28

Hertfordshire Way
HALL BARNS
THE STREET

4

Shirley
Bradley Spring

3

Hoare's La
Bozengreen Farm
Rotten Row
High Wood
Patient End Farmhouse

27

Hertfordshire Way
Patient End
Bozen Green

2

SG11

1

THE CAUSEWAY
Hole Farm Cott
Hole Farm

26

40 **A** 41 **B** 41 **C** 42 **D** **E** **F**

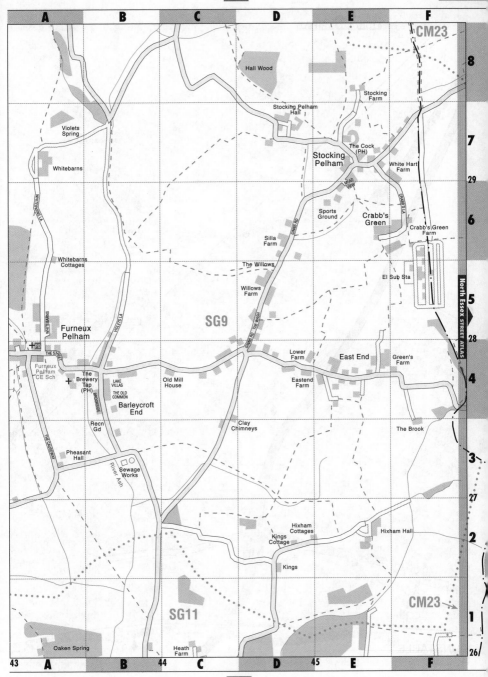

CM23

A B C D E F

8

Hall Wood

Stocking
Farm

Violets
Spring

Stocking Pelham
Hall

7

Whitebarns

The Cock
(PH)

Stocking
Pelham

White Hart
Farm

29

Whitebarns
Cottages

Sports
Ground

Crabb's
Green

Crabb's Green
Farm

6

Silla
Farm

The Willows

El Sub Sta

North Essex Street Atlas

SG9

Willows
Farm

5

Furneux
Pelham

28

Furneux
Pelham
CE Sch

Lower
Farm

East End

Green's
Farm

4

The
Brewery
Tap
(PH)

LAKE
VILLAS

Old Mill
House

Eastend
Farm

THE STREET

THE OLD
COMMON

Barleycroft
End

Recn
Gd

Clay
Chimneys

The Brook

3

Pheasant
Hall

River Ash

Sewage
Works

27

THE CAUSEWAY

Hixham
Cottages

Kings
Cottage

Hixham Hall

2

SG11

Kings

CM23

1

Oaken Spring

Heath
Farm

26

43 A B 44 C D 45 E F

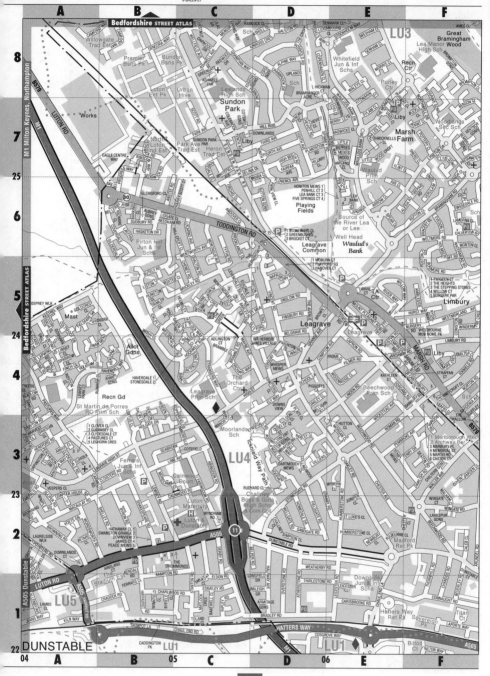

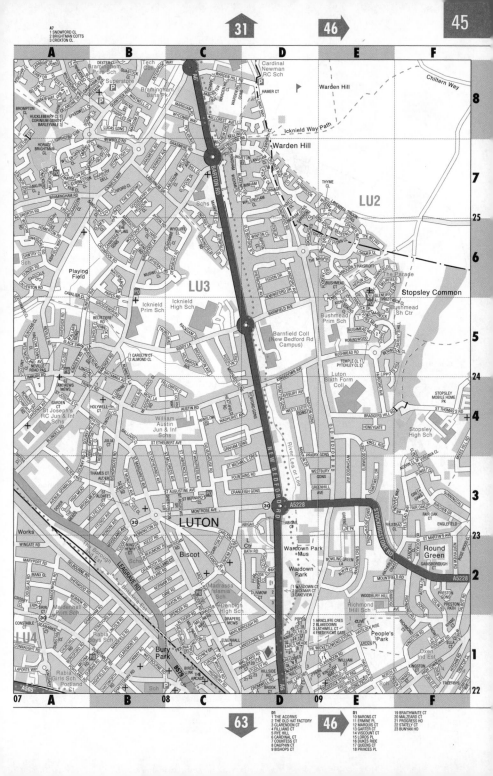

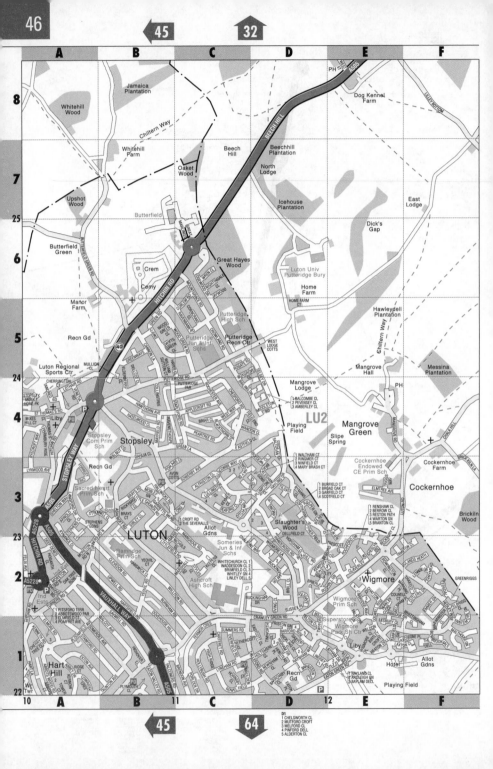

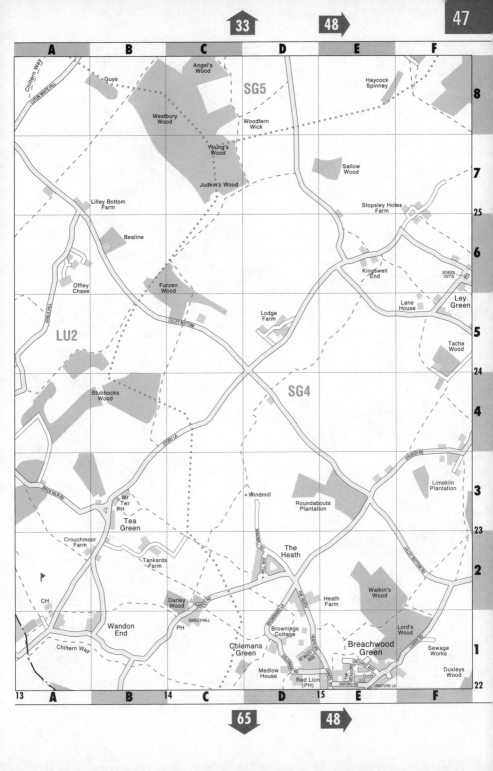

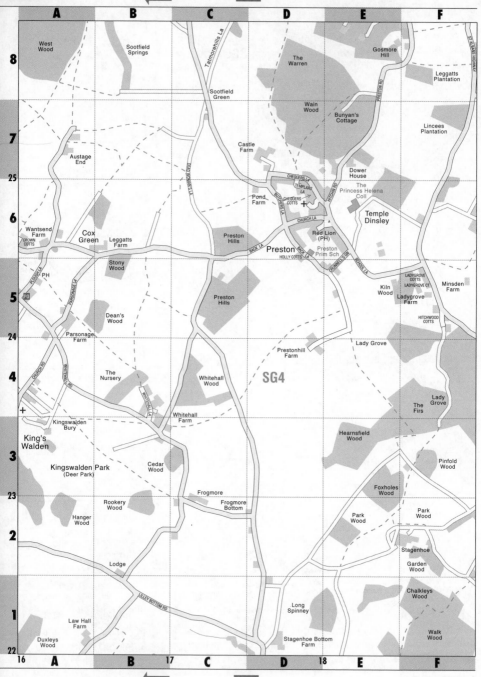

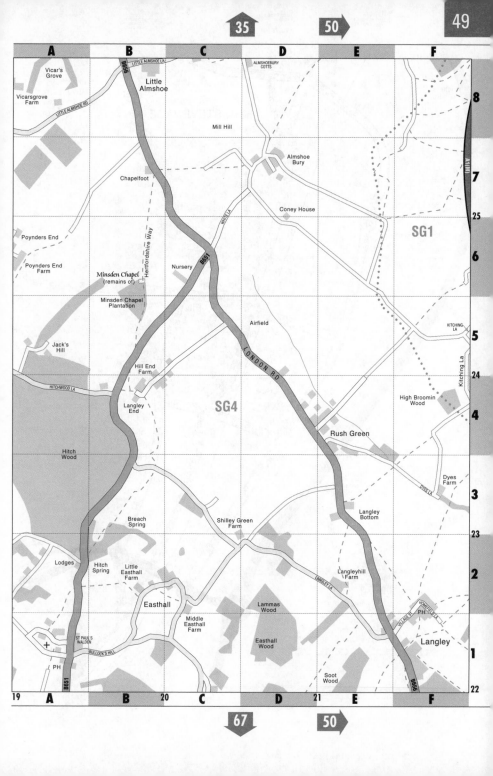

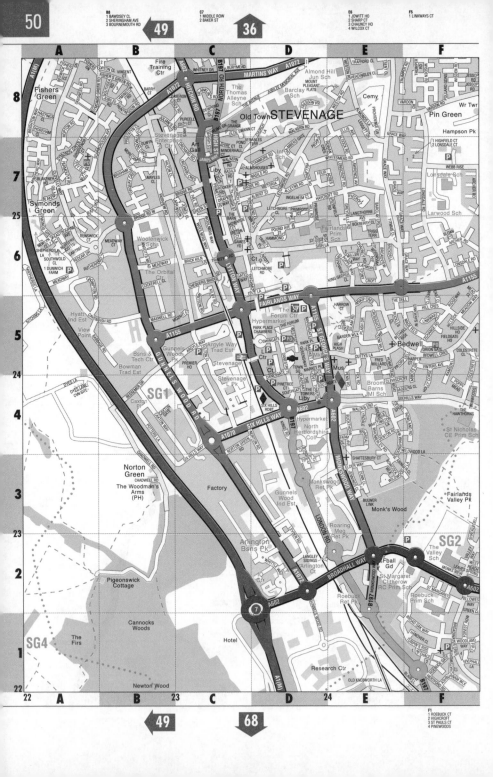

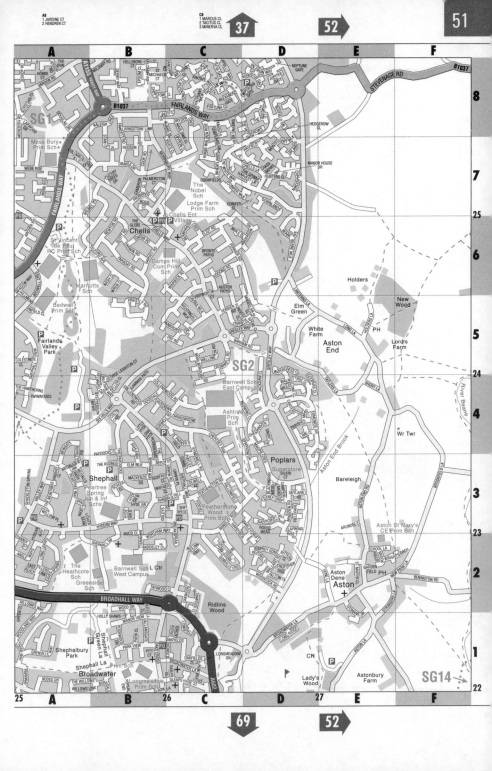

51
38

| | A | B | C | D | E | F |

B1037
STEVENAGE RD B1037
WENHAM CT
Rooks Nest Farm
Walkern Prim Sch
WRIGHTS MDW

8

Brickfield

Bassus Green

St John's Wood

The Bushes

Coble's Spring

7

Jubilee Plantation

River Beane

The Croft

WALKERN RD

25

Walkern Hall Farm

Clay End

Baron's Grove

Walkern Hall

Walman's Green

6

Farm Wood

Walman's Wood

Bridge Farm

Box Hall

Cabbage Green

5

WALKERN RD

OLD SCHOOL GN

24

SG2

Haily Park Wood

Lordship Farm

Benington Bury

Benington CE Prim Sch

Wr Twr

Cole's Green

Benington

Benington Park

4

Hubbert's Grove

Benington Lordship Gdns

DUCK LA

OAK TREE CL

CHURCH GN

TRIPLE STILES

BLACKSMITHS HILL

High Wood

The Bell (PH)

TOWN LA

3

FORD LA

WALKERN RD

Park Wood

Finches Farm

23

2

BENINGTON RD

BRACEYS

HEBING END

GOODEY MEADOW

PH

Burn's Green

HIGH STREET

WHEMPSTEAD RD

Holbrook Farm

SG14

Bawne Hook

High Grove

1

Cotton La

Small Hopes

Chain Wlk

HIGH ELMS LA

Oxshott Hill

Landing Strip

22

| 28 | A | B | 29 | C | D | 30 | E | F |

51
70

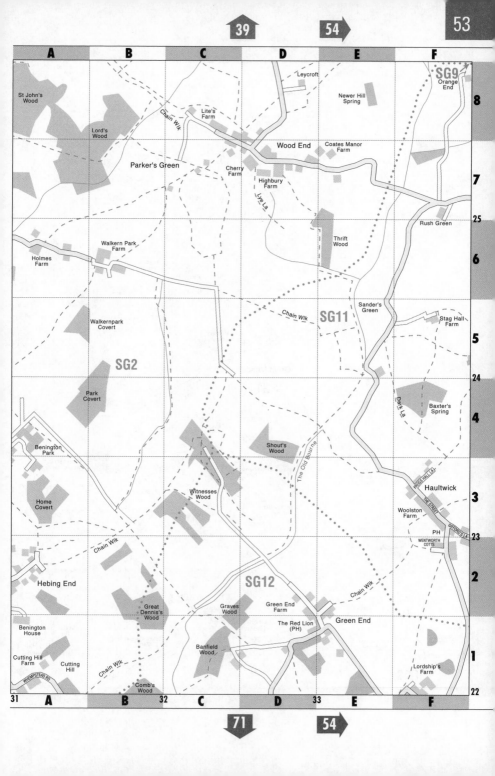

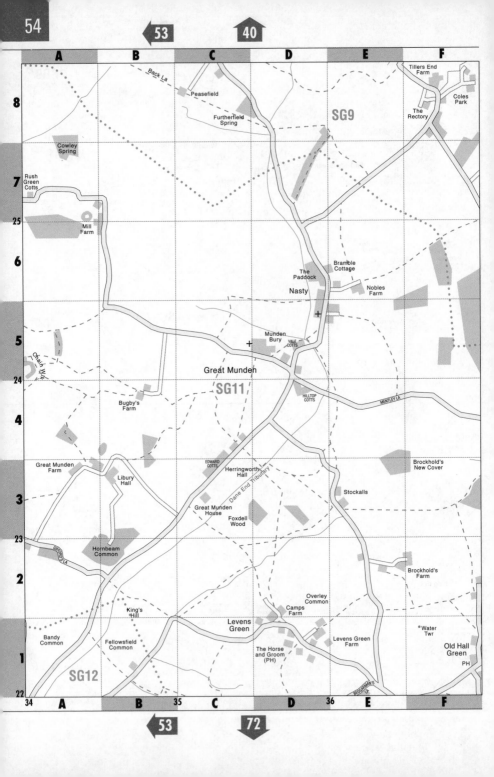

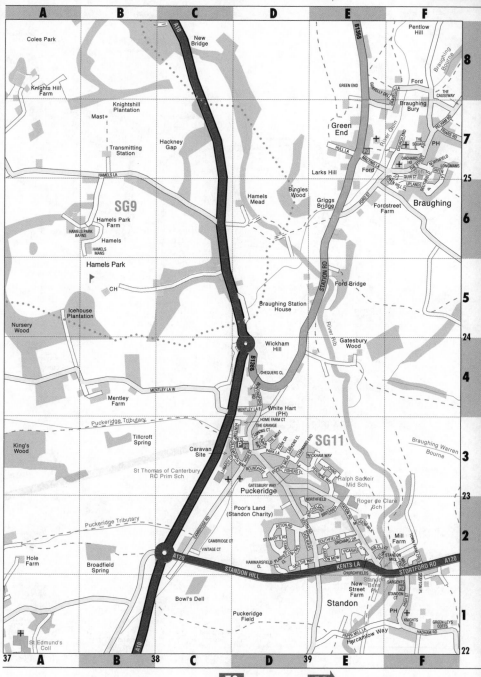

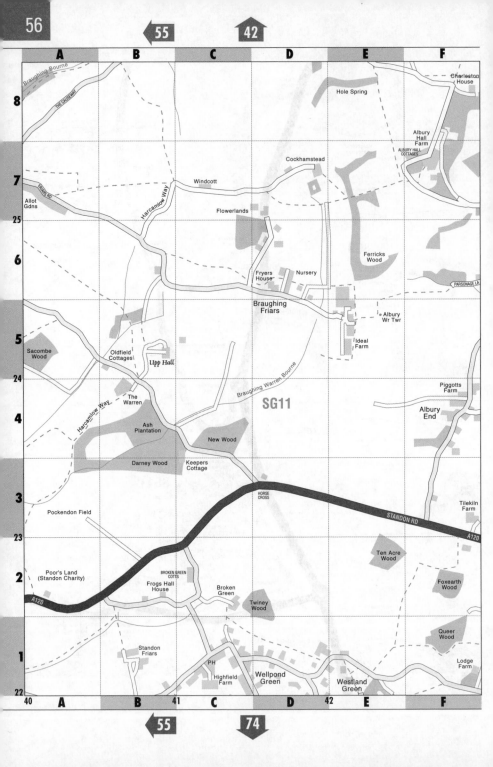

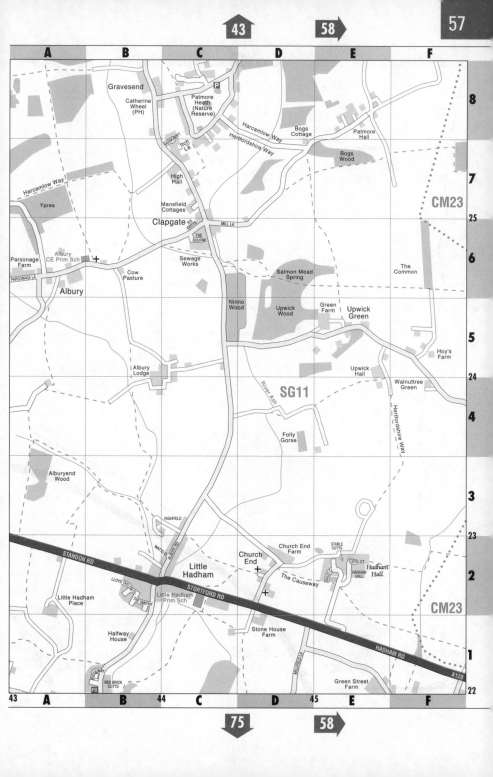

Map Labels

Gravesend

Catherine Wheel (PH)

Patmore Heath (Nature Reserve)

Harcamlow Way

Bogs Cottage

Patmore Hall

Hertfordshire Way

Bogs Wood

Briercroft

Itch La

High Hall

CM23

Harcamlow Way

Ypres

Mansfield Cottages

Clapgate

COTTS

MILL LA

25

THE BOURNE

Parsonage Farm

Albury CE Prim Sch

PARSONAGE LA

Albury

Cow Pasture

Sewage Works

Salmon Mead Spring

The Common

6

Ninno Wood

Upwick Wood

Green Farm

Upwick Green

5

Albury Lodge

Hoy's Farm

River Ash

SG11

Upwick Hall

24

Walnuttree Green

4

Folly Gorse

Hertfordshire Way

Alburyend Wood

3

HIGHFIELD

23

STANDON RD

WATTS PL

ALBURY RD

Church End Farm

STABLE COTTS

CAPEL CT

HADHAM HALL

Hadham Hall

Little Hadham

Church End

BURY LA

The Causeway

LLOYD TAYLOR CL

STORTFORD RD

CM23

Little Hadham Place

THE SMITHY

Little Hadham Prim Sch

Halfway House

Stone House Farm

HADHAM RD

RIDGEWAY

PO

RED BRICK COTTS

MILL FIELD LA

Green Street Farm

A120

22

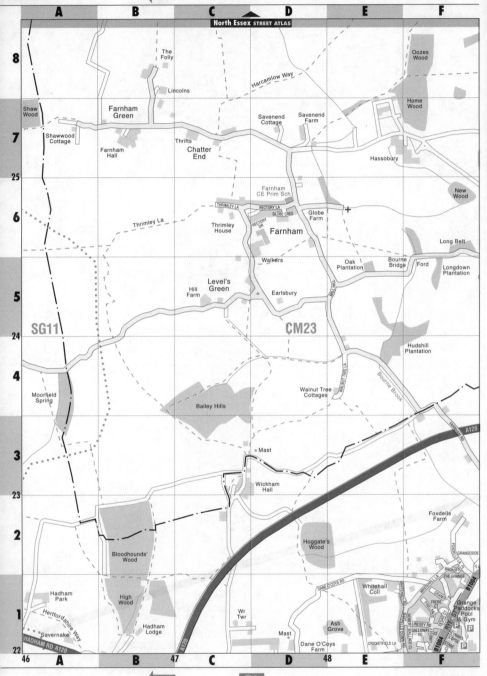

57

North Essex STREET ATLAS

A B C D E F

8

The Folly

Lincolns

Oozes
Wood

Harcamlow Way

Home
Wood

Shaw
Wood

Farnham
Green

Savenend
Cottage

Savenend
Farm

7

Shawwood
Cottage

Thrifts

Chatter
End

Hassobury

Farnham
Hall

Farnham
CE Prim Sch

25

New
Wood

6

Thrimley La

Thrimley La

Thrimley
House

THRIMLEY LA

RECTORY LA

GLOBE CRES

RECTORY
DR

Farnham

Globe
Farm

Long Belt

Walkers

Oak
Plantation

Bourne
Bridge

Ford

Longdown
Plantation

Level's
Green

Hill
Farm

Earlsbury

5

SG11

CM23

24

Hudshill
Plantation

4

Moorfield
Spring

Bailey Hills

Walnut Tree
Cottages

WALNUT TREE LA

Bourne Brook

A120

3

Mast

Wickham
Hall

THEYDON RD

A120

23

Foxdells
Farm

2

Bloodhounds'
Wood

Hoggate's
Wood

GRANGESIDE

THE GRANGE

BROADLEY

Hadham
Park

Hertfordshire Way

High
Wood

Whitehall
Coll

DANE O'COYS RD

WHITEHALL LA

WHITEHALL LA

FRERE
CT

THE GRANGE

Grange
Paddocks
Pool
& Gym

1

Savernake

HADHAM RD A120

A120

Hadham
Lodge

Wr
Twr

Mast

Ash
Grove

Dane O'Coys
Farm

CRICKETFIELD LA

LINDSEY RD

GALLOWAY
RD

RYE ST

B1004

22

46 A 47 B C 48 D E F

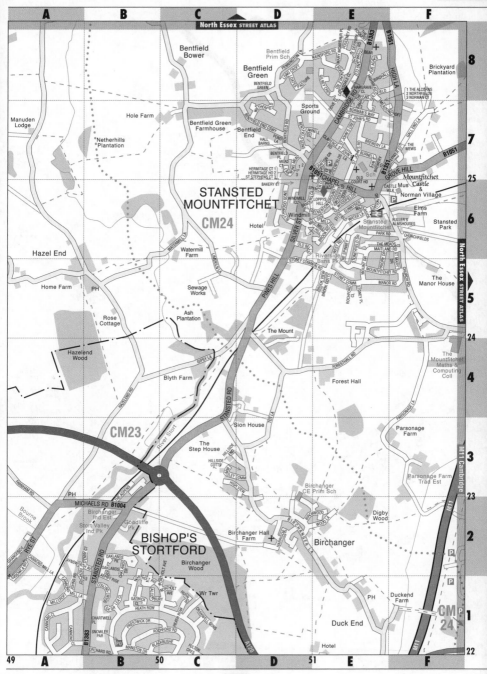

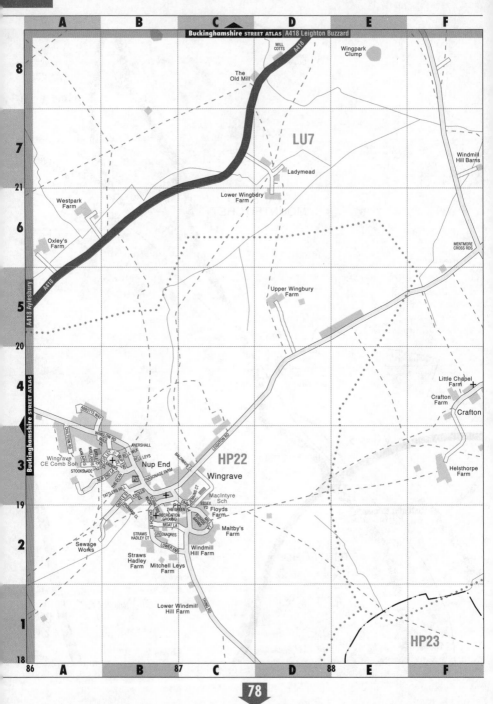

A

B

C

D

E

F

8

7

21

6

5

20

4

3

19

2

1

18

LU7

Wingpark
Clump

Windmill
Hill Barns

The Old Mill

MILL
COTTS

A418

Ladymead

Lower Wingbury
Farm

Westpark
Farm

Oxley's
Farm

A418 Aylesbury

A418

MENTMORE
CROSS RDS

Upper Wingbury
Farm

Little Chapel
Farm

Crafton
Farm

Crafton

Helsthorpe
Farm

HP22

Wingrave

LEIGHTON RD

BALDWINS CL

ABBOTTS MEAD

WINSLOW RD

MILL
CL

CHILTERN RD

NAP HILL RD

Wingrave
CE Comb Sch

Nup End

TATTLERS HILL

PARSONAGE FARM

STOOKSMEAD

BELL LEYS

ANNERSHALL

NUP END LA

THE GLEBE

CHURCH ST

CASTLE CT

KNOLL

LOWER END

CHURCH ST

CHURCH ST

MacIntyre
Sch

ESSEX
YD

Floyds
Farm

Maltby's
Farm

Windmill
Hill Farm

THE GREEN

RECREATION
GROUND

MOAT LA

GREENACRES

STRAWS
HADLEY CT

Sewage
Works

Straws
Hadley
Farm

Mitchell Leys
Farm

Lower Windmill
Hill Farm

FURSE RD

HP23

86

87

88

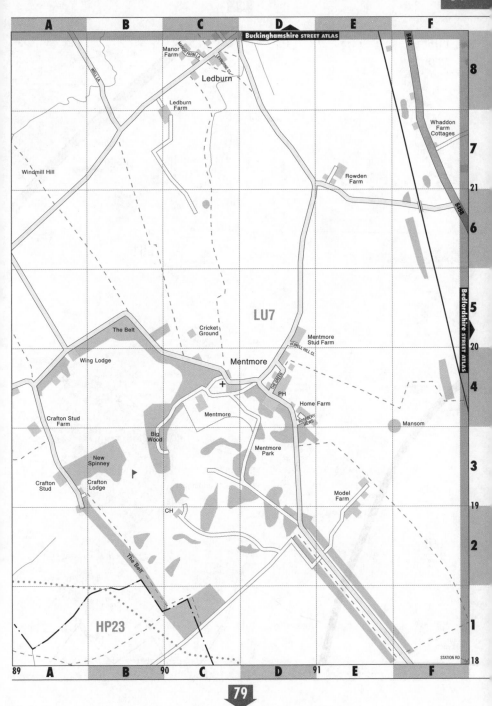

Buckinghamshire STREET ATLAS

Bedfordshire STREET ATLAS

Ledburn

Manor Farm

Ledburn Farm

Whaddon Farm Cottages

Windmill Hill

Rowden Farm

LU7

The Belt

Cricket Ground

Wing Lodge

Mentmore Stud Farm

Mentmore

PH

Home Farm

Mansom

Crafton Stud Farm

Big Wood

Mentmore

Mentmore Park

New Spinney

Crafton Stud

Crafton Lodge

Model Farm

CH

The Belt

HP23

STATION RD

89   90   91

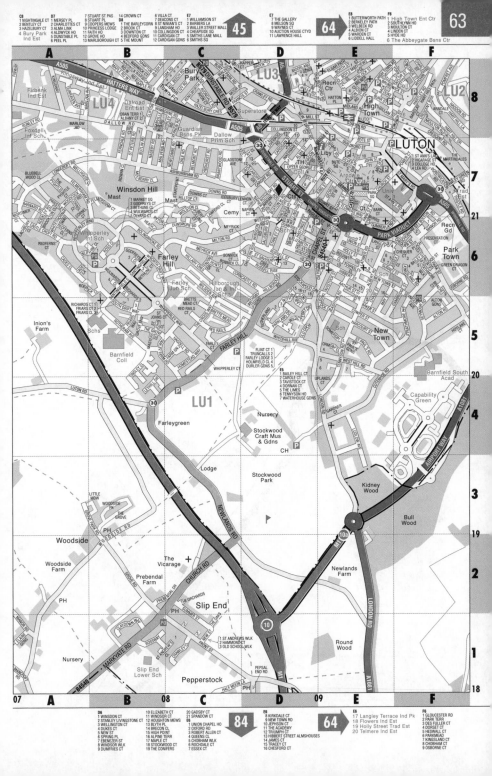

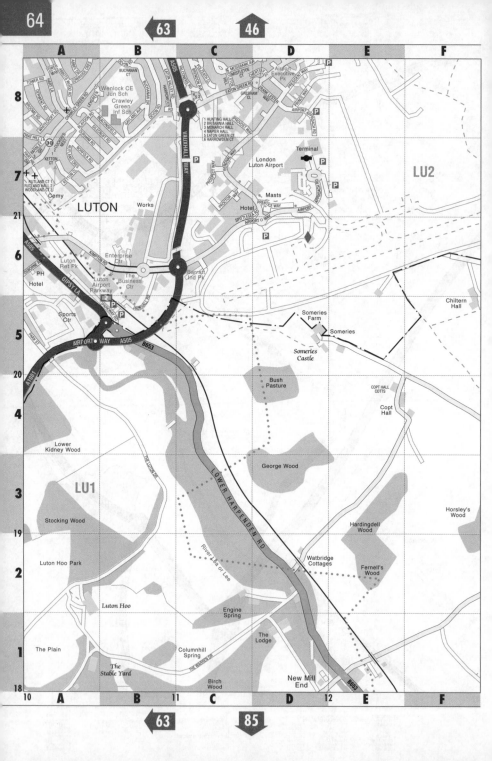

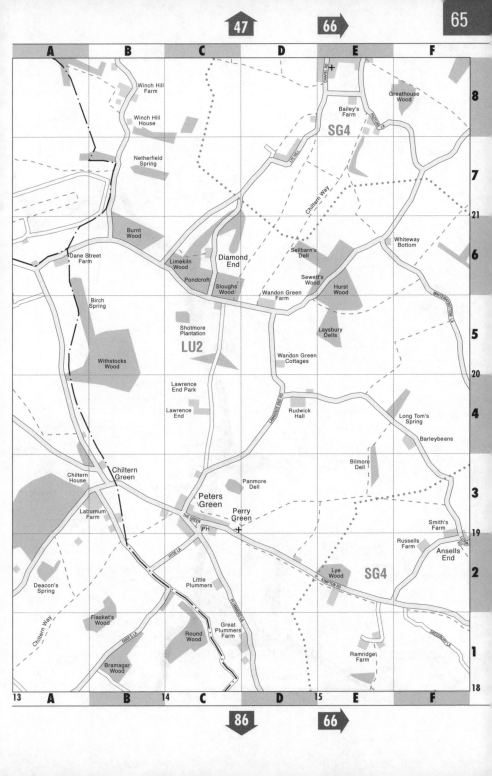

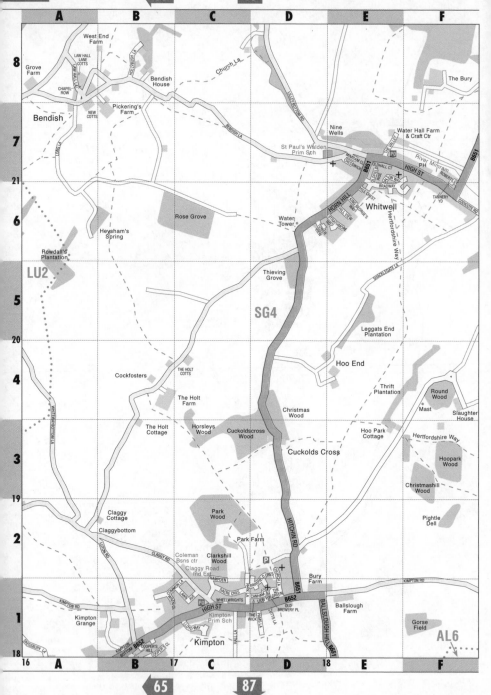

A   B   C   D   E   F

8   Grove Farm   West End Farm   LAW HALL LANE COTTS   Church La.   The Bury

Bendish House

Bendish   NEW COTTS   Pickering's Farm   Nine Wells   Water Hall Farm & Craft Ctr

7   St Paul's Walden Prim Sch   MINRAM CL   River Minram   HIGH ST   B651

CRESSWICK   OLDHALL CT   PO

21   WISH   HORN HILL   TANNERY YD   COCKCOTE RD

6   Rose Grove   Heysham's Spring   Water Tower   Whitwell

Rowdall's Plantation   Thieving Grove   Hertfordshire Way

LU2

5   SG4   BRACKENDALE LA

20   Leggats End Plantation

4   Cockfosters   THE HOLT COTTS   Hoo End

The Holt Farm   Thrift Plantation   Round Wood   Mast   Slaughter House

The Holt Cottage   Horsleys Wood   Cuckoldscross Wood   Christmas Wood   Hoo Park Cottage   Hertfordshire Way

3   Cuckolds Cross   Hoopark Wood

Christmashill Wood

19   Claggy Cottage   Park Wood   Pightle Dell

2   Claggybottom   CLAGGY RD   Park Farm

HITCHIN RD

Coleman Bsns ctr   Clarkshill Wood   Claggy Road Ind Est   HAMPDEN   Bury Farm   KIMPTON RD

KIMPTON RD   WHEELWRIGHTS   B651   B652

1   Kimpton Grange   HIGH ST   Kimpton Prim Sch   OLD BREWERY PL   Ballslough Farm   Gorse Field

LLOYD WAY   THE WICK   BALLSLOUGH HILL B651

18   COOPER'S HILL   Kimpton   AL6

16   A   B   17   C   D   18   E   F

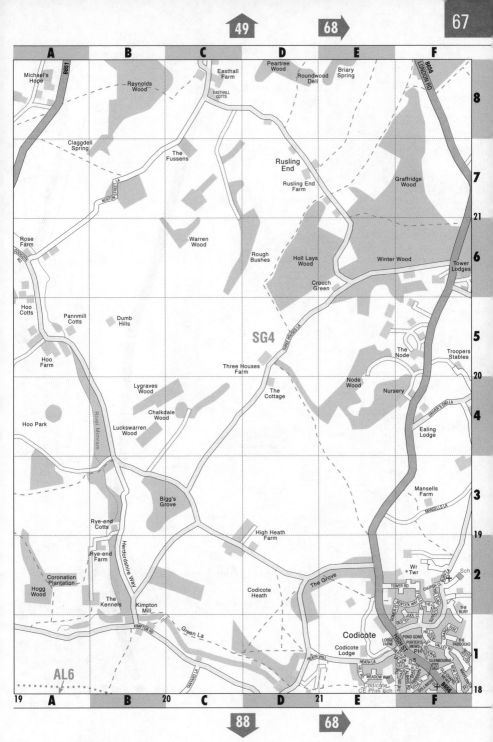

A B C D E F

8

Michael's Hope

B651

B656
LONDON RD

Easthall
Farm

Peartree
Wood

Roundwood
Dell

Briary
Spring

Reynolds
Wood

EASTHALL
COTTS

7

Claggdell
Spring

The
Fussens

Rusling
End

Graffridge
Wood

Rusling End
Farm

NORTON STREET LA

21

Rose
Farm

Warren
Wood

Rough
Bushes

Holl Lays
Wood

Winter Wood

Tower
Lodges

6

CODICOTE RD

SG4

Crouch
Green

Hoo
Cotts

Pannmill
Cotts

Dumb
Hills

THREE HOUSES LA

The
Node

Troopers
Stables

5

Hoo
Farm

Three Houses
Farm

Node
Wood

Nursery

20

Lygraves
Wood

The
Cottage

DRIVER'S END LA

Hoo Park

Chalkdale
Wood

River Mimram

Luckswarren
Wood

Ealing
Lodge

4

Mansells
Farm

3

Bigg's
Grove

MANSELLS LA

Rye-end
Cotts

High Heath
Farm

19

Rye-end
Farm

Hertfordshire Way

Wr
Twr

Sch

2

Coronation
Plantation

The Grove

TOWER RD

Hogg
Wood

The Kennels

Kimpton
Mill

Codicote
Heath

Codicote

AL6

KIMPTON RD

Green La

TEWIN RD LA

Codicote
Lodge

HEATH LA

HEATH HILL

HIGH ST

B656

MEADOW WAY

Codicote
CE Prim Sch

1

18

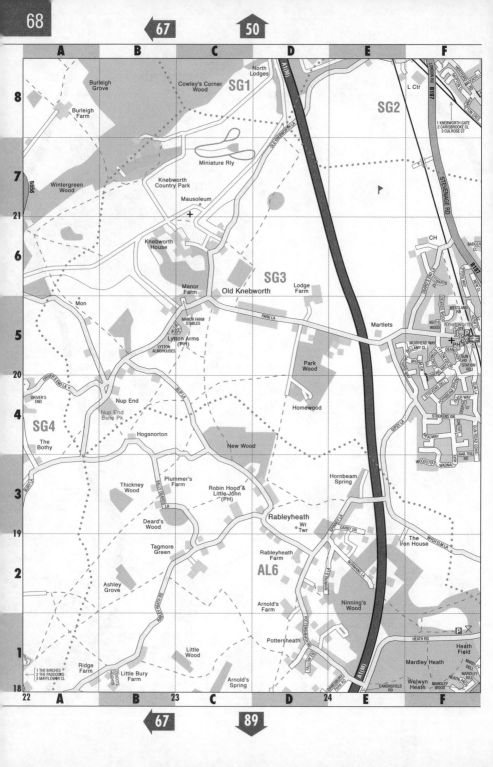

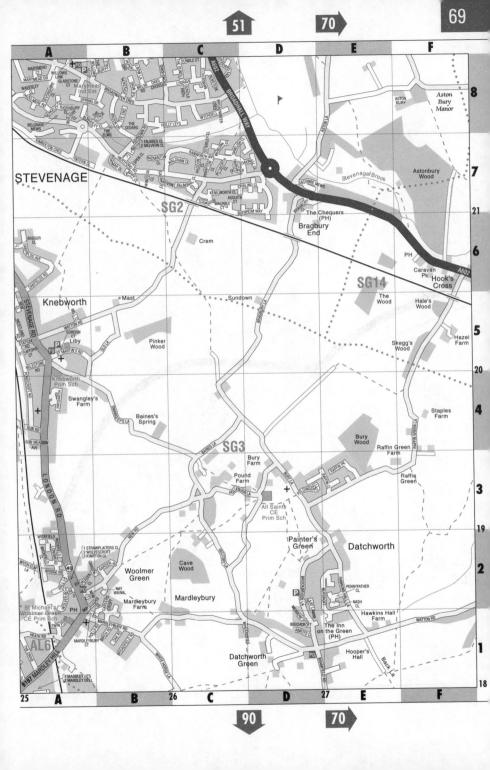

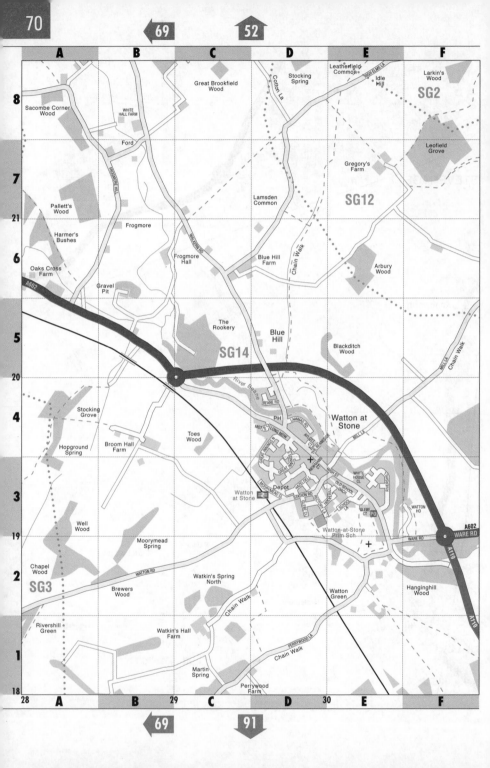

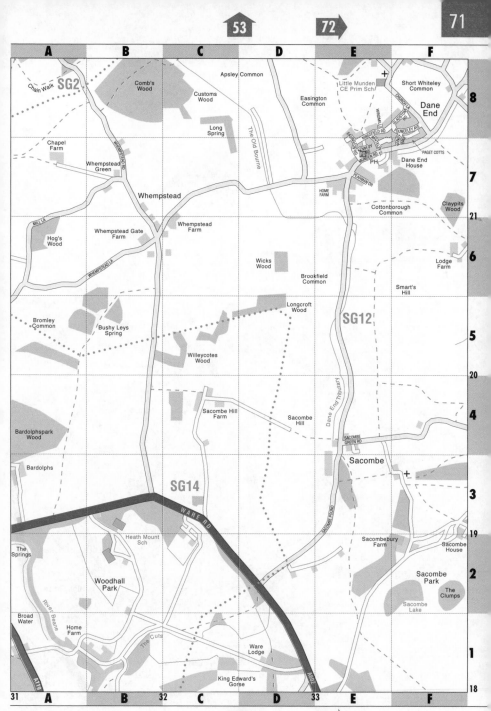

71 54

8

Fullar's Common

Moorfield Common

High Trees Farm

Hatchett Farm

Hatchett Poultry Farm

Beggarman's Wood

BEGGARMAN'S LA

Trenchern Hills

Hill Farm

7

Whitehill Farm

Langton's La

Shelly's Wood

Roughground Wood

21

CH

Cock's Wood

Rigery Farm

6

Potter's Hall Farm

Potter's Green

POTTER'S WOOD CL

Labdens Farm

Black Grove

5

ROWNEY LA

Rowney Priory

Standon Green End Farm

Willowtree Farm

20

Rowney Wood

LOWGATE LA

Knoll Farm

SG12

4

LOWGATE LA

Sacombe Green

Standon Green End

SG11

Mott's Wood

Barwick Tributary

A10

3

Church Wood

Dilly Wood

The Bourne

Salmonsley Wood

LANE END RD

19

Low Wood

Home Wood

2

Home Farm

Gages Wood

MARSHALL'S LA

Marshall's Farm PH

CAMBRIDGE COTTS

Pullar Memorial CE Prim Sch

High Cross

Sutes

1

Furzeground Wood

Marshall's

NORTH LDG

ISCAR CL

PASSFIELD COTTS

Hazelwood Farm

Mark's Wood

Rennesley Garden Wood

Highcross Hill

Gravelpit Wood

A10

SG12

18

71 93

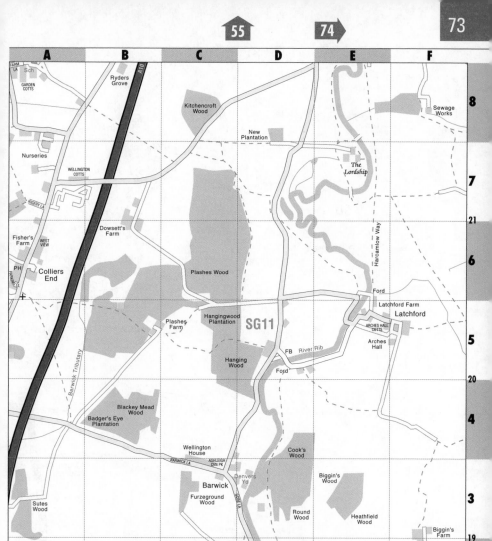

| A | B | C | D | E | F |

8 Sewage Works

FARM LA Sch
GARDEN COTTS
Ryders Grove
Kitchencroft Wood

21

Nurseries
WELLINGTON COTTS
New Plantation
The Lordship

7

RIGERY LA
Dowsett's Farm
Harcamlow Way

6
Fisher's Farm
WEST VIEW
Plashes Wood
Ford
Latchford Farm
Latchford

PH
PH
Colliers End
+

Plashes Farm
Hangingwood Plantation
SG11
ARCHES HALL COTTS
Arches Hall

5

Barwick Tributary
Hanging Wood
FB River Rib
Ford

20

Blackey Mead Wood
Badger's Eye Plantation

4

Wellington House
BARWICK LA
ASHLEIGH CVN PK
Cook's Wood
Biggin's Wood

Denvers Yd
Barwick
Furzeground Wood
Round Wood
Heathfield Wood

3

Sutes Wood
Biggin's Farm

19

Barwick Ford
Great Barwick

Ash Plantation
Tyler's Hill
Little Barwick Farm
New Plantation
Gutteridge Lye
SG10

2

Great Southey Wood
Harcamlow Way
Round Wood
Sawtrees Wood

Aldeck Spring
SG12
Steere Wood
Rush Green

1

18

| A | B | C | D | E | F |

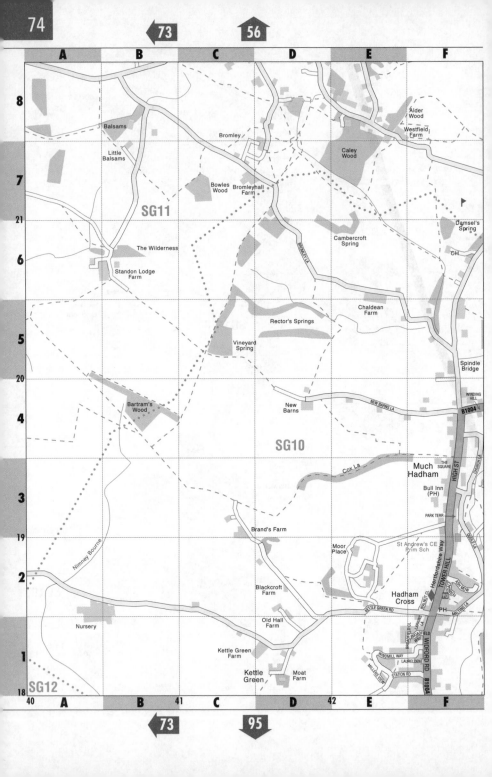

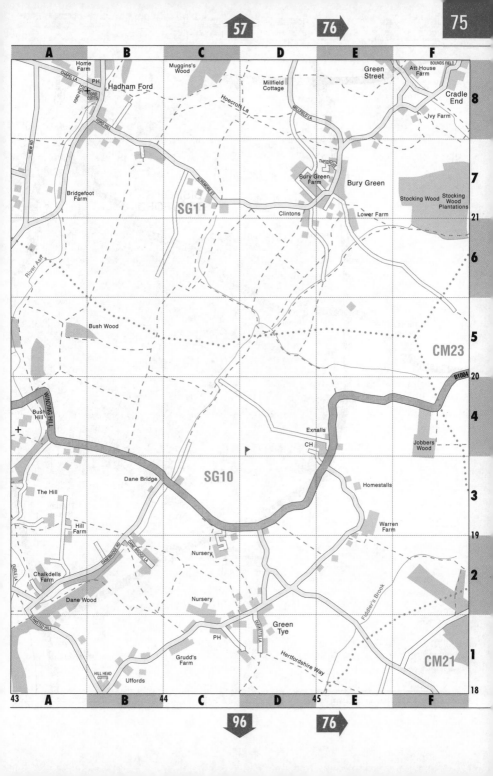

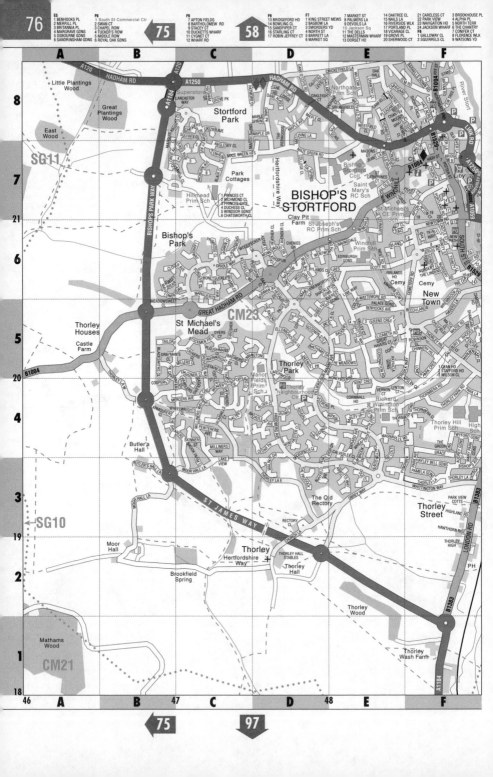

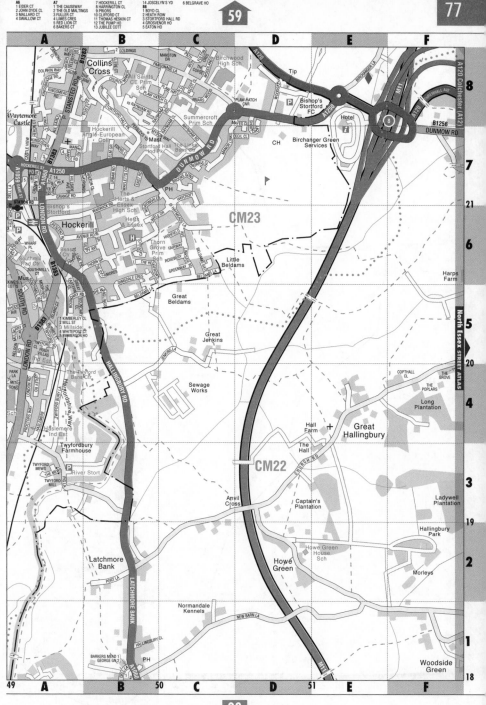

A6	A7	7 HOCKERILL CT	14 JOSCELYN'S YD	6 BELGRAVE HO
1 EIDER CT	1 THE CAUSEWAY	8 HARRINGTON CL	B8	
2 JOHN DYDE CL	2 THE OLD MALTINGS	9 PRIORS	1 BOYD CL	
3 MALLARD CT	3 FULLER CT	10 CLIFFORD CT	2 HEATH ROW	
4 SWALLOW CT	4 LIMES CRES	11 THOMAS HESKIN CT	3 STORTFORD HALL RD	
	5 RED LION CT	12 THE PUMP HO	4 GROSVENOR HO	
	6 BAKERS CT	13 JUBILEE COTT	5 EATON HO	

CM23

CM22

North Essex STREET ATLAS

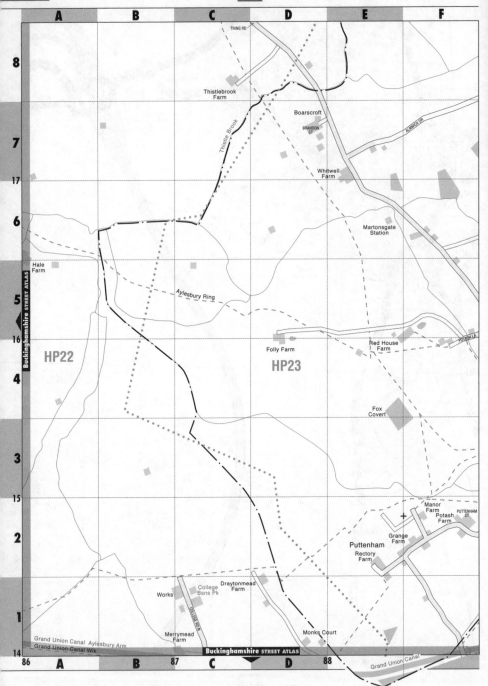

60

A   B   C   D   E   F

8

7

17

6

5

16

4

3

15

2

1

14

86   A   B   87   C   D   88   E   F

Buckinghamshire STREET ATLAS

TRING RD

Thistlebrook
Farm

Thistle Brook

Boarscroft

BRANDON
CT

ALNWICK DR

Whitwell
Farm

Martonsgate
Station

Hale
Farm

Aylesbury Ring

HP22

HP23

Folly Farm

Red House
Farm

POTASH LA

Fox
Covert

Manor
Farm

Potash
Farm

PUTTENHAM
CT

Grange
Farm

Puttenham

Rectory
Farm

Works

College
Bsns Pk

Draytonmead
Farm

COLLEGE RD

Monks Court

Merrymead
Farm

Grand Union Canal Aylesbury Arm
Grand Union Canal Wlk

Buckinghamshire STREET ATLAS

Grand Union Canal

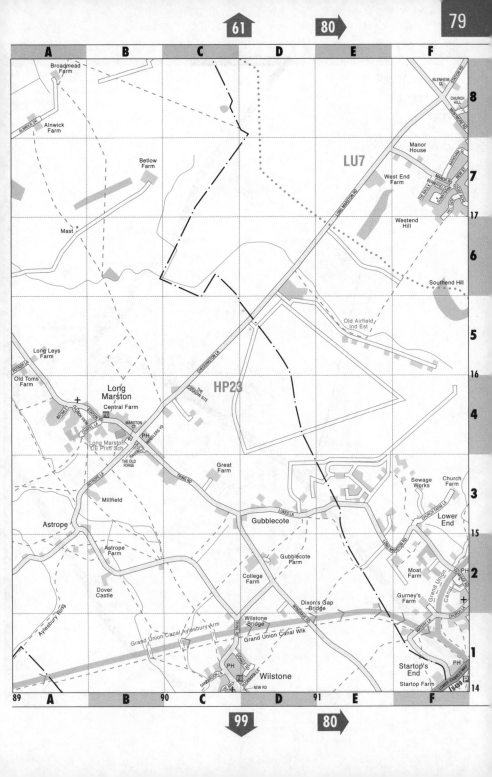

Bedfordshire STREET ATLAS

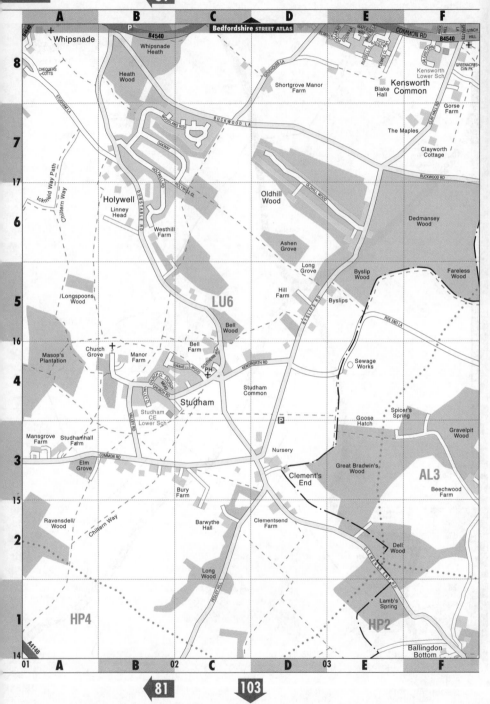

Bedfordshire STREET ATLAS

8

Whipsnade

CHEQUERS
COTTS

Whipsnade
Heath

Heath
Wood

B4540

Shortgrove Manor
Farm

COMMON RD

B4540

LYNCH
HILL

KICK HILL

GREENACRES
CVN PK

Kensworth
Lower Sch

Blake
Hall

Kensworth
Common

7

BUCKWOOD LA

WOODLAND RISE

OAKWAY

The Maples

Gorse
Farm

Clayworth
Cottage

BUCKWOOD RD

17

Holywell

Linney
Head

Westhill
Farm

Oldhill
Wood

OLDHILL WOOD

Dedmansey
Wood

6

Ashen
Grove

Long
Grove

Byslip
Wood

Fareless
Wood

5

Longspoons
Wood

LU6

Bell
Wood

Hill
Farm

Byslips

B5 SI2 7E RD

ROE END LA

16

Mason's
Plantation

Church
Grove

Manor
Farm

Bell
Farm

SWANELLS WOOD

KENSWORTH RD

Sewage
Works

4

Studham
Common

CHURCH RD

MEAD
C OF E CHURCH

VALLEY RD

PH

Studham

Spicer's
Spring

Gravelpit
Wood

Mansgrove
Farm

Studhamhall
Farm

Studham
CE
Lower Sch

VALLEY RD

Goose
Hatch

AL3

Beechwood
Farm

3

Elm
Grove

COMMON RD

Nursery

Clement's
End

Great Bradwin's
Wood

15

Bury
Farm

2

Ravensdell
Wood

Chiltern Way

Barwythe
Hall

Clementsend
Farm

Dell
Wood

1

HP4

Long
Wood

PEGLEY HILL

CLEMENTS END RD

Lamb's
Spring

HP2

14

A4146

Ballingdon
Bottom

01   A   B   02   C   D   03   E   F

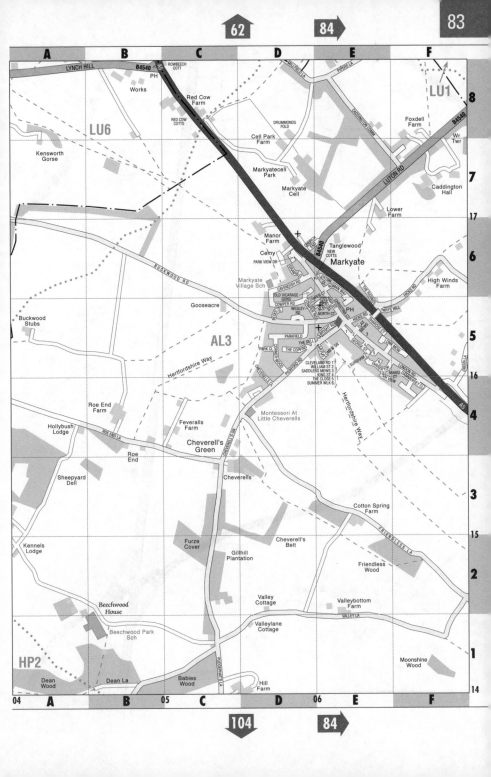

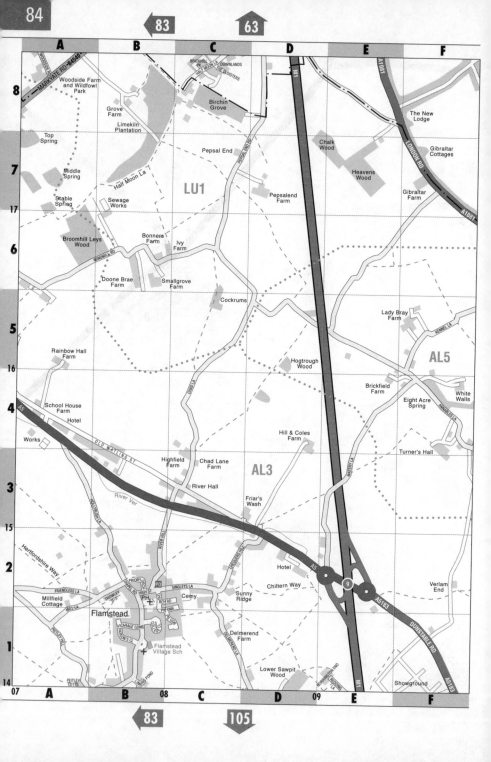

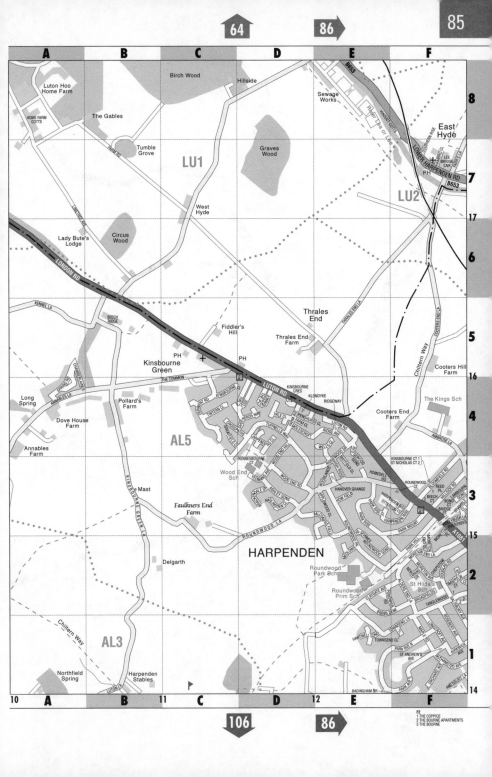

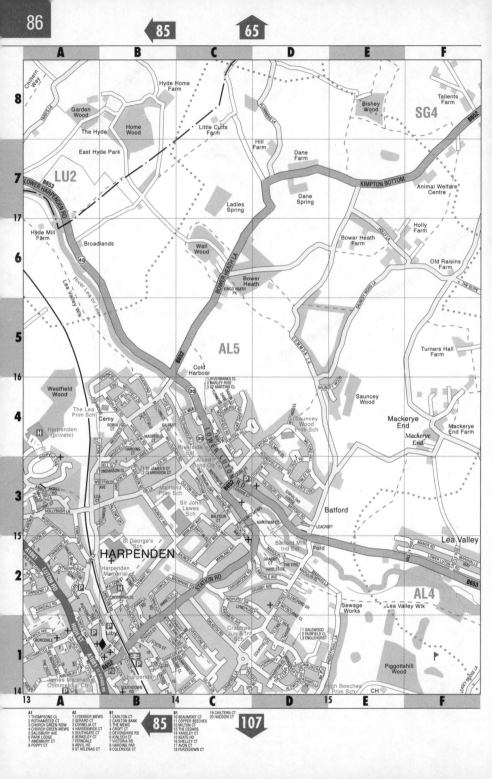

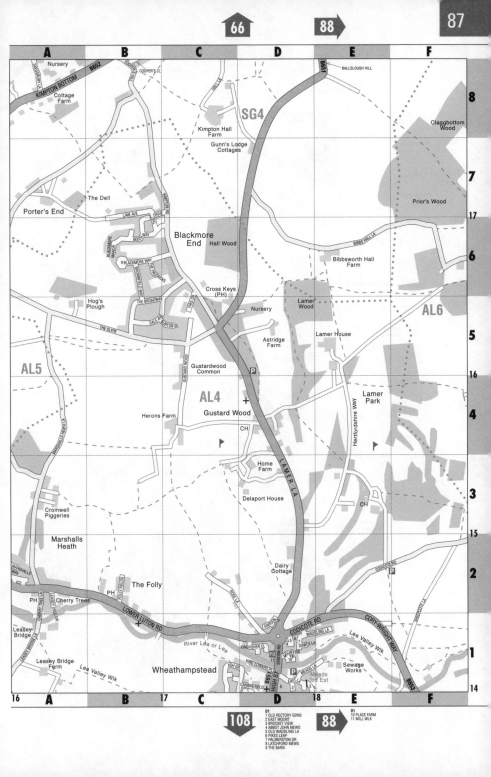

D1
1 OLD RECTORY GDNS
2 EAST MOUNT
3 BROCKET VIEW
4 ABBOT JOHN MEWS
5 OLD WADDLING LA
6 PIKES LEAP
7 PALMERSTON DR
8 LATCHFORD MEWS
9 THE BARN

D1
10 PLACE FARM
11 MILL WLK

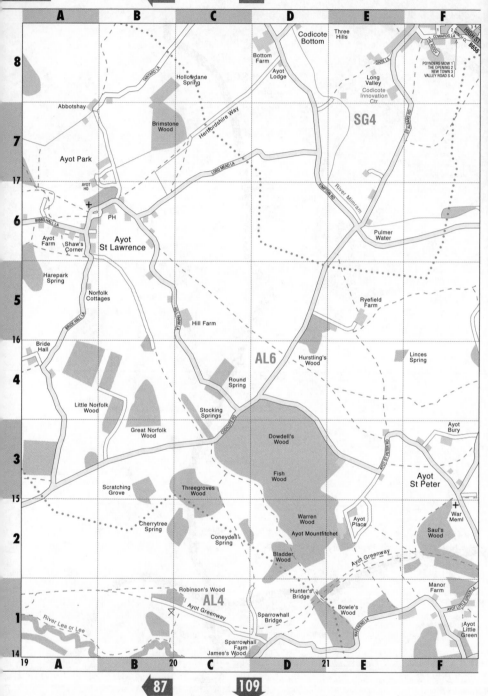

87
67

A B C D E F

8

Codicote
Bottom

Three
Hills

HIGH ST

B656

COWARDS LA

POYNDERS MDW 1
THE OPENING 2
NEW TOWN 3
VALLEY ROAD S 4

DARK LA

Bottom
Farm

Ayot
Lodge

Hollowdane
Spring

TANYARD LA

Long
Valley
Codicote
Innovation
Ctr

Abbotshay

Brimstone
Wood

Hertfordshire Way

7

SG4

ST ALBANS RD

Ayot Park

LORD MEAD LA

17

River Mimram

AYOT
HO

KIMPTON RD

PH

6

BIBBS HALL LA

Ayot
St Lawrence

Pulmer
Water

Ayot
Farm

Shaw's
Corner

Harepark
Spring

Norfolk
Cottages

Ryefield
Farm

5

HILL FARM LA

Hill Farm

BRIDE HALL LA

16

Bride
Hall

AL6

Hurstling's
Wood

Linces
Spring

4

Little Norfolk
Wood

Round
Spring

Great Norfolk
Wood

Stocking
Springs

CODICOTE RD

Dowdell's
Wood

Ayot
Bury

3

Scratching
Grove

Threegroves
Wood

Fish
Wood

AYOT ST PETER RD

Ayot
St Peter

War
Meml

15

Cherrytree
Spring

Coneydell
Spring

Warren
Wood

Ayot Mountfitchet

Ayot
Place

Saul's
Wood

2

Bladder
Wood

Ayot Greenway

Manor
Farm

Robinson's Wood

AL4

Hunter's
Bridge

Bowle's
Wood

WATERS LANE

AYOT LITTLE GREEN LA

1

Ayot Greenway

Sparrowhall
Bridge

Ayot
Little
Green

River Lea or Lee

Sparrowhall
Farm
James's Wood

14

19 A B 20 C D 21 E F

87
109

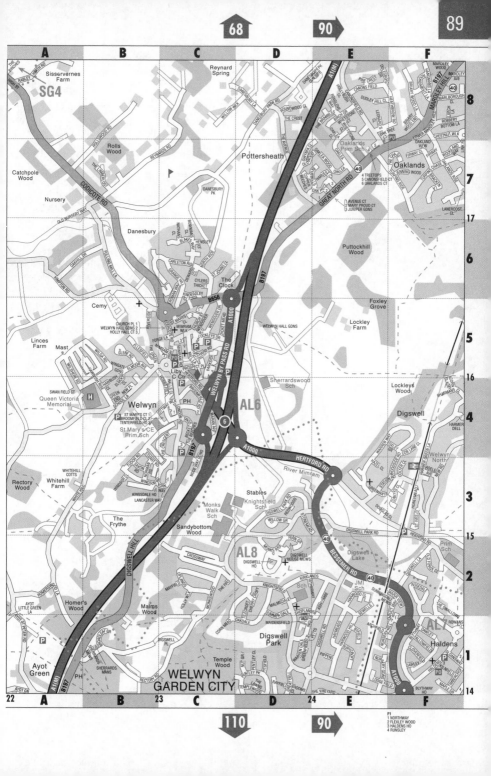

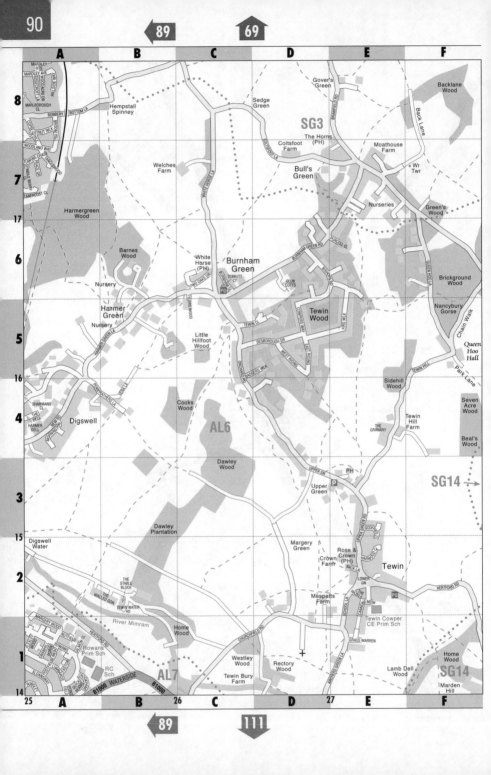

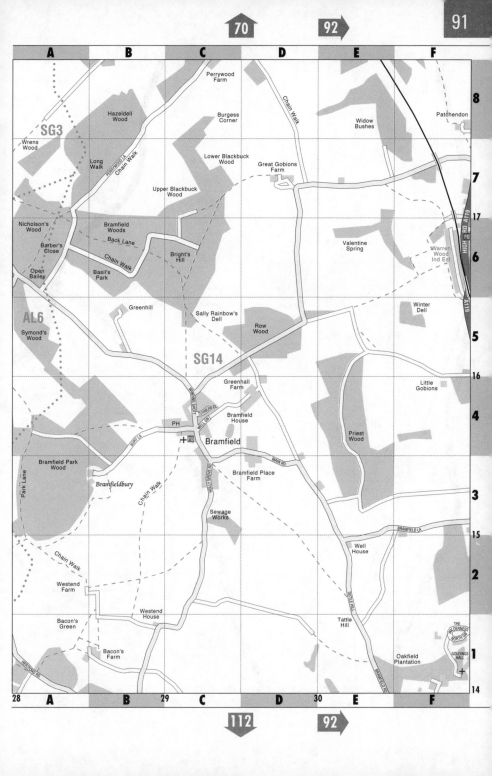

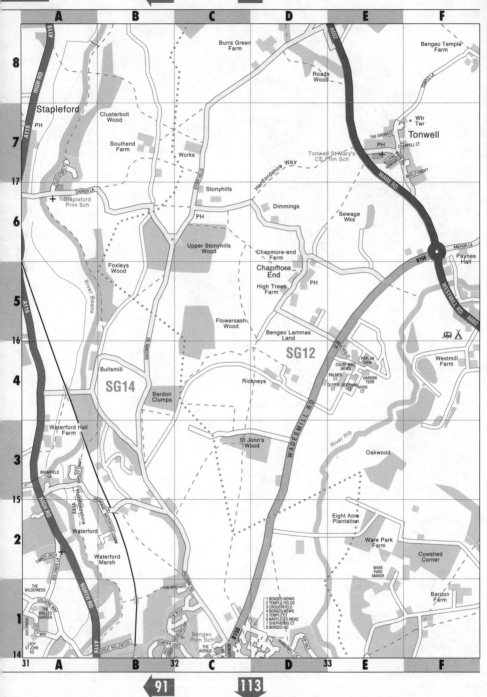

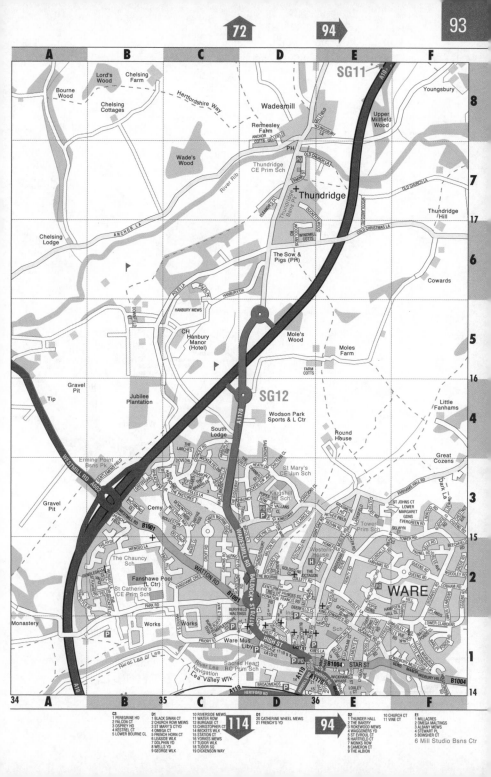

SG11

Youngsbury

Lord's Wood
Chelsing Farm
Bourne Wood
Chelsing Cottages
Hertfordshire Way
Wadesmill
Upper Millfield Wood

Wade's Wood
Renmesley Farm
Thundridge CE Prim Sch
Thundridge
Thundridge Hill

Chelsing Lodge
ANCHOR LA
River Rib
WINDMILL COTTS
COLD CHRISTMAS LA

17

The Sow & Pigs (PH)
Cowards

Chelsing Lodge

6

HANBURY MEWS
CH Hanbury Manor (Hotel)
Mole's Wood
Moles Farm

FARM COTTS

5

16

Tip
Gravel Pit
Jubilee Plantation
SG12
Wodson Park Sports & L Ctr
Little Fanhams

4

Gravel Pit
Ermine Point Bsns Pk
South Lodge
Round House
Great Cozens

St Mary's CE Jun Sch

3

WESTMILL RD
A602
Cemy
The Lanches
Kingshill Inf Sch
St Johns Ct
Lower Margaret Gdns
Evergreen Rd
Selwyn
Tower Prim Sch

15

The Chauncy Sch
St Catherine's CE Prim Sch
Fanshawe Pool (L Ctr)
Western House
The Octagon
H

WARE

2

Monastery
Works
Works
PARK RD
Ware Mus
Liby
Buryfield Maltings
Sacred Heart RC Prim Sch
HIGH ST
STAR ST
B1004

Kibes La

River Lea or Lee
River Lea Navigation
Lea Valley Wlk
HERTFORD RD
A119
LOXLEY
B1004

1

14

A **B** **C** **D** **E** **F**

8

HOME FARM
YOUNGSBURY

Hanley
Spring

Goss
Covert

Sawtrees
Farm

Halfyards
Common

The
Arboretum

Harecroft
Brow

Burleigh
Common

Castlebury
Farm

Nursery

Fabdens

7

River Rib

Timber
Hall

OLD CHURCH LA

MEADOWS VIEW
COTTS

17

COLD CHRISTMAS LA

Cold
Christmas

Buckney
Wood

Hertfordshire Way

Baker's
End

Swangles
Farm

6

Nimney
Wood

Ashridge
Common

Harcamlow Way

Legges
Cottage

Appleton
Green

Cook's
Farm

5

*New Hall
Farm*

ABBOTTSFIELD
COTTS

Hogtrough
La

SG12

Milletts

Newhall
Green

Babbs
Green

APPLETON LA

WADESMILL RD

HELHAM
GN

SCHOLAR'S
HILL

16

Noah's
Ark

COANWOOD
COTTS

Nimney Bourne

4

FANHAMS
HALL

Fanhams
Grange

Long La

Wareside

RED LION
YD

HIGHFIELD
COTTS

B1004

LABURNHAM
COTTS

FANHAMS
HALL

Reeves
Green

THE CRUFT

White Horse
(PH)

The
Lodge

Morley
Ponds

Wareside CE
Prim Sch

3

ASH RD

Priors Wood
Prim Sch

Morley
Hall

Newhouse
Farm

GREENFIELD RD

BEACON RD

Swades
Farm

15

ELMS RD

Wood La

Newhole
Farm

Mardocks
Mill

2

THE VINEYARD

Butlers
Hall

1

WIDBURY
HO

Priorswood
Cottages

Watersplace
Farm

Ford

Young
Wood

River Ash

Mardocks
Farm

Harcamlow Way

B1004 WIDBURY HILL

Brokengall
Hill

14

37 **A** **38** **B** **C** **D** **39** **E** **F**

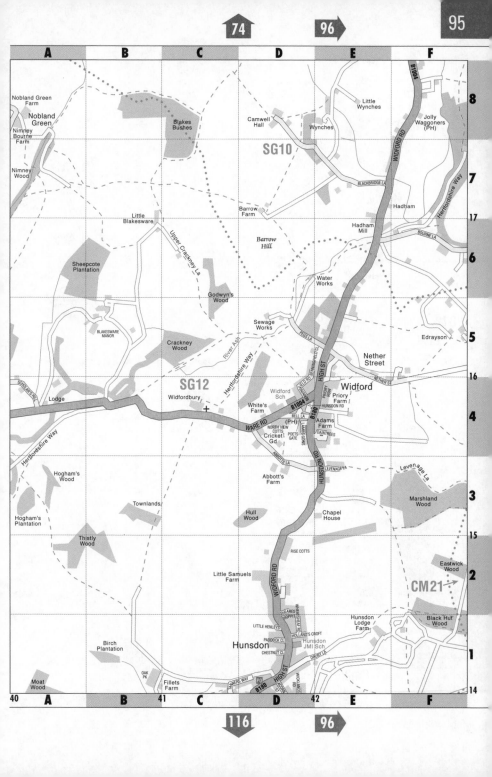

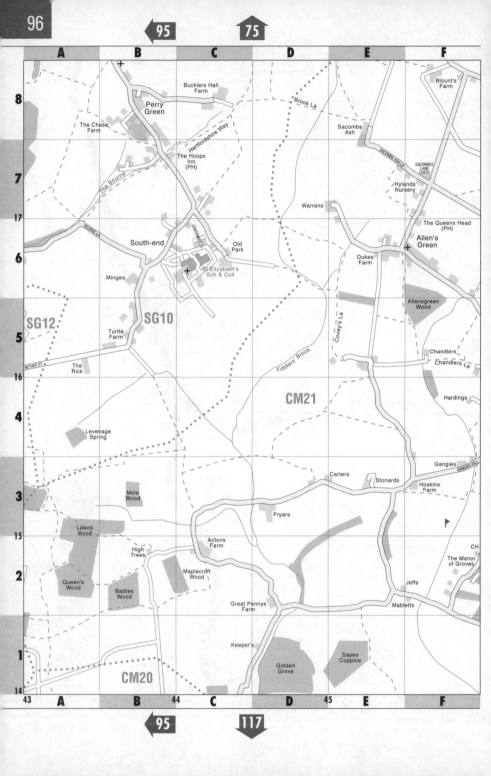

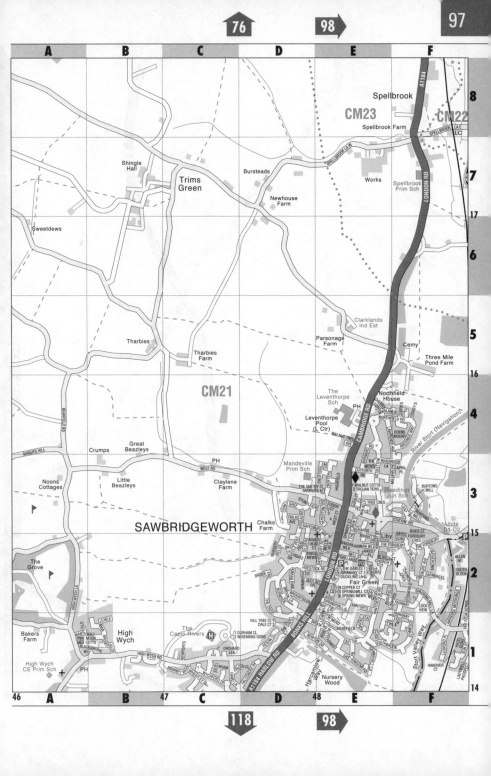

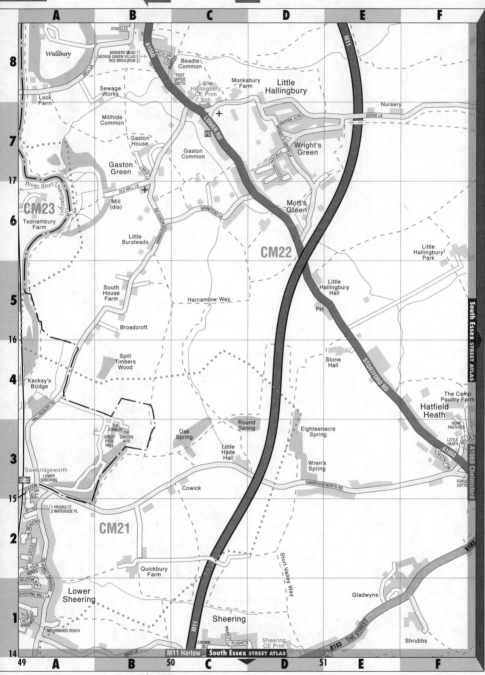

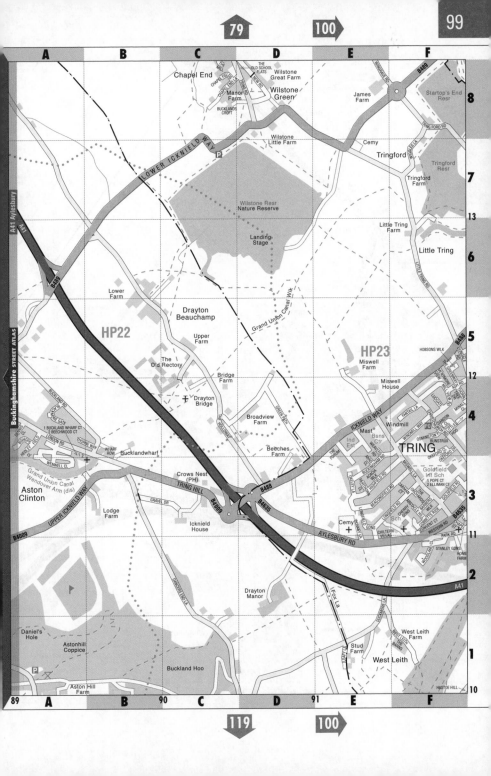

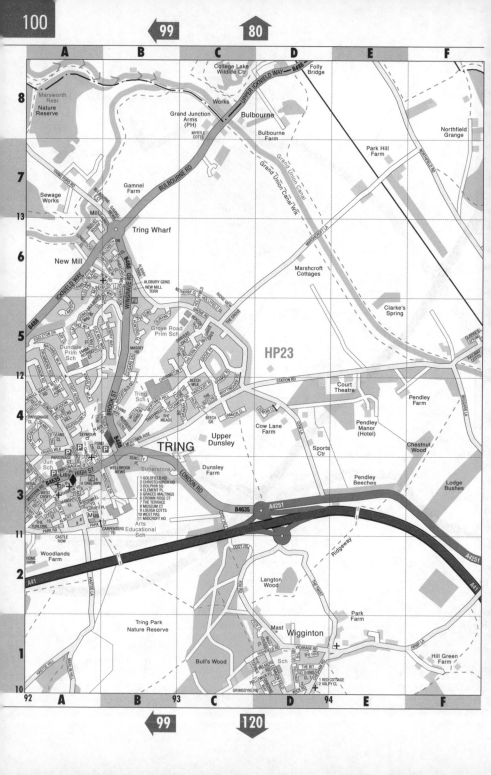

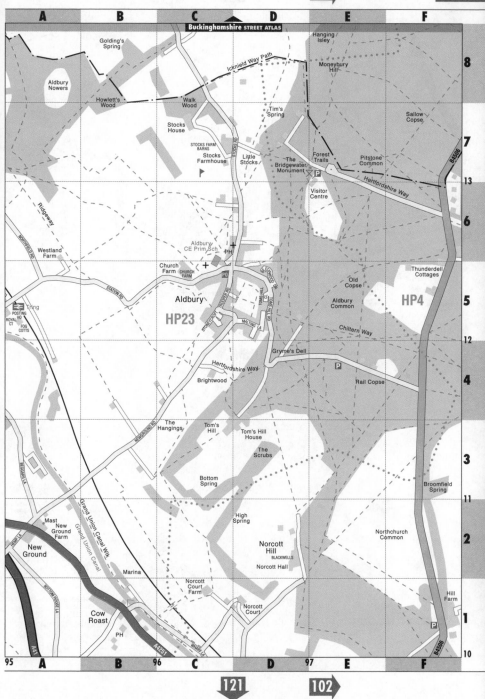

Buckinghamshire STREET ATLAS

Golding's Spring

Aldbury Nowers

Howlett's Wood

Walk Wood

Stocks House

STOCKS FARM BARNS

Stocks Farmhouse

Little Stocks

Tim's Spring

Icknield Way Path

Hanging Isley

Moneybury Hill

Sallow Copse

Forest Trails

The Bridgewater Monument

Pitstone Common

Hertfordshire Way

Visitor Centre

Ridgeway

Westland Farm

NORTHFIELD RD

Aldbury CE Prim Sch
PH

Church Farm

CHURCH FARM

PO

STATION RD

Tring

POSTING HO
ROYAL
CT

FOG COTTS

Aldbury

HP23

MALTING LA

Old Copse

Aldbury Common

Thunderdell Cottages

HP4

Chiltern Way

Gryme's Dell

Hertfordshire Way

Brightwood

Rail Copse

NEWGROUND RD

The Hangings

Tom's Hill

Tom's Hill House

The Scrubs

Broomfield Spring

Bottom Spring

High Spring

Norcott Hill

BLACKWELLS

Norcott Hall

Northchurch Common

Mast
New Ground Farm

New Ground

Grand Union Canal Wlk

Grand Union Canal

Marina

Norcott Court Farm

Norcott Court

BISGRAVE LA

BOTTOM HOUSE LA

A41

Cow Roast

PH

A4251

Hill Farm

B4506

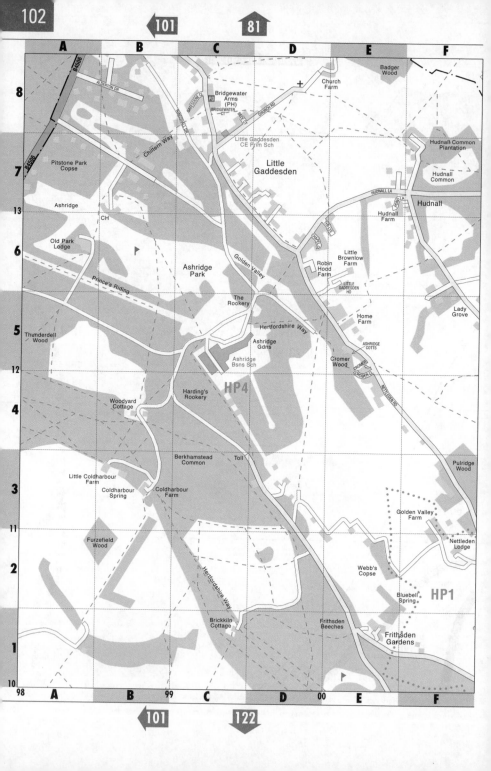

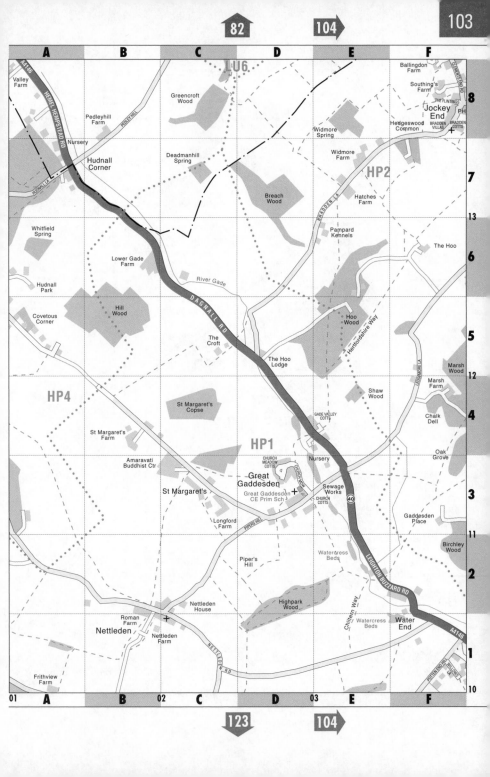

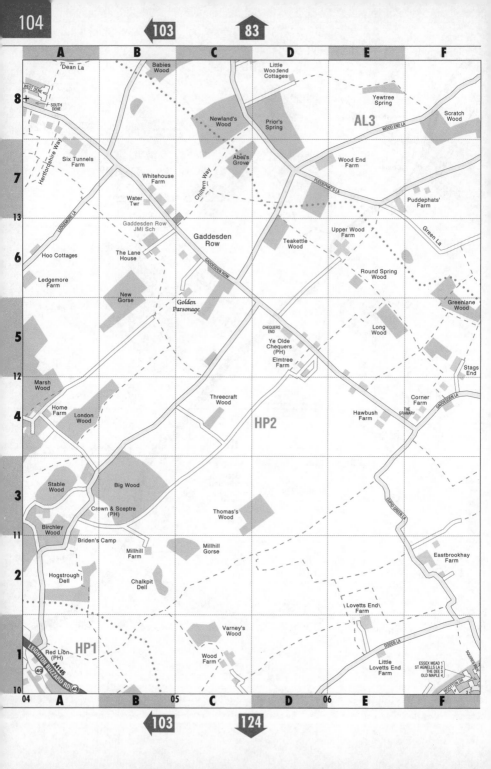

103
83

Dean La

Babies Wood

Little Woodend Cottages

Yewtree Spring

Scratch Wood

WEST DENE
SOUTH DENE

Newland's Wood

Prior's Spring

AL3

Hertfordshire Way

Six Tunnels Farm

Whitehouse Farm

Chiltern Way

Abel's Grove

Wood End Farm

PUDDEPHAT'S LA

Water Twr

Puddephats' Farm

Green La

LEIGHTON LA

Gaddesden Row JMI Sch

Gaddesden Row

Teakettle Wood

Upper Wood Farm

Hoo Cottages

The Lane House

GADDESDEN ROW

Round Spring Wood

Greenlane Wood

Ledgemore Farm

New Gorse

Golden Parsonage

CHEQUERS END

Ye Olde Chequers (PH)

Long Wood

Stags End

Elmtree Farm

Marsh Wood

Threecraft Wood

HP2

Hawbush Farm

Corner Farm

THE GRANARY

GADDESDEN LA

Home Farm

London Wood

Stable Wood

Big Wood

Crown & Sceptre (PH)

Thomas's Wood

CAPEL GREEN LA

Birchley Wood

Briden's Camp

Millhill Farm

Millhill Gorse

Eastbrookhay Farm

Hogstrough Dell

Chalkpit Dell

Varney's Wood

Lovetts End Farm

HP1

Red Lion (PH)

LEIGHTON BUZZARD RD

A4146

Wood Farm

DODDS LA

Little Lovetts End Farm

ESSEX MEAD 1
ST AGNELLS LA 2
THE DEE 3
OLD MAPLE 4.

WOOTTON DR

SQUIRES RIDE

04
05
06

103
124

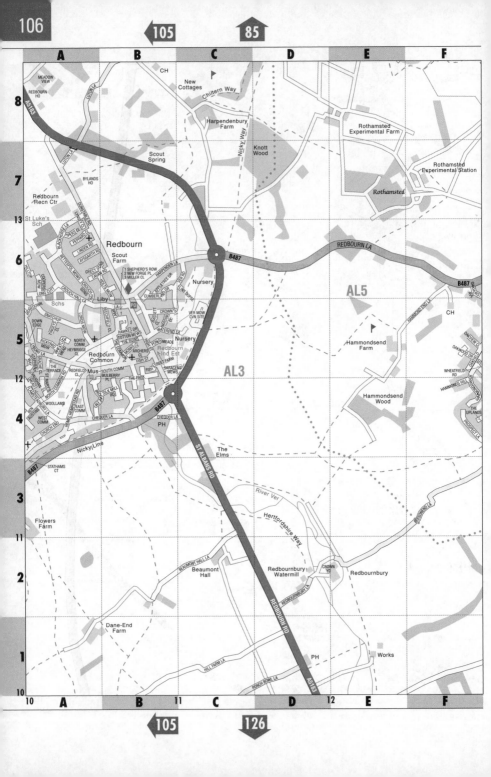

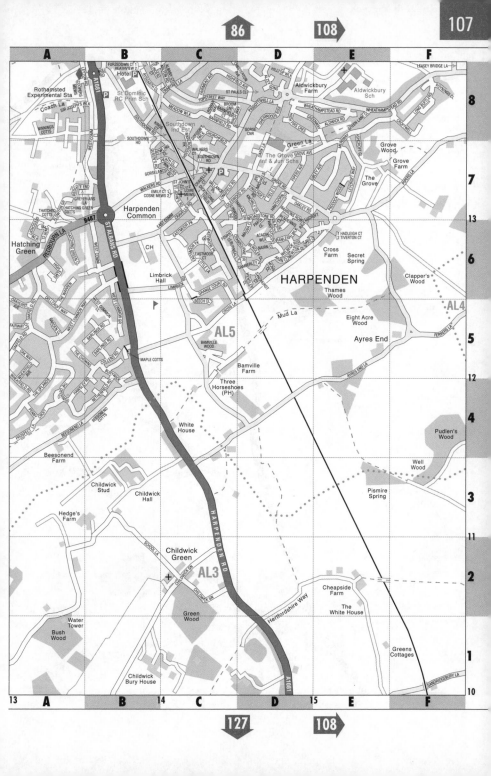

107
87

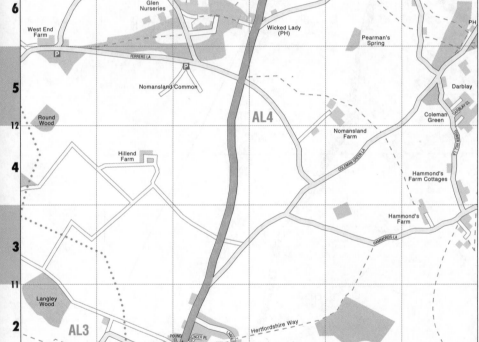

A · B · C · D · E · F

8

Wheathampstead Rd
Pipers La
CH
AL5
Pipers

Down Green House
Harpenden Rd
Amwell La

Lea Valley Wlk
Old Rectory Gdns 2
Thomas Sparrow Ho 3
Brewhouse Hill
Lettuce Barton Rd
Wick Ave
Matlings Dr
Butterfield Rd
Hilltop View
High Ash Rd

Bury La
Church St
St Thomas
Granary Cl
The Hill
B651
Town
Four Limes
Walnut Ct
Offas Way
Caesars Rd
Saxon Rd
Riddie's Rd
Housden Cl
Smallwood Cl
Lamb Ct
Wright Cl
Vale Ct
Ovys Cl
Hill Dyke Rd
Beech Cres
Garrard Way
Tudor Rd
Battlefield
Marford Rd

Prim Sch
Liby
Sch

Marford Farm
The Nelson (PH)
Fort-Wright Way
B653

Belgic Oppidum

7
Little Piggotts Wood
Amwell
The Elephant & Castle (PH)
Down Green La
13
Stocking Wood
Bull La
Amwell La

PH
Nomansland
Glen Nurseries

Wicked Lady (PH)
Beech Hyde Farm
Cherry La

PH
Pearman's Spring

6
West End Farm
P
Ferrers La
P
Nomansland Common

5
AL4
Nomansland Farm
Coleman Green La

Darblay
Coleman Green
Darblay Cl
Oliver Hill
PH

12
Round Wood

4
Hillend Farm
Hammond's Farm Cottages
Hammond's Farm
Hammonds La

3

11
Langley Wood
AL3
Sandridgebury La

2
Hertfordshire Way
Pound Cl
High St
Spencer Pl
Langley End
Langley Gr
Sweetbriar
Lyndon Mead
Sandridge Sch
Fairshot Ct
Harlowdell Spring

The Green Man (PH)
Sandridgebury
Sandridgebury Farm
Church End
Giles Cl
B651
Sch
Cemy
St Leonards Cres
House La
Harefield
Woodcock Hill
Mast
Fairfolds

1
Northside
Royance Cres
Highfield Rd
B651
Reynolds Cres
Sandridge
Bessey La
Fairfold's Farm

10
16 · A · B · 17 · C · D · 18 · E · F

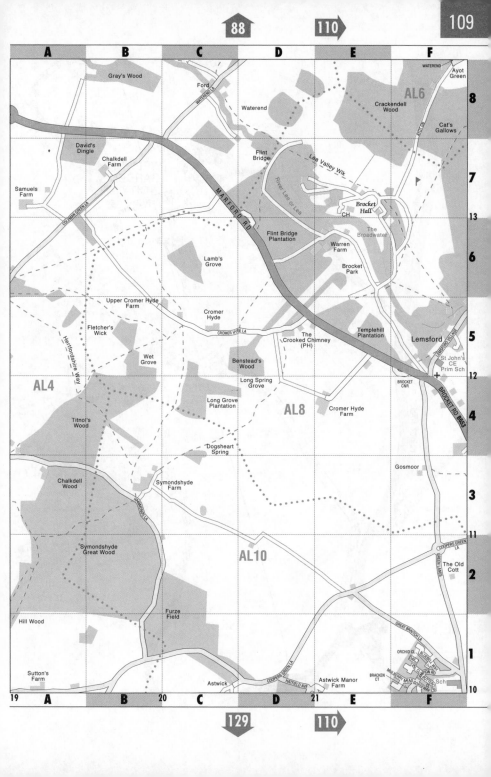

Map labels

Column markers (top): A B C D E F

Grid / page references (right side): 8, 13, 6, 5, 12, 4, 3, 11, 2, 1, 10

WATEREND
Ayot Green
AL6
Gray's Wood
Ford
Crackendell Wood
Waterend
Cat's Gallows
David's Dingle
AYOT DR
Chalkdell Farm
Flint Bridge
Lea Valley Wlk
Samuels Farm
River Lee or Lea
Brocket Hall
CH
COLEMAN GREEN LA
MARFORD RD
Flint Bridge Plantation
The Broadwater
Lamb's Grove
Warren Farm
Brocket Park
Upper Cromer Hyde Farm
Cromer Hyde
Templehill Plantation
Lemsford
Fletcher's Wick
CROMER HYDE LA
LEMSFORD VILLAGE
St John's CE Prim Sch
Hertfordshire Way
The Crooked Chimney (PH)
Wet Grove
AL4
Benstead's Wood
BROCKET CNR
Long Spring Grove
Titnol's Wood
Long Grove Plantation
AL8
Cromer Hyde Farm
BROCKET RD B653
Dogsheart Spring
Gosmoor
Chalkdell Wood
Symondshyde Farm
COOPERS GREEN LA
HAMMONDS LA
GREEN LANES
The Old Cott
Symondshyde Great Wood
AL10
GREAT BRAUGH LA
Furze Field
ORCHID CL
Hill Wood
BRACKEN CT
MULBERRY MEAD
Sutton's Farm
Astwick
COOPERS GREEN LA
HATFIELD AVE
Astwick Manor Farm
Sch

Column markers (bottom): A B C D E F

Numbers (bottom): 19, 20, 21

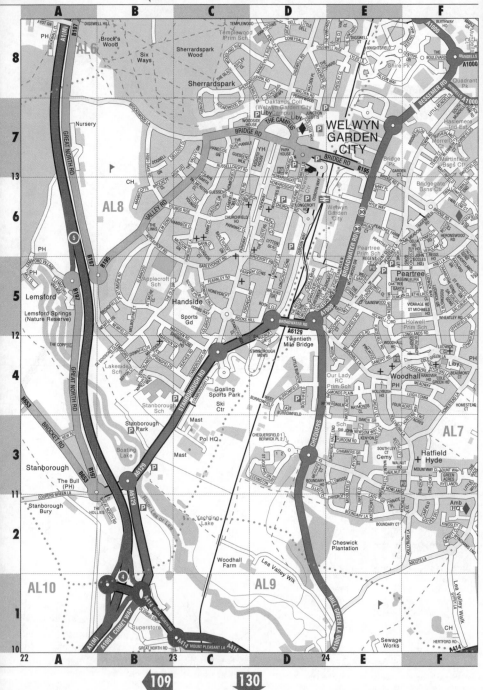

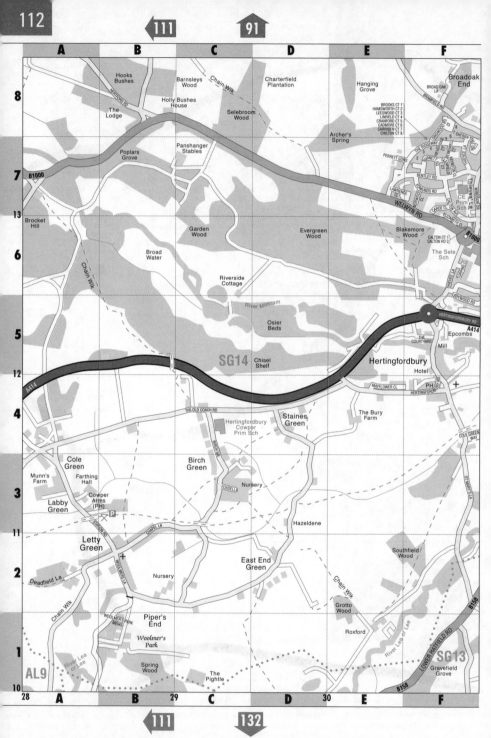

111
91

	A	B	C	D	E	F

8

Hooks Bushes

Barnsleys Wood

Chain Wlk

Charterfield Plantation

Hanging Grove

Broadoak End

BROAD OAK LA

BROOKS CT 1
HAMSWORTH CT 2
LEESWOOD CT 3
LINFIELD CT 4
CRANFORD CT 5
CADMORE CT 6
CARRIDEN CT 7
CHILTON CT 8

Holly Bushes House

The Lodge

Selebroom Wood

Archer's Spring

THE RIDGEWAY

PERRETT GDNS

BARNET

NEWTON CL

7

B1000

Poplars Grove

Panshanger Stables

WELWYN RD

BENTLEY RD

LAWRENCE

EDMUNDS RD

CARDE CL

CE Prim Sch

WINDSOR DR

13

Brocket Hill

Garden Wood

Evergreen Wood

Blakemore Wood

B1000

CALTON CT 1
CALTON HO 2

The Sele Sch

6

Broad Water

Chain Wlk

Riverside Cottage

PIERCE VILLA

DRYWOOD RD

5

River Mimram

Osier Beds

SG14

Chisel Shelf

HERTINGFORDBURY RD

A414

Epcombs

THE COURTYARD

Mill

Hertingfordbury

12

A414

Chisel Shelf

Hotel

MAYFLOWER CL

PH

HERTINGFORD

4

THE OLD COACH RD

Hertingfordbury Cowper Prim Sch

Staines Green

The Bury Farm

COLE GREEN WAY

BIRCH GR

3

Cole Green

Munn's Farm

Farthing Hall

Birch Green

Nursery

Hazeldene

Southfield Wood

ST MARY'S LA

COXDELLS

Labby Green

Cowper Arms (PH)

P

STATION RD

11

Letty Green

CHISEL LA

2

Deadfield La

WOOD MEAD LA

Nursery

East End Green

Chain Wlk

Grotto Wood

Southfield Wood

B158

1

Chain Wlk

WOOLMER'S PARK MEWS

Piper's End

Woolmer's Park

Roxford

River Lea or Lee

LOWER HATFIELD RD

SG13

Gravefield Grove

10

AL9

River Lea or Lee

Spring Wood

The Pightle

B158

	A	B	C	D	E	F

111
132

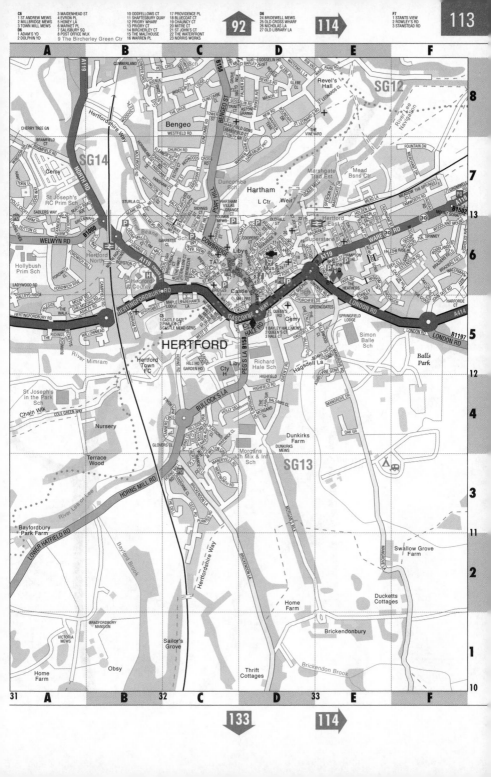

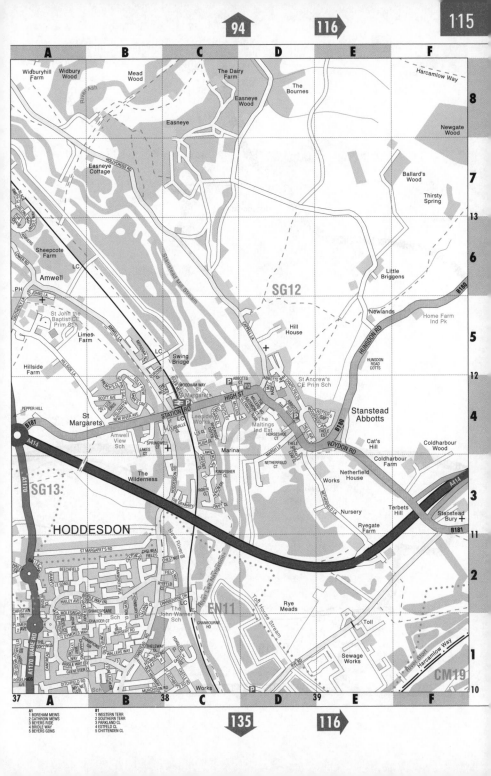

94
116

A B C D E F

8

7

13

6

5

12

4

3

11

2

1

10

Harcamlow Way

Widburyhill Farm
Widbury Wood
Mead Wood
The Dairy Farm
The Bournes
Newgate Wood

River Ash
Easneye Wood
Easneye
Ballard's Wood
Thirsty Spring

Easneye Cottage
HOLLYCROSS RD

Sheepcote Farm
LC
Amwell
PH
JOHNS LA
St John the Baptist CE Prim Sch

Limes Farm
Swing Bridge
Little Briggens
Newlands
Home Farm Ind Pk

SG12

Hillside Farm
Hill House
St Andrew's CE Prim Sch
HUNSDON ROAD COTTS

HUNSDON RD

PEPPER HILL
B181
A414
St Margarets
STATION RD
HIGH ST
Stanstead Abbotts
Cat's Hill
Coldharbour Wood

Amwell View Sch
Leeside Works
The Maltings Ind Est
HORSESHOE CT
Marina
ROYDON RD
Coldharbour Farm

A1170
SG13
The Wilderness
Netherfield CT
NETHERFIELD LA
Netherfield House
Works
Nursery
A414
Terbets Hill
Stanstead Bury
B181

HODDESDON
The Granary
KINGFISHER CL
ROBIN CL
SWIFT CL
Ryegate Farm
B180

ST MARGARET'S RD
CHELSEA FIELDS
CHESTNUT GR
New River Navigation

BEECHFIELD
HAILEY AVE
EN11
The John Warner Sch
CRANBOURNE HO
Rye Meads
Toll

River Lea Navigation

CHRISTIAN
A1170 WARE RD
Sch
Works
Sewage Works
Harcamlow Way
River Stort
CM19
Toll House Stream
RYE RD

135
116

A1
1 BOREHAM MEWS
2 CATHROW MEWS
3 BEYERS RIDE
4 BRIDLE WAY
5 BEYERS GDNS

B1
1 WESTERN TERR
2 SOUTHERN TERR
3 PARKLAND CL
4 ESTFELD CL
5 CHITTENDEN CL

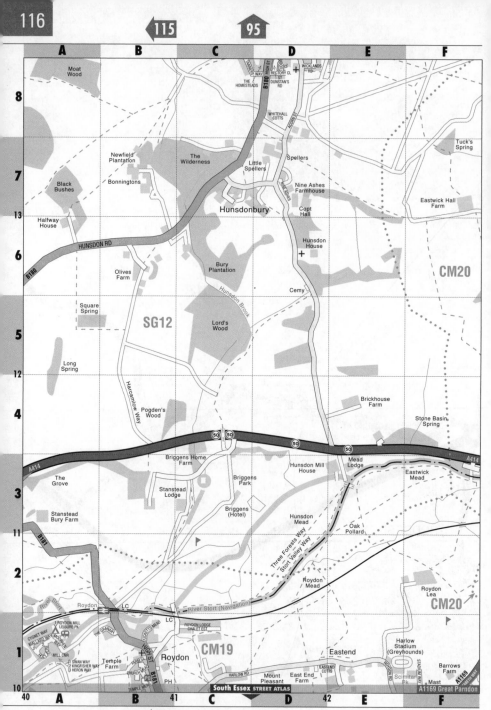

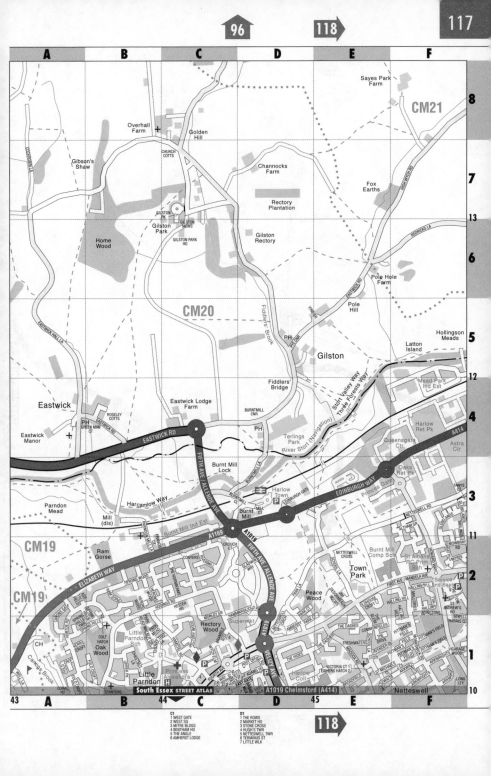

C1
1 WEST GATE
2 WEST SQ
3 MITRE BLDGS
4 BENTHAM HO
5 THE ANGLE
6 AMHERST LODGE

D1
1 THE ROWS
2 MARKET HO
3 STONE CROSS
4 HUGH'S TWR
5 NETTESWELL TWR
6 TERMINUS ST
7 LITTLE WLK

South Essex STREET ATLAS

A1019 Chelmsford (A414)

Netteswell

117 97

	A	B	C	D	E	F

8
Rowney Wood
WYCHFORD DR
Pishiobury Park Walks
Rowney Farm
Harcamlow Way / Three Forests Way
The Osier Bed
CM21
Pishiobury Park
Union Wood
SEYMOUR MEWS
Durrington Hall

7
PH
Rowneybury
River Stort (Navigation)
Stort Valley Way
13
Ashplant
The Italstyle Bldg
RIVERSIDE CT
Aylmers Farm
Redericks Farm
PH
Harlow Mill Bridge
Wyldwood Farm
Gibberd Garden
Princey Brook

6
Maple River Ind Est
WHEAT...
B183
Stort Valley Way / Three Forests Way
River Walk
Sarbir Ind Est
CAMBRIDGE RD
MARRIOTS
Harlowbury
CAMPIONS

5
Harlow Mill
PRIORY AVE
Harlowbury
SHEERING RD
12
A414
Chapel
Temple Fields
EDINBURGH WAY
Ascent Pk
Athena Est
MANOR RD
Harlowbury Prim Sch
DRAKES MDW 1
FITZWILLIAMS CT 2
CHURCH MILL GRANGE 3
GILDEN WAY
South Essex STREET ATLAS

4
A414 MILL HATCH
St James Ctr
Superstore
Shenval Ind Est
STATION RD
JOCELYNS
FAIRCROFT
Old Harlow
COWLINS
MULBERRY GN
FERVINS
GILDEN CL
B183
Churchgate Street
CM20
Astra Ctr
SOUTH LA
MULBERRY TERR
Oakwood Est
BROMLEY LA
Libry
HIGH ST
THE MAYNE
Hotel
Churchgate CE Prim Sch

3
Mark Hall North
STACKFIELD
THE TAWN
PARK HILL
HURST LA
BRUMMELL PL
Sch
L Ctr
Nursery
CM17
St Nicholas Sch
11
Mus
FIRST AVE MANDELA AVE
B183
EAST PK
WALFORDS
Mark Hall Sch
Hubbard's Hall
THE GOWERS
DOVEHOUSE CROFT
Playing Field

2
THE STOW
ORCHARD
Libry
Spinney Jun Schs
Playing Field
Sports Gd
HARLOW
Gravel Pit Spring
Newpond Spring
Hotel
Hubbard's Hall Farm
Roundhouse

1
Mark Hall South
A414
Works
ALEXANDRA RD
MILESTONE RD
HOLLAND WAY
THE CHASE
ALBA...
New Hall Farm
Hubbard's Hall Farm
LADYSHOT

10
Markhall Wood
A414 Chelmsford
South Essex STREET ATLAS
Brenthall Wood
Barnsley Wood
M11 Woodford

M11 Bishop's Stortford

46	A	47	B	C	47	C	48	D	E	F

A1
1 THE SPINNEY

C1
1 BASIL MEWS
2 SOPER SQ
3 SQUARE ST
4 REGINALD MEWS
5 ALLIS MEWS
6 TATTON ST
7 HARROWBAND RD

C4
1 ROSEMARY CL
2 GARDEN TERRACE RD
3 CHERRY BLOSSOM CL
4 DELLFIELD CT
5 OAKWOOD MEWS
6 DARLINGTON CT

D1
1 ST NICHOLAS GN
2 GREEN ST
3 CROSS WAY
4 GREAT AUGUR ST
5 RAMBLERS LA
6 SIMPLICITY LA
7 HONOR ST

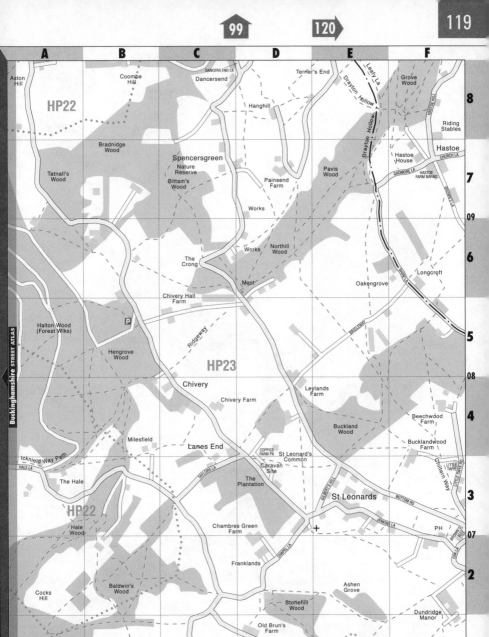

A B C D E F

HP22

Aston Hill

Coombe Hill

Dancersend

DANCERS END LA

Terrier's End

Grove Wood

8

Hanghill

Drayton Hollow

Lety LA

Riding Stables

Bradnidge Wood

Spencersgreen

Painsend Farm

Pavis Wood

Hastoe House

Hastoe

HASTOE HILL

CHURCH LA

7

Tatnall's Wood

Nature Reserve

Bittam's Wood

GADMORE LA

HASTOE FARM BARNS

BROWNS LA

Works

09

The Crong

Works

Northill Wood

Mast

Oakengrove

Longcroft

SHIRE LA

6

Chivery Hall Farm

BRIDLEWAY

5

Halton Wood (Forest Wlks)

P

Ridgeway

HP23

Leylands Farm

08

Hengrove Wood

Chivery

Chivery Farm

Buckland Wood

Beechwood Farm

Bucklandwood Farm

4

Milesfield

Lanes End

COPPICE FARM PK

St Leonard's Common

Caravan Site

Chiltern Way

LITTLE TWYE

LITTLE TWYE RD

Icknield Way Path

HALE LA

TAYLORS LA

The Plantation

GILBERT'S HILL

St Leonards

BOTTOM RD

PH

3

The Hale

HP22

Hale Wood

JENKINS LA

CHAPEL LA

BROWN'S LA

OAK LA

07

Chambres Green Farm

Ashen Grove

Dundridge Manor

2

Cocks Hill

Baldwin's Wood

Franklands

Stonehill Wood

Old Brun's Farm

ARREWIG LA

Lady Grove

HP5

1

HP16

Great Wildmoor Wood

Brun Grange

06

A 89 B 90 C D 91 E F

← 119
100

8

Bishop's
Wood

Marlin Hill
Farm

CHURCH LA

MAIN HILL

HASTOE
CROSS

Ridgeway

Wick
Farm

Sheep
Walk

COLEBARNE WAY

WICK RD

Wigginton
Bottom

Geary's
Hill

CATHERINE
COTTS

HOLLYBUSH
ROW

Lewin's Farm

Lower
Wood

Harding's
Wood

CLAYHILL

A   **B**   **C**   **D**   **E**   **F**

7

Wick
Wood

Grim's Ditch

Chiltern Way

CHESHAM RD

WIGGINTON BOTTOM

Wood
Row

Woodrow Farm

Icknield Way Path

GRAVEL LA

09

Kiln Farm

6

Shrubb's
Wood

KILN RD

Champneys

5

High Scrubs

Roundhill
Wood

HP23

Abbey Dawn
Kennels

The Flats

08

Drayton
Wood

DUNN LA

Langly
Farm

CHOLESBURY RD

BEECH LA

HERITAGE
GN

HP4 ⊹

4

Shirelane
Farm

Ambers
Farm

Redwing
Farm

Tring Grange
Farm

PARROTT'S LA

Parrott's
Farm

Purple Heather
Farm

Cholesbury Bottom

Hillside
Farm

HP4

3

Buckland
Common

+

Cholesbury
Common

Heath End
Farm

07

OAK LA

1 CHERRY TREE LA
2 LITTLE TWYE RD
3 BOTTOM RD

CHILTERN
COTTS

CHOLESBURY LA

SANDPIT HILL
COTTS

Cholesbury

PH
The
Windmill

HORSEBLOCK LA

THE
ROW

Hawridge
Common

2

Braziersend
Farm

Ray's
Hill

TWYE RD

Rays Hill/
Farm

Hawridge &
Cholesbury
CE Sch

+

Hawridge

Bottom Farm
House

HAWRIDGE VALE

STONEY LA

1

OAK LA

Little Braziers
End

BRAZIERS RD

HP5

Works

Hawridge
Place

Hawridge

Rose and
Crown
(PH)

HAWRIDGE LA

Gyles
Croft

06

← PEPPETT'S GN

92   **A**   **B**   93   **C**   **D**   94   **E**   **F**

← 119

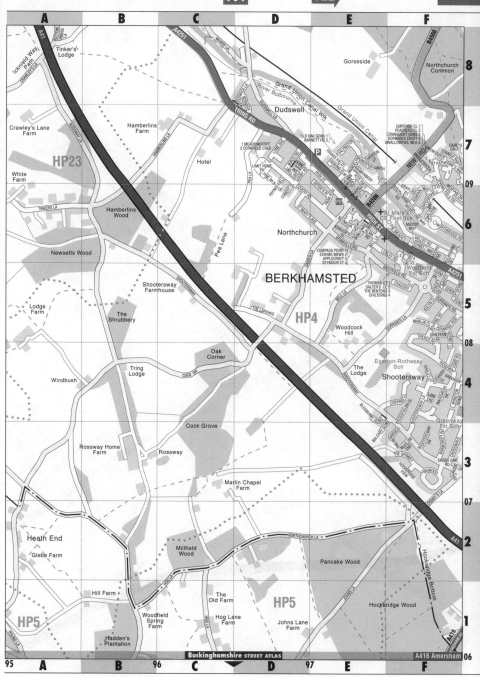

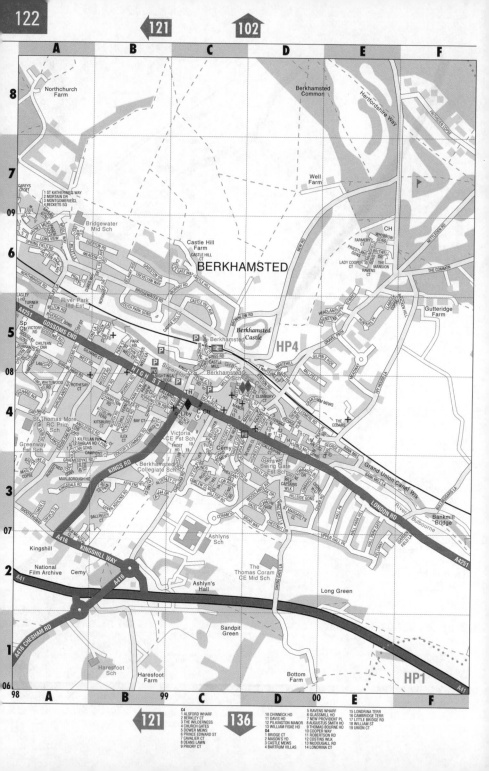

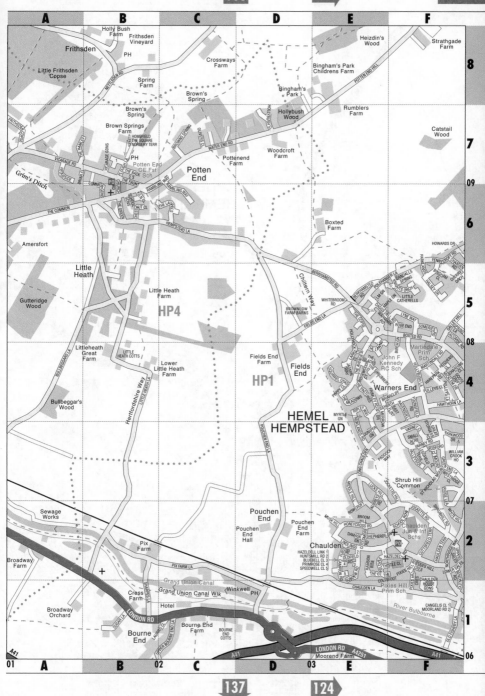

Frithsden
Holly Bush Farm
Frithsden Vineyard
PH
Little Frithsden Copse
Crossways Farm
Heizdin's Wood
Strathgade Farm

8

Spring Farm
Brown's Spring
Bingham's Park Childrens Farm
Potten End Hill

Brown's Spring
Bingham's Park

Brown Springs Farm
1 HOMEFIELD
2 THE SQUARE
3 NURSERY TERR
PH
BROWN'S SPRING
DUKES CL
WATER END RD
Hollybush Wood
Rumblers Farm

7

Catstail Wood

VICARAGE RD
THE HAM LL
VICARAGE GDNS
Potten End CE Fst Sch
THE BACK
THE FRONT
Pottenend Farm
Woodcroft Farm

Grim's Ditch
BRIARS CROFT
RAMBLING WAY
RAMBLING RD
Potten End

09

THE COMMON
COMMON
CHESTNUT CL
THE LANE
HEMPSTEAD LA
Boxted Farm

HOWARDS DR

6

Amersfort

Little Heath

Little Heath Farm

Chiltern Way
BERKHAMSTED RD
WHITEBROOM RD

09

PARK RISE
SANDALS
LITTLE CATHERELLS

5

Gutteridge Wood
Littleheath Great Farm
LITTLE HEATH COTTS
Lower Little Heath Farm

BROWNLOW FARM BARNS
FIELDS END LA
LYNE WAY
ROBE END
SOMERIES
BOXTED RD

08

Hertfordshire Way
LITTLE HEATH LA
Fields End Farm
Fields End

HP1

John F Kennedy RC Sch
Martindale Prim Sch

4

Bullbeggar's Wood

HP4

HEMEL
HEMPSTEAD
MYRTLE GN

Warners End

HAWTHORN LA

PARKWOOD DR

WILLIAM CROOK HO

3

Shrub Hill Common

07

Sewage Works

ROUGHER END LA

Pouchen End

Pouchen End Farm

ST THOMAS MORE RD
SPRINGHILL RD
WHITE HILL

Pix Farm

Pouchen End Hall
Chaulden
HAZELDELL LINK
HUNTSMILL RD
BLUEBELL CL
PRIMROSE CL
SPEEDWELL CL
MISS HILL
HONEYCROSS RD
SHEPHERDS
DAMASK
OLDFIELD
HAZELDELL RD
Chaulden Jun & Inf Schs

2

Broadway Farm

Cress Farm
Hotel
Grand Union Canal
Grand Union Canal Wlk
Winkwell PH
LONDON RD
PIX FARM LA

CHAULDEN LA
Pixies Hill Prim Sch
CHAULDEN HOUSE GDNS

River Bulbourne
CANGELIS CL
MOORLAND RD

07

Broadway Orchard

Bourne End
LONDON RD
Bourne End Farm
BOURNE END COTTS

A41
LONDON RD
Moorend Farm
A4251
A41

1

06

← 123
↑ 104

← 123
↑ 138

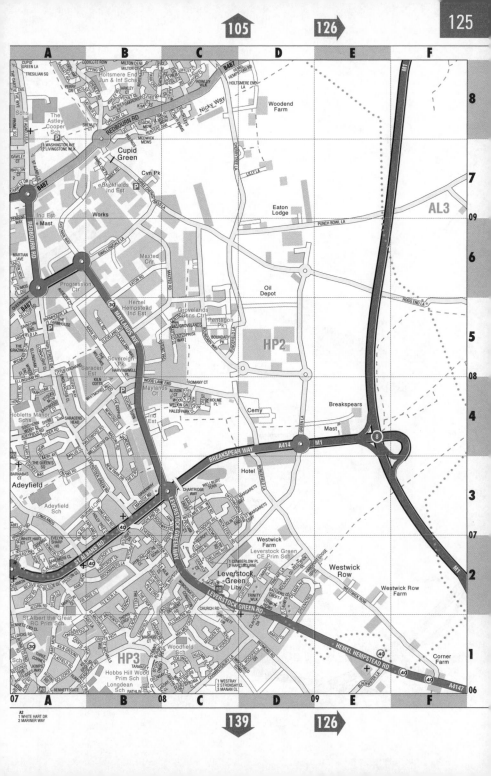

125
106

A B C D E F

8

7

09

6

5

08

4

HP2

3

07

2

1

06

10 A B 11 C D 12 E F

HILL FARM LA
Hill Farm
PUNCH BOWL LA
New Jerome Cottage
Baker's Farm
Hertfordshire Way
Shafford Farm
Southend Farm
Whitehedge Spring
Hogg End
REDBOURN RD
Beech Hyde
HOGG END LA
SHAFFORD COTTS
Bow Bridge
Old Jeromes
River Ver
A5183
Butlers Farm
Maynes Farm
Kettlewell's Farm
AL3
Kentish Wood
Windmillhill Wood
Gorhambury
Shepherds Cottages
The Vistas
Bruce's Plantation
Old Gorhambury House (remains of)
Cypress Wood
Brickkiln Wood
Temple Cottage
Lord Bacon's Mount
Prae Wood House
Temple Wood
Praewood Farm
Stud Cottages
A4147
Prae Wood
Westwick Hall
M1
Square Wood
REDBOURN LA
HP3
Hill End Farm
M10
A4147
M1
HEMEL HEMPSTEAD RD
AL2
AKEMAN CL
MEAUTYS

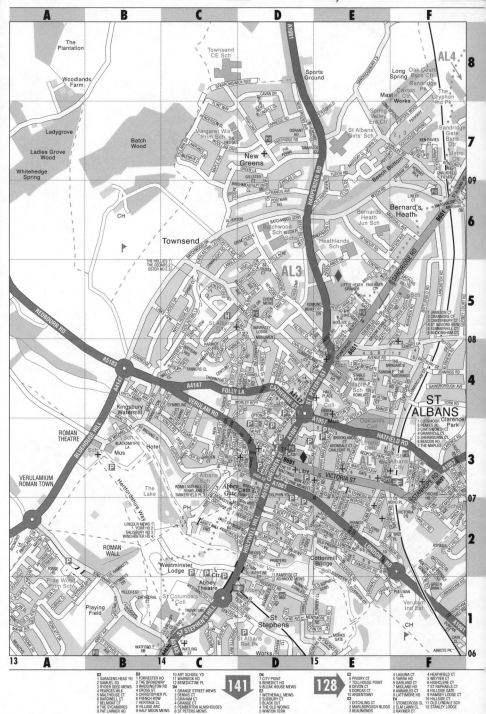

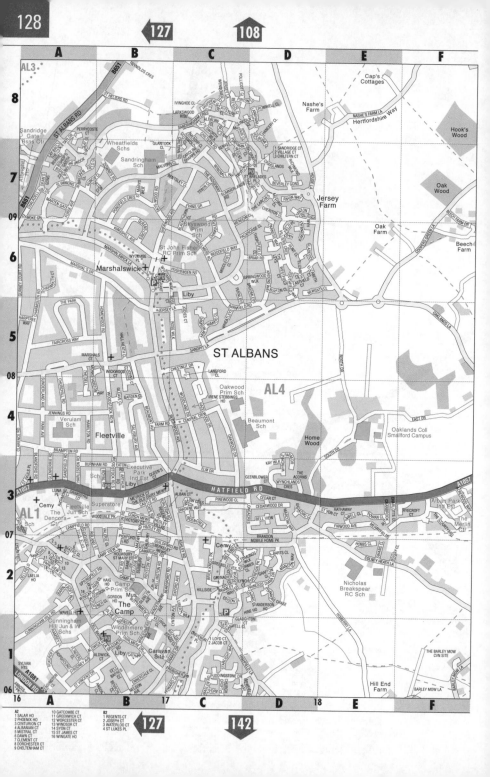

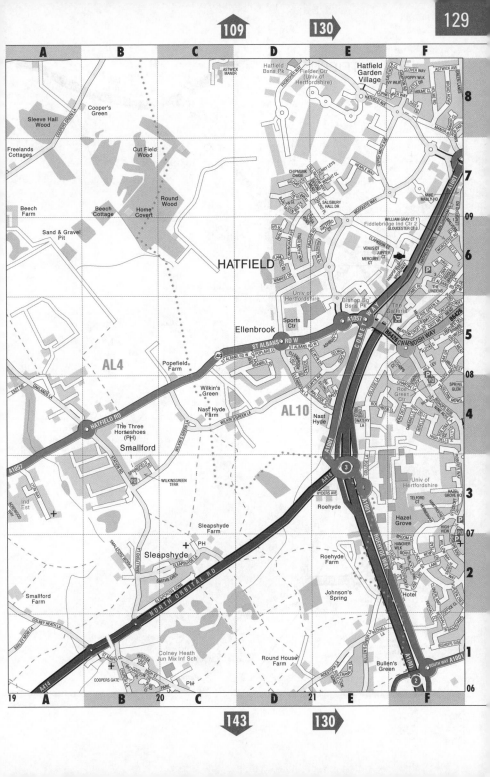

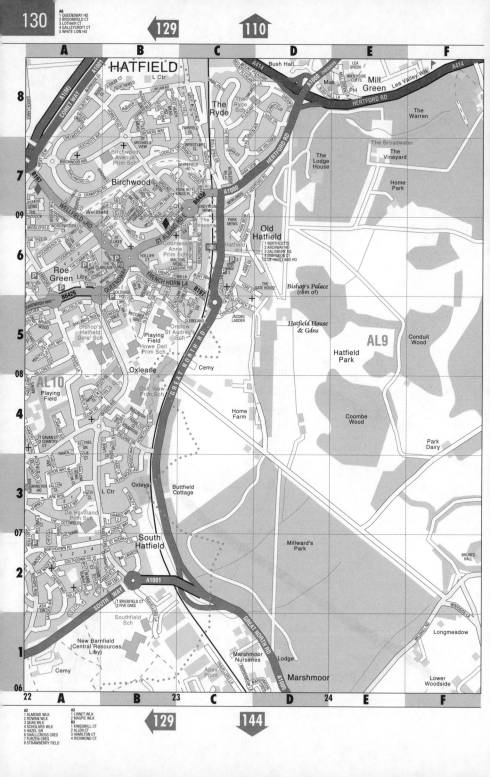

131
112

| A | B | C | D | E | F |

8

B158

Water Hall Farm

Spring Wood

River Lea or Lee

LOWER HATFIELD RD

B158

Sandpit Danes

Broadgreen Wood

BROAD GREEN WOOD

Bunkers Hill

Howe Green

7

WATERHALL COTTS

Pollard Wood

Kennel Hall Farm

Stocking La

Bayford Hall Farm

Bayford Hall

Longacre Wood

09

Chain Wlk

Culver Wood

Great Stockings

Chain Wlk

6

Ashfield Farm

Chain Wlk

Culverwood House

Culverwood Farm

Stocking La

Bayford

WILLOW CNR

Furze Field

Manor House

5

CH

AL9

Breach La

SG13

Twr

Chain Wlk

Bayford Wood

Caravan Pk

Bayford CE Prim Sch

Bayford Grange

Bayford House

08

Danes Farm

ORCHARD CL

Five Horse Shoes (PH)

The Gage

CHURCH RD

CHURCH

ORCHARD

4

Berkhamsted Lane Plantation

Little Berkhamsted

BUCK'S ALLEY

Bell's Wood

ASHENDENE RD

LITTLE BERKHAMSTED LA

3

Chain Wlk

Bush Farm

Buck's Alley Wood

Bucks Farm

The Wilderness

WHITE STUBBS LA

07

The Beehive (PH)

2

WOODCOCK LODGE

Mast

HENDERSON PL

Epping Green

Ashendene Farm

Ashen Grove

Wr Twr

Epping Green Farm

Calves Grove

1

Chain Wlk

Woodcock Lodge Farm

Chain Wlk

DULWICH LA

Birch Wood

TYLERS CSWY

Tylers Causeway

06

| 28 | A | B | 29 | C | D | 30 | E | F |

133
114

A
B
C
D
E
F
8
7
09
6
5
08
4
3
07
2
1
06
34
35
36
Mast
ELBOW LA
B1197
The Woodman (PH)
A10
Cutthroat La
THE CHALET
Woollensbrook
HERTFORD RD
Elbowlane Farm
Box Wood
SG13
Bramble La
Westfield Com Prim Sch
Woollens Brook
B1197
Dalmonds
Dalmond's Wood
Wr Twr
Goose Green
The Huntsman (PH)
Lanthorn's Wood
A10
HIGH LEIGH BARNS
BOX LA
High Leigh Farm
EN11
MANGROVE LA
HIGHFIELD FARM
LORD ST
High Leigh
Beech Wlk
Highfield Wood
Red Hills
Hoddesdonpark Wood
Hoddesdon Lodge
Recn Gd
Spital Brook
Sheredes Sch
Sheredes Prim Sch
COCK LA
Danemead Wood
P
Nursery Grove
Chestnut Grove
Great Grove
BROXBOURNEBURY MEWS
Icehouse Grove
Broxbourne
Broxbournebury Mansion
CH
PEMBRIDGE LA
Edgewood Farm
EN10
Lower White Stubbs
WOOD HOUSE LA
WHITE STUBBS LA
Cold Hall
Baas Hill
BAAS HILL
P
Sports Gd
Broxbourne CE Prim Sch
WHITE STUBBS FARM
Cozens Grove
The Broxbourne Sch
SPRING WLK
Baas Manor Farm
Carneles Green
CHURCH LA
New River
HIGH ROAD BROXBOURNE
A1170
WENTWORTH COTTS
Tudor Farm
WEST END RD
Manor House
Bury Farm
A10
Ley Park Prim Sch
HIGH RD
B194
STATION RD
A1170

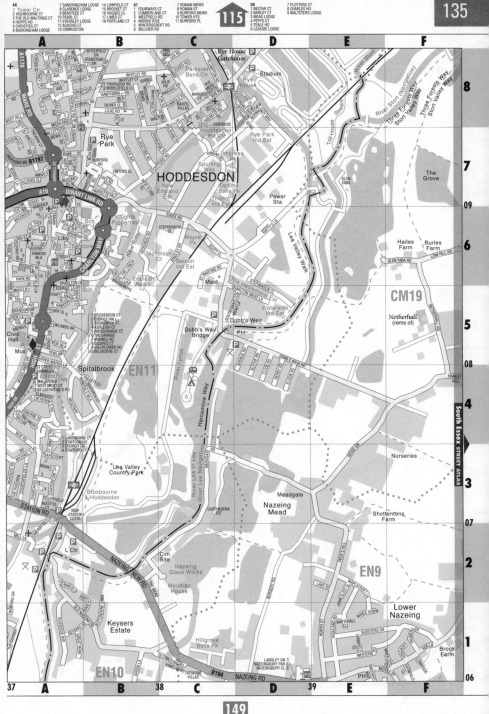

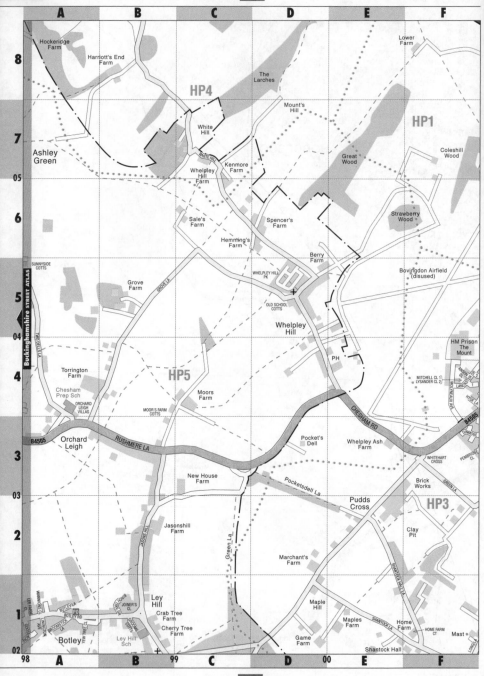

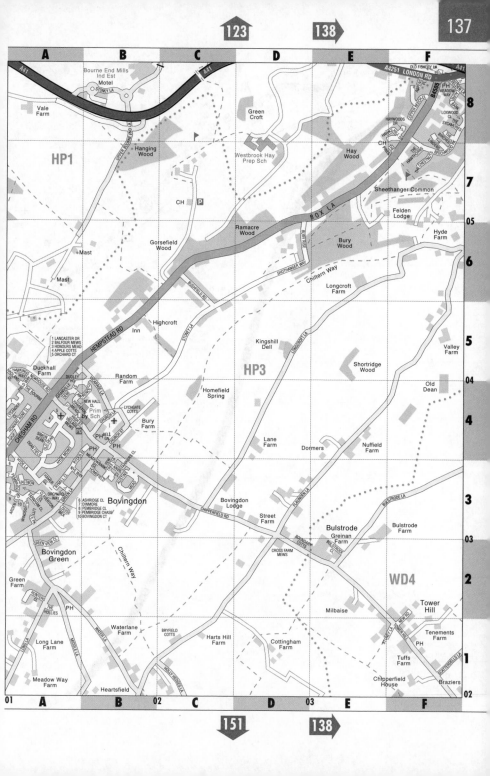

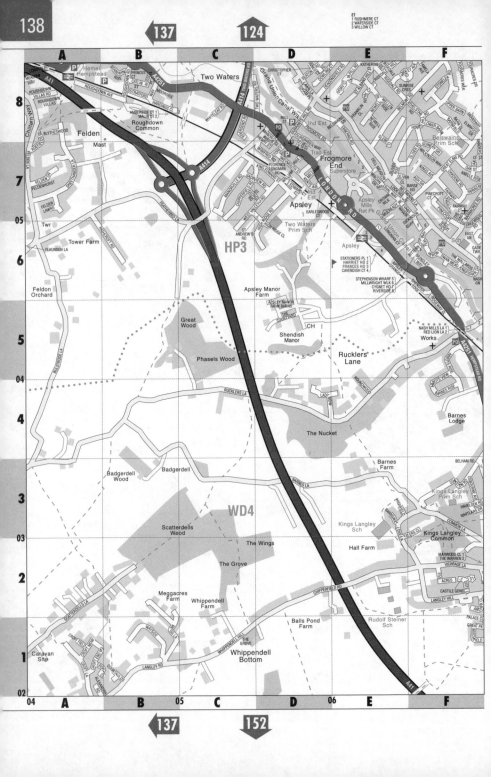

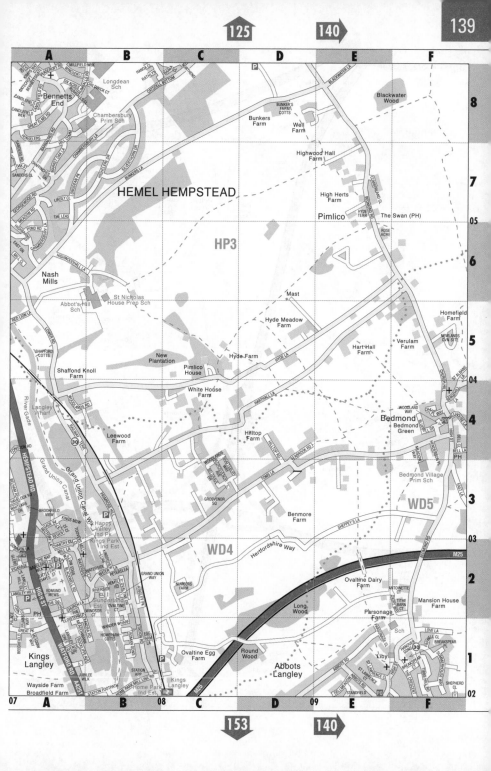

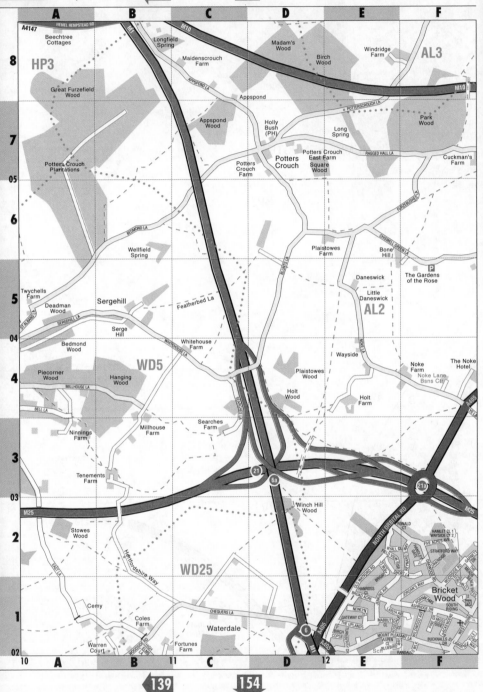

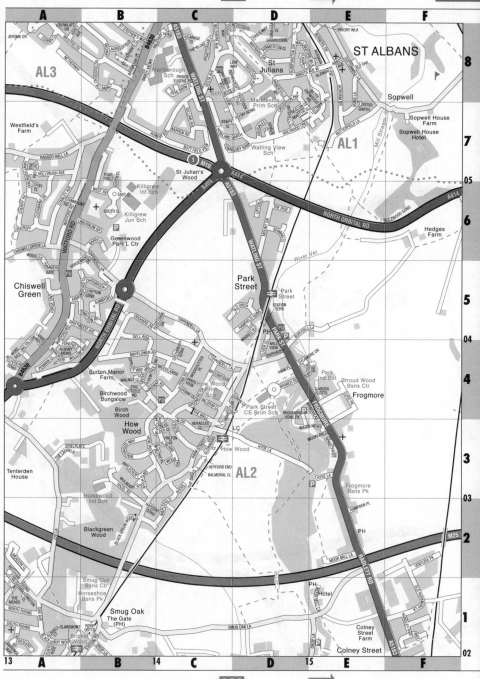

| | A | B | C | D | E | F |

8

ADMIRALS WLK
NELSON AVE
MOUNTBATTEN
SWALLOW LA
ASHBOURNE CT
CROSBY CL
ASHFIELD PARK DR
BARLEY MOW LA
Barley Mow (PH)

1 MASLEN RD
2 HOUSEFIELD WAY
3 CHUCH CROFT
4 HONEYCROFT DR
5 MARTIN'S CT

KETTLEHANGER GN
Tyttenhanger
L Ctr
Francis Bacon Sch
Mast
ST ALBANS
Knight's Wood

PINE RIDGE 1
LANSDOWNE PL 2
CADOGEN PL 3
ASHOK HO 4
AL1
Highfield Farm
AL4

7
Cemy
Highfield Hall
Highfield Manor
Blout Spring

THE ALMONDS
POPLARS

05
A414
NORTH ORBITAL RD

6
Nursery
North Cotts
B5378
Caravan Site
Coppice Wood

5
Strawberry Cres
WISTARIA DR
ORCHARD HO
Napsbury Park
FARM CRES
FARM CRES
COOMBES RD
MAPSBURY AVE
HARVEY RD
KING'S RD
Bens Ctr
London Colney
Bowmansgreen Farm

04
ROSEMARY
MARRIX CRES
GOLDRING WAY
BENNING WAY
BOYES CRES
AZALEA
SHENLEY LA
THE BIRCHES
MANOR RD
SUMMERFIELD RD
Liby
Sch
CHESTER RD
JUBILEE
WILLOUGHMT CT

1 TUDOR CT
2 MILLFIELD CL
3 CYRIL DUMBLETON HO

Riverside Ind Est

4
RUSH LEYS CT 1
LITTLE CROFT CT 2
CASSON CT 3
SPINNEY ROW 4

1 THE CLOCK TOWER
2 JAMES CT
3 HYDE CT
4 LOGAN CT
5 ACORN CT
6 WILDE CT
7 THE BROWNINGS
8 GREAT LEYS CT

AL2
COLVER RD
WALSINGHAM WAY CHICKEN LA
FIELDFARES
St Bernadette RC Prim Sch
ARMSTRONG CL
WATERSPLASH CT 1
SEVERNVALE 2
TYNEDALE 3
THE BELL RDBT
A1081
Colney Fields Shopping Pk

3
SOUTH FARM COTTS
Fir Tree Farm
ROMAN HO 1
THE GREEN 2
HEATHER CT 3
COULSON CT 4
THOMAS GOULD HO 5
M25
B556
Barley-Mo-Farm
River Colne
Broad Colney Bridge
Broad Colney
22

03
All Saints Pastoral Ctr
BELL LA

2
M25

1
Springfield Farm
Colney Park
HARPER LA
STAFF COTTS
HADLEIGH CL
WD7
SHENLEYBURY

1 LIME WAY
2 HEATH WAY
3 MEADOW AVE
4 MEADOW CL

02
Harperbury
B5378
H
SHENLEYBURY FARM COTTS
B5378
FARM LA
Clore Shalom Sch

| 16 | A | B | 17 | C | D | 18 | E | F |

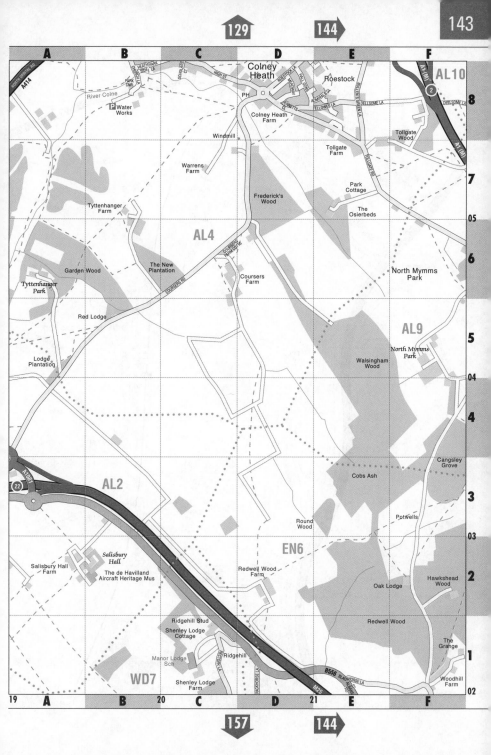

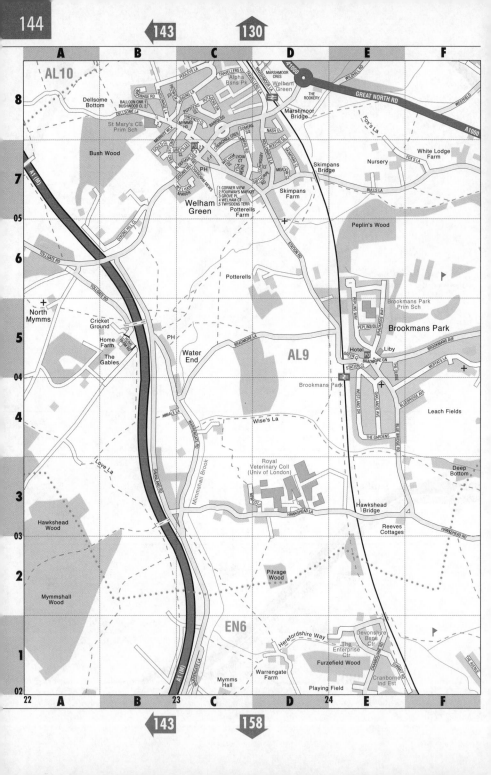

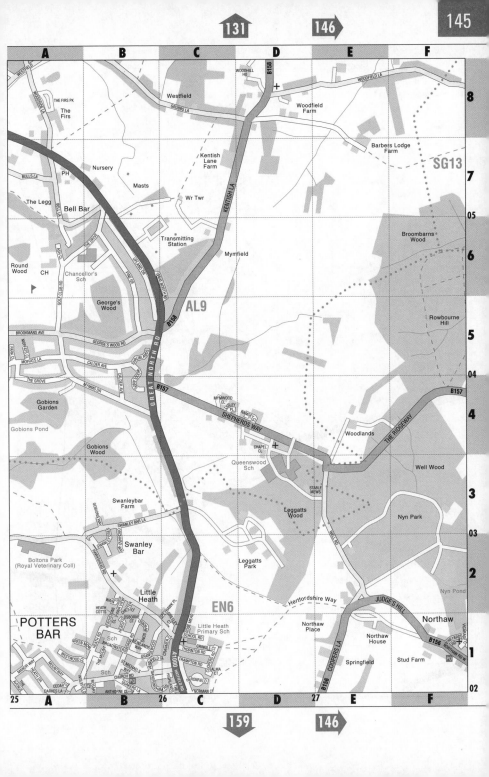

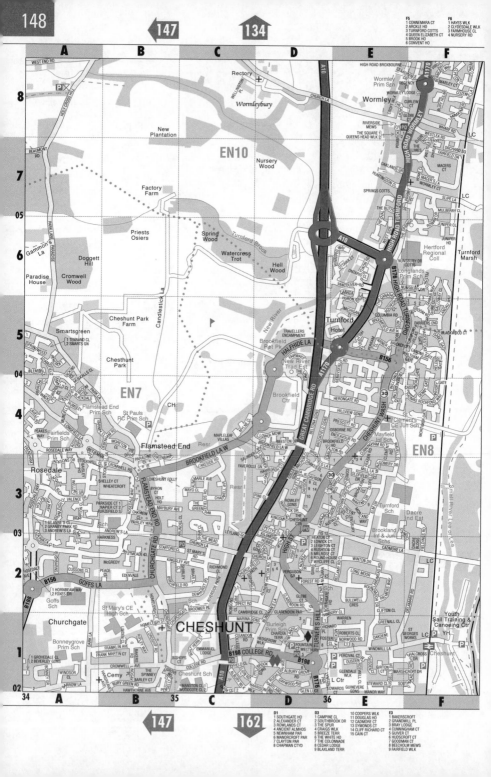

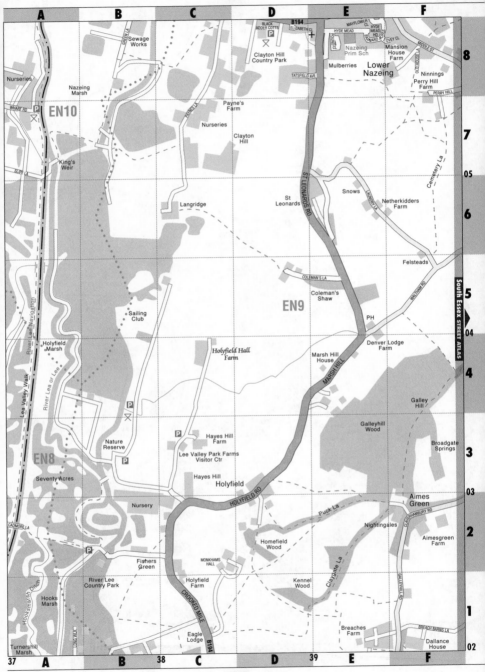

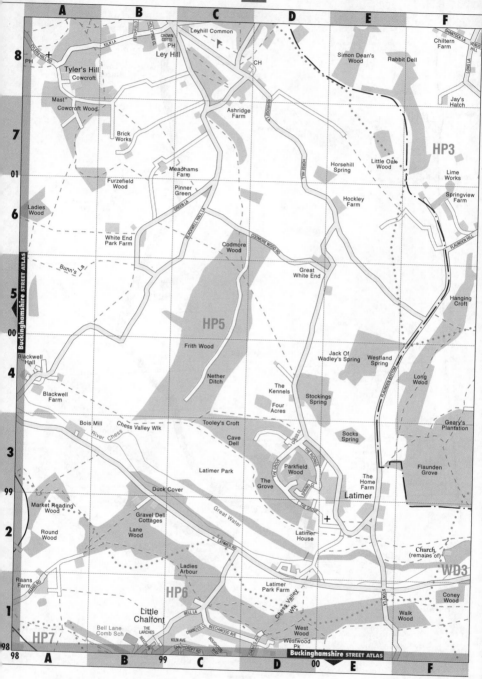

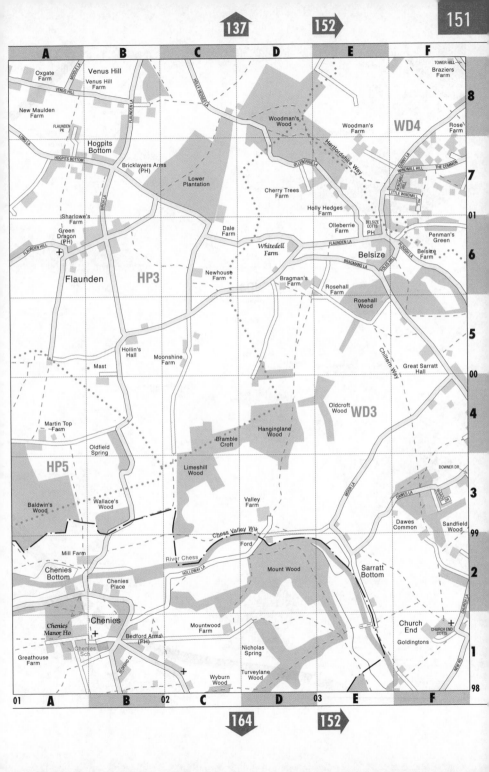

151 138

A B C D E F

8

Croft La
Chapel Croft
Didsbury Cotts
Langley Rd
Tower Hill
Dunny La
Forge La
The Street
Blackwells
Harpersfield
PH
Kings Cl
The Common
St Paul's CE Prim Sch
Green La
P

Chipperfield

Rookery Wood

Berrybush Farm

Mast
Langley Lodge La
Middle Farm

7

Manor House

Hertfordshire Way

Langley Lodge Farm

Langley Lodge

01

Chipperfield Common

Topcommon

Hunterswood

6

Callipers Hall

Gyfres Farm

Berrybushes Wood

Penmans

Hillmeads Farm

Cart & Horses (PH)

Quickmoor La

WD4

Baytree Farm

Bucks Hill

Model Farm

Commonwood

5

Bucks Hill

Commonwood Common

Bucks Hill Farm

Plough La

00

Red Lion Farm

Bucks Hill House

Little Westwood Farm

Great Westwood Farm

Old House La

4

Wheatsheaf Cotts
Red Lion La

The Boot (PH)

Sarratt

Briar Cottage

Bottom La

High Spring

Juniper Hill

WD3

Dawes La
Alexandra Rd
Dimmocks La
Church La
Myrtle Cotts
Carpenders
Seaman's End La
Dunny La

3

Newhall Farm

Bucks Hill Bottom

Templepan Wood

Sarratt CE Prim Sch

99

Green End Bsns Ctr

White House

Templepan La

Yew Court Farm

Chandler's La

M25

2

Potten Farm

Long Fighter Mobile Home Pk

White Shack La

Micklefield Green Cotts

Micklefield Green

Great Wood

Chandler's Farm

Clarendon Arms (PH)

Chandler's Cross

Scrubbs Farm

Micklefield Green Farm

Great Wood Cottages

Cottage Farm

Fir Tree Hill

1

Scrubbs Wood

M25

Sarratt Rd 1
Sarratt La 2

Coltspring School of Riding

98

04 05 06

A B C D E F

151 165

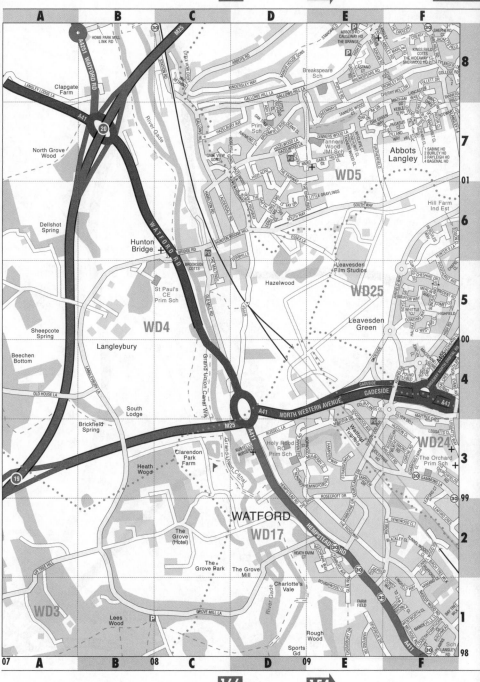

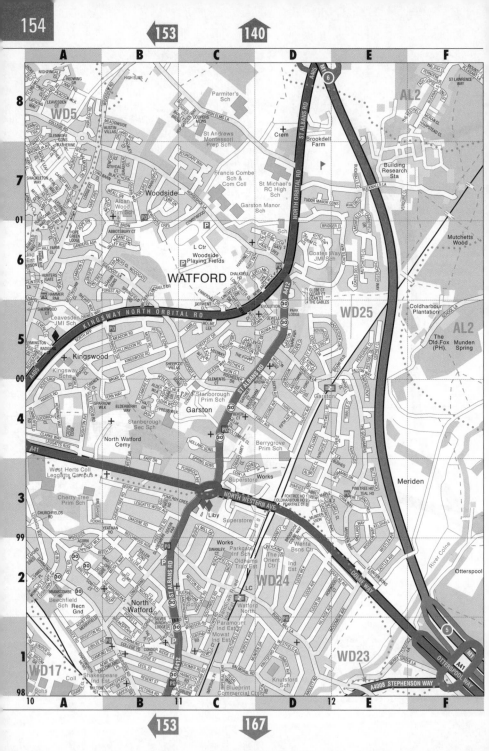

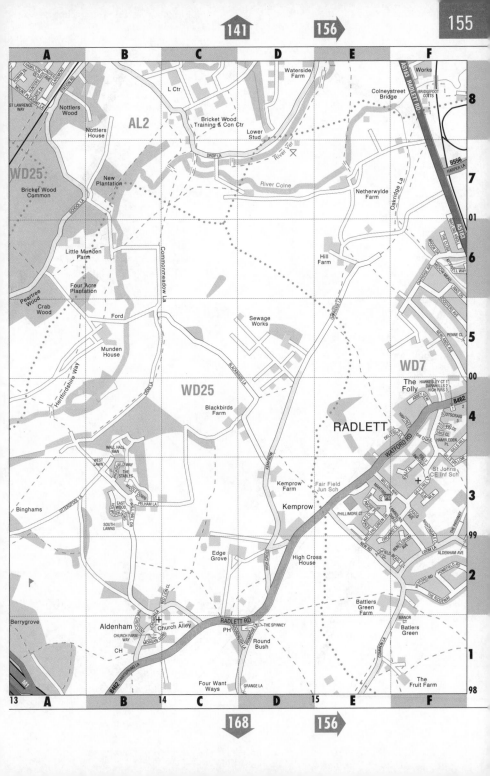

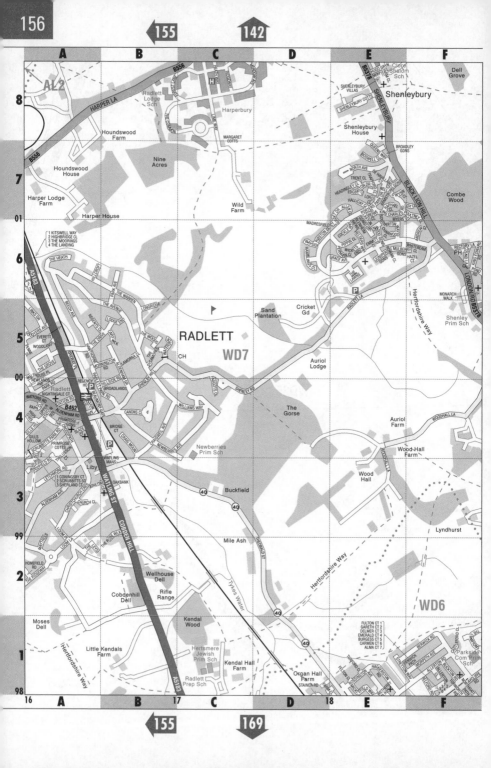

RADLETT

WD7

WD6

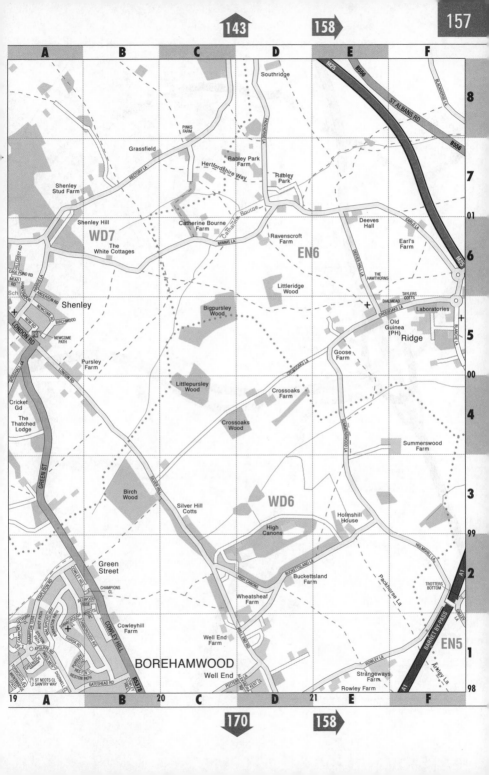

157 144

8

South
Mimms

Hertfordshire Way

CECIL RD

Mimms
Hall

Warrengate
Cottages

The
Furzefield
Ctr

Playing
Field

WINDMORE
HALL

The
Wroxham
Sch

DEEPDENE

MUTTON LA

Cranborne
Prim Sch

PH

B556
ST ALBANS RD

GASCOYNE
CL

PH

7

St Giles'
CE Prim
Sch

ST GILES' AVE

GREYHOUND LA

SWANLAND RD

Mimmshall Brook

EN6

LEXINGTON CT 1
ORCHARD CT 2
KNIFTON CT 3

ORMESBY DR

TEMPLE
CT

SUFFOLK RD

VICARAGE

BROOKLANDS GDNS

Potters
Bar

B556

Bridgefoot

BRIDGEFOOT LA

Dugdale
Hill

STEVENS LA

SANTERS LA

6

Hotel

Grasmere

Dame Alice
Owen's Sch

RYDAL
MOUNT

Pope Paul
RC Prim
Sch

M25

Lorry
Pk

South Mimms
Motorway
Service Area

Playing
Field

RIDER RD

SANTERS LA

5

Blanche Lane
Farm

Motel

1 23

M25

FB

Elm Farm

BENTLEY HEATH LA

00

A1081

Bentley
Heath

4

A1(M)

BLANCHE LA

Dancers Hill
Farm

Norfolk Lodge
Farm

BARNET BY-PASS

DANCERS LA

Dancers Hill
House

DANCERS HILL RD

Norfolk
Lodge

3

The
Cottage

Dyrham Park
Farm

Dancers
Hill

Laurel Lodge La

ST ALBANS RD

Wrotham
Park

99

EN5

A1

TROTTERS BOTTOM

Home
Farm

2

The
Green Dragon
(PH)

KITT'S END RD

Lower
Kitt's End
Farm

Wrotham
Bens Pk

BARNET RD

A1000

Valentine's
Farm

CH

Dyrham
Park

Knightsland
Farm

Kitt's End

Kitt's End
Farm

GALLEY LA

1

A1081

A1000

A1000

98

157 171

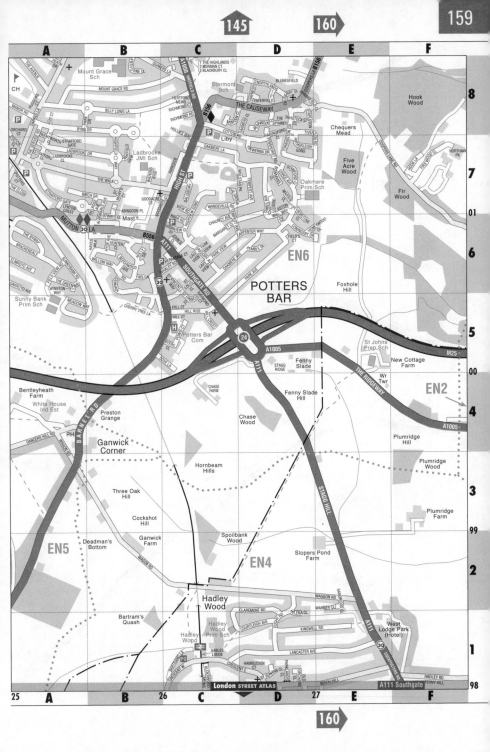

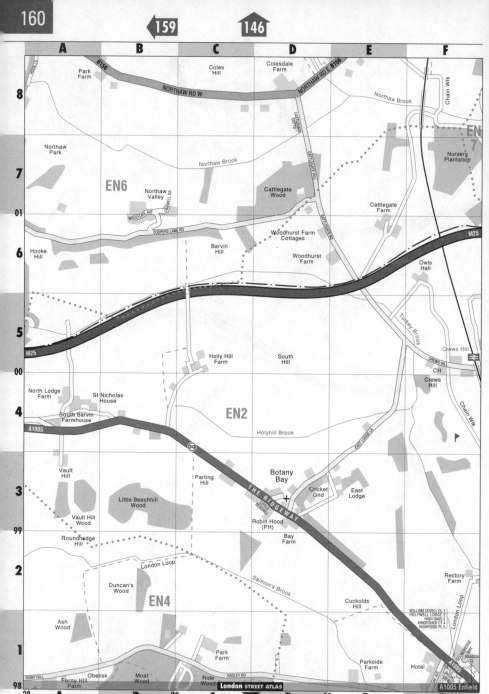

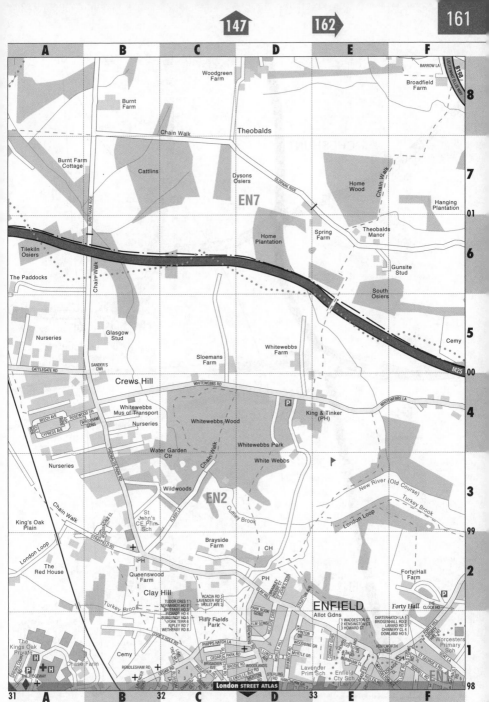

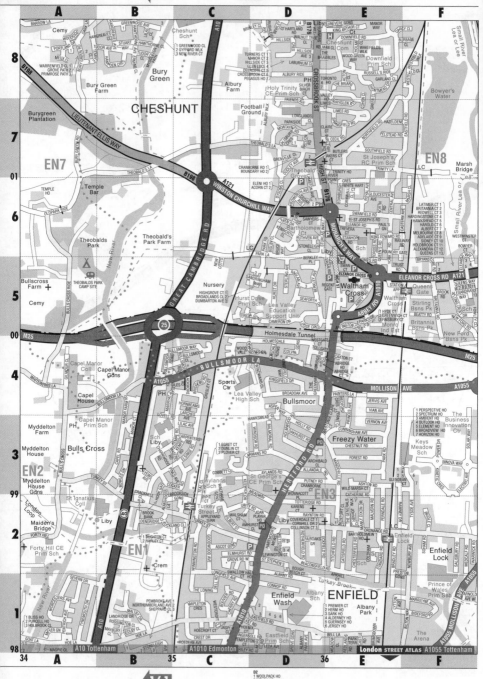

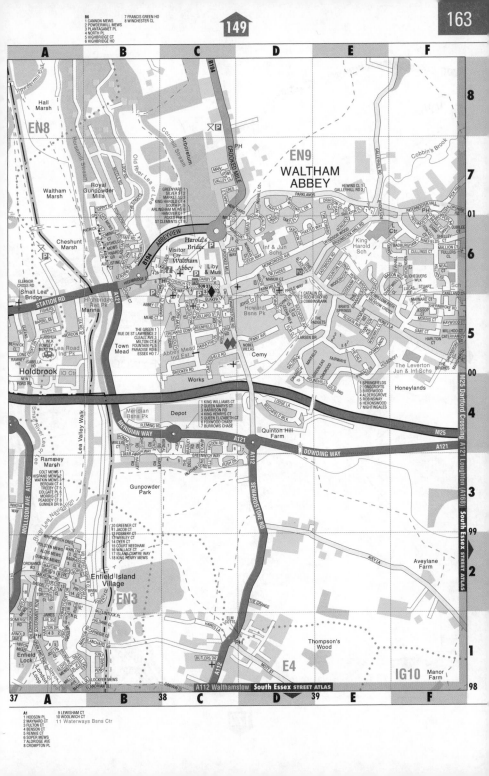

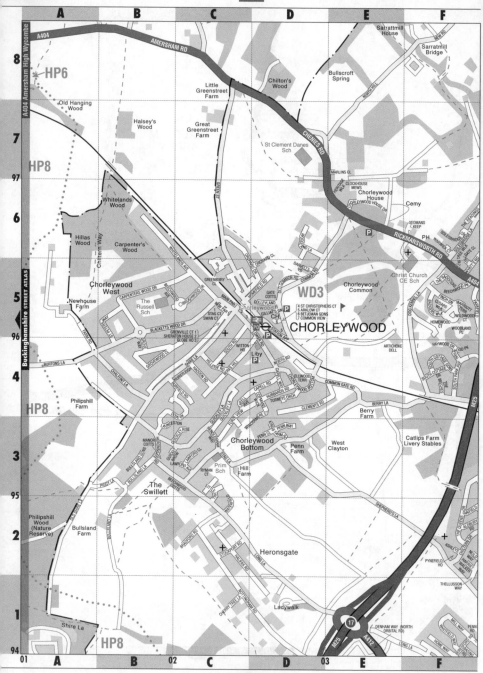

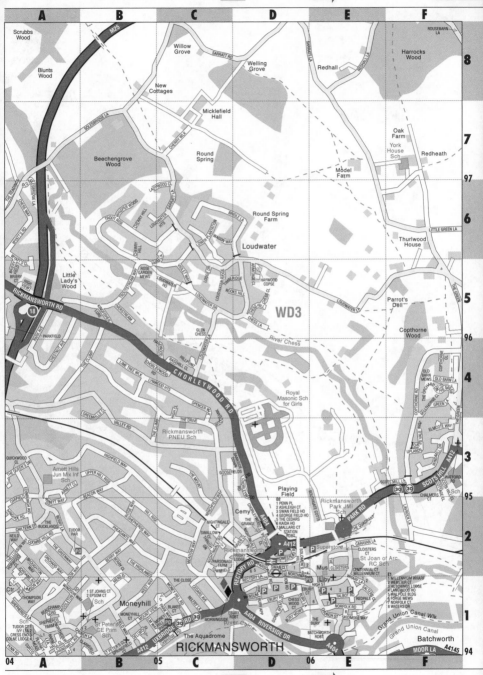

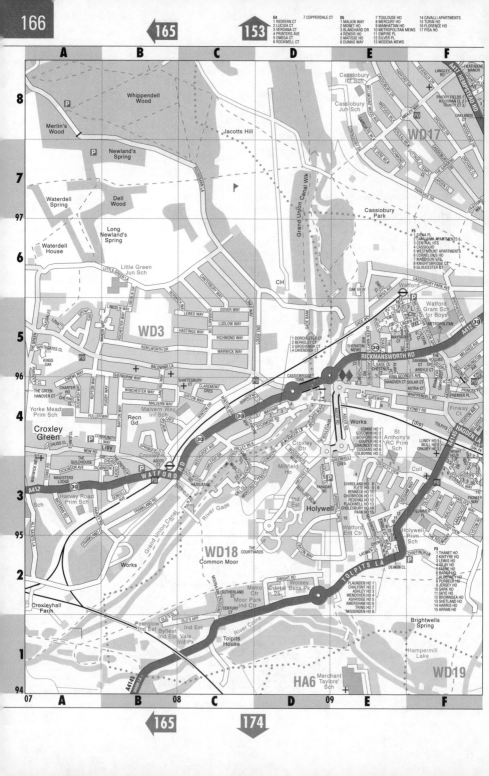

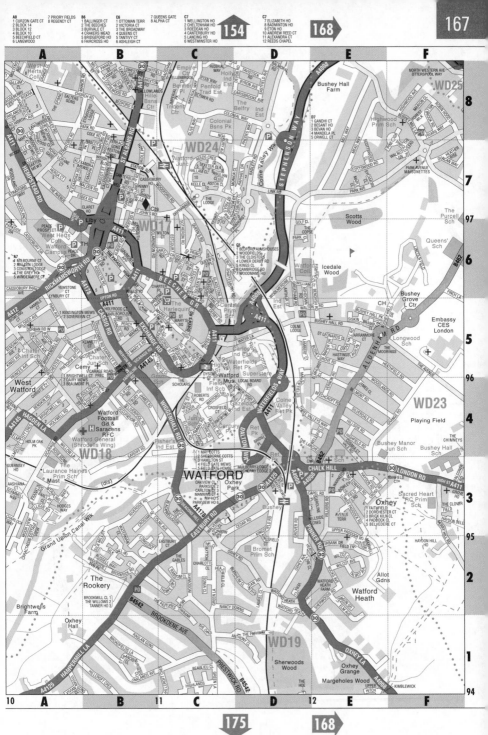

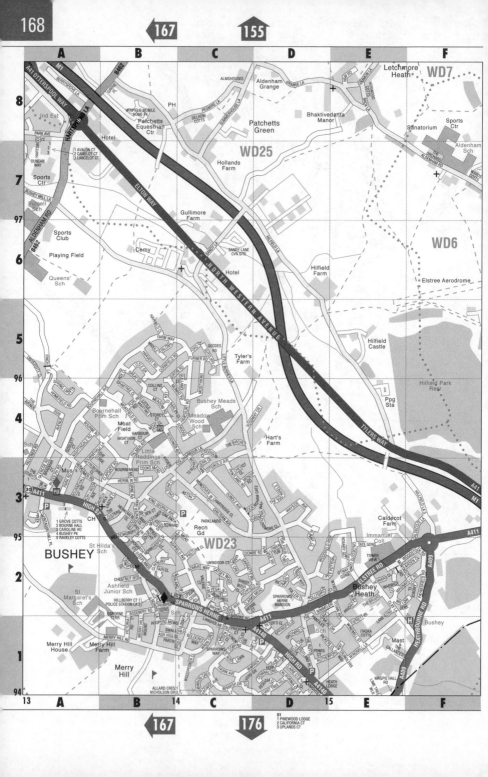

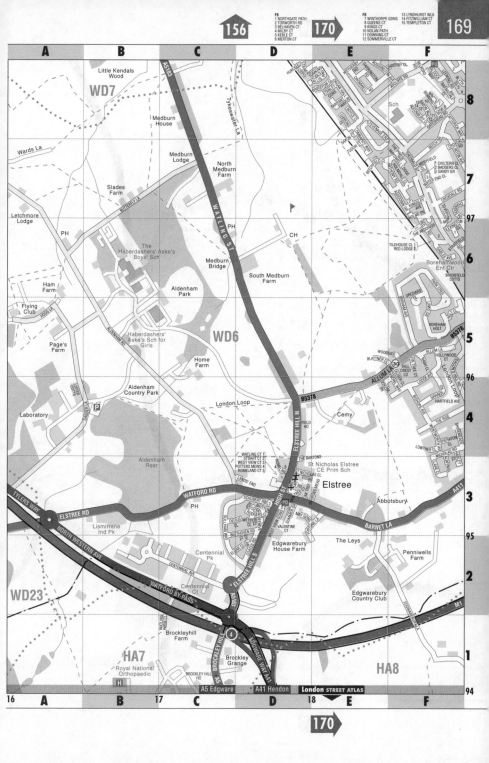

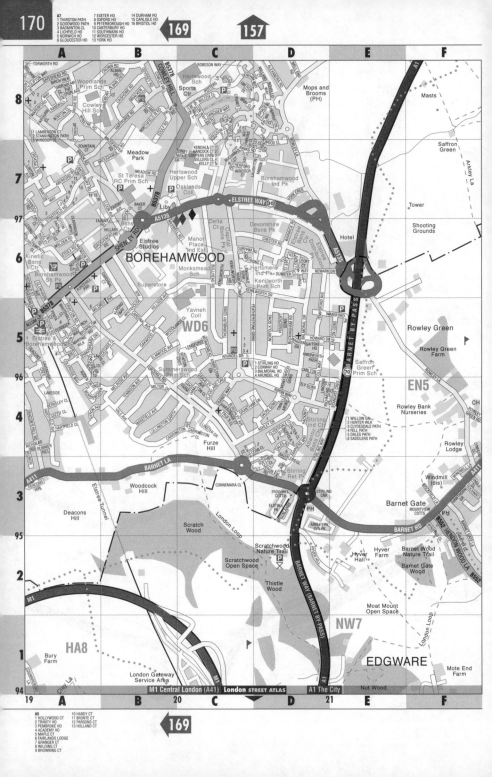

158

E5
1 COE'S ALLEY
2 HERTSWOOD CT
3 SUNBURY CT
4 MERIDEN HO
5 NORFOLK CT
6 VANBURGH CT

7 MORRISON CT
8 KINGSHILL CT
9 BARONSMERE CT
10 CHARTWELL CT

E6
1 RICHARD CT
2 ALSTON CT
3 RIDGELEIGH CT
4 BARLETTS COTTS
5 NURSERY ROW
6 HADLEY PAR

7 EXCHANGE BLDGS
8 CHIPPING CL
9 BRUCE RD
10 HART LODGE
11 HOLKHAM HO
12 LEATHERSELLERS CL
13 BRADDON CT

14 LEINSTER MEWS

D6
1 BIRNBECK CT
2 WILBURY LODGE
3 CHAUCER HO
4 PINERIDGE CT
5 BYFORD HO
6 OAKMEDE
7 WESSEX CT

F5
1 OLIVIA CT
2 VANTAGE CT
3 GRASEBY HO
4 WINCHESTER CT
5 MONTAGUE CL
6 ROCHESTER CT
7 GORDON MANS
8 LAWN MANS
9 AVENUE MANS

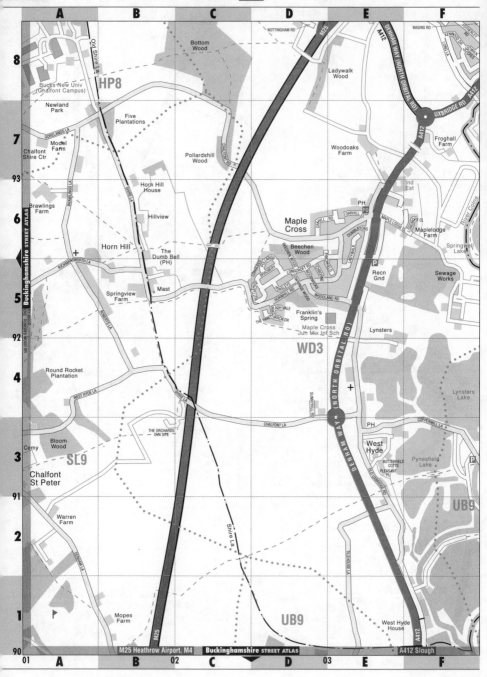

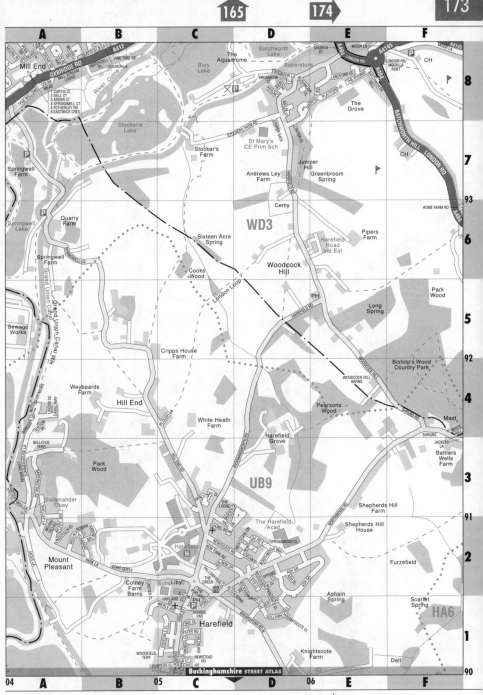

Buckinghamshire STREET ATLAS

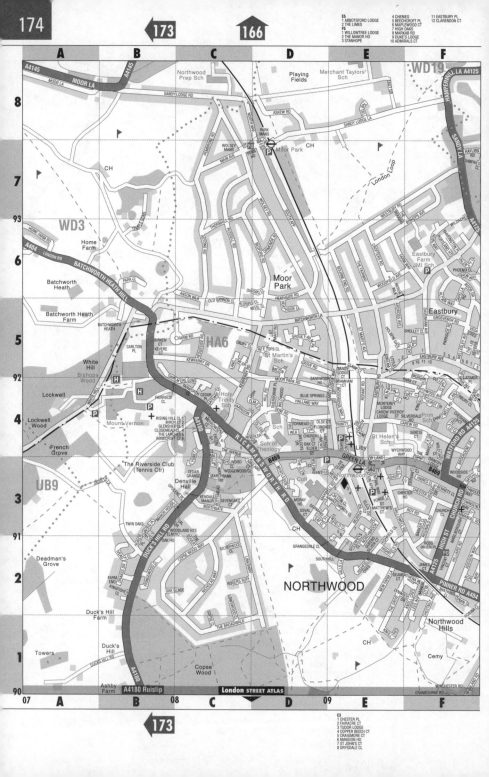

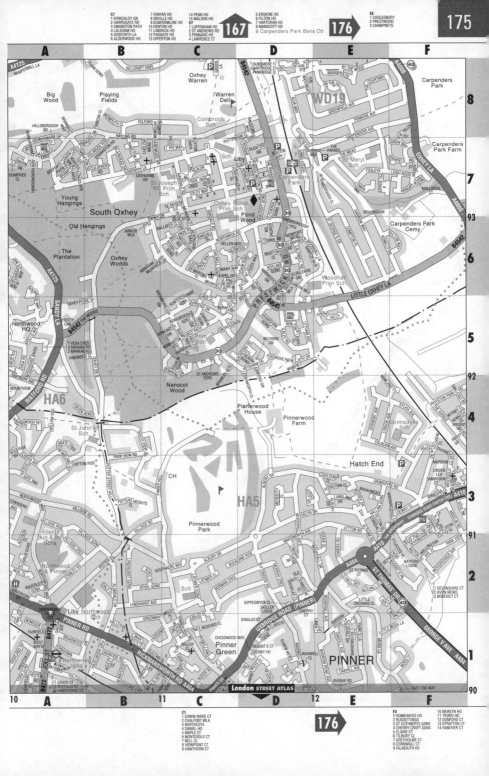

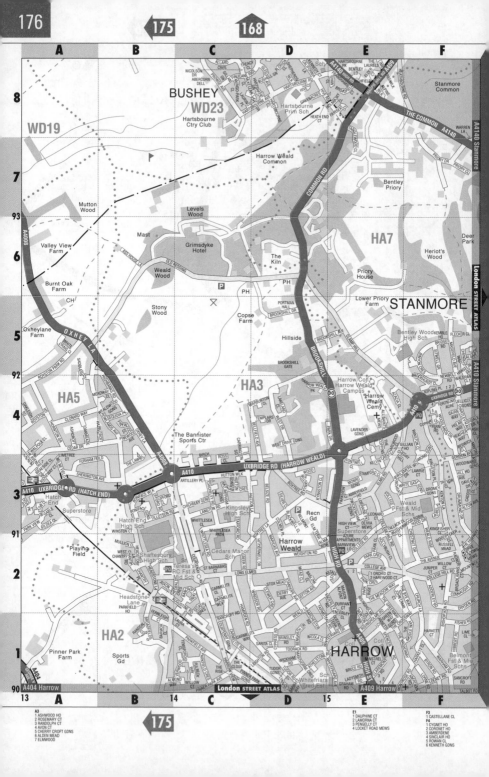

Index

Place name May be abbreviated on the map

Location number Present when a number indicates the place's position in a crowded area of mapping

Locality, town or village Shown when more than one place has the same name

Postcode district District for the indexed place

Page and grid square Page number and grid reference for the standard mapping

Church Rd **6** Beckenham BR2..........**53** C6

Cities, towns and villages are listed in CAPITAL LETTERS Public and commercial buildings are highlighted in magenta
Places of interest are highlighted in blue with a star★

Abbreviations used in the index

Acad	**Academy**	Comm	**Common**	Gd	**Ground**	L	**Leisure**	Prom	**Promenade**
App	**Approach**	Cott	**Cottage**	Gdn	**Garden**	La	**Lane**	Rd	**Road**
Arc	**Arcade**	Cres	**Crescent**	Gn	**Green**	Liby	**Library**	Recn	**Recreation**
Ave	**Avenue**	Cswy	**Causeway**	Gr	**Grove**	Mdw	**Meadow**	Ret	**Retail**
Bglw	**Bungalow**	Ct	**Court**	H	**Hall**	Meml	**Memorial**	Sh	**Shopping**
Bldg	**Building**	Ctr	**Centre**	Ho	**House**	Mkt	**Market**	Sq	**Square**
Bsns, Bus	**Business**	Ctry	**Country**	Hospl	**Hospital**	Mus	**Museum**	St	**Street**
Bvd	**Boulevard**	Cty	**County**	HQ	**Headquarters**	Orch	**Orchard**	Sta	**Station**
Cath	**Cathedral**	Dr	**Drive**	Hts	**Heights**	Pal	**Palace**	Terr	**Terrace**
Cir	**Circus**	Dro	**Drove**	Ind	**Industrial**	Par	**Parade**	TH	**Town Hall**
Cl	**Close**	Ed	**Education**	Inst	**Institute**	Pas	**Passage**	Univ	**University**
Cnr	**Corner**	Emb	**Embankment**	Int	**International**	Pk	**Park**	Wk, Wlk	**Walk**
Coll	**College**	Est	**Estate**	Intc	**Interchange**	Pl	**Place**	Wr	**Water**
Com	**Community**	Ex	**Exhibition**	Junc	**Junction**	Prec	**Precinct**	Yd	**Yard**

Index of towns, villages, streets, hospitals, industrial estates, railway stations, schools, shopping centres, universities and places of interest

A

Aashiana Ct WD18 ...... 167 A3
Abbey Ave AL3 ....127 B1
Abbey CE Prim Sch The
AL1........................ 127 D2
Abbey Ct
  St Albans AL1 ....127 D2
  Waltham Abbey EN9 ....163 B5
Abbey Dr
  Abbots Langley WD5 .....154 A7
  Luton LU2 ....46 A1
Abbeyfield Ho HA3 .....176 E3
Abbeygate Bsns Ctr The **5**
  LU2.......................63 F8
Abbey Mead Ind Est
  EN9 ....163 C5
Abbey Mill End AL3 .....127 C2
Abbey Mill La AL3 .....127 C2
Abbey Rd EN8 ....162 E5
Abbey Sta AL1.........127 D1
Abbey Theatre AL1..... 127 C1
Abbeyview EN9........163 C6
Abbey View
  Radlett WD7 ....155 F4
  St Albans AL1 ....127 D1
  Watford WD25.........154 D3
Abbey View Rd AL3 ...127 C3
Abbis Orch SG5 ....21 E5
Abbot John Mews **5**
  AL4.......................87 D1
Abbots Ave AL1........141 E8
Abbots Ave W AL1.....141 D8
Abbotsbury Ct WD25.....154 B7
Abbots Cl SG3.........69 D1
Abbots Ct LU2.........46 A1
Abbotsford Lo **1**
  HA6.......................174 E5
Abbots Gr SG1 ....50 F5
Abbot's Hill Sch HP3 ...139 B5
ABBOTS LANGLEY 153 F7
Abbots Langley Sch
  WD5......................139 F1
Abbots Pk AL1.........128 A1
Abbots Pl WD6 ....157 B2
Abbots Rd WD5 ....139 E1
Abbots Rise WD4 ....138 D4
Abbots View WD4......138 E4
Abbotswood Par LU2 ....46 A1
Abbots Wood Rd LU2 ....64 A8
Abbotts Ct SG12.........115 D4

Abbottsfield Cotts
SG12......................94 E5
Abbotts La SG12.........95 D3
Abbotts Rd SG6 ....22 D6
Abbotts Rise SG12.....115 D4
Abbotts Way
  Bishop's Stortford
  CM23 ....76 E3
  Stanstead Abbotts
  SG12......................115 D4
  Wingrave HP22 ....60 A4
Abbotts Yd **1** SG8 ....7 D6
Abdale La SG9 ....144 C4
Abel Cl HP2 ....125 A3
Abel Smith Sch SG13 ...113 D6
Abercorn Dell WD23 ...176 C8
Aberdale Gdns EN6 ...158 F7
Aberdeen Rd HA3 ......176 F1
Aberford Rd WD6......170 A7
Abigail Cl LU3 ....45 D3
Abigail Ct LU3.........45 D3
Abinger Cl SG1.........50 E3
Aboyne Lodge Jun Mix Inf
  Sch AL3 ....127 D4
Abraham Cl WD19 ......175 B6
Abridge Cl EN8 ....162 D4
Abridge Ct EN8 ....162 D4
Abridge Ho EN8 ....162 D4
Abstacle Hill HP23......99 F3
Acacia Cl
  Hammond Street EN7 ....147 E4
  Stanmore HA7 ....176 E4
Acacia Gr HP4.........122 B3
Acacia Rd EN2 ....161 D1
Acacias Ct SG12 EN11 ....135 A6
Acacia St AL10 ....130 A2
Acacia Wlk
  Harpenden AL5 ....107 D6
  Tring HP23 ....99 E3
Academy Ct AL2........142 B5
Academy Ho AL4 WD6...170 C4
Academy The **11** LU1....63 E6
Acers AL2 ....141 C3
Achilles Cl HP2.........124 F5
Ackroyd Rd SG8 ....7 E8
Acme Rd WD24 ....154 B1
Acorn Cl
  Cheshunt EN8 ....162 D6
  London Colney AL2 ....142 B4

Acorn Glade AL6 ....89 F4
Acorn La EN6 ....146 E2
Acorn Pl WD24 ....154 A2
Acorn Rd HP3 ....125 A2
Acorn St SG12...........116 D8
Acorns The
  1 Luton LU2...........45 D1
  St Albans AL4 ....128 D3
Acremore St SG11.....75 C7
Acre Piece SG4...........35 A6
Acre Way HA6..........174 F2
Acre Wood HP2 ....124 E2
Acrewood Way AL4 ....128 F3
Acton Cl EN8............162 E8
Acworth Cres LU4 ......44 C5
Acworth Ct **2** LU4......44 C5
Adamsfield EN7 ....148 A5
Adams Ho CM20 ....117 D1
Adams Way HP23 ......100 B6
Adam's Yd **1** SG14 ....113 D6
Adderley Rd
  Bishop's Stortford
  CM23 ....76 F7
  Harrow HA3.............176 F2
Addington Way LU4.....44 D3
Addiscombe Rd
  WD18.....................167 B5
Addison Cl HA6.........175 A2
Addison Way HA6......174 F2
Adelaide Cl EN1 ....161 F1
Adelaide Ct EN8 ....162 F5
Adelaide St
  Luton LU1 ....63 D7
  St Albans AL3 ....127 D4
Adele Ave AL6...........89 F3
ADEYFIELD 125 A3
Adeyfield Gdns HP2.....124 F4
Adeyfield Rd HP2........124 F3
Adeyfield Sch HP2.....125 A3
Adhara Rd HA6 ....176 A8
Adingtons CM20 ....117 F2
Adlington Ct LU4 ....44 C4
Admirals Cl AL4 ....143 E8
Admirals Ct **10** HA6 ....174 F5
Admiral St SG13 ....114 A6
Admirals Wlk
  Hoddesdon EN11.........135 B4
  St Albans AL1 ....142 A8
Admiral Way HP4.......121 F6
Adrian Cl
  Barnet EN5 ....171 D3
  Harefield UB9 ....173 D2
Adrian Ho WD5..........153 E8

Adrian Rd WD5.........153 E8
Adstone Rd LU1.........62 F3
Ailsworth Rd LU3........45 A7
AIMES GREEN 149 F2
Ainsdale Rd WD19 ....175 C7
Ainsland Ct LU4 ....44 B2
Aintree Rd SG8 ....7 F6
Aintree Way SG1 ....51 C8
Airedale
  Hemel Hempstead
  HP2.......................124 E6
  7 Luton LU4............44 C5
Airfield Way WD25.....153 F5
Airport Approach Rd
  Luton LU2 ....64 D7
  Luton LU2 ....64 D8
Airport Executive Pk
  LU2.......................64 D8
Airport Way LU1, LU2....64 A5
Aitken Rd EN5 ....171 C4
Akeman Cl AL3 ....126 F1
Akeman St HP23.........100 A3
Akers Ct SG13 ....162 E7
Akrill Ho AL5 ....86 A3
Alamein Cl EN10..........134 E3
Alandale Dr HA5........175 B2
Alan Dr EN5 ....171 E3
Alban Ave AL3 ....127 D5
Alban Cres WD6........170 B8
Alban Ct
  Barnet EN5 ....171 D5
  St Albans AL1 ....128 C3
Alban Ho WD6...........170 B8
Albanian Ct **4** AL1 ....128 A2
Alban Pk Ind Est AL4 ....128 F3
Alban Rd SG6 ....23 C3
Albans View SG2.......154 B6
Alban Wood Prim Sch
  WD25.....................154 B7
Albany Cl WD23 ....168 D3
Albany Ct
  Harpenden AL5 ....107 C8
  Luton LU1 ....63 B8
Albany Mews
  Chiswell Green AL2.....141 A4
  3 Ware SG12...........93 E1
Albany Park Ave EN3 ....162 D1
Albany Pl AL7 ....110 E6
Albany Rd EN3 ....162 D1
Albany Sch EN3 ....162 D1
Albany Terr HP23 ......100 B6
Alba Rd CM17 ....118 C1
Albatross Ct SG13 .....114 B7

Albemarle Ave
  Cheshunt EN8 ....148 C3
  Potters Bar EN6 ....159 B7
Albemarle Gate AL1 ...127 D2
Albert Ct EN8 ....162 F5
Albert Rd
  Arlesey SG15...........11 A4
  Luton LU1 ....63 E6
Albert Rd N WD17 ......167 B6
Albert Rd S WD17 ......167 B6
Albert St
  Markyate AL3 ....83 E5
  St Albans AL1 ....127 D2
  Stevenage SG1 ....50 D7
  Tring HP23 ....100 A3
Albion Cl SG13 ....113 E7
Albion Ct **4** LU2.........63 E8
Albion Hill HP2 ....124 D2
Albion Rd
  Luton LU2 ....63 E8
  Pitstone LU7 ....80 D5
  St Albans AL1 ....127 F3
Albion The **9** SG12 ....93 D2
Albright Ho AL4 ....128 A7
ALBURY 57 A6
Albury CE Prim Sch
  SG11......................57 A6
Albury Cl LU3 ....31 A1
Albury Dr
  Pinner HA5 ....175 D3
  Pinner HA5 ....175 E3
ALBURY END 56 F4
Albury Grove Rd EN8 ...148 D1
Albury Hall Cotts SG11...56 F7
Albury Rd SG11..........57 C2
Albury Ride EN8 ....162 D8
Albury Wlk EN8..........148 C1
Albury Ho **2** HP2.......124 D3
Alconbury
  Bishop's Stortford
  CM23 ....59 B1
  Welwyn Garden City
  AL7.......................111 E6
Alconbury Cl WD6 ......169 F8
Alcorns The CM24 ......59 E7
ALDBURY 101 C5
Aldbury CE Prim Sch
  HP23......................101 C6
Aldbury Cl
  St Albans AL4 ....128 C8

Aldbury Cl continued
Watford WD25. . . . . .154 D3
Aldbury Gdns HP23 . . . . . . .100 B6
Aldbury Gr AL7 . . . . .111 B6
Aldbury Rd WD3. . . . . .164 F2
Aldeburgh Cl SG1 . . . . .36 A1
ALDENHAM 155 B1
Aldenham Ave WD7. . . . . . .156 A4
Aldenham Ctry Pk*
WD6. . . . . .169 B4
Aldenham Gr WD7. . . . . . . .156 B5
Aldenham Rd
Bushey WD23 . . . . .168 A6
Elstree WD6, WD25. . . . . .169 B1
Radlett WD7 . . . . .156 A4
Watford WD23. . . . . .167 E5
Aldenham Sch WD6. . . . . . .168 F7
Alden Mead **6** HA5. . . . .176 A3
Alderbury Rd CM24. . . . . . .59 E8
Alder Cl
Baldock SG7 . . . . .23 F7
Bishop's Stortford CM23. . . .76 D4
Chiswell Green AL2 . . . . . .141 C3
Hoddesdon EN11. . . . . . . .135 B8
Alder Cres LU3 . . . . .45 A3
Alder Ct LU2 . . . . .45 B3
Alderley Ct HP4 . . . . .122 C3
Alderman Cl AL9 . . . . .144 C7
Alderney Ho
Enfield EN3 . . . . .162 D1
7 Watford WD18. . . . . . .166 F3
Alders Ct AL7 . . . . .111 A6
Alders End La AL5. . . . . .85 F2
Aldersgrove EN9. . . . . .163 E5
Alders Wlk CM21 . . . . .97 E2
Alderton Cl **3** LU2. . . . . . .46 D1
Alderton Dr HP4. . . . . .102 B8
Alder Wlk WD25. . . . . .154 B4
Alderwood Ho **6**
EN4 . . . . .159 C1
Aldhous Cl LU3 . . . . .45 B5
Aldis Mews EN3 . . . . .163 A2
Aldock AL7. . . . . .111 A3
Aldock Rd SG1 . . . . .50 E7
Aldridge Ave **7** EN3 . . . .163 A1
Aldridge Ct SG12 . . . . .12 E1
Aldwick AL1 . . . . .128 B1
Aldwickbury Cres AL5 . . . . .86 D1
Aldwickbury Sch AL5 . . . . .107 E8
Aldwick Ct AL1. . . . . .128 A3
Aldwick Rd AL5 . . . . .107 E8
Aldwyck Ct HP1. . . . . .124 C4
Aldwyck Ho **4** LU1 . . . . . .63 D7
Aldwyke Rise SG12 . . . . .93 C3
Aldykes AL10 . . . . .129 F5
Alesia Rd LU3 . . . . .44 F6
Alexander Ct **2** EN8 . . . . .148 D1
Alexander Gate SG1 . . . . . . .51 C8
Alexander Rd
Hertford SG14 . . . . .113 A6
London Colney AL2 . . . . . .142 D6
Stotfold SG5 . . . . .11 F6
Alexandra Ave LU3. . . . . . . .45 C2
Alexandra Ct
Cheshunt EN8 . . . . .162 F5
11 Watford WD24. . . . . .167 C7
Alexandra Mews
WD17. . . . . .167 A7
Alexandra Rd
Borehamwood WD6. . . . . .170 D8
Chipperfield WD4. . . . . . . .138 A1
Harlow CM17. . . . . .118 C2
Hemel Hempstead HP2. . . .124 D4
Hitchin SG5 . . . . .21 F1
Kings Langley WD4 . . . . . .139 B1
Sarratt WD3. . . . . .152 A3
St Albans AL1 . . . . .127 E3
Watford WD17. . . . . .167 A7
Alexandra Way EN8. . . . . . .162 F5
Alex Ct HP2 . . . . .124 E6
ALEY GREEN 62 E1
Aleyn Way SG7 . . . . .13 B1
Alfriston Cl LU2 . . . . .46 C3
Aigar Cl HA7 . . . . .176 F5
Alington La SG6 . . . . .22 F3
Alison Ct HP2 . . . . .125 C4
Allandale
Hemel Hempstead
HP2. . . . . .124 D5
St Albans AL3 . . . . .141 B8
Allandale Cres EN6. . . . . . .158 E2
Allandale Rd EN3 . . . . .162 D3
Allard Cl EN7 . . . . .147 F4
Allard Cres WD23. . . . . .168 C1
Allard Way LU10. . . . . .134 E2
Alldicks Rd HP3 . . . . .124 F1
Allenby Ave LU5 . . . . .44 A1
Allen Cl
Shenley WD7 . . . . .156 E7
Wheathampstead AL4 . . . .108 D7
Allen Ct **2** AL10 . . . . .130 B3
Allendale LU3 . . . . .31 A1
Allen Ho CM21 . . . . .97 F2
ALLEN'S GREEN 96 F6
Allerton Cl WD6 . . . . .156 F1
Allerton Rd WD6 . . . . .156 F1
Alleyns Rd SG1. . . . . .50 D7
Allied Bsns Ctr AL5. . . . . . . .86 C3
Allis Mews **5** CM17. . . . .118 C1
Allison SG6. . . . . .23 C5
All Saints CE Prim Sch
Bishop's Stortford
CM23. . . . . .77 B8

All Saints CE Prim Sch
continued
Datchworth SG3 . . . . .69 D3
All Saints Cl CM23 . . . . .77 A8
All Saints Cres WD25 . . . . .154 D6
All Saints La WD3 . . . . .166 A3
All Saints Mews HA3. . . . . . .76 E4
Allton Rd SG16. . . . . .10 A4
Allum La WD6. . . . . .169 E5
Allwood Rd EN7 . . . . .147 F4
Alma Ct
Borehamwood WD6. . . . . .156 F1
Potters Bar EN6 . . . . .145 C1
Alma Cut AL1. . . . . .127 E2
Alma Link **3** LU1. . . . . . . .63 D7
Alma Rd
Berkhamsted HP4 . . . . . . .121 E6
St Albans AL1 . . . . .127 E2
Alma Row HA3 . . . . .176 D2
Alma St LU1. . . . . .63 D7
Almond Cl LU3 . . . . .45 B4
Almond Hill Jun Sch
SG1. . . . . .50 E8
Almonds La SG1. . . . . .50 E8
Almonds The AL1 . . . . .142 B7
Almond Way
Borehamwood WD6. . . . . .170 B5
Harrow HA2. . . . . .176 C1
Almond Wlk **1** AL10. . . .130 A2
Almshoebury Cotts
SG4 . . . . .49 D8
Almshouse La EN1. . . . . . . .162 B2
Almshouses
Radlett WD25 . . . . .168 C8
Stevenage SG1 . . . . .50 C7
Alms La SG7 . . . . .4 D4
Alnwick Dr HP23 . . . . .78 F7
Alpha Bsns Pk AL9 . . . . . . .144 C8
Alpha Ct **8** WD17 . . . . . .167 C6
Alpha Pl **4** CM23. . . . . . . .76 F8
Alpine Cl SG4. . . . . .35 A5
Alpine Terr **16** LU1. . . . . . .63 D6
Alpine Way LU3 . . . . .44 D8
Alpine Wlk HA7 . . . . .176 E8
Alsford Wharf **1** HP4. . .122 C4
Alsop Cl AL2 . . . . .142 E3
Alston Ct **2** EN5. . . . . . . .171 E6
Alston Rd
Barnet EN5 . . . . .171 E6
Hemel Hempstead HP1. . . .124 A2
Alswick Hall Cotts SG9. . . . .41 B8
Altair Way HA6 . . . . .174 F5
Altham Gdns WD19 . . . . . .175 D6
Altham Gr CM20. . . . . .117 F3
Altham Rd HA5 . . . . .175 E3
Althorp Ct EN5 . . . . .171 A2
Althorp Rd
Luton LU3 . . . . .45 C1
St Albans AL1 . . . . .127 F4
Alton Ave HA7. . . . . .176 F3
Alton Gdns LU1. . . . . .63 F5
Alton Rd LU1 . . . . .63 F5
Altwood AL5 . . . . .86 D1
Alva Way WD19. . . . . .175 D8
Alverton AL3 . . . . .127 C6
Alwin Pl WD18 . . . . .166 E5
Alwyn Cl
Borehamwood WD6. . . . . .169 F3
Luton LU2 . . . . .45 E2
Alyngton HP4 . . . . .121 E7
Alzey Gdns AL5. . . . . .107 D8
Amberden **3** HA7 . . . . . .176 F4
Amberley Cl
Harpenden AL5 . . . . .86 B2
Luton LU2 . . . . .46 D4
Amberley Gn SG12 . . . . .93 C4
Amberry Ct CM20 . . . . .117 D1
Amberside Ct HP3 . . . . .138 B8
Ambient Ho EN3. . . . . .162 F3
Ambleside
Harpenden AL5 . . . . .86 D2
Luton LU3 . . . . .44 F5
Ambrose La AL5 . . . . .85 F4
Amenbury Ct **7** AL5. . . . .86 A1
Amenbury La AL5. . . . . .86 A1
Amersham Ho WD18. . . . . .166 E2
Amersham Rd WD3. . . . . . .164 B8
Ames Ct
Luton LU3 . . . . .31 A1
Luton LU3 . . . . .44 F8
Amethyst Wlk AL8 . . . . .110 B4
Amherst Lo **6** CM20 . . . .117 C1
Amhurst Ct EN3 . . . . .162 D2
Amor Way SG6 . . . . .23 B6
AMWELL. 115 A6
Amwell Cl WD25. . . . . .154 E4
Amwell Comm AL7 . . . . . . .111 C5
Amwell Ct
Hoddesdon EN11. . . . . . . .135 A7
Waltham Abbey EN9 . . . . .163 E6
Amwell End SG12. . . . . .93 D1
Amwell Hill SG12 . . . . .114 F6
Amwell La
Stanstead Abbotts
SG12. . . . . .115 B5
Wheathampstead AL4. . . .108 B7
Amwell Pl SG13 . . . . .114 C4
Amwell St SG12 . . . . .135 A7
Amwell View Sch
SG12. . . . . .115 B4
Anchor Cl EN8. . . . . .148 D3
Anchor Cotts SG12. . . . . . . .93 D7
Anchor La
Hemel Hempstead
HP1. . . . . .124 B1
Hemel Hempstead HP1. . . .124 C2
Tonwell SG12. . . . . .93 B6
Anchor Rd SG7 . . . . .23 F7

Anchor St CM23 . . . . .77 A6
Ancient Almhos **4**
EN8 . . . . .148 D1
Anderson Cl LU9 . . . . .173 A2
Anderson Ho AL4. . . . . .128 D2
Anderson Rd
Shenley WD7 . . . . .157 A6
Stevenage SG2 . . . . .51 D6
Anderson's Ho **3** SG5. . . .34 F8
Anderson's La SG9 . . . . .29 A1
Andover Cl LU4. . . . . .44 C6
Andrew Cl WD7 . . . . .156 F6
Andrew Reed Ct **10**
WD24. . . . . .167 C7
Andrews Cl HP22 . . . . .124 D5
Andrewsfield AL7. . . . . .111 C6
Andrew's La
Cheshunt EN7 . . . . .148 B3
Goff's Oak EN7 . . . . .147 F3
Andrews Lane Prim Sch
EN7 . . . . .148 B3
Anelle Rise HP3 . . . . .138 F7
Anershall HP22. . . . . .60 B3
Angel Cl LU4. . . . . .44 D3
Angel Cotts SG5 . . . . .33 D2
Angell's Mdw SG7 . . . . .4 D4
Angel Pavement **7** SG8. . .7 D6
Anglefield Rd HP4. . . . . . . .122 A4
Anglesey Cl CM23. . . . . .76 C7
Anglesey Rd WD19. . . . . . .175 C5
Angle The **6** CM20 . . . . .117 C1
Angle Ways SG2. . . . . .51 B1
Anglian Cl WD24 . . . . .167 C7
Angotts Mead SG1. . . . . . . .50 B6
Angus Cl LU4. . . . . .44 A3
Anmer Gdns LU4. . . . . .44 B4
Annables Ct **8** AL1 . . . . .127 E3
Annables La AL5. . . . . .85 A4
Annette Cl HA3 . . . . .176 E1
Anns Cl HP23. . . . . .99 E3
Ansell Cl SG1. . . . . .36 B1
Ansells Ho HA5. . . . . .175 D1
Ansells End SG4 . . . . .66 A6
Anson Cl
Bovingdon HP3 . . . . .136 F4
Sandridge AL4 . . . . .108 C1
St Albans AL1 . . . . .128 B1
Anson Wlk HA6. . . . . .174 C6
Anstee Rd LU4 . . . . .44 B6
ANSTEY 29 B6
Anstey Fst Sch SG9. . . . . . . .29 A6
Anthony Cl WD19. . . . . . . .167 D1
Anthony Gdns LU1 . . . . .63 D6
Anthony Rd WD6 . . . . .169 F7
Anthorne Ct EN6. . . . . .159 B8
Antoin Mews HA6. . . . . . . .174 E3
Antoinette Ct WD5. . . . . . . .139 F2
Antoneys Cl HA5. . . . . .175 D1
Antonine Gate AL1 . . . . . . .127 A2
Anvil Cl HP3. . . . . .137 B3
Anvil Ct
Buntingford SG9 . . . . .40 E8
Luton LU3 . . . . .44 E5
Anvil Ho **8** AL5 . . . . .86 A2
Apex Point AL9. . . . . .130 C1
Aplins Cl AL5. . . . . .86 A2
Apollo Ave HA6. . . . . .175 A5
Apollo Way
Hemel Hempstead
HP2. . . . . .124 F5
Apperfield Ind Est EN7 . . . .147 E5
Apple Cotts HP3 . . . . .137 A4
Applecroft
Berkhamsted HP4 . . . . . . .121 E6
Chiswell Green AL2. . . . . .141 B3
Lower Stondon SG16. . . . . .10 B3
Applecroft Rd
Luton LU2 . . . . .46 C4
Welwyn Garden City
AL8 . . . . .110 B6
Applecroft Sch AL8. . . . . . .110 B5
Appleford's Cl EN11 . . . . . .134 F8
Apple Orch The HP2 . . . . . .124 F5
Appleton Ave SG12 . . . . . . .94 E5
Appleton Fields CM23. . . . . .76 E4
Appletree Gr AL3 . . . . .106 B6
Appletrees SG5 . . . . .34 D6
Applewood Wlk WD25 . . . .154 B4
Applewood Cl AL5. . . . . . . .85 E3
Appleyard Terr EN3 . . . . . .162 C2
Approach Rd AL1 . . . . .127 E2
Approach The EN6 . . . . . . .158 F7
Appspond La AL2 . . . . .140 C8
April Pl CM21. . . . . .97 F3
Apsley Cl CM23 . . . . .76 F4
APSLEY END 10 B3
Apsley End Rd SG5 . . . . .19 E6
Apsley Grange HP3 . . . . . . .138 E6
Apsley Ind Est HP3 . . . . . . .138 D7
Apsley Manor Farm Barns
HP3 . . . . .138 D5
Apsley Mills Ret Pk
HP3 . . . . .138 D5
Apsley Sta HP3 . . . . .138 E6
Apton Cotts CM23 . . . . .76 F7
Apton Fields **7** CM23. . . .76 F6
Apton Rd CM23. . . . . .76 F7
Aquarius Way HA6 . . . . . . .175 A6
Aragon Cl
Enfield EN2 . . . . .160 F1
Hemel Hempstead HP2. . . .125 C8
Aran Cl AL5 . . . . .107 D6
Arbour Cl LU3 . . . . .31 A1
Arbour The SG13 . . . . .113 D4
Arbroath Gn WD19. . . . . . .175 B7

Arcade **5** SG5. . . . . .34 E7
Arcade The
Hatfield AL10. . . . . .130 B6
Letchworth Garden City
SG6 . . . . .22 F6
Luton LU4 . . . . .45 C1
Arcade Wlk **4** SG5 . . . . . .34 E7
Arcadian Cl AL5 . . . . .86 A2
Archer Cl WD4 . . . . .138 F2
Archer Rd SG1 . . . . .51 A6
Archers SG9. . . . . .40 F8
Archers Cl
Hertford SG14 . . . . .113 C7
Redbourn AL3 . . . . .106 B5
Archers Fields AL1 . . . . . . .127 F5
Archers Green La
AL6. . . . . .111 E8
Archers Ride AL7 . . . . .111 B4
Archers Way SG6. . . . . .22 D6
Arches Hall Cotts SG11 . . . .73 E5
Archfield AL7 . . . . .89 E1
Archibald Cl EN3 . . . . .162 D3
Arch Rd SG4 . . . . .35 E4
Archway Ho AL9. . . . . .130 C6
Archway Par LU3 . . . . .44 F4
Archway Rd LU3. . . . . .44 E4
Arckle Ho **2** EN10 . . . . . .148 F5
ARDELEY. 38 F3
Ardeley St Lawrence CE
Prim Sch SG2 . . . . .38 F3
Arden Cl
Bovingdon HP3 . . . . .137 A3
Bushey WD23 . . . . .168 F2
Arden Ct WD3 . . . . .173 A8
Arden Gr AL5. . . . . .86 B1
Arden Pl LU2 . . . . .45 E1
Arden Press Way SG6. . . . . .23 B6
Ardens Way AL4 . . . . .128 C5
Ardentinny **8** AL1 . . . . . .127 E2
Ardleigh Gn LU2. . . . . .46 E1
Ardross Ave HA6. . . . . .174 E5
Arena Par SG6 . . . . .22 F6
Arena The EN3 . . . . .162 F1
Arena The WD25 . . . . .154 D5
Argent Ho HA5 . . . . .175 F4
Argent Way EN7 . . . . .147 D5
Argyle Ct WD18. . . . . .166 F5
Argyle Rd EN5. . . . . .171 C5
Argyle Way SG1 . . . . .50 C5
Argyle Way Trad Est
SG1. . . . . .50 C5
Argyll Ave LU3. . . . . .45 C2
Argyll Rd HP2. . . . . .124 E8
Arkhill Ct EN3 . . . . .162 E2
ARKLEY. 171 A4
Arkley Ct HP2 . . . . .125 B8
Arkley Dr EN5. . . . . .171 B4
Arkley La EN5 . . . . .171 B5
Arkley Pk Cvn Pk
EN5 . . . . .170 D3
Arkley Rd HP2. . . . . .125 B8
Arkley View EN5. . . . . .171 B5
Arklow Ct WD3. . . . . .164 D5
Arkwrights CM20 . . . . .117 F1
ARLESEY. 11 A4
Arlesey Ho SG15. . . . . .11 A8
Arlesey New Rd SG15, SG5,
SG6 . . . . .22 B7
Arlesey Rd
Henlow SG16. . . . . .10 D8
Henlow SG16. . . . . .10 D8
Ickleford SG5 . . . . .21 F5
Stotfold SG5 . . . . .11 A8
Arlesey Sta SG15 . . . . .11 A8
Arlingham Cotts EN6 . . . . .158 A7
Arlington Cres EN8 . . . . . . .162 E5
Arlington Ct SG1 . . . . .50 D2
Armand Cl WD17 . . . . .153 F1
Armitage Cl WD3. . . . . .165 D5
Armitage Gdns LU4 . . . . . . .44 D3
Armourers Ct CM23 . . . . . . .76 B4
Armour Rise SG12. . . . . . . .22 B2
Armstrong Cl
Borehamwood WD6. . . . . .170 C6
London Colney AL2 . . . . . .142 E4
Armstrong Gdns WD7. . . . .156 E7
Armstrong Rd **1** HP1 . . .124 D4
Arncliffe Cres LU2 . . . . .45 E1
Arndale Ct LU2. . . . . .63 F8
Arndale Ctr LU1. . . . . .63 E7
Arnett Cl WD3. . . . . .165 A3
Arnett Hills Jun Mix Inf
Sch WD3 . . . . .165 A3
Arnett Way WD3. . . . . .165 A2
Arnold Ave E EN3 . . . . .163 A1
Arnold Ave W EN3. . . . . . . .162 F1
Arnold Cl
Hitchin SG4 . . . . .35 B8
Luton LU2 . . . . .46 A3
Stevenage SG1 . . . . .36 D2
Arnold Rd EN9 . . . . .163 C4
Arnolds La SG7. . . . . .3 F6
Arran Cl HP3 . . . . .125 C1
Arran Ct LU1 . . . . .63 A2
Arran Ho **16** WD18 . . . . .166 F3
Arranmore Ct WD23 . . . . . .167 E5
Arretine Cl AL3 . . . . .126 F1
Arrewig La HP5, HP23 . . . . .119 D1
Arrow Cl LU3 . . . . .44 E6
Arthur Gibbens Ct SG1. . . . .37 A1
Arthur Rd AL1 . . . . .128 B3
Arthur St
Luton LU1 . . . . .63 E6
Watford WD23. . . . . .167 D5
Artichoke Dell WD3. . . . . . .164 E4
Artillery Pl HA3. . . . . .176 C3

Artisan Cres AL3. . . . . .127 C4
Art School Yd **10** AL1 . . .127 D3
Arts Educational Sch
HP23 . . . . .100 B3
Arundel Cl
Aston SG2 . . . . .51 E3
Cheshunt EN8 . . . . .148 C3
Hemel Hempstead HP2. . . .125 B4
Arundel Gr AL3. . . . . .127 C7
Arundel Ho WD6 . . . . .170 C5
Arundel Ho WD6 . . . . .170 C5
Arundel Rd WD5 . . . . .154 A7
Arundel Rd LU4 . . . . .44 F2
Arwood Mews SG7 . . . . .23 F7
Ascent Pk CM20 . . . . .118 B5
Ascot Cl
Bishop's Stortford
CM23 . . . . .77 C8
Borehamwood WD6. . . . . .170 A4
Ascot Cres SG1 . . . . .37 B1
Ascot Ct WD3 . . . . .166 B3
Ascot Gdns EN3 . . . . .162 C2
Ascot Ind Est SG6 . . . . .23 B7
Ascot Rd
Luton LU4 . . . . .45 B2
Royston SG8 . . . . .7 F6
Watford WD18. . . . . .166 E4
Ascots La AL7 . . . . .110 F2
Ascot Terr SG12 . . . . .114 F7
Ashanger La SG7 . . . . .24 D4
Ashbourne Cl SG6 . . . . .23 B3
Ashbourne Ct AL4 . . . . . . .142 C8
Ashbourne Gdns
SG13 . . . . .113 E5
Ashbourne Rd EN10 . . . . . .134 F2
Ashbourne Sq HA6 . . . . . . .174 E4
Ashbrook La SG4 . . . . .35 B3
Ashburnam Wlk SG2. . . . . . .50 F1
Ashburnham Cl
WD19. . . . . .175 A7
Ashburnham Dr
WD19. . . . . .175 A7
Ashburnham Rd LU1 . . . . . .63 C7
Ashbury Cl AL10. . . . . .129 E5
Ashby Ct HP2. . . . . .105 B1
Ashby Gdns AL1 . . . . .141 D7
Ashby Rd
Berkhamsted HP4 . . . . . . .121 D7
Watford WD24. . . . . .154 A1
Ashby Rise CM23 . . . . .59 B1
Ash Cl
Abbots Langley WD5 . . . . .153 D7
Brookmans Park AL9 . . . . .145 A6
Harefield UB9 . . . . .173 D2
Harrow HA7. . . . . .176 F4
Oxhey WD05. . . . . .154 B4
Ashcombe AL8 . . . . .89 E2
Ash Copse AL2 . . . . .154 F8
Ashcroft HA5. . . . . .176 A4
Ashcroft Cl AL5. . . . . .107 E8
Ashcroft Ct EN10 . . . . .134 F1
Ashcroft High Sch LU2. . . . .46 C2
Ashcroft Rd LU2 . . . . .46 B3
Ashdale CM23 . . . . .76 D4
Ashdale Gdns LU3 . . . . .31 A1
Ashdale Dr HA7 . . . . .176 F4
Ashdales AL1. . . . . .141 D7
Ashdon Ho EN5. . . . . .171 F6
Ashdown SG6 . . . . .11 F1
Ashdown Cres EN8 . . . . . . .148 E3
Ashdown Dr WD6. . . . . .169 F7
Ashdown Rd
Stevenage SG2 . . . . .69 B8
Watford WD23. . . . . .167 D6
Ash Dr
Hatfield AL10. . . . . .130 A2
Hitchin SG4 . . . . .35 A4
Ashendene Rd SG13 . . . . . .132 F4
Ashfield Ave WD23. . . . . . .168 C2
Ashfield Jun Sch
WD23. . . . . .168 B2
Ashfields WD24, WD25. . . .153 F4
Ashfield Way LU3 . . . . .45 A4
Ashford Gn WD19. . . . . . . .175 D5
Ashfords SG9. . . . . .40 D4
Ash Gr
Harefield UB9 . . . . .173 D2
Hemel Hempstead HP3 . . .138 F7
Wheathampstead AL4 . . . . .87 C1
Ash Groves CM21. . . . . .98 A2
Ash Hill Vil WD23 . . . . .168 B1
Ashleigh SG2. . . . . .51 B4
Ashleigh Ct
Hoddesdon EN11. . . . . . . .135 A5
2 Rickmansworth
WD3 . . . . .165 D2
6 Watford WD17 . . . . . .167 C6
Ashleigh Cvn Pk SG11 . . . . .73 C3
Ashley Cl
Cheddington LU7 . . . . .80 A8
Hemel Hempstead HP3. . . .124 F1
Pinner HA5 . . . . .175 B1
Welwyn Garden City
AL8 . . . . .110 C8
Ashley Ct AL10 . . . . .130 B6
Ashley Dr WD6 . . . . .170 D4
Ashley Gdns AL5. . . . . .85 D3
ASHLEY GREEN 136 A7
Ashley Ho WD18. . . . . .166 E2
Ashley Rd
Hertford SG14 . . . . .113 B5
St Albans AL1 . . . . .128 C2
Ashleys WD3 . . . . .164 F2
Ashlyn Cl WD23 . . . . .167 E5
Ashlyns Ctr HP4 . . . . .122 B3
Ashlyns Rd HP4 . . . . .122 B3
Ashlyns Sch HP4 . . . . .122 C2
Ash Mdw SG10 . . . . .74 F2

Ash Mill SG8 . . . . .17 C3
Ashmore Rise HP3 . . . . .125 B2
Ashok Ho AL1 . . . . 142 A8
Ash Rd
Luton LU4 . . . . .63 B8
Tring HP23 . . . . .99 F4
Ware SG12 . . . . .94 A3
Ash Ride EN2 . . . . .161 A4
Ashridge Bsns Sch
HP4 . . . . 102 C3
Ashridge Cl HP3 . . . . .137 A3
Ashridge Cotts HP4 . . . . . . .102 C5
Ashridge Dr
Bricket Wood AL2 . . . . .140 F1
South Oxhey WD19 . . . . . . .175 C5
Ashridge Estate Visitor
Ctr★ HP4 . . . . 101 C6
Ashridge Gdns★ HP4 . . . 102 D5
Ashridge Ho WD18 . . . . .166 E2
Ashridge La HP5 . . . . .150 D7
Ashridge Rise HP4 . . . . .121 F5
Ash Shams Sch LU1 . . . . . . .63 D6
Ashton Rd
Enfield EN3 . . . . .162 A3
Luton LU1 . . . . .63 E5
Ashton's La SG7 . . . . .23 E6
Ashtree Ct AL1 . . . . .127 F3
Ash Tree Field CM20 . . . . . 117 A2
Ashtree Prim Sch SG2 . .51 C4
Ash Tree Rd WD24 . . . . . . .154 B3
Ashtree Way HP3 . . . . .124 A2
Ashurst Cl HA6 . . . . .174 E3
Ash Vale WD3 . . . . .172 D5
Ashville Trad Est SG7 . . . .12 F1
Ashville Way SG7 . . . . .13 A1
Ash Way SG8 . . . . 7 F6
ASHWELL 4 D3
Ashwell SG1 . . . . .36 C2
Ashwell Ave LU3 . . . . .44 C8
Ashwell Cl SG4 . . . . .36 B4
Ashwell Comm SG4 . . . . . .36 B4
ASHWELL END 4 A5
Ashwell & Morden Sta
SG7 . . . . 5 D2
Ashwell Par LU3 . . . . .44 C8
Ashwell Pk AL5 . . . . .86 D1
Ashwell Pl WD24 . . . . 154 A2
Ashwell Prim Sch SG7 . . 4 D4
Ashwell Rd
Bygrave SG7 . . . . .13 C4
Guilden Morden SG8 . . . . . . 1 F1
Hinxworth SG7 . . . . 3 E5
Newnham SG7 . . . . .12 F8
Ashwell St
Ashwell SG7 . . . . 4 D4
Kneesworth SG8 . . . . 2 A3
St Albans AL1 . . . . .127 A4
Ashwell Village Mus★
SG7 . . . . 4 C3
Ashwood Ho 🔢 HA5 . . . .176 A3
Ashwood Mews AL1 . . . . . .127 D1
Ashwood Pl SG4 . . . . .35 A5
Ashwood Rd EN6 . . . . .159 B6
Askew Rd HA6 . . . . .174 D8
Aspasia Cl AL1 . . . . .127 F2
Aspen Cl
Bricket Wood AL2 . . . . .140 E1
Stevenage SG2 . . . . .69 B7
ASPENDEN 40 D5
Aspenden Ho SG9 . . . . .40 E5
Aspenden Rd SG9 . . . . .40 E6
Aspen Park Dr WD25 . . . . 154 B4
Aspens Pl HP3 . . . . .137 F8
Aspens The
Bishop's Stortford
CM23 . . . . .59 B3
Hitchin SG4 . . . . .35 A6
Aspen Way
Enfield EN3 . . . . .162 D4
Welwyn Garden City
AL7 . . . . .111 C5
Aspfield Row HP1 . . . . .124 B5
Asquith Ct SG2 . . . . .69 C7
Asquith Ho AL3 . . . . .110 D7
Ass House La HA3 . . . . .176 B6
Astall Cl HA3 . . . . .176 E2
Aster Cl CM23 . . . . .76 D6
Asters The EN7 . . . . .147 F5
Astley Cooper Sch The
HP2 . . . . .125 A8
Astley Gn LU2 . . . . .46 D2
Astley Rd HP1 . . . . .124 C3
ASTON 51 E2
Aston Cl
Bushey WD23 . . . . .168 C3
Stevenage SG2 . . . . .36 C2
Watford WD24 . . . . .99 A3
ASTON CLINTON 99 A3
ASTON END 51 E5
Aston End Rd SG2 . . . . .51 E3
Aston Grange LU4 113 D8
Astonia Ho SG7 . . . . .23 F7
Aston La SG2 . . . . .69 E8
Aston Rd SG11 . . . . .55 D2
Aston Rise SG2 . . . . .35 B6
Aston St Mary's CE Prim
Sch SG2 . . . . .51 E2
Astons Rd HA4 . . . . .174 C6
Aston View HP2 . . . . .105 A1
Aston Way EN6 . . . . .159 D7
Astra Ct
Luton LU2 . . . . .45 F2
Watford WD18 . . . . .166 F4
Astra Ctr CM20 . . . . .117 F4
Astral Cl SG16 . . . . .10 B3
ASTROPE 99 B3
Astrope La HP23 . . . . .79 B3

Astwick Ave AL10 . . . . . . .129 F8
Astwick Manor AL10 . . .129 C8
Astwick Rd
Stotfold SG5 . . . . 3 A2
Stotfold SG5 . . . . 11 F8
Athelstan Rd HP3 . . . . .138 F8
Athelstan Wlk N AL7 . . . . . .110 E5
Athelstan Wlk S AL7 . . . . . .110 D5
Athelstone Rd HA3 . . . . . . .176 D1
Athena Est CM20 . . . . .118 B4
Athena Pl HA6 . . . . .174 F2
Athenia Cl EN7 . . . . .147 C5
Atherstone Rd LU4 . . . . .44 D1
Atherton End CM21 . . . . . . .97 E3
Athlone Cl WD7 . . . . .156 B3
Athol Cl HA5 . . . . .175 B2
Athol Gdns HA5 . . . . .175 B2
Atholl Cl LU3 . . . . .44 D8
Atlantic Bsns Ctr
WD6 . . . . .170 A7
Atlantic Lo 🔢 SG4 . . . . . . .35 A8
Atria Rd HA6 . . . . .175 A5
Attenborough Cl
WD19 . . . . .175 E7
Attimore Cl AL8 . . . . .110 B5
Attimore Rd AL8 . . . . .110 B5
Auber Cl EN11 . . . . .114 F1
Aubretia Ho AL7 . . . . .111 B4
Aubrey Ave AL2 . . . . .142 C5
Aubrey Gdns LU4 . . . . .44 B6
Aubrey La AL3 . . . . .105 C2
Aubreys SG6 . . . . .23 A2
Aubreys Rd HP1 . . . . .123 E3
Aubries SG2 . . . . .38 B1
Auckland Cl EN1 . . . . .162 B4
Auckland Rd SG8 . . . . 7 E8
Auction House Ctyd 🔢
LU1 . . . . .63 E7
Auden Dr WD6 . . . . .170 A4
Audley Ct WD6 . . . . .170 A6
Audley Dr HA6 . . . . .174 D4
Audley Gdns LU4 . . . . .175 C1
Audrey Gdns CM23 . . . . . . .76 F4
Audwick Cl EN8 . . . . .148 E3
Augustine Ct EN9 . . . . .163 B6
Augustine Rd HA3 . . . . .176 C2
Augustus Cl AL3 . . . . .127 A2
Augustus Gate SG2 . . . . . . .51 D8
Augustus Smith Ho 🔢
HP4 . . . . .122 D4
Austen Paths SG2 . . . . .51 C3
Austen Mews 🔢 HP1 . . . .124 D4
Austin Cl LU3 . . . . .45 C4
Austins Mead HP3 . . . . .137 B3
Austins Pl 🔢 HP2 . . . . .124 D4
Austin Villas WD25 . . . . . . .154 B8
Autumn Glades HP3 . . . . . .125 C1
Autumn Gr AL7 . . . . .111 B4
Avalon Cl WD25 . . . . .154 E7
Avalon Ct WD23 . . . . .168 A7
Avebury Cl LU2 . . . . .45 D4
Avebury Ct HP2 . . . . .125 A5
Aventine Ct AL1 . . . . .127 D2
Avenue App WD4 . . . . .139 A1
Avenue Ct AL6 . . . . .89 E7
Avenue Grimaldi LU2 . . . . . .45 A3
Avenue Mans 🔢 EN5 . . . .171 F5
Avenue One SG6 . . . . .23 C6
Avenue Rd
Bishop's Stortford
CM23 . . . . .77 B6
Hoddesdon EN11 . . . . .135 D5
Pinner HA5 . . . . .175 E1
St Albans AL1 . . . . .127 C4
Avenue Rise WD23 . . . . . . .168 A4
Avenue St Nicholas
AL5 .86 A1
Avenue Terr WD19 . . . . . . .167 E3
Avenue The
Barnet EN5 . . . . .171 E6
Bushey WD23 . . . . .167 F5
Harrow HA3 . . . . .176 F2
Hemel Hempstead HP1 . . . .123 E4
Hertford SG14 . . . . .113 B8
Hitchin SG4 . . . . .35 A4
Hoddesdon EN11 . . . . .135 A4
Luton LU4 . . . . .44 D5
Northwood HA6 . . . . .174 C4
Oaklands AL6 . . . . .89 D7
Pinner HA5 . . . . .175 F4
Potters Bar EN6 . . . . .145 A1
Radlett WD7 . . . . .156 B5
Stevenage SG1 . . . . .50 D8
Stotfold SG5 . . . . 11 F4
Watford WD17 . . . . .167 A7
Avey La EN9 . . . . .163 E2
Avia Cl HP3 . . . . .138 D7
Avior Dr HA6 . . . . .174 F4
Avocet Cl AL10 . . . . .129 F6
Avocet Cl AL3 . . . . .11 E1
Avocet Cl LU3 . . . . .45 F3
Avon Chase SG16 . . . . .10 C3
Avon Cl WD25 . . . . .154 C5
Avon Cotts SG12 . . . . .46 B3
Avon Ct
🔢 Harpenden AL5 . . . . .86 B1
Luton LU1 . . . . .63 C8
🔢 Pinner HA5 . . . . .175 F3
Avondale Ct AL1 . . . . .127 E3
Avondale Rd LU1 . . . . .63 C8
Avon Dr LU2 . . . . .37 A3
Avon Mews HA5 . . . . .175 F2
Avon Rd SG16 . . . . .10 B4
Avon Sq HP2 . . . . .124 F8
Axe Cl LU3 . . . . .44 E6
Aycliffe Dr HP2 . . . . .124 D7
Aycliffe Drive Prim Sch
HP2 . . . . .124 E7
Aycliffe Rd WD6 . . . . .156 F1

Aydon Rd LU3 . . . . .45 B6
Aylands Rd EN3 . . . . .162 D3
Aylands Sch EN3 . . . . .162 C3
Aylesbury Rd HP23 . . . . .99 E3
Aylott Cl SG14 . . . . .70 D4
Aylotts Cl SG9 . . . . .40 D8
Aylsham Rd EN11 . . . . .135 C8
Aylward Dr SG2 . . . . .51 B4
Aynho St WD18 . . . . .167 B4
Aynsworth Ave CM23 . . . . . .59 B2
Ayot Gn
Ayot St P AL6 . . . . .89 A1
Hatfield AL10 . . . . .109 F8
Welwyn Garden City
AL6 . . . . .109 F8
AYOT GREEN 89 A1
Ayot La AL6 . . . . .88 A6
Ayot Little Green La
AL6 .88 F1
Ayot Path WD6 . . . . .157 A1
AYOT ST LAWRENCE 88 B6
AYOT ST PETER 88 F3
Ayot St Peter Rd AL6 . . . . . .88 C3
Ayr Cl SG1 . . . . .51 C8
AYRES END 107 E5
Ayres End La AL3, AL5 . . . .107 C5
Aysgarth Cl AL5 . . . . .107 B8
Aysgarth Rd AL3 . . . . .106 A6
Azalea Cl AL2 . . . . .142 B4
Azure Appartments
HA3 . . . . .176 E2

B

Baas Hill EN10 . . . . .134 D2
Baas Hill Cl EN10 . . . . .134 E2
Baas La EN10 . . . . .134 E3
Babbage Rd SG1 . . . . .50 B5
BABBS GREEN 94 C5
Back La
Buckland SG9 . . . . .27 D8
Little Hallingbury CM22 . . . . .98 B7
Preston SG4 . . . . .48 D6
Radlett WD25 . . . . .168 E8
Sheering CM22 . . . . .98 B1
Tewin AL6 . . . . .90 C2
Back St
Ashwell SG7 . . . . 4 C3
Luton LU2 . . . . .63 E8
Back The HP4 . . . . .123 B7
Bacons Dr EN6 . . . . .146 E2
Bacon's Yd SG7 . . . . 4 D4
Badburgham Ct EN9 . . . . . .163 F6
Baddeley Cl
Holdbrook EN3 . . . . .163 A2
Stevenage SG2 . . . . .51 B2
Bader Cl
Stevenage SG2 . . . . .36 F1
Welwyn Garden City
AL7 . . . . .111 C6
Badger Cl SG3 . . . . .69 A6
Badgers CM23 . . . . .76 E5
Badgers Cl
Borehamwood WD6 . . . . . . .169 F7
Hertford SG13 . . . . .114 B6
Stevenage SG2 . . . . .50 A4
Badgers Croft
Hemel Hempstead
HP2 . . . . .125 D3
Hoddesdon EN10 . . . . .134 E2
Totteridge N20 . . . . .171 D1
Badgers Ct WD25 . . . . .154 A5
Badgers Wlk
Burnham Green AL6 . . . . . . .90 C5
Chorleywood WD3 . . . . .164 F5
Badger Way AL10 . . . . .130 B3
Badington Dr AL5 . . . . .85 C1
Badminton Cl
🔢 Borehamwood
WD6 . . . . .170 A7
Stevenage SG2 . . . . .69 B7
Badminton Ho 🔢
WD24 . . . . .167 C7
Badminton Pl EN10 . . . . . . .134 E3
Bagenal Ho WD5 . . . . .153 F7
Bagwicks Cl LU4 . . . . .44 E2
Bailey Hill Ct 🔢 LU1 . . . . . .63 E5
Bailey Mews HP1 . . . . .124 D4
Bailey St LU1 . . . . .63 F6
Baines La SG4 . . . . .69 C4
Baird Cl WD23 . . . . .168 B3
Bairstow Cl WD6 . . . . .169 E8
Baisley Ho EN7 . . . . .148 A3
Bakehouse Ct SG9 . . . . .40 E8
Baker Cl WD6 . . . . .170 B7
Bakercroft 🔢 EN8 . . . . . . .148 E3
Bakers Ct 🔢 CM23 . . . . . . .77 A7
BAKER'S END 94 E7
Bakers Gr AL7 . . . . .111 C7
Bakers La
Barley SG8 . . . . 8 F2
Kensworth Common LU6 . . . .82 E8
Baker's La SG4 . . . . .67 F1
Bakers Rd EN7 . . . . .148 B1
Baker St
Enfield EN1 . . . . .161 E1
Hertford SG13 . . . . .113 D6
Luton LU1 . . . . .63 E5
Potters Bar EN6 . . . . .158 E5
🔢 Stevenage SG1 . . . . .50 C7
Bakers Wlk CM21 . . . . .97 E2
Bakery Ct CM24 . . . . .59 D6
Bakery The 🔢 SG12 . . . . . . .93 D2
Bakewell Cl LU4 . . . . .44 C5
Balcary Gdns HP4 . . . . .121 F4
Balcombe Cl LU2 . . . . .46 D4
Balcon Way WD6 . . . . .170 C8

BALDOCK 23 E8
Baldock Ind Est SG7 . . . . . .23 F7
Baldock La SG6 . . . . .23 D4
Baldock Rd
Aspenden SG9 . . . . .40 B8
Letchworth Garden City
SG6 .23 B5
Royston SG8 . . . . 6 C4
Stotfold SG5 . . . . .12 A5
Baldock St
Royston SG8 . . . . 7 C6
Ware SG12 . . . . .93 D2
Baldock Sta SG7 . . . . .12 F1
Baldock Way AL10 . . . . .169 F8
Baldways Cl HP22 . . . . .60 C3
Baldwins AL7 . . . . .111 C6
Baldwins La WD3 . . . . .166 B5
Balfour Cl AL5 . . . . .86 C3
Balfour Mews HP3 . . . . .137 A4
Balfour St SG14 . . . . .113 C7
Baliol Rd SG5 . . . . .34 F8
Ballater Cl WD19 . . . . .175 C6
BALLINGDON BOTTOM
. . . . .82 F1
Ballinger Ct
Berkhamsted HP4 . . . . .122 B3
🔢 Watford WD18 . . . . .167 B6
Balloon Car AL9 . . . . .144 B8
Balmer Cl LU4 . . . . .44 B5
Balmoral Cl
Chiswell Green AL2 . . . . . . .141 C1
Stevenage SG2 . . . . .69 C7
Balmoral Dr WD6 . . . . .170 D5
Balmoral Ho WD6 . . . . .170 C5
Balmoral Rd
Abbots Langley WD5 . . . . . .154 A7
Enfield EN1 . . . . .162 D3
Hitchin SG5 . . . . .21 E1
Watford WD24 . . . . .154 C1
Balmore Wood LU1 . . . . .31 B5
Balsams AL3 . . . . .113 D4
Bampton Rd LU4 . . . . .44 B2
Bamville Wood AL5 . . . . . . .107 C5
Banbury Cl LU4 . . . . .44 F4
Banbury St WD18 . . . . .167 B4
Bancroft SG5 . . . . .34 F7
Bancroft Gdns HA3 . . . . . . .176 C2
Bancroft Rd
Harrow HA3 . . . . .45 B5
Luton LU1 . . . . .63 B5
Bandley Rise SG2 . . . . .51 C3
Banes Down EN9 . . . . .135 E1
Bank Cl LU4 . . . . .44 C4
Bank Ct HP1 . . . . .124 C2
Bank Mill HP4 . . . . .122 C4
Bank Mill La HP4 . . . . .122 B4
Bankside CI UB9 . . . . .173 A4
Bankside Down WD3 . . . . . .165 D3
Banks Rd WD6 . . . . .170 C2
Bannister Gdns SG8 . . . . 7 E8
Bantel Villas EN11 . . . . .135 C8
Barbel Cl EN8 . . . . .163 A5
Barberry Rd HP1 . . . . .124 A3
Barbers La 🔢 LU1 . . . . .63 E7
Barchester Rd HA3 . . . . . . .176 D1
Barclay Cl
Hertford Heath SG13 . . . . .114 B4
Watford WD18 . . . . .167 A3
Barclay Cres SG2 . . . . .51 C3
Barclay Ct
Hoddesdon EN11 . . . . .135 A5
Luton LU2 . . . . .63 F8
Barclay Rd SG9 . . . . .50 D8
Barden Cl UB9 . . . . .173 C3
Bards Cnr HP1 . . . . .124 B4
Bardwell Ct 🔢 AL1 . . . . . . .127 D2
Bardwell Rd AL1 . . . . .127 D2
Barfolds AL3 . . . . .144 C8
Barford Rise LU2 . . . . .46 D1
Bargrove Ave HP2 . . . . .138 E7
Bargrove Ave HP1 . . . . .124 A2
Barham Ave WD6 . . . . .169 F5
Barham Rd SG2 . . . . .51 C5
Barker Cl HA6 . . . . .174 E4
Barkers Mead CM22 . . . . . . .77 B1
Barkham Cl LU7 . . . . .79 F2
Barking Cl LU4 . . . . .44 B6
Barkston Path WD6 . . . . . . .157 A1
BARKWAY 17 C4
Barkway CE Fst Sch
SG8 .17 C4
Barkway Hill SG8 . . . . .17 E6
Barkway Rd SG8 . . . . 7 E5
Barkway St SG8 . . . . 7 D5
BARLEY 8 F1
Barley Brow WD25 . . . . .154 C8
Barley CE Fst Sch SG8 . . . 9 A1
Barleycorn The 🔢 LU3 . . . .63 D8
Barleycroft
Buntingford SG9 . . . . .40 E6
Stevenage SG2 . . . . .51 B3
Tonwell SG12 . . . . .92 F7
Barley Croft
Hemel Hempstead
HP2 . . . . .125 C3
Hertford SG14 . . . . .113 D8
Stapleford SG14 . . . . .92 A3
BARLEYCROFT END 43 B4
Barleycroft Gn AL8 . . . . .110 C6
Barleycroft Rd AL8 . . . . .110 C5
Barley Ct
Cheshunt EN7 . . . . .148 B1
🔢 Hoddesdon EN11 . . . . .135 D8
Barley Hills CM23 . . . . .76 E4
Barley La LU4 . . . . .44 C5

Barley Mow Cvn Site The
AL4 .128 F1
Barley Mow La AL4 . . . . . . .142 F8
Barley Ponds Cl SG12 . . . . . .93 F1
Barley Ponds Rd SG12 . . . . .93 F1
Barley Rd
Barley SG8 . . . . 9 A7
Great Chishill SG8 . . . . 9 C2
Barley Rise
Baldock SG7 . . . . .24 B8
Harpenden AL5 . . . . .86 C4
Barleyvale LU3 . . . . .45 A8
Barlings Rd AL5 . . . . .107 B5
Barlow Cl AL10 . . . . .129 D7
Barmor Cl HA2 . . . . .176 B1
Barmouth Row 🔢
HP2 . . . . .124 E6
Barnack Gr SG8 . . . . 7 C7
Barnacres Rd HP3 . . . . .139 A8
Barnard Acres EN9 . . . . . . .149 E8
Barnard Gn AL7 . . . . .110 F5
Barnard Rd
Hemel Hempstead
HP3 . . . . .138 F8
Radlett WD7 . . . . .156 A4
Welwyn Garden City
AL8 .110 C6
Barncroft SG11 . . . . .57 C7
Barncroft Prim Sch
HP2 . . . . .124 D8
Barncroft Rd HP4 . . . . .121 F6
Barncroft Way AL1 . . . . .128 A2
Barn Ct
Luton LU1 . . . . .63 E7
Sawbridgeworth CM21 . . . . .97 E3
Barndell Cl SG5 . . . . .11 F6
Barndicott AL7 . . . . .111 C6
Barndicott Ho AL7 . . . . .111 C6
Barnes La W04 . . . . .138 D3
Barnes Rise WD4 . . . . .138 F4
BARNET 171 F4
Barnet By-Pass
Borehamwood WD6 . . . . . . .170 E5
Dancers Hill EN5 . . . . .158 A3
Barnet Coll EN5 . . . . .171 F5
BARNET GATE 170 F3
Barnet Gate La EN5 . . . . . .170 F3
Barnet Hill EN5 . . . . .171 F5
Barnet Hill Jun Mix Inf
Sch EN5 . . . . .171 F4
Barnet Hospl EN5 . . . . .171 D5
Barnet La
Borehamwood WD6 . . . . . . .170 B3
Totteridge N20, N20 . . . . . .171 F2
Barnet Mus★ EN5 . . . . .171 E5
Barnet Rd
Barnet EN5 . . . . .170 E3
Ganwick Corner EN6,
EN5 . . . . .159 A4
London Colney AL2 . . . . . . .142 E4
Barnet Stall Market
EN5 .171 E6
Barnet Ho HP4 . . . . .121 F7
Barnet Trad Est EN5 . . . . . .171 F6
Barnet Way (Barnet By-
Pass) WD7 . . . . .170 D2
Barnet Wood Nature
Trail★ EN5 . . . . .170 F2
Barnfield HP3 . . . . .138 F8
Barnfield Ave LU2 . . . . .45 D5
Barnfield Cl
Hoddesdon EN11 . . . . .135 A8
Lower Nazeing EN9 . . . . . . .135 F1
Barnfield Coll (New
Bedford Rd Campus)
LU2 .45 D3
Barnfield Coll (Rotherham
Avenue Campus) LU1 . . . .63 B5
Barnfield Coll (York Street
Campus) LU2 . . . . .63 E6
Barnfield Ct AL5 . . . . .107 C8
Barnfield Rd
Harpenden AL5 . . . . .107 C8
St Albans AL4 . . . . .128 C5
Welwyn Garden City
AL7 .110 E4
Barnfield South Acad
LU1 .63 B5
Barnfield Tech Coll
LU3 .45 B8
Barnfield West Acad
LU4 .44 A3
Barnhurst Path WD19 . . . . .175 C5
Barnsdale Cl WD6 . . . . .169 F8
Barns Dene AL5 . . . . .85 C4
Barnside Ct AL8 . . . . .110 C6
Barns The HP23 . . . . .99 F1
Barnston Cl LU2 . . . . .46 D1
Barnsway WD4 . . . . .138 C3
Barn The
Stevenage SG2 . . . . .50 C6
🔢 Wheathampstead
AL4 .87 D1
Barnview Lo HA3 . . . . .176 E2
Barnwell SG2 . . . . .51 B2
Barnwell Sch East Campus
SG2 .51 C4
Barnwell Sch West
Campus SG2 . . . . .51 B2
Barnwood Cl N20 . . . . .171 F1

Baron Ct SG1. . . . . .36 B1
Barons Ct **10** LU2. . . . . .45 D1
Baronsmere Ct **9**
 EN5. . . . . .171 E5
Barons Row AL5. . . . . .107 D7
Barra Cl HP3 . . . . .139 C8
Barra Ho **6** WD18. . . . . .166 F3
Barrass Cl EN3 . . . . .163 A2
Barratt Ind Pk LU2. . . . . .64 C6
Barratt Way HA3. . . . . .176 D1
Barrells Down Rd
CM23. . . . . .58 E1
Barrett La **5** CM23. . . . . . . .76 F7
Barrington Dr UB9. . . . . .173 A3
Barrington Mews AL7. . . . . .111 B5
Barrington Rd SG6. . . . . .22 F4
Barrons Row AL5. . . . . .107 D7
Barrowby Cl LU2 . . . . .46 D1
Barrowdene Cl HA5. . . . . . . .175 E1
Barrow La EN7 . . . . .147 F1
Barrow Point Ave
HA5. . . . . .175 E1
Barrow Point La HA5 . . . . . . .175 E1
Barr Rd EN6. . . . . .159 C6
Barry Cl AL2. . . . . .141 B6
Barry Ct SG1. . . . . .50 B8
Bartel Cl HP3. . . . . .125 D1
Bartholomew Court Sh
Pavilion EN8 . . . . .162 E6
Bartholomew Gn AL3. . . . . . .83 E5
Bartholomew Ho EN3. . . . . .162 C2
Bartholomew Rd **8**
CM23. . . . . .76 F6
Bartletts Cotts **4**
EN5. . . . . .171 E6
Bartletts Mead SG14. . . . . . . .92 D1
Barton Cl AL3. . . . . .86 C3
Barton Rd
Hexton SG5 . . . . .19 A1
Luton LU3 . . . . .45 C7
Wheathampstead AL4 . . . . . .108 C8
Bartons The WD6. . . . . .169 D3
Barton Way
Borehamwood WD6. . . . . . . .170 A7
Croxley Green WD3. . . . . .166 B4
Bartrams La EN4 . . . . .159 C1
Bartrop Cl EN7 . . . . .147 D3
Bartrum Villas **4**
HP4. . . . . .122 D4
BARWICK 73 C3
Barwick La SG11 . . . . .73 C3
Basbow La **2** CM23. . . . . . .76 F7
Baschurch Cl WD18. . . . . . . .166 C3
Basildon Sq HP4. . . . . .124 F7
Basil Mews **1** CM17. . . . . .118 C1
Basils Rd SG1. . . . . .50 D7
Baslow Cl HA3. . . . . .176 D2
Bassett Cl AL3. . . . . .106 B5
Bassil Rd HP2 . . . . .124 D2
Bassingbourne Cl
EN10 . . . . .134 F3
Bassingham Wlk AL7. . . . . . .110 F5
BASSUS GREEN 52 F8
Batchelors SG11. . . . . .55 E2
Batchwood Dr AL3. . . . . .127 C6
Batchwood Gdns AL3. . . . . . .127 D6
Batchwood Sch AL3. . . . . . . .127 D6
Batchwood View AL3. . . . . . .127 D5
BATCHWORTH 165 F1
Batchworth Heath
WD3. . . . . .174 B5
Batchworth Heath Hill
WD3. . . . . .174 A6
Batchworth Hill WD3. . . . . . .173 F7
Batchworth La HA6. . . . . . . .174 D5
Batchworth Rdbt
WD3. . . . . .165 E1
Bateman Rd WD3. . . . . .166 A3
BATFORD 86 D3
Batford Cl AL7. . . . . .111 B5
Batford Mill Ind Est
AL5. .86 D2
Batford Rd AL5. . . . . .86 D3
Bath Pl EN5 . . . . .171 F6
Bath Rd LU3 . . . . .45 D2
Bathurst Rd HP2. . . . . .124 E6
Batterdale AL9. . . . . .130 C6
Battlefield Rd AL1. . . . . .127 F5
Battlers Green Dr
WD7. . . . . .155 E3
Battleview AL4 . . . . .108 E8
Baud Cl SG11. . . . . .57 E2
Baulk The
Cheddington LU7. . . . . .79 F7
Ivinghoe LU7 . . . . .80 F5
Lilley LU2 . . . . .32 D2
Bawdsey Cl **1** SG1. . . . . . . .50 B8
Bay Cl LU4 . . . . .44 B6
Bay Tr HP4. . . . . .122 B4
BAYFORD 133 F6
Bayford Cl
Hemel Hempstead
HP2. . . . . .125 C8
Hertford SG13 . . . . .113 C4
Bayford CE Prim Sch
SG13. . . . . .132 F5
Bayford Gn SG13. . . . . .133 A6
Bayford La SG13. . . . . .132 F7
Bayford Lo HA5. . . . . .175 D2
Bayford Sta SG13. . . . . .133 B5
Bayhurst Dr HA6. . . . . .174 F4
Baylam Cl LU2. . . . . .46 E1
Bayley Hall Mews
SG14 . . . . .113 D5
Baylie Ct HP2 . . . . .124 E4

Baylie La HP2 . . . . .124 E4
Bay Tree Cl
Chiswell Green AL2. . . . . . . .141 C3
Hammond Street EN7 . . . . . .147 F4
Bay Tree Wlk WD17 . . . . .154 A1
Bayworth SG2. . . . . .23 B5
Beacon Ct SG13 . . . . .114 C3
Beacon Ho AL1. . . . . .127 F3
Beacon Rd
Ringshall HP4 . . . . .81 A1
Ware SG12 . . . . .94 A2
Beaconsfield LU2. . . . . .64 B8
Beaconsfield Rd
Enfield EN3 . . . . .162 D2
Hatfield AL10. . . . . .130 C6
St Albans AL1 . . . . .127 E3
Tring HP23. . . . . .99 E3
Beacons The AL10. . . . . .130 C6
Beacons The SG1. . . . . .37 B3
Beacon Way
Rickmansworth WD3. . . . . . .165 B3
Tring HP23. . . . . .100 C5
Beadles The CM22. . . . . .98 B8
Beadlow Rd LU4. . . . . .44 A4
Beagle Cl WD7 . . . . .155 F2
Beale Cl SG2 . . . . .51 C6
Bear La SG2 . . . . .4 D4
Bearton Ave SG5. . . . . .34 E8
Bearton Ct SG5 . . . . .21 E1
Bearton Ct SG5. . . . . .21 E1
Bearton Gn SG5. . . . . .21 D1
Bearton Rd SG5. . . . . .21 E1
Bearwood Cl EN6. . . . . .159 D8
Beatty Rd EN8. . . . . .162 F5
Beauchamp Gdns
WD3. . . . . .165 A1
Beauchamps AL7 . . . . .111 B5
Beaulieu Cl WD19 . . . . .167 C1
Beaulieu Dr EN6. . . . . .163 B6
Beaumayes Cl HP1 . . . . .124 B2
Beaumonds **3** AL1 . . . . . . .127 E3
Beaumont Ave AL1. . . . . .128 B4
Beaumont Ct **3** SG5. . . . . .34 D8
Beaumont Ct
8 Harpenden AL5 . . . . .86 B1
Welwyn Garden City
AL7. . . . . .110 F5
Beaumont Gate WD7 . . . . . . .156 A4
Beaumont Hall La
AL3. . . . . .106 C2
Beaumont Pl
Barnet EN5 . . . . .171 E5
Watford WD18. . . . . .167 A4
Beaumont Rd
Hammond Street EN7 . . . . . .147 F7
Luton LU3 . . . . .45 A2
Beaumont Sch AL4 . . . . .128 C4
Beaumont View EN7 . . . . . . .147 D5
Beazley Cl SG12 . . . . .93 E2
Beckbury Ct LU2. . . . . .46 E2
Becket Gdns AL6 . . . . .89 C4
Beckets Sq HP4 . . . . .122 A6
Beckets Wlk **14** SG12. . . . . .93 D1
Becketts SG14 . . . . .113 A5
Beckett's Ave SG5 . . . . .127 C6
Beckfield La SG9 . . . . .26 D7
Beckham Cl LU2. . . . . .45 D7
Becks Cl AL3 . . . . .83 D5
Bedale Rd EN2 . . . . .161 C1
Bede Cl HA5 . . . . .175 E1
Bede Ct HP4 . . . . .102 C8
Bedford Almshouses **11**
WD18. . . . . .167 C5
Bedford Ave EN5 . . . . .171 A4
Bedford Cl WD3. . . . . .151 B1
Bedford Cres EN3 . . . . .162 A4
Bedford Gdns **4** LU2. . . . . .63 D8
Bedford Park Rd AL1. . . . . . .127 E3
Bedford Rd
Hitchin SG5 . . . . .34 E7
Ickleford SG5 . . . . .21 D5
Letchworth Garden City
SG6. . . . . .22 D7
Lower Stondon SG16. . . . . . . .10 B3
Moor Park HA6 . . . . .174 D6
St Albans AL1 . . . . .127 E2
Bedford St
Berkhamsted HP4 . . . . .122 D4
Hitchin SG5 . . . . .34 D7
Watford WD24. . . . . .167 B8
BEDMOND 139 F4
Bedmond La
Bricket Wood AL3,
WD5. . . . . .140 B6
St Albans AL3 . . . . .126 F1
Bedmond Rd
Abbots Langley WD5 . . . . . . .139 F2
Hemel Hempstead HP3. . . . . .125 D1
Pimlico HP3. . . . . .139 E2
Bedmond Village Prim
Sch WD5 . . . . .139 F3
BEDWELL. 50 E5
Bedwell Ave AL9,
SG13 . . . . .132 A4
Bedwell Cl AL7. . . . . .110 E5
Bedwell Cres SG1 . . . . .50 E5
Bedwell Prim Sch SG1. . . . . .51 A5

Bedwell Rise SG1. . . . . .50 E5
Beesonend Cotts AL5 . . . . . .107 B4
Beesonend La AL3,
AL5. . . . . .106 F3
Beeston Cl WD19 . . . . .175 D6
Beeston Dr EN8 . . . . .148 D4
Beetham Ct SG12. . . . . .92 E4
Beethoven Rd WD6. . . . . . . .169 D3
Beeton Cl HA5. . . . . .176 A3
Beggarman's La SG11. . . . . . .72 D8
Beggars Bush La WD18,
WD3. . . . . .166 D4
Beggars La HP23 . . . . .101 A3
Beken Ct WD25. . . . . .154 C4
Belcher Rd **8** EN11 . . . . . . .135 A7
Belcon Ind Est EN11 . . . . . . .135 C6
Beldam Ave SG8. . . . . .7 E5
Beldams Gate CM23. . . . . . . .77 B5
Beldams La CM23. . . . . .77 B5
Belfairs Gn WD19. . . . . .175 D5
Belford Rd WD6. . . . . .156 F1
Belfry Ave UB9 . . . . .173 B2
Belfry La WD3. . . . . .165 C1
Belfry The LU2. . . . . .45 E6
Belfry The WD24. . . . . .167 D8
Belfry Villas UB9. . . . . .173 A2
Belgrave Ave WD18. . . . . . . .166 F4
Belgrave Cl AL4 . . . . .128 C2
Belgrave Dr WD4 . . . . .139 C3
Belgrave Ho **6** CM23 . . . . . .77 B8
Belgrave Mews SG1 . . . . .69 A8
Belgrave Rd LU4. . . . . .44 D5
Belgravia Cl EN5 . . . . .171 F6
Belham Rd WD4 . . . . .139 A3
Belhaven Ct **3** WD6. . . . . . .169 F8
Bell Acre SG6 . . . . .23 B4
Bell Acre Gdns SG6. . . . . .23 B4
Bellamy Cl
Knebworth SG3. . . . . .68 F5
Watford WD17 . . . . .167 A8
Bellamy Rd EN8 . . . . .148 E2
BELL BAR 145 A7
Bellchambers Cl AL2. . . . . . .142 C5
Bell Cl
Bedmond WD5. . . . . .139 F4
Hitchin SG4 . . . . .35 B6
Knebworth SG3. . . . . .69 A5
7 Pinner HA5. . . . . .175 D1
Bellefield Rd EN3. . . . . .162 E1
Bellefield Rd WD24. . . . . . . .154 D2
Belle Vue La WD23. . . . . .168 D1
Belle Vue Rd SG12. . . . . .93 F1
Bellevue Terr UB9. . . . . .173 A3
Bell Farm Ind Pk SG8. . . . . . .18 A2
Bellfield Ave HA3 . . . . .176 D4
Bellgate HP2 . . . . .124 E6
Bellgate Prim Sch
HP2. . . . . .124 E5
Bell Gn HP3 . . . . .137 B4
Bell Ho AL7 . . . . .37 B3
Bellingdon WD19 . . . . .175 E7
Bellis Ho AL7. . . . . .111 B4
Bell La
Abbots Langley WD5 . . . . . . .140 A4
Berkhamsted HP4 . . . . .121 E5
Brookmans Park AL9 . . . . . . .145 A7
Enfield EN3 . . . . .162 E1
Hertford SG14 . . . . .113 D6
Hoddesdon, Broxbourne
EN11. . . . . .134 E2
Hoddesdon EN11 . . . . .135 A6
Little Chalfont HP6 . . . . .150 C1
Nuthampstead SG8 . . . . .18 B2
Shenley AL2 . . . . .142 E2
Stevenage SG1 . . . . .50 C7
Widford SG12 . . . . .95 D4
Bell Leys Comb Sch
HP6 . . . . .150 B1
Bell Leys HP22 . . . . .60 B3
Bell Mead CM21 . . . . .97 C3
Bellmount Wood Ave
WD17. . . . . .166 E8
Bell Rdbt The AL2 . . . . .142 F4
Bell Row **8** SG7 . . . . .23 B8
Bells Hill
Barnet EN5 . . . . .171 D5
Bishop's Stortford CM23. . . . . .76 F7
Bell St CM21. . . . . .97 E2
Bells Wlk CM21. . . . . .97 E2
Bell View AL4. . . . . .128 D3
Bell Wlk HP22 . . . . .60 B3
Belmers Rd HP23. . . . . .100 D1
Belmont Ct **7** AL1 . . . . .127 D2
Belmont Fst Sch HA3 . . . . . .176 F1
Belmont Hill AL1 . . . . .127 D2
Belmont Lo HA3 . . . . .176 D3
Belmont Mid Sch
HA3. . . . . .176 F1
Belmont Rd
Hemel Hempstead
HP3. . . . . .138 E8
Luton LU1 . . . . .63 C7
Watford WD23. . . . . .167 E4
Belmor Rd AL3 . . . . .170 A3
Belper Rd LU4. . . . . .44 D2
Belsham Pl LU2. . . . . .46 E2
BELSIZE. 151 E6
Belsize Cl
Hemel Hempstead
HP3. . . . . .125 A2
St Albans AL4 . . . . .128 C8
Belsize Cotts WD3. . . . . .151 E6
Belsize Rd
Harrow HA3. . . . . .176 D3
Hemel Hempstead HP3. . . . . .125 A2
Belswains Gn WD19 . . . . . . .138 E8
Belswains La HP3. . . . . .138 F7
Belswains Prim Sch
HP3. . . . . .138 F7
Beltona Gdns EN8. . . . . .148 D4

Belton Rd HP4. . . . . .122 A5
Belvedere Ct
Hoddesdon EN11. . . . . .135 A5
Watford WD19. . . . . .167 E3
Belvedere Gdns AL2 . . . . . . .141 A4
Belvedere Rd LU3 . . . . .45 B5
Bembridge Gdns LU3 . . . . . . .44 F7
Ben Austins AL3 . . . . .106 A4
Benbow Cl AL1. . . . . .128 B1
Benbroke Pl SG1 . . . . .37 B4
Benchley Hill SG4. . . . . .35 C8
Benchleys Rd HP1 . . . . .123 F2
Bencroft EN7. . . . . .148 A5
Bencroft Rd HP2 . . . . .124 E3
Bencroft Wood*
EN10 . . . . .133 D1
BENDISH. 66 A7
Bendish La SG4 . . . . .66 C7
Bendysh Rd WD23. . . . . .167 E5
Benedict Ct HA5. . . . . .175 E1
Benedict Ho **8** AL3. . . . . . . .127 D4
Benedictine Gate
EN8. . . . . .148 E4
Benedictine Pl **12**
AL1. .127 D3
Benford Rd EN11 . . . . .134 F4
Bengarth Dr HA3 . . . . .176 D1
BENGEO 113 C8
Bengeo Ho SG14 . . . . .92 C1
Bengeo Mdws SG14. . . . . . . .92 C1
Bengeo Mdws SG14. . . . . . . .92 C1
Bengeo Prim Sch
SG14. . . . . .92 C1
Bengeo St SG14 . . . . .113 C8
Benhooks Ave CM23 . . . . . . .76 F5
Benhooks Pl **1** CM23. . . . . .76 F5
Beningfield Dr AL2. . . . . .142 B4
BENINGTON 52 E4
Benington CE Prim Sch
SG2. . . . . .52 D4
Benington Cl LU2. . . . . .45 F5
Benington Lordship
Gdns* SG2. . . . . .52 D4
Benington Rd
Aston SG2 . . . . .51 F2
Benington SG2. . . . . .52 A7
Benneck Ho WD18. . . . . .166 E3
Bennett Cl
Northwood HA6. . . . . .174 F3
Welwyn Garden City
AL7. . . . . .110 F2
Bennett Ct
Letchworth Garden City
SG6. . . . . .22 F6
Letchworth Garden City
SG6. . . . . .23 A5
Bennetts Cl AL4 . . . . .143 D8
BENNETTS END 139 A8
Bennetts End Cl HP3. . . . . . .124 F1
Bennetts End Rd HP3. . . . . . .125 A1
Bennettsgate HP3 . . . . .139 A8
Bennetts La SG9. . . . . .25 F4
Benningfield SG12 . . . . .95 D5
Benningfield Gdns
HP4. . . . . .122 E6
Benningfield Rd SG14 . . . . . .92 B4
Bennington Dr WD6. . . . . . . .169 F8
Benskin Rd WD18. . . . . .167 A4
Benslow La SG4 . . . . .35 A7
Benslow Rise SG4 . . . . .35 A8
Benson Cl LU3. . . . . .44 F7
Benson Ct **4** EN3 . . . . .163 A1
Bensted SG2 . . . . .69 C8
Bentfield Bower CM24 . . . . . .59 C8
Bentfield End Cswy
CM24. . . . . .59 D7
Bentfield Gdns CM24. . . . . . .59 D7
Bentfield Gn CM24. . . . . .59 D7
BENTFIELD GREEN 59 D7
Bentfield Pl CM24 . . . . .59 D7
Bentfield Prim Sch
CM24. . . . . .59 D7
Bentfield Rd CM24. . . . . .59 D7
Bentham Ho **4** CM20 . . . . . .117 C1
Bentick Way SG4. . . . . .67 F2
Bentley Cl CM23. . . . . .76 F5
Bentley Ct **2** LU1 . . . . .63 C8
BENTLEY HEATH 158 F4
Bentley Heath La EN5. . . . . .158 E8
Bentley Lo WD23 . . . . .176 E8
Bentley Rd SG14. . . . . .112 F1
Bentley Wood High Sch
HA7. . . . . .176 F5
Benton Rd WD19. . . . . .175 D5
Bentons The HP4 . . . . .121 F6
Bentsley Cl AL4. . . . . .128 C7
Berceau Wlk WD17 . . . . .166 E8
Berdan Ct EN3 . . . . .163 A2
Berefield HP2 . . . . .124 D5
Beresford Rd
Luton LU4 . . . . .45 A1
Rickmansworth WD3. . . . . . .164 F1
St Albans AL1 . . . . .128 C2
Bericot Gn AL9 . . . . .111 E7
Bericot Way AL7 . . . . .111 D6
Berkeley Cl SG5. . . . . .23 A4
Berkeley Cl
Abbots Langley WD5 . . . . . . .153 F5
Borehamwood WD6. . . . . . . .170 A4
6 Hitchin SG5 . . . . .34 D8
Potters Bar EN6. . . . . .158 F7
Stevenage SG2 . . . . .69 A8
Ware SG12 . . . . .93 C2
Berkeley Ct
Croxley Green WD3. . . . . . . .166 D4
6 Harpenden AL5 . . . . .86 A2

Berkeley Mews AL1 . . . . . . 128 B2
Berkeley Path 2 LU2 . . . .63 E8
Berkeley Sq HP2 . . . . 105 C3
BERKHAMSTED 122 C6
Berkhamsted Castle*
HP4 . . . . 122 D5
Berkhamsted Collegiate
Sch
Berkhamsted HP4 . . . . . .122 B4
Berkhamsted HP4 . . . . . .122 C4
Berkhamsted Rd HP1 . . .123 E5
Berkhamsted Sta
HP4 . . . . 122 C5
Berkley Ave EN8 . . . . . . .162 D5
Berkley Cl
Pitstone LU7 . . . . .80 D3
St Albans AL4 . . . . .128 C7
Berkley Ct 2 HP4 . . . . . .122 C4
Berkley PI EN8 . . . . .105 C3
Berkley Wlk WD3 . . . . . . .164 C4
Bermer PI WD24 . . . . .167 C8
Bermer Rd WD24 . . . . . . .167 C8
Bernard Gr EN9 . . . . .163 B6
BERNARD'S HEATH 127 F6
Bernards Heath Inf Sch
AL1 . . . . .127 F5
Bernards Heath Jun Sch
AL1 . . . . .127 E6
Bernard St AL3 . . . . .127 D4
Berners Dr AL1 . . . . .141 E8
Berners Way EN10 . . . . . .148 F8
Bernhardt Cres SG2 . . . . .51 C6
Berries The AL4 . . . . .128 A7
Berrow Cl LU2 . . . . .46 E2
Berry Ave WD24 . . . . .154 B3
Berry Cl WD3 . . . . .165 B2
Berryfield LU7 . . . . .79 F7
Berrygrove La WD25 . . . .168 A8
Berry Grove La WD24,
WD25 . . . . .154 E1
Berrygrove Prim Sch
WD25 . . . . .154 D4
Berry La WD3 . . . . .165 A2
Berry Leys LU3 . . . . .44 E7
Berrymead HP2 . . . . .124 F5
Berry Way WD3 . . . . .165 B2
Bert Collins Ct LU1 . . . . . .63 C7
Berthold Mews EN9 . . . . .163 B6
Berwick Cl
Harrow HA2 . . . . .176 F4
Holdbrook EN8 . . . . .163 A5
Stevenage SG1 . . . . .50 A8
Berwick PI AL7 . . . . .110 D3
Berwick Rd WD6 . . . . . . .156 F1
Besant Ho 2 WD24 . . . . .167 D7
Besford Cl LU2 . . . . .46 E2
Bessemer Cl SG5 . . . . .21 E2
Bessemer Dr SG1 . . . . .50 B4
Bessemer Rd AL7, AL8 . . .89 E2
Bethune Cl LU1 . . . . .63 B6
Bethune Ct LU1 . . . . .63 B6
Betjeman Cl
Cheshunt EN7 . . . . .148 A3
Harpenden AL5 . . . . .86 C2
Betjeman Gdns WD3 . . . .164 D5
Betjeman Rd SG8 . . . . .2 D1
Betjeman Way HP1 . . . . .124 B4
Betony Vale SG8 . . . . .7 F5
Bettespool Mdws AL3 . . .106 A6
Betty Entwistle Ho
AL1 . . . . .141 E8
Betty's La HP2 . . . . .100 A4
Bevan Cl HP3 . . . . .124 E1
Bevan Ho 3 WD24 . . . . .167 D7
Beverley Cl SG8 . . . . .7 88
Beverley Gdns
Cheshunt EN7 . . . . .148 A1
St Albans AL4 . . . . .128 D7
Welwyn Garden City
AL7 . . . . .111 C6
Beverley Rd
Luton LU4 . . . . .44 F1
Stevenage SG1 . . . . .37 B2
Beverly Cl EN10 . . . . .134 E2
Bevil Ct EN11 . . . . .115 A1
Bewdley Cl AL5 . . . . .107 D6
Bewley Cl EN8 . . . . .162 D8
Beyers Gdns 5 EN11 . . .115 A1
Beyers Prospect
EN11 . . . . .115 A1
Beyers Ride 3 EN11 . . . .115 A1
Bibbs Hall La SG4, SG6, AL6 . .87 E6
Biddenham Turn
WD25 . . . . .154 C4
Bideford Gdns LU3 . . . . . .45 D4
Bideford Rd EN3 . . . . . . .162 F1
Bidwell Cl SG6 . . . . .23 B5
Biggin Hill SG9 . . . . .28 D7
Biggin La SG5 . . . . .34 F7
Biggs Grove Rd EN7 . . . .147 E4
Bignells Corner EN6 . . . .158 B5
Billet La HP4 . . . . .122 A6
Bill Miller Ct SG6 . . . . .22 F8
Billy Lows La EN6 . . . . . . .159 B8
Bilton Ct LU1 . . . . .44 F1
Bilton Rd SG4 . . . . .21 F2
Bilton Way
Enfield EN3 . . . . .162 F1
Luton LU1 . . . . .44 F1
Bilton Way Ind Est LU1 . .62 F8
Bingen Rd SG5 . . . . .21 C1
Bingham Cl HP1 . . . . .123 F3
Bingham's Park Childrens
Farm* HP1 . . . . .123 E8
Bingley Rd LU3 . . . . .135 C6
Binham Cl LU2 . . . . .45 D7
Binyon Cres HA7 . . . . . . .176 F5

Birchall La SG14 . . . . .111 E4
Birchalls CM24 . . . . .59 E8
Birchall Wood AL7 . . . . . .111 C5
BIRCHANGER 59 E2
Birchanger CE Prim Sch
CM23 . . . . .59 D2
Birchanger Ind Est
CM23 . . . . .59 B2
Birchanger La CM23 . . . . .59 D2
Birch Ct HA6 . . . . .174 C4
Birch Dr
Hatfield AL10 . . . . .130 A4
Maple Cross WD3 . . . . . .172 D5
Birchen Gr LU2 . . . . .45 F3
Bircherley Ct 14
SG14 . . . . .113 D6
Bircherley Green Ctr The
8 SG14 . . . . .113 D6
Bircherley St SG14 . . . . . .113 D6
Birches The
Bushey WD23 . . . . .168 C4
Codicote SG4 . . . . .89 A8
Hemel Hempstead HP3 . .137 F8
Letchworth Garden City
SG6 . . . . .22 E8
London Colney AL2 . . . . .142 C4
Waltham Abbey EN9 . . . .163 F5
Birchfield Rd EN8 . . . . . . .148 C2
Birch Gn
Hemel Hempstead
HP1 . . . . .123 F5
Hertingfordbury SG14 . . .112 C4
Birch Gr
Lower Stondon SG16 . . . . .10 B3
Oaklands AL6 . . . . .89 E8
Potters Bar EN6 . . . . .159 E7
BIRCH GREEN 112 C3
Birch La HP3 . . . . .151 B7
Birch Leys HP2 . . . . .125 C8
Birch Link LU4 . . . . .45 C1
Birchmead AL1 . . . . .153 F1
Birchmead Cl AL3 . . . . . .127 D6
Birch Pk HA3 . . . . .176 C3
Birch Rd
Berkhamsted HP4 . . . . . .121 D7
Woolmer Green SG3 . . . . .69 B1
Birch Tree Gr HP5 . . . . . .136 B1
Birch Tree Wlk WD17 . . .153 F2
Birchway AL10 . . . . .130 B7
Birch Way
Harpenden AL5 . . . . .107 C8
London Colney AL2 . . . . .142 D4
Birch Wlk WD6 . . . . .170 A8
BIRCHWOOD 130 B7
Birchwood
Birchanger CM23 . . . . . . .59 D2
Shenley WD7 . . . . .157 A5
Waltham Abbey EN9 . . . .163 E5
Birchwood Ave AL10 . . . .130 A7
Birchwood Avenue Prim
Sch AL10 . . . . .130 B7
Birchwood Cl AL10 . . . . .130 A7
Birchwood High Sch
CM23 . . . . .77 C8
Birchwood Ho AL7 . . . . . .111 B6
Birchwood Way AL2 . . . .141 B3
Birdcroft Rd AL8 . . . . . . .110 D5
Birdie Way SG13 . . . . . . .114 B7
Birds Cl AL7 . . . . .111 B4
Birdsfoot La LU3 . . . . .45 B6
Birds Hill SG6 . . . . .23 A6
Birkbeck Rd EN2 . . . . . . .161 D1
Birken Ct HA6 . . . . .174 B5
Birklands AL1 . . . . .142 B7
Birklands La AL1 . . . . .142 B7
Birling Dr LU2 . . . . .46 C4
Birsley Ct 1 EN5 . . . . . . .171 D5
Birstal Gn WD19 . . . . . . .175 C3
Birtley Croft LU2 . . . . .46 E1
BISCOT 45 C2
Biscot Rd LU3 . . . . .45 C2
Bishop Ct WD5 . . . . .153 F8
Bishop Ken Rd HA3 . . . . .176 F1
Bishops Ave
Borehamwood WD6 . . . . .169 F4
Moor Park HA6 . . . . .174 F7
Bishop's Ave CM23 . . . . . .76 F3
Bishops Cl
Cheshunt EN8 . . . . .148 B1
9 Luton LU3 . . . . .45 D1
Bishops Field HP22 . . . . . .99 A4
Bishop's Hatfield Girls'
Sch AL10 . . . . .130 A5
Bishops Mead HP4 . . . . . .124 B1
Bishop's Palace (rem of)*
AL9 . . . . .130 D6
BISHOP'S PARK 76 C6
Bishops Park Way
CM23 . . . . .76 B7
Bishop Sq Bsns Pk
AL10 . . . . .129 C5
Bishops Rd AL6 . . . . .90 D6
Bishops Rise AL10 . . . . . .129 F2
BISHOP'S STORTFORD
. . . . .76 D7
Bishop's Stortford Bsns
Ctr CM23 . . . . .77 A6
Bishop's Stortford Coll
CM23 . . . . .76 E7

Bishop's Stortford High
Sch The CM23 . . . . .76 F4
Bishop's Stortford Sta
CM23 . . . . .77 A6
Bishop's Wood Ctry Pk*
WD3 . . . . .173 F4
Bishops Wood Hospl
HA6 . . . . .174 B4
Bishop Wood CE Jun Sch
HP23 . . . . .100 A3
Biskra WD17 . . . . .167 A8
Bisley Cl EN8 . . . . .162 D6
Bittern Cl
Hammond Street EN7 . . .147 C6
Hemel Hempstead HP3 . .138 F6
Stevenage SG2 . . . . .51 D2
Bittern Way SG6 . . . . .11 E1
Bit The HP23 . . . . .100 D1
Black Adder Cotts
EN9 . . . . .149 D8
Blackberry Mead SG2 . . . .51 D3
Blackbirds La WD25 . . . . .155 C5
Black Boy Wood AL2 . . . .141 A1
Blackbridge La SG10 . . . . .95 E7
Blackbury Cl EN6 . . . . . . .159 C8
Blackbushe CM23 . . . . . . .59 C1
Blackbush Spring
CM20 . . . . .118 A1
Black Cut 3 AL1 . . . . . . .127 E2
Blackdale EN7 . . . . .148 A4
Blackdown Cl SG1 . . . . . . .37 B3
Blackett-Ord Ct SG8 . . . . . .7 D7
Blacketts Wood Dr
WD3 . . . . .164 B5
Black Fan Rd
Welwyn Garden City
AL7 . . . . .110 F7
Welwyn Garden City
AL7 . . . . .111 B6
Blackford Rd WD19 . . . . .175 D5
Black Green Wood Cl
AL2 . . . . .141 B2
BLACKHALL 30 B4
Blackhorse Cl SG4 . . . . . . .35 A5
Blackhorse La
Hitchin SG4 . . . . .35 A5
Redbourn AL3 . . . . .106 A6
Ridge EN6 . . . . .157 F8
Blackhorse Rd SG6 . . . . . .23 C8
Blackley Cl WD17 . . . . . . .153 F2
Black Lion Cl CM17 . . . . .118 C4
Black Lion Hill WD7 . . . . .156 F7
Blackmoor La WD18 . . . .166 D4
Blackmore Cl SG1 . . . . . . .51 A8
BLACKMORE END 87 C6
Blackmore Gate HP22 . . . .99 A4
Blackmore Manor AL4 . . .87 B6
Blacksmith Cl SG5 . . . . . . .11 F7
Blacksmiths Cl CM23 . . . .76 B5
Black Smiths Cl SG12 . . .115 A7
Blacksmiths Hill SG2 . . . . .52 E4
Blacksmith's La
Reed SG8 . . . . .16 C5
St Albans AL3 . . . . .127 B3
Blacksmiths Way
CM21 . . . . .97 A1
Black Swan Ct 1
SG12 . . . . .93 D1
Black Swan La LU3 . . . . . .45 A5
Blackthorn Cl
St Albans AL4 . . . . .128 C6
Watford WD25 . . . . .154 B7
Blackthorn Dr LU2 . . . . . .46 C4
Blackthorne Cl AL10 . . . .129 F2
Blackthorn Rd AL7 . . . . . .111 A5
Blackwater La HP3 . . . . . .125 E1
Blackwell Ct HA3 . . . . . . .176 D3
Blackwell Dr WD19 . . . . .167 C3
Blackwell Hall La
HP5 . . . . .150 C6
Blackwell Rd WD4 . . . . . .139 A2
Blackwells HP23 . . . . .101 D2
Blackwood Ct EN7 . . . . . .148 F5
Bladon Cl SG4 . . . . .35 F3
Blaine Ct LU2 . . . . .100 A6
Blair Cl
Bishop's Stortford
CM23 . . . . .76 C7
Hemel Hempstead HP2 . .105 B1
Stevenage SG2 . . . . .51 D1
Blairhead Dr WD19 . . . . .175 B7
Blake Cl
Royston SG8 . . . . .2 D1
St Albans AL1 . . . . .142 A8
Blakedown LU2 . . . . .45 E1
Blakedown Rd AL8 . . . . . .110 D8
Blakemore End Rd
SG4 . . . . .35 D3
Blakeney Dr LU2 . . . . .45 C7
Blakeney Ho SG1 . . . . .50 A7
Blakeney Rd SG1 . . . . .50 A7
Blakes Ct
Rickmansworth WD3 . . . .165 C1
Sawbridgeworth CM21 . . .97 E2
Blakesware Manor
SG12 . . . . .95 B5
Blakes Way AL4 . . . . .89 C6
Blanchard Dr 3
WD18 . . . . .166 E5
Blanchard Gr EN3 . . . . . .163 B1
Blanche La EN6 . . . . .157 F5
Blandford Ave LU2 . . . . . .45 D6
Blandford Rd AL1 . . . . . . .128 B3
Blanes The SG12 . . . . .93 C3
Blattner Cl WD6 . . . . .169 E5
Blaxland Terr 9 EN8 . . . .148 D3
Blaydon Rd LU2 . . . . .64 A8

Bleak House Mews 9
AL3 . . . . .127 D4
Blegberry Gdns HP4 . . . .121 E4
Blenheim Cl
Cheddington LU7 . . . . . . .79 F8
Sawbridgeworth CM21 . . .118 C8
Watford WD19 . . . . .167 D2
Blenheim Cres LU3 . . . . . .45 C2
Blenheim Ct
Bishop's Stortford
CM23 . . . . .76 C7
Welwyn Garden City
AL7 . . . . .110 F7
Blenheim Mews WD7 . . .156 E6
Blenheim Rd
Barnet EN5 . . . . .171 D5
St Albans AL1 . . . . .127 F4
Blenheim Way SG2 . . . . . .69 D7
Blenheim Rd WD5 . . . . . .154 A7
Blenkin Cl AL2 . . . . .127 C7
Blind La SG2, SG9 . . . . . . .38 F5
Blindman's La EN8 . . . . . .148 D2
Bliss Ho EN1 . . . . .162 A1
Block 10 4 WD17 . . . . . .167 A8
Block 12 3 WD17 . . . . . .167 A8
Block 14 2 WD17 . . . . . .167 A8
Bloomfield Ave LU2 . . . . . .45 E6
Bloomfield Rd
Hammond Street EN7 . . .147 C6
Harpenden AL5 . . . . .85 F3
Blossom La EN2 . . . . .161 C1
Bluebell Cl
Hemel Hempstead
HP1 . . . . .123 E2
Hertford SG13 . . . . .114 A6
Bluebell Dr
Bedmond WD5 . . . . .139 F4
Goff's Oak EN7 . . . . .147 D3
Lower Stondon SG16 . . . .10 A3
Bluebells AL6 . . . . .89 D7
Bluebell Way AL10 . . . . . .109 F1
Bluebell Wood Cl LU1 . . . .63 A7
Blueberry Cl AL3 . . . . .127 D7
Bluebird Way AL2 . . . . . . .140 E1
Bluebridge Ave AL9 . . . . . .144 F4
Blue Bridge Rd AL9 . . . . .144 E4
Bluecoat Ct 18 SG14 . . . .113 D6
Bluecoats Ave SG14 . . . . .113 D6
Bluecoat Yd SG12 . . . . . . .93 D1
Bluehouse Hill AL3 . . . . . .127 B3
Blueprint Commercial Ctr
WD24 . . . . .154 C1
Blue Springs HA6 . . . . . . .174 E4
Bluett Rd AL2 . . . . .142 D4
Blundell Cl AL3 . . . . .127 D7
Blundell Rd LU3 . . . . .45 A4
Blunesfield EN6 . . . . .159 D8
Blunts La AL2 . . . . .140 D5
Blyth Cl
Borehamwood WD6 . . . . .170 A8
Stevenage SG1 . . . . .50 A7
Blythe Rd EN11 . . . . .135 D5
Blythewood HP3 . . . . .138 A8
Blyth PI 8 LU1 . . . . .63 D6
Blythway AL7 . . . . .89 F1
Blythway Ho AL7 . . . . .89 F1
Blythway Gdns CM24 . . . .59 D6
Blythwood Rd HA5 . . . . . .175 D2
Boardman Ct EN5 . . . . . . .171 E4
Bockings SG2 . . . . .38 C1
Bodmin Rd LU4 . . . . .44 F3
Bodwell Cl HP1 . . . . .124 A4
Bogmoor Rd SG8 . . . . .18 A8
Bognor Gdns WD19 . . . . .175 C5
Bohemia HP2 . . . . .124 E4
Boissy Cl AL4 . . . . .128 E2
Boleyn Cl HP2 . . . . .125 C8
Boleyn Ct EN10 . . . . .134 E2
Bolingbroke Rd LU1 . . . . .63 B6
Boling Brook AL4 . . . . . . .128 A7
Bolney Gn LU2 . . . . .46 C4
Bolton Cl LU1 . . . . .63 F7
Boltons Park (Royal
Veterinary Coll)
EN6 . . . . .145 A2
Bond Ct AL5 . . . . .85 F3
Bondor Bsns Ctr SG7 . . . .23 F7
Boniface Gdns HA3 . . . . . .176 B3
Boniface Wlk HA3 . . . . . . .176 B3
Bonks Hill CM21 . . . . .97 D1
Bonney Gr EN7 . . . . .148 A1
Bonneygrove Prim Sch
EN7 . . . . .148 A1
Bonnick Cl LU1 . . . . .63 C6
Bonnick Ct LU1 . . . . .63 C6
Booths Cl AL9 . . . . .144 D7
Boreham Holt WD6 . . . . . .169 F5
Boreham Mews 1
EN11 . . . . .115 A1
BOREHAMWOOD 170 B4
Borehamwood Ent Ctr
WD6 . . . . .169 F6
Borehamwood Ind Pk
WD6 . . . . .170 B7
Borehamwood Sh Pk
WD6 . . . . .169 F6
Bornedene EN6 . . . . .158 E8
Borodale AL5 . . . . .86 A1
Borough Ind Est The
LU3 . . . . .45 B2
Borough Way EN6 . . . . . . .158 E7
Borrell Cl EN10 . . . . .134 F3
Borrowdale Ct 4
HP2 . . . . .124 E6
Borton Ave SG16 . . . . .10 B8
Bosanquet Rd EN11 . . . . .135 C8
Boscombe Ct SG6 . . . . . . .23 B6

Bosmore Rd LU3 . . . . .44 F5
Boswell Cl WD7 . . . . .156 E7
Boswell Dr SG5 . . . . .21 E7
Boswell Gdns SG1 . . . . . . .36 D1
Boswick La HP4 . . . . .121 D8
BOTANY BAY 160 D3
Botany Lo SG1 . . . . .37 B3
BOTLEY 136 A1
Botley La HP5 . . . . .136 A1
Botley Rd
Botley HP5 . . . . .136 A1
Hemel Hempstead HP22 . .125 B8
Bottom House La
HP23 . . . . .101 A3
Bottom La WD3, WD4 . . .152 C4
Bottom Rd HP23 . . . . . . .119 F3
Bough Beech Ct EN3 . . . .162 D2
Boughton Way HP6 . . . . . .150 C1
Boulevard The
Watford WD18 . . . . .166 D4
Welwyn Garden City
AL7 . . . . .110 F8
Boulton Rd SG1 . . . . .37 C2
Bounce The HP2 . . . . .124 D5
Boundary Cl
Barnet EN5 . . . . .171 F8
Bishop's Stortford CM23 . .77 A5
Boundary Cotts HP3 . . . .137 D2
Boundary Ct AL7 . . . . .110 F2
Boundary Dr SG14 . . . . . .113 D8
Boundary Ho
Cheshunt EN8 . . . . .162 D7
Welwyn Garden City
AL7 . . . . .110 D3
Boundary La AL7 . . . . .110 E2
Boundary Pk HP2 . . . . . . .125 C5
Boundary Rd
Bishop's Stortford
CM23 . . . . .77 A5
St Albans AL1 . . . . .127 E5
Boundary Way
Hemel Hempstead
HP2 . . . . .125 C5
Watford WD25 . . . . .154 C7
Bounds Field SG11 . . . . . .75 F8
Bourne Apartments The 2
AL5 . . . . .85 F2
Bourne Cl
Hoddesdon EN10 . . . . . . .134 F3
Ware SG12 . . . . .93 D2
BOURNE END 123 B1
Bourne End Cotts
HP1 . . . . .123 C1
Bourne End Mills Ind Est
HP1 . . . . .137 B8
Bourne End Rd HA6 . . . . .174 E6
Bourne Hall WD23 . . . . . .168 A3
Bournehall Ave WD23 . . .168 A4
Bournehall La WD23 . . . .168 A4
Bournehall Prim Sch
WD23 . . . . .168 B4
Bournehall Rd WD23 . . . .168 A3
Bourne Honour SG12 . . . .92 E7
Bourne La SG12 . . . . .96 A6
Bournemead WD23 . . . . .168 B3
Bournemouth Rd 3
SG1 . . . . .50 B8
Bourne Rd
Berkhamsted HP4 . . . . . .121 F5
Bushey WD23 . . . . .168 A4
Bourne The
Bishop's Stortford
CM23 . . . . .77 A8
Bovingdon HP3 . . . . .137 A4
Clapgate SG11 . . . . .57 C6
3 Harpenden AL5 . . . . . . .85 F2
Ware SG12 . . . . .93 D2
Bouvier Rd EN3 . . . . .162 C1
BOVINGDON 137 B3
Bovingdon Cres
WD25 . . . . .154 D5
Bovingdon Ct HP3 . . . . . .137 A3
BOVINGDON GREEN 137 A2
Bovingdon Prim Sch
HP3 . . . . .137 B4
Bowbrook LU2 . . . . .46 F1
Bowcock Wlk SG1 . . . . . . .50 E3
Bower Heath La AL5 . . . . .86 C6
Bowershott SG6 . . . . .23 A4
Bower's Par AL5 . . . . .86 A1
Bowers Way AL5 . . . . .86 A1
Bowes Lyon Mews
AL3 . . . . .127 D3
Bowgate AL1 . . . . .127 E4
Bowlers Mead SG9 . . . . . .40 D7
Bowles Gn EN1 . . . . .162 B3
Bowling Cl
14 Bishop's Stortford
CM23 . . . . .76 F6
Harpenden AL5 . . . . .107 C7
Bowling Ct WD18 . . . . . . .167 A5
Bowling Gn SG1 . . . . .50 C8
Bowling Green La
Buntingford SG9 . . . . .40 D8
Luton LU2 . . . . .45 E2
Bowling Rd SG12 . . . . .93 E1
Bowmans Ave SG4 . . . . . . .35 B6
Bowmans Cl
Potters Bar EN6 . . . . .159 D7
Welwyn AL6 . . . . .89 C6
Bowmans Ct HP2 . . . . . . .124 E5
Bowmans Gn WD25 . . . . .154 E3
Bowmansgreen Prim Sch
AL2 . . . . .142 C4
Bowman Trad Est SG1 . . .50 B5

Bowring Gn WD19 .... 175 C5
Bowsher Ct 5 SG12 .... 93 E1
Bowyer Ct EN8 .... 162 F6
Bowyers 6 HP2 .... 124 D5
Bowyer's Cl SG5 .... 21 D1
Boxberry Cl SG1 .... 50 E6
Boxfield AL7 .... 111 B3
Boxgold Gn SG2 .... 51 D8
Boxgrove Cl LU2 .... 46 C5
Boxhill 3 HP2 .... 124 D5
Box La
  Hemel Hempstead
  HP3 .... 137 E7
  Hoddesdon EN11 .... 134 E6
BOXMOOR 124 A2
Boxmoor Prim Sch
  HP1 .... 124 A2
Boxted Cl LU4 .... 44 C5
Boxted Rd HP1 .... 123 F5
Boxtree La HA3 .... 176 D3
Boxtree Rd HA3 .... 176 D3
Boxwell Rd HP4 .... 122 B4
Boyce Cl WD6 .... 169 E8
Boyd Cl 1 LU2 .... 77 B8
Boyes Cres AL2 .... 142 B5
Boyle Cl LU2 .... 63 E8
Bracely Cl LU3 .... 44 F6
Brace Cl EN7 .... 147 B6
Braceys SG2 .... 52 F2
Brache Cl AL3 .... 106 A5
Brache Ct LU1 .... 63 F6
Bracken Cl WD6 .... 170 B8
Bracken Ct AL10 .... 109 F1
Brackendale EN6 .... 159 A6
Brackendale Gr
  Harpenden AL5 .... 85 D3
  Luton LU3 .... 45 B5
Brackendene AL2 .... 140 F1
Bracken Hill HP4 .... 122 F5
Bracken La AL6 .... 89 F7
Brackens The HP2 .... 124 D4
Bracklesham Gdns
  LU2 .... 46 D3
Bracknell Pl HP2 .... 124 F7
Bradbery WD3 .... 172 D5
Bradbury Cl WD6 .... 170 B8
Bradcot Cotts SG2 .... 39 C2
Bradden Cotts HP2 .... 103 F8
Bradden La HP1, HP2 .... 103 E7
Bradden Villas HP2 .... 103 F8
Bradden Ct 15 EN5 .... 171 C6
Bradfordbury Mansion
  SG13 .... 113 B1
Bradford Rd WD3 .... 164 C2
Bradgate EN6 .... 146 D4
Bradgate Cl EN6 .... 146 D3
Bradgers Hill Rd LU2 .... 45 E4
Bradley Comm CM23 .... 76 F8
Bradley Rd
  Enfield EN3 .... 162 E2
  Luton LU4 .... 44 D1
  Waltham Abbey EN9 .... 163 C4
Bradleys Cnr SG4 .... 35 C8
Bradman Way SG1 .... 37 A1
Bradmore Gn AL9 .... 144 E5
Bradmore La AL9 .... 144 C5
Bradmore Way AL9 .... 144 E5
Bradshaw Rd WD24 .... 154 C1
Bradshaws AL10 .... 129 F1
Bradway SG4 .... 66 E6
Braeburn Wlk SG8 .... 7 C7
Braemar Cl SG2 .... 69 B7
Braemar Ct WD23 .... 168 A3
Braemar Turn HP2 .... 105 B1
Braeside Cl HA5 .... 176 A3
Bragbury Cl SG2 .... 69 D7
BRAGBURY END 69 D6
Bragbury La SG2, SG3 .... 69 D5
Bragmans La WD3 .... 151 E6
Braham Ct 2 SG5 .... 34 E7
Brain Cl AL10 .... 130 B6
Braithwaite Ct 19 LU3 .... 45 D1
Brake Shear Ho EN5 .... 171 F6
Brakynbery HP4 .... 121 F7
Bramble Cl
  Harpenden AL5 .... 85 F3
  Luton LU4 .... 44 C4
  Watford WD25 .... 154 A5
Bramble Rd
  Hatfield AL10 .... 129 D5
  Luton LU4 .... 44 C4
Bramble Rise CM20 .... 117 C1
Brambles The
  Bishop's Stortford
  CM23 .... 76 C6
  Cheshunt EN8 .... 162 D8
  Oaklands AL6 .... 89 E8
  Royston SG8 .... 7 E5
  St Albans AL1 .... 127 D1
  Stevenage SG1 .... 36 D2
  Ware SG12 .... 93 C3
Brambling Cl WD23 .... 167 E5
Brambling Rise HP2 .... 124 E6
BRAMFIELD 91 C4
Bramfield
  Hitchin SG4 .... 35 B6
  Watford WD25 .... 154 E5
Bramfield Cl SG14 .... 113 A7
Bramfield La SG14 .... 91 F3
Bramfield Pl HP2 .... 105 A1
Bramfield Rd
  Datchworth SG3 .... 90 E8
  Hertford SG14 .... 112 F8
Bramham Ct HA6 .... 174 E4
Bramhanger Acre LU3 .... 44 D7

Bramingham Bsns Pk
  LU3 .... 45 B8
Bramingham Prim Sch
  LU3 .... 45 B8
Bramingham Rd LU3 .... 44 F6
Bramleas WD18 .... 166 F5
Bramley Cl SG7 .... 12 F1
Bramley Ct WD25 .... 154 B8
Bramley Gdns WD19 .... 175 C5
Bramley House Ct
  EN2 .... 161 D2
Bramley Shaw EN9 .... 163 F6
Bramley Way AL4 .... 128 C2
Brampton Cl
  Cheshunt EN7 .... 148 A3
  Harpenden AL5 .... 86 D1
Brampton Park Rd
  SG5 .... 21 E1
Brampton Rd
  Royston SG8 .... 7 C5
  South Oxhey WD19 .... 175 A7
  St Albans AL1 .... 128 A4
Brampton Terr WD6 .... 157 A1
Bramshaw Gdns
  WD19 .... 175 D5
Bramshott Cl SG4 .... 34 F5
Bramshot Way WD19 .... 175 A8
Branch Cl AL10 .... 130 C7
Branch Rd
  Park Street AL2 .... 141 D4
  St Albans AL3 .... 127 B4
Brandles Rd SG6 .... 23 A3
Brandles Sch SG7 .... 23 E7
Brandon Cl EN7 .... 147 F5
Brandon Ct HP23 .... 78 D7
Brandon Mobile Home Pk
  AL4 .... 128 D2
Brand St SG5 .... 34 E7
Branksome Cl HP2 .... 125 A4
Branscombe Ho
  WD24 .... 154 A2
Branton Cl LU2 .... 46 E2
Brantwood Rd LU1 .... 63 C7
BRAUGHING 55 F6
BRAUGHING FRIARS 56 D5
Brawlings La SL9 .... 172 A6
Bray Cl WD6 .... 170 C8
Bray Dr SG1 .... 37 A3
Brayes Manor SG5 .... 11 F6
Bray Lo 3 EN8 .... 148 E3
Brays Ct SG12 .... 46 B3
Brays Rd LU2 .... 46 B3
Brays Springs EN9 .... 163 E5
Braziers End HP5 .... 120 C1
Braziers Field SG13 .... 113 F6
Braziers Quay CM23 .... 77 A6
Breach Barns La EN9 .... 149 F1
BREACHWOOD GREEN 47 E1
Breachwood Green Jun
  Mix & Inf Sch SG4 .... 47 E1
Bread & Cheese La
  EN7 .... 147 D6
Breadcroft La AL5 .... 86 B1
Breakmead AL7 .... 111 B4
Breakspear SG1 .... 51 C3
Breakspear Ave AL1 .... 127 F2
Breakspear Ct WD5 .... 139 F1
Breakspear Ct WD24 .... 154 B1
Breakspeare Rd WD5 .... 153 E8
Breakspeare Sch
  WD5 .... 153 E8
Breakspear Pl WD5 .... 139 F1
Breakspear Rd N UB9 .... 173 D1
Breakspear Way HP2 .... 125 C4
Breaks Rd AL10 .... 130 B6
Brecken Cl AL4 .... 128 A7
Brecon Cl 14 LU1 .... 63 D6
Breeze Terr 5 EN8 .... 148 D3
Bren Ct EN3 .... 163 A2
Brendon Ave LU2 .... 46 C1
Brent Ct SG1 .... 50 E5
BRENT PELHAM 30 B2
Brent Pl WD24 .... 154 A2
Brett Pl WD24 .... 154 A2
Brett Rd EN5 .... 171 C4
Bretts Mead LU1 .... 63 C5
Bretts Mead Ct LU1 .... 63 C5
Brewers Cl CM23 .... 76 C5
Brewery Ct SG7 .... 12 E1
Brewery La
  1 Baldock SG7 .... 23 E8
  Stansted Mountfitchet
  CM24 .... 59 E7
Brewery Rd EN11 .... 135 B6
Brewery Yd CM24 .... 59 F7
Brewhouse Hill AL4 .... 108 C8
Brewhouse La SG14 .... 113 C6
Briants Cl HA5 .... 175 F1
Briar Cl
  Cheshunt EN8 .... 148 C2
  Luton LU2 .... 46 C4
  Potten End HP4 .... 123 A7
Briarcliff HP1 .... 123 E4
Briardale
  Stevenage SG1 .... 50 E4
  Ware SG12 .... 93 C3
Brierley Cl EN10 .... 134 F1
Briar Patch La SG6 .... 22 D3
Briar Rd
  St Albans AL4 .... 128 D6
  Watford WD25 .... 154 B4
Briars Cl AL10 .... 130 A5
Briars La AL10 .... 130 A5
Briars The
  Bushey WD23 .... 168 E2
  Cheshunt EN8 .... 162 E8
  Hertford SG13 .... 114 A6

Briars The continued
  Sarratt WD3 .... 152 A3
Briarswood EN7 .... 147 E3
Briars Wood AL10 .... 130 A5
Briar Way HP4 .... 122 D3
Briarwood Dr HA6 .... 175 A1
Briary La SG8 .... 7 C5
Briary Wood End AL6 .... 89 F8
Briary Wood La AL6 .... 89 F8
Brick Cotts SG7 .... 27 D8
Brickcroft EN10 .... 148 E5
Brickenden Ct EN9 .... 163 F6
BRICKENDON 133 C4
Brickendon Ct EN11 .... 135 A5
Brickendon La
  Brickendon SG13 .... 133 D6
  Hertford SG13 .... 113 C3
Bricket Rd AL1 .... 127 D3
BRICKET WOOD 140 F1
Bricket Wood Sta
  AL2 .... 141 A1
Brickfield AL10 .... 130 A2
Brickfield Ave HP3 .... 125 B2
Brickfield Cotts WD6 .... 169 F6
Brickfield Ct AL10 .... 130 B2
Brickfield La EN5 .... 170 F3
Brickfields Ind Est
  HP2 .... 125 B2
Brickfields The SG12 .... 93 B2
Brickhill Pk LU1 .... 84 C8
Brick Kiln Cl WD19 .... 167 E3
Brick Kiln La SG4 .... 34 E5
Brick Kiln Rd
  Cockernhoe LU2 .... 47 A3
  Stevenage SG1 .... 50 C6
Brick Knoll Pk AL1 .... 128 C2
Brickley Rd LU4 .... 44 C5
Brickmakers La HP3 .... 125 B2
Brickwall Ct AL6 .... 110 A8
Brickyard La SG8 .... 16 E5
Bride Hall La AL6 .... 88 A5
Bridewell Cl SG9 .... 40 E8
Bridewell Mews 24
  SG14 .... 113 D6
Bridge Cl
  1 Berkhamsted HP4 .... 122 D4
  Harpenden AL5 .... 85 F3
  Radlett WD7 .... 156 B4
  Welwyn Garden City
  AL7 .... 110 F6
Bridge End AL4 .... 108 B8
Bridgefields AL7 .... 110 F7
Bridge Foot SG9 .... 40 E7
Bridge Foot SG12 .... 93 D1
Bridge Gate Cotts AL2 .... 155 F8
Bridgefoot La EN6 .... 158 D6
Bridgeford Ho
  13 Bishop's Stortford
  CM23 .... 76 F6
  5 Watford WD18 .... 167 B6
Bridgegate Bsns Ctr
  AL7 .... 110 F6
Bridgend Rd EN1 .... 162 C4
Bridgenhall Rd EN1 .... 161 F1
Bridge Pk AL7 .... 110 E7
Bridge Pl WD17 .... 167 D4
Bridger Ct WD25 .... 154 E6
Bridge Rd
  Abbots Langley WD4 .... 153 C6
  Letchworth Garden City
  SG6 .... 22 F6
  Stevenage SG2 .... 50 C7
  Welwyn Garden City
  AL8 .... 110 C7
Bridge Rd E AL7 .... 110 F6
Bridge Rd W SG1 .... 50 B7
Bridges Cl SG14 .... 113 C6
Bridges Rd HA7 .... 176 F5
Bridge St
  Berkhamsted HP4 .... 122 D4
  Bishop's Stortford CM23 .... 76 F7
  Hemel Hempstead HP1 .... 124 C2
  Hitchin SG5 .... 34 E6
  Kneesworth SG8 .... 2 B8
  Luton LU1 .... 63 E8
Bridgewater Ct HP4 .... 102 C8
Bridgewater Hill HP4 .... 121 F7
Bridgewater Mid Sch
  HP4 .... 122 A6
Bridgewater Monument
  The* HP4 .... 101 E7
Bridgewater Rd HP4 .... 122 B5
Bridgewater Way
  WD23 .... 168 B3
Bridgeways EN11 .... 135 B6
Bridle Cl
  Enfield EN3 .... 162 F2
  Hoddesdon EN11 .... 115 A2
  St Albans AL3 .... 127 E5
Bridle La WD3 .... 165 D6
Bridle Path WD17 .... 167 B7
Bridleway HP23 .... 119 C5
Bridle Way
  Berkhamsted HP4 .... 122 A6
  Great Amwell SG12 .... 115 A6
  4 Hoddesdon EN11 .... 115 A2
Bridle Way (N) EN11 .... 115 B2
Bridle Way (S) EN11 .... 115 A1
Bridlington Rd WD19 .... 175 D7
Brierley Cl LU2 .... 46 D2
Briery Cl WD3 .... 165 A5
Briery Field WD3 .... 165 A5
Briery Way HP2 .... 125 A4
Brigadier Ave EN2 .... 161 C1
Brigadier Hill EN2 .... 161 C1
Brightman Cotts 2
  LU3 .... 45 A7

Brighton Rd WD24 .... 154 A1
Brighton Way SG1 .... 50 A8
Brightview Cl AL2 .... 140 C2
Brightwell Ct WD18 .... 167 A4
Brightwell Rd WD18 .... 167 A4
Brill Cl LU2 .... 46 D2
Brimfield Cl LU2 .... 46 D2
Brimsdown Ave EN3 .... 162 E1
Brimstone Way HP4 .... 121 F6
Brindley Way HP3 .... 138 F6
Brinklow Ct AL3 .... 141 B8
Brinley Cl EN8 .... 162 D8
Brinsley Rd HA3 .... 176 D1
Brinsmead AL2 .... 141 E4
Briscoe Cl EN11 .... 134 F8
Briscoe Rd EN11 .... 134 F8
Bristol Ho 16 WD6 .... 170 A7
Bristol Rd LU3 .... 45 B4
Britannia Sq SG11 .... 55 E2
Britannia Ave LU3 .... 45 B4
Britannia Bsns Pk
  EN8 .... 162 F5
Britannia Ct EN8 .... 162 F5
Britannia Est LU3 .... 45 B2
Britannia Hall LU2 .... 64 C8
Britannia Pl 3 CM23 .... 76 E5
Britannia Rd EN8 .... 162 F5
Brittain Way SG2 .... 51 B4
Britten Cl WD6 .... 169 D3
Britton Ave AL3 .... 127 D3
Britwell Dr HP4 .... 122 E6
Brixham Cl SG1 .... 50 B7
Brixton Rd WD24 .... 167 B8
Broad Acre AL2 .... 140 E1
Broadacres LU2 .... 45 D6
Broad Acres AL10 .... 129 F8
Broad Baulk SG9 .... 40 D8
Broadcroft
  2 Hemel Hempstead
  HP2 .... 124 D5
  Letchworth Garden City
  SG6 .... 22 C3
Broad Ct AL7 .... 110 E6
Broadfield
  Bishop's Stortford
  CM23 .... 58 F2
  Harlow CM20 .... 117 E1
Broadfield Cl SG10 .... 74 E1
Broadfield Ct WD23 .... 176 E8
Broadfield Pl AL8 .... 110 B5
Broadfield Prim Sch
  CM20 .... 117 E1
Broadfield Way
  Much Hadham SG10 .... 74 F1
  Radlett WD25 .... 155 B3
Broadgate EN9 .... 163 F7
Broad Gn SG13 .... 132 F8
Broadgreen Rd EN7 .... 147 D5
BROADGREEN WOOD 132 F8
Broad Green Wood
  SG13 .... 133 A8
Broadhall Way SG2 .... 51 B2
Broadlake Cl AL2 .... 142 D4
Broadlands WD7 .... 156 B4
Broadlands Cl EN8 .... 162 D5
Broadlawns Ct HA3 .... 176 F2
Broad Mdw SG13 .... 114 B3
Broadleaf Gr AL8 .... 89 B1
Broadley Gdns WD7 .... 156 F7
Broadmead SG4 .... 35 B5
Broad Mead LU3 .... 45 A3
Broadmead Ct HA5 .... 175 C3
Broadmeadow Ride
  SG4 .... 35 A4
Broadmeads SG12 .... 93 D1
Broadoak Ave EN3 .... 162 D4
Broad Oak Ct LU2 .... 46 D3
BROADOAK END 112 F8
Broad Oak La SG14 .... 112 F8
Broad Oak Way SG2 .... 50 F1
Broad St HP2 .... 124 D4
Broadstone Rd AL5 .... 107 D7
Broadview SG1 .... 50 E6
Broadview Ho EN3 .... 162 F3
Broadwalk The HA6 .... 174 C1
BROADWATER 51 A1
Broadwater
  Berkhamsted HP4 .... 122 C5
  Potters Bar EN6 .... 145 B1
Broadwater Ave SG6 .... 22 C5
Broadwater Cres
  Stevenage SG2 .... 69 C8
  Welwyn Garden City
  AL7 .... 110 D5
Broadwater Dale SG6 .... 22 C5
Broadwater La SG2 .... 51 D1
Broadwater Rd AL7 .... 110 C6
Broadway SG6 .... 22 C5
Broadway Ave CM17 .... 118 A4
Broadway Ct SG6 .... 22 C5
Broadway The
  Blackmore End AL4 .... 87 B5
  Harrow HA3 .... 176 F1
  Hatfield AL9 .... 130 C6

Broadway The continued
  Pinner HA5 .... 175 F3
  2 St Albans AL1 .... 127 D3
  8 Watford WD17 .... 167 C6
Broad Wlk CM20 .... 117 D1
Brocket Cnr AL8 .... 109 F4
Brocket Ct
  18 Hoddesdon EN11 .... 135 A6
  Luton LU4 .... 44 D5
Brocket Rd
  Hatfield AL8 .... 110 A3
  Hoddesdon EN11 .... 135 A6
Brockett Cl AL8 .... 110 B6
Brocket View AL4 .... 108 D8
Brockhurst Cl HA7 .... 176 F4
Brocklesbury Cl
  WD24 .... 167 D7
Brockley Hill HA7 .... 169 C1
Brockley Hill Ho HA7 .... 169 C1
Brockswood La AL8 .... 110 B7
Brockswood Prim Sch
  HP2 .... 105 C3
Brockton Cl LU1 .... 63 A7
Brockwell Shott SG2 .... 38 B1
Brodewater Rd WD6 .... 170 B7
Brodie Rd EN2 .... 161 C1
Broken Green Cotts
  SG11 .... 56 C2
Bromborough Gn
  WD19 .... 175 C5
Bromet Cl WD17 .... 153 F1
Bromet Prim Sch
  WD19 .... 167 D2
Bromleigh Cl EN8 .... 148 E3
Bromley HP23 .... 79 A4
Bromley Cl CM20 .... 118 B4
Bromley La SG10, SG11 .... 74 D6
Brompton Cl LU3 .... 44 F8
Brompton Gdns LU3 .... 44 F8
Bronte Ave SG5 .... 11 C2
Bronte Cres HP2 .... 105 B1
Bronte Ct 11 WD6 .... 170 A5
Bronte Paths SG2 .... 51 C6
Brook Bank EN1 .... 162 B2
Brookbridge La SG3 .... 69 D2
Brook Cl WD6 .... 170 B7
Brook Cotts CM24 .... 59 E5
Brook Ct LU3 .... 45 D1
Brookdene Ave WD19 .... 167 C1
Brookdene Dr HA6 .... 174 F4
Brook Dr
  Radlett WD7 .... 155 F6
  Stevenage SG2 .... 69 B8
Brooke Cl WD23 .... 168 C2
Brooke End AL3 .... 106 A4
Brooke Gdns CM23 .... 77 C7
Brooke Ho WD23 .... 168 C1
BROOK END 11 E5
Brook End CM21 .... 97 D2
Brookend La SG4 .... 35 B3
Brooke Rd SG8 .... 7 D8
Brooker Rd EN9 .... 163 C5
Brooke Way WD23 .... 168 C2
Brook Farm Cl CM23 .... 76 C3
Brook Field SG2 .... 51 E2
Brookfield Ct HP23 .... 100 B4
Brookfield Ctr EN8 .... 148 D4
Brookfield Gdns EN8 .... 148 C4
Brookfield Ho
  Cheshunt EN8 .... 148 D4
  Hemel Hempstead HP2 .... 124 D2
Brookfield La E SG8 .... 51 F3
Brookfield La E EN8 .... 148 D3
Brookfield La W EN8 .... 148 C4
Brookfield Ret Pk
  EN8 .... 148 D5
Brookfields CM21 .... 97 D2
Brookfield View WD4 .... 139 A3
Brookhill SG2 .... 68 F8
Brook Ho 5 EN10 .... 148 F5
Brookhouse Pl 3
  CM23 .... 76 F8
Brook La
  Berkhamsted HP4 .... 122 B5
  Sawbridgeworth CM21 .... 97 C2
Brookland Inf Sch
  EN8 .... 148 E3
Brookland Jun Sch
  EN8 .... 148 E3
Brooklands Cl LU4 .... 44 C6
Brooklands Ct AL1 .... 127 E3
Brooklands Gdns EN6 .... 158 E7
Brookmans Ave AL9 .... 144 E5
BROOKMANS PARK 144 E5
Brookmans Park Prim Sch
  AL9 .... 144 E5
Brookmans Park Sta
  AL9 .... 144 E5
Brookmead Sch LU7 .... 80 E5
Brookmill Cl WD19 .... 167 B2
Brook Rd
  Borehamwood WD6 .... 170 A7
  Cheshunt EN8 .... 162 F6
  Sawbridgeworth CM21 .... 97 C1
  Stansted Mountfitchet
  CM24 .... 59 E5
Brooks Ct SG14 .... 112 F7
Brooksfield AL7 .... 111 B7
Brookshill HA3 .... 176 D5
Brookshill Ave HA3 .... 176 D5
Brookshill Dr HA3 .... 176 D5
Brookshill Gate HA3 .... 176 D5
Brookside
  Buckland SG9 .... 27 D5
  Furneux Pelham SG9 .... 43 B4
  Hatfield AL10 .... 129 D5
  Hertford SG13 .... 113 C5
  Hoddesdon EN11 .... 135 A6

Brookside continued

Letchworth Garden City
SG6...................22 F5
South Mimms EN6........158 A7
Waltham Abbey EN9.....163 E7
Watford WD24...........154 D3
Brookside Cl EN1 173 E3
Brookside Cotts WD4...153 C5
Brookside Cres EN6...146 E4
Brookside Cvn Pk
WD19...................167 B2
Brookside Gdns EN1...162 C2
Brookside Rd WD19...167 B2
Brook St
Luton LU3...............63 D8
Stotfold SG5............11 E6
Tring HP23.............100 B4
Brook View
Hitchin SG4.............35 C6
Stansted Mountfitchet
CM24..................59 E5
Broom Barns Jun Mix Inf
Sch SG1................50 E4
Broom Cl
Hammond Street EN7....148 A4
Hatfield AL10..........129 F4
Broom Cnr AL5.........107 C8
Broomer Pl EN8........148 C2
Broomfield
Chiswell Green AL2.....141 C4
Harlow CM20...........118 A3
Broomfield Ave EN10..148 E5
Broomfield Cl AL6....89 C4
AL10.................130 A6
Broomfield Ct [2]
AL10...................89 C4
Broomfield Rise WD5..153 D7
Broom Gr
Knebworth SG3..........68 F5
Watford WD17..........154 A1
Broom Hall
Hemel Hempstead
HP1..................123 E2
Welwyn AL6.............90 A8
Broomhills AL2......111 B7
Broomleys AL4.......128 D6
Brooms Cl AL8.........89 D1
Brooms Rd LU2........64 A8
Broomstick Hall Rd
EN9...................163 E6
Broomstick La HP5...136 K1
Broom Wlk SG1.........50 E5
Broughinge Rd WD6...170 B7
Broughinge Rd WD6...170 B7
Broughmills AL3......45 C5
Broughton Hill SG6...23 B6
Broughton Way WD3...165 A2
Brownfields AL7.....110 F7
Brownfields Ct AL7...111 A7
Brownfield Way AL4..87 B6
Browning Ct [9] WD6...170 A5
Browning Dr SG4.......35 B8
Browning Rd
Enfield EN2............161 D1
Harpenden AL5..........86 C2
Luton LU4..............44 A2
Brownings La SG4......47 D1
Brownings Rd SG4....142 B4
Brownlow Farm Barns
HP1..................123 D5
Brownlow Gate HP4...81 B1
Brownlow La LU7......80 A7
Brownlow Rd
Berkhamsted HP4........122 C5
Borehamwood WD6.......170 A5
Brown's Cl LU4........44 D5
Brown's Rise HP23....119 E3
Browne Ho [12]
WD18..................166 F3
Browns Hedge LU7.....80 C7
Brown's La HP23......119 F7
Browns Rise HP23....119 E3
Browns Spring HP4...122 E7
Brow The WD25........154 B6
BROXBOURNE..........134 F3
Broxbournebury Mews
EN10..................134 C3
Broxbourne CE Prim Sch
EN10..................134 F2
Broxbourne & Hoddesdon
Sta EN10..............135 A3
Broxbourne Sch The
EN10..................134 C2
Broxdell SG1.........50 E6
Broxley Mead LU4.....44 D5
Bruce Gr WD24........154 C1
Bruce Rd
[3] Barnet EN5.........171 E4
Harrow HA3............176 E1
Bruce Way EN8........162 D6
Brummell Pl CM17....118 C3
Brunel Dr HP23.......124 D1
Brunel Rd SG2.........51 B7
Brunel Wlk SG5.......11 C2
Brunswick Ct EN11...135 A5
Brunswick Rd EN3...163 A1
Brunts Hall AL9......130 F2
Brushrise WD24.......154 A3
Brushwood Dr WD3....164 C5
Brussels Way LU3.....44 D8
Bryan Rd CM23........76 F8
Bryanstone Rd EN8...162 F5
Bryant Cl EN5........171 F4
Bryant Ct AL5.........86 A3
Bryce Cl SG12........93 D3
Bryfield Cotts HP3...137 C1
Buchanan Ct
Borehamwood WD6......170 C7

Buchanan Ct continued
Luton LU2..............64 B8
Buchanan Dr LU2......64 B8
Bucketsland La WD6...157 D2
Buckingham Cl AL1...127 F4
Buckingham Dr LU2...46 D2
Buckingham Lo [6]
EN11.................135 A6
Buckingham Rd
Borehamwood WD6.....170 D5
Tring HP23.............99 E3
Watford WD24..........154 C2
BUCKLAND.............27 D8
BUCKLAND COMMON.....120 B3
Buckland Rise HA5...175 D2
Bucklands Croft HP23..99 C8
Bucklands The WD3...165 A2
Buckland Wharf Ct
HP22.................99 A4
Buckle Cl LU3.........44 F7
Bucklersbury SG5.....34 E6
Bucklers Cl EN10.....134 F1
Bucknalls Cl WD25...154 E7
Bucknalls Dr AL2....154 F8
Bucknalls La WD25...154 E7
Bucks Alley SG13....132 D4
Bucks Ave WD19.......167 E2
Buck's Head Cotts SG4..35 E3
BUCKS HILL..........152 C5
Bucks Hill WD4......152 C5
Bucks New Univ (Chalfont
Campus) HP8...........172 A8
Buckthorn Ave SG1...50 E4
Buckton Rd WD6......156 F1
Buckwood La LU6......82 C7
Buckwood Rd AL3......83 C6
Buddcroft AL7........111 B7
Bude Cres SG1.........50 A7
BULBOURNE...........100 C8
Bulbourne Cl
Berkhamsted HP4......121 F6
Hemel Hempstead HP1...124 A2
Bulbourne Ct HP23...100 A7
Bulbourne Rd HP23...100 B7
Bullace Cl HP1.......124 A4
Bullbeggars La HP4...123 A4
Bullen's Green La
AL4..................143 E8
Bullfields CM21......97 E3
Bullhead Rd WD6......170 C6
Bull La
Cottered SG9...........39 C8
Wheathampstead AL4....108 A6
Bullock's Hill SG4...49 B1
Bullock's La SG13....113 C4
Bull Plain SG14......113 D6
Bull Rd AL5..........107 B8
Bullrush Cl AL10....130 B4
BULLS CROSS.........162 A3
Bull's Cross EN2.....162 A3
Bulls Cross Ride EN7..162 A3
BULL'S GREEN.........90 D7
Bulls La AL9.........144 E7
Bullsland Gdns WD3..164 B3
Bullsland La WD3....164 B3
BULLSMOOR............162 D4
Bullsmoor Cl EN8.....162 C4
Bullsmoor Gdns EN8..162 B4
Bullsmoor La
EN1....................162 C4
EN3....................162 C4
Bullsmoor Ride EN8..162 C4
Bullsmoor Way EN8...162 C4
Bull Stag Grn AL9...130 C7
Bullwell Cres EN8...148 C2
BULSTRODE...........137 E3
Bulstrode Cl WD4....137 E2
Bulstrode La
Chipperfield WD4......137 F3
Hemel Hempstead HP3...138 A5
Bulwer Lane SL1......50 E3
Buncefield La HP2...125 C5
Bungalows The
Essendon AL9..........131 F7
Harpenden AL5..........86 C3
Bungalow The SG11....41 E1
Bunker's Farm Cotts
HP3..................139 D8
Bunkers La HP3.......139 B7
Bunnsfield AL7.......111 C7
Bunstrux HP23.......100 A4
BUNTINGFORD..........40 F7
Buntingford Bsns Pk
SG9...................40 C8
Buntingford Rd SG11..55 D4
Bunting Rd LU4.......44 A4
Bunyan Cl
Pirton SG5.............20 D4
Tring HP23............100 B5
Bunyan Ho [22] LU2...45 D1
Bunyan Rd SG5........34 F8
Bunyans Cl LU3.......45 A5
BUPA Bushey Hospl
WD23.................168 F1
Burbage Cl EN10......162 F8
Burchell Ct WD23....168 C2
Burfield AL10.........130 A7
Burfield Ct LU2.......46 D3
Burfield Rd WD3......164 C4
Burford Cl LU3.......31 A1
Burford Gdns EN11...135 B7
Burford Rd EN11......135 B7
Burford Mews [9]
EN11.................135 A7
Burford Pl [11] EN11..135 A7
Burford St EN11......135 A7
Burford Way SG5......21 D2

Burgage Ct [12] SG12..93 D1
Burgage La SG12......93 D1
BURGE END............20 D5
Burge End La SG5.....20 C5
Burgess Cl EN7.......147 C6
Burgess Ct WD6......156 F1
Burghley Ave
Bishop's Stortford
CM23................76 C7
Borehamwood WD6.....170 C4
Burghley Cl SG2.......69 B8
Burgoyne Hatch
CM20.................118 A1
Burgundy Croft AL7...110 F4
Burgundy Ho EN2.....161 C1
Burhill Gr HA5.......175 E1
Burleigh Mead AL9...130 C7
Burleigh Prim Sch
EN8..................148 D1
Burleigh Rd
Cheshunt EN8..........162 E7
Hemel Hempstead HP2..125 C2
Hertford SG13.........114 A7
St Albans AL1.........128 B3
Burleigh Way EN6....146 E1
Burley SG6...........11 F2
Burley Ho WD5........153 F7
Burley Rd CM23.......77 A4
Burnell Rise SG6.....22 D5
Burnells Way CM24...59 E7
Burnett Cl HP3.......124 E2
Burnett Sq SG14.....112 F7
Burnham
Burnham Green AL6......90 C6
Enfield EN1...........161 E1
BURNHAM GREEN........90 C6
Burnham Green Rd AL6,
SG3....................90 D6
Burnham Rd
Luton LU2..............46 B2
St Albans AL1..........128 B3
Burnley Cl WD19......175 C5
Burnsall Pl AL5.....107 C6
Burns Cl
Hitchin SG4............35 B8
Stevenage SG2.........51 C8
Burns Dr HP2........105 B1
BURN'S GREEN.........52 F2
Burnside
Hertford SG14.........113 A5
Hoddesdon EN11.......134 F6
Sawbridgeworth CM21...97 D2
St Albans AL1.........128 B1
Burnside Cl AL10.....130 A8
Burnside Terr CM17..118 F3
Burns Rd SG8..........7 D8
Burnt Cl LU3..........44 F7
Burntfarm Ride EN2,
EN7..................161 B7
Burntmill Cl CM20...117 C3
Burntmill Cnr CM20..117 D4
Burnt Mill Comp Sch
CM20.................117 C2
Burnt Mill Ind Est
CM20.................117 C3
Burntmill La CM20...117 D3
Burr Cl AL2..........142 E4
Burrowfield AL7.....110 D4
Burrows Chase EN9...163 E4
Burrs La SG8..........17 C3
Burrs Pl LU2.........63 E6
Burr St LU2...........63 E8
Bursland SG6.........22 D6
Burston Dr AL2......141 C3
Burton Ave WD18.....167 A5
Burton Dr EN3........163 A2
Burton Grange EN7...147 E4
Burton La EN7........147 E3
Burtons La WD3.......164 A4
Burtons Mill CM21....97 E3
Burvale Ct [3] WD18..167 B6
Burwell Rd SG2.......51 B4
Bury Cotts AL3......105 E5
Burycroft AL8........89 E1
Burydale SG2.........69 B8
Buryfield La AL1.....141 D5
Bury End SG5.........20 D4
Bury Field SG9........29 B7
Buryfield Maltings
SG12.................93 C2
Buryfield Terr SG12..93 C1
Buryfield Way SG12..93 C1
Bury Gn
Hemel Hempstead
HP1..................124 C4
Wheathampstead AL4...108 C8
BURY GREEN
Bishop's Stortford....75 E7
Cheshunt.............162 B8
Bury Green Rd
Cheshunt EN7..........162 A7
Cheshunt EN7..........162 A8
Bury Hill HP1.......124 C4
Bury Hill Cl HP1....124 C4
Bury Holme EN10.....148 F8
Bury La
Bramfield SG14.........91 B4
Codicote SG4...........67 F2
Datchworth SG3.........69 D3
Rickmansworth WD3.....165 D1
Streatley LU3.........82 B3
Bury Mdws WD3.......165 D1
Bury Mead SG15.......11 A7
Bury Mead Rd SG5....21 F1

BURY PARK.............45 B1
Bury Park Ind Est [4]
LU1....................63 C8
Bury Park Rd LU1....63 C8
Bury Plantation SG8..7 F6
Bury Rd
Harlow CM17...........118 D4
Hatfield AL10.........130 C6
Hemel Hempstead HP1...124 C3
Bury Rise HP3........137 D6
Bury The
Codicote SG4...........67 F2
Rickmansworth WD3.....165 E1
Burywick AL5........107 B5
Bushbarns EN7.......148 A3
Bushby Ave EN10.....134 F1
Bushell Gn WD23....176 D8
Bushell Wharf HP23..100 A6
BUSHEY..............168 C3
Bushey Cl AL7.......111 B5
Bushey Gn AL7.......111 B5
Bushey Grove Rd
WD23.................167 E8
Bushey Hall Dr WD23..167 E5
Bushey Hall Pk WD23..167 E5
Bushey Hall Rd WD23..167 E5
Bushey Hall Sch
WD23.................167 F4
BUSHEY HEATH........168 E2
Bushey Heath Prim Sch
WD23.................168 D1
Bushey Ley AL7......111 B5
Bushey Manor Jun Sch
WD23.................167 F4
Bushey Meads Sch
WD23.................168 C4
Bushey Mill Cres
WD24.................154 D3
Bushey Mill La
Watford, North Watford
WD24.................154 D1
Watford WD23.........167 E8
Bushey Mus * WD23...168 A3
Bushey & Oxhey Inf Sch
WD23.................167 F8
Bushey Pk WD23......168 A3
Bushey Sta WD19.....167 D3
Bushfield Rd HP3....137 C6
Bush Hall La AL9....130 D6
Bushmead Cl LU2.....45 E6
Bushmead Prim Sch
LU2....................45 E5
Bushmead Rd LU2.....45 E6
Bushmead Sh Ctr LU2..45 E5
Bush Spring SG7.....13 A1
Bushwood Cl AL9....144 B8
Business Ctr E SG6...23 C6
Business Ctr The LU2..64 B6
Business Ctr W SG6...23 C6
Business Innovation Ctr
The EN3..............162 F3
Butchers La SG4......48 D6
Butely Rd LU4........44 B5
Bute Sq LU1..........63 E7
Bute St LU1..........63 E7
Butlers Ct EN8.......162 E7
Butlers Dr E4.......163 C1
Butler's Hall La CM23..76 B3
Butlers Yd SG7.......12 E1
Butlin Rd LU1........63 B7
Buttercup Ct AL10...109 F1
Butterfield LU2......46 B7
Butterfield Cotts
WD3..................172 E3
Butterfield Ct SG7...23 E8
Butterfield Green Rd
LU2....................46 A6
Butterfield Rd AL4...141 E4
Butterfly La WD6.....108 C2
Butterfly Wlk WD6...169 B7
Buttermere Cl AL1...128 B2
Buttersweet Rise
CM21.................97 E1
Butterwick WD25....154 E3
Butterworth Path [1]
LU2....................63 C8
Butt Field View AL1..141 C7
Buttlehide WD3.......172 D5
Buttondene Cres
EN10.................135 B1
Butts End HP1.......124 A5
Buttsmead HA6.......174 C3
Butts The EN10......148 E7
Buttway SG7...........1 F3
Buxton Cl AL4........128 D6
Buxton Path WD19....175 C7
Buxton Rd LU1........63 D7
Buxtons La SG8........1 F3
Buzzard Rd LU4.......44 A4
Byde St SG14.........113 C7
Byers Cl EN6.........159 C5
Byewaters WD18......166 C3
Byeway The WD3......173 E8
Bye Way The HA3.....176 F2
Byfield AL8..........89 E1
Byfield Cl LU4.......44 B1
Byfleet Ind Est WD18..166 B1
Byford Ho [5] EN5...171 D5
BYGRAVE..............13 C5
Bygrave SG1..........36 C2
Bygrave Rd SG7.......12 F1
Bylands CM23.........76 D6
Bylands Ho AL3......106 A7
Byng Dr EN6.........159 A8
Byng Rd EN5..........171 D6
Byrd Cl SG1...........50 D4
Byrd Wlk SG7.........23 F7

Byron Ave
Borehamwood WD6......170 A4
Watford WD24.........167 D8
Byron Cl
Hammond Street EN7....147 F4
Hitchin SG4............35 B8
Stevenage SG2.........51 C7
Byron Ct EN8........148 B3
Byron Pl HP2........105 B1
Byron Rd
Harpenden AL5..........86 A2
Harrow HA3...........176 F1
Luton LU4.............44 B2
Royston SG8............7 B8
Byslips Rd LU6.......82 D5
By The Mount AL7....110 D5
By The Wood WD19....175 E8
Byways HP4..........122 E5
Byway The EN6.......159 A6
By-Wood End SL9.....172 A5

C

Cabot Cl SG2..........51 A7
CADDINGTON...........62 D3
Caddington Comm AL3..83 E8
Caddington Pk LU1....44 B1
Caddis Cl HA7........176 F3
Cade Cl SG6..........12 C1
Cades Cl LU1.........63 A6
Cades La LU1.........63 A6
Cadia Cl LU1.........62 E4
Cadmore Ct
[2] Cheshunt EN8......148 D3
Hertford SG14........112 F7
Cadmore La EN8......148 D2
Cadogan Pl AL1......142 A8
CADWELL..............21 F5
Cadwell Cl SG4.......22 A2
Cadwell Gn SG4.......22 A2
Cadwell La SG4.......22 A2
Caernarvon Cl
Hemel Hempstead
HP2..................124 D3
Stevenage SG2.........69 B7
Caernarvon Ct HP2...124 D3
Caesars Ct AL4......108 E2
Cage Pond Rd WD7....156 F6
Cain Cl AL1..........127 F1
Cain Ct [8] EN8.....148 D3
Cairns Cl AL4........128 D2
Cairn Way HA7.......176 F4
Caishowe Rd WD6.....170 B8
Caister Cl
Hemel Hempstead
HP2..................124 E2
Stevenage SG2.........36 A1
Calais Cl EN7.......147 D5
Calbury Cl AL1......128 B2
Caldbeck EN9.........163 D5
Caldecot Ave EN7....147 F2
CALDECOTE.............3 D1
Caldecote Gdns
WD23.................168 E2
Caldecote Rd SG7.....12 E8
Caldecote Way EN10...134 F1
Calder Ave AL9......145 B5
Calder Way SL3......172 E3
Caldicott Cl SG4.....34 F7
Caldwell Rd WD19....175 D6
Caleb Cl LU4.........44 F2
Caledonian Ct WD17..167 B7
Caledon Rd AL2......142 D5
California SG7.......12 F1
California Ct [2]
WD23.................168 D1
California La WD23...168 D1
Callaghan Ct HP4....122 D4
Callanders The WD23..168 E1
Callard Ho HP4......122 D4
Callisto Ct HP2.....124 F6
Callowland Pl WD24..154 B1
Callowlands WD24....167 B8
Calnwood Ct LU4......44 C3
Calnwood Rd LU4.....44 C3
Calton Ave SG14.....112 F7
Calton Ct SG14......112 F6
Calton Ho SG14......112 F6
Calverley Cl CM23....76 E4
Calverton Rd LU3.....45 A6
Calvert Rd EN5......171 D7
Camberley Pl AL5....107 D8
Camborne Dr HP2.....124 E7
Cambrian Way HP2....124 F6
Cambridge Cl EN8....148 C3
Cambridge Cotts SG11..72 E1
Cambridge Cres SG8..2 A8
Cambridge Ct
Barnet EN5............171 F6
Standon SG11..........55 C2
Cambridge Dr EN6....158 E8
Cambridge Ho CM17...118 C5
Cambridge Rd
Barkway SG8...........17 D5
Barley SG8.............9 A3
Harlow CM20...........118 C6
Hitchin SG4............22 C2
Sawbridgeworth CM21...97 E4
St Albans AL1.........128 B2
Standon SG11..........55 C2
Stansted Mountfitchet
CM24..................59 E8
[6] Watford WD18......167 C5

Cambridge St LU1 .... 63 F6
Cambridge Terr **16**
HP4 .... 122 D4
Cam Ctr SG4 .... 22 A3
Camelot Ct WD23 .... 168 A7
Cameron Ct SG2 .... 51 B7
Cameron Ct **3** SG12 .... 93 D2
Cameron Dr EN6 .... 162 C5
Camfield AL7 .... 110 F2
Camford Way LU3 .... 44 A8
Camlet Way AL3 .... 127 B4
Campana Ct EN5 .... 171 D6
Campania Gr LU3 .... 45 A8
Campbell Cl
 Buntingford SG9 .... 40 E7
 Hitchin SG4 .... 35 B8
Campers Ave SG6 .... 22 E5
Campers Rd SG6 .... 22 E5
Campers Wlk SG6 .... 22 E5
Campfield Rd
 Hertford AL9 .... 113 B5
 St Albans AL1 .... 128 A3
Campfield Way SG6 .... 22 D5
Campion Cl **1** EN8 .... 148 D3
Campion Cl WD25 .... 154 A6
Campion Ct SG1 .... 50 C8
Campion Rd
 Hatfield AL10 .... 129 F8
 Hemel Hempstead HP1 .... 123 E2
Campions Ct HP4 .... 122 B3
Campions The
 Borehamwood WD6 .... 157 A1
 Stansted Mountfitchet
 CM24 .... 59 E8
Campion Way SG8 .... 7 E5
Campkin Mead SG2 .... 51 D3
Camp Rd AL1 .... 128 B2
Camps Hill Com Prim Sch
 SG2 .... 51 C6
CAMP THE 128 B2
Campus Five SG6 .... 23 C7
Campus The AL8 .... 110 D7
Camp View Rd AL1 .... 128 B2
Cam Sq SG4 .... 22 A3
Canada La EN10 .... 148 E6
Canadas The EN10 .... 148 E6
Canal Ct HP4 .... 122 E4
Canalside HP4 .... 121 F6
Canal Way UB9 .... 173 A4
Canberra Cl
 Kneesworth SG8 .... 2 B5
 St Albans AL3 .... 127 B4
Canberra Gdns LU3 .... 45 B6
Candlefield Cl HP3 .... 139 A8
Candlefield Rd HP3 .... 139 A8
Candlefield Wlk HP3 .... 139 A8
Caneland Ct EN9 .... 163 F5
Canfield CM23 .... 76 F5
Cangels Cl HP1 .... 124 A1
Canham Ct SG4 .... 66 D1
Cannix Cl SG2 .... 51 A7
Cannon Ho **1** SG4 .... 34 F6
Cannon La LU2 .... 46 B5
Cannon Mews **1** EN9 .... 163 B6
Cannon Rd WD18 .... 167 C4
Cannons Ct CM23 .... 59 A1
Cannon's Cl SG8 .... 1 F5
Cannons Ct SG11 .... 55 D3
Cannons Mdw AL6 .... 90 E2
Cannons Mead CM24 .... 59 D7
Cannons Mill La CM23 .... 59 A1
Cannon St AL3 .... 127 D4
Canons Cl WD7 .... 156 B4
Canons Field
 Oaklands AL6 .... 89 E8
 Wheathampstead AL4 .... 87 D1
Canonsfield Ct AL6 .... 89 E7
Canonsfield Rd AL6 .... 89 E8
Canons Gate
 Cheshunt EN8 .... 148 F5
 Harlow CM20 .... 117 A2
Canons Rd SG12 .... 93 C2
Canopus Way HA6 .... 175 A6
Canopy La CM17 .... 118 C1
Cantelowes Rd EN5 .... 171 D4
Canterbury Cl
 Luton LU3 .... 44 F4
 Northwood HA6 .... 174 F4
Canterbury Ct AL1 .... 127 E4
Canterbury Ho
 10 Borehamwood
 WD6 .... 170 A7
 4 Watford WD17 .... 167 C7
Canterbury Rd
 Borehamwood WD6 .... 170 A7
 Watford WD17 .... 167 B7
Canterbury Way
 Croxley Green WD3 .... 166 C6
 Stevenage SG1 .... 36 F2
Capability Gn LU1 .... 63 F7
Capel Ct SG11 .... 57 E2
Capel Ho WD19 .... 175 D6
Capella Rd HA6 .... 174 F6
Capell Ave WD3 .... 164 C4
Capell Rd WD3 .... 164 D4
Capell Way WD3 .... 164 D4
Capel Manor Coll
 EN1 .... 162 A4
Capel Manor Gdns* EN1,
 EN7 .... 162 B4
Capel Manor Prim Sch
 EN1 .... 162 B4

Capel Rd
 Enfield EN1 .... 162 B3
 Watford WD17 .... 167 E3
Capelvere Wlk WD17 .... 166 E8
Cape Rd AL1 .... 128 B3
Capio Rivers Hospl The
 CM21 .... 97 C1
Capital Bsns Pk WD6 .... 170 C6
Caponfield AL7 .... 111 B4
Cappell La SG12 .... 115 D5
Capron Rd LU4 .... 44 E4
Captains Wlk HP4 .... 122 D3
Caractacus Cottage View
 WD18 .... 166 E5
Caractacus Gn WD18 .... 166 F3
Caravan La WD3 .... 165 E2
Caravan Site The HP23 .... 79 C4
Carbone Hill EN6,
 SG13 .... 146 D5
Carde Cl SG14 .... 112 F7
Cardiff Cl SG2 .... 69 B7
Cardiff Gr LU1 .... 63 D7
Cardiff Rd WD18 .... 2 A8
Cardiff Rd
 Luton LU1 .... 63 D7
 Watford WD18 .... 167 A4
Cardiff Way WD5 .... 154 A7
Cardigan Cl **1** LU1 .... 63 D8
Cardigan Gdns **2** LU1 .... 63 D8
Cardigan St LU1 .... 63 D7
Cardinal Ave WD6 .... 170 B5
Cardinal Cl EN7 .... 147 F5
Cardinal Ct
 Borehamwood WD6 .... 170 B6
 6 Luton LU2 .... 45 D1
Cardinal Gr AL3 .... 127 B1
Cardinal Newman RC Sch
 A Specialist Science Coll
 LU3 .... 31 C1
Cardinals Gate SG8 .... 7 C6
Cardy Rd HP1 .... 124 B3
Careless Ct **21** CM23 .... 76 F7
Carew Lo HA6 .... 174 E4
Carew Rd HA6 .... 174 F4
Carew Way WD19 .... 175 F7
Careys Croft HP4 .... 122 A7
Carisbrooke Ave
 WD24 .... 167 D8
Carisbrooke Cl SG2 .... 68 F8
Carisbrooke Rd
 Harpenden AL5 .... 86 C2
 Luton LU4 .... 44 E1
Carisbrook Rd AL2 .... 141 B5
Carleton Rd EN8 .... 148 E4
Carleton Rise AL6 .... 89 C6
Carlisle Ave AL3 .... 127 D4
Carlisle Ho **15** WD6 .... 170 A7
Carlos Ind Est WD17 .... 167 D5
Carlton Bank **2** AL5 .... 86 B1
Carlton Cl
 Borehamwood WD6 .... 170 D5
 Luton LU3 .... 45 C2
Carlton Cres LU3 .... 45 C2
Carlton Ct
 1 Harpenden AL5 .... 86 B1
 Watford WD19 .... 167 C3
Carlton Pl HA6 .... 174 E5
Carlton Rd AL5 .... 86 B2
Carman Ct HP23 .... 99 F3
Carmelite Cl HA3 .... 176 C2
Carmelite Rd
 Harrow HA3 .... 176 C1
 Luton LU4 .... 44 A3
Carmelite Way HA3 .... 176 C1
Carmelite Wlk HA3 .... 176 C1
Carmen Ct WD6 .... 156 F1
Carnaby Rd EN10 .... 134 E3
Carnarvon Rd EN5 .... 171 E6
Carnegie Ct EN3 .... 163 B1
Carnegie Gdns LU3 .... 45 A8
Carnegie Rd AL3 .... 127 D7
CARNELES GREEN 134 B1
Caro La HP3 .... 125 B1
Carol Cl LU3 .... 45 A4
Carole Ct **2** LU1 .... 63 E5
Caroline Ho WD23 .... 168 A3
Caroline Pl WD19 .... 167 E3
Caroline Sharpe Ho
 AL4 .... 128 C7
Carolyn Ct LU1 .... 45 A4
Caroon Dr WD3 .... 152 B3
Carpenders Ave
 WD19 .... 175 E8
Carpenders Cl AL5 .... 85 D4
Carpenders Park Bsns Ctr
 WD19 .... 175 D7
Carpenders Park Sta
 WD19 .... 175 D7
Carpenters Rd EN1 .... 162 C3
Carpenters The CM23 .... 76 B5
Carpenters Wood Dr
 WD3 .... 164 B5
Carpenters Yd HP23 .... 100 B3
Carpenter Way EN6 .... 159 D6
Carriages The SG12 .... 114 E8
Carrigans CM23 .... 76 F8
Carrington Ave WD6 .... 170 C4
Carrington Cl
 Arkley EN5 .... 171 A4
 Borehamwood WD6 .... 170 C4
Carrington Pl HP23 .... 100 C5
Carrington Sq HA3 .... 176 C3
Carsdale Cl LU3 .... 45 A6
Carteret Rd LU2 .... 46 C1
Carterhatch La EN1 .... 161 F1
Carters Cl
 Arlesey SG15 .... 11 A7

Carters Cl continued
 Aston SG2 .... 51 D4
Cartersfield Rd EN9 .... 163 C5
Carters La (Wibbly
 Wobbley La) SG5 .... 34 A6
Carters Leys CM23 .... 76 D8
Carters Way SG15 .... 11 A7
Carters Wlk SG15 .... 11 A7
Carthagena Est EN9 .... 135 C3
Cart Path WD25 .... 154 C6
Cartref SG1 .... 50 A6
Cart Tk The HP3 .... 138 F6
Cartwright Rd
 Royston SG8 .... 7 D5
 Stevenage SG1 .... 37 C2
Carve Ley AL7 .... 111 B5
Carvers Croft SG3 .... 69 B2
Cary Wlk WD7 .... 156 B5
Cashio La SG6 .... 23 A8
Caslon Way SG6 .... 11 F1
Cassandra Gate EN8 .... 148 F4
Cassiobridge Rd
 WD18 .... 166 E5
Cassiobridge Terr
 WD3 .... 166 D4
Cassiobury Dr WD17 .... 166 F7
Cassiobury Ho WD17 .... 167 B7
Cassiobury Inf Sch
 WD17 .... 166 E8
Cassiobury Jun Sch
 WD17 .... 166 E8
Cassiobury Park Ave
 WD17 .... 166 F6
Cassio Ho **4** WD18 .... 166 F5
Cassio Pl WD18 .... 166 E5
Cassio Rd WD18 .... 167 B5
Casson Ct AL2 .... 142 A8
Castano Ct WD5 .... 153 E8
Castellane Cl **1** HA6 .... 174 F3
Castings Ho SG6 .... 23 A7
Castle Cl
 Bushey WD23 .... 168 B3
 Hoddesdon EN11 .... 115 C1
 Pitstone LU7 .... 80 D3
Castle Cotts SG9 .... 29 B7
Castle Croft Rd LU1 .... 63 A6
Castle Gate SG5 .... 21 D1
Castle Gdns SG14 .... 113 C5
Castle Gate Way HP4 .... 122 C5
Castle Hill HP4 .... 122 C6
Castle Hill Ave HP4 .... 122 C5
Castle Hill Cl HP4 .... 122 C5
Castle Hill Ct HP4 .... 122 C6
Castle Mead HP1 .... 124 B1
Castle Mead Gdns **3**
 SG14 .... 113 C5
Castle Mews **3** HP4 .... 122 D4
Castle Mill EN2 .... 122 C5
Castle Rd
 Enfield EN3 .... 162 E1
 Hoddesdon EN11 .... 115 C1
 Sawbridgeworth CM21 .... 97 C1
 St Albans AL1 .... 128 B3
Castle Rise AL4 .... 86 F2
Castle Row HP23 .... 100 A3
Castles Cl SG5 .... 11 F3
Castle St
 Berkhamsted HP4 .... 122 C4
 Bishop's Stortford CM23 .... 76 E8
 Hertford SG14 .... 113 D5
 Luton, High Town LU1 .... 63 E7
 Luton, New Town LU1 .... 63 E6
Castle View CM23 .... 77 A7
Castle Wlk CM24 .... 59 E6
Catalin Ct EN9 .... 148 D3
Catalonia Apartments **2**
 SG12 .... 93 D1
Caterham Ct EN9 .... 163 F5
Catesby Gn LU3 .... 31 A1
Catham Cl AL1 .... 128 B1
Cathedral & Abbey Church
 of St Alban* AL3 .... 127 D3
Cathedral Ct AL3 .... 127 B1
Catherall Rd LU3 .... 45 B6
Catherine Cl HP2 .... 125 B8
Catherine Cotts HP23 .... 120 C8
Catherine Ho WD19 .... 175 B7
Catherine Rd EN3 .... 162 E3
Catherine St AL3 .... 127 D4
Catherine Wheel Mews **20**
 EN11 .... 115 A1
Catisfield Rd EN3 .... 162 E2
Catkin Cl HP1 .... 124 B4
Catlin St HP3 .... 138 E8
Catsbrook Rd LU3 .... 45 B6
Catsdell Bottom HP3 .... 139 B8
Catsey La WD23 .... 168 C2
Catsey Wood WD23 .... 168 C2
Catterick Way WD6 .... 169 F8
Cattlegate Cotts EN6 .... 160 D8
Cattlegate Hill EN6 .... 160 D7
Cattlegate Rd
 Crews Hill EN2 .... 161 A5
 Northaw EN6 .... 160 D6
Cattley Cl EN5 .... 171 E5
Cattlins Cl EN7 .... 147 F2
Causeway EN6 .... 159 D8
Causeway Ho WD5 .... 153 E8
Causeway The
 1 Bishop's Stortford
 CM23 .... 77 A7
 Braughing SG9, SG11 .... 42 D1
 Brent Pelham SG9 .... 30 B1

Causeway The continued
 Buntingford SG9 .... 40 F8
 Furneux Pelham SG9 .... 43 A3
 Kneesworth SG8 .... 2 A5
 Potters Bar EN6 .... 159 D8
 Therfield SG8 .... 15 F7
Cautherly La SG12 .... 115 A5
Cavalier Cl LU3 .... 45 A5
Cavalier Ct
 7 Berkhamsted HP4 .... 122 C4
 Stevenage SG1 .... 36 B1
Cavalli Apartments **14**
 WD18 .... 166 E5
Cavan Cl AL10 .... 130 A4
Cavan Dr AL3 .... 127 D8
Cavan Rd AL3 .... 106 A6
Cave Gate SG9 .... 28 D6
Cavell Ct CM23 .... 77 B6
Cavell Dr CM23 .... 77 B6
Cavell Rd EN7 .... 148 A4
Cavell Wlk SG2 .... 51 C5
Cavendish Cres WD6 .... 170 A5
Cavendish Ct
 Croxley Green WD3 .... 166 D4
 Hemel Hempstead HP3 .... 138 E6
Cavendish Rd
 Barnet EN5 .... 171 C6
 Luton LU3 .... 45 B2
 Markyate AL3 .... 83 D6
 St Albans AL1 .... 127 F3
 Stevenage SG1 .... 50 B5
Cavendish Sch The
 HP1 .... 124 B4
Cavendish Way AL10 .... 129 F5
Cawkell Cl CM24 .... 59 D7
Caxton Ct
 Enfield EN3 .... 162 E4
 Luton LU3 .... 44 F4
Caxton Ctr AL3 .... 127 F8
Caxton Gate SG1 .... 50 B4
Caxton Hill SG13 .... 113 F6
Caxton Pl SG1 .... 50 B4
Caxton Rd EN11 .... 115 B2
Caxton Way
 Stevenage SG1 .... 50 B4
 Watford WD18 .... 166 D2
Cecil Cl CM23 .... 77 D7
Cecil Cres AL10 .... 130 B7
Cecil Ct EN5 .... 171 D6
Cecil Rd
 Cheshunt EN8 .... 162 E7
 Hertford SG13 .... 113 C3
 Hoddesdon EN11 .... 135 C8
 South Mimms EN6 .... 158 B7
 St Albans AL1 .... 127 F3
Cecil St WD24 .... 154 B1
Cedar Ave
 Cheshunt EN8 .... 162 D6
 Ickleford SG5 .... 21 E4
Cedar Cl
 Hertford SG14 .... 113 B6
 Potters Bar EN6 .... 145 A1
 Sawbridgeworth CM21 .... 97 C1
 Ware SG12 .... 114 D8
Cedar Cres SG8 .... 7 B6
Cedar Ct
 Bishop's Stortford
 CM23 .... 58 F1
 St Albans AL4 .... 128 C4
 Watford WD25 .... 154 D6
Cedar Dr HA5 .... 176 A4
Cedar Gn EN11 .... 135 A5
Cedar Grange HA6 .... 174 C3
Cedar Lawn Ave EN5 .... 171 E4
Cedar Lo **8** EN8 .... 148 D3
Cedar Park Rd EN2 .... 161 C1
Cedar Pk CM23 .... 76 D4
Cedar Pl HA6 .... 174 C4
Cedar Rd
 Berkhamsted HP4 .... 122 E3
 Enfield EN2 .... 161 C1
 Hatfield AL10 .... 130 A4
 Watford WD19 .... 167 D3
Cedars Ave WD3 .... 165 C1
Cedars Cl WD6 .... 170 B5
Cedars Manor Sch
 HA3 .... 176 C2
Cedars The
 Berkhamsted HP4 .... 122 E4
 1 Harpenden AL5 .... 86 B1
 5 Rickmansworth
 WD3 .... 165 D2
 St Albans AL3 .... 127 C5
 Stevenage SG2 .... 69 B8
Cedars Wlk WD3 .... 164 F5
Cedar Way HP4 .... 122 D3
Cedar Wlk
 Hemel Hempstead
 HP3 .... 124 D1
 Waltham Abbey EN9 .... 163 D5
 Welwyn Garden City
 AL7 .... 111 B5
Cedarwood Dr AL4 .... 128 D3
Cedar Wood Dr
 WD25 .... 154 B4
Celandine Dr LU3 .... 45 A8
Celia Ho AL7 .... 110 F6
Cell Barnes Cl EN1 .... 128 B1
Cell Barnes La AL1 .... 128 B1
Cemetery Hill HP1 .... 124 C2
Cemetery Rd CM23 .... 76 F6
Cemmaes Court Rd
 HP1 .... 124 C3
Cemmaes Mdw HP1 .... 124 C3
Centenary Ct SG10 .... 75 F6
Centenary Ave WD6 .... 169 C2
Centennial Ct WD6 .... 165 E2
Centennial Ct WD6 .... 169 C2

Centennial Pk WD6 .... 169 C2
Central App SG6 .... 22 F6
Central Ave
 Cheshunt EN8 .... 162 E6
 Lower Stondon SG16 .... 10 B3
 Whipsnade LU6 .... 81 E8
Central Dr
 St Albans AL4 .... 128 C4
 Welwyn Garden City
 AL7 .... 110 F8
Central Hts **3** WD18 .... 166 F5
Central Prim Sch
 WD18 .... 167 C5
Central Rd CM20 .... 118 A4
Central Way HA6 .... 174 E3
Centrium AL1 .... 127 C1
Centro HP2 .... 125 C5
Centurion Ct **3** AL1 .... 128 A2
Century Ct **1** AL3 .... 127 C4
Century Ct WD18 .... 166 C2
Century Ho HP1 .... 124 C4
Century Pk WD17 .... 167 C4
Century Rd
 Hoddesdon EN11 .... 135 A7
 Ware SG12 .... 93 D2
Cervantes Ct HA6 .... 174 F3
Chace Ave EN6 .... 159 D7
Chace The SG2 .... 50 F1
Chad La AL3 .... 84 C4
Chadwell SG12 .... 114 C8
Chadwell Ave EN8 .... 148 C3
Chadwell Cl LU2 .... 45 F1
Chadwell Rd SG1 .... 50 B3
Chadwell Rise SG12 .... 114 B8
Chaffinches Gn HP3 .... 139 A7
Chaffinch La WD18 .... 166 F2
Chaffinch Way SG6 .... 22 E6
Chalet Cl HP4 .... 121 F4
Chalet The EN11 .... 134 E8
Chalfont Cl HP2 .... 125 B8
Chalfont Ho WD18 .... 166 F5
Chalfont La
 Chorleywood WD3 .... 164 B4
 Maple Cross WD3 .... 172 D3
Chalfont Pl AL1 .... 127 E3
Chalfont Rd WD3, SG9,
 HP8 .... 172 C7
CHALFONT ST PETER 172 A3
Chalfont Shire Ctr*
 HP8 .... 172 A7
Chalfont Way LU2 .... 46 D2
Chalfont Wlk **2** HA5 .... 175 C1
Chalgrove AL7 .... 111 D7
Chalk Dale AL7 .... 111 B7
Chalkdell Fields AL4 .... 128 E3
Chalkdell Hill HP2 .... 124 E3
Chalkdell Ho WD25 .... 154 C6
Chalkdell Path **8** SG5 .... 34 D8
Chalkdown
 Luton LU2 .... 45 E6
 Stevenage SG2 .... 51 D7
Chalk Hill
 Cockernhoe LU2 .... 47 A5
 Watford WD19 .... 167 E3
Chalk Hills SG7 .... 23 F5
Chalks Ave CM21 .... 97 C3
Challney Boys High Sch &
 Com Coll LU4 .... 44 D2
Challney Ct LU4 .... 44 D2
Challney Girls High Sch
 LU4 .... 44 C3
Chalmers Ct WD3 .... 165 F3
Chalton Rd LU4 .... 44 C5
Chamberlaines AL5 .... 85 A5
Chambersbury La
 HP3 .... 139 A7
Chambersbury Prim Sch
 HP3 .... 139 B8
Chambers Gate SG1 .... 50 D7
Chambers Gr AL7 .... 110 E3
Chambers La SG5 .... 21 E4
Chambers' St SG14 .... 113 C6
Champions Cl WD6 .... 157 B2
Champions Gn EN11 .... 115 A1
Champions Way
 EN11 .... 115 A1
Champneys **8** WD19 .... 175 E8
Chancellors SG15 .... 11 B7
Chancellors Rd SG1 .... 36 D3
Chancellor's Sch AL9 .... 145 A4
Chancery Cl AL4 .... 128 D8
Chandlers Cl CM23 .... 76 C4
CHANDLER'S CROSS 152 E2
Chandler's La WD3 .... 152 E2
Chandlers Rd AL4 .... 128 C6
Chandlers Way SG14 .... 113 A6
Chandos Cl HP6 .... 150 C1
Chandos Rd
 Borehamwood WD6 .... 170 A7
 Luton LU4 .... 44 C4
Chantry Cl
 Bishop's Stortford
 CM23 .... 76 E8
 Edgware NW7 .... 170 F2
 Enfield EN2 .... 161 C1
 Kings Langley WD4 .... 139 A2
Chantry Ct AL10 .... 130 A4
Chantry La
 Hatfield AL10 .... 129 F4
 Hatfield AL10 .... 130 A4
 Little Wymondley SG4 .... 35 F2
 London Colney AL2 .... 142 D5
Chantry Mount CM23 .... 76 F8
Chantry Pl HA3 .... 176 B2

Chantry Rd
Bishop's Stortford
CM23 . . . . **76** E8
Harrow HA3. . . . . **176** B2
Chantry The
6 Bishop's Stortford
CM23 . . . . **76** F8
Harlow CM20. . . . . **118** A2
Chaomans SG1 . . . . **50** F6
Chapel Cl
Brookmans Park AL9 . . . **145** D4
Little Gaddesden HP4 . . **102** D6
Luton LU2 . . . . **45** C8
St Albans AL1 . . . . **141** D8
Chapel Cotts HP2 . . . . . **124** D4
Chapel Croft WD4 . . . . . **152** A8
Chapel Crofts HP4 . . . . **121** E6
Chapel Dr SG15 . . . . **11** A4
CHAPEL END **99** C8
Buntingford SG9 . . . . . . **40** E7
Hoddesdon EN11 . . . . . **135** A5
Chapel End La HP23 . . . . **99** E3
Chapelfields SG12 . . . . **115** D4
Chapel Fields HP23 . . . . **99** E3
Chapel Hill CM24 . . . . . . **59** E6
Chapel La
Letty Green SG14 . . . . . **112** B3
Little Hadham SG11 . . . . **75** D8
Long Marston HP23 . . . . **79** B4
St Leonards HP23 . . . . . **119** D2
Chapel Pl SG5 . . . . **11** F6
Chapel Rd
Breachwood Green
SG4 . . . . **65** E8
Flamstead AL3. . . . . **84** B2
Chapel Row
Bendish SG4 . . . . **66** A8
3 Bishop's Stortford
CM23 . . . . **76** F8
Harefield UB9 . . . . **173** C2
Hitchin SG5 . . . . **34** F8
Chapel St
Berkhamsted HP4 . . . . . **122** D4
Hemel Hempstead HP2 . . **124** D4
Hinxworth SG7 . . . . **3** D6
Luton, High Town LU1 . . . **63** E7
Luton, New Town LU1 . . . **63** F8
Tring HP23 . . . . **99** F3
Chapel Viaduct LU1 . . . . **63** E7
Chapel Way WD5 . . . . . **139** F4
Chapman Ctyd 8
EN8 . . . . **148** C1
Chapman Rd SG1 . . . . . . **36** B1
Chapmans End SG11 . . . . **55** D3
CHAPMORE END **92** D5
Chappell Ct SG12 . . . . . . **92** E7
Chapter House Rd LU4 . . **44** A3
Chard Dr LU3 . . . . **31** B1
Chardia Terr EN8 . . . . . **148** D1
Charding Cres SG8 . . . . . . **7** C7
Charham Mews AL9 . . . . **144** C7
Charles Ho 8 EN11 . . . . **135** D8
Charles St
Berkhamsted HP4 . . . . . **122** B4
Hemel Hempstead HP1 . . **124** C2
Luton LU2 . . . . **63** F8
Tring HP23 . . . . **99** F3
Charlesworth Cl 4
HP3 . . . . **124** D1
Charlock Way WD18 . . . **166** F3
Charlotte Cl
St Albans AL1 . . . . **128** E3
Watford WD19 . . . . **167** C2
Charlottes Ct 2 LU1 . . . . **63** E7
CHARLTON **34** D5
Charlton Cl EN11 . . . . . . **135** A6
Charlton Mead La
EN11 . . . . **135** D5
Charlton Rd SG5 . . . . . . **34** D5
Charlton Way EN11 . . . . **135** D6
Charlwood Cl HA3 . . . . . **176** E4
Charlwood Rd LU4 . . . . . . **44** B1
Charmbury Rise LU2 . . . . **46** A4
Charmouth Ct AL1 . . . . . **128** A6
Charmouth Rd AL1 . . . . . **128** A5
Charndon Cl LU3 . . . . **31** B1
Charnwood Rd EN1 . . . . **162** B3
Charter Ho WD3 . . . . . . **166** A4
Charter Pl WD17. . . . . . . **167** C6
Chartley Ave HA7 . . . . . **176** F4
Chartridge WD19 . . . . . **175** D8
Chartridge Cl
Arkley EN5 . . . . **171** A4
Bushey WD23 . . . . **168** C3
Chartridge Way HP2 . . . **125** C3
Chartwell Cl 10 EN5 . . . **171** E5
Chartwell Dr LU2 . . . . . . **45** E1
Chartwell Pl CM23 . . . . . **58** B8
Chartwell Rd HA6 . . . . . **174** E3
Charwood Cl WD7. . . . . **156** E6
Chasden Rd HP1. . . . . . . **123** F5
Chase Cl SG15 . . . . **11** A8
Chase Farm EN6 . . . . . . **159** C4
Chase Farm Hospl
EN2 . . . . **161** A1
Chase Hill Rd SG15 . . . . . **11** A7
Chaseside CL LU7. . . . . . . **80** A7
Chase St LU1. . . . . **63** E6
Chase The
Arlesey SG15. . . . . **11** A4
Bishop's Stortford CM23 . **76** F6
Goff's Oak EN7 . . . . **147** B3
Great Amwell SG12 . . . . **115** A6
Harlow CM17. . . . . **118** C1

Chase The continued
Hemel Hempstead HP2 . . **124** E2
Hertford SG13. . . . . **113** F6
Oaklands AL6. . . . . **89** F7
Radlett WD7 . . . . **155** F4
Watford WD18. . . . . **166** E5
Chaseways CM21 . . . . . **118** C8
Chasten Hill SG6 . . . . **22** D7
Chater Inf Sch WD18. . . **167** A5
Chater Jun Sch WD18. . . **167** B5
Chatsworth Cl
Bishop's Stortford
CM23 . . . . **76** C7
Borehamwood WD6. . . . **170** A6
Chatsworth Ct
St Albans AL1 . . . . **127** F3
Stevenage SG2 . . . . **50** F1
Chatsworth Mews
WD24. . . . . **154** A1
Chatsworth Rd LU4 . . . . . **45** B1
CHATTER END **58** C7
Chatter End CM23 . . . . . . **58** C7
Chatteris Cl LU4 . . . . **44** D4
Chatterton SG6 . . . . **23** C5
Chatton Cl LU2 . . . . **46** E2
Chaucer Cl HP4 . . . . **121** F5
Chaucer Ct EN11 . . . . . . **115** A1
Chaucer Gr WD6 . . . . . . **170** A5
Chaucer Ho 3 EN5 . . . . **171** D5
Chaucer Rd
Luton LU3 . . . . **45** C2
Royston SG8 . . . . **7** C8
Chaucer Way
Hitchin SG4 . . . . **35** C7
Hoddesdon EN11 . . . . . **115** A2
Chaucer Wlk HP2. . . . . . **105** B3
CHAULDEN **123** E2
Chaulden House Gdns
HP1 . . . . **123** F1
Chaulden Jun & Inf Schs
HP1 . . . . **123** F2
Chaulden La HP1 . . . . . . **123** C1
Chaulden Terr HP1. . . . . **123** F2
CHAUL END **62** C7
Chaul End La LU4. . . . . . . **44** E1
Chaul End Rd
Caddington LU1 . . . . **62** D2
Luton LU1 . . . . **44** C1
Chauncey Ho WD18. . . . **166** F3
Chauncy Ave EN6 . . . . . **159** C6
Chauncy Cl SG12 . . . . . . **93** D3
Chauncy Ct 19 SG14 . . . **113** D6
Chauncy Gdns SG7 . . . . . **13** B1
Chauncy Ho 3 SG1 . . . . . **50** E6
Chauncy Rd SG1. . . . . **50** E6
Chauncy Sch The SG12 . . **93** B2
Chaworth Gn 11 LU4 . . . . **44** C5
CHEAPSIDE **29** B7
Cheapside LU1 . . . . **63** E7
Cheapside Sq 4 LU1 . . . . **63** E7
Cheapside AL7. . . . . **111** D7
Cheddington Comb Sch
LU7 . . . . **80** A7
Cheddington La HP23 . . . **79** C5
Cheddington Rd LU7 . . . . **80** C4
Cheffins Rd EN11 . . . . . . **114** F1
CHELLS **51** B6
Chells Ent Village SG2 . . **51** C6
Chells La SG2 . . . . **51** D7
Chells Way SG2 . . . . **51** B6
Chelmsford Rd SG14 . . . **113** B5
Chelsea Fields EN11 . . . . **115** B2
Chelsing Rise HP2 . . . . . **125** C3
Cheltenham Ct 9 LU2 . . . **46** D1
Cheltenham Ct 9
AL1. . . . . **128** A2
Cheltenham Ho 2
WD24. . . . . **167** C7
Chelveston Cl LU3 . . . . . **111** D7
Chelwood Ave AL10. . . . **130** A8
Chelwood Cl HA6. . . . . . **174** C3
Chenduit Way HA7. . . . . **176** F5
Chene Dr AL3 . . . . **127** D5
Chene Mews AL3 . . . . . . **127** D5
Cheney Rd LU4 . . . . **44** C5
CHENIES **151** B1
Chenies 4 HA6. . . . . **174** F5
Chenies Ave HA6 . . . . . . **174** F4
CHENIES BOTTOM **151** A2
Chenies Cl HP2. . . . . **125** B8
Chenies Gn CM23. . . . . . . **76** D6
Chenies Manor Ho*
WD3. . . . . **151** A1
Chenies Rd WD3. . . . . . . **164** D7
Chenies Sch WD3. . . . . . **151** B1
Chennells AL10. . . . . **129** F4
Chennells Cl SG4. . . . . **22** B2
Chepstow AL5 . . . . **85** F2
Chepstow Cl SG1 . . . . **51** B8
Chequer Ct LU1. . . . . **63** F6
Chequer La AL3 . . . . **106** B4
Chequers
Bishop's Stortford
CM23 . . . . **76** C8
Hatfield AL9 . . . . **130** D8
Welwyn Garden City
AL7 . . . . **110** D3
Chequers Bridge Rd
SG1 . . . . **50** C6
Chequers Cl
Buntingford SG9 . . . . . . **40** D8
Pitstone LU7 . . . . **80** C4
Standon SG11 . . . . **55** D4
Stotfold SG5 . . . . **12** A6
Chequers Cotts
Preston SG4 . . . . **48** D6

Chequers Cotts continued
Whipsnade LU6 . . . . **82** A8
Chequers End HP2. . . . . **104** D5
Chequersfield AL7 . . . . . **110** D3
Chequers Hill AL3 . . . . . . **84** C2
Chequers La
Abbots Langley WD2 . . . **140** C1
Pitstone LU7 . . . . **80** C5
Preston SG4 . . . . **48** D7
Chequer St
Luton LU1 . . . . **63** F6
St Albans AL1 . . . . **127** D3
Chequers Wlk EN9. . . . . **163** F6
Cheriton Cl AL4 . . . . **128** D7
Cherrington Ct LU2 . . . . . **46** A4
Cherry Bank HP2 . . . . . . **124** D5
Cherry Blossom Cl 3
CM17 . . . . **118** C4
Cherry Cl SG3 . . . . **68** F4
Cherry Croft
Croxley Green WD3 . . . . **166** B3
Welwyn Garden City AL8 . **89** D2
Cherry Croft Gdns 4
HA5 . . . . **175** F3
Cherry Ct HA5 . . . . **175** D2
Cherrydale WD18 . . . . . **166** F5
Cherry Dr SG8 . . . . **7** E7
Cherry Gdns
Bishop's Stortford
CM23 . . . . **77** A8
Sawbridgeworth CM21 . . **97** E4
Tring HP23 . . . . **99** F3
CHERRY GREEN **40** C1
Cherry Green Barns
SG9 . . . . **40** C1
Cherry Green La SG9 . . . . **40** D3
Cherry Hill
Chiswell Green AL2 . . . . **141** A6
Harrow HA3. . . . . **176** E4
Rickmansworth WD3 . . . **165** B6
Cherry Hills WD19 . . . . . **175** C5
Cherry Hollow WD5. . . . **153** F8
Cherry Orch HP1 . . . . . . **124** A5
Cherry Orchard La
SG9 . . . . **28** A3
Cherry Rd EN3 . . . . **162** C1
Cherry Tree Ave AL2 . . . **142** D5
Cherrytree La HP2 . . . . . **125** C7
Cherry Tree La
Arlesey SG15. . . . . **11** A4
Luton LU3 . . . . **46** A1
Chorleywood WD3 . . . . **164** C1
Harlow CM20. . . . . **117** B1
Potters Bar EN6 . . . . . . **159** B5
Wheathampstead AL4 . . . **87** A2
Cherry Tree Prim Sch
WD24. . . . . **154** A3
Cherry Tree Rd
Hoddesdon EN11 . . . . . **135** A7
Watford WD24. . . . . **154** B3
Cherry Tree Rise SG8 . . . . **38** B1
Cherry Trees SG16 . . . . . **10** B3
Cherry Trees Dr SG2 . . . . **51** B7
Cherry Way AL10 . . . . . . **130** A2
Cherry Wlk WD3 . . . . . . **165** C7
Chertsey Cl LU2 . . . . **64** D8
Chertsey Rise SG2 . . . . . . **51** C4
Cherwell Cl WD3 . . . . . . **166** A4
Cherwell Dr SG1. . . . . **37** A3
Chesfield Cl CM23 . . . . . . **76** F5
Chesford Cl 10 LU1 . . . . . **63** E6
Chesford Rd LU2 . . . . **46** C4
Chesham Ct HA6 . . . . . . **174** E4
Chesham Prep Sch
HP5 . . . . **136** A4
Chesham Rd
Berkhamsted HP4 . . . . . **122** C3
Bovingdon HP3, HP3 . . . **136** E3
Wigginton HP23. . . . . . . **120** E7
Chesham Way WD18 . . . **166** F3
Cheshire Dr WD25 . . . . . **153** F5
CHESHUNT **148** C1
Cheshunt Centre The
EN8 . . . . **148** D3
Cheshunt Com Hospl
EN8 . . . . **162** E8
Cheshunt Folly EN8. . . . **148** B3
Cheshunt Sch EN8 . . . . . **148** C1
Cheshunt Sta EN8 . . . . . **148** F1
Cheshunt Wash EN8 . . . **148** E4
Cheslyn Cl LU2 . . . . **46** E2
Chess Cl
Latimer HP5. . . . . **150** D3
Luton LU2 . . . . **46** A4
Chess Hill WD3 . . . . **165** D5
Chess La WD3 . . . . **165** D5
Chess Vale Rise WD3 . . . **165** A3
Chesswood Ct WD3. . . . **165** D1
Chesswood Way HA5 . . . **175** D1
Chester Ave LU4 . . . . **44** E3
Chester Cl
Luton LU4 . . . . **44** E2
Potters Bar EN6 . . . . . . **145** B2
Chesterfield Flats
EN5 . . . . **171** D4
Chesterfield Prim Sch
EN3 . . . . **162** E2
Chesterfield Rd
Barnet EN5 . . . . **171** D4
Enfield EN3 . . . . **162** E2
Chester Gibbons Gn
AL2 . . . . **142** D5
Chester Ho HA6 . . . . **174** E3
Chester Pl 11 HA6. . . . . **174** E3

Chester Rd
Borehamwood WD6. . . . **170** D6
Northwood HA6. . . . . . . **174** F3
Stevenage SG1 . . . . **37** A1
Watford WD18. . . . . **167** A5
Chesterton Ave AL5. . . . . **86** D1
Chestnut Ave
Lower Stondon SG16. . . . **10** C3
Luton LU3 . . . . **44** C8
Northwood HA6. . . . . . . **174** F2
Rickmansworth WD3 . . . **165** A4
Ware SG12 . . . . **93** F3
Chestnut Cl
Bishop's Stortford
CM23 . . . . **76** E6
Dagnall HP4. . . . . **81** C5
Hunsdon SG12 . . . . **95** D1
Potten End HP4 . . . . . . **123** B6
Chestnut Ct
Hitchin SG5 . . . . **34** D8
Watford WD18. . . . . **166** E5
Chestnut Dr
Berkhamsted HP4 . . . . . **122** D3
Harrow HA3. . . . . **176** F2
Hatfield Heath CM22. . . . **98** F3
St Albans AL4 . . . . **128** C5
Chestnut Gr EN11. . . . . . **115** C2
Chestnut La
Harlow CM20. . . . . **117** B1
Kneesworth SG8 . . . . **2** B6
Totteridge N20. . . . . **171** E1
Chestnut Rd EN3 . . . . . . **162** E3
Chestnut Rise WD23 . . . **168** B2
Chestnuts The
Codicote SG4. . . . . **67** D2
Hemel Hempstead HP3 . . **137** F7
Hertford SG13. . . . . **113** D5
Chestnut Wlk
Hitchin SG4 . . . . **35** A4
Royston SG8 . . . . **7** E5
Stevenage SG1 . . . . **36** D1
Watford WD24. . . . . **154** A2
Welwyn AL6. . . . . **90** A8
Cheverells Cl AL3. . . . . . . **83** D4
Cheverell's Gn
Cheverell's Green AL3. . . **83** C4
Markyate AL3 . . . . **83** C4
CHEVERELL'S GREEN . . **83** C4
Cheviot Cl
Bushey WD23 . . . . **168** C3
Luton LU3 . . . . **44** D7
Cheviot Rd LU3. . . . . **44** D7
Cheviots
Hatfield AL10. . . . . **130** A3
Hemel Hempstead HP2 . . **124** F6
Cheviot Way SG1 . . . . **37** A3
Cheyne Cl
Pitstone LU7 . . . . **80** D4
Ware SG12 . . . . **93** D3
Cheynes Inf Sch LU3 . . . . **44** D8
Chicheley Gdns HA3 . . . **176** C3
Chicheley Rd HA3 . . . . . **176** C3
Chichester Way
WD25. . . . . **154** E6
Chicken La AL2. . . . . **142** D4
Chidbrook Rd WD18 . . . **166** E3
Chilcott Rd WD24. . . . . . **153** F3
Chilcourt SG8 . . . . **7** C6
Childs Ave UB9 . . . . **173** C1
Childwick Ct HP3 . . . . . . **139** B8
Childwick Gn AL3 . . . . . . **107** C2
CHILDWICK GREEN . . . **107** C2
Childwick Way SG6. . . . . **22** E8
Chilham Cl HP2 . . . . **124** E2
Chiltern Ave WD23 . . . . **168** C3
Chiltern Cl
Berkhamsted HP4 . . . . . **121** F5
Borehamwood WD6. . . . **169** F3
Goff's Oak EN7 . . . . **147** B4
St Albans AL4 . . . . **128** D7
Watford WD18. . . . . **166** F5
Chiltern Cnr HP4 . . . . . . **122** A5
Chiltern Cotts HP23. . . . . **80** A2
Chiltern Ct
19 Harpenden AL5 . . . . . **86** B1
St Albans AL4 . . . . **128** D7
Chiltern Dr WD3. . . . . . . **165** A2
Chiltern Gdns LU4 . . . . . . **44** F3
CHILTERN GREEN **65** B3
Chiltern Park Ave
HP4 . . . . **122** A6
Chiltern Rd
Baldock SG7 . . . . **23** F6
Hitchin SG5 . . . . **35** A7
St Albans AL4 . . . . **128** C7
Wingrave HP22 . . . . **60** A3
Chiltern Rise LU1. . . . . . . **63** D6
Chilterns
Berkhamsted HP4 . . . . . **121** F6
Hatfield AL10. . . . . **130** A3
Hemel Hempstead HP2 . . **124** D5
Chilterns The
Hitchin SG4 . . . . **35** A6
Kensworth Common LU6. . **82** F8
Chiltern View SG6 . . . . . . **22** D5
Chiltern Villas HP23. . . . . **99** E3
Chiltern Way HP23. . . . . **100** C5
Chilton Cl SG14 . . . . **112** B8
Chilton Gn AL7 . . . . **111** C6
Chilvers Bank SG7. . . . . . **23** C3
Chilwell Gdns WD19 . . . **175** C6
Chilworth Gate EN10. . . **134** F1
Chime Sq AL1 . . . . **127** E4
Chimneys The WD23 . . . **167** F4
Chindit Cl EN10. . . . . **134** E3
Chinneck Ho 10 HP4 . . . **122** C4

Chinnery Cl EN1. . . . . . . **161** F1
Chinnery Hill CM23 . . . . . **76** F5
Chipmunk Chase
AL10. . . . . **129** D7
CHIPPERFIELD **152** B8
Chipperfield Rd
Bovingdon HP3 . . . . **137** C3
Hemel Hempstead HP3 . . **138** C7
Kings Langley WD4 . . . . **138** D2
CHIPPING **27** D5
CHIPPING BARNET **171** E5
Chipping Cl 8 EN5 . . . . . **171** E6
Chippingfield HP17. . . . . **118** C3
Chipping Hall Cotts
SG9 . . . . **27** D4
Chirdland Ho WD18. . . . **166** E3
Chishill Rd
Barley SG8. . . . . **9** A2
Great Chishill SG8 . . . . . . **9** F3
Chishill Windmill* SG8 . . . **9** C2
Chiswell Cl WD24. . . . . . **154** C1
CHISWELL GREEN **141** A5
Chiswell Green La
AL2. . . . . **140** E6
Chittenden Cl 5
SG13. . . . . **115** B1
Chivenor Pl AL4 . . . . **128** C1
CHIVERY **119** C4
Chobham Ct 8 LU1. . . . . . **63** F6
Chobham Dr SG1. . . . . **63** F6
Chobham St 5 LU1 . . . . . **63** E6
CHOLESBURY **120** C2
Cholesbury 1 WD19 . . . . **175** E8
Cholesbury La HP23 . . . . **120** E3
Cholesbury Rd HP23 . . . **120** B2
Cholesbury Rd HP23 . . . **120** D5
CHORLEYWOOD **164** D5
CHORLEYWOOD BOTTOM
. . . . **164** D3
Chorleywood Bottom
WD3. . . . . **164** D4
Chorleywood Cl WD3 . . . **165** D2
Chorleywood House Dr
WD3. . . . . **164** C3
Chorleywood Prim Sch
WD3. . . . . **164** C3
Chorleywood Rd
WD3. . . . . **165** C4
Chorleywood Sta
WD3. . . . . **164** D5
CHORLEYWOOD WEST
. . . . **164** B5
Chouler Gdns SG1. . . . . . **36** C3
Chowns The AL5. . . . . . . **107** A5
Christ Church CE Prim
Sch SG12 . . . . **93** E1
Christ Church CE Sch
WD3. . . . . **164** F5
Christchurch Cl AL3 . . . . **127** D4
Christchurch Cres
WD7 . . . . **156** A3
Christchurch Ho
HP23 . . . . **100** A3
Christ Church La EN5 . . . **171** D7
Christchurch Pl SG14 . . . **113** C6
Christ Church Prim Sch
EN5 . . . . **171** D7
Christchurch Rd
Hemel Hempstead
HP2. . . . . **124** D4
Tring HP23 . . . . **99** F4
Christian Cl EN11. . . . . . **114** F2
Christie Cl EN10. . . . . . . **134** F3
Christie Ct WD18 . . . . . . **167** A4
Christie Rd
Stevenage SG2 . . . . **51** D5
Waltham Abbey EN9 . . . **163** B4
Christies Ct 8 EN11 . . . . **135** A4
Christina Ct AL3 . . . . **83** E5
Christopher Ct
Hemel Hempstead
HP3. . . . . **138** D8
13 Ware SG12. . . . . **93** D1
Christopher Pl 5
AL3. . . . . **127** D3
Christy's Yd SG7. . . . . **3** D6
Chrysalis Sch for Autism
SG4 . . . . **67** F2
Church Cl
Codicote SG4. . . . . **67** F2
Cuffley EN6 . . . . **146** E2
Little Berkhamsted
SG13. . . . . **132** C4
Northwood HA6. . . . . . . **174** F3
Radlett WD7 . . . . **156** A3
Reed SG8. . . . . **16** C4
Studham LU6 . . . . **82** B4
Church Cotts
Essendon AL9 . . . . **131** E6
Gilston CM20. . . . . **117** C7
Great Gaddesden HP1. . . **103** D3
Church Cres
Sawbridgeworth CM21 . . . **97** F2
St Albans AL3 . . . . **127** C4
Church Ct
Hoddesdon EN10. . . . . . **135** A3
12 Ware SG12. . . . . **93** D2
CHURCH END **11** B7
CHURCH END **24** D1
Church End
Sandon SG9 . . . . **9** A1
Braughing SG11. . . . . . . **55** F7
CHURCH END **57** D2
Church End AL3 . . . . **83** D6

CHURCH END
Pitstone 80 D3
Redbourn 105 F4
Church End
Redbourn AL3 . . . . .106 A4
Sandridge AL4 . . . . .108 C2
CHURCH END 151 F1
Church End SG2 . . . . .38 C2
Church End Cotts
WD3 . . . . .151 F1
Church Farm HP23 . . . . . .101 C5
Church Farm La HP23 . . . .79 F3
Church Farm Way
WD25 . . . . .155 B1
Churchfield
Barley SG8 . . . . .9 A1
Harlow CM20 . . . . .118 B2
Harpenden AL5 . . . . .107 C8
Church Field SG12 . . . . .93 B3
Churchfield Ho AL8 . . . . . .110 C6
Church Field Path
EN8 . . . . .148 C2
Churchfield Rd AL6 . . . . .90 C1
Churchfields
Hertford SG13 . . . . .113 D5
Hoddesdon EN10 . . . . .135 A3
Standon SG11 . . . . .55 E2
Stansted Mountfitchet
CM24 . . . . .59 F6
Churchfields La EN10 . . . .135 A3
Churchfields Rd
WD24 . . . . .153 F3
CHURCHGATE 148 A1
Churchgate
Cheshunt EN8 . . . . .148 B1
7 Hitchin SG5 . . . . .34 E7
Churchgate CE Prim Sch
CM17 . . . . .118 F3
Churchgate Rd EN8 . . . . . .148 B2
Church Gates **4** HP4 . . . .122 C4
Churchgate St CM17 . . . . .118 F4
CHURCHGATE STREET
. . . . .118 F3
Church Gn
Benington SG2 . . . . .52 D4
Great Wymondley SG4 . . . . . .35 E6
Harpenden AL5 . . . . .86 A1
Church Green Mews **4**
AL5 . . . . .86 A1
Church Green Row **3**
AL5 . . . . .86 A1
Church La
Arlesey SG15 . . . . .11 A7
Ashwell SG7 . . . . .4 D4
Barkway SG8 . . . . .17 C4
Berkhamsted HP4 . . . . .122 C4
Bishop's Stortford CM23 . . . .76 D3
Bovingdon HP3 . . . . .137 B4
Cheddington LU7 . . . . .80 A8
Dane End SG12 . . . . .71 F8
Graveley SG4 . . . . .36 C4
Guilden Morden SG8 . . . . .1 F5
Harrow HA3 . . . . .176 F2
Hatfield AL9 . . . . .130 C5
Hoddesdon EN10 . . . . .134 C1
Kimpton SG4 . . . . .66 D1
Kings Langley WD4 . . . . .139 A2
Letchworth Garden City
SG6 .12 C1
Marsworth HP23 . . . . .79 F1
Much Hadham SG10 . . . . .74 F3
Northaw EN6 . . . . .146 A1
Preston SG4 . . . . .48 D6
Radlett WD25 . . . . .155 B1
Reed SG8 . . . . .16 E5
Rickmansworth WD3 . . . . . .165 B1
4 Royston SG8 . . . . .7 C6
Sarratt WD3 . . . . .152 A2
Stapleford SG14 . . . . .92 A6
Stevenage SG1 . . . . .50 D8
Therfield SG8 . . . . .15 F7
Tring HP23 . . . . .120 A7
Weston SG4 . . . . .24 D1
Church Manor CM23 . . . . . .77 B8
Church Mead
Roydon CM19 . . . . .116 B1
Studham LU6 . . . . .82 B4
Church Meadow Cotts
HP1 .103 D3
Church Mill Grange
CM17 . . . . .118 E4
Church Path
Great Amwell SG12 . . . . .114 F6
Ickleford SG5 . . . . .21 E4
Little Wymondley SG4 . . . . . . .35 F3
Church Pl AL6 . . . . .89 C5
Church Rd
Flamstead AL3 . . . . .84 B2
Great Hallingbury CM22 . . . . .77 D3
Hemel Hempstead HP3 . . . . .125 C2
Hertford SG14 . . . . .113 C7
Ivinghoe LU7 . . . . .80 F5
King's Walden SG4 . . . . .47 F3

Church Rd continued
Little Berkhamsted
SG13 . . . . .132 C4
Little Gaddesden HP4 . . . . . .102 D8
Northwood HA6 . . . . .174 F3
Pitstone, Church End
LU7 .80 E3
Potten End HP4 . . . . .123 B6
Potters Bar EN6 . . . . .145 B1
Slip End LU1 . . . . .63 C2
Stansted Mountfitchet
CM24 . . . . .59 F5
Stotfold SG5 . . . . .11 F6
Streatley LU3 . . . . .31 A6
Studham LU6 . . . . .82 B4
Watford WD17 . . . . .167 B8
Welwyn Garden City
AL8 .110 D6
Church Row Mews **2**
SG12 . . . . .93 D1
Church St
Baldock SG7 . . . . .12 E1
Bishop's Stortford CM23 . . . .76 F7
Bovingdon HP3 . . . . .137 B4
Buntingford SG9 . . . . .40 E8
Essendon AL9 . . . . .131 E6
Guilden Morden SG8 . . . . .1 F5
Hatfield AL9 . . . . .130 C5
Hemel Hempstead HP2 . . . . .124 D5
Hertford SG14 . . . . .113 D6
Luton, High Town LU2 . . . . . .63 F8
Luton LU2 . . . . .63 E7
Rickmansworth WD3 . . . . . .165 E1
Sawbridgeworth CM21 . . . . . .97 E2
Shillington SG5 . . . . .19 E8
St Albans AL3 . . . . .127 D4
Waltham Abbey EN9 . . . . . . .163 C6
Ware SG12 . . . . .93 D1
Watford WD18 . . . . .167 C5
Welwyn AL6 . . . . .89 C5
Wheathampstead AL4 . . . . . .108 B7
Wingrave HP22 . . . . .60 B2
Church Street Ind Est
SG12 . . . . .93 D1
Church View
Hoddesdon EN10 . . . . .134 F3
Long Marston HP23 . . . . .79 A4
Church Wlk
Bushey WD23 . . . . .168 C1
Sawbridgeworth CM21 . . . . . .97 F2
Churchyard Wlk **6**
SG5 .34 E7
Church Yd
Hitchin SG5 . . . . .34 E7
Tring HP23 . . . . .100 A3
Cicero Dr LU3 . . . . .45 A8
Cillocks CI EN11 . . . . .135 A7
City Point **7** AL1 . . . . .127 C4
Claggy Rd SG4 . . . . .66 B2
Claggy Road Ind Est
SG4 .66 C2
Claire Ct
Bushey WD23 . . . . .168 D1
Cheshunt EN8 . . . . .162 D7
8 Pinner HA5 . . . . .175 F3
Clamp Hill HA7 . . . . .176 E5
CLAPGATE 57 C6
Clapgate Rd WD23 . . . . . . .168 B3
Clare CI WD6 . . . . .169 F3
Clare Cres SG7 . . . . .23 E6
Clare Ct
Enfield EN3 . . . . .162 E4
Northwood HA6 . . . . .174 E5
St Albans AL1 . . . . .127 C4
Clare Gdns SG4, SG5 . . . . . .34 E7
Claremont
Bricket Wood AL2 . . . . .155 A8
Goff's Oak EN7 . . . . .147 A2
Claremont Cres WD3 . . . .166 C4
Claremont Rd
Hadley Wood EN4 . . . . .159 D2
Harrow HA1 . . . . .176 E1
Luton LU4 . . . . .45 B1
Clarence CI WD23 . . . . .168 D2
Clarence Lo **8** EN11 . . . . .135 A6
Clarence Rd
Berkhamsted HP4 . . . . .122 C4
Harpenden AL5 . . . . .86 A3
St Albans AL1 . . . . .128 A4
Stansted Mountfitchet
CM24 . . . . .59 E7
Clarendon CI **1** HP2 . . . . .124 C8
Clarendon Ct
Harpenden AL5 . . . . .86 B3
3 Luton LU2 . . . . .45 D1
12 Northwood HA6 . . . . . . .174 E3
Clarendon Fields
WD3 . . . . .152 F1
Clarendon Mews
WD6 . . . . .170 A6
Clarendon Par EN8 . . . . . .148 D2
Clarendon Rd
Borehamwood WD6 . . . . .170 A6
Cheshunt EN8 . . . . .148 D2
Harpenden AL5 . . . . .86 B3
Luton LU2 . . . . .45 E1
Watford WD17 . . . . .167 B6
Claret Ho WD17 . . . . .167 B7
Clarion CI SG1 . . . . .33 C2
Clarion Ho SG5 . . . . .33 C2
Clarke's Rd AL10 . . . . .130 B7
Clarke's Spring HP23 . . . . .100 C3
Clarke Way WD25 . . . . .154 A4
Clarkfield WD3 . . . . .165 B1
Clarklands Ind Est
CM21 . . . . .97 E5
Clark Rd SG8 . . . . .7 D7
Clarks CI SG12 . . . . .93 D3

Clarks Mead WD23 . . . . . .168 D2
Clarkson Ct AL10 . . . . .129 E6
Claudian PI AL3 . . . . .127 A1
Claughton Ct AL4 . . . . .128 C2
Claverhambury Rd
EN9 .149 F2
Claverley Gn LU2 . . . . .46 E2
Claverton CI HP3 . . . . .137 A3
Claybury WD23 . . . . .168 B2
Claybush Rd SG7 . . . . .4 D3
Claycroft AL7 . . . . .111 B7
Claydon CI LU3 . . . . .45 C7
Claydown Way LU1 . . . . . . .63 B1
CLAY END 52 F7
Claygate Ave AL5 . . . . .85 E2
Clay Hall Rd LU6 . . . . .82 F7
Clayhill HP23 . . . . .120 E7
CLAY HILL 161 B2
Clay Hill EN2 . . . . .161 D2
Clay La WD23 . . . . .168 B4
Claymore HP2 . . . . .124 E7
Claymore Dr SG5 . . . . .21 F5
Claymores SG1 . . . . .50 E6
Claypits CM23 . . . . .77 B7
Clayton Dr HP3 . . . . .125 D1
Clayton Hill Ctry Pk*
EN9 .149 D8
Clayton Par **7** EN8 . . . . . .148 D1
Cleall Ave EN8 . . . . .163 C5
Cleave The AL5 . . . . .86 C2
Clement Ct **7** AL1 . . . . . . .128 A2
Clementine Way **4**
HP1 .124 B1
Clement PI HP23 . . . . .100 A3
Clement Rd EN8 . . . . .148 E4
Clementsbury SG13 . . . . . . .133 C8
Clements Cl WD25 . . . . .154 C4
CLEMENT'S END 82 D3
Clements End Rd LU6,
HP2 . . . . .82 E2
Clements Rd WD3 . . . . .164 D4
Clements St SG12 . . . . .93 E1
Clevedon Rd LU2 . . . . .46 B2
Cleveland Cres WD6 . . . . . .170 C4
Cleveland Rd
Hemel Hempstead
HP2 .125 B5
Markyate AL3 . . . . .83 C5
Cleveland Way
Hemel Hempstead
HP2 .125 B5
Stevenage SG1 . . . . .37 C3
Cleves Rd HP2 . . . . .125 B8
Cleviscroft SG1 . . . . .50 E4
Clewer Cres HA3 . . . . .176 D2
Clifford Cres LU4 . . . . .44 D1
Clifford Ct **10** CM23 . . . . . .77 A7
Cliff Richard Ct **14**
EN8 .148 D3
Clifton CI EN8 . . . . .148 E2
Clifton Ct HP3 . . . . .124 D1
Clifton Rd
Luton LU1 . . . . .63 B8
Watford WD17 . . . . .167 B4
Clifton St AL1 . . . . .127 E4
Clifton Way
Borehamwood WD6 . . . . .170 A8
Ware SG12 . . . . .93 D3
Climb The WD3 . . . . .165 B8
Clump The WD3 . . . . .165 B4
Clinton Ave LU2 . . . . .45 F3
Clinton End HP2 . . . . .125 C3
Clitheroe Gdns WD19 . . . .175 D7
Clive CI EN6 . . . . .158 F8
Clive Ct LU1 . . . . .45 E1
Clive Par HA5 . . . . .174 E3
Clive Way WD24 . . . . .167 C8
Clock Ho The EN2 . . . . .161 F2
Clockhouse Mews
WD3 . . . . .164 E6
Clock Tower The AL2 . . . . .142 B4
Cloister Garth
Berkhamsted HP4 . . . . .122 C4
St Albans AL1 . . . . .141 E7
Cloister Lawns SG6 . . . . . . .22 F4
Cloisters Ct WD3 . . . . .165 E1
Cloisters Rd
Letchworth Garden City
SG6 .23 A4
Luton LU4 . . . . .44 B3
Cloisters The
Bushey WD23 . . . . .168 B3
Kings Langley WD4 . . . . .139 A2
Rickmansworth WD3 . . . . . .165 E2
Slip End LU1 . . . . .84 C8
3 Watford WD18 . . . . .167 C5
Welwyn Garden City
AL8 .110 D6
Cloister Wlk HA7 . . . . .176 A4
Clonard Way HA5 . . . . .176 A4
Clone Shalom Sch
London Colney WD7 . . . . . . .142 E1
Shenleybury WD7 . . . . .156 E8
Closemead Ct HA6 . . . . . . .174 C4
Close The
Baldock SG7 . . . . .23 E7
Brookmans Park AL9 . . . . . . .144 E5
Bushey WD23 . . . . .168 A4
Codicote SG4 . . . . .67 F1
Harpenden AL5 . . . . .85 D4
Harrow HA2 . . . . .176 C1
Hinxworth SG7 . . . . .3 D6
Luton LU3 . . . . .45 A5
Markyate AL3 . . . . .83 E5
Potters Bar EN6 . . . . .159 A7
Radlett WD7 . . . . .155 F6
Rickmansworth WD3 . . . . . .165 E1
Royston SG8 . . . . .7 B1
St Albans AL1 . . . . .141 C8

Close The continued
Stevenage SG1 . . . . .36 C1
Wallington SG9 . . . . .25 E6
Ware SG12 . . . . .93 E1
CLOTHALL 24 E4
Clothall Rd
Baldock SG7 . . . . .23 F8
Clothall SG7 . . . . .24 C6
Clovelly Way SG1 . . . . .50 A7
Clover Ave CM23 . . . . .76 B6
Clover CI LU4 . . . . .44 A3
Cloverfield AL7 . . . . .89 F1
Clover Field The
WD23 . . . . .167 F3
Cloverland AL10 . . . . .129 F2
Clover Way
Hatfield AL10 . . . . .129 F8
Hemel Hempstead HP1 . . . . .124 B4
Club Cotts AL6 . . . . .90 D6
Clump The WD25 . . . . .165 B4
Clunbury Ct HP4 . . . . .122 D4
Cluny Way SG15 . . . . .11 A5
Clusterbolts SG14 . . . . .92 A7
Clutterbucks WD3 . . . . .152 A3
Clyde Rd EN11 . . . . .135 D5
Clydesdale CI LU4 . . . . .44 A3
Clydesdale Ct LU4 . . . . .44 A3
Clydesdale Path WD6 . . . . .170 C4
Clydesdale Rd
Luton LU4 . . . . .44 A3
Royston SG8 . . . . .7 E5
Clydesdale Wlk **2**
EN10 . . . . .148 F6
Clyde Sq HP2 . . . . .124 F8
Clyde Terr SG13 . . . . .114 A6
Clyfton CI EN10 . . . . .148 F8
Clyston Rd WD18 . . . . .166 F3
Coach Dr SG4 . . . . .34 F5
Coach Ho Cloisters **2**
SG7 .23 E8
Coach House Cloisters
SG7 .23 E7
Coachman's La SG7 . . . . . . .23 D8
Coach Mews AL1 . . . . .128 B3
Coanwood Cotts SG4 . . . . . .66 C1
Coates Dell WD25 . . . . .154 E6
Coates Rd WD6 . . . . .169 D2
Coates Way WD25 . . . . .154 E6
Coates Way Jun Mix Inf
Sch WD25 . . . . .154 E6
Cobb CI WD6 . . . . .170 C4
Cobbett CI EN3 . . . . .162 C3
Cobbetts Ride HP23 . . . . . . .99 F3
Cobble Gn WD25 . . . . .153 B7
Cobbinsbank EN9 . . . . .163 D6
Cobbins The EN9 . . . . .163 E6
Cobbins Way CM17 . . . . . . .118 E4
Cobblers Wick HP22 . . . . . . .60 B3
Cobb Rd HP4 . . . . .121 F4
Cobden Hill WD7 . . . . .156 B2
Cobden St LU2 . . . . .45 F1
Cobham Rd SG12 . . . . .93 F2
Cob Lane CA6 . . . . .89 F4
Cobmead AL10 . . . . .130 B7
Cockhush Ave SG13 . . . . . . .114 B7
Cockerell CI SG1 . . . . .50 B6
COCKERNHOE 46 F3
Cockernhoe Endowed CE
Prim Sch LU2 . . . . .46 E3
Cocker Rd EN1 . . . . .162 C3
Cockfosters Rd EN4 . . . . . . .159 E1
Cock Gr HP23 . . . . .121 C4
Cock La
Brent Pelham, SG11 . . . . .30 F3
Hoddesdon EN11 . . . . .134 D4
Cockle Way WD7 . . . . .156 E6
Cockrobin La CM20 . . . . . . .117 A7
CODICOTE 67 E1
CODICOTE BOTTOM 88 D8
Codicote CE Prim Sch
SG4 .67 E1
Codicote Dr WD25 . . . . .154 D5
Codicote Ho SG1 . . . . .36 C1
Codicote Hts SG4 . . . . .68 B1
Codicote Innovation Ctr
SG4 .88 D2
Codicote Rd
Ayot St L AL4, AL6, SG4 . . . .88 C3
Welwyn AL6 . . . . .89 B7
Wheathampstead AL4 . . . . . . .87 D1
Whitwell SG4 . . . . .66 F6
Codicote Row HP2 . . . . .105 B1
Codmore Wood Rd
HP5 .150 D6
Coe's Alley **1** EN5 . . . . .171 E5
Cohen CI EN8 . . . . .162 E8
Colborne Ho WD18 . . . . . . .166 E3
Colbron CI SG7 . . . . .4 C4
Colburn Ave HA5 . . . . .175 E4
Colchester Rd HA6 . . . . .175 A1
COLD CHRISTMAS 94 B6
Cold Christmas La
SG12 . . . . .93 E6
Coldham Gr EN3 . . . . .162 E2
Coldharbour La
Bushey WD23 . . . . .168 C4
Harpenden AL5 . . . . .86 C4
Colebrook Ave LU3 . . . . .44 C7
COLE GREEN
Brent Pelham 29 F3
Letty Green 112 A3
Cole Green Ho AL7 . . . . . . .110 F4
Cole Green La AL7 . . . . .111 B4
Cole Green Way
SG14 . . . . .113 A4
Cole Green Way
Cole Green, Stains ctr SG4 . . .66 C2
Coleman Green La
Sandridge AL4 . . . . .108 E4

Coleman Green La
continued
Wheathampstead AL4 . . . . . .109 A7
Colemans CI SG5 . . . . .20 D4
COLEMANS GREEN 47 D1
Coleman's La EN9 . . . . .149 E5
Colemans Rd SG4 . . . . .47 D1
Cole Rd WD17 . . . . .167 B8
Coleridge CI
Hammond Street EN7 . . . . . .147 F4
Hitchin SG4 . . . . .35 B8
Coleridge Cres HP2 . . . . . . .105 B1
Coleridge Ct **9** AL5 . . . . . . .86 B1
Coleridge Way WD6 . . . . . .170 A5
Colesdale EN6 . . . . .146 E1
Coles Gn WD23 . . . . .168 C1
Colestrete SG1 . . . . .50 F5
Colestrete CI SG1 . . . . .50 F5
Coleswood Rd AL5 . . . . .107 C7
Colgate Ct EN5 . . . . .171 E4
Colgate PI EN3 . . . . .163 A2
Colgrove AL8 . . . . .110 C5
Colindale Ave AL1 . . . . .127 F1
Colin Rd LU2 . . . . .45 F2
College Ave HA3 . . . . .176 E2
College Bsns Pk HP22 . . . . .78 C1
College Ct
Bishop's Stortford
CM23 . . . . .76 D7
Flamstead AL3 . . . . .84 B1
Harrow HA3 . . . . .176 E3
Ware SG12 . . . . .114 D8
College Ct
Cheshunt EN8 . . . . .148 C1
Hoddesdon EN11 . . . . .134 F8
College Hill Rd HA3 . . . . . . .176 E3
College Ho LU1 . . . . .63 F7
College La AL10 . . . . .129 C4
College Lake Wildlife
Ctr* HP23 . . . . .100 C8
College PI AL3 . . . . .127 C3
College Rd
Abbots Langley WD5 . . . . . . .154 A8
Cheshunt EN8 . . . . .148 D1
Harrow HA3 . . . . .176 E2
Hertford Heath SG13 . . . . . .114 D2
Hitchin SG5 . . . . .34 F8
Hoddesdon EN11 . . . . .134 F8
St Albans AL1 . . . . .128 B2
College Rd N HP22 . . . . .78 C1
College St AL3 . . . . .127 D3
College Way
Northwood HA6 . . . . .174 D4
Welwyn Garden City
AL8 .110 D7
College Yd WD24 . . . . .154 B1
Collens Rd AL5 . . . . .107 B5
Collenswood Rd SG2 . . . . . .51 B4
Collet Ct EN8 . . . . .148 D3
Collet Gdns EN8 . . . . .148 D3
Collett Rd
Hemel Hempstead
HP1 .124 C3
Ware SG12 . . . . .93 D2
Collett Sch The HP1 . . . . . .124 B4
Colleyland WD3 . . . . .164 D5
COLLIERS END 73 A6
Collingdon Ct **10** LU1 . . . . .63 D8
Collingdon St LU1 . . . . .63 D8
Collings Wells CI LU1 . . . . . .62 E4
Collingtree LU2 . . . . .46 B4
Collingwood CI LU4 . . . . .44 D3
Collingwood Ct SG8 . . . . . . .7 D7
Collingwood Dr AL2 . . . . . . .142 D6
COLLINS CROSS CM23 . . . . .59 B1
Collins Cross CM23 . . . . .59 B1
Collins Ct WD23 . . . . .168 B4
Collinson Ct EN8 . . . . .162 E2
Collinson CI SG4 . . . . .22 C2
Collyer Rd AL2 . . . . .142 D4
Colmer PI HA3 . . . . .176 D3
Colnbrook CI AL2 . . . . .142 E4
Colnbrook Sch WD19 . . . . .175 C2
Colne Ave
Rickmansworth WD3 . . . . . .173 A8
Watford WD19 . . . . .167 C3
Colne Bridge Ret Pk
WD17 . . . . .167 D4
Colne Gdns AL2 . . . . .142 E4
Colne Lo
Rickmansworth WD3 . . . . . .165 A1
Watford WD17 . . . . .167 D5
Colne Mead WD3 . . . . .173 A8
Colne Valley Ret Pk
WD17 . . . . .167 C4
Colne Way
Hemel Hempstead
HP2 .124 F8
Watford WD24, WD25 . . . . . .154 D3
Colne Way Ct WD24 . . . . . .154 D3
Colney Fields Shopping Pk
AL2 .142 F2
COLNEY HEATH 143 D8
Colney Heath Jun Mix Inf
Sch AL4 . . . . .129 C1
Colney Heath La AL4 . . . . . .128 E2
COLNEY STREET 141 E1
Colonial Bsns Pk
WD24 . . . . .167 C8
Colonial Way WD24 . . . . . .167 C8
Colonnade The **7**
EN8 .148 D3
Colston CI SG1 . . . . .125 C1
Colston Cres EN7 . . . . .147 B4
Colt Hatch CM20 . . . . .117 D3
Colthurst Gdns EN11 . . . . .135 D8
Colt Mews EN3 . . . . .163 A2

Colts Cnr SG2 . . . . .51 B4
Colts Croft SG8 . . . . .9 E2
Coltsfield CM24 . . . . .59 E8
Coltsfoot AL7 . . . . .111 B4
Coltsfoot Dr SG8 . . . . .7 E6
Coltsfoot Gn LU4 . . . . .44 A5
Coltsfoot La SG3 . . . . .90 D7
Coltsfoot Rd SG12 . . . . . . .93 E3
Coltsfoot The HP1 . . . . . . .123 E2
Colts The CM23 . . . . .76 E4
Columbia Rd EN10 . . . . . . .148 E5
Columbus Ct SG2 . . . . .51 A7
Columbus Gdns HP4 . . . . .175 A2
Colvin Gdns EN8 . . . . .162 D4
Colwell Ct LU2 . . . . .46 E2
Colwell Rd SG2 . . . . .51 C3
Colwell Rise LU2 . . . . .46 E2
Colwyn Cl SG1 . . . . .50 B7
Colyer Cl AL6 . . . . .89 F3
Combe Ho WD18 . . . . .166 E3
Combe Rd WD18 . . . . .166 F3
Combe St HP1 . . . . .124 C3
Combewood WD25 . . . . . . .154 C7
Comet Cl WD25 . . . . .153 F5
Comet Rd AL10 . . . . .129 F6
Comet Way AL10 . . . . .129 E5
Commerce Way SG6 . . . . . .22 F6
Common Field HP23 . . . . . .100 D1
Commonfields CM20 . . . . . .117 E1
Common Gate Rd
 WD3 . . . . .164 A4
Common Gdns HP4 . . . . . .123 B6
Common La
 Ashwell SG7 . . . . .4 B6
 Harpenden AL5 . . . . .86 D5
 Kimpton SG4 . . . . .68 B1
 Kings Langley WD4 . . . . .138 F3
 Radlett WD7, WD25 . . . . .155 E1
Common Rd
 Chorleywood WD3 . . . . . .164 D5
 Kensworth Common LU6 . .82 F8
 Stanmore HA7 . . . . .176 D7
 Stotfold SG5 . . . . .11 F7
 Studham LU6 . . . . .82 B3
Common Rise SG4 . . . . . . .22 A1
Commons La HP2 . . . . .124 E4
Commons The AL7 . . . . . . .111 B3
Commonswood Sch
 AL7 . . . . .111 B3
Common The
 Chipperfield WD4 . . . . . . .152 B8
 Harpenden AL5 . . . . .85 C4
 Hatfield AL10 . . . . .130 A6
 London Colney WD7 . . . . .156 B8
 Potten End HP4 . . . . .123 A6
 Redbourn AL3 . . . . .106 B5
 Stanmore HA7 . . . . .176 F8
Common View
 Chorleywood WD3 . . . . . .164 D5
 Letchworth Garden City
  SG6 . . . . .23 A8
Common View Sq SG6 . . . .23 A8
Common Wharf SG12 . . . . .93 E1
COMMONWOOD 152 E8
Community Way WD18 . . . .166 B4
Compass Point HP4 . . . . . .121 E6
Compton Ave LU4 . . . . .44 D4
Compton Gdns AL2 . . . . . .141 B5
Compton St CM23 . . . . . . .76 E4
Comroston 13 EN11 . . . . . .135 A6
Comyne Rd WD24 . . . . . . .153 F3
Comyns The WD23 . . . . . . .168 C1
Concorde Dr HP2 . . . . .124 D3
Concorde St LU2 . . . . .63 F8
Condor Ct WD24 . . . . .154 B1
Conduit La
 Great Hormead SG9 . . . . . .29 B1
 Hoddesdon EN11 . . . . . . .135 A4
Conduit La E EN11 . . . . . . .135 B6
Coney Cl AL10 . . . . .130 B3
Coneydale AL8 . . . . .110 D8
Coney Gree CM21 . . . . .97 D3
Congreve Rd EN9 . . . . .163 E6
Conifer Cl
 Goff's Oak EN7 . . . . .147 F2
 Stevenage SG2 . . . . .51 D7
Conifer Ct 7 CM23 . . . . . . .76 E4
Conifer 19 Luton LU1 . . . . . .63 D6
 Watford WD25 . . . . .154 C4
Conifer Wlk SG2 . . . . .51 D7
Coningsby Dr WD17 . . . . . .166 E7
Coningsby Bank AL1 . . . . . .141 D7
Coningsby Cl AL9 . . . . .144 D7
Coningsby Ct WD7 . . . . . . .156 A3
Coningsby Dr EN6 . . . . .159 D6
Coniston Cl HP3 . . . . .125 C1
Coniston Lo 8 WD17 . . . . . .167 A7
Coniston Rd
 Kings Langley WD4 . . . . .138 F3
 Luton LU3 . . . . .44 F5
Connaught Cl LU2 . . . . .46 B3
Connaught Gdns HP4 . . . . .121 F7
Connaught Rd
 Barnet EN5 . . . . .171 D3
 Harpenden AL5 . . . . .86 B2
 Harrow HA3 . . . . .176 F8
 Luton LU4 . . . . .44 F1
 St Albans AL3 . . . . .127 C6
Connelly La SG5 . . . . .11 D2
Connemara Ct WD6 . . . . . .170 D3
Connemara Ct 1
 EN10 . . . . .148 F5
Conner's Cl SG8 . . . . .1 F4
Connop Rd EN3 . . . . .162 F1
Conquerors Hill AL4 . . . . . .108 E8
Conquest Ct LU4 . . . . .34 F5
Constable Ct LU4 . . . . .45 A1

Constantine Cl SG1 . . . . . .36 F1
Constantine Pl SG7 . . . . . . .13 B1
Convent Cl SG5 . . . . .34 F8
Convent Cl HP23 . . . . .99 F3
Convent Ho 8 EN10 . . . . . .148 F5
Conway Gdns EN2 . . . . . . .161 E1
Conway Ho WD6 . . . . .170 C5
Conway Rd LU4 . . . . .45 B1
Cony Ct 7 EN7 . . . . .147 E5
Conyers CM20 . . . . .117 C2
Cook Rd SG2 . . . . .51 B7
Cook's Hole Rd EN2 . . . . . .161 C1
Cooks Mead WD23 . . . . . .168 B3
Cooks Spinney CM20 . . . . .118 A2
Cooks Vennel HP1 . . . . . . .124 B5
Cooks Way
 Hatfield AL10 . . . . .130 B3
 Hitchin SG4 . . . . .22 A1
Coombe Gdns HP4 . . . . . . .121 F5
Coombe Hill Rd WD3 . . . . .165 A2
Coombelands Rd WD3 . . . . .2 E1
Coombe Rd
 Bushey WD23 . . . . .168 D2
 Kelshall SG8 . . . . .6 A1
Coombes Rd AL2 . . . . .142 C5
Coopers Cl
 Aston SG2 . . . . .51 D4
 Bishop's Stortford CM23 . .76 B4
Cooper's Cl SG4 . . . . .66 B1
Coopers Cres WD6 . . . . . . .170 C8
Coopers Ct SG14 . . . . .113 D6
Coopers Field SG6 . . . . . . .22 D7
Coopers Gate AL4 . . . . .129 B1
Coopers Green La AL4,
 AL10 . . . . .109 D1
Cooper's Hill SG4 . . . . .87 B8
Coopers La EN6 . . . . .145 E1
Coopers Lane Rd EN6 . . . .160 B6
Coopers Mdw AL3 . . . . . . .106 A6
Coopers Mews
 Harpenden AL5 . . . . .107 A8
 9 Luton LU1 . . . . .63 D7
 Watford WD25 . . . . .154 C8
Coopers Rd SG2 . . . . .145 C1
Coopers Wlk 10 EN8 . . . . .148 D3
Cooper Way 10 HP4 . . . . . .122 D4
Cooters End La AL5 . . . . . . .85 E2
Copenhagen Cl LU3 . . . . . .44 D8
Copmans Wick WD3 . . . . . .164 D4
Coppens The SG5 . . . . .12 A5
Copper Beech Cl HP3 . . . . .137 F8
Copper Beech Ct 4
 HA6 . . . . .174 E3
Copper Beeches
 11 Harpenden AL5 . . . . . . .86 B1
 Oaklands AL4 . . . . .89 D7
Copper Ct CM21 . . . . .97 E2
Copperdale Ct 7
 WD18 . . . . .166 E4
Copperfield Cl SG5 . . . . . . .11 C2
Copperfields
 Luton LU4 . . . . .44 C3
 Royston SG8 . . . . .7 C6
 Welwyn Garden City
  AL7 . . . . .111 C5
Coppermill La WD3,
 UB9 . . . . .172 F3
Copperwood SG13 . . . . . . .113 F6
Coppice Cl
 Harrow HA7 . . . . .176 F4
 Hatfield AL10 . . . . .129 F1
Coppice Farm Pk
 HP23 . . . . .119 D4
Coppice Mead SG5 . . . . . . .11 E5
Coppice The
 Bishop's Stortford
  CM23 . . . . .76 D5
 1 Harpenden AL5 . . . . . . .85 F3
 Hemel Hempstead HP2 . . .125 B4
 Watford WD19 . . . . .167 C3
 Wigginton HP23 . . . . . . .100 D1
Coppings The EN11 . . . . . .115 A1
Coppins Cl HP4 . . . . .121 F4
Coppins The
 Harrow HA3 . . . . .176 A4
 Hatfield AL8 . . . . .110 A4
 Markyate AL3 . . . . .83 D5
Copse Cl HA6 . . . . .174 C1
Copse The
 Bishop's Stortford
  CM23 . . . . .77 C8
 Hemel Hempstead HP1 . . .123 E5
 Hertford SG13 . . . . .114 A6
 Watford WD17 . . . . .167 D6
Copse Way LU3 . . . . .44 D8
Copsewood Rd WD24 . . . . .167 B8
Copse Wood Way
 HA6 . . . . .174 C2
Copthall Cl CM22 . . . . .77 F4
Copt Hall Cotts LU2 . . . . . .64 E4
Copthorne Cl LU2 . . . . .46 D3
Copthorne Ave EN10 . . . . .134 F3
Copthorne Rd WD3 . . . . . .165 F4
Coral Gdns HP2 . . . . .124 F3
Coral Ho CM20 . . . . .117 A1
Corals Mead AL1 . . . . .110 D5
Coram Ct HP4 . . . . .122 C3
Corbridge Dr LU2 . . . . .46 E1
Corby Cl AL7 . . . . .141 A6
Cordell Cl EN8 . . . . .148 E3
Cordell Ct AL3 . . . . .141 A8
COREY'S MILL 36 B2
Coreys Mill La SG1 . . . . . . .36 C1
Corfe Cl
 Borehamwood WD6 . . . . .170 D6

Corfe Cl continued
 4 Hemel Hempstead
  HP2 . . . . .124 E2
Corinium Gate AL3 . . . . . . .127 A1
Corinium Gdns LU3 . . . . . . .45 A8
Corncastle Rd LU1 . . . . . . .63 D6
Corncrake Cl LU2 . . . . .46 E3
Corncroft AL10 . . . . .130 B7
Cornel Cl LU1 . . . . .63 A7
Cornel Ct LU1 . . . . .63 A7
Cornelia St 3 AL5 . . . . .86 A2
Cornelious Ho 6
 WD18 . . . . .166 F5
Corner Cl SG6 . . . . .22 E6
Cornerfield AL10 . . . . .130 B8
Corner Hall HP3 . . . . .124 D1
Corner Hall Ave HP3 . . . . .124 D1
Corners AL7 . . . . .111 A7
Corner View AL9 . . . . .144 C7
Corner Wood AL3 . . . . .83 D5
Cornfield Cres HP4 . . . . . . .121 D7
Cornfield Rd WD23 . . . . . . .168 B5
Cornfields SG2 . . . . .51 C7
Cornfields The HP1 . . . . . . .124 B2
Cornflower Way AL10 . . . . .129 E8
Cornhill Dr EN3 . . . . .162 E2
Corn Mead AL8 . . . . .89 C1
Cornmill EN9 . . . . .163 B6
Cornwall Cl EN8 . . . . .162 E6
Cornwall Ct 8 HA6 . . . . . . .175 F3
Cornwall Ho CM23 . . . . . . .76 E4
Cornwall Rd
 Harpenden AL5 . . . . .86 B2
 Pinner AL5 . . . . .175 F3
 St Albans AL1 . . . . .127 E1
Coronation Ave SG8 . . . . . . .7 C5
Coronation Rd
 Bishop's Stortford
  CM23 . . . . .76 E5
 Ware SG12 . . . . .93 D2
Coronet Ho 2 HA7 . . . . . . .176 F4
Corringham Ct AL1 . . . . . . .127 F4
Corton Cl SG1 . . . . .50 B8
Corvus Cl SG8 . . . . .7 E8
Cory-Wright Way AL4 . . . . .87 E1
Cosgrove Way LU4 . . . . . . .44 D1
Cosmo Rd SG12 . . . . .114 D1
Cosne Mews AL5 . . . . .107 C7
Costins Wlk 8 HP4 . . . . . . .122 D4
Cotefield LU4 . . . . .44 C3
Cotesmore Rd HP1 . . . . . . .123 E2
Cotlandswick AL2 . . . . .142 C5
Cotney Croft SG2 . . . . .51 D3
Cotsmoor AL1 . . . . .127 F3
Cotswold HP2 . . . . .124 E6
Cotswold Cl LU3 . . . . .44 F7
Cotswold Bsns Pk LU1 . . . .62 D2
Cotswold Cl AL4 . . . . .128 C8
Cotswold Dr SG1 . . . . .37 A3
Cotswold Gdns LU3 . . . . . .44 C7
Cotswolds AL10 . . . . .130 A3
Cottage Cl
 Croxley Green WD3 . . . . .165 F3
 Watford WD17 . . . . .166 F7
Cottage Gdns EN8 . . . . . . .148 D2
Cottage Rd LU2 . . . . .64 C2
Cottered SG9 . . . . .26 F1
Cotterells HP1 . . . . .124 B3
Cotterells Hill HP1 . . . . . . .124 C3
Cotter Ho SG1 . . . . .37 A3
Cotton Dr SG13 . . . . .114 B7
Cotton Field AL10 . . . . .130 B7
Cottonmill Cres AL1 . . . . . .127 D2
Cottonmill La AL1 . . . . .127 D1
Cotton Rd EN6 . . . . .159 C8
Coulser Cl HP1 . . . . .124 A6
Coulson Ct
 London Colney AL2 . . . . .142 D4
 Luton LU1 . . . . .62 F8
Coulter Cl EN6 . . . . .146 D4
Council Cotts
 Great Wymondley SG4 . . .35 F6
 Letchworth Garden City
  SG6 . . . . .23 B2
 Radwell SG7 . . . . .12 C4
Council Hos LU2 . . . . .32 D3
Counters Cl HP1 . . . . .124 A3
COUNTER'S END 124 A3
Countess Anne CE Prim
 Sch AL9 . . . . .130 C6
Countess Cl UB9 . . . . .173 C1
Countess Ct 7 LU2 . . . . . . .45 D1
Couper Ho UB10 . . . . .166 E3
Coursers Farm Cotts
 AL4 . . . . .143 C6
Coursers Rd AL2, AL4 . . . .143 C6
Courtaulds WD4 . . . . .138 B1
Court CM23 . . . . .76 E5
Courtenay Ave HA3 . . . . . .176 D2
Courtenay Gdns HA3 . . . . .176 C1
Courtfield Cl EN10 . . . . . . .135 A3
Courtfields AL5 . . . . .86 D1
Courtlands WD24 . . . . .153 E4
Courtlands Dr WD17 . . . . . .153 E3
Courtleigh Ave EN4 . . . . . .159 C4
Court Needham EN3 . . . . . .163 A2
Courtway The WD19 . . . . . .175 E8
Courtyard Mews SG12 . . . .92 E4
Courtyards The
 WD18 . . . . .166 E5
Courtyard The
 Harlow CM17 . . . . .118 D4
 Hemel Hempstead HP3 . . .138 D5
 Hertingfordbury SG14 . . . .112 F5
 St Albans AL4 . . . . .128 F3
Covent Garden Cl LU4 . . . .44 F3
Coventry Cl SG1 . . . . .37 B1

Coverdale
 Hemel Hempstead
  HP2 . . . . .124 E6
 Luton LU4 . . . . .44 B6
Coverdale Ct EN3 . . . . .162 E2
Covert Cl HP4 . . . . .121 D6
Covert Rd HP4 . . . . .121 D6
Covert The HA6 . . . . .174 C2
Cowards La SG4 . . . . .88 F8
Cowbridge SG14 . . . . .113 C6
Cowdray Cl LU2 . . . . .46 C3
Cow La
 Bushey WD23 . . . . .168 A3
 Tring HP23 . . . . .100 D4
 Watford WD25 . . . . .154 C3
Cowles EN7 . . . . .147 F4
Cowley Hill WD6 . . . . .157 B1
Cowley Hill Sch WD6 . . . . .170 A8
Cowlins CM17 . . . . .118 D4
Cowper Cres AL4 . . . . .92 B1
Cowper Ct
 Markyate AL3 . . . . .83 D5
 Watford WD24 . . . . .154 A2
Cowper Rd
 Berkhamsted HP4 . . . . . .122 B4
 Harpenden AL5 . . . . .86 C1
 Hemel Hempstead HP1 . . .124 B2
 Markyate AL3 . . . . .83 D5
 Welwyn Garden City
  AL7 . . . . .110 F4
Cowper Rise AL3 . . . . .83 D5
Cowper St LU1 . . . . .63 E5
Cowpers Way AL6 . . . . .90 C5
Cowridge Cres LU2 . . . . . . .64 A8
COW ROAST 101 B1
Cowslip Cl SG8 . . . . .7 F5
Cowslip Hill SG6 . . . . .22 E7
Cowslips AL7 . . . . .111 C5
Cox Cl WD7 . . . . .156 F7
Coxfield Cl HP2 . . . . .124 E2
COX GREEN 48 A6
Cox's Gdns CM23 . . . . .76 B5
Cox's Way SG15 . . . . .11 A6
Coyney Gn SG13 . . . . .45 C1
Cozens La E EN10 . . . . . . .134 F1
Cozens La W EN10 . . . . . . .134 F1
Crabbes Cl SG5 . . . . .34 E7
CRABB'S GREEN 43 E6
Crabb's La SG9 . . . . .43 F6
Crab La WD25 . . . . .155 B4
Crabtree Cl
 Bushey WD23 . . . . .168 A3
 Hemel Hempstead HP3 . . .124 D1
Crabtree Cl 3 HP3 . . . . . . .124 D1
Crabtree La
 Harpenden AL5 . . . . .86 C1
 Hemel Hempstead HP3 . . .124 D1
Crabtree Jun & Inf Sch
 AL5 . . . . .86 C1
Crab Tree La SG5 . . . . .20 D4
Crab Tree Rd SG3 . . . . .68 F4
Crabtree Wlk EN10 . . . . . . .134 E4
Crackley Mdw HP2 . . . . . . .125 B8
Cracknell Cl EN1 . . . . .162 B2
CRADLE END 75 F8
Cradock Rd LU4 . . . . .44 B1
CRAFTON 60 F4
Crafton Gn CM24 . . . . .59 E7
Cragg Ave WD7 . . . . .155 F3
Cragside SG2 . . . . .69 C7
Craigmore Rd SG3 . . . . . . .68 F2
Craigavon Rd HP2 . . . . . . .124 F7
Craiglands AL5 . . . . .128 D7
Craigmore Ct 5 HA6 . . . . .174 E3
Craig Mount AL7 . . . . .156 B4
Craigs Wlk 8 EN8 . . . . . . .148 D3
Craigweil Ave WD7 . . . . . . .156 B4
Crakers Mead 4
 WD18 . . . . .167 B4
Cranborne Cl
 Hertford SG13 . . . . .113 C3
 Potters Bar EN6 . . . . .158 E8
Cranborne Cres EN6 . . . . . .158 E8
Cranborne Rd EN3 . . . . . . .162 D3
Cranborne Gdns AL7 . . . . .110 F5
Cranborne Ind Est
 EN6 . . . . .144 E1
Cranborne Par EN6 . . . . . .158 E8
Cranborne Prim Sch
 EN6 . . . . .158 E8
Cranborne Rd
 Cheshunt EN8 . . . . .162 D7
 Hatfield AL10 . . . . .130 B6
 Hoddesdon EN11 . . . . . . .135 C7
Cranbourne Ct SG1 . . . . . . .36 B1
Cranbourne Dr
 Harpenden AL5 . . . . .107 D6
 Hoddesdon EN11 . . . . . . .115 C2
Cranbourne Ho EN11 . . . . .115 C2
Cranbourne Prim Sch The
 EN11 . . . . .115 B2
Cranbourne Rd
 Northwood HA6 . . . . .174 F4
 Potters Bar EN6 . . . . .144 E1
Cranbrook Cl SG12 . . . . . . .93 D3
Cranbrook Dr
 Luton LU3 . . . . .44 D8
 St Albans AL4 . . . . .128 E3
Cranefield Dr WD25 . . . . . .154 E6
Crane Mead SG12 . . . . . . .114 D8
Crane Mead Bsns Pk
 SG12 . . . . .114 D8
Cranes Way WD6 . . . . .170 C4
Cranfield Cres EN6 . . . . . . .146 E2
Cranford HP2 . . . . .124 E5

Cranford Ct
 Harpenden AL5 . . . . .86 C1
 Hertford SG14 . . . . .112 F7
Cranleigh Ct EN7 . . . . .148 A3
Cranleigh Gdns LU3 . . . . . .45 D3
Cranmer Cl EN6 . . . . .145 C1
Cranmore Cl AL1 . . . . .127 F4
Cranwell Cl AL4 . . . . .128 C1
Cranwell Gdns CM23 . . . . .59 C1
Craster Cl AL5 . . . . .107 C7
Cravells Rd AL5 . . . . .107 C7
Crawford Rd AL10 . . . . .130 A7
Crawley Cl LU1 . . . . .63 C1
Crawley Dr HP2 . . . . .124 F7
Crawley Green Inf Sch
 LU2 . . . . .64 B8
Crawley Green Rd
 Luton, Hart Hill LU2 . . . . .64 A8
 Luton LU2 . . . . .46 D1
Crawley Rd LU1 . . . . .63 D8
Creasey Ct SG6 . . . . .23 C3
Creasy Cl WD5 . . . . .153 E1
Crecy Gdns AL3 . . . . .106 A6
Creighton Ave AL3 . . . . . . .141 D8
Crescent E EN4 . . . . .159 C1
Crescent Rd
 Bishop's Stortford
  CM23 . . . . .77 A6
 Hemel Hempstead HP2 . . .124 D3
 Luton LU2 . . . . .63 F8
Crescent Rise LU2 . . . . . . .63 F8
Crescent The
 Abbots Langley WD5 . . . .139 F1
 Ardeley SG2 . . . . .38 F2
 Bricket Wood AL2 . . . . . .141 A1
 Caddington LU1 . . . . .62 E3
 Cottered SG9 . . . . .39 D7
 Croxley Green WD3 . . . . .166 B3
 Harlow CM17 . . . . .118 C6
 Hitchin SG5 . . . . .21 D1
 Letchworth Garden City
  SG6 . . . . .23 A5
 Lower Stondon SG16 . . . .10 C4
 Marsworth HP23 . . . . . . .84 A4
 Pitstone LU7 . . . . .80 C4
 Radlett WD7 . . . . .155 B1
 St Ippolyts SG4 . . . . .35 A3
 Watford WD18 . . . . .167 C5
 Welwyn AL6 . . . . .89 C4
Crescent W EN4 . . . . .159 C1
Cress End WD3 . . . . .165 A1
Cressex Cl AL2 . . . . .141 A1
Cresswell Gdns 4 LU3 . . . .31 B1
Cresswick SG4 . . . . .66 E7
Cresta Cl LU5 . . . . .44 A2
Crest Dr EN3 . . . . .162 C1
Crest Pk HP2 . . . . .125 C4
Crest The
 Goff's Oak EN7 . . . . .147 B4
 Luton LU3 . . . . .45 B7
 Oaklands AL6 . . . . .89 D8
 Sawbridgeworth CM21 . . .97 D2
 Ware SG12 . . . . .93 D3
Creswick Ct AL7 . . . . .110 D5
Creswick Prim Sch
 AL7 . . . . .110 E3
Crew Curve HP4 . . . . .121 E7
CREWS HILL 161 B4
Crews Hill End 160 F5
Crews Hill Sta 1 EN2 . . . . .160 E5
Crib St SG12 . . . . .93 D2
Cricketers Ct AL3 . . . . .127 E4
Cricketer's Rd SG15 . . . . . .11 A4
Cricketfield La CM23 . . . . . .76 D4
Cringle Ct EN6 . . . . .145 C1
Crispin Field LU7 . . . . .80 C4
Croasdaile Rd CM24 . . . . . .59 E8
Croasdale Ct CM24 . . . . . . .59 E8
Crocus Field EN5 . . . . .171 F3
Croft Cl WD4 . . . . .138 A1
Croft Ct
 Borehamwood WD6 . . . . .170 D6
 4 Harpenden AL5 . . . . . . .86 B1
 Hitchin SG5 . . . . .34 E7
Croft End Rd WD4 . . . . . . .138 A1
Crofters CM21 . . . . .97 E3
Crofters End CM21 . . . . . . .97 E3
Crofters Rd HA6 . . . . .174 E6
Croft Field
 Chipperfield WD4 . . . . . . .138 A1
 Hatfield AL10 . . . . .130 A5
Croft La
 Chipperfield WD4 . . . . . . .138 A1
 Letchworth Garden City
  SG6 . . . . .12 B1
Croft Mdw WD4 . . . . .138 A1
Croft Mdws LU7 . . . . .80 C4
Croft Rd
 Luton LU2 . . . . .46 B3
 Ware SG12 . . . . .93 C2
Crofts Path HP3 . . . . .125 B1
Crofts The
 Hemel Hempstead
  HP3 . . . . .125 B2
 Stotfold SG5 . . . . .11 F6
Croft The
 Barnet EN5 . . . . .171 E5
 Chiswell Green AL2 . . . . .141 A6
 Hoddesdon EN10 . . . . . . .148 E8
 Luton LU3 . . . . .44 D8
 Wareside SG12 . . . . .94 E4
 Welwyn Garden City
  AL7 . . . . .110 F3
Croftwell AL5 . . . . .107 F8

Croft Wlk EN10 . . . . 148 E8
Cromdale Wlk SG1 . . . . 37 B4
CROMER 38 D5
Cromer Cl HP4 . . . . 102 E5
Cromer Hyde La AL8 . . . 109 C5
Cromer Rd WD24 . . . . 154 C1
Cromer Way
  Luton, Stopsley Common
  LU2 . . . . 45 E6
  Luton, Warden Hill LU2 . . 45 D7
Cromer Windmill★
  SG2 . . . . 38 E6
Crompton Pl 8 EN3 . . . 163 A1
Crompton Rd SG1 . . . . 50 A6
Cromwell Ave EN7 . . . . . 148 B1
Cromwell Cl
  Bishop's Stortford
  CM23 . . . . 76 B7
  St Albans AL4 . . . . 128 D8
Cromwell Gn SG6 . . . . 23 B8
Cromwell Hill LU2 . . . . 45 D1
Cromwell Rd
  Borehamwood WD6 . . . . 169 E8
  Cheshunt EN7 . . . . 148 B3
  Hertford SG13 . . . . 114 A7
  Letchworth Garden City
  SG6 . . . . 23 D8
  Luton LU3 . . . . 45 D1
  Stevenage SG2 . . . . 51 C5
  Ware SG12 . . . . 93 F2
Cromwell Way SG5 . . . . . . 20 D4
Crooked Mile
  Waltham Abbey EN9 . . . 163 C6
  Waltham Abbey EN9 . . . 163 C7
Crooked Way EN9 . . . . . . 135 C7
Crookhams AL7 . . . . 90 A1
Crop Comm AL10 . . . . 130 B7
Crosby Cl
  Luton LU2 . . . . 45 A2
  St Albans AL4 . . . . 142 C8
Crosfield Ct WD17 . . . . . . 167 D4
Crossbrook AL10 . . . . 129 E4
Crossbrook St EN8 . . . . . 162 E8
Crossbrook St EN8 . . . . . 162 D8
Crossett Sp HP3 . . . . 125 C1
Cross Farm Mews
  HP3 . . . . 137 D2
Crossfell Rd HP3 . . . . 125 C2
Crossfield Rd EN11 . . . . . 135 B8
Crossfields AL3 . . . . 141 B8
Crossfields CI HP4 . . . . . . 121 F4
Crossgates SG1 . . . . 50 E5
Cross La
  Harpenden AL5 . . . . 107 C5
Crosslands LU1 . . . . 62 E3
Crossleys SG6 . . . . 11 F2
Crossmead WD19 . . . . 167 B3
Cross Oak Rd HP4 . . . . . . 122 A4
Crossoaks La EN6 . . . . 157 F5
Crosspaths AL5 . . . . 85 C4
Crosspath The WD7 . . . . 156 A4
Cross Rd
  Cheshunt EN8 . . . . 162 E6
  Hertford SG14 . . . . 113 C7
  Watford WD19 . . . . 167 E3
Cross St
  Letchworth Garden City
  SG6 . . . . 22 F7
  Luton LU2 . . . . 63 E8
  4 St Albans AL3 . . . . 127 D3
  Ware SG12 . . . . 93 E1
  Watford WD17 . . . . 167 C6
Crossway
  Pinner HA5 . . . . 175 B1
  Welwyn Garden City AL8 . . 89 C2
Cross Way
  3 Harlow CM17 . . . . . . 118 D1
  Harpenden AL5 . . . . 86 C3
Crossways
  Barley SG8 . . . . 8 F1
  Berkhamsted HP4 . . . . . . 122 B6
  Hemel Hempstead HP3 . . 125 B3
Crossway The LU1 . . . . 63 C3
Cross Way The LU1 . . . . . . 63 C3
Crosthwaite Ct AL5 . . . . . 86 B2
Crouch Cl CM20 . . . . 117 C3
Crouchfield
  Hemel Hempstead
  HP1 . . . . 124 B2
  Hertford SG12 . . . . 92 C1
Crouchfield La SG12 . . . . 92 E4
Crouch Hall Gdns
  AL3 . . . . 106 A6
Crouch Hall La AL3 . . . . . 106 A6
Crouch La EN7 . . . . 147 C4
Crowborough Path
  WD19 . . . . 175 D5
Crow Furlong SG5 . . . . . . 34 D7
Crow La SG8 . . . . 16 F5
Crowland Rd LU2 . . . . 46 C5
Crown Cl CM22 . . . . 98 C1
Crown Cotts
  Botley HP5 . . . . 150 B8
  King's Walden SG4 . . . . . 48 A6
Crown Ct 14 LU1 . . . . 63 D7
Crownfield EN10 . . . . 135 A2
Crown Lo SG15 . . . . 11 A4
Crown Rd WD6 . . . . 170 B8
Crown Rise WD25 . . . . . . 154 D5
Crown St AL3 . . . . 106 B5
Crown Terr CM23 . . . . 77 A7
Crown Wlk HP3 . . . . 138 E7
Crown Yd AL3 . . . . 106 D2

Croxdale Rd WD6 . . . . 170 A7
Croxley Ctr WD18 . . . . . . 166 D4
CROXLEY GREEN 166 A4
Croxley Sta WD3 . . . . 166 B3
Croxley View WD18 . . . . 166 E3
Croxton 3 LU3 . . . . 45 A1
Crozier Ave AL3 . . . . 76 C8
Crunnell's Gn SG4 . . . . . . 48 E5
Crusader Way WD18 . . . 166 F3
Cubbington Cl LU3 . . . . . . 45 A7
Cubitt Cl SG4 . . . . 35 C7
Cubitts Cl AL6 . . . . 89 F3
Cublands SG13 . . . . 114 B6
Cuckmans Dr AL2 . . . . . . 141 A6
CUCKOLDS CROSS 66 D3
Cuckoo's Nest LU2 . . . . . 64 A7
Cucumber La AL9,
  SG13 . . . . 132 A1
CUFFLEY 146 E3
Cuffley Ave WD25 . . . . . . 154 D5
Cuffley Cl LU3 . . . . 44 F4
Cuffley Ct HP2 . . . . 125 C8
Cuffley Hill EN7 . . . . 147 B2
Cuffley Sch EN6 . . . . 146 F1
Cuffley Sta EN6 . . . . 146 F2
Cullera Cl HA6 . . . . 174 F3
Cullings Cl EN9 . . . . 163 F6
Culrose Cl SG2 . . . . 68 F8
Culverden Rd WD19 . . . . 175 B7
Culverhouse Rd LU3 . . . . 45 C3
Culver Lo AL1 . . . . 127 E5
Culver Rd AL1 . . . . 127 E5
Culworth Cl LU1 . . . . 62 E3
Cumberland Ct
  Hertford SG14 . . . . 113 C8
  Pimlico HP3 . . . . 139 E7
Cumberland Ct
  2 Hoddesdon EN11 . . . 135 A7
  St Albans AL3 . . . . 127 E4
Cumberland Dr AL3 . . . . 106 B6
Cumberland St LU1 . . . . . 63 E6
CUMBERLOW GREEN . . . 25 E1
Cunnday Pl HP2 . . . . 125 C2
Cundalls Rd SG12 . . . . 93 E2
Cunningham Ave
  Enfield EN3 . . . . 162 E3
  Hatfield AL10 . . . . 129 D6
  St Albans AL1 . . . . 127 E7
Cunningham Ct 4
  EN8 . . . . 148 E3
Cunningham Hill Inf Sch
  AL1 . . . . 128 A1
Cunningham Hill Jun Sch
  AL1 . . . . 128 A1
Cunningham Hill Rd
  AL1 . . . . 128 A1
Cunningham Rd EN8 . . . 148 E4
CUPID GREEN 125 B7
Cupid Green La
  Flamstead HP2 . . . . 104 E3
  Hemel Hempstead HP2 . 105 A1
Curlew Cl
  Berkhamsted HP4 . . . . . 122 C3
  Letchworth Garden City
  SG6 . . . . 11 C1
Curlew Cres SG8 . . . . 7 E8
Curlew Ct EN10 . . . . 148 F8
Curlew Rd LU2 . . . . 46 C5
Curo Pk AL2 . . . . 141 E4
Currie St SG13 . . . . 113 E6
Curteys CM17 . . . . 118 D5
Curtis Rd WD3 . . . . 165 A1
Curtis Rd HP3 . . . . 125 D2
Curtis Dr WD25 . . . . 153 F5
Curtis Way HP4 . . . . 122 D3
Curzon Gate Ct 1
  WD7 . . . . 167 A8
Curzon Rd LU3 . . . . 45 C1
Cussans Ho WD18 . . . . . 166 F3
Cussons Cl EN7 . . . . 148 A2
Cutforth Rd CM21 . . . . 97 E3
Cuthbert Ct EN7 . . . . 147 F2
Cutlers Cl CM23 . . . . 76 C4
Cutlers Gn LU2 . . . . 46 F2
Cutmore Dr AL4 . . . . 129 B1
Cut Throat Ave HP4,
  LU6 . . . . 81 C7
Cuttsfield Terr HP1 . . . . . 123 F2
Cutts La SG1 . . . . 66 D1
Cuttys La SG1 . . . . 50 E5
Cwmbran Cl HP2 . . . . 124 F7
Cygnet Cl
  Borehamwood WD6 . . . 170 C8
  Northwood HA6 . . . . 174 C4
Cygnet Ct 11 CM23 . . . . . 76 F5
Cygnet Ho
  Hemel Hempstead
  HP3 . . . . 138 F6
  1 Stanmore HA7 . . . . . . 176 F4
Cygnet Hospl SG1 . . . . . . 36 B2
Cygnet Way CM19 . . . . . 116 A1
Cylers Thicket AL6 . . . . . 89 C6
Cymbeline Ct AL3 . . . . . . 127 C4
Cypress Ave
  Crews Hill EN2 . . . . 161 A4
  Welwyn Garden City
  AL7 . . . . 111 C5
Cypress Cl EN9 . . . . 163 D6
Cypress Rd HA3 . . . . 176 D1
Cypress Wlk WD25 . . . . . 154 B4
Cyril Dumpleton Ho
  AL2 . . . . 142 D5
Cyrils Way AL1 . . . . 141 D8

D

Dacorum Way HP1 . . . . . . 124 C3
Dacre Bldgs EN8 . . . . 148 F2
Dacre Cres SG4 . . . . 66 C1
Dacre Gdns WD6 . . . . 170 D4
Dacre Rd SG8 . . . . 7 F6
Dacre Ind Est EN8 . . . . . 148 F3
Dacre Rd SG5 . . . . 35 A8
Daffodil Cl AL10 . . . . 109 F1
Dagger La WD6 . . . . 169 B4
Daggs Dell Rd HP1 . . . . . 123 E5
DAGNALL 81 C6
Dagnall Rd
  Great Gaddesden
  HP1 . . . . 103 C5
  Whipsnade HP4, LU6 . . . 81 D8
Dagnalls SG6 . . . . 22 F7
Dagnall Sch HP4 . . . . 81 C5
Dahlia Cl
  Hammond Street EN7 . . 147 C6
  Luton LU2 . . . . 46 B4
Daintrees SG12 . . . . 95 A4
Daintry Lo HA6 . . . . 174 F3
Dairy Cotts SG5 . . . . 19 B2
Dairyglen Ave EN8 . . . . . 162 E7
Dairy Mews WD18 . . . . . 167 A4
Dairy Way WD5 . . . . 139 F2
Daisy Cl SG6 . . . . 23 A8
Daisy Dr AL10 . . . . 129 F8
Dalby Cl LU4 . . . . 44 B3
Dale Ave AL4 . . . . 87 B5
Dale Cl
  Hitchin SG4 . . . . 34 F4
  Pinner HA5 . . . . 175 B2
Dale Ct CM21 . . . . 97 D2
Dale Rd LU3 . . . . 63 C7
Daleside Dr DN6 . . . . 158 F6
Dales Path WD6 . . . . 170 A5
Dales Rd WD6 . . . . 170 A5
Dale The
  Letchworth Garden City
  SG6 . . . . 22 E5
  Waltham Abbey EN9 . . . 163 E5
Dalewood
  Harpenden AL5 . . . . 86 D1
  Welwyn Garden City
  AL7 . . . . 111 D5
Dalkeith Rd AL5 . . . . 86 C1
Dallow Prim Sch LU1 . . . 63 C8
Dallow Rd LU1 . . . . 63 B8
Dalroad Ent Est LU1 . . . 63 B8
Dalton Cl LU3 . . . . 31 B1
Dalton Gdns CM23 . . . . . 76 E4
Dalton St AL3 . . . . 127 D4
Dalton Way
  Watford WD17 . . . . 167 A4
  Whitwell SG4 . . . . 66 E7
Daltry Cl SG1 . . . . 36 C2
Daltry Rd SG1 . . . . 36 C2
Damask Cl
  Tring HP23 . . . . 100 C4
  Weston SG4 . . . . 37 B8
Damask Gn HP1 . . . . 123 E2
DAMASK GREEN 37 B8
Damask Green Rd SG4 . . 37 B8
Dame Alice Owen's Sch
  EN6 . . . . 158 E6
Dammersey Cl AL3 . . . . . 83 F4
Damson Way AL4 . . . . . . 128 C5
Damson Wlk SG7 . . . . 5 A3
Dancers End La HP23 . . . 99 C2
DANCERS HILL 158 C5
Dancers Hill Rd EN5 . . . 158 D3
Dancers La EN5 . . . . 158 C4
Dancote SG3 . . . . 68 F5
Dane Acres CM23 . . . . 76 D8
Dane Bridge La SG10 . . . 75 B2
Danebridge Rd SG10 . . . 75 B2
Dane Cl
  Harpenden AL5 . . . . 86 C4
  Stotfold SG5 . . . . 11 B8
Dane Ct AL1 . . . . 128 B2
DANE END 71 E8
Dane End SG8 . . . . 16 B4
Dane End Ho SG1 . . . . 36 C1
Dane End La SG4 . . . . 37 E5
Dane End Rd SG11 . . . . . . 72 E3
Danefield Rd SG5 . . . . 20 C4
Dane Ho CM23 . . . . 76 D8
Danemead EN11 . . . . 115 A1
Dane O'Coys Rd CM23 . . 58 E1
Dane Pk CM23 . . . . 76 D8
Dane Rd AL3 . . . . 45 C2
Danesbury La AL6 . . . . . . 89 D8
Danesbury Park Rd
  AL6 . . . . 89 D8
Danesbury Pk Cvn Site
  AL6 . . . . 89 D8
Danescroft SG6 . . . . 12 A1
Danesgate SG1 . . . . 50 D4
Danes The AL2 . . . . 141 C3
Danestrete SG1 . . . . 50 D5
Daniel Ho 4 HA5 . . . . . . 175 C1
Daniells AL7 . . . . 111 A7
Danvers Croft HP23 . . . . 100 C5
Danvers Dr LU3 . . . . 31 C1
Danziger Way WD6 . . . . . 170 C8
Darblay Cl AL4 . . . . 108 C5
Darby Dr
  Waltham Abbey EN9 . . . 163 C6
  Welwyn AL6 . . . . 90 A4
Darcy Cl EN8 . . . . 162 E8

Darkes La EN6 . . . . 159 A8
Dark La
  Cheshunt EN7 . . . . 148 A1
  Codicote SG4 . . . . 88 E8
  Harpenden AL5 . . . . 107 D7
  Sandon SG9 . . . . 15 B1
  Wingrave HP22 . . . . 60 C3
Darlands Dr EN5 . . . . 171 D4
Darleyhall LU2 . . . . 47 C1
Darley Rd LU2, SG4 . . . . . 47 C2
Darlington Ct 6
  CM17 . . . . 118 C4
Darnhills WD7 . . . . 155 F4
Darnicle Hill EN7 . . . . . . 147 A6
Darrington Rd WD6 . . . . 169 E8
Darr's La HP4 . . . . 121 D6
Dartmouth Mews LU4 . . 44 D3
Dartons Ho SG7 . . . . 12 E1
Dart The HP2 . . . . 125 A8
Darvells Yd WD3 . . . . 164 D5
Darwin Cl
  Hemel Hempstead
  HP2 . . . . 105 B1
  St Albans AL3 . . . . 127 E7
Darwin Gdns WD19 . . . . 175 C5
Darwin Rd SG2 . . . . 51 B6
Dashes The CM20 . . . . . . 117 E1
DASSELS 41 E3
Datchet Cl HP2 . . . . 125 B8
DATCHWORTH 69 E2
DATCHWORTH GREEN
  . . . . 69 C3
Datchworth Turn
  HP2 . . . . 125 C3
Dauphin Ct 8 LU2 . . . . . . 45 D1
Dauphine Ct 1 HA3 . . . . 176 E1
Davenham Ave HA6 . . . . 174 F5
Daventer Dr HA7 . . . . 176 E4
David Evans Ct SG6 . . . . 22 D7
Davidson Ho 11 HP2 . . . 124 D4
Davies St SG13 . . . . 113 E6
Davis Cl AL1 . . . . 127 E3
Davis Ho 11 HP4 . . . . 122 C4
Davison Ct EN8 . . . . 148 D3
Davison Dr EN8 . . . . 148 D3
Davis' Row SG15 . . . . 11 A4
Davys Cl AL4 . . . . 108 E7
Dawes La
  Sarratt WD3 . . . . 151 F3
  Wheathampstead AL4 . . 87 D1
Dawley AL7 . . . . 89 F1
Dawley Ct HP2 . . . . 125 A7
Dawlish Cl SG2 . . . . 69 C7
Dawlish Rd LU4 . . . . 44 F3
Dawn Ct 8 AL1 . . . . 128 A2
Dawson Cl SG6 . . . . 10 C5
Dayemead AL7 . . . . 111 B3
Days Cl AL10 . . . . 129 F5
Day's Cl SG2 . . . . 7 C5
Days Mead AL10 . . . . 129 F5
Deacon Cl AL1 . . . . 141 D7
Deacons Cl
  Borehamwood WD6 . . . 170 A5
  Pinner HA5 . . . . 175 B1
Deacons Ct 7 AL1 . . . . . . 128 B2
Deaconsfield Rd HP3 . . . 138 E8
Deacons Hill WD19 . . . . . 167 C3
Deacon's Hill Rd
  WD6 . . . . 170 A4
Deacons Hts WD6 . . . . . . 170 A3
Deacons Way WD6 . . . . . 170 A5
Deadman's Ash La
  WD3 . . . . 152 B1
Dead Woman's La SG4 . . 48 C7
Deakin Cl WD18 . . . . 166 E3
Dean Cl WD25 . . . . 154 D6
Deane Ct HA6 . . . . 174 E3
Dean Field HP3 . . . . 137 A4
Dean Mead CM23 . . . . 76 F5
Dean Moore Ct AL1 . . . . 127 D2
Deans Ct
  Abbots Langley WD5 . . . 153 D7
  Tring HP23 . . . . 100 A4
Deanscroft SG3 . . . . 68 F5
Deans Furlong HP23 . . . . 100 A4
Dean's Gdns AL4 . . . . 128 A2
Deans Lawn 8 HP4 . . . . . 122 C4
Deans Mdw HP4 . . . . 81 C5
Deansway AL7 . . . . 138 F8
Dean The HP22 . . . . 60 A8
Deard's End La SG3 . . . . 68 F5
Deards Wood SG3 . . . . . . 68 F5
Debenham Ct EN5 . . . . . 171 C4
Debenham Rd EN7 . . . . . 148 B4
Deepdene EN6 . . . . 158 D8
Deep Denes LU2 . . . . 46 A2
Deeping Cl SG3 . . . . 68 F4
Deercote Cl SG3 . . . . 68 F4
Deerfield Cl SG12 . . . . 93 D2
Deerings The AL5 . . . . . . 107 A4
Deer Park Way EN9 . . . . 163 B4
Deerswood Ave AL10 . . 130 B3
Dee The HP2 . . . . 124 F8
Deene Ave HA6 . . . . 174 E3
de Havilland Aircraft
  Heritage Mus The★
  AL2 . . . . 143 B2
De Havilland Cl AL10 . . . 129 F6
De Havilland Ct WD7 . . . 156 E7
De Havilland Ho AL10 . . 130 C6
De Havilland Prim Sch
  AL10 . . . . 130 A3
De Havilland Way
  WD5 . . . . 153 F7
Deimos Dr HP2 . . . . 125 A6
Delahay Rise HP4 . . . . . . 122 B6

Delamere Rd EN8 . . . . . . 148 F2
Delamere Rd WD6 . . . . . . 170 B8
Delcroft SG12 . . . . 93 C2
Delfield Gdns LU1 . . . . 62 E4
Delius Cl WD6 . . . . 169 C3
Dell Cl AL5 . . . . 86 B3
Dellcot Cl LU2 . . . . 46 B4
Dellcott Cl AL8 . . . . 110 C7
Dellcroft Way AL5 . . . . . . 107 A5
Dell Ct WD3 . . . . 173 A8
Dellcut Rd HP2 . . . . 125 A5
Dellfield
  St Albans AL1 . . . . 127 F2
  Thundridge SG12 . . . . . . 93 D8
Dell Field Ave HP4 . . . . . 122 B6
Dellfield Cl
  Berkhamsted HP4 . . . . . 122 A6
  Radlett WD7 . . . . 155 F4
  Watford WD17 . . . . 167 A7
Dellfield Ct
  4 Harlow CM17 . . . . . . 118 C4
  Luton LU2 . . . . 46 D2
Dellfield Rd AL10 . . . . . . 130 A5
Dell La
  Bishop's Stortford
  CM23 . . . . 77 A7
  Spellbrook CM22 . . . . . . 98 A8
Dell Mdw HP3 . . . . 138 C7
Dellmeadow WD5 . . . . . . 139 E1
Dellors Cl EN5 . . . . 171 D4
Dell Rd
  Berkhamsted HP4 . . . . . 121 D7
  Enfield EN3 . . . . 162 C1
  Watford WD24 . . . . 154 A2
Dell Rise AL2 . . . . 141 B5
Dell Side WD24 . . . . 154 A2
Dellsome La
  Colney Heath AL4 . . . . . 143 E8
  Welham Green AL9 . . . . 144 B8
Dell Spring SG9 . . . . 40 E8
Dells The
  Bishop's Stortford
  CM23 . . . . 76 F7
Dellswood Cl SG13 . . . . . 113 E5
Dells Wood Cl EN11 . . . . 114 F1
Dell The
  Baldock SG7 . . . . 23 E6
  Caddington LU1 . . . . 62 E3
  Hertford SG13 . . . . 113 C3
  Luton LU2 . . . . 46 F1
  Markyate AL3 . . . . 83 D5
  Moor Park HA6 . . . . 174 E8
  Pinner HA5 . . . . 175 D1
  Radlett WD7 . . . . 156 A4
  Royston SG8 . . . . 7 C5
  St Albans AL1 . . . . 128 A4
  Stevenage SG1 . . . . 50 E5
  Waltham Abbey EN9 . . . 163 C3
  Welwyn AL6 . . . . 90 A4
Dellwood WD3 . . . . 165 B1
Delmar Ave HP2 . . . . 125 D2
Delmer Ct WD6 . . . . 156 F1
Delmerend La AL3 . . . . . . 84 C1
Delphine Cl LU1 . . . . 63 A6
Delrow Cotts WD25 . . . . 168 C8
Delta Ct WD6 . . . . 170 C6
Delta Gain WD19 . . . . . . 175 D1
Demontfort Rise SG12 . . 93 C3
Denbigh Cl 2 HP2 . . . . . . 124 E2
Denbigh High Sch LU3 . . 45 C2
Denbigh Inf Sch LU3 . . . 45 B2
Denbigh Jun Sch LU3 . . . 45 B2
Denbigh Rd LU3 . . . . 45 C2
Denby SG6 . . . . 23 B4
Dencora Ctr The AL1 . . . 128 A3
Dencora Way LU3 . . . . . . 44 B8
Dendridge Cl EN1 . . . . . . 162 B2
Dene La SG2 . . . . 51 E2
Dene Rd HA6 . . . . 174 D4
Denes The HP3 . . . . 138 F7
Denewood Ct WD17 . . . . 153 F2
Denham Cl
  Hemel Hempstead
  HP2 . . . . 125 A8
  Luton LU3 . . . . 44 E8
Denham La SL9 . . . . 172 A2
Denham Way WD6 . . . . . 170 C8
Denham Way (North
  Orbital Rd) WD3 . . . . . 172 E4
Denmark Cl LU3 . . . . 44 E8
Denmark St WD7 . . . . 167 B7
Dennis Cl HP2 . . . . 99 A4
Dennis Ct 2 AL3 . . . . 127 D4
Denny Ave EN9 . . . . 163 D5
Denny Ct CM23 . . . . 59 B2
Denny Gate EN8 . . . . 148 F4
Denny's La HP4 . . . . 121 F3
De Novo Pl AL1 . . . . 127 F3
Densley Cl AL8 . . . . 110 D8
Denton Cl
  Barnet EN5 . . . . 171 C4
  Luton LU4 . . . . 44 B3
Denton Ho 10 WD19 . . . 175 C7
Denton Rd SG1 . . . . 50 E4
Dents Cl SG6 . . . . 23 C3
Denvers Yd SG11 . . . . 73 D3
Derby Ave HA3 . . . . 176 D2
Derby Ho HA5 . . . . 175 D1
Derby Rd
  Hoddesdon EN11 . . . . . 135 D5
  Luton LU4 . . . . 44 C2
  Watford WD18 . . . . 167 C5
Derby Way SG1 . . . . 51 B8
Derry Leys AL10 . . . . 129 E2
Derwent Ave
  Luton LU3 . . . . 45 B7
  Pinner HA5 . . . . 175 E4

Derwent Cl WD25........ 154 C5
Derwent Lower Sch
SG16 ....10 B5
Desborough Cl
Hertford SG14 ....92 C1
Welwyn Garden City
AL7 ....11 B3
Desborough Dr AL6.......90 D5
Desborough Rd SG4.......35 C8
Des Fuller Ct 3 LU1......63 F6
Desmond Rd WD24......153 F3
De Soissons Cl AL8......110 A4
De Tany Ct AL1 ....127 D2
Deva Cl AL3..............127 A1
Devereux Dr WD17......153 E1
De Vere Wlk WD17......166 E7
Devey Way SG14..........92 A1
Devoils La 8 CM23.......76 F7
Devon Ct 8 AL1..........127 C2
Devon Mead AL10.......129 E2
Devon Rd
Luton LU2................64 B8
Watford WD24..........167 D8
Devonshire Bsns Ctr
EN6...................144 E1
Devonshire Bsns Pk
WD6..................170 D6
Devonshire Cl SG2........69 A8
Devonshire Ct HA5.....175 F2
Devonshire Rd
5 Harpenden AL5........86 B1
Pinner HA5..............175 F2
DEWES GREEN 30 F1
Dewes Green Rd CM23....30 F1
Dewgrass Gr EN8.........162 D4
Dewhurst Rd EN8........148 C2
Dewhurst St Mary CE Prim
Sch EN8................148 C2
Dewpond Cl SG1...........50 C8
Dewsbury Rd LU3..........45 C6
Dexter Cl
Luton LU3................31 B1
St Albans AL1..........128 A2
Dexter Rd
Barnet EN5.............171 D3
Harefield UB9..........173 C1
Dialmead EN6............157 F5
DIAMOND END.............65 C6
Diamond Ind Ctr SG6......23 C7
Diamond Rd WD24.......154 A1
Dickens Byd SG5.........11 C2
Dickens Ct AL3..........127 D4
Dickens Ct
Hatfield AL10...........130 B7
Hemel Hempstead HP2...105 B1
Dickenson Way 19
SG12 ....93 D1
Dicker Mill SG13........113 C9
Dicket Mead AL6.........89 E3
Dickins Cl EN7..........148 A5
Dickinson Ave WD3......166 A3
Dickinson Quay HP3.....138 F7
Dickinson Sq WD3.......166 A3
Dickson EN7.............147 F4
Didsbury Cotts WD4.....152 A8
Dig Dag Hill EN7........147 F4
DIGSWELL 89 E4
Digswell Cl WD6.........157 A1
Digswell Ct AL8.........110 E8
Digswell Ho AL8..........89 B2
Digswell Ho AL8..........89 D2
Digswell House Mews
AL8...................89 B2
Digswell La AL7..........89 F2
DIGSWELL PARK 89 D1
Digswell Park Rd
Welwyn Garden City
AL8...................89 D3
Welwyn Garden City AL8...89 E3
Digswell Pl AL8..........89 C1
Digswell Rd AL8..........89 E1
Digswell Rise AL8.......110 E8
Dimmocks La WD3........152 B3
Dimsdale Cotts SG9......29 B7
Dimsdale Cres CM23......77 B6
Dimsdale St SG14........13 C6
Dinant Link Rd EN11.....135 B7
Dingle Ct HA5...........175 D1
Dingles Ct HA5..........175 D1
Dinmore HP3............136 F3
Dione Rd HP2...........124 F6
Dixon Pl SG9.............40 E7
Dixon's Ct SG12.........114 E8
Dixons Hill Cl AL9......144 B6
Dixons Hill Rd AL9......144 A6
Dobb's Weir Rd EN11....135 D5
Docklands SG5...........20 D4
Doctor's Commons Rd
HP4...................122 B4
Dodds La HP2...........104 E1
Dodwood AL7............111 B5
Doggetts Way AL1.......127 C1

Dog Kennel La
Chorleywood WD3......164 D5
Hatfield AL10...........130 A6
Royston SG8.............7 D6
Dognell Gn AL8.........110 B7
Dolesbury Dr AL6........89 E8
Dollimore Cl SG4.........67 F1
Dollis Brook Wlk EN5...171 E3
Dollis Valley Dr EN5...171 F4
Dollis Valley Way
EN5...................171 F3
Dolphin Sq HP23........100 A3
Dolphin Way CM23.......77 A8
Dolphin Yd
2 Hertford SG14........113 D6
St Albans AL1..........127 D3
7 Ware SG12.............93 D1
Dominic Ct EN9.........163 B6
Doncaster Cl SG1.........51 C8
Doncaster Gn WD19.....175 C5
Donkey La EN9...........99 E2
Donne Cl SG8............7 C8
Dorant Ho AL3..........127 D7
Dorcas Ct 9 AL1.........127 E2
Dorchester Ave EN11....135 A8
Dorchester Ct
Croxley Green WD3......166 D4
8 St Albans AL1........128 A2
Watford WD19..........167 E3
Dordans Rd LU4..........44 F4
Dorel Cl LU2............45 F2
Dorian Cl HP23.........100 D4
Dormans Cl HA6........174 D3
Dormer Ct EN5..........171 D4
Dormie Cl AL3...........127 C5
Dornan Ct 4 LU1.........63 E5
Dorrien's Croft HP4....121 D7
Dorrington Cl LU3......45 C1
Dorrofield Cl WD3......166 D4
Dorset Cl HP4...........121 F5
Dorset Ct 4 LU1.........63 F6
Dorset Ho
13 Bishop's Stortford
CM23 ....76 F7
3 Enfield EN3.........162 D2
Douglas Ave WD24......154 E2
Douglas Cl AL6..........89 E3
Douglas Dr SG1.........51 A8
Douglas Ho 11 EN8......148 D3
Douglas Rd
Harpenden AL5..........85 F2
Luton LU4...............45 A2
Douglas Way AL7.......111 C6
Dove Cl
Bishop's Stortford
CM23 ....76 D3
Stansted Mountfitchet
CM24 ....59 E8
Dovecote The SG7.........4 D4
Dove Ct AL10...........130 A3
Dovedale
Luton LU2...............45 E6
Stevenage SG2...........51 B4
Ware SG12...............93 C3
Dovehouse Cl UB9......173 C1
Dovehouse Croft
CM20 ....118 A2
Dove House Dr SG16.....10 D8
Dovehouse Hill LU2......46 B1
Dovehouse La LU6........82 D8
Dove La EN6............159 C5
Dove Pk
Chorleywood WD3......164 C4
Pinner HA5.............176 A3
Dover Cl
St Albans AL1...........45 A3
Pitstone LU7............80 D2
Dove Rd SG1............36 F3
Doverfield EN7..........147 C2
Dover Way WD3.........166 C5
Dowding Way
Waltham Abbey EN9....163 E3
Watford WD25..........153 F5
Dower Ct SG4............34 F5
Dower Mews 5 HP4......122 C4
Dowland Ho EN1........161 F1
Dowley Wood AL7.......111 B5
Dowling Ct 4 HA3......138 D8
Downalong WD23.......168 D1
Downe Edge AL3........168 C5
Downer Dr WD3.........152 A3
Downes Rd AL4..........128 B7
Downfield Cl SG13......114 C4
Downfield Ct SG12.......93 B5
Downfield Prim Sch
EN8...................162 E8
Downfield Rd
Cheshunt EN8...........162 E8
Hertford Heath SG13....114 C5
Downfields AL8.........110 B4
Down Green La AL4......108 A7
Downhall Ley SG9........40 E7
Downing Ct 11 WD6....169 F8
Downings Wood
WD3..................172 D5
Downlands
Baldock SG7.............13 A1
Luton LU3...............45 B8
Royston SG8.............7 C6
Slip End LU1.............84 C8
Stevenage SG2...........51 D1
Waltham Abbey EN9.....163 E5
Downlands Ct LU4.......44 A2
Downs Ct LU1............63 C7
Downsfield AL10........130 B2
Downside HP2...........124 E4
Downside Inf Sch LU4....44 E1

Downside Jun Sch LU4...44 E1
Downs La AL10..........130 A3
Downs Rd LU1............63 C7
Downs The AL10.........130 A3
Downs View LU4.........44 D4
Downsway Cl SG8........7 C6
Downton Ct 3 LU3.......63 D8
Downview LU4...........44 B2
Dowry Wlk WD17........153 F1
Dragon Rd AL10........129 D6
Drakes Ct EN8..........148 D3
Drakes Dr
Northwood HA6.........174 B2
St Albans AL1..........128 C1
Stevenage SG2..........51 B7
Drakes Mdw CM17......118 E4
Drakes Way AL10........130 B3
Drapers Mews LU3......45 C1
Drapers Way SG1.........50 C7
Drayman's Ct CM23.....76 B5
Drayson Ct EN9.........163 E7
Drayton Ave EN6.......158 E7
DRAYTON BEAUCHAMP
.......................99 C5
Drayton Rd
Borehamwood WD6.....170 A5
Luton LU4...............44 A3
Driftway SG8.............16 E4
Driftway The HP2.......124 F3
Driftwood Ave AL2......141 B5
Driver's End La SG4,
SG3...................68 A4
Drive The
Barnet EN5.............171 E6
Blackmore End AL4........87 B7
Brookmans Park AL9....145 B6
Cheshunt EN7..........148 B3
Goff's Oak EN7.........147 B3
Harlow CM20...........117 E1
Harpenden AL5..........86 A1
Hertford SG14..........113 C8
Hoddesdon EN11.......135 A8
London Colney AL2.....142 A6
Northwood HA6.........174 E2
Oaklands AL6............69 A1
Potters Bar EN6.......158 F7
Radlett WD7...........156 A5
Rickmansworth WD3....165 C3
Sawbridgeworth CM21...97 E2
Watford WD17..........153 E2
Driveway The
Hemel Hempstead HP3...124 B1
Dromey Gdns HA3.......176 F3
Drop La AL2.............155 C7
Drovers Way
Bishop's Stortford
CM23 ....76 C5
Hatfield AL10...........130 B8
St Albans AL1..........127 D3
Drummond Dr HA7......176 F3
Drummond Ride
HP23..................100 A5
Drummonds Fold AL3....83 D8
Drummonds The LU4.....44 C2
Drury La SG12............95 E1
Drycroft AL7...........110 E2
Dryden Cres SG2.........51 C8
Dryden Rd HA3..........174 E3
Drysdale Ct 8 HA6......174 F3
Dubbs Knoll Rd SG8.....1 F5
Dubrae Cl AL3..........127 A1
Duchess Cl CM23........76 C2
Duchy Rd EN4...........159 D1
DUCK END...............59 E1
Duck End CM23..........59 E1
Ducketts La SG10........75 D1
Ducketts Mead CM19...116 B1
Ducketts Wharf 10
CM23 ....76 F6
Ducketts Wood SG12....93 E6
Duck La SG2.............52 E4
Duckling La CM21........97 E2
Duckmore La HP23.......99 E2
Duck's Hill Rd HA6......174 B1
Dudley Ave EN8.........162 D7
Dudley Hill Cl AL6......89 E8
Dudley Ho HP3..........137 A4
Dudley St LU2............63 E8
DUDSWELL 121 D7
Dudswell La HP4........121 D7
Dugdale Ct SG5..........21 C1
Dugdale Hill La EN6....158 E7
Dugdales WD3...........166 A5
Dukes Ave LU6...........81 E8
Dukes Ct 4 LU1.........63 D6
Duke's La SG5...........34 F8
Duke's Lo 9 HA6........174 F5
Dukes Ride
Bishop's Stortford
CM23 ....76 C7
18 Luton LU3...........45 C1
Duke St
Hoddesdon EN11.......135 A7
Luton LU2...............63 E8
Watford WD17..........167 C6

Duncombe Cl
Hertford SG14 ....113 C8
Luton LU3 ....45 C6
Duncombe Rd
Berkhamsted HP4......121 E6
Hertford SG14 ....113 C8
Duncombe Sch SG14....113 C7
Duncots Cl SG5..........21 E3
Dundale Prim Sch
HP23..................100 A5
Dundale Rd HP23.......100 A4
Dundas Mews EN3......163 A2
Dundri Ho SG8..........7 C6
East Cl
Chiswell Green AL2....141 B6
Hitchin SG4.............22 B1
Stevenage SG1..........50 F5
East Comm
Harpenden AL5.........107 C7
Redbourn AL3..........106 A4
Eastcote Dr AL5.........107 D6
Eastcott Ct LU2..........46 D1
East Ct
Moor Park WD1........174 E8
Sawbridgeworth CM21...97 E1
St Albans AL4..........128 F4
Watford WD25.........154 B3
EASTEND 116 C1
Eastend Cotts CM19....116 D1
EAST END GREEN 112 D2
East End Way HA5......175 F1
Eastern Ave
Cheshunt EN8..........162 F6
Lower Stondon SG16....10 C3
Eastern Way SG6........12 A1
Eastfield Ave WD24....167 D8
Eastfield Cl LU2.........46 C4
Eastfield Ct AL4.........128 D6
Eastfield Prim Sch
EN3...................162 D1
Eastfield Rd
Cheshunt EN8..........162 F6
Enfield EN3............162 D1
Royston SG8............7 E6
East Flint HP1..........123 F4
Eastgate SG1............50 D5
East Gate CM20.........117 D1
Eastglade HA6.........174 F5
East Gn HP3............139 A6
EASTHALL 49 B2
Easthall Ho SG1.........36 C1
Eastham Ct EN5.........171 F4
East Hill LU3.............45 B6
Eastholm SG6...........23 A8
Eastholm Gn SG6........23 A8
EAST HYDE.............85 F8
East La
Abbots Langley WD5....140 A2
Wheathampstead AL4....87 D1
Eastlea Ave WD25......154 E2
East Lodge La EN2.....160 E4
Eastman Way
Hemel Hempstead
HP2...................125 A6
Stevenage SG1..........37 C2
East Mead AL7.........111 B3
East Mimms 4 HP2....124 E4
Eastmoor Ct AL5........107 C6
Eastmoor Pk AL5.......107 C6
East Mount 2 AL4.......87 D1
Eastor HP3............137 A3
East Pk
Harlow CM17...........118 C3
Sawbridgeworth CM21...97 E1
East Rd
Bishop's Stortford
CM23 ....77 B7
Enfield EN3............162 C1
Harlow CM20...........118 B4
East Reach SG2.........51 A2
East Ridgeway EN6.....146 E3
East Riding AL6.........90 D5
East St
Hemel Hempstead
HP2...................124 D3
Lilley LU2...............32 D2
Ware SG12..............93 D1
East View
Barnet EN5.............171 F6
Essendon AL9..........131 F6
St Ippolyts SG4.........35 C2
EASTWICK 117 A4
Eastwick Cres WD3....172 F3
Eastwick Hall La
CM20 ....117 A5
Eastwick Rd
Eastwick CM20.........117 B4
Hunsdon CM20.........117 C6
Eastwick Row HP2......125 A2
East Wlk CM20..........117 D1
East Wood WD25......155 B3
Eastwood Ct HP2.......125 A4
Eaton Gate HA6........174 C4
Eaton Gdns EN10......134 C2
Eaton Grn Ct LU2........64 C8
Eaton Green Rd LU2.....64 C8
Eaton Ho 8 CM23........77 B8
Eaton Pl LU2............46 D1
Eaton Rd
Hemel Hempstead
HP2...................125 B6
St Albans AL1..........128 B3
Eaton Valley Rd LU2....64 B8
Eaton Way WD6........169 F8
Ebberns Rd HP3........138 E8

Eastbury Ct continued
Watford WD19..........167 C2
Eastbury Farm Jun Mix Inf
Sch HA6...............174 F6
Eastbury Pl 11 HA6....174 F5
Eastbury Rd
Northwood HA6........174 E4
Watford WD19..........167 C3
Eastcheap SG6..........22 F6

Eagle Centre Way LU4...44 B2
Eagle Cl LU4.............44 A4
Eagle Ct
Baldock SG7............12 C1
Hertford SG13..........114 B7
Eagle Way AL10.........130 A3
Ealing Cl WD6..........170 D8
Earlswood Ct WD3.....138 D7
Earls Cl CM23...........76 D5
Earls Hill Gdns SG8......7 C6
Earls La EN6............157 F6
Earlsmead SG6..........22 F3
Earls Meade LU2........45 D1
Earl St WD17...........167 B6
Easington Rd SG2.......71 E7
Easingwold Gdns LU1....62 F8
Eastbourne Ave SG1.....50 A6
Eastbrook Rd EN9......163 A6
East Burrowfield AL7....110 D4
EASTBURY 174 F5
Eastbury Ave HA6......174 F5
Eastbury Ct
St Albans AL1..........127 F4

Ebeneezer Ct SG14 ..... 113 C6
Ebeneezer St 7 LU1 .....63 D6
Ebury App WD3 ..... 165 D1
Ebury Cl HA6 ..... 174 C5
Ebury Ct WD3 ..... 165 D1
Ebury Rd
 Rickmansworth WD3 ..... 165 D1
 Watford WD17 ..... 167 C6
Ebury Rdbt WD3 ..... 165 D1
Echo Hill SG8 .....7 C5
Eddington Cres AL7 ..... 110 D3
Eddy St HP4 ..... 122 A5
Eden Cl EN3 ..... 163 A1
Edenhall Cl HP2 ..... 125 D2
Edens Cl CM23 .....77 B7
Edens Mount CM21 .....97 F4
Edenvale EN7 ..... 148 B2
Edgars Ct AL7 ..... 110 E5
Edgbaston Dr WD7 ..... 156 E7
Edgbaston Rd WD19 ..... 175 E7
Edgcott Cl LU3 .....31 B1
Edgecote Cl LU1 .....62 E3
Edgehill Gdns LU3 .....44 C8
Edgewood Dr LU2 .....46 C6
Edgeworth Cl SG2 .....51 C1
EDGWARE 170 E1
Edgwarebury La WD6,
 HA8 ..... 169 F1
Edgware Way HA8 ..... 169 D1
Edinburgh Ave WD25 ..... 165 A2
Edinburgh Cres EN8 ..... 162 E6
Edinburgh Dr WD5 ..... 154 A7
Edinburgh Gate
 CM20 ..... 117 D3
Edinburgh Gdns CM23 ...76 E6
Edinburgh Pl CM20 ..... 118 A4
Edinburgh Sq SG8 .....2 A6
Edinburgh Way CM20 ... 117 E3
Edison Cl AL4 ..... 128 C2
Edison Rd SG2 .....51 B6
Edkins Cl LU2 .....45 E5
Edlyn Cl HP4 ..... 121 F5
Edmonds Dr SG2 .....51 D4
Edmund Beaufort Dr
 AL3 ..... 127 E5
Edmund Mews WD4 ..... 139 A2
Edmunds Rd SG14 ..... 112 F7
Edridge Cl WD23 ..... 168 C4
Edson Cl WD25 ..... 153 F6
Edulf Rd WD6 ..... 170 B8
Edward Amey Cl
 WD25 ..... 154 C3
Edward Cl
 Abbots Langley WD5 ..... 153 F7
 St Albans AL1 ..... 127 F2
Edward Cotts SG11 .....54 C3
Edward Ct
 Hemel Hempstead
 HP3 ..... 138 D7
 Waltham Abbey EN9 ..... 163 F6
Edwards Ct EN8 ..... 148 E1
Edward St LU2 .....45 F1
Edwick Ct EN8 ..... 148 D2
Edwinstree CE Mid Sch
 SG9 .....40 D8
Edwin Ware Ct 1
 HA5 ..... 175 C1
EDWORTH 3 A6
Edwyn Cl EN5 ..... 171 D3
Egdon Dr LU2 .....45 D6
Egerton Rd HP4 ..... 122 B6
Egerton-Rothesay Sch
 HP4 ..... 121 E4
Egg Farm La WD4 ..... 139 B1
Egglesfield Cl HP4 ..... 121 E6
Eggleton Dr HP23 ..... 100 A5
Egret Ct EN3 ..... 162 C3
Eider Ct 1 CM23 .....77 A6
Eight Acres HP3 ..... 100 A4
Eighth Ave LU3 .....44 D7
Eisenberg Cl SG7 .....13 B1
Elaine Gdns LU1 .....63 A1
Elbow La
 Hertford Heath EN11,
 SG13 ..... 134 B7
 Stevenage SG2 .....51 B1
Eldefield SG6 .....22 D7
Elderbeck Cl EN7 ..... 148 A2
Elderberry Cl LU2 .....46 B4
Elderberry Dr SG4 .....35 A4
Elderberry Way
 WD25 ..... 154 B4
Elder Ct
 Bushey WD23 ..... 176 E8
 Northwood HA6 ..... 174 D4
Elderfield
 Harlow CM17 ..... 118 D3
 Welwyn Garden City
 AL7 ..... 111 B6
Elderflower Ct 6 SG6 ...34 F7
Elder Rd SG12 .....93 F3
Elder Way SG1 .....50 E3
Eldon Ave WD6 ..... 170 B7
Eldon Rd
 Hoddesdon EN11 ..... 135 D4
 Luton LU4 .....44 C1
Eldrig Turn HP2 ..... 124 E7
Eleanor Ave AL3 ..... 127 D5
Eleanor Cross Rd
 Cheshunt EN8 ..... 162 F5
 Holdbrook EN8 ..... 163 A5
Eleanor Gdns EN5 ..... 171 D4
Eleanor Rd
 Cheshunt EN8 ..... 162 E6
 Hertford SG14 ..... 113 C6

Eleanor's Cl SG12 .....93 D7
Eleanor Way EN8 ..... 162 F5
Electric Ave EN3 ..... 162 F3
Element Ho EN3 ..... 162 F3
Eleni Rd EN3 ..... 162 D6
Elfrida Rd WD18 ..... 167 C4
Elgar Cl WD6 ..... 169 D2
Elgar Path LU2 .....62 E8
Elgin Dr HA6 ..... 174 E3
Elgin Ho SG4 .....35 A6
Elgin Rd
 Cheshunt EN8 ..... 148 C1
 Hoddesdon EN10 ..... 148 F8
Elgood Ave HA6 ..... 175 A3
Eliot Rd
 Royston SG8 .....7 D8
 Stevenage SG2 .....51 C6
Elizabeth Cl
 Barnet EN5 ..... 171 D6
 Hertford SG14 ..... 112 F6
 Lower Nazeing EN9 ..... 149 D8
 Welwyn Garden City
 AL7 ..... 111 C6
Elizabeth Ct
 10 Luton LU1 .....63 D6
 St Albans AL4 ..... 128 D6
 Watford WD17 ..... 153 F1
Elizabeth Dr HP23 ..... 100 B6
Elizabeth Ho
 12 Hemel Hempstead
 HP1 ..... 124 D4
 7 Watford WD24 ..... 167 C7
 Welwyn Garden City
 AL7 ..... 111 B6
Elizabeth Rd CM23 .....76 E5
Elizabeth St LU1 .....63 D6
Elizabeth Way CM20 ... 117 B2
Ella Ct LU2 .....45 F1
Ellenborough Cl CM23 ...76 D5
ELLENBROOK 129 D5
Ellenbrook Cl WD4 ..... 167 C8
Ellenbrook Cres AL10 ... 129 D5
Ellenbrook La AL10 ..... 129 D4
Ellen Cl HP2 ..... 124 F4
Ellenhall Cl LU3 .....45 C1
Ellerdine Cl LU3 .....45 B4
Ellesborough Cl
 WD19 ..... 175 C5
Ellesfield AL6 .....89 B5
Ellesmere Gr EN5 ..... 171 F4
Ellesmere Rd HP4 ..... 122 D4
Ellice SG6 .....23 B4
Elliman Ct HP23 .....99 F3
Ellingham Cl HP2 ..... 125 A5
Ellingham Rd HP2 ..... 124 F4
Elliott Cl AL7 ..... 110 D3
Elliott Ct CM23 .....77 A8
Ellis Ave SG1 .....50 E8
Ellis Cl EN11 ..... 114 F2
Ellis Fields AL3 ..... 127 E6
Elliswick Rd AL5 .....86 B2
Ellwood Gdns WD25 ..... 154 C5
Ellwood Terr WD3 ..... 164 D4
Elm Ave
 Caddington LU1 .....62 E3
 Watford WD19 ..... 167 E2
Elmbank Ave EN5 ..... 171 C5
Elmbridge CM17 ..... 118 F3
Elmbrook Dr CM23 .....76 E3
Elm Cl EN9 ..... 163 D5
Elmcote HA5 ..... 175 C1
Elmcote Way WD3 ..... 165 F3
Elm Cotts
 Meesden SG9 .....29 F6
 Waltham Abbey EN9 ..... 163 D1
Elm Dr
 Cheshunt EN8 ..... 148 E3
 Hatfield AL10 ..... 130 A4
 St Albans AL4 ..... 128 C3
Elmfield Cl EN6 ..... 158 E6
Elmfield Ct LU2 .....46 A1
Elmfield Rd EN6 ..... 158 E6
Elm Gdns
 Enfield EN2 ..... 161 D1
 Welwyn Garden City
 AL8 ..... 110 B6
Elm Gn HP1 ..... 123 E5
Elm Gr
 Berkhamsted HP4 ..... 122 C4
 Bishop's Stortford CM23 ...77 B7
 Watford WD24 ..... 154 A2
Elm Hatch HA5 ..... 174 B3
Elm Ho HA6 ..... 174 D4
Elmhurst EN10 ..... 135 A4
Elmhurst Cl WD23 ..... 167 E5
Elmhurst Rd EN3 ..... 162 C2
Elm Lawn Cl 2 AL1 ..... 127 E4
Elmoor Ave AL6 .....89 B5
Elmoor Cl AL6 .....89 B4
Elmore Rd
 Enfield EN3 ..... 162 D1
 Luton LU2 .....46 A1
Elm Park Rd HA5 ..... 175 D1
Elm Pk SG7 .....23 F8
Elm Rd
 Barnet EN5 ..... 171 F5
 Bishop's Stortford CM23 ...76 E8
Elmroyd Ave EN6 ..... 158 F6
Elmroyd Cl EN6 ..... 158 F6
Elms Cl SG4 .....35 E3
Elmscroft Gdns EN6 ..... 158 F7
Elmside HL6 .....82 E8
Elmside Wlk SG5 .....34 E7
Elms Rd
 Harrow HA3 ..... 176 E3
 Ware SG12 .....94 A2
Elms The
 Codicote SG4 .....67 F2

Elms The continued
 Hertford SG13 ..... 114 A6
 Stevenage SG2 .....69 B8
Elmswell St SG14 ..... 112 F7
Elm Terr HA3 ..... 176 D2
Elmtree Ave LU2 .....45 F6
Elm Tree Farm Cl SG5 ....20 C4
Elm Tree Wlk
 Chorleywood WD3 ..... 164 F5
 Tring HP23 ..... 100 A5
Elm Way WD3 ..... 165 B1
Elm Wlk
 Radlett WD7 ..... 155 F3
 Royston SG8 .....7 F7
Elmwood
 7 Pinner HA5 ..... 176 A3
 Sawbridgeworth CM21 ....97 F1
 Welwyn Garden City
 AL8 ..... 110 B5
Elmwood Ave
 Baldock SG7 .....23 F7
 Borehamwood WD6 ..... 170 B5
Elmwood Cres LU2 .....45 E3
Elmwood Ct SG2 .....23 F8
Elm Yd SG4 .....35 E3
Elppin Ct EN10 ..... 134 F3
Elsinge Rd EN1 ..... 162 C3
Elsons Mews AL7 ..... 111 B6
ELSTREE 169 E3
Elstree & Borehamwood
 Sta WD6 ..... 170 A5
Elstree Bsns Ctr WD6 ... 170 D6
Elstree Distribution Pk
 WD6 ..... 170 D6
Elstree Hill N WD6 ..... 169 D4
Elstree Hill S WD6 ..... 169 D2
Elstree Pk WD6 ..... 170 D3
Elstree Way WD6 ..... 170 C7
Elton Ave EN5 ..... 171 F4
Elton Ct SG14 ..... 113 C7
Elton Pk WD17 ..... 167 B7
Elton Rd SG14 ..... 113 C7
Elton Way WD25 ..... 168 B7
Elvaston Ct EN5 ..... 171 C4
Elveden Cl LU2 .....45 E6
Elvington Gdns LU3 .....31 B1
Ely Cl
 Hatfield AL10 ..... 129 F6
 Stevenage SG1 .....37 B1
Ely Gdns WD6 ..... 170 D4
Ely Ho AL7 ..... 110 F6
Ely Rd AL1 ..... 128 A3
Ely Way LU4 .....44 D4
Embleton Rd WD19 ..... 175 A7
Emerald Cl WD6 ..... 156 F1
Emerald Rd LU4 .....44 A3
Emerton St HP4 ..... 121 E7
Emerton Garth HP4 ..... 121 E7
Emily Ct AL5 ..... 107 C7
Emmanuel Lo EN6 ..... 148 C1
Emmanuel Rd HA6 ..... 174 E5
Emma Rothschild Ct
 HP23 ..... 100 A5
Emma's Cres SG12 ..... 115 B4
Emmer Gn LU2 .....46 F2
Emmerson Ho CM23 .....77 A5
Emmitt St HP4 ..... 156 E6
Emperor Cl HP4 ..... 121 F7
Emperors Gate HP2 .....51 D8
Empire Ctr WD24 ..... 167 C8
Empire Pl 1 WD18 ..... 166 E5
Empress Rd LU3 .....44 E4
Endeavour Rd EN8 ..... 148 E4
Enderby Rd LU3 .....45 C6
Enderley Cl HA3 ..... 176 E2
Enderley Rd HA3 ..... 176 E2
Endersby Rd EN5 ..... 171 C4
Endymion Cl AL10 ..... 130 C6
Endymion Mews
 AL10 ..... 130 C6
Endymion Rd AL10 ..... 130 C6
ENFIELD 161 E2
Enfield Cty Sch (Lwr)
 EN2 ..... 161 E1
ENFIELD ISLAND VILLAGE
 ..... 163 B2
ENFIELD LOCK 162 F2
Enfield Lock Sta EN3 ... 162 E2
ENFIELD WASH 162 D1
Englefield LU2 .....45 F3
Englehurst AL5 .....86 D1
Enid Cl AL2 ..... 154 F8
Enjakes Cl SG2 .....69 B7
Ennerdale Cl AL1 ..... 128 B3
Ennerdale Dr WD25 ..... 154 C5
Ennis Cl AL5 ..... 107 D6
Ennismore Cl SG6 .....23 C3
Ennismore Gn LU2 .....46 F1
Enslow Cl LU1 .....62 E3
Enterprise Ctr AL1 ..... 128 B3
Enterprise Ctr The
 EN6 ..... 144 C1
Enterprise Way
 Hemel Hempstead
 HP2 ..... 125 C5
 Luton LU3 .....45 B8
Enville Ho 8 WD19 ..... 175 C7
Epping Forest District
 Mus* EN9 ..... 163 C6
Epping Gn HP2 ..... 125 B8
EPPING GREEN 132 D2
Epping Way LU3 .....44 C8

Epsom Cl SG1 .....51 B8
Epsom Ct WD3 ..... 165 B1
Ereswell Rd LU3 .....45 A7
Eric Steele Ho AL2 ..... 141 B4
Erin Cl LU4 .....45 A2
Erin Ct LU4 .....45 A2
Ermine Cl
 Cheshunt EN7 ..... 162 B8
 Royston SG8 .....7 D8
 St Albans AL3 ..... 127 A2
Ermine Ct SG9 .....40 E8
Ermine Mews 8 LU2 .....45 D1
Ermine Pl 11 LU2 .....45 D1
Ermine Point Bsns Pk
 SG12 .....93 B3
Ermine St
 Buckland SG9 .....27 D6
 Thundridge SG12 .....93 D7
Errington Cl AL10 ..... 129 E6
Erskine Ho 5 WD19 ..... 175 D7
Escarpment Ave HP4,
 LU6 .....81 D8
Escot Way EN5 ..... 171 C4
Esdaile Hall EN11 ..... 135 A5
Esdaile La EN11 ..... 135 A5
Eskdale
 London Colney AL2 ..... 142 F4
 Luton LU4 .....44 C5
Eskdale Ct 3 HP2 ..... 124 E6
Eskdale Rd EN11 ..... 131 F6
ESSENDON 131 F6
Essendon CE Prim Sch
 AL9 ..... 131 F6
Essendon Gdns AL7 ..... 110 F5
Essendon Hill AL9 ..... 131 F7
Essex Cl AL10 ..... 129 F6
Essex Ct 7 LU1 .....63 F6
Essex Ho EN9 ..... 163 C5
Essex La WD4 ..... 153 D6
Essex Mead HP2 ..... 105 A1
Essex Rd
 Borehamwood WD6 ..... 170 A6
 Hoddesdon EN11 ..... 135 C6
 Stevenage SG1 .....50 B8
 Watford WD17 ..... 167 B7
Essex St AL1 ..... 127 E4
Essex Yd HP22 .....60 C3
Estcourt Rd WD17 ..... 167 C6
Estfeld Cl 4 EN11 ..... 115 B1
Ethelred Cl AL7 ..... 110 F5
Ethorpe Cl AL3 ..... 127 D4
Etonbury Mid Sch
 SG15 .....11 C3
Eton Ho 9 WD24 ..... 167 C7
Europa Rd HP2 ..... 124 F6
Euston Ave WD18 ..... 166 F4
Evans Ave WD25 ..... 153 F4
Evans Cl SG8 .....7 D7
Evan's Cl WD3 ..... 166 A4
Evans Gr AL4 ..... 128 C7
Evans Way HP23 ..... 100 B4
Evans Wharf HP3 ..... 138 E7
Evedon Cl LU3 .....44 F6
Evelyn Dr HA5 ..... 175 D3
Evelyn Rd LU5 .....44 A1
Evelyn Sharp Ho HP2 ... 125 A2
Evensyde WD18 ..... 166 D3
Everall Cl HP1 ..... 124 C3
Everard Cl AL1 ..... 127 D1
Everest Cl SG15 .....11 B5
Everest Gdns CM23 .....76 E5
Everest Way HP2 ..... 125 A3
Everett Cl
 Bushey WD23 ..... 168 E1
 Hammond Street EN7 ..... 147 C6
Everett Ct WD7 ..... 156 A5
Everett Rd SG13 .....69 A2
Evergreen Rd SG2 .....93 F3
Evergreen Way LU3 .....45 A8
Evergreen Wlk 2
 HP3 ..... 124 E1
Everlasting La AL3 ..... 127 C5
Eversden Ct HP2 ..... 105 B1
Eversley Lo 11 EN11 ..... 135 A6
Everard Cl AL1 ..... 127 D1
Everon Pl 5 SG14 ..... 113 D6
Evolution WD25 ..... 154 D5
Exchange Bldgs 7
 EN5 ..... 171 E6
Exchange Rd
 Stevenage SG1 .....50 F5
 Watford WD18 ..... 167 B5
Executive Pk Ind Est
 AL1 ..... 128 B3
Exeter Cl
 Stevenage SG1 .....37 B2
 Watford WD24 ..... 167 C7
Exeter Ho 7 WD6 ..... 170 A7
Exhims Mews HP4 ..... 121 E6
Explorer Dr WD18 ..... 166 F3
Extension Rd SG13 ..... 113 F6
Exton Ave LU2 .....46 A1
EYEWORTH 1 A8
Eynsford Ct SG4 .....34 F6
Eynsford Rd LU4 .....44 D3

F

Faggots Cl WD7 ..... 156 C4
Faints Cl EN7 ..... 147 F2
Fairacre HP3 ..... 138 F7
Fairacre Ct 3 HA6 ..... 174 E3
Fairacres Cl EN6 ..... 158 F6
Fairburn Cl WD6 ..... 170 A8
Fair Cl WD23 ..... 168 B2
Faircroft CM17 ..... 118 C4
Faircross Ho 6
 WD17 ..... 167 B6
Faircross Way AL1 ..... 128 A5
Fairfax Ave LU3 .....44 D7

Fairfax Rd SG13 ..... 113 F7
Fairfield
 Buntingford SG9 .....40 F6
 Northwood HA6 ..... 175 A1
 Pinner HA6 ..... 175 A1
 Welwyn Garden City WD19 ... 175 D7
Fairfield Cl
 Harpenden AL5 .....86 D1
 Hatfield AL10 ..... 130 C8
 Northwood HA6 ..... 174 B4
 Radlett WD7 ..... 155 E2
Fairfield Cres SG1 .....37 B4
Fairfield Dr EN10 ..... 148 F7
Fair Field Jun Sch
 WD7 ..... 155 E3
Fairfield Lower Sch
 SG5 .....11 C2
Fairfield Rd EN11 ..... 135 A8
Fairfields Prim Sch
 EN7 ..... 148 A4
Fairfield Way
 Hitchin SG4 .....35 D8
 Stevenage SG1 .....37 C3
Fairfield Wlk 8 EN8 ..... 148 E3
Fairfolds WD25 ..... 154 E4
Fairford Ave LU2 .....45 E4
Fairgreen Rd LU1 .....62 F3
Fairhaven AL2 ..... 141 D4
Fairhaven Cres WD19 ... 175 A7
Fairhill HP3 ..... 138 F7
Fairlands Lo 6 WD6 ..... 170 A5
Fairlands Prim Sch
 SG1 .....50 D6
Fairlands Way SG1 .....51 A7
Fairlawns
 Pinner HA5 ..... 175 D1
 Watford WD17 ..... 153 F1
Fairley Way EN7 ..... 148 B3
Fairmead Ave AL5 ..... 107 C8
Fair Oak Ct LU2 .....45 F3
Fair Oak Dr LU2 .....45 F3
Fairoaks Gr EN3 ..... 162 D2
Fairseat Cl WD23 ..... 176 E8
Fairshot Ct AL4 ..... 108 D2
Fairthorn Cl HP23 .....99 E3
Fair View EN6 ..... 145 B2
Fairview Dr WD17 ..... 153 E3
Fairview Rd SG1 .....50 B7
Fairway
 Bishop's Stortford
 CM23 .....77 C6
 Hemel Hempstead HP3 ... 138 F7
 Sawbridgeworth CM21 ....97 F2
 Ware SG12 ..... 114 C8
Fairway Ave WD6 ..... 170 B7
Fairway Cl
 Chiswell Green AL2 ..... 141 C4
 Harpenden AL5 ..... 107 A5
Fairway Ct HP3 ..... 138 F7
Fairway Ho WD6 ..... 170 B6
Fairways
 Cheshunt EN8 ..... 148 D5
 Waltham Abbey EN9 ..... 163 E5
Fairway The
 Abbots Langley WD5 ..... 153 D7
 Moor Park HA6 ..... 174 E6
Faithfield WD19 ..... 167 E3
Faith Ho 1 LU1 .....63 D7
Falcon Cl
 Hatfield AL10 ..... 130 A3
 Northwood HA6 ..... 174 E6
 Sawbridgeworth CM21 ....97 C1
 Stevenage SG2 .....51 D2
Falcon Ct 8 SG12 .....93 D3
Falconer Rd WD23 ..... 168 A3
Falconer Sch WD23 ..... 168 A4
Falconers Field AL5 .....85 E3
Falconers Pk CM21 .....97 D1
Falconers Rd LU2 .....46 B1
Falconer St CM23 .....76 C5
Falcon Ridge HP4 ..... 122 C3
Falcon Way
 Watford WD25 ..... 154 E5
 Welwyn Garden City
 AL7 ..... 110 E8
Falkirk Gdns WD19 ..... 175 D5
Falkland Rd EN5 ..... 171 E7
Fallow End AL6 .....68 C1
Fallowfield
 Luton LU3 .....45 C4
 Stevenage SG2 .....51 C3
 Welwyn Garden City AL7 ...89 F1
Fallowfield Cl UB9 ..... 173 C2
Fallowfield Wlk HP1 ..... 124 A6
Fallow Rise SG13 ..... 113 F6
Fallows Gn AL5 .....86 B3
Falmouth Cl AL3 ..... 127 D5
Falmouth Ho 9 HA5 ..... 175 F3
Falstaff Gdns AL1 ..... 141 C8
Falstone Gn LU2 .....46 E1
Fanhams Hall SG12 .....94 A4
Fanhams Hall Rd SG12 ...93 F3
Fanhams Rd SG12 .....93 E2
Fanshaw Ct SG14 ..... 113 C7
Fanshawe Cres SG12 .....93 C2
Fanshawe St SG14 ..... 113 D7
Fanshaws La SG13 ..... 133 C5
Fantail La HP23 .....99 F4
Faraday Cl
 Luton LU4 .....44 C1
 Watford WD18 ..... 166 D3
Faraday Gdns SG5 .....11 C1
Faraday Ho WD18 ..... 166 D3
Faraday Rd SG2 .....51 B6
Fareham Ho HP2 ..... 124 D2
Far End AL10 ..... 130 B2
Faringdon Rd LU4 .....44 C1
Faringford Cl EN6 ..... 159 D8

Farland Rd HP2 ...125 B3
Farley Ct LU1 ...63 C5
Farley Farm Rd LU1 ...63 B5
FARLEY HILL ...63 C5
Farley Hill LU1 ...63 C5
Farley Jun Sch LU1 ...63 C6
Farley Lo LU1 ...63 D5
Farm Ave AL5 ...85 D4
Farmbrook LU2 ...45 D7
Farm Cl
 Barnet EN5 ...171 C4
 Borehamwood WD6 ...156 E1
 Cheshunt EN8 ...148 C1
 Cuffley EN6 ...146 E4
 Harpenden AL5 ...85 D4
 Hertford LU2 ...113 A6
 Letchworth Garden City SG6 ...12 A1
 London Colney WD7 ...142 E1
 Roydon CM19 ...116 B1
 Shenleybury WD7 ...156 E8
 Stevenage SG1 ...50 E4
 Welwyn Garden City AL8 ...110 C6
Farm Cotts LU2 ...93 D5
Farm Cres AL2 ...142 E1
Farm End HA6 ...174 B2
Farmers Cl WD25 ...154 B6
Farmery Ct HP4 ...122 E6
Farm Field WD17 ...153 E1
Farm Gn LU1 ...63 C5
Farm Hill Rd EN9 ...163 D6
Farmhouse Cl EN10 ...148 F6
Farmhouse La HP2 ...125 A5
Farmhouse The HP2 ...125 A5
Farm La
 Hoddesdon EN11 ...135 C8
 Rickmansworth WD3 ...165 C6
 Standon SG11 ...73 A8
Farm Pl HP4 ...121 F5
Farm Rd
 Little Chalfont WD3 ...164 A5
 Northwood HA6 ...174 C5
 Slip End LU1 ...85 B7
 St Albans AL1 ...128 B4
Farmstead Rd HA3 ...176 D1
Farm Way
 Bushey WD23 ...168 B3
 Moor Park HA6 ...174 F6
Farne Ho WD18 ...166 F3
FARNHAM ...58 D6
Farnham CE Prim Sch CM23 ...58 D6
Farnham Cl
 Bovingdon HP3 ...137 A3
 Sawbridgeworth CM21 ...97 C1
Farnham Gn CM23 ...58 B7
FARNHAM GREEN ...58 B7
Farnley Gr LU2 ...64 A7
Farquhar St SG14 ...113 C7
Farraline Rd WD18 ...167 B5
Farrant Way WD6 ...169 E8
Farr Top AL3 ...83 E5
Farriday Cl AL3 ...127 E7
Farrier Ct SG8 ...7 C7

Felden Lawns HP3 ...138 A7
Felix La LU2 ...46 A2
Fellowes La AL4 ...143 E8
Fellowes Way SG2 ...51 A2
Fell Path WD6 ...170 D4
Felmersham La LU1 ...63 B7
Felmersham Rd LU1 ...63 A7
Felmongers CM20 ...118 B2
Felstead Cl LU2 ...45 F3
Felstead Rd EN8 ...162 E7
Felstead Way LU2 ...45 F3
Felton Cl
 Borehamwood WD6 ...156 C1
 Cheshunt EN10 ...148 F6
 Luton LU2 ...46 D1
Fen End SG5 ...11 F8
Fennycroft Rd HP1 ...124 A6
Fensomes Alley HP2 ...124 D4
Fensom's Cl HP2 ...124 D4
Fenswick Cl LU3 ...45 B5
Fenwick Path WD6 ...156 F1
Ferguson Gr EN8 ...148 D2
Fermor Cres LU2 ...46 C1
Fern Ct EN10 ...148 F8
Fern Ct HP4 ...122 B4
Ferndale
 Harpenden AL5 ...86 A2
 Much Hadham SG10 ...74 F2
Ferndale Rd
 Enfield EN3 ...162 E2
 Luton LU3 ...63 B7
Fern Dells AL10 ...129 F4
Ferndene AL2 ...154 F8
Ferndown HA6 ...175 A1
Ferndown Cl HA5 ...175 E3
Ferndown Rd WD19 ...175 C6
Fern Dr HP3 ...124 E2
Ferncroft AL1 ...141 D8
Ferney Rd EN7 ...147 D5
Fern Gr AL8 ...89 D2
Fernheath LU3 ...31 A1
Fern Ho HA7 ...176 F4
Fernleigh Ct HA2 ...176 B1
Fernleys AL4 ...128 D3
Ferns Cl EN3 ...162 E3
Ferns The AL3 ...127 D7
Fernville La HP2 ...124 D3
Fern Way WD25 ...154 B4
Ferny Hill EN4 ...159 F1
Ferrars Cl LU4 ...44 B1
Ferrars Inf Sch LU4 ...44 B3
Ferrars Jun Sch LU4 ...44 B3
Ferrars La AL4 ...108 B5
Ferrier Rd SG2 ...51 C6
Ferryhills Cl WD19 ...175 C7
Feryngs Cl CM17 ...118 C4
Fesants Croft CM20 ...118 B3
Fetherstone Cl EN6 ...159 D7
Fiddlebridge Ind Ctr AL10 ...129 F6
Fiddle Bridge La AL10 ...129 F6
Fidler Pl WD23 ...168 B3
Field Cl
 Harpenden AL5 ...107 D7
 St Albans AL4 ...128 A7
Field Cres SG8 ...7 F7
Field End EN5 ...171 B5
Field End Cl
 Luton LU2 ...46 C4
 Watford WD19 ...167 E2
 Wigginton HP23 ...100 D1
Fielder Ctr (Univ of Herts) AL10 ...129 D8
Fielders Way WD7 ...156 E6
Fieldfare
 Letchworth Garden City SG6 ...11 G1
 Stevenage SG2 ...51 D3
Fieldfare Gn LU4 ...44 A5
Fieldfares AL2 ...142 D4
Fieldfare Way SG8 ...7 E8
Fieldgate Ho SG1 ...50 F5
Field Gate Mews WD17 ...167 C4
Fieldgate Rd LU4 ...44 D2
Field Ho WD6 ...169 D4
Field Inf Sch WD18 ...167 C4
Fieldings Rd EN8 ...148 F2
Field Jun Sch WD18 ...167 C4
Field La SG6 ...22 F4
Field Rd
 Hemel Hempstead HP2 ...125 A3
 Watford WD19 ...167 E3
Fields End HP23 ...100 A6
Fields End La HP1 ...123 E5
Field View Rd EN6 ...159 D6
Field View Rise AL2 ...140 E2
Fieldway
 Berkhamsted HP4 ...122 C2
 Stansted Abbotts SG12 ...115 B4
 Wigginton HP23 ...100 D1
Field Way
 Bovingdon HP3 ...137 A4
 Hoddesdon EN11 ...115 C2
 Rickmansworth WD3 ...165 B1
Fifth Ave
 Letchworth Garden City SG6 ...23 C6
 Watford WD25 ...154 D4

Fifth Ave / Allende Ave CM20 ...117 C3
Figtree Hill HP2 ...124 D4
Filey Cl SG1 ...50 A7
Filiano Ct LU2 ...45 D1
Fillingham Way AL10 ...129 E2
Filmer Rd LU4 ...44 E4
Filton Ho WD19 ...175 D7
Finbracks SG1 ...37 A4
Finch Cl
 Hatfield AL10 ...130 A3
 Luton LU4 ...44 A4
Finchdale HP1 ...124 A3
Finche's End SG2 ...52 B8
Finches The
 Hertford SG13 ...114 B6
 Hitchin SG4 ...35 A7
Finch Gn WD3 ...164 F5
Finch La WD23 ...168 A5
Finchley Rd LU4 ...44 A6
Finley Rd AL5 ...86 D3
Finsbury Ct EN8 ...162 E5
Finsbury Rd LU4 ...44 D5
Finucane Rise WD23 ...176 C8
Finway LU3 ...63 A8
Finway Ct WD18 ...166 F4
Finway Rd HP2 ...125 B7
Firbank Dr WD19 ...167 E2
Firbank Ind Est LU1 ...63 A8
Firbank Rd AL3 ...127 F7
Fir Cl SG2 ...50 F1
Firecrest SG6 ...11 E1
Fire Station Alley EN5 ...171 E7
Firlands AL10 ...130 A4
Firlands Ho CM23 ...76 E6
Firs Cl
 Hatfield AL10 ...130 B4
 Hitchin SG5 ...34 D8
Firs Dr AL4 ...87 C5
Firs La EN6 ...159 B6
Firs Pk The AL9 ...145 A8
First Ave WD25 ...154 D4
First Ave / Mandela Ave CM20 ...117 F2
First Garden City Heritage Mus* SG6 ...23 A5
Firs The
 Hammond Street EN7 ...147 E4
 Harpenden AL5 ...86 D2
 St Albans AL1 ...142 B7
 Welwyn Garden City AL8 ...89 C2
 Wigginton HP23 ...100 D1
Firs Wlk
 Burnham Green AL6 ...90 E5
 Northwood HA6 ...174 D4
Firs Wood Cl EN6 ...159 F7
Firsthdens Vinyard* HP4 ...123 B8
Fir Tree Cl HP3 ...125 B2
Fir Tree Cl WD6 ...169 F5
Fir Tree Hill WD3 ...153 A2
Firway AL6 ...89 F7
Firway Cl AL6 ...89 F7
Firwood Ave AL4 ...128 E3
Fisher Cl
 Holdbrook EN3 ...163 B2
 Kings Langley WD4 ...139 A2
Fishermans Way EN11 ...135 D8
Fisher Rd HA3 ...176 F1
Fishers Cl
 Holdbrook EN8 ...163 A5
 Standon SG11 ...55 D3
Fishers Ct WD17 ...167 E6
FISHERS GREEN ...36 A1
Fisher's Green Rd SG1 ...50 B8
Fishers Hatch CM20 ...117 C1
Fisher's Ind Est WD18 ...167 C4
Fishers Hoo SG14 ...113 D6
Fishers Mead SG1 ...55 D3
Fishery Cotts HP1 ...124 A1
Fishery Pas HP1 ...124 B1
Fishery Rd HP1 ...124 A1
Fish Hill SG8 ...7 D6
Fishponds Rd SG5 ...34 E8
Fishpool St AL3 ...127 C3
Fish St AL3 ...127 D3
Fish Street Farm AL3 ...106 B5
Fitzjohn Ave EN5 ...171 F5
Fitzroy Ave LU3 ...45 B3
Fitzwarin Cl LU3 ...44 E8
Fitzwilliam Ct WD6 ...169 F8
Fitzwilliams Ct CM17 ...118 E4
Five Acres
 Kings Langley WD4 ...138 F2
 London Colney AL2 ...142 D6
 Stansted Mountfitchet CM24 ...59 E8
Five Acres Ave AL2 ...140 F2
Five Fields Cl WD19 ...175 F7
Five Oaks
 Caddington LU1 ...62 F4
 Luton LU1 ...62 F4
Five Oaks Mid Sch LU1 ...62 F3
Five Springs LU3 ...44 E6
Five Springs Ct LU3 ...44 E6
Flackwell Ho WD18 ...166 E3
Flagstaff Cl EN9 ...163 B6
Flagstaff Rd EN9 ...163 B6
Flags The HP2 ...125 B3
Flamingo Cl AL10 ...129 D6
FLAMSTEAD ...84 B1
Flamsteadbury La AL3 ...106 A4
FLAMSTEAD END ...148 B4

Flamstead End Prim Sch EN7 ...148 A4
Flamstead End Rd EN8 ...148 B3
Flamstead Village Sch AL3 ...84 B1
Flandrian Cl EN3 ...163 B1
Flash La EN2 ...161 C3
Flatfield Rd HP3 ...125 A1
FLAUNDEN ...151 A6
Flaunden Bottom HP3, HP5 ...150 E4
Flaunden Hill HP3 ...151 A6
Flaunden Ho WD18 ...166 E2
Flaunden La
 Bovingdon HP3 ...137 D3
 Sarratt WD3 ...151 E6
Flaunden Pk HP3 ...151 A8
Flavian Cl AL3 ...126 F1
Flax Mews AL3 ...83 E5
Flecker Cl HA7 ...176 F5
Fleet The SG8 ...7 C6
FLEETVILLE ...128 B3
Fleetville Inf Sch AL1 ...128 B3
Fleetville Jun Sch AL1 ...128 A3
Fleetwood SG6 ...23 D8
Fleetwood Cres SG1 ...50 B7
Fleetwood Way WD19 ...175 C6
Fleming Cl EN7 ...148 A5
Fleming Cres SG14 ...113 A6
Fleming Dr SG5 ...11 D2
Fleming Rd EN9 ...163 B4
Fletcher Way HP2 ...124 D5
Flete Ho WD18 ...166 E3
Flexley Wood AL7 ...90 A1
Flight Path SG16 ...10 B3
Flinders Cl
 St Albans AL1 ...128 A1
 Stevenage SG2 ...51 D5
Flint Cl LU3 ...44 E7
Flint Copse AL3 ...106 C6
Flint Cotts SG5 ...33 A2
Flint Ct LU1 ...63 D5
Flintings The HP2 ...103 F8
Flint Rd SG6 ...23 C8
Flint Way AL3 ...127 C7
Flora Gr AL1 ...127 E5
Floral Dr AL2 ...142 D5
Florence Ave LU3 ...44 D6
Florence Cl WD25 ...154 A4
Florence Ct HA6 ...174 E4
Florence Ho WD18 ...166 F6
Florence Longman Ho HP3 ...138 D7
Florence St SG5 ...34 F8
Florence Wlk CM23 ...76 F8
Florida Cl WD23 ...176 D8
Flowers End LU1 ...63 E6
Flowers Way LU1 ...63 E7
Flowton Gr AL5 ...107 A7
Floyds Barns HP22 ...66 C2
Fog Cotts HP23 ...101 A5
Fogerty Cl EN3 ...163 B2
Fold Croft CM20 ...117 A1
Foldingshott SG3 ...69 D3
Follett Dr WD5 ...153 F8
Folly Ave AL3 ...127 C4
Folly Cl
 Hitchin SG4 ...35 A5
 Radlett WD7 ...155 F3
Folly Fields AL4 ...87 B2
Folly La
 Caddington LU1 ...62 E4
 St Albans AL3 ...127 C4
Folly Path SG4 ...35 A5
Folly Pathway WD7 ...155 F3
Folly The
 Buntingford SG9 ...40 D7
 Hertford SG14 ...113 D6
FOLLY THE
 Radlett ...155 F3
 Wheathampstead ...87 B2
Folly View SG12 ...115 B4
Fontmell Cl AL3 ...127 E5
Fontwell Cl HA3 ...176 F5
Football Cl SG7 ...12 E1
Forbes Ave EN6 ...159 D7
Ford Cl WD23 ...168 C5
Ford Cotts SG11 ...79 F8
FORD END ...30 E4
Ford End Watermill* LU7 ...80 E6
Ford Field SG11 ...75 A8
Fordham Cl SG7 ...4 D4
Fordham Rd SG8 ...7 E5
Fordhams Terr SG8 ...15 F7
Fordhams Wood (Nature Reserve)* SG8 ...6 E4
Ford La SG2 ...52 A3
Ford St SG11 ...55 A5
Fordwich Cl SG14 ...113 A6
Fordwich Rd AL8 ...110 C5
Fordwich Rise SG14 ...113 A6
Forebury Ave CM21 ...97 F2
Forebury Cres CM21 ...97 F2
Forebury The CM21 ...97 F2
Forefield AL2 ...141 A4
Forelands Pl CM21 ...97 E2
Fore St
 Harlow CM17 ...118 C4
 Hatfield AL9 ...130 C6
 Hertford SG14 ...113 D6
 Weston SG4 ...24 B1
Forest Ave HP3 ...124 D1

Foresters Cl EN7 ...147 E4
Foresthall Rd CM24 ...59 E4
Forest La WD7 ...156 B8
Forest Rd
 Cheshunt EN8 ...148 D2
 Enfield EN3 ...162 E3
 Watford WD25 ...154 B6
Forest Row SG2 ...50 E1
Forest Wlk WD23 ...167 F8
Forfar Ho WD19 ...175 C7
Forge Cl
 Chipperfield WD4 ...152 A8
 Hitchin SG5 ...34 F8
Forge Cotts
 Essendon AL9 ...131 E8
 Hatfield Heath CM22 ...98 F3
Forge End
 Chiswell Green AL2 ...141 A5
 Weston SG4 ...24 C1
Forge La
 Northwood HA6 ...174 E3
 Welwyn AL6 ...89 C5
Forge Mews WD3 ...165 E1
Forres Cl EN11 ...135 A8
Forres Prim Sch LU1 ...115 B1
Forrest Cres LU2 ...46 A3
Forrester Ho AL1 ...127 D3
Forresters Dr AL7 ...111 C5
Fortnums Acre HA7 ...176 F4
Fortuna Cl SG1 ...51 C8
Fortune La WD6 ...169 D3
Forty Hall* EN2 ...161 F2
Forty Hill EN2 ...161 F1
Forty Hill CE Prim Sch EN2 ...162 A2
Forty Hill Ho EN2 ...161 F1
Forum Ctr The SG1 ...50 D5
Forum The
 Stevenage SG1 ...50 D5
 Tring HP23 ...99 E4
Fosberry Ct EN3 ...163 A2
Foskett Ho SG5 ...34 D8
Fosse Ho AL3 ...127 A2
Foster Cl
 Cheshunt EN8 ...148 E1
 Stevenage SG1 ...36 D1
Foster Dr SG4 ...35 A5
Foster Rd HP4 ...124 B1
Foston Cl LU3 ...44 F6
Fotherley Rd WD3 ...172 F8
Foulds Sch EN5 ...171 D6
Founceley Ave SG12 ...71 F4
Founders Rd EN11 ...115 B1
Foundry Gate EN8 ...162 E6
Fountain Ct
 Borehamwood WD6 ...170 A7
 Cheshunt EN8 ...148 D1
Fountain Dr SG13 ...113 F7
Fountain Pl EN7 ...163 C5
Fountain Row SG4 ...35 B6
Fountains Rd LU3 ...45 D3
Fouracres SG6 ...23 A3
Four Acres
 Stevenage SG1 ...50 D7
 Welwyn Garden City AL7 ...110 F4
Fouracres Dr HP3 ...124 F1
Four Acres The CM21 ...98 A2
Fouracres Wlk HP3 ...124 F1
Fourdrinier Way HP3 ...138 D8
Four Lanes AL4 ...108 D4
Four Swannes Prim Sch EN8 ...162 E6
Fourth Ave
 Harlow CM20 ...117 C1
 Letchworth Garden City SG6 ...23 C7
 Luton LU3 ...44 D7
 Watford WD25 ...154 D4
Four Trees AL2 ...141 B7
Four Tubs The WD23 ...168 C3
Fourways SG13 ...133 A5
Fourways Ct EN11 ...135 A7
Fourways Market AL9 ...144 C7
Fovant Cl AL5 ...107 C6
Fovant Ct SG1 ...36 B1
Fowley Cl EN8 ...162 F5
Fowley Mead Pk EN8 ...163 A5
Fowlmere Rd LU2 ...45 D6
Foxbury Cl LU2 ...45 D6
Fox Cl
 Bushey WD23 ...168 B5
 Elstree WD6 ...169 D3
 Wigginton HP23 ...100 D1
Fox Cnr SG8 ...1 F5
Foxcroft AL1 ...128 A1
Foxdell HA6 ...174 D4
Foxdell Inf Sch LU1 ...63 A8
Foxdell Jun Sch LU1 ...62 E8
Foxdells CM23 ...112 C3
Foxdells La LU1 ...58 F2
Foxes Cl SG13 ...114 B6
Foxes Dr EN7 ...148 A2
Foxes La EN6 ...146 E3
Foxes Par EN9 ...163 C6
Foxfield SG2 ...51 C3
Foxfield Cl HA6 ...174 F4
Foxglove Bank SG8 ...7 F5
Foxglove Cl
 Bishop's Stortford CM23 ...76 C6
 Hatfield AL10 ...130 B4
 Hoddesdon EN11 ...115 C1

Foxgloves The HP1 . . . . .123 E2
Foxglove Way
  Luton LU3 . . . . .45 D2
  Oaklands AL6 . . . . .89 E8
Foxgrove Path WD19 . . . .175 D5
Foxhill
  Luton LU2 . . . . .45 E5
  Watford WD24 . . . . .154 A3
Fox Hill SG8 . . . . .1 F5
Fox Hill Rd SG8 . . . . .1 F5
Foxholes Ave SG13 . . . . . .113 F6
Foxhollows
  Hatfield AL10 . . . . .130 B7
  London Colney AL2 . . . . . .142 C5
Fox La SG8 . . . . .15 F7
Foxlands Cl WD25 . . . . . . .154 A5
Foxley Dr CM23 . . . . .77 B8
Foxley Gr AL6 . . . . .89 F4
Foxleys WD19 . . . . .175 E7
Fox Rd
  Stevenage SG1 . . . . .50 E4
  Wigginton HP23 . . . . .100 C2
Fox's La AL9 . . . . .144 F7
Foxton Rd EN11 . . . . .135 A6
Foxtree Ho WD25 . . . . . . .154 E3
Foxwood Chase EN9 . . . .163 C4
Foyle Cl SG1 . . . . .37 C3
Frampton Rd EN6 . . . . . . .145 C1
Frampton St SG14 . . . . . . .113 D6
Frances Ho HP3 . . . . .138 E6
Francis Ave AL3 . . . . .127 D6
Francis Bacon Sch
  AL1 . . . . .142 B8
Francis Cl
  Hitchin SG4 . . . . .35 A5
  Stotfold SG5 . . . . .11 E6
Francis Combe Sch & Com
  Coll WD25 . . . . .154 C7
Francis Ct
  Harlow CM20 . . . . .117 B2
  St Albans AL1 . . . . .127 E2
Francis Green Ho [7]
  EN9 . . . . .163 B6
Francis House Prep Sch
  HP3 . . . . .99 F3
Francis Rd
  Hinxworth SG7 . . . . .3 C6
  Ware SG12 . . . . .93 D2
  Watford WD18 . . . . .167 B5
Francis St LU1 . . . . .63 D8
Francis Wks EN11 . . . . . . .135 B6
Frankland Cl WD3 . . . . . . .166 A2
Frankland Rd WD3 . . . . . .166 B3
Frank Lester Way LU2 . . . .64 D8
Franklin Ave
  Cheshunt EN7 . . . . .148 B1
  Watford WD18 . . . . .167 A3
Franklin Cl
  Colney Heath AL4 . . . . . . .129 E1
  Hemel Hempstead HP3 . . .138 E8
  Pirton SG5 . . . . .20 D4
Franklin Gdns SG4 . . . . . . .22 B1
Franklin Rd WD17 . . . . . . .167 B7
Franklin's Rd SG1 . . . . .50 C8
Frank Martin Ct EN7 . . . . .148 B1
Franks Cl SG16 . . . . .10 B5
Frank Young Ct SG5 . . . . . .21 D1
Franshams WD23 . . . . . . .176 D8
Fraser Rd EN6 . . . . .148 E3
Fredericks Gate LU2 . . . . . .45 E1
Frederick St LU2 . . . . .45 E1
Frederick Street Pas
  LU2 . . . . .45 E1
Fred Millard Ct SG1 . . . . . .50 E5
Freeman Ave LU3 . . . . .45 B8
Freemans Cl SG5 . . . . .21 D1
Freewaters Cl SG5 . . . . . . .21 E4
FREEZY WATER 162 E3
Freezywater St George's
  CE Prim Sch EN1 . . . . . . .162 D3
Freman Coll SG9 . . . . .40 D8
Freman Dr SG9 . . . . .40 D8
French Horn Ct [5]
  SG12 . . . . .93 D1
French Horn La AL10 . . . .130 B6
French Lo SG5 . . . . .34 F8
French Row [4] AL3 . . . . .127 D3
French's Cl SG12 . . . . .115 B4
French's Yd [2] SG12 . . . . .93 D1
Frensham EN7 . . . . .148 A4
Frensham Dr SG4 . . . . .22 C2
Frere Ct CM23 . . . . .58 F1
Freshwater Cl LU3 . . . . .44 F7
Freshwaters CM20 . . . . . .117 C1
Fresson Rd SG1 . . . . .50 D8
Fretherne Rd AL8 . . . . . . .110 D6
Friars Cl LU1 . . . . .63 B5
Friarscroft EN10 . . . . .135 A3
Friars Ct LU1 . . . . .63 B5
Friars Field HP4 . . . . .121 E7
Friars Rd
  Braughing SG11 . . . . .56 A7
  Weston SG4 . . . . .24 B1
Friars Way
  Kings Langley WD4 . . . . . .139 A1
  Luton LU1 . . . . .63 B5
  Watford WD23 . . . . .167 F8
Friars Wlk HP23 . . . . .100 A4
Friars Wood CM23 . . . . . . .77 C8
Friday Furlong SG5 . . . . . . .34 C8
Friedberg Ave CM23 . . . . . .76 D4
Friendless La AL3 . . . . .83 F2
Friends Ave EN8 . . . . .162 D7
Friern Cl [6] EN7 . . . . .147 E5
Friesian Cl LU4 . . . . .44 A3

Frimley Rd HP1 . . . . .123 E4
Fringewood Cl HA6 . . . . . .174 E2
Frinton Cl WD19 . . . . .175 B8
Friston Gn LU2 . . . . .46 D1
FRITHSDEN 122 D4
Frithsden Copse HP4 . . . .122 F8
FRITHSDEN GARDENS
  . . . . .102 F1
Frithwood Ave HA6 . . . . . .174 F4
Frithwood Prim Sch
  HA6 . . . . .174 F4
Frobisher Dr WD23 . . . . . .168 A3
Frobisher Dr SG2 . . . . .51 B7
Frobisher Rd AL1 . . . . . . .128 C1
Frobisher Way AL10 . . . . .129 D8
Froghall Cotts WD6 . . . . .170 D3
Froghall La SG2 . . . . .38 B1
Frogmoor Ct WD3 . . . . . .173 D8
Frogmoor La WD3 . . . . . .173 D8
FROGMORE 141 E4
Frogmore AL2 . . . . .141 E4
Frogmore Bsns Pk
  AL2 . . . . .141 E3
FROGMORE END 138 E7
Frogmore Hill SG14 . . . . . .70 B7
Frogmore Ho SG1 . . . . .36 C1
Frogmore Home Pk
  AL2 . . . . .141 D4
Frogmore Rd Ind Est
  HP3 . . . . .138 D8
Frogmore St HP23 . . . . . .100 A3
Frogs Hall La SG12 . . . . . . .53 F3
Frome Cl LU4 . . . . .44 E4
Frome Sq HP2 . . . . .125 A8
Front St LU1 . . . . .63 C1
Front The HP4 . . . . .123 B7
Frost Ho HP4 . . . . .122 C3
Frowick Cl AL9 . . . . .144 B8
Frowycke Cres EN6 . . . . . .158 A7
Fry Rd SG2 . . . . .51 C5
Fryth Mead AL3 . . . . .127 B4
Fulbeck Way HA2 . . . . . . .176 C1
Fulbourne Cl LU4 . . . . .44 E2
Fulford Gr WD19 . . . . .175 B8
Fuller Cl WD23 . . . . .168 D2
Fuller Cl [8] CM23 . . . . . . .77 A7
Fuller Gdns WD24 . . . . . .154 B2
Fuller Rd WD24 . . . . .154 B2
Fuller's Almshouses
  CM24 . . . . .59 F6
Fullers Cl EN9 . . . . .163 F6
Fullers Cl SG6 . . . . .22 E7
Fullerton Cl AL3 . . . . .83 E6
Fuller Way WD3 . . . . .166 A4
Fulling Mill La AL6 . . . . . . .89 B6
Fulmar Cres HP1 . . . . .124 A3
Fulmore Cl AL5 . . . . .86 D4
Fulton Cl SG1 . . . . .50 C5
Fulton Cres CM23 . . . . .77 C8
Fulton Ct
  Borehamwood WD6 . . . . .156 F1
  [3] Holdbrook EN3 . . . . . .163 A1
Furham Feild HA5 . . . . . . .176 A3
Furlay Cl SG6 . . . . .22 D7
Furlongs HP1 . . . . .124 A4
Furlong The HP23 . . . . . . .100 A3
Furlong Way SG12 . . . . . . .115 A7
Furmston Ct SG6 . . . . .23 A7
FURNEUX PELHAM 43 A4
Furneux Pelham CE Sch
  SG9 . . . . .43 A4
Furriers Cl CM23 . . . . .76 C5
Furrowfield AL10 . . . . .130 B7
Furrows The LU3 . . . . .45 B7
Furse Ave AL4 . . . . .128 A7
Furtherfield WD5 . . . . .153 E7
FURTHER FORD END 30 D6
Furtherground [1]
  HP2 . . . . .124 E2
Furzebushes La AL2 . . . . .140 F6
Furze Cl
  Luton LU2 . . . . .45 D2
  South Oxhey WD19 . . . . . .175 C5
Furzedown SG2 . . . . .51 B4
Furzedown Ct [18] AL5 . . . .86 B1
Furzefield EN8 . . . . .148 B3
Furzefield Ct EN6 . . . . .158 E8
Furzefield Ctr The
  EN6 . . . . .158 D8
Furzefield Rd AL7 . . . . . . .110 E4
Furze Gr SG8 . . . . .7 E5
Furzehill Par WD6 . . . . . . .170 A6
Furzehill Rd WD6 . . . . .170 B5
Furzen Cres AL10 . . . . . . .129 F2
Furze Rd HP1 . . . . .123 E2
Furze View WD3 . . . . .164 C4
Fyffes Cl SG5 . . . . .34 F8

G

Gable Cl
  Abbots Langley WD5 . . . .153 E7
  Pinner HA5 . . . . .176 A3
Gables Ave EN4 . . . . .169 F6
Gables Lo EN4 . . . . .159 C1
Gables The
  [3] Hemel Hempstead
    HP1 . . . . .124 D4
  Sawbridgeworth CM21 . . . .97 E2
  Watford WD17 . . . . .167 C2
  Watford, Woodside
    WD25 . . . . .154 D6
Gaddesden Cres
  WD25 . . . . .154 E5
Gaddesden Gr AL7 . . . . . .111 B6
Gaddesden La AL3 . . . . . .105 C4

GADDESDEN ROW 104 C6
Gaddesden Row HP2 . . . .104 C6
Gaddesden Row Jun Mix
  Inf Sch HP2 . . . . .104 B6
Gade Ave WD18 . . . . .166 B5
Gade Bank WD1 . . . . .166 D5
GADEBRIDGE 124 A5
Gadebridge Ct HP1 . . . . . .124 C4
Gadebridge La
  Hemel Hempstead,
    Gadebridge HP1 . . . . . . .124 B5
  Hemel Hempstead HP1 . . .124 C5
Gadebridge Rd HP1 . . . . . .124 B4
Gadebridge Hts HP1 . . . .124 C3
Gade Cl
  Hemel Hempstead
    HP1 . . . . .124 B4
  Watford WD18 . . . . .166 C5
Gadeside WD24, WD25 . . .153 E4
Gade Twr HP3 . . . . .138 F6
Gade Valley Cl WD4 . . . . .139 A3
Gade Valley Cotts
  HP1 . . . . .103 C4
Gade View Gdns
  WD4 . . . . .153 C5
Gadeview Rd HP3 . . . . . . .138 D7
Gadmore La HP23 . . . . . . .119 F7
Gadsby Ct [20] LU1 . . . . . . .63 D6
Gadswell Cl WD25 . . . . . .154 E3
Gage Cl SG8 . . . . .7 D7
Gainsborough Ave
  AL1 . . . . .127 E4
Gainsborough Cl LU2 . . . . .45 F2
Gainsford Cres SG4 . . . . . .22 C2
Gainswood AL7 . . . . .110 E5
Gaitskell Ho WD6 . . . . . . .170 D5
Gall End La CM24 . . . . .59 F7
Galleria The AL10 . . . . . . .129 F5
Gallery The
  Letchworth Garden City
    SG6 . . . . .22 F6
  [7] Luton LU1 . . . . .63 E7
Galleycroft Cl [4]
  AL10 . . . . .130 A6
Galley Gn SG13 . . . . .115 A2
Galley Hill HP1 . . . . .124 B6
Galleyhill Rd EN9 . . . . . . .163 E7
Galley La EN5 . . . . .171 B6
Galleywood SG5 . . . . .21 D4
Galliard Cl LU3 . . . . .45 A4
Galloway Cl
  [1] Bishop's Stortford
    CM23 . . . . .76 F8
  Cheshunt EN10 . . . . .148 F5
Galloway Rd CM23 . . . . . . .58 F1
Gallows Hill WD4 . . . . . . .153 C7
Gallows Hill La WD5 . . . . .153 B6
Galston Rd LU3 . . . . .44 D8
Games Yd SG1 . . . . .50 E4
Gammon Cl HP3 . . . . .125 A2
Gammons Farm Cl
  WD24 . . . . .153 F3
Gammons La WD17,
  WD24 . . . . .154 A2
Gamnel HP23 . . . . .100 B6
Gamnel Mews HP23 . . . . .100 B7
Ganders Ash WD25 . . . . . .154 A6
Gandhi Ct [1] WD24 . . . . .167 D7
Gangies Hill CM21 . . . . . . .97 A4
Gant Ct EN9 . . . . .163 F5
Garden Wlk WD19 . . . . . . .175 E6
GANWICK CORNER 159 B4
Ganymede Pl HP2 . . . . . . .124 F6
Gaping La SG5 . . . . .34 D7
Garden Ave AL10 . . . . .130 A2
Garden Cl
  Barnet EN5 . . . . .171 C5
  Harpenden AL5 . . . . .107 A5
  Royston SG8 . . . . .7 C6
  St Albans AL1 . . . . .128 B4
  Watford WD17 . . . . .166 F7
  Woolmer Green SG3 . . . . . .69 B2
Garden Cotts
  Park Street AL2 . . . . .141 E4
  Standon SG11 . . . . .73 A8
Garden Ct
  Hoddesdon EN10 . . . . . . .134 F4
  Luton LU3 . . . . .45 A4
  Welwyn Garden City
    AL7 . . . . .110 E7
  Wheathampstead AL4 . . . . .87 D1
Garden Field SG2 . . . . .51 E2
Garden Field La HP4 . . . . .122 F2
Garden Fields Jun Mix Inf
  Sch AL3 . . . . .127 D6
Garden Ho SG13 . . . . .113 C5
Garden Hos The CM21 . . . .96 B3
Gardenia Ave LU3 . . . . .45 A4
Garden La SG8 . . . . .7 D5
Garden Rd
  Abbots Langley WD5 . . . .153 E8
  Buntingford SG9 . . . . .40 E8
  Woolmer Green SG3 . . . . . .69 B2
Garden Row [6] SG5 . . . . . .34 F8
Gardens of the Rose The*
  AL2 . . . . .140 F5
Gardens The
  Baldock SG7 . . . . .23 E8
  Brookmans Park AL9 . . . .144 E4
  Henlow SG16 . . . . .10 D8
  Stotfold SG5 . . . . .11 E6
  Watford WD17 . . . . .166 F7
Garden Terr SG12 . . . . .92 E4
Garden Terrace Rd [2]
  CM17 . . . . .118 C4

Garden Wlk
  Royston SG8 . . . . .7 E7
  Stevenage SG1 . . . . .50 E5
Gardiners La SG7 . . . . .4 D4
Gardner Ct
  Luton LU1 . . . . .63 E4
  Watford WD25 . . . . .154 C4
GARDNERS END 39 B3
Gareth Ct WD6 . . . . .156 F1
Garfield Ct LU2 . . . . .46 D3
Garfield St WD24 . . . . .154 B1
Garland Cl
  Hemel Hempstead HP2 . . .124 D4
Garland Ct [6] AL1 . . . . . .127 E3
Garland Rd SG12 . . . . .93 E1
Garnault Rd EN1 . . . . .161 F1
Garner Dr EN10 . . . . .148 E5
Garnett Cl WD24 . . . . .154 D3
Garnett Dr AL2 . . . . .140 F2
Garrard Way AL4 . . . . .108 D8
Garratts Rd WD23 . . . . . . .168 C2
Garretts Cl SG14 . . . . .113 C6
Garretts Mead LU2 . . . . . . .46 B3
Garrison Ct [2] SG4 . . . . . .34 F7
Garrowsfield EN5 . . . . . . .171 F4
Garsmouth Way
  WD25 . . . . .154 D3
GARSTON 154 C4
Garston Cres WD25 . . . . . .154 C5
Garston Dr WD25 . . . . . . .154 D5
Garston La WD25 . . . . . . .154 D5
Garston Manor Sch
  WD25 . . . . .154 C7
Garston Park Par
  WD25 . . . . .154 D4
Garston Sta WD25 . . . . . . .154 D4
Garter Ct [18] AL1 . . . . . . .45 D1
Garthland Dr EN5 . . . . . . .171 C4
Garth Rd SG6 . . . . .22 E3
Garth The WD5 . . . . .153 D6
Gartlet Rd WD17 . . . . .167 C6
Gascoyne Cl EN6 . . . . .158 A7
Gascoyne Way SG13,
  SG14 . . . . .113 D5
Gas La SG8 . . . . .17 C3
Gaskarth Cl SG12 . . . . . . .114 E8
Gaskin's Gallop SG12 . . . .115 B4
Gaskin's Ride HP4 . . . . . .122 E5
Gilroy Rd [10] HP2 . . . . . . .124 D4
Gisland Ct LU3 . . . . .163 E4
GILSTON 117 E5
Gilston Mews CM20 . . . . .117 C6

Gibbons Cl
  Borehamwood WD6 . . . . .169 E8
  Sandridge AL4 . . . . .108 C1
Gibbons Way SG3 . . . . .68 F5
Gibbs Cl EN6 . . . . .148 D2
Gibbs Couch WD19 . . . . . .175 D7
Gibbs Field CM23 . . . . .76 D5
Gibraltar Lo AL5 . . . . .86 D3
Gibson Cl SG4 . . . . .35 B7
Gidian Ct AL2 . . . . .141 D4
Gifford's La SG11 . . . . .54 A2
Gilbert Burnet Ho
  HP1 . . . . .124 F1
Gilbert Ct AL5 . . . . .86 B4
Gilbert Ho WD25 . . . . .154 D4
Gilbert's Hill HP23 . . . . . .119 E3
Gilbert St EN3 . . . . .162 C4
Gilbert Way HP4 . . . . .122 A4
Gilbey Ave CM23 . . . . .77 B6
Gilbey Cres CM24 . . . . .59 E8
Gildea Cl HA5 . . . . .176 C4
Gilden Cl CM17 . . . . .118 E4
Gilden Way CM17 . . . . . . .118 D3
Gilder Cl LU3 . . . . .45 A8
Gilderdale LU4 . . . . .44 B6
Gilders CM21 . . . . .97 D2
Giles Cl AL4 . . . . .108 C1
Giles Inf Sch The SG1 . . . . .37 A1
Giles Jun Sch SG1 . . . . .37 A1
Gilhams Ct HP4 . . . . .122 B5
Giliam St LU2 . . . . .63 E8
Gillan Gn WD23 . . . . .176 C8
Gill Cl WD18 . . . . .166 C3
Gillian Ave AL1 . . . . .141 C7
Gillian Ho HA3 . . . . .176 E4
Gilliat's Gn WD3 . . . . .164 D5
Gilliflower Ho EN11 . . . . . .135 A5
Gillings Ct EN5 . . . . .171 E5
Gillison Cl SG6 . . . . .23 B5
Gills Hill WD7 . . . . .155 F4
Gills Hill La WD7 . . . . .155 F3
Gills Hollow WD7 . . . . . . .155 F3
Gillsted Ct AL3 . . . . .127 D7
Gilmour Cl EN2 . . . . .162 A4
Gilpin Gn AL5 . . . . .86 C1
Gilpin Rd SG12 . . . . .114 E8
Gilpin's Gallop SG12 . . . .115 B4
Gilpin's Ride HP4 . . . . . . .122 E5
Gilson Park Ho
  CM20 . . . . .117 C6
Gilston Pk CM20 . . . . .117 C6
Ginns Rd SG9 . . . . .43 D6
Gippeswyck Cl HA5 . . . . . .175 D2
Gipsy La
  Bishop's Stortford CM23,
    CM24 . . . . .59 C4
  Knebworth AL6, SG3 . . . . . .68 E4
  Luton LU1 . . . . .64 A4
Girdle Rd SG4 . . . . .22 A2
Girons Cl SG4 . . . . .35 B7
Girtin Rd WD23 . . . . .168 C5
Girton Ct EN8 . . . . .148 E1
Girton Way WD3 . . . . .166 C4
Gisburne Way WD24 . . . . .147 B6
Gladding Rd EN7 . . . . .147 E5
Gladeside AL4 . . . . .128 D6
Gladesmere Ct WD24 . . . .154 B2
Glades The HP1 . . . . .123 E4
Glade The
  Baldock SG7 . . . . .23 E7
  Letchworth Garden City
    SG6 . . . . .22 F6
  Welwyn Garden City
    AL8 . . . . .110 C8
Gladeway The EN9 . . . . . .163 D6
Gladsmuir Rd EN5 . . . . . . .171 E7
Gladstone Ave LU1 . . . . . . .63 C7
Gladstone Ct SG2 . . . . .69 A8
Gladstone Dr SG5 . . . . .11 D2
Gladstone Pl EN5 . . . . .171 D5
Gladstone Rd
  Dane End SG12 . . . . .71 F8
  Hoddesdon EN11 . . . . . . .135 B7
  Ware SG12 . . . . .93 C2
  Watford WD17 . . . . .167 C6
Gladwin Way CM20 . . . . . .117 D2
Glaisdale LU4 . . . . .44 C5
Glamis Cl
  Cheshunt EN7 . . . . .148 A2
  Hemel Hempstead HP2 . . .105 B1
Glamis Pl HP2 . . . . .124 E4
Glanfield HP2 . . . . .124 E6
Glassmill Ho [6] HP4 . . . . .122 C4
Gleave Cl AL1 . . . . .128 B4
Glebe Ave SG15 . . . . .11 A7
Glebe Cl
  Essendon AL9 . . . . .131 F6
  Hemel Hempstead HP3 . . .138 E7
  Hertford SG14 . . . . .113 D8
  Pitstone LU7 . . . . .80 D5
  Watton at St SG14 . . . . . . .70 D3
Glebe Cotts AL9 . . . . .131 F6
Glebe Ct
  Bishop's Stortford
    CM23 . . . . .77 B8
  Cheshunt EN8 . . . . .148 D2
  Hatfield AL10 . . . . .130 C6
  Watford WD25 . . . . .154 D6
  Watton at St SG14 . . . . . . .70 E3
Glebe Ho AL9 . . . . .131 F6
Glebe La EN5 . . . . .171 A3
Glebeland AL10 . . . . .130 C5
Glebelands CM20 . . . . . . .117 E3

Glebe Rd
Hertford SG14 . . . . 113 D8
Letchworth Garden City
  SG6 . . . . 23 B8
Welwyn AL6 . . . . 89 B5
Glebe The
Ardeley SG2 . . . . 38 F3
Harlow CM20 . . . . 117 E1
Kings Langley WD4 . . . . . 139 A2
Stevenage SG2 . . . . 51 B6
St Ippolyts SG4 . . . . 35 C2
Watford WD15 . . . . 154 D6
Glebe View SG2 . . . . 38 C2
Gleed Ave WD23 . . . . . . 176 D8
Glemsford Cl LU4 . . . . . . 44 B6
Glemsford Dr AL5 . . . . . . 86 D2
Glenblower Ct AL4 . . . . . 128 D3
Glenbourne SG4 . . . . 67 F1
Glen Chess WD3 . . . . . . 165 C5
Glencoe Rd WD23 . . . . . 168 A3
Glencorse Gn WD19 . . . . 175 D6
Glendale HP1 . . . . 124 B3
Glendale Wlk EN8 . . . . . 148 E1
Glendean Ct EN3 . . . . . . 162 F3
Gleneagles Cl WD19 . . . . 175 D6
Gleneagles Dr LU2 . . . . . . 45 E6
Glenester Cl LU1 . . . . . . 115 A1
Glen Faba CM19 . . . . . . 135 E7
Glen Faba Rd CM19 . . . . 135 F6
Glenferrie Rd AL1 . . . . . 128 A3
Glenfield St SG14 . . . . . 112 F7
Glenfield Rd LU3 . . . . 45 C6
Glengall Pl AL1 . . . . 141 E8
Glenhaven Ave WD6 . . . 170 A6
Glen Luce EN8 . . . . 148 D1
Glenlyn Ave AL1 . . . . . . 128 B2
Glenmire Terr SG12 . . . . 115 D4
Glenmore Gdns WD5 . . . 154 A7
Glenshee Cl HA6 . . . . . . 174 C4
Glen The
Caddington LU1 . . . . 62 E3
Hemel Hempstead HP2 . . 124 E4
Northwood HA6 . . . . 174 B3
Glenview Gdns HP1 . . . . 124 B3
Glenview Rd HP1 . . . . . . 124 B3
Glenville Ave EN2 . . . . . 161 D1
Glen Way WD17 . . . . . . 153 E1
Glenwood
Hoddesdon EN10 . . . . . . 134 F4
Welwyn Garden City
  AL7 . . . . 111 D5
Glenwood Cl SG2 . . . . . . 51 C2
Glevum Cl AL3 . . . . 126 C1
Globe Cl AL5 . . . . 86 B1
Globe Cres CM23 . . . . . . 58 D6
Globe Ct
Hertford SG14 . . . . 113 C8
Hoddesdon EN10 . . . . . . 148 C8
Globe Ho WD3 . . . . 164 C5
Glossop Way SG15 . . . . . 11 B7
Gloucester Ave EN8 . . . . 162 E2
Gloucester Cl SG1 . . . . . . 36 E2
Gloucester Ct
Hatfield AL10 . . . . 129 F6
2 Watford WD18 . . . . . . 166 F5
Gloucester Ho 6
  WD6 . . . . 170 A7
Gloucester Rd
Enfield EN2 . . . . 161 C1
1 Luton LU1 . . . . 63 F6
Glover Cl EN7 . . . . 147 F4
Glovers Cl SG13 . . . . . . 113 C4
Glovers Cl SG5 . . . . 21 F1
Glynde The SG2 . . . . 69 B8
Glynswood Pl HA6 . . . . . 174 B3
Goat La EN1 . . . . 161 F1
Gobions Way AL6 . . . . . 145 B3
Goblins Gn AL7 . . . . 110 D5
Goddard End SG2 . . . . . . 69 C8
Goddards Cl SG13 . . . . . 132 C4
Godfrey Cl SG2 . . . . 51 B3
Godfreys Cl LU1 . . . . 63 B6
Godfreys Ct LU1 . . . . 63 B6
Godfries Cl AL6 . . . . 90 E3
Godsafe SG14 . . . . 118 E4
Godwin Cl EN3 . . . . 163 C1
Goffs Cres EN7 . . . . 147 C2
Goffs La EN7 . . . . 148 A2
Goffs La EN7 . . . . 147 E2
GOFF'S OAK 147 C3
Goff's Oak Ave EN7 . . . . 147 C3
Goffs Sch EN7 . . . . 148 A3
Golda Cl EN5 . . . . 171 D3
Gold Cl EN10 . . . . 134 E3
Goldcrest Cl LU4 . . . . 44 A5
Goldcrest Way WD23 . . . 168 C1
Goldcroft HP3 . . . . 125 A1
Golden Dell AL7 . . . . 110 F2
Goldens Way SG14 . . . . . 92 A1
Golden Willows SG5 . . . . 21 E6
Goldfield Inf Sch HP23 . . . 99 F3
Goldfield Rd HP23 . . . . . 99 F3
Goldfinch Way WD6 . . . 170 A6
Goldings
Bishop's Stortford
  CM23 . . . . 77 B8
Hertford SG13 . . . . 92 A1
Goldings Cres AL10 . . . . 130 B6
Goldings Hall SG14 . . . . . 91 F1
Goldings Ho AL10 . . . . . 130 B6
Goldings La SG14 . . . . . . 92 A2
Goldington Cl EN11 . . . . 114 F1
Goldon SG6 . . . . 23 C6
Goldring Way AL2 . . . . . 142 B5
Goldsmith Way AL3 . . . . 127 C4
Goldstone Cl SG12 . . . . . 93 D2

Golf Cl WD23 . . . . 167 D6
Golf Club Rd AL9 . . . . . 145 A6
Golf Ride EN2 . . . . 161 A4
Gombards AL3 . . . . 127 D4
Gomer Cl SG4 . . . . 67 E2
Gonnerston AL3 . . . . . . 127 B4
Gonville Ave WD3 . . . . . 166 B3
Gonville Cres SG2 . . . . . . 51 C2
Goodacre Cl EN6 . . . . . . 159 C7
Goodacre Cl EN6 . . . . . . 159 C7
Goodey Meade SG2 . . . . . 52 F2
Goodison Cl WD23 . . . . . 168 C4
Goodliffe Pk CM23 . . . . . 59 B2
Goodman Ct 7 EN8 . . . . 148 E3
Goodrich Cl WD25 . . . . . 154 A4
Goodwin Ho WD18 . . . . 166 E3
Goodwins Mead LU 80 A7
Goodwin Stile CM23 . . . . 76 D5
Goodwood Ave
Enfield EN3 . . . . 162 C2
Watford WD24 . . . . 153 E3
Goodwood Cl EN11 . . . . 135 A2
Goodwood Par WD24 . . . 153 E3
Goodwood Path 2
  WD6 . . . . 170 A7
Goodwood Rd SG8 . . . . . . 7 F6
Goodyers Ave WD7 . . . . 155 F5
Gooseacre AL7 . . . . 110 F4
Goose Acre
Botley HP5 . . . . 136 A1
Cheddington LU7 . . . . 80 A7
Gooseberry Hill LU3 . . . . 45 B7
Goosecroft HP1 . . . . 123 F4
Goosefields WD3 . . . . . . 165 C3
GOOSE GREEN 134 C7
Goose La CM22 . . . . 98 E7
Goral Mead WD3 . . . . . . 165 D1
Gordian Way SG2 . . . . . . 37 C1
Gordon Ave HA7 . . . . . . 176 F4
Gordon Cl AL1 . . . . 128 B2
Gordon Ho SG3 . . . . 69 A5
Gordon Mans 7 EN5 . . . 171 F5
Gordon Rd EN9 . . . . 163 A5
Gordon's Wlk AL5 . . . . . 107 C8
Gordon Way EN5 . . . . . . 171 F5
Gore La SG11 . . . . 73 D3
Gorelands La HP8 . . . . . 172 A7
Gorhambury★ AL3 . . . . 126 C4
Gorham Dr AL1 . . . . 141 E8
Gorle Cl WD25 . . . . 154 A4
Gorleston Cl SG1 . . . . . . 36 A1
Gorse Cl AL10 . . . . 129 F2
Gorse Cnr
Harpenden AL5 . . . . 107 C8
St Albans AL3 . . . . 127 D5
Gorselands AL5 . . . . 107 B7
Gorseway AL10 . . . . 109 F1
Gorst SG6 . . . . 22 E5
Gosford Ho WD18 . . . . . 166 E3
Gosforth La
South Oxhey WD19 . . . . . 175 B7
1 South Oxhey WD19 . . 175 A7
Gosforth Path WD19 . . . 175 A7
Goshawk Cl LU4 . . . . 44 A4
Goslett Ct WD23 . . . . . . 168 A4
Gosling Ave SG5 . . . . 33 C2
Gosling Ski Ctr★ AL3 . . 110 C4
Gosmore SG1 . . . . 36 A4
Gosmore Ley Cl SG4 . . . . 34 E3
Gosmore Rd SG4 . . . . 34 F5
Gossamers The WD25 . . 154 E4
Gosse Cl LU4 . . . . 114 F1
Gosselin Ho SG14 . . . . . 113 D8
Gosselin Rd SG14 . . . . . 113 C8
Gossoms End HP4 . . . . . 122 A5
Gossoms Ryde HP4 . . . . 122 A5
Gothic Mede Lower Sch
  SG15 . . . . 11 A5
Gothic Way SG15 . . . . . . 11 B5
Gould Cl AL9 . . . . 144 B7
Government Row
  EN3 . . . . 163 A2
Gower Field EN6 . . . . . . 158 A7
Gower Rd SG8 . . . . 7 C7
Gowers The CM20 . . . . . 118 B2
Gowar Gn SG6 . . . . 156 E6
Grace Cl WD6 . . . . 170 D8
Grace Ct HA6 . . . . 175 A1
Grace Gdns CM23 . . . . . . 76 F4
Grace Maltings
  HP23 . . . . 100 A3
Grace Way SG1 . . . . 36 B3
Graemesdyke Rd HP4 . . . 122 A3
Grafton Cl LU4 . . . . 44 B3
Grafton Pl SG11 . . . . 55 F1
Graham Ave EN10 . . . . . 134 E2
Graham Cl AL1 . . . . 127 D1
Graham Ct 3 AL3 . . . . . 127 D4
Graham Gdns LU3 . . . . . . 45 C4
Graham Ho HA3 . . . . . . 176 E1
Grailands CM23 . . . . 58 F3
Grammar School Wlk
  SG5 . . . . 34 E7
Grampian Pl SG1 . . . . . . 37 B4
Grampian Way AL3 . . . . . 44 C8
Granaries The EN9 . . . . . 163 E5
Granary Cl AL4 . . . . 108 D8
Granary Ct CM21 . . . . . . 97 E2
Granary La SG4 . . . . 86 C1
Granary The
Arlesey SG15 . . . . 11 A5
Flamstead HP2 . . . . 104 F4
Hemel Hempstead HP1 . . 124 B7
Roydon CM19 . . . . 116 B1

Granary The continued
Stanstead Abbotts
  SG12 . . . . 115 C3
Tewin AL6 . . . . 90 E4
Granby Ave AL5 . . . . 86 D2
Granby Cl AL5 . . . . 86 D2
Granby Rd
Luton LU4 . . . . 44 E2
Stevenage SG1 . . . . 36 C2
Grandfield Ave WD17 . . . 167 A8
Grandmill Pl 2 EN8 . . . 148 E3
Grand Union Way
  WD4 . . . . 139 B2
Grange Ave
Luton LU4 . . . . 44 D4
Totteridge N20 . . . . 171 E2
Grange Bottom SG8 . . . . . 7 E5
Grange Cl
Hemel Hempstead
  HP2 . . . . 125 A2
Hertford SG14 . . . . 113 B6
Hitchin SG4 . . . . 35 A4
Markyate AL3 . . . . 83 D6
Watford WD17 . . . . 167 A8
Grange Court Rd AL5 . . . 107 C6
Grange Ct
Hertford SG13 . . . . 113 C7
Letchworth Garden City
  SG6 . . . . 12 A1
4 St Albans AL3 . . . . . . 127 D4
Waltham Abbey EN9 . . . 163 C5
Grangedale Cl HA6 . . . . . 174 E2
Grange Dr SG5 . . . . 11 F5
Grange Gdns SG12 . . . . . 114 E8
Grange Hill AL6 . . . . 89 C6
Grange Jun Sch SG6 . . . . 12 A2
Grange Pk CM23 . . . . 58 F1
Granger Ct 7 WD6 . . . . 170 A5
Grange Rd
Bishop's Stortford
  CM23 . . . . 77 A7
Borehamwood WD6 . . . . 169 F4
Letchworth Garden City
  SG6 . . . . 22 F8
Pitstone LU7 . . . . 80 D5
Tring HP23 . . . . 100 C5
Watford WD17 . . . . 167 A4
Wilstone HP23 . . . . 79 D1
Grange Rise SG4 . . . . 67 F1
Grangeside CM23 . . . . . . 59 A2
Grange St 4 AL3 . . . . . . 127 D4
Grange Street Mews 1
  AL3 . . . . 127 D4
Grange The
Abbots Langley WD5 . . . 153 E8
Bishop's Stortford CM23 . . 58 F1
Hoddesdon EN11 . . . . . . 135 A5
Rickmansworth WD3 . . . 165 D2
Standon SG11 . . . . 55 D3
Stevenage SG8 . . . . 50 C8
Therfield SG8 . . . . 16 F6
Grange Wlk CM23 . . . . . . 77 A7
Grangewood EN6 . . . . . . 145 B1
Gransden Cl LU3 . . . . 45 A7
Grant Gdns AL5 . . . . 86 B2
Grantham Cl SG8 . . . . 7 B8
Grantham Gdns SG2 . . . . 93 E2
Grantham Gn WD6 . . . . 170 C4
Grantham Mews CM23 . . 122 D4
Grantham Rd LU4 . . . . . . 45 B1
Granville Ct AL1 . . . . . . 127 F3
Granville Dene HP3 . . . . 137 A4
Granville Gdns EN11 . . . 115 A2
Granville Rd
Barnet EN5 . . . . 171 D6
Berkhamsted HP4 . . . . . 121 E6
Hitchin SG4 . . . . 35 A4
Luton LU1 . . . . 63 B8
St Albans AL1 . . . . 127 F3
Watford WD18 . . . . 167 C5
Graseby Ho 3 EN5 . . . . 171 F5
Grasmere SG2 . . . . 37 C3
Grasmere Ave
Harpenden AL5 . . . . 86 C1
Luton LU3 . . . . 45 B7
Grasmere Cl
Hemel Hempstead
  HP3 . . . . 125 B1
Watford WD25 . . . . 154 B7
Grasmere Rd
Luton LU3 . . . . 45 C7
St Albans AL1 . . . . 128 B1
Ware SG12 . . . . 93 E3
Grassington Cl AL2 . . . . . 141 A1
Grass Mdws SG2 . . . . 51 D7
Grass Warren AL6 . . . . . . 90 E1
Grassy Cl HP1 . . . . 124 A4
Gravel Dr HP23 . . . . 99 B3
Gravel Hill AL10 . . . . . . 130 A8
Gravelhill Terr HP1 . . . . 124 A2
Gravel La HP1 . . . . 124 A3
Gravelly Dell SG11 . . . . . 55 F8
Gravelly La SG11 . . . . . . 55 F8
Gravel Path
Berkhamsted HP4 . . . . . 122 C5
Hemel Hempstead HP1 . . 124 A3

Gravely Ct HP2 . . . . 125 C2
GRAVESEND 57 B8
Grayling Cl HP4 . . . . 121 F6
Graylings The WD5 . . . . 153 D6
Grays Cl SG3 . . . . 7 C8
Grays Ct CM23 . . . . 76 E4
Graysfield AL7 . . . . 111 A3
Gray's La SG5 . . . . 34 D7
Grazings The HP2 . . . . . 124 F5
GREAT AMWELL 114 F5
GREAT ASHBY 37 D3
Great Ashby Way SG1 . . . 37 B3
Great Augur St 4
  CM17 . . . . 118 D1
Great Braitch La AL10 . . 109 F1
Great Bramingham La
  LU3 . . . . 31 B2
Great Break AL7 . . . . . . 111 B5
Great Cambridge Rd
Cheshunt EN8 . . . . 148 D4
Enfield EN1 . . . . 162 C6
GREAT CHISHILL 9 F2
Great Conduit AL7 . . . . 111 C7
Great Dell AL8 . . . . 89 D1
Great Eastern Cl CM23 . . 77 A6
Great Elms Rd HP3 . . . . 138 F7
Greatfield Cl AL5 . . . . . . 85 C4
Great Gables SG1 . . . . . . 37 B4
GREAT GADDESDEN . . . 103 D3
Great Gaddesden CE Prim
  Sch HP1 . . . . 103 D3
Great Ganett AL7 . . . . . . 111 C4
GREATGAP 80 D6
Great Gn SG5 . . . . 20 D4
Great Gr WD23 . . . . 168 B5
Great Groves EN7 . . . . . 147 E3
Great Hadham Rd
  CM23 . . . . 76 C5
GREAT HALLINGBURY
  . . . . 77 E4
Greatham Rd WD23 . . . 167 D5
Greatham Road Ind Est
  WD23 . . . . 167 D5
Great Havers Ct CM23 . . 76 E5
Great Heart HP2 . . . . . . 124 E5
Great Heath AL10 . . . . . 130 B8
GREAT HORMEAD 42 B8
Great Hyde Hall CM21 . . 98 B3
Great Innings N SG14 . . . 70 D4
Great Innings S SG14 . . . 70 D3
Great Lawne SG3 . . . . . . 69 D2
Great Ley AL7 . . . . 110 E4
Great Leys Ct AL2 . . . . . 142 B4
Great Marlings SG2 . . . . . 46 C6
Great Mdw EN10 . . . . . 135 A1
Great Molewood SG14 . . 92 B1
GREAT MUNDEN 54 C5
Great North Rd
Barnet EN5 . . . . 171 E6
Brookmans Park AL9,
  EN6 . . . . 145 B5
Hatfield AL9 . . . . 130 C5
Oaklands AL6 . . . . 89 E7
Radwell SG7 . . . . 12 D3
Welwyn Garden City
  AL8 . . . . 110 A7
GREAT OFFLEY 33 D2
Great Palmers HP2 . . . . 124 F8
Great Pk WD4 . . . . 139 A4
Great Plumtree CM20 . . . 117 F2
Great Rd HP2 . . . . 124 F4
Great Slades EN6 . . . . . 158 F6
Great Stockwood Rd
  EN7 . . . . 147 D5
Great Sturgess Rd
  HP1 . . . . 123 F3
Great Whites Rd HP3 . . . 124 F1
Great Wood Ctry Pk★
  EN6 . . . . 146 B5
GREAT WYMONDLEY . . . 35 F6
Greenacre Cl EN5 . . . . . 158 F1
Greenacres
Bushey WD23 . . . . 176 D8
Hemel Hempstead HP2 . . 125 D2
Pitstone LU7 . . . . 80 C4
Wingrave HP22 . . . . 60 B2
Green Acres
Lilley LU2 . . . . 32 D2
Stevenage SG2 . . . . 51 C1
Welwyn Garden City
  AL7 . . . . 110 F3
Greenacres Cvn Pk
  LU6 . . . . 82 F8
Greenall Cl EN8 . . . . 148 E1
Greenbank EN8 . . . . 148 B3
Greenbank Rd WD17 . . . 153 D5
Greenbanks AL1 . . . . . . 127 F1
Greenbushes LU4 . . . . . . 44 D6
Green Cl
Brookmans Park AL9 . . . 144 E5
Cheshunt EN8 . . . . 162 E8
Luton LU4 . . . . 44 C5
Stevenage SG2 . . . . 50 F2
Greencoates SG13 . . . . . 113 E5
Green Croft AL10 . . . . . 130 A8
Green Ct 6 LU4 . . . . 44 C5
Green Dell Way HP3 . . . 125 D2
Green Dragon Ct LU1 . . . 63 F6
Green Drift SG8 . . . . 7 C7
Green Edge WD25 . . . . . 154 A4
Greene Field Rd HP4 . . . 122 E7
GREEN END 55 E7
Green End SG11 . . . . 55 E8
GREEN END
Dane End 53 E1

GREEN END continued
Hemel Hempstead 124 A2
Sandon 26 D7
Green End AL6 . . . . 89 B4
GREEN END 24 C2
Green End Bsns Ctr
  WD3 . . . . 152 A2
Green End Gdns HP1 . . . 124 A2
Green End La HP1 . . . . . 123 F3
Green End Rd HP1 . . . . . 124 A2
Greener Ct EN3 . . . . 163 A2
Greenes Ct HP4 . . . . 122 C5
Greene Wlk HP4 . . . . . . 122 D3
Greenfield
Hatfield AL9 . . . . 130 D8
Royston SG8 . . . . 7 B7
Welwyn Garden City AL8 . . 89 D1
Greenfield Ave
Ickleford SG5 . . . . 21 D4
South Oxhey WD19 . . . . . 175 E8
Greenfield La SG5 . . . . . 21 E4
Greenfield Rd SG1 . . . . . 50 E7
Greenfields
Cuffley EN6 . . . . 146 E1
Stansted Mountfitchet
  CM24 . . . . 59 E7
Greenfields Prim Sch
  WD19 . . . . 175 C5
Greenfield St EN9 . . . . . 163 C5
Greengate LU3 . . . . 44 C8
Greenheys Cl HA6 . . . . . 174 E2
Greenhill Ave LU2 . . . . . 45 E3
Green Hill Cl SG11 . . . . . 55 F7
Greenhill Cres WD18 . . . 166 E3
Greenhill Ct HP1 . . . . . . 124 B2
Greenhill Pk CM23 . . . . . 76 D5
Greenhills SG12 . . . . 93 C3
Greenhills Cl WD3 . . . . . 165 B4
Green La
Ashwell SG7 . . . . 4 E5
Bovingdon HP3 . . . . 137 A3
Bovingdon, Pudds Cross
  HP3 . . . . 136 F3
Braughing SG11 . . . . 55 F7
Croxley Green WD3 . . . . 165 F4
Hemel Hempstead 125 D4
Hitchin SG4 . . . . 22 B1
Hoddesdon EN10 . . . . . . 149 B8
Ivinghoe LU7 . . . . 80 E5
Kensworth Common LU6 . . 82 E8
Latimer HP5 . . . . 152 F2
Letchworth Garden City
  SG6 . . . . 23 C8
Luton LU2 . . . . 46 C4
Markyate AL3 . . . . 83 F5
Northwood HA6 . . . . 174 E3
St Albans, New Greens
  AL3 . . . . 127 D7
St Albans, Sopwell AL1 . . 142 A7
Watford WD19 . . . . 167 C2
Welwyn Garden City
  AL7 . . . . 111 D5
Greenland Rd EN5 . . . . . 171 C3
Greenlands WD6 . . . . . . 170 D3
Green Lane Cl AL5 . . . . . 107 E8
Greenlane Ind Est SG6 . . 23 C7
Green Lane Cl AL10 . . . . 109 F2
Green Lanes Prim Sch
  AL10 . . . . 109 F1
Greenleas SG1 . . . . 36 F1
Green Leys Cotts SG13 . . 55 F1
Green Man Ct CM20 . . . . 117 A4
Green Mdw EN6 . . . . . . 145 A1
Green Oaks LU2 . . . . 45 F3
Green Path HP22, HP23 . . 99 D4
Greeniggs LU2 . . . . 46 F2
Greenside WD6 . . . . 157 A1
Greenside Dr SG5 . . . . . . 34 D8
Greenside Pk LU2 . . . . . . 45 E3
Greenside Sch SG2 . . . . . 51 B2
Greensleeves Cl AL4 . . . 128 C6
Green St
Chorleywood WD3 . . . . . 164 C6
2 Harlow CM17 . . . . . . 118 D1
Royston SG8 . . . . 7 D8
Shenley WD6, WD7 . . . . 157 A3
Stevenage SG1 . . . . 50 C7
Greenstead CM21 . . . . . . 97 E1
GREEN STREET
Borehamwood 157 B2
Little Hadham 75 E8
GREENSWARD WD23 . . . 168 B3
GREEN THE 81 F8
Green The
Bishop's Stortford
  CM23 . . . . 76 F4
Caddington LU1 . . . . 62 E4
Cheddington LU7 . . . . 80 A7
Cheshunt EN8 . . . . 148 C3
Codicote SG4 . . . . 67 F1
Harefield UB9 . . . . 173 C2
Kimpton SG4 . . . . 66 D1
London Colney AL2 . . . . 142 D4
Luton LU4 . . . . 44 C5
Mentmore LU7 . . . . 61 D4
Newnham SG7 . . . . 12 E7
Old Knebworth SG3 . . . . . 68 C5
Peters Green LU2 . . . . . . 65 F2
Pitstone LU7 . . . . 80 D4
Potten End HP4 . . . . 123 B6
Royston SG8 . . . . 7 D6
Sarratt WD3 . . . . 152 A3
Stotfold SG5 . . . . 11 F7
Waltham Abbey EN9 . . . 163 C5
Ware SG12 . . . . 93 D3

Green The continued
Welwyn AL6 . . . . .89 B5
Welwyn Garden City
AL7 . . . . .111 A4
Wingrave HP22 . . . . .60 B2
GREEN TYE 75 D1
Green Vale AL7 . . . . .111 A5
Green View Cl HP3 . . . . . .137 A2
Greenway
Berkhamsted HP4 . . . . . .122 A4
Bishop's Stortford CM23 . .77 C6
Harpenden AL5 . . . . .107 E8
Hemel Hempstead HP2 . .125 B3
Letchworth Garden City
SG6 . . . . .23 A2
Pinner HA5 . . . . .175 B1
Walkern SG2 . . . . .52 B8
Greenway Fst Sch
HP4 . . . . .121 F4
Greenway Gdns HA3 . . . .176 E1
Greenways
Abbots Langley WD5 . . . .153 E7
Buntingford SG9 . . . . .40 D8
Goff's Oak EN7 . . . . .147 B2
Hertford SG14 . . . . .113 B6
Luton LU2 . . . . .46 A6
Stevenage SG1 . . . . .50 E6
Welwyn AL6 . . . . .89 C3
Greenway The
Enfield EN3 . . . . .162 D4
Harrow HA3 . . . . .176 E1
Potters Bar EN6 . . . . . . .159 A6
Rickmansworth WD3 . . . .165 A2
Tring HP23 . . . . .99 F5
Greenwich Ct
Cheshunt EN8 . . . . .162 E5
11 St Albans AL1 . . . . . . .128 A2
Greenwich Way EN9 . . . .163 C3
Greenwood Ave EN7 . . . .162 B8
Greenwood Cl EN7 . . . . .162 B8
Greenwood Court Ind Est
LU2 . . . . .46 A2
Greenwood Dr WD25 . . .154 B5
Greenwood Gdns
WD7 . . . . .156 E6
Greenyard EN9 . . . . .163 C6
Greer Rd HA3 . . . . .176 C2
Gregories Cl LU3 . . . . . . .45 D1
Gregory Ave EN6 . . . . . .159 C6
Gregory Mews EN9 . . . .163 B7
Gregson Cl WD6 . . . . . . .170 C8
Grenadier Cl AL4 . . . . . . .128 C2
Grenadine Cl EN7 . . . . . .147 F4
Grenadine Way HP23 . . .100 A5
Greneway Sch The SG8 . . .7 E7
Grenfell Cl WD6 . . . . .170 C8
Grenville Ave EN10 . . . . .134 F2
Grenville Cl EN8 . . . . .162 D7
Grenville Ct WD3 . . . . . . .164 C5
Grenville Way SG2 . . . . . .51 A1
Gresford Cl AL4 . . . . .128 D3
Gresham Cl LU2 . . . . .64 D8
Gresham St HP4 . . . . .122 B3
Gresley Cl AL8 . . . . .110 E8
Gresley Ct
Enfield EN1 . . . . .162 C4
Potters Bar EN6 . . . . . . .145 C1
Gresley Way SG2 . . . . . . .51 D5
Greville Cl AL9 . . . . .144 C7
Greycaine Rd WD24 . . . .154 D2
Greydells Rd SG1 . . . . . . .50 E6
Greyfriars SG12 . . . . .93 B3
Greyfriars La AL5 . . . . . . .107 A7
Greyholme Ct 7 HA6 . . . .157 F4
Greyhound La EN6 . . . . .158 A6
Grey House The 4
WD7 . . . . .167 A7
Greystoke Cl HP4 . . . . . .122 A3
Griffiths Way AL1 . . . . . . .127 C1
Griffon Way WD25 . . . . .153 F5
Grimsdyke Cres EN5 . . . .171 C6
Grimsdyke Fst & Mid Sch
HA5 . . . . .175 F4
Grimsdyke Lo AL1 . . . . . .128 A3
Grimsdyke Rd
Pinner HA5 . . . . .175 E3
Wigginton HP23 . . . . . . .100 D1
Grimstone Rd SG4 . . . . . .35 E4
Grimston Rd AL1 . . . . . . .127 F2
Grimthorpe Cl AL3 . . . . . .127 D6
Grindcobbe AL1 . . . . .141 D8
Grinders End SG4 . . . . . . .36 B4
Grinstead La CM22 . . . . . .98 C6
Groom Ct AL1 . . . . .127 E5
Groom Rd EN10 . . . . .148 F5
Groomsby Dr LU2 . . . . . . .80 E5
Grooms Cotts HP5 . . . . . .136 B1
Grosvenor Ave WD4 . . . .139 C3
Grosvenor Cl CM23 . . . . .76 D4
Grosvenor Ct
Croxley Green WD3 . . . . .166 D4
Stevenage SG1 . . . . .50 A7
Hemel H 4 CM23 . . . . . . .77 B8
Grosvenor Rd
Baldock SG7 . . . . .12 F1
Borehamwood WD6 . . . .170 B6
Hoddesdon EN10 . . . . . .134 F3
Luton LU3 . . . . .45 B5
Moor Park HA6 . . . . .174 F5
St Albans AL1 . . . . .127 E2
Watford WD17 . . . . .167 C6
Grosvenor Rd W SG2 . . . .12 F1
Grosvenor St WD4 . . . . . .139 C3
Grosvenor Terr HP1 . . . . .124 A3
Grotto The SG12 . . . . . . .114 D8

Ground La AL10 . . . . .130 B7
Grove Ave AL5 . . . . .107 D7
Grovebury Gdns AL2 . . . .141 C4
Grove Cotts WD23 . . . . . .168 A3
Grove Cres WD3 . . . . .166 A5
Grove Ct
Arlesey SG15 . . . . .11 A8
Barnet EN5 . . . . .171 E6
Waltham Abbey EN9 . . . .163 B6
Grovedale Cl EN7 . . . . . . .147 F1
Grove End LU1 . . . . .63 B5
Grove Farm Pk HA6 . . . .174 D5
Grove Gdns
Enfield EN3 . . . . .162 D1
Tring HP23 . . . . .100 B5
Grove Hall Rd WD23 . . . .167 C8
GROVEHILL 124 E8
Grove Hill CM24 . . . . .59 E7
Grove Ho
Bushey WD23 . . . . .167 F3
Cheshunt EN8 . . . . .148 B1
Hitchin SG4 . . . . .22 A2
12 Luton LU1 . . . . .63 D7
Grove Inf Sch The
AL5 . . . . .107 D7
Grove Jun Sch The
AL5 . . . . .107 D7
Grove La HP5 . . . . .136 B5
Grove Lea AL10 . . . . .130 A2
Grove Mdw AL7 . . . . .111 C6
Grove Mead AL10 . . . . . .129 F5
Grove Mill Ct SG4 . . . . . . .22 A2
Grove Mill La WD3,
WD17 . . . . .153 C1
Grove Park Rd LU1 . . . . . .63 B3
Grove Path EN7 . . . . .162 A8
Grove Pk
Bishop's Stortford
CM23 . . . . .76 C8
Tring HP23 . . . . .100 C5
Grove Pl 1 Bishop's Stortford
CM23 . . . . .76 F7
Bushey WD25 . . . . .168 B8
Welham Green AL9 . . . . .144 C7
Grover Cl HP2 . . . . .124 D4
Grove Rd
Borehamwood WD6 . . . .170 A8
Harpenden AL5 . . . . .107 D7
Hemel Hempstead HP1 . .124 A2
Hitchin SG4 . . . . .21 F1
Luton LU1 . . . . .63 D7
Northwood HA6 . . . . .174 D5
Rickmansworth WD3 . . . .173 A8
Slip End LU1 . . . . .63 B2
St Albans AL1 . . . . .127 D2
Stevenage SG1 . . . . .50 D7
Tring HP23 . . . . .100 C5
Ware SG12 . . . . .93 F2
Grove Rd W EN3 . . . . .162 C2
Grove Road Prim Sch
HP23 . . . . .100 C5
Grover Rd WD19 . . . . . . .167 F2
Grove The
Brookmans Park AL9 . . . .145 A4
Chipperfield WD4 . . . . . .138 C1
Great Hallingbury CM22 . .77 F4
Latimer HP5 . . . . .150 D3
Little Hadham SG11 . . . . .75 E7
Luton LU1 . . . . .63 B5
Potters Bar EN6 . . . . . . .159 C7
Radlett WD7 . . . . .156 A5
Tring HP23 . . . . .100 C5
Woodside LU1 . . . . .63 B3
Grove Way WD3 . . . . .164 B4
Grove Wlk SG14 . . . . . . .113 C8
Grovewood Cl WD3 . . . . .164 B4
Grubbs La AL9 . . . . .145 C8
Gryphon Ind Pk The
AL3 . . . . .127 F8
Guardian Bsns Pk LU1 . . .63 C8
GUBBLECOTE 79 D3
Guernsey Cl LU4 . . . . .44 A3
Guernsey Ho
Enfield EN1 . . . . .162 D1
Watford WD18 . . . . .167 A3
Guessens Ct AL8 . . . . . . .110 C5
Guessens Gr AL8 . . . . . . .110 C6
Guessens Rd AL8 . . . . . . .110 C6
Guessens Wlk AL8 . . . . . .110 C7
GUILDEN MORDEN 1 F4
Guilden Morden CE Prim
Sch SG8 . . . . .1 F5
Guildford Cl SG1 . . . . .36 F2
Guildford Rd AL1 . . . . . . .128 B2
Guildford St LU1 . . . . .63 E7
Guildhouse The WD3 . . .166 B3
Guilfords CM17 . . . . .118 C5
Guinevere Gdns EN8 . . . .162 E8
Guiver Ct 8 EN8 . . . . .148 E3
Gulland Cl WD23 . . . . . . .168 C4
Gullbrook HP1 . . . . .124 A3
Gullet Wood Rd
WD25 . . . . .154 A4
Gullicot Way LU7 . . . . .80 D4
Gulphs The SG13 . . . . . . .113 D5
Gun Ho SG3 . . . . .68 F5
Gun La SG3 . . . . .68 F5
Gun Meadow Ave SG3 . . .69 A4
Gunnels Wood Ind Est
SG1 . . . . .50 D3

Gunnels Wood Pk SG1 . . .50 B5
Gunnels Wood Rd SG1 . . .50 B5
Gunner Dr EN3 . . . . .163 A2
Gunpowder Pk* EN9 . . . .163 B3
Gun Rd SG3 . . . . .69 A4
Gun Road Gdns SG3 . . . . .68 F4
Gurney Court Rd AL1 . . . .127 F5
Gurney's La SG5 . . . . .21 B7
GUSTARD WOOD 87 D4
Gustard Wood AL4 . . . . . . .87 C5
Gwent Cl WD25 . . . . .154 D5
Gwynfa Cl AL6 . . . . .89 D7
Gwynne Cl HP23 . . . . .100 A5
Gwynns Wlk SG13 . . . . . .113 E6
Gyfford Wlk EN7 . . . . . . .162 B8
Gypsy Cl SG12 . . . . .114 F4
Gypsy La
Abbots Langley WD4 . . . .153 D5
Great Amwell SG12 . . . . .114 F4
Welwyn Garden City
AL7 . . . . .110 C1
Gypsy Moth Ave AL10 . . .129 E7

H

Haberdashers' Aske's Boys'
Sch WD6 . . . . .169 B6
Haberdashers' Aske's Sch
for Girls WD6 . . . . .169 B5
Hackforth EN5 . . . . .171 B4
Hackney Cl WD6 . . . . .170 D4
Haddenham Ct HP2 . . . . .105 B1
Haddestoke Gate EN8 . . .148 F5
Haddon Cl
Borehamwood WD6 . . . .170 A6
Stevenage SG2 . . . . .69 C7
Haddon Ct 20 AL5 . . . . . .86 B1
Haddon Rd
Chorleywood WD3 . . . . .164 C4
Luton LU2 . . . . .63 F8
HADHAM CROSS 74 F2
Hadham Ct CM23 . . . . . . .76 B8
HADHAM FORD 75 B8
Hadham Gr CM23 . . . . . . .76 C8
Hadham Hall SG11 . . . . . .57 E2
Hadham Rd
Bishop's Stortford
CM23 . . . . .76 D8
Little Hadham SG11 . . . . .57 F1
Standon SG11 . . . . .55 F1
Hadland Cl HP3 . . . . .137 A5
Hadleigh SG6 . . . . .23 B4
Hadleigh Ct
Harpenden AL5 . . . . .107 E6
Hoddesdon EN10 . . . . . .134 F1
HADLEY 171 F6
Hadley Cl WD6 . . . . .169 F3
Hadley Ct LU3 . . . . .45 D1
Hadley Gn EN5 . . . . .171 E6
Hadley Gn W EN5 . . . . . .171 E7
Hadley Green Rd EN5 . . .171 F7
Hadley Highstone
EN5 . . . . .171 E8
Hadley Par 8 EN5 . . . . . .171 E6
Hadley Rd EN2, EN4 . . . .160 C1
Hadley Ridge EN5 . . . . . .171 F6
HADLEY WOOD 159 C2
Hadley Wood Prim Sch
EN4 . . . . .159 C1
Hadley Wood Sta
EN4 . . . . .159 C1
Hadlow Down Cl LU3 . . . .45 A5
Hadrian Cl AL3 . . . . .127 A1
Hadrians Wlk SG1 . . . . . . .51 C8
Hadrian Way SG7 . . . . . . .23 D7
Hadwell Cl SG2 . . . . .51 A3
Hagdell Rd LU1 . . . . .63 C5
Hagden La WD18 . . . . . . .167 A4
Haggerston Rd WD6 . . . .156 F1
Hagsdell Rd SG13 . . . . . .113 D5
Haig Cl AL1 . . . . .128 B2
Haig Ho AL1 . . . . .128 B2
HAILEY 114 F2
Hailey Ave EN11 . . . . .115 A2
Haileybury & Imperial
Service Coll SG13 . . . . .114 D2
Hailey Cl SG13 . . . . .114 F2
Hailey Hall Sch SG13 . . .114 F2
Hailey La
Hertford Heath SG13 . . . .114 E2
Hoddesdon SG13 . . . . . .114 F2
Hailey Pl CM21 . . . . .97 E2
Haines Way WD25 . . . . . .154 A5
Halcroft Ho EN7 . . . . .147 F4
Haldane Cl EN3 . . . . .163 B1
HALDENS 89 F1
Haldens Ho 3 AL7 . . . . . . .89 F1
Hale Cl SG13 . . . . .113 D5
Hale Ho EN3 . . . . .162 D2
Hale La HP22 . . . . .119 A3
Hale Rd SG13 . . . . .113 D5
Hales Mdw AL5 . . . . .86 A2
Hales Park Cl HP2 . . . . . .125 C4
Hales Pk HP2 . . . . .125 C4
Haleswood Rd HP2 . . . . .125 B4
Half Acre SG5 . . . . .34 D6
Half Acres CM23 . . . . .76 F8
Halfhide La EN8 . . . . .148 D5
Halfhides EN9 . . . . .163 D6
Half Moon Cotts CM21 . . .97 B1
Half Moon La LU1 . . . . . . .84 C8
Half Moon Mdw HP2 . . . .125 C8
Half Moon Mews 9
AL1 . . . . .127 D3

Halford Ct AL10 . . . . .129 E6
Halfway Ave LU4 . . . . .44 D1
Halifax Cl
Bricket Wood AL2 . . . . . .154 F8
Watford WD25 . . . . .153 F5
Halifax Rd WD3 . . . . .164 C2
Halifax Way AL7 . . . . .111 E6
Hallam Cl WD24 . . . . .167 C7
Hallam Gdns HA5 . . . . . . .175 E3
Halland Way HA6 . . . . . . .174 D4
Hall Barns
Furneux Pelham SG9 . . . .42 F4
Stansted Mountfitchet
CM24 . . . . .59 D7
Hall Dr AL3 . . . . .165 A1
Hall Cotts SG9 . . . . .29 A1
Hall Dr UB9 . . . . .173 C2
Halley Rd EN9 . . . . .163 B3
Halleys Ridge SG14 . . . . .113 A5
Hall Gdns AL4 . . . . .143 D8
Hall Heath Cl AL1 . . . . . . .128 B5
Halliday Cl WD7 . . . . .156 E7
Hallingbury Cl CM22 . . . . .77 B1
Hallingbury Rd
Bishop's Stortford
CM22 . . . . .77 B4
Sawbridgeworth CM21 . . .98 A4
Halling Hill CM20 . . . . . . .117 F2
Hall La
Blackmore End SG4 . . . . .87 C8
Great Chishill SG8 . . . . . . .9 F2
Great Hormead SG9 . . . . .29 A1
Woolmer Green SG3 . . . . .69 A2
Hall Mead SG6 . . . . .22 D6
Hallmores EN10 . . . . .135 A4
Hall North Rd HA6 . . . . . .174 F8
Hallowes Cres WD19 . . . .175 A7
Hall Park Gate HP4 . . . . .122 E3
Hall Park Hill HP4 . . . . . .122 E3
Hall Pk HP4 . . . . .122 E3
Hall Place Cl AL1 . . . . . . .127 E4
Hall Place Gdns AL1 . . . .127 E4
Hall Rd HP2 . . . . .125 B5
Halls Cl AL6 . . . . .89 C4
HALL'S GREEN 37 F6
Hallside Rd EN1 . . . . .161 F1
Hallwicks Rd LU2 . . . . . . .46 B3
Hallworth Dr SG5 . . . . . . .11 E6
Hallworth Ho SG5 . . . . . . .11 E6
Halsey Dr
Hemel Hempstead
HP1 . . . . .123 F5
Hitchin SG4 . . . . .35 B7
Halsey Pk AL2 . . . . .142 F4
Halsey Pl WD24 . . . . .154 B1
Halsey Rd WD18 . . . . . . .167 B6
Halstead Hill EN7 . . . . . . .147 E1
Halter Cl WD6 . . . . .170 D4
Halton Cl AL2 . . . . .141 C3
Halton Wood (Forest
Wlks)* HP23 . . . . .119 A5
Haltside AL10 . . . . .129 E4
Halwick Cl 11 HP1 . . . . . .124 A2
Halyard Cl LU3 . . . . .45 B6
Halyard End Est SG6 . . . . .23 B6
Hamberlins La HP4 . . . . . .121 C7
Hamble St WD18 . . . . . . .167 A5
Hamblen Pl WD7 . . . . . . .155 F4
Hambleden Ct EN4 . . . . . .159 D1
Hamblings Cl WD7 . . . . . .156 D6
Hambridge Way SG5 . . . . .20 D4
Hambro Cl LU2 . . . . .85 F7
Hamburgh Ct EN8 . . . . . .148 D3
Hamels Dr SG13 . . . . .114 B7
Hamels La SG9 . . . . .55 B7
Hamels Mans SG11 . . . . . .55 B6
Hamels Park Barns
SG11 . . . . .55 B6
Hamer Cl HP3 . . . . .137 A3
Hamer Ct LU2 . . . . .45 D8
Hamilton Ave EN11 . . . . .135 A8
Hamilton Cl
Bricket Wood AL2 . . . . . .155 A8
Dagnall HP4 . . . . .81 C5
South Mimms EN6 . . . . .158 A6
Hamilton Ct 3 AL10 . . . . .130 B3
Hamilton Mead HP3 . . . . .137 A4
Hamilton Rd
Abbots Langley WD4 . . . .153 C6
Berkhamsted HP4 . . . . . .122 B4
South Oxhey WD19 . . . . .175 B7
St Albans AL1 . . . . .128 A4
Hamilton St WD18 . . . . . .167 C6
Hamlet Cl AL2 . . . . .140 F1
Hamlet Hill CM19 . . . . . . .135 F4
Hamlet The HP4 . . . . .123 A7
Hammarsfield Cl SG11 . . .55 D2
Hammarsfjord Rd
CM20 . . . . .117 D2
Hammerdell SG2 . . . . .51 A6
HAMMERFIELD 124 A3
Hammer La HP2 . . . . .124 F6
Hammer Par WD25 . . . . .154 A6
Hammers Gate AL2 . . . . .141 A5
Hammond Cl
Barnet EN5 . . . . .171 E4
Hammond Street EN7 . . .147 F5
Stevenage SG2 . . . . .50 D6
Hammond Ct LU1 . . . . . . .63 C1
Hammond End La
AL5 . . . . .106 F5
Hammond Prim Sch The
HP2 . . . . .124 F6
Hammonds Hill AL5 . . . . .106 F4
Hammonds La AL10 . . . . .109 B3
HAMMOND STREET 147 D5

Hammondstreet Rd
EN7 . . . . .147 D5
Hammondswick AL5 . . . . .106 F4
Hamonde SG6 . . . . .23 C4
Hampden Cl AL4 . . . . .66 C1
Hampden Cl SG6 . . . . .23 B8
Hampden Cres EN7 . . . . .162 B8
Hampden Hill SG12 . . . . . .93 F2
Hampden Hill Cl SG12 . . .93 F2
Hampden Pl AL2 . . . . .141 E2
Hampden Rd
Harrow HA3 . . . . .176 C3
Hitchin SG4 . . . . .22 C1
Hampden Rise SG8 . . . . . . .7 D4
Hampden Way WD17 . . . .153 E3
Hampermill La WD19 . . .167 A1
Hampstead Cl AL2 . . . . . .154 F8
Hampton Cl
Borehamwood WD6 . . . .170 C4
Stevenage SG2 . . . . .69 C7
Hampton Gdns CM21 . . . .118 C7
Hampton Ho SG13 . . . . . .113 E6
Hampton Rd LU4 . . . . .63 B8
Hamstel Rd CM20 . . . . . .117 C1
Hamsworth Ct SG14 . . . .112 F7
Hanaper Dr SG8 . . . . .8 F2
Hanbury Cl
Cheshunt EN8 . . . . .148 E2
Ware SG12 . . . . .93 E1
Hanbury Cotts AL9 . . . . .131 E6
Hanbury Dr SG12 . . . . . . .93 C6
Hanbury Mews SG12 . . . .93 C5
Hancock Cl WD6 . . . . .170 C5
Hancock Dr LU2 . . . . .45 E5
Hancroft Rd HP3 . . . . . . .124 F1
Handa Cl HP3 . . . . .139 B8
Handcross Rd LU2 . . . . . . .46 D2
Hand La CM21 . . . . .97 C1
Handley Gate AL2 . . . . . .140 F2
Handley Page Way
AL2 . . . . .141 F1
Handleys Cl HP22 . . . . . . .124 D2
Handpost Lodge Gdns
HP2 . . . . .125 D2
HANDSIDE 110 C5
Handside Cl AL8 . . . . .110 C6
Handside La AL8 . . . . .110 C6
Handsworth Way
WD19 . . . . .175 A7
Hangar Ruding WD19 . . .175 F7
Hanger Cl HP1 . . . . .124 B2
Hangmans La AL6 . . . . . . .89 F8
Hanover Cl SG2 . . . . .50 F1
Hanover Ct
Croxley Green WD3 . . . . .166 A4
Hoddesdon EN11 . . . . . .135 A7
Luton LU4 . . . . .44 D5
14 Pinner HA5 . . . . .175 F3
Sawbridgeworth CM21 . . .97 F1
Waltham Abbey EN9 . . . .163 C6
Watford WD18 . . . . .166 E5
Hanover Gdns WD5 . . . . .139 F1
Hanover Gn HP1 . . . . .124 A1
Hanover Grange AL5 . . . . .85 E3
Hanover Ho AL7 . . . . .110 F4
Hanover Wlk AL10 . . . . . .129 F2
Hanross Cl AL2 . . . . .140 E1
HANSCOMBE END 19 D8
Hanscombe End Rd
SG5 . . . . .19 D7
Hanselin Cl HA7 . . . . .176 F5
Hanswick Cl LU2 . . . . .46 B2
Hanworth Cl LU2 . . . . .45 D7
Hanyards End SG6 . . . . . .146 E3
Hanyards La EN6 . . . . . . .146 E3
Happy Valley Ind Pk
WD4 . . . . .139 B3
Harbert Gdns AL2 . . . . . .141 C2
Harborne Cl WD19 . . . . . .175 C5
Harbour Ct WD23 . . . . . .168 B4
Harbury Dell LU3 . . . . .45 B7
Harcourt Rd
Bushey WD23 . . . . .168 C4
Tring HP23 . . . . .100 C3
Harcourt St 4 AL5 . . . . . . .63 E5
Hardenwick Ct 4 AL5 . . . .86 A2
Harding Cl
Luton LU3 . . . . .44 E7
Redbourn AL3 . . . . .106 B5
Watford WD25 . . . . .154 C6
Harding Cl AL5 . . . . .86 B4
Harding Par 8 AL5 . . . . . . .86 B1
Harding Cl HP3 . . . . .138 B8
Hardings CM22 . . . . .98 C6
Hardingstone Ct EN8 . . . .162 F5
Hardwick Cl SG2 . . . . .69 C7
Hardwick Pl AL2 . . . . .142 D4
Hardwicke Pl AL2 . . . . . . .142 D4
Hardwicke Gn LU3 . . . . . . .45 B7
Hardy Cl
Barnet EN5 . . . . .171 E4
Hitchin SG4 . . . . .35 C7
Hardy Ct 10 WD6 . . . . . . .170 A5
Hardy Dr SG8 . . . . .7 D4
Hardy Rd HP2 . . . . .124 F4
Harebell Cl AL7 . . . . .110 E3
Harebell SG13 . . . . .114 B6
Harebreaks The
WD24 . . . . .154 B2
Hare Cres WD25 . . . . . . .154 A7
HAREFIELD 173 C1
Harefield
Harlow CM20 . . . . .118 A1
Stevenage SG2 . . . . .51 C3
Harefield Acad The
UB9 . . . . .173 D2
Harefield Cl LU1 . . . . .62 F8
Harefield Hospl UB9 . . . .173 C2

Harefield Inf Sch
UB9 . . . . 173 C2
Harefield Jun Sch
UB9 . . . . 173 C2
Harefield Pl AL4 . . . . 128 D6
Harefield Rd
Luton LU1 . . . . 62 F8
Rickmansworth WD3 . . . . . . 173 D7
Harefield Road Ind Est
WD3 . . . . 173 E6
Hare La AL1 . . . . 130 B3
Harepark Cl HP1 . . . . 123 F4
Haresfoot Sch HP4 . . . . . . 122 B1
HARE STREET
Buntingford 41 D7
Cottered 38 F6
Hare Street Rd SG9 . . . . 41 B8
Harewood WD3 . . . . 165 C4
Harewood Ct HA3 . . . . 176 E2
Harewood Rd WD19 . . . . . . 175 B7
Harford Dr WD17 . . . . 166 E8
Harforde Ct SG13 . . . . 114 A6
Hargrave Cl CM24 . . . . 59 E8
Hargreaves Ave EN7 . . . . . 162 B8
Hargreaves Cl EN7 . . . . . . 162 B8
Hargreaves Rd SG8 . . . . 7 D5
Harkett Cl HA3 . . . . 176 F1
Harkett Ct HA3 . . . . 176 F1
Harkness EN7 . . . . 148 B2
Harkness Ct SG4 . . . . 22 B1
Harkness Rd **9** HP2 . . . . . 124 D4
Harkness Way SG4 . . . . 22 C2
Harland Ct UB9 . . . . 173 C1
Harlech Rd WD5 . . . . 154 A8
Harlequin Ho WD17 . . . . . . 167 C5
Harlesden Rd AL1 . . . . 128 A3
Harlestone Cl LU3 . . . . 31 A1
Harley Ct
Enfield EN1 . . . . 162 B2
St Albans AL4 . . . . 128 D7
Harlings The SG13 . . . . 114 C2
HARLOW 118 C2
Harlowbury Prim Sch
CM17 . . . . 118 D4
Harlow Coll CM20 . . . . 117 D1
Harlow Ct HP2 . . . . 125 D8
Harlow Mill Sta CM20 . . . . 118 C5
Harlow Rd
Roydon CM19 . . . . 116 C1
Sawbridgeworth CM17 . . . . 118 C6
Harlow Ret Pk CM20 . . . . . 117 F4
Harlow Stad (Greyhounds)
CM19 . . . . 116 E1
Harlow Town Sta
CM20 . . . . 117 D3
Harlton Ct EN9 . . . . 163 F5
Harmer Dell AL6 . . . . 89 F4
HARMER GREEN 90 B5
Harmony Cl AL10 . . . . 130 A7
Harmsworth Way N20 . . . . 171 F1
Harness Way AL4 . . . . 128 D6
Harold Cres EN9 . . . . 163 C7
Harold Ct LU4 . . . . 162 F5
HARPENDEN 86 B2
HARPENDEN COMMON
. . . . 107 B7
Harpenden Hospl (private)
AL5 . . . . 86 A4
Harpenden La AL3 . . . . 106 B6
Harpenden Meml Hospl
AL5 . . . . 86 B2
Harpenden Rd
St Albans AL3 . . . . 127 E6
Wheathampstead AL5,
AL4 . . . . 108 B8
Harpenden Rise AL5 . . . . . . 85 F3
Harpenden Sta AL5 . . . . 86 B1
Harperbury Hospl
WD7 . . . . 156 C8
Harper Ct SG1 . . . . 50 F5
Harper La WD7 . . . . 156 B8
Harpsfield Broadway
AL10 . . . . 129 F6
Harps Hill AL3 . . . . 83 E5
Harptree Way AL1 . . . . 128 A5
Harriet Ho HP3 . . . . 138 E6
Harriet Walker Way
WD3 . . . . 164 F2
Harriet Way WD23 . . . . 168 D2
Harrington Cl **8** CM23 . . . . . 77 A7
Harrington Ct SG13 . . . . . . 114 C3
Harriot Hts AL1 . . . . 127 C4
Harris Ho **14** WD18 . . . . . . 166 F3
Harris La
Great Offley SG5 . . . . 33 D2
Shenley WD7 . . . . 157 A6
Harrison Cl
3 Hitchin SG4 . . . . 34 F7
Northwood HA6 . . . . 174 C4
Harrison Rd EN9 . . . . 163 C4
Harrisons CM23 . . . . 59 D2
Harrison Wlk EN8 . . . . 148 D1
Harris Rd WD25 . . . . 154 A4
Harris's La SG12 . . . . 93 C1
Harrogate Rd **2**
WD19 . . . . 175 C7
HARROW 176 E1
Harrowband Rd **7**
CM17 . . . . 118 C1
Harrow Coll, Harrow
Weald Campus HA3 . . . 176 E4
Harrow Ct SG1 . . . . 50 E5
Harrowden Ct LU2 . . . . 64 C8
Harrowden Rd LU2 . . . . 64 B8
Harrow View HA2 . . . . 176 C1
Harrow Way WD19 . . . . 175 E6

HARROW WEALD 176 D2
Harrow Weald Pk
HA3 . . . . 176 D4
Harrow Yd HP23 . . . . 100 A3
Harry Scott Ct LU4 . . . . 44 C6
Harston Dr EN3 . . . . 163 A1
Hartcran Ho **7** WD19 . . . . 175 D7
Hartcroft Cl HP3 . . . . 125 B2
Hartfield Ave WD6 . . . . 170 A4
Hartfield Ct **8** SG12 . . . . 93 D2
Hartforde Rd WD6 . . . . 170 B8
Harthall La WD4, HP3 . . . . 139 D4
HARTHAM 113 D7
Hartham La SG14 . . . . 113 D6
Hartham Villas SG14 . . . . . 113 C7
HART HILL 46 A1
Hart Hill Dr LU2 . . . . 63 F8
Hart Hill La LU2 . . . . 63 F8
Hart Hill Path LU2 . . . . 63 F8
Hart La LU2 . . . . 64 A8
Hartland Ct SG5 . . . . 34 D7
Hartland Rd EN8 . . . . 148 D1
Hartley Rd LU2 . . . . 63 F8
Hart Lo **10** EN5 . . . . 171 E6
Hartmoor Mews EN3 . . . . . 162 D2
Hart Rd
Harlow CM17 . . . . 118 C6
St Albans AL1 . . . . 127 D2
Hartsbourne Ave
WD23 . . . . 176 D8
Hartsbourne Cl WD23 . . . . 176 D8
Hartsbourne Pk
WD23 . . . . 176 D8
Hartsbourne Prim Sch
WD23 . . . . 176 D8
Hartsbourne Rd
WD23 . . . . 176 D8
Hartsbourne Way
HP2 . . . . 125 C2
Hartsfield Jun Mix Inf Sch
SG7 . . . . 12 F1
Hartsfield Rd LU2 . . . . 46 B2
Hartspring La WD23,
WD25 . . . . 168 A8
Hartswood Gn WD23 . . . . . 176 D8
Hartwell Gdns AL5 . . . . 85 E1
Harvest Cl LU4 . . . . 44 A3
Harvest Ct
Letchworth Garden City
SG6 . . . . 23 A2
Oaklands AL6 . . . . 89 E7
St Albans AL4 . . . . 128 D7
Harvest End WD25 . . . . 154 D3
Harvest La SG2 . . . . 51 D7
Harvest Mead AL10 . . . . . . 130 B7
Harvest Rd WD23 . . . . 168 B5
Harveyfields EN9 . . . . 163 C5
Harvey Rd
Croxley Green WD3 . . . . . . 166 A3
London Colney AL2 . . . . . . 142 C5
Stevenage SG2 . . . . 50 F8
Harvey Road Prim Sch
WD3 . . . . 166 A3
Harvey's Hill LU2 . . . . 45 F5
Harvington Pk LU7 . . . . 80 D3
Harvingwell Pl HP2 . . . . . . 125 B5
Harwood Cl
Tewin AL6 . . . . 90 E2
Welwyn Garden City AL8 . . 89 E1
Harwood Hill AL8 . . . . 89 E1
Harwood Hill Jun Mix Inf
Sch AL8 . . . . 89 E2
Harwoods Rd WD18 . . . . . . 167 A5
Hasedines Rd HP1 . . . . 124 A4
Haseldine Mdws AL10 . . . . 129 F4
Haseldine Rd AL2 . . . . 142 D5
Haselfoot SG6 . . . . 22 E6
Hasketon Dr LU4 . . . . 44 B6
Haslemere CM23 . . . . 77 A4
Haslemere Est The
EN11 . . . . 135 C6
Haslemere Ind Est
Bishop's Stortford
CM23 . . . . 77 A4
Welwyn Garden City
AL7 . . . . 110 F7
Haslewood Ave EN11 . . . . 135 A3
Haslingden Cl AL5 . . . . 85 D3
Hastings Cl SG1 . . . . 50 A8
Hastings St LU1 . . . . 63 D7
Hastings Way
Croxley Green WD3 . . . . . . 166 C5
Watford WD23 . . . . 167 E5
HASTOE 119 F7
Hastoe Cross HP23 . . . . . . 120 A7
Hastoe Farm Barns
HP23 . . . . 119 F7
Hastoe La HP23 . . . . 100 A2
HATCH END 175 E3
Hatch End High Sch
HA3 . . . . 176 B2
Hatch End Sta HA5 . . . . . . 176 A3
Hatch Gn CM22 . . . . 98 B8
HATCHING GREEN 107 A6
Hatching Green Cl
AL5 . . . . 107 A6
Hatching Green Cotts
AL5 . . . . 107 A7
Hatch La SG4 . . . . 24 A3
HATFIELD 130 B8
Hatfield Ave AL10 . . . . 129 E8
Hatfield Bsns Pk
AL10 . . . . 129 D8
Hatfield Cres HP2 . . . . 124 F7
HATFIELD GARDEN
VILLAGE 129 E8

HATFIELD HEATH 98 F4
Hatfield House & Gdns*
AL9 . . . . 130 D5
HATFIELD HYDE 110 F3
Hatfield Rd
Essendon AL9 . . . . 111 E1
Potters Bar EN6 . . . . 159 C8
St Albans AL1, AL4 . . . . . . 128 C3
Watford WD24 . . . . 167 B8
Hatfield Sta AL10 . . . . 130 C6
Hatfield Tunnel AL10 . . . . . 129 F6
Hathaway Cl LU4 . . . . 44 B2
Hathaway Ct AL4 . . . . 128 E3
Hatherleigh Gdns
EN6 . . . . 159 D7
Hatherley Chase LU2 . . . . . . 45 E2
Hatters Cl AL4 . . . . 166 D3
Hatters Way LU1, LU4 . . . . . 44 D1
Hatters Way Ret Pk
LU4 . . . . 44 E1
Hatton Pl LU2 . . . . 63 E8
Hatton Rd EN8 . . . . 148 D2
HAULTWICK 53 F3
Havelock Rd
Kings Langley WD4 . . . . . . 138 F3
Luton LU2 . . . . 45 E1
Havelock Rise LU2 . . . . 45 E1
Haven Cl AL10 . . . . 129 F6
Havensfield WD4 . . . . 152 B8
Haven The SG5 . . . . 11 F6
Havercroft Cl AL3 . . . . 127 C1
Haverdale LU4 . . . . 44 C4
Havers La CM23 . . . . 76 F5
Haward Rd EN11 . . . . 135 C8
Hawbush Cl AL6 . . . . 89 B4
Hawbush Rise HA6 . . . . 174 F3
Hawes La SG4 . . . . 63 C1
Haweswater Dr
WD25 . . . . 154 C6
Hawfield Gdns AL2 . . . . . . 141 D5
Hawkes Dr AL3 . . . . 106 B5
Hawkesley Ct WD7 . . . . 155 F4
Hawkesworth Cl HA6 . . . . 174 E3
Hawkfield SG6 . . . . 23 C8
Hawkfields LU2 . . . . 45 E6
Hawkins Way HP3 . . . . 137 A5
Hawkins Cl WD6 . . . . 170 C7
Hawkins Hall La SG3 . . . . . 69 E2
Hawkshead Ct EN8 . . . . . . 162 F5
Hawkshead La AL9 . . . . 144 D3
Hawkshead Rd EN6 . . . . . . 145 B2
Hawkshill AL1 . . . . 128 A2
Hawkshill Dr HP3 . . . . 137 F8
Hawksmead Cl EN3 . . . . . . 162 D3
Hawksmoor WD7 . . . . 157 A6
Hawkwell Dr HP23 . . . . 100 C4
HAWRIDGE 120 C1
Hawridge & Cholesbury
CE Sch HP5 . . . . 120 C2
Hawridge La HP5 . . . . 120 F1
Hawridge Vale HP5 . . . . . . 120 F1
Hawsley Rd AL5 . . . . 107 A4
Hawthorn Ave LU2 . . . . 46 B4
Hawthorn Cl
Abbots Langley WD5 . . . . . 154 A1
Harpenden AL5 . . . . 107 D7
Hertford SG14 . . . . 113 A7
Hitchin SG5 . . . . 34 E6
Royston SG8 . . . . 7 F7
Watford WD17 . . . . 153 F1
Hawthorn Cres **5** LU5 . . . 175 C1
Hawthorn Ct **5** HA6 . . . . . 174 E3
Hawthorne Ave EN7 . . . . . 162 B8
Hawthorne Cl EN7 . . . . 162 B8
Hawthorne Ct HA6 . . . . 175 A1
Hawthorne Rd WD7 . . . . . . 156 A5
Hawthornes AL10 . . . . 129 F3
Hawthorn Gr
Barnet EN5 . . . . 170 F3
Enfield EN2 . . . . 161 D1
Hawthorn Hill SG6 . . . . 22 F7
Hawthorn La HP1 . . . . 123 F4
Hawthorn Rd EN11 . . . . . . 135 B8
Hawthorn Rise CM23 . . . . . 76 A3
Hawthorns AL3 . . . . 110 D8
Hawthorns The
Berkhamsted HP4 . . . . 122 A5
Hemel Hempstead HP3 . . . 137 F7
Maple Cross WD3 . . . . 172 D5
Ridge EN6 . . . . 157 E6
Stevenage SG1 . . . . 51 A4
Ware SG12 . . . . 93 C3
Hawthorn Way
Chiswell Green AL2 . . . . . . 141 A7
Royston SG8 . . . . 7 F7
Haybourne Mead HP4 . . . . 124 B2
Hay Cl WD6 . . . . 170 C7
Haycroft
Bishop's Stortford
CM23 . . . . 77 C7
Luton LU2 . . . . 45 E6
Haycroft Rd SG1 . . . . 50 D7
Haydon Rd EN9 . . . . 163 C4
Haydock Rd SG8 . . . . 7 F6
Haydock Round SG1 . . . . . . 37 A4
Haydon Dell AL2 . . . . 167 F3
Haydon Hill Ho WD23 . . . . 167 F3
Haydon Rd WD19 . . . . 167 E3
Hayes Cl LU2 . . . . 46 C5
Hayes Hill Farm*
EN9 . . . . 149 C3
Hayes Wlk
1 Cheshunt EN10 . . . . . . 148 F6
Potters Bar EN6 . . . . 159 B6
Hayfield SG2 . . . . 51 D7

Hayfield Cl WD23 . . . . 168 B5
Haygarth SG3 . . . . 69 A4
Hay Gn SG8 . . . . 15 F6
HAY GREEN 15 F6
Hayhurst Rd LU4 . . . . 44 B1
Hay La AL5 . . . . 86 A1
Hayley Bell Gdns CM23 . . . 76 F3
Hayley Comm SG2 . . . . 51 C3
Hayling Dr LU2 . . . . 46 D3
Hayling Rd WD19 . . . . 175 B8
Haymeads AL8 . . . . 89 E1
Haymeads La CM23 . . . . 77 C6
Haymoor SG6 . . . . 22 E7
Haynes Cl AL7 . . . . 111 A5
Haynes Mead HP4 . . . . 122 A6
Haysman Cl SG6 . . . . 23 B7
HAY STREET 41 E1
Hayton Cl LU3 . . . . 31 B2
Hay Wains SG3 . . . . 69 B2
Haywards The EN10 . . . . . . 134 F2
Haywood Cl HA5 . . . . 175 D1
Haywood Copse WD3 . . . . 165 D5
Haywood Ct EN9 . . . . 163 F5
Haywood Dr WD3 . . . . 164 F4
Haywood Grove Sch
HP2 . . . . 125 A8
Haywood La SG8 . . . . 16 A6
Haywood Pk WD3 . . . . 164 F4
Haywoods Dr HP3 . . . . 137 F8
Haywoods La SG8 . . . . 7 E7
Hazelbank WD3 . . . . 166 C3
Hazelbury Ave WD5 . . . . . 153 C7
Hazelbury Cres LU1 . . . . . . 63 C8
Hazelbury Ct **3** LU1 . . . . . 63 C8
Hazel Cl
3 Hammond Street
EN7 . . . . 147 E5
Hemel Hempstead HP1 . . . 89 E3
Hazelcroft HA5 . . . . 176 B4
Hazel Ct
Hitchin SG4 . . . . 35 A7
Shenley WD7 . . . . 156 F6
Hazeldell SG1 . . . . 70 D3
Hazeldell Link HP1 . . . . 123 E2
Hazeldell Rd HP1 . . . . 123 F2
Hazeldene EN8 . . . . 162 E7
HAZEL END 59 A6
Hazel End CM23 . . . . 59 A5
Hazelend Rd CM23 . . . . 59 B4
Hazel Gdns CM21 . . . . 97 F1
Hazel Gr
Hatfield AL10 . . . . 129 F2
Stotfold SG5 . . . . 11 E5
Watford WD25 . . . . 154 B4
Welwyn Garden City
AL7 . . . . 111 C7
Hazel Grove Ho AL10 . . . . 129 F3
Hazel Mead EN5 . . . . 171 B4
Hazelmere Rd
St Albans AL4 . . . . 128 C6
Stevenage SG2 . . . . 69 A8
Hazel Rd
Berkhamsted HP4 . . . . 122 D3
Chiswell Green AL2 . . . . . . 141 B3
Hazels The AL6 . . . . 90 E2
Hazel Tree Rd WD24 . . . . . 154 B3
Hazelwood Cl
Hitchin SG5 . . . . 34 F8
Luton LU2 . . . . 46 B4
Hazelwood Dr
Pinner HA5 . . . . 175 B1
St Albans AL4 . . . . 128 C4
Hazelwood La WD5 . . . . . . 153 D7
Hazelwood Rd WD3 . . . . . . 166 C3
Hazely HP23 . . . . 100 C4
Heacham Cl LU4 . . . . 44 B4
Headingley Cl
Hammond Street EN7 . . . . 147 F5
Shenley WD7 . . . . 156 F7
Stevenage SG1 . . . . 50 E8
Headlands Dr HP4 . . . . 122 E5
Headstone La HA3 . . . . 176 B2
Headstone Lane Sta
HA3 . . . . 176 B2
Healey Rd WD18 . . . . 166 F3
Healy Ct EN5 . . . . 171 D3
Hearle Way AL10 . . . . 129 E7
Heath Ave
Royston SG8 . . . . 7 C6
St Albans AL3 . . . . 127 D5
Heathbourne Rd
WD23 . . . . 168 D5
Heath Brow HP1 . . . . 124 C1
Heathbrow Rd AL6 . . . . 89 F8
Heath Cl
Harpenden AL5 . . . . 107 C7
Hemel Hempstead HP1 . . . 124 C2
Luton LU1, LU2 . . . . 63 B6
Potters Bar EN6 . . . . 145 B1
Heathcliff Ave SG5 . . . . 11 B2
Heathcote Ave AL10 . . . . . 130 A7
Heathcote Sch The
SG2 . . . . 51 A2
Heath Cotts EN6 . . . . 145 B1
Heathcroft AL7 . . . . 111 C6
Heathdene Manor
WD17 . . . . 166 F8
Heather Cl
Abbots Langley WD5 . . . . . 154 A7
Bishop's Stortford CM23 . . . 76 D6
Heather Ct AL2 . . . . 142 D4
Heather Gdns EN6 . . . . 163 C3
Heathermere SG6 . . . . 11 F1

Har–Hem 195

Heather Rd AL8 . . . . 110 C4
Heather Rise WD23 . . . . . . 167 F7
Heathers The SG13 . . . . . . 113 C6
Heather Way
Harrow HA7 . . . . 176 F4
Hemel Hempstead HP2 . . . 124 D4
Potters Bar EN6 . . . . 158 F7
Heath Farm Ct WD17 . . . . 153 D2
Heath Farm La AL1,
AL3 . . . . 127 E5
Heathfield SG8 . . . . 7 B6
Heathfield Cl
Caddington LU1 . . . . 62 F4
Potters Bar EN6 . . . . 145 B1
Watford WD13 . . . . 167 C2
Heathfield Ct **4** AL1 . . . . . 127 E4
Heathfield Lower Sch
LU1 . . . . 62 E4
Heathfield Rd
Hitchin SG5 . . . . 21 F1
Luton LU3 . . . . 45 C4
Watford WD3 . . . . 167 F5
Heathgate SG13 . . . . 114 B2
Heath Hall SG7 . . . . 23 F7
Heath Hill SG4 . . . . 67 D1
Heath La
Codicote SG4 . . . . 68 E8
Hemel Hempstead HP1 . . . 124 C2
Hertford Heath SG13 . . . . . 114 C2
Heathlands AL6 . . . . 68 F1
Heathlands Dr AL3 . . . . 127 E5
Heathlands Sch AL3 . . . . . . 127 E6
Heath Lo WD23 . . . . 168 D1
Heath Mount Sch SG14 . . . 71 B2
Heath Park Ho HP2 . . . . . . 124 C1
Heath Rd
Breachwood Green
SG4 . . . . 47 D1
Oaklands AL6 . . . . 68 F1
Potters Bar EN6 . . . . 145 B1
St Albans AL3 . . . . 127 E5
Watford WD19 . . . . 167 E2
Heath Row CM23 . . . . 59 B1
Heathside
Colney Heath AL4 . . . . 143 B8
St Albans AL1 . . . . 127 E5
Heathside Cl HA6 . . . . 174 D5
Heathside Rd HA6 . . . . 174 D6
HEATH THE 47 D2
Heath The
Breachwood Green
SG4 . . . . 47 D1
Radlett WD7 . . . . 156 A6
Heathview AL5 . . . . 107 B8
Heath Way WD7 . . . . 156 C8
Heaton Ct EN8 . . . . 148 D2
Heaton Dell LU2 . . . . 46 E1
Heay Fields AL7 . . . . 111 C7
Hebden Cl LU4 . . . . 44 B4
HEBING END 53 A2
Hebing End SG2 . . . . 52 F2
Heckford Cl WD18 . . . . 166 C3
Hedgebrooms AL7 . . . . 111 C7
Hedge Row HP1 . . . . 124 A5
Hedgerow SG2 . . . . 51 D8
Hedgerow La EN5 . . . . 171 B4
Hedgerows The SG2 . . . . . . 97 F2
Hedgerows The
Bishop's Stortford
CM23 . . . . 77 B6
Stevenage SG2 . . . . 51 B4
Hedgerow The LU4 . . . . 44 D6
Hedgerow Wlk EN8 . . . . . . 148 D1
Hedges Cl AL10 . . . . 130 B6
Hedgeside HP4 . . . . 123 A7
Hedgeside Rd HA6 . . . . 174 C5
Hedges The AL3 . . . . 127 C7
Hedley Cl HP22 . . . . 99 A3
Hedley Rd AL1 . . . . 128 B3
Hedley Rise LU2 . . . . 46 F2
Hedley Villas AL1 . . . . 128 B3
Hedworth Ave EN8 . . . . . . 162 D6
Heights The
Hemel Hempstead
HP2 . . . . 124 F6
Luton LU3 . . . . 44 E5
Helena Cl EN4 . . . . 159 D4
Helena Pl **5** HP2 . . . . 124 D5
Helens Gate SG1 . . . . 148 E5
Helham Gn SG12 . . . . 94 F4
Hellards Rd SG1 . . . . 50 D7
Hellebore Cl SG1 . . . . 51 B8
Hellen Way WD19 . . . . 175 D6
Helmsley Cl LU4 . . . . 44 C5
Helston Cl HA5 . . . . 175 F3
Helston Gr HP2 . . . . 124 D8
Helston Pl WD5 . . . . 153 F7
HEMEL HEMPSTEAD
. . . . 124 D6
Hemel Hempstead General
Hospl HP2 . . . . 124 D3
Hemel Hempstead Ind Est
HP2 . . . . 125 B5
Hemel Hempstead
Montessori Sch HP1 . . . 124 B1
Hemel Hempstead Rd
Great Gaddesden HP4 . . . . . 81 F1
Hemel Hempstead HP2,
HP3 . . . . 125 E1
Redbourn AL3, HP2 . . . . . . 105 E2
St Albans HP3, AL2,
AL3 . . . . 126 D1
Hemel Hempstead Sch
The HP1 . . . . 124 C2

Hemel Hempstead Sta HP3 ....138 A8
Hemingford Dr LU2....45 D6
Hemingford Rd WD17...153 C3
Hemmings The HP4....121 F3
Hemming Way WD25 ...154 A4
Hemp La HP23....100 F1
Hempstall Al7.......111 B4
Hempstead La HP4 ....123 C6
Hempstead Rd
  Bovingdon HP3 .....137 B5
  Kings Langley WD4 ....139 A3
  Watford WD17........153 C2
Hemsley Rd WD4 .....139 B2
Henbury Way WD19....175 D7
Henderson Cl Al3 ....127 C7
Henderson Pl
  Bedmond WD5.......139 F4
  Little Berkhamsted SG13........132 C2
Hendon Wood La NW7........171 A1
Hendren Ct 2 SG1 ....51 A8
Henge Way LU3 .....44 E7
HENLOW...........10 D8
Henlow Ind Est SG16...10 B4
Henry Cl EN2........161 E1
Henry St
  Hemel Hempstead HP3........138 D7
  Tring HP23 ....100 A3
Hensley Cl
  Hitchin SG4 ....35 B6
  Welwyn AL6.........89 C6
Henstead Pl LU2.......46 D1
Hepburn Ct EN6.......158 A7
Hepworth Ct SG2.......51 C6
Heracles Cl Al2 ......141 C3
Herald Cl CM23.........76 D6
Herbert St HP2 ......124 D4
Hercules Way WD25 ...153 F6
Hereford Rd LU4......44 A3
Hereward Cl EN9......163 C7
Herga Ct WD17.......167 A7
Heritage Cl 7 AL3 ....127 D3
Heritage Gn HP23 ....120 F5
Heritage Wlk WD3....164 E6
Herkomer Cl WD23 ...168 B3
Herkomer Rd WD23 ...168 B3
Herm Ho EN3 ....162 D1
Hermitage Cl
  Potters Bar EN6 ......159 C6
  Stansted Mountfitchet CM24........59 D7
Hermitage Ho CM24....59 D7
Hermitage Rd SG5....34 F7
Hermitage The SG15...11 B8
Herne Ct WD23 ......168 C2
Herne Rd
  Bushey WD23 ....168 B3
  Stevenage SG1 ......36 B1
Herneshaw AL10......129 F3
Herns La AL7........111 B8
Herns Way AL7 ......111 A8
Heron Cl
  Hemel Hempstead HP3........138 F6
  Rickmansworth WD3 ...173 D8
  Sawbridgeworth CM21 ...97 D1
Heron Ct CM23 ....77 A7
Heron Dr
  Luton LU2 ....45 E6
  Stansted Abbotts SG12.........115 C3
Heronfield EN6 .....145 C1
Herongate Rd EN4...148 E4
Heron Mead EN3 ....163 A1
Heron Pl LU89.......173 A4
Herons Elm HP4 .....121 E7
HERONSGATE.......164 D2
Heronsgate Rd WD3 ..164 B3
Heronslea WD25.....154 C3
Herons Way AL1.......142 B8
Heronswood EN9....163 E5
Herons Wood CM20...117 B2
Heronswood Pl AL7 ..111 A5
Heronswood Rd AL7...111 A5
Heron Trad Est LU3 ...44 C7
Heron Way
  Hatfield AL10........130 A3
  Roydon CM19........116 A1
  Royston SG8 ....7 E8
  Stotfold SG5........11 E6
Heron Wlk HP4......174 E6
HERTFORD.........113 C5
Hertford Castle*
  SG14............113 B6
Hertford County Hospl
  SG14............113 B6
Hertford East Sta SG13............113 E6
HERTFORD HEATH...114 B3
Hertford Heath Prim Sch SG13 ....114 C4
Hertford Mews EN6...159 C8
Hertford Mus* SG14 ...113 D6
Hertford North Sta SG14............113 B6
Hertford Rd
  Enfield EN3 ....162 D3
  Great Amwell SG12....114 F4
  Hatfield AL9.........111 B1
  Hoddesdon EN11.....134 E8
  Stevenage SG2 ......69 B7
  Tewin AL6 ....90 F2

Hertford Rd continued
  Welwyn AL6.........89 D3
Hertford Regional Coll
  Cheshunt EN10 ......148 F6
  Ware SG12 ....114 D8
Hertford St Andrew CE
  Prim Sch SG14 ......112 E7
Hertfordshire Bsns Ctr
  AL2.............142 D5
Hertfordshire & Essex
  Bishop's Stortford CM23........77 B7
Hertfordshire Theatre Sch
  SG4 ....34 F6
HERTINGFORDBURY ...112 E5
Hertingfordbury Cowper
  Prim Sch SG14 ......112 F4
Hertingfordbury Rd
  Hertford SG14.......113 B5
  Hertingfordbury SG14 ..112 F4
Herts & Essex Hospl
  CM23............77 B6
Hertsmere Ind Pk WD6.............170 D1
Hertsmere Jewish Prim
  Sch WD7 ....156 C1
Hertswood Ct 2 EN5 ...171 E5
Hertswood Sch WD6...170 D2
Hertswood Upper Sch WD6.............170 C7
Hester Ho CM20.....117 C2
Heswall Ct 6 LU1 ....63 F6
Heswall Gn WD19....175 A7
Hetchleys HP1.......124 A6
Hever Cl LU7........80 D2
Hewins Cl EN9......163 E7
Hewitt Cl AL4 ....108 D7
Hewlett Rd LU3......44 E5
HEXTON..........19 B2
Hexton Jun Mix Inf Sch SG5 ....19 A1
Hexton Rd
  Great Offley SG5......33 E8
  Lilley LU2 ....32 C4
Heybridge Ct SG14....112 F7
Heybrigge Cl AL3 ....106 A5
Heybridge Rd SG8.....9 E3
Heydons Cl AL3......127 D5
Heyford End AL2.....141 C3
Heyford Rd WD7.....155 F2
Heyford Way AL10 ...130 C7
Heysham Dr WD19...175 D5
Heywood Dr LU2......42 F2
Hibbert Ave WD24 ...154 D1
Hibbert Rd HA3......176 F1
Hibberts Ct SG6......22 E7
Hibbert St LU1 ......45 D3
Hibbert Street
  Almshouses 13 LU1....63 E6
Hickling Cl LU2.......46 D1
Hickling Way AL5......86 C3
Hickman Cl EN10 ....134 D3
Hickman St LU1......44 D8
Hickman's Hill SG7....24 D4
Hicks Rd AL3........83 E6
Hidalgo Ct HP2.......124 F6
Hideaway The WD5...153 F8
Hides The CM20 .....117 D1
Higgins Rd EN7.....147 D4
High Acres WD5.....153 D7
Higham Dr LU2.......46 D1
HIGHAM GOBION 19 A6
High Ash Rd AL4 ....108 C7
High Ave SG6........22 E4
Highbanks Rd HA5...176 B4
HIGH BARNET.......171 E6
High Barnet Sta EN5...171 F5
Highbarns HP3 ......139 A6
High Beeches Prim Sch
  AL5.............86 D1
High Beech Rd LU3...44 D7
Highbourne Ct 2
  EN11............135 A6
Highbridge Cl WD7...164 A6
Highbridge Cl 5 EN9..163 B6
Highbridge Ho 6 EN9............163 B6
Highbridge Ret Pk
  EN9 ....163 B5
Highbridge St EN9...163 B6
Highbury Ave LU1....135 A8
Highbury Ho (North Herts
  Music Sch) SG4......35 A7
Highbury Inf Sch SG4...34 F6
Highbury Rd
  Hitchin SG4 ....35 A7
  Luton LU1 ....45 C1
Highbush Rd SG5....11 E5
High Canons WD6....157 D2
High Cl WD3 ....165 C4
Highclere 6 AL1.....127 E4
Highclere 2 SG2......50 F1
Highcroft Rd HP3....138 B6
HIGH CROSS........72 F2
High Cross WD25....155 D2
High Dane SG4.......22 A2
High Dells AL10.....129 F4
High Elms
  Harpenden AL5 ......107 A6
  Watford WD25.......154 B8
High Elms Cl HA6....174 D4
High Elms La
  Abbots Langley WD25,
  WD5............154 C8
  Benington SG2......52 F1
HIGHFIELD........124 F6

Highfield
  Bushey WD23.....176 E8
  Kings Langley WD4 ...138 E3
  Letchworth Garden City
  SG6............22 E4
  Little Hadham SG11....57 C3
  Sawbridgeworth CM21...97 E3
  South Oxhey WD19 ...175 F7
  Watford WD25.......153 F5
Highfield Ave
  Bishop's Stortford CM23........77 C6
  Harpenden AL5 ......107 C8
Highfield Cl HA6.....174 E2
Highfield Cres HA6....174 E2
Highfield Ct
  Hertford SG13.......113 D4
  Stevenage SG1 ......50 F7
Highfield Dr EN10...134 E2
Highfield Farm SG13...134 A6
Highfield Hall AL4...142 E7
Highfield Ho HP2....124 F5
Highfield La
  Colney Heath AL4 ....142 E8
  Hemel Hempstead HP2...124 F5
Highfield Manor AL4...142 E7
Highfield Oval AL5....86 A4
Highfield Park Dr
  AL4.............142 C8
Highfield Rd
  Berkhamsted HP4 ....122 D4
  Hammond Street EN7...147 E5
  Hertford SG13.......113 D4
  Luton LU4 ....45 B1
  Northwood HA6 .....174 E2
  Sandridge AL4.......108 B1
  Tring HP23.........99 E3
  Watford WD23.......167 E4
  Wigginton HP23......100 D1
Highfields
  Cuffley EN6 ....146 E3
  Radlett WD7........155 F4
Highfield Sch The SG6...22 D4
Highfields Cl LU5.....44 A2
Highfield Way
  Potters Bar EN6 .....159 B7
  Rickmansworth WD3 ..165 B3
High Firs WD7.......156 A4
High Firs Cres AL5...107 D8
Highgate Gr CM21....97 D2
High Gr
  St Albans AL3 ......127 D5
  Welwyn Garden City
  AL8............110 C7
Highgrove Ct EN8....162 D5
High House Est CM17...118 F4
High La CM24.......59 F8
Highland Dr
  Bushey WD23 ....168 C2
  Hemel Hempstead HP3...125 B3
Highland Rd
  Bishop's Stortford CM23........76 F3
  Lower Nazeing EN9...135 E1
  Northwood HA6 .....175 A1
Highlands
  Hatfield AL9........130 C8
  Royston SG8 ....7 E6
  Watford WD19.......167 C1
Highlands The
  Potters Bar EN6 .....145 C1
  Rickmansworth WD3 ..165 B2
High Leigh Barns
  EN11............134 E6
Highmead CM24......59 E8
High Mead LU3.......45 A3
High Meads AL4.....108 C8
Highmill SG12.......93 D3
Highmoor AL5.......86 A4
High Oak Rd SG12....93 E3
High Oaks
  Enfield EN2 ....160 F1
  7 Northwood HA6 ...174 F5
  St Albans AL3 ......127 D7
High Oaks Rd AL8...110 B7
Highover Cl LU2......46 B1
Highover Jun Mix Inf Sch
  SG4 ....22 C1
Highover Rd SG6......22 C5
Highover Way SG4....22 B1
High Plash SG1......50 E5
High Point 15 LU1....63 D6
High Rd
  Bushey WD23 ....168 D1
  Essendon AL9 ......131 E5
  Harrow HA3........176 E3
  Hoddesdon EN10....134 F3
  Shillington SG5......19 E8
  Stapleford SG14.....92 A2
  Watford WD25.......154 A7
High Ridge
  Cuffley EN6 ....146 E4
  Harpenden AL5 ......85 E3
  Luton LU2 ....46 C1
High Ridge Cl HP3...138 D6
Highridge Pl EN2....160 F1
High Ridge Rd HP3...138 D7
High Road Broxbourne
  EN10............134 F1
High Road Turnford
  EN10............148 E6
High Road Wormley
  EN10............148 F8
High St
  Abbots Langley WD5...139 F1
  Arlesey SG15.......11 A5
  Ashwell SG7........4 D4
  Baldock SG7........23 F8

High St continued
  Barkway SG8........17 C3
  Barley SG8..........8 F2
  Barnet EN6.........171 F5
  Bedmond WD5......139 F4
  Berkhamsted HP4 ....122 B4
  Berkhamsted, Northchurch
  HP4............121 E6
  Bishop's Stortford CM23...76 F7
  Bovingdon HP3 .....137 A4
  Buntingford SG9 .....40 E8
  Bushey WD23 ....168 A3
  Cheddington LU7.....80 A7
  Cheshunt EN8 ......148 D2
  Cheshunt, Waltham Cross
  EN8............162 D7
  Cheshunt, Waltham Cross
  EN8............162 E5
  Codicote SG4........67 F1
  Colney Heath AL4 ....129 B1
  Elstree WD6........169 D3
  Eyeworth SG19 ......1 A8
  Flamstead AL3.......84 B2
  Graveley SG4........36 C4
  Great Offley SG5......33 C3
  Guilden Morden SG8 ...1 F4
  Harefield UB9 ......173 C1
  Harlow CM17........118 C4
  Harpenden AL5 ......86 A1
  Harrow HA3........176 E1
  Hemel Hempstead HP1,
  HP3............124 D4
  Hinxworth SG7.......3 D6
  Hitchin, Gosmore SG4 ...34 F3
  Hitchin SG5 ....34 E7
  Hoddesdon EN11.....135 A5
  Hunsdon SG12......95 D1
  Ivinghoe LU7.......80 E5
  Kimpton SG4........66 C1
  Kings Langley WD4 ...139 A2
  London Colney AL2 ...142 D5
  Luton LU4 ....44 C4
  Markyate AL3 ....83 E5
  Much Hadham SG10 ...74 F3
  Northwood HA6 .....174 F2
  Pirton SG5.........20 D4
  Potters Bar EN6 .....159 C7
  Redbourn AL3 ....106 B5
  Reed SG8..........16 E5
  Rickmansworth WD19...116 B1
  Roydon CM19.......116 B3
  Royston SG8 ....7 D6
  Sandridge AL4.......108 C2
  St Albans AL3 ......127 D3
  Standon, Puckeridge
  SG11............55 D3
  Standon SG11.......55 F1
  Stanstead Abbotts
  SG12............115 C4
  Stevenage SG1 ......50 C7
  Stotfold SG5........11 F6
  Tring HP23.........100 A3
  Walkern SG2 ....38 B1
  Ware SG12 ....93 D1
  Watford WD18.......167 B6
  Watford WD17.......167 C5
  Watton at S SG14 ....70 E3
  Welwyn AL6.........66 F7
  Wheathampstead AL4 ...87 D1
  Whitwell SG4........66 F7
  Widford SG12.......95 E5
High Street Gn HP2...125 A5
HIGH TOWN.........63 E8
High Town Ent Ctr 1
  LU2............63 F8
High Town Rd LU2....45 F1
High View
  Birchanger CM23......59 D3
  Chorleywood WD3 ...165 A5
  Hatfield AL10........130 A2
  Park St SG4.........30 D7
  St Albans AL3 ......83 E5
  Watford WD18.......166 F3
Highview EN6........159 C6
High View Ct HA3....176 E3
Highview Gdns
  Potters Bar EN6 .....159 C6
  St Albans AL4 ......128 C8
Highway The HA7....176 F2
High Wickfield AL7 ...111 C5
Highwood Ave WD23...167 F8
High Wood Cl LU1....62 F7
Highwoodhall La HP3...139 A6
Highwood Prim Sch
  WD23............167 E8
High Wood Rd EN11...114 F1
HIGH WYCH........97 B1
High Wych CE Prim Sch
  CM21............97 A1
High Wych La CM21 ...97 A2
High Wych Rd
  Gilston CM21.......117 F7
  High Wych CM21......97 B1
High Wych Way HP2 ...105 A1
Hilbury AL10.........129 F4
Hilfield La WD25.....168 D6
Hilary Cl LU3........44 D7
Hilary Cres LU1......63 C6
Hilary Ho WD6......170 B6
Hilary Rd HP2 ......125 A4
Hilary Rise SG15.....11 B5
Hilberry Ct WD23...168 B2
Hillborough Inf Sch
  LU1............63 C6
Hillborough Jun Sch
  LU1............63 C6
Hillborough Rd LU1....63 B6
Hillbrow SG6........22 D5

Hill Cl
  Barnet EN5 ....171 C4
  Harpenden AL5 ......86 C4
  Luton LU3 ....45 C7
Hill Comm HP3 .....139 A8
Hill Cres SG1........50 F5
Hillcrest
  Baldock SG7........23 F7
  Hatfield AL10........130 A5
  St Albans AL3 ......127 B1
Hill Crest
  Potters Bar EN6 .....159 C5
  Welwyn SG6........66 E6
Hillcrest Ave LU2.....45 C8
Hillcrest Cl EN7.....147 C2
Hillcrest Cvn Pk LU1...62 F2
Hill Crest Lo WD6....169 F5
Hillcrest Rd WD7....157 A6
Hillcroft WD7.......156 A6
Hill Croft Cl LU4......44 C6
Hillcroft Cres WD19...175 B8
Hill Cl EN6.........159 C5
Hilldown Rd HP1....124 A5
Hill Dyke Rd AL4....108 E7
HILL END.........173 B4
Hille Bsns Ctr WD24...167 B8
HILL END.........173 B4
Hill End La AL4......128 C2
Hill End Rd UB9.....173 C3
Hill Farm Ave WD25...154 A6
Hill Farm Cl WD25...154 A6
Hill Farm Ind Est
  WD25............154 A6
Hill Farm La
  Ayot St L AL6.......88 C5
  Redbourn AL3 ......106 C1
Hillfield AL10........130 C8
Hillfield Ave SG4......22 A2
Hillfield Cl HP2......124 E3
Hillfield La S WD23 ...168 F3
Hillfield Rd HP2 .....124 E3
Hillgate SG4.........22 A3
Hillgrove Bsns Pk
  EN10............135 C1
Hill Head Cotts SG10...75 B1
Hill Ho
  Harefield UB9 ......173 C1
  Hertford SG13.......113 C5
Hillhouse EN9 ......163 F6
Hill House Ave HA7...176 F3
Hillhouse CE Prim Sch
  EN9 ....163 F6
Hilliard Rd HA6......174 F2
Hillingdon Rd WD25...154 B5
Hill La SG4..........35 A2
Hill Ley AL10........129 F5
Hill Leys EN6 ....146 E3
Hillmead SG1.........51 A6
Hill Mead HP4......122 A3
Hillmead Prim Sch
  CM23............76 C7
Hillpath SG6.........23 B6
Hillpoint WD3 ......165 C4
Hill Rd
  Codicote SG4........67 E1
  Northwood HA6 .....174 D4
Hill Rise
  Cuffley EN6 ....146 E3
  Luton LU3 ....44 D7
  Potters Bar EN6 .....159 C5
  Rickmansworth WD3 ..165 B2
Hillrise Ave WD24 ...154 D2
Hillshott SG6........175 A7
Hillshott Inf Sch SG6 ...23 A6
Hillside
  Codicote SG4........67 F1
  Hatfield AL10........130 A5
  Hoddesdon EN11.....134 F7
  Royston SG8 ....7 D5
  St Albans AL3 ......128 C2
  Stevenage SG1 ......50 F5
  Ware SG12 ....114 D8
  Welwyn Garden City
  AL7............111 B3
Hill Side LU7.........79 F7
Hillside Ave
  Bishop's Stortford
  CM23............77 A7
  Borehamwood WD6...170 B5
  Cheshunt EN8 ......162 D8
Hillside Cl WD5.....153 E7
Hillside Cotts
  Birchanger CM23......59 C3
  Wareside SG12 ......94 F4
Hillside Cres
  Cheshunt EN8 ......162 D8
  Enfield EN2 ....161 D1
  Northwood HA6 .....175 A2
  Stansted Abbotts
  SG12............115 B4
  Watford WD19.......167 D3
Hillside Ct
  Cheshunt EN8 ......162 D8
  St Albans AL1.......127 E4
Hillside End AL3......59 C3
Hillside Gate 8 AL1...127 E4
Hillside Gdns
  Barnet EN5 ....171 E5
  Berkhamsted HP4 ....122 D3
  Pinner HA5.........175 B2
Hillside Ho SG1......50 F5
Hillside Jun & Inf Schs
  HA6............175 A3
Hillside La SG12......115 A5
Hillside Mans EN5....171 F5
Hillside Rd
  Chorleywood WD3 ...164 C4

Hillside Rd continued
  Harpenden AL5 ....85 F3
Luton LU3 ....45 D1
Pinner HA5 ....175 B3
Radlett WD7 ....156 B4
St Albans AL1 ....127 C4
Watford WD17 ....167 A4
Hillside Rise HA6 ....175 A3
Hillside Terr SL13 ....113 C4
Hillside Way AL6 ....90 A8
Hills La HA6 ....174 E2
Hill St AL3 ....127 C3
Hill The
  Harlow CM17 ....118 C4
  Wheathampstead AL4 ....108 D8
Hilltop AL3 ....105 F6
Hill Top SG7 ....23 E7
Hilltop Cl EN7 ....63 C7
Hilltop Cotts
  Great Munden SG11 ......54 D4
  Great Offley SG5 ....33 C3
Hilltop Ct LU1 ....63 C7
Hilltop Rd
  Bedmond WD4 ....139 D4
  Berkhamsted HP4 ....122 C3
Hilltop View AL4 ....108 D7
Hilltop Wlk AL5 ....107 D8
Hill Tree Cl CM21 ....97 D1
Hill View
  Berkhamsted HP4 ....122 A6
  Buckland SG9 ....27 D8
  Whitwell SG4 ....66 E6
Hillview Cl HA5 ....175 B3
Hillview Cres LU2 ....45 C8
Hillview Gdns EN8 ....148 A4
Hillview Rd HA5 ....175 F4
Hilly Fields AL7 ....111 C1
Hilmay Dr HP1 ....124 C2
Hilton Cl SG1 ....50 B7
Himalaya Way WD18 .....166 F3
Hindhead Gn WD19 .....175 C5
Hine Ho AL4 ....128 D2
Hine Way SG5 ....21 C1
Hinwick Cl SG15 ....11 B7
HINXWORTH 4 B8
Hinxworth Rd
  Ashwell SG7 ....4 B4
  Hinxworth SG7 ....3 D3
Hipkins CM23 ....76 E4
Hipkins Pl EN10 ....134 E3
Hispano Mews EN3 ......163 A4
Hitchens Cl HP1 ....123 F4
HITCHIN 34 E8
Hitchin Boys' Sch SG4 ...34 E8
Hitchin British Schools
  Mus* SG5 ....34 F6
Hitchin Bsns Ctr The
  SG4 ....22 A3
Hitchin Girls' Sch SG4 ...34 F7
HITCHIN HILL 34 F5
Hitchin Hill SG4 ....34 F5
Hitchin Hill Path SG4 ....34 F5
Hitchin Hospl SG5 ....34 D8
Hitchin Mus* SG5 ....34 E7
Hitchin Rd
  Arlesey SG15 ....15 D6
  Great Wymondley SG4 ...35 D6
  Hexton SG5 ....19 E1
  Hitchin SG4 ....34 F3
  Kimpton SG4 ....66 D2
  Letchworth Garden City
    SG6 ....22 E3
  Lower Stondon SG16 ....10 C6
  Luton LU2 ....46 A4
  Pirton SG5 ....20 E2
  Preston SG4 ....48 E6
  Stevenage SG1 ....36 B2
  Stotfold SG5 ....11 E5
  Weston SG4 ....24 B1
Hitchin Road Ind & Bsns
  Ctr SG15 ....11 A3
Hitchin St SG7 ....23 E8
Hitchin Sta SG4 ....35 A8
Hitchwood Cotts SG4 ....48 F5
Hitchwood La SG4 ....49 C4
Hitherbaulk AL7 ....110 E4
Hitherfield La AL5 ....86 A2
Hitherway AL8 ....89 D2
Hitherwell Dr HA3 ....176 D2
Hive Cl WD23 ....176 D8
Hive Rd WD23 ....176 D8
Hixberry La AL4 ....128 E1
Hobart Wlk AL3 ....127 F7
Hobbs Cl
  Cheshunt EN8 ....148 D2
  St Albans AL4 ....128 F8
Hobbs Cross Rd CM17 ...118 F3
Hobbs Ct SG1 ....51 A8
Hobbs Hayes SG6 ....16 E5
Hobbs Hill AL6 ....89 C4
Hobbs Hill Rd HP3 ......138 F8
Hobbs Hill Wood Prim Sch
  HP3 ....125 B1
Hobbs Way AL8 ....110 C5
Hobby Horse Cl EN7 .....147 D5
Hobletts Manor Inf Sch
  HP2 ....125 A4
Hobletts Manor Jun Sch
  HP2 ....125 A4
Hobletts Rd HP2 ....124 F4
Hobsons Cl EN11 ....114 F1
Hobsons Wlk HP23 ......99 F5
Hobtoe Rd CM20 ....117 A4
Hockeridge View HP4 ...121 F3
HOCKERILL 77 A6
Hockerill SG14 ....70 E3

Hockerill Anglo-European
  Coll CM23 ....77 B7
Hockerill Ct [7] CM23 ....77 A7
Hockerill St CM23 ....77 A7
Hocklands AL7 ....111 C7
Hockwell Ring LU4 ....44 C4
HODDESDON 135 C7
Hoddesdon Ind Ctr
  EN11 ....135 C7
Hoddesdon Rd SG12 .....115 C3
Hodges Way WD18 ......167 A3
Hodings Rd CM20 ....117 C2
Hodson Pl [1] EN3 ....163 A1
Hodwell SG7 ....4 D4
Hoecroft EN9 ....135 F1
Hoecroft Ct EN11 ....162 C1
Hoe La
  Enfield EN1, EN3 ....162 B1
  Lower Nazeing EN9 .....135 F1
  Ware SG12 ....114 D7
Hoestock Rd CM21 ....97 D2
Hoe The WD19 ....175 D8
Hogarth Cl LU2 ....46 A2
Hogarth Rd WD23 ....168 B2
Hogg End La AL3 ....126 C6
Hogges Cl [16] EN11 .....135 A6
Hoggs La WD6 ....169 A5
Hog Hall La HP4 ....81 A5
Hog La HP5 ....121 C1
HOGPITS BOTTOM 151 B7
Hogpits Bottom HP3 .....151 B7
Hogsdell La SG13 ....114 B4
Holbeck La EN7 ....147 F5
Holbein Gate HA6 ....174 E5
Holborn Cl AL4 ....128 D8
Holbrook Cl EN1 ....162 A1
Holbrook Gdns WD25 ...155 B3
Holcroft Rd AL5 ....86 D3
HOLDBROOK 163 A5
Holdbrook Cl EN8 ....162 F5
Holdbrook Prim Sch
  EN8 ....162 F5
Holden Cl
  Hertford SG13 ....113 E7
  Watford WD18 ....35 C7
Holders La SG12 ....51 E5
Holdings The AL9 ....130 D7
Holecroft EN9 ....163 E5
Holford Way LU3 ....31 B1
Holgate Dr LU4 ....44 B3
Holkham Cl LU4 ....44 A4
Holkham Ho [11] EN5 ...171 C4
Holland Ct
  [B] Borehamwood
    WD6 ....170 A5
  Luton LU2 ....45 C2
Holland Gdns WD25 .....154 C4
Holland Rd LU3 ....45 B2
Holland's Croft SG12 ....95 D1
Holland Way CM17 ......118 D1
Holliday St LU4 ....122 D4
Hollier Cl AL10 ....130 B6
Hollies Ave AL10 ....130 A5
Hollies Cl SG8 ....7 E6
Hollies The
  Bovingdon HP3 ....137 A2
  St Albans AL1 ....127 E4
  St Albans, Townsend
    AL3 ....127 C5
  Watford WD18 ....166 F5
Hollies Way SG6 ....159 C8
Holloway La WD3 ....151 C2
Holloways La AL9 ....144 D7
Holloway The WD23,
  HP22 ....99 C4
Hollybush Cl
  Harrow HA3 ....176 E2
  Oaklands AL6 ....89 E8
  Potten End HP4 ....123 D7
  Watford WD17 ....167 C2
Hollybush Hill LU2, LU6 ..32 F1
Hollybush La
  Bendish SG4 ....68 B8
  Datchworth SG3 ....69 C3
  Flamstead AL3 ....84 B3
  Harpenden AL5 ....86 A3
  Hemel Hempstead HP1 .123 F4
  Welwyn Garden City
    AL7 ....110 E5
Hollybush Prim Sch
  SG14 ....113 A6
Hollybush Rd LU2 ....46 C1
Hollybush Row HP22 ....120 D8
Hollybush Way EN7 .....148 A3
Holly Cl AL10 ....129 F4
Holly Copse SG1 ....50 F4
Holly Cotts SG4 ....48 D6
Holly Croft SG14 ....113 A7
Hollycross Rd SG12 .....115 B7
Holly Dell SG13 ....113 C4
Holly Dr
  Berkhamsted HP4 ......122 D3
  Potters Bar EN6 ....159 B6
Hollyfield
  Hatfield AL10 ....130 A2
  Tring HP23 ....100 C5
Hollyfield Cl HP23 ....100 C5
Hollyfields EN10 ....148 C5
Holly Gr HA5 ....175 E2
Hollygrove WD23 ....168 D2

Holly Grove Rd SG14 ....91 C3
Holly Hall Cl AL4 ....89 C5
Holly Hedges La HP3 ....151 C8
Hollyhock Cl HP1 ....123 E4
Holly Ho WD24 ....167 C8
Holly La AL5 ....86 E6
Holly Leys SG2 ....69 C8
Holly Rd
  Enfield EN3 ....162 D3
  Woolmer Green SG3 ...69 B1
Holly Shaws SG2 ....51 B1
Holly St LU1 ....63 E6
Holly Street Trad Est [10]
  LU1 ....63 E6
Hollytree Cl HP5 ....150 B8
Holly Tree Ct HP2 ......125 B3
Hollytree Ho WD24 .....153 E3
Holly Wlk
  Harpenden AL5 ....86 D1
  Welwyn Garden City AL8 .89 C2
Hollywood Gr WD6 ......169 F5
Holmbrook Ave LU3 .....45 C5
Holmbury Ct WD23 .....176 E8
Holmbury St Mary Ct
  AL1 ....128 B2
Holmdale SG6 ....23 B5
Holmdale Rd WD6 ....169 F7
Holme Cl
  Cheshunt EN8 ....162 E8
  Hatfield AL10 ....129 F8
Holme Lea WD25 ....154 C5
Holme Pk WD6 ....169 F7
Holme Pl HP2 ....125 C4
Holme Rd AL10 ....129 F8
Holmes Cl AL3 ....127 E4
Holmesdale EN8 ....162 D4
Holme Way HA7 ....176 A5
Holmfield Cl LU1 ....63 D5
Holm Oak Pk WD18 ....167 A4
Holmscroft Rd LU3 .....44 F6
Holmshill La EN5,
  WD6 ....157 F2
Holmside Rise WD19 ...175 B7
Holmwood Rd EN3 .....162 D3
Holroyd Cres SG7 ......23 F7
Holt Cl WD6 ....169 F5
Holt Cotts The SG4 .....66 C4
Holt Ho EN8 ....148 B3
Holts Mdw AL3 ....106 B6
Holtsmere Cl
  Luton LU2 ....46 D1
  Watford WD25 ....154 C4
Holtsmere End Inf Sch
  HP2 ....125 B8
Holtsmere End Jun Sch
  HP2 ....125 B8
Holtsmere End La
  HP2 ....105 C1
Holt The
  Hemel Hempstead
    HP2 ....124 E2
  Welwyn Garden City
    AL7 ....111 D5
HOLWELL 21 B7
Holwell Cl LU6 ....36 C2
Holwell Ct AL9 ....111 F1
Holwell Cvn Pk AL9 .....111 B1
Holwell Hyde AL7 ....111 C4
Holwell Hyde La AL7 ....113 C3
Holwell La AL9 ....131 F8
Holwell Prim Sch AL7 ...110 F5
Holwell Rd
  Holwell SG5 ....21 C7
  Pirton SG5 ....20 E6
  Welwyn Garden City
    AL7 ....110 E5
Holy Acre CM19 ....116 A1
Holy Cross Hill EN10 ...148 A8
Holy Family RC Jun Mix &
  Inf Sch The AL7 ......90 A1
HOLYFIELD 149 C3
Holyfield Hall Farm*
  EN9 ....149 C4
Holyfield Rd EN9 ....149 D2
Holyrood Cres AL1 ......141 D7
Holyrood Ct WD18 ......167 B5
Holy Rood RC Prim Sch
  WD17 ....153 D3
Holy Trinity CE Prim Sch
  Cheshunt EN10 ....162 D7
  Northwood HA6 ....174 C4
HOLYWELL 166 D3
Holywell Cl LU6 ....82 C6
Holywell Ct LU4 ....45 B4
Holywell Hill AL1 ......127 D2
Holywell Ho LU2 ....160 F1
Holywell Prim Sch
  WD18 ....166 F3
Holywell Rd
  Studham LU6 ....82 B6
  Watford WD18 ....167 A4
Home Cl
  Cheshunt EN10 ....148 F7
  Luton LU4 ....44 C4
  Stotfold SG5 ....11 F7
Homedale Dr LU4 ......44 D2
Homedell Ho AL5 ......85 E3
Home Farm AL9 ....100 A2
Home Farm Cotts
  Newgate Street SG13 .146 F8
  Slip End LU1 ....85 A8
Home Farm Ct
  Bovingdon HP3 ....136 F1
  Cockernhoe LU2 .....46 D5
  Standon SG11 ....55 D3
Home Farm Ind Pk
  SG12 ....115 F5

Home Farm Rd
  Berkhamsted HP4 .....121 D7
  Brookmans Park AL9 ..144 B5
  Rickmansworth WD3 ..174 A6
Home Farm Youngsbury
  SG12 ....94 A8
Homefield
  Bovingdon HP3 ....137 B3
  Hinxworth SG7 ....3 D6
  Potten End HP4 ....123 B7
Home Field EN5 ....171 F4
Homefield La SG4 ....49 F2
Homefield Rd
  Bushey WD23 ....168 A4
  Chorleywood WD3 ....164 D5
  Hemel Hempstead HP2 .125 A2
  Radlett WD7 ....155 F2
  Ware SG12 ....93 E2
Homehayes Ho [1]
  HA5 ....175 F3
Homeleigh Ct EN8 .....148 B1
Homeleigh St EN8 ......148 B1
Home Ley AL7 ....110 E6
Home Mdw AL7 ....110 F6
Homepark Cotts WD4 ..139 B1
Home Park Ind Est
  WD4 ....139 B1
Home Park Mill Link Rd
  WD4 ....139 B1
Home Pastures CM22 ...98 F3
Homerfield AL8 ....110 C7
Homerswood La AL6 ...89 A2
Homerswood Prim Sch
  AL8 ....89 D2
Homerton Rd LU2 ......45 A6
Homestead Cl AL2 .....141 C4
Homestead Ct AL7 .....110 F4
Homestead La AL7 .....110 F4
Homestead Moat SG2 ..50 E1
Homestead Rd
  Hatfield AL10 ....130 B8
  Rickmansworth WD3 ..165 D1
Homesteads The
  SG12 ....116 D8
Homestead Way LU1 ...63 C5
Home Way WD3 ....164 F1
Homewood Ct WD3 ....164 F1
Homewood Ind Sch
  AL2 ....141 B3
Homewood La EN6 .....146 C4
Homewood Rd AL1 ....128 C3
Homewood Venue
  EN6 ....146 E4
Honeybourne CM23 ....76 E4
Honey Brook EN9 ......163 E6
Honeycroft AL8 ....110 C5
Honeycroft Dr AL4 .....142 C8
Honeycross Rd HP1 ....123 C2
Honeygate LU2 ....45 E4
Honey La
  Brent Pelham CB11 ....30 F3
  Buntingford SG9 ......40 F3
  [B] Hertford SG14 ....111 D5
  Waltham Abbey EN9 ..163 E5
Honeymead AL6 ....89 F3
Honeymeade CM21 ....118 C7
Honeysuckle Cl
  Bishop's Stortford
    CM23 ....76 C6
  Hertford SG13 ....114 A6
Honeysuckle Gdns
  AL10 ....130 B4
Honeyway SG8 ....7 E6
Honeywood Cl EN6 ....159 D6
Honilands Prim Sch
  EN1 ....162 B3
Honiton Mews LU3 ....44 E6
Honor St [7] CM17 ....118 C4
Honours Mead HP3 ....137 A4
Hoo Cotts SG5 ....33 D1
HOO END 66 E4
Hoo Farm Cotts SG5 ..33 D1
Hook Gate EN1 ....162 B3
Hook La
  Northaw EN6 ....159 F7
  Northaw EN6 ....160 A8
Hook's Cross SG14 ....69 F6
Hoopers Mews WD23 ..168 B1
Hoops La SG8 ....9 C5
Hoo St LU1 ....63 E5
Hoo The CM17 ....118 C5
Hope Gn WD20 ....154 A6
Hope Green Lo WD25 ..154 A6
Hopewell Rd SG7 ......23 D8
Hop Garden Way
  WD25 ....154 C8
Hopground Cl AL10 .....128 A1
Hopkins Cres AL1 ......108 B1
Hopkins Yd AL1 ....127 E2
Hoppit Rd EN9 ....163 B7
Hopps Ho [4] EN11 ....135 A6
Hopton Rd SG1 ....50 A8
Hopwood Cl WD17 .....153 D3
Horace Brightman Cl
  LU3 ....45 A7
Horace Gay Gdns SG6 ..22 C6
Hordle Gdns AL1 ....127 C2
Horizon Ho EN3 ....162 F3
Hormead CE Prim Sch
  SG9 ....41 F8
Hornbeam Cl
  Borehamwood WD6 ...170 A8
  Hertford SG13 ....113 B7
Hornbeam La AL2 .....35 C5
Hornbeam La AL9 .....131 C2
Hornbeams
  Bricket Wood AL2 .....140 F1

Hornbeams continued
  Welwyn Garden City
    AL7 ....111 B5
Hornbeams Ave EN1 ...162 C4
Hornbeam Spring 68 F4
Hornbeams The
  Harlow CM20 ....117 C2
  Stevenage SG2 ....51 B4
Hornbeam Way EN7 ...147 F2
Hornets The WD18 ....167 B5
HORN HILL 172 B6
Horn Hill SG4 ....66 E6
Hornhill Rd WD3 ......172 D5
Hornsby Cl LU2 ....46 C1
Hornsfield AL7 ....111 C7
Horns Mill Rd SG13 ...113 C3
Horns Rd SG13 ....113 C3
Horrocks Cl SG12 .....93 C3
Horsa Gdns AL10 .....129 E7
Horseblock La HP5 ....120 E2
Horsecroft Rd HP1 ....124 A1
Horse Cross SG11 .....56 D3
Horse Hill HP5 ....150 D7
Horselers HP3 ....139 A8
Horsemans Dr AL2 ....141 B6
Horseshoe Bsns Pk
  AL2 ....141 B1
Horseshoe Cl
  Barley SG8 ....8 F1
  Cheddington LU7 ......80 A7
Horseshoe Ct
  Hitchin SG4 ....34 E6
  Stanstead Abbotts
    SG12 ....115 D4
Horseshoe Hill SG9 ...42 A8
Horseshoe La
  Great Hormead SG9 ...42 A8
  Totteridge N20 ....171 D7
  Watford WD25 ....154 C7
Horseshoe The HP3 ...125 C1
Horsham Cl LU2 ......46 D2
Horsleys WD3 ....172 D5
Horton Gdns HP2 .....105 A1
Horwood Cl WD3 .....165 A2
Horwood Cotts WD25 .168 E8
Horwood Rd AL2 .....154 E2
Hospital Rd SG15 .....11 A4
Houghton Mews [12]
  LU1 ....63 D6
Houlton Cl AL4 ....108 E7
Housefield Way AL4 ...142 C8
House La
  Arlesey SG15 ....11 A7
  Sandridge AL4 ....108 C1
  St Albans AL1 ....128 D7
Housemans End HP1 ...124 B6
Housman Ave SG8 .....2 C1
Howard Agne Cl HP3 ...137 A4
Howard Bsns Pk EN9 ...163 D6
Howard Cl
  Bushey WD23 ....168 E2
  Luton LU2 ....45 A4
  St Albans AL1 ....128 C1
  Stotfold SG5 ....11 E5
  Waltham Abbey EN9 ..163 D5
  Watford WD24 ....154 A2
Howard Ct
  Enfield EN1 ....161 E1
  Letchworth Garden City
    SG6 ....23 B4
Howard Ctr The AL8 ...110 D6
Howard Dr
  Borehamwood WD6 ...170 D5
  Letchworth Garden City
    SG6 ....23 B3
Howarde Ct SG1 ......50 C6
Howard Gate SG6 .....23 B4
Howard Park Cnr SG6 ..23 A6
Howards Cl HA5 ....175 B3
Howards Dr HP1 ......124 A5
Howardsgate AL8 .....110 D6
Howards Wood SG6 ...23 B3
Howard Way
  Barnet EN5 ....171 D4
  Harlow CM20 ....117 F2
Howberry Gn SG15 ....11 A3
Howe Cl WD7 ....156 E7
Howe Dell AL10 ......130 B5
Howe Dell Prim Sch
  AL10 ....130 B5
HOWE GREEN 77 D2
Howe Green House Sch
  CM22 ....77 D2
Howell Hill Cl LU7 ....61 D5
Howe Rd HP3 ....125 A1
How Field AL5 ....85 E3
Howfield Gn EN11 ...115 A1
Howicks Gn AL7 .....111 A3
Howland Garth AL1 ...141 A3
Howlands AL7 ....111 A3
Howlands Ho AL7 ....111 A3
Howse Rd EN9 ......163 B4
Howton Pl WD23 ....168 D1
HOW WOOD 141 B3
How Wood AL2 ....141 B3
How Wood Prim Sch
  AL2 ....141 C4
How Wood Sta AL2 ..141 C3
Hoylake Cl LU3 .....63 F5
Hoylake Gdns WD19 .175 D6
Hubbards Rd WD3 ...164 D4
Huckleberry Cl LU3 ..45 A8

HUDNALL 102 F7
HUDNALL CORNER 103 B7
Hudnall La HP4...............102 F7
Hudscroft Ct ⑥ EN8 ...148 E3
Hudson Cl
  St Albans AL1 ....141 D8
  Watford WD24............153 F13
Hudson Rd SG2 ....51 B7
Hudsons Ct EN6 ....159 A8
Huggins La AL9 ....144 C8
Hughenden Rd AL4 ......128 C6
Hugh's Twr ④ CM20 ....117 D1
Hugh Villas CM23 ....77 A5
Hugo Cl WD18 ....166 E3
Hugo Gryn Way WD7 ...156 E8
Hull Cl SG13 ....55 E7
Humber Ct SG1...............36 F3
Humberstone Cl LU4......44 E2
Humberstone Rd LU4.....44 E2
Humphrey Talbot Ave
  LU6............................81 F7
HUNSDON 95 D1
Hunsdon AL7 ....111 D6
HUNSDONBURY 116 C7
Hunsdon Jun Mix Inf Sch
  SG12..........................95 D1
Hunsdon Rd
  Stanstead Abbotts
  SG12........................115 E5
  Widford SG12 ....95 F3
Hunsdon Road Cotts
  SG12........................115 C5
Hunston Cl LU4..............44 E5
Hunt Cl AL4 ....128 D6
Hunter Cl
  Borehamwood WD6 .....170 D4
  Potters Bar EN6 ....159 B6
Huntercombe Gdns
  WD19........................175 C5
Hunters Cl
  Bovingdon HP3 ....137 A2
  Stevenage SG2 ....51 D7
  Stotfold SG5 ....11 E6
  Tring HP23.................100 B5
Hunters Gate WD25 ......154 A6
Hunter's La WD25 ....153 F6
Hunters Oak HP2 ....125 B8
Hunters Pk HP4 ....122 E5
Hunters Reach EN7.......147 F2
Hunters Ride AL2..........155 A8
Hunters Way
  Royston SG8 ....7 E6
  Welwyn Garden City
  AL7 ....110 E3
Hunter Wlk WD6 ....170 D4
Huntingdon Cl EN10 .....148 E7
Huntingdon Ct EN5 ......171 F6
Huntingdon Rd SG1......50 B8
Hunting Gate
  Hemel Hempstead
  HP2..........................124 E7
  Hitchin SG4 ....22 A3
Hunting Hall LU2............64 C8
HUNTON BRIDGE 153 B6
Hunton Bridge Hill
  WD4..........................153 C6
Hunts Cl LU1 ....63 C6
Huntsman Cl SG11 ....55 D3
Huntsmans Cl HP4.........81 C5
Huntsmill Rd HP1........123 E2
Hurlock Way LU4 ....44 C5
Huron Gr CM23...............59 C1
Huron Rd EN10 ....148 E5
Hurricane Way WD5 .....154 A7
Hurst Cl
  Baldock SG7 ....13 A1
  Bishop's Stortford CM23...76 E7
  Welwyn Garden City
  AL7 ....111 C5
Hurst Dr EN8 ....162 D5
Hurst Drive Prim Sch
  EN8 ....162 D5
Hurstleigh WD3 ....164 C4
Hurstlings AL7 ....111 B5
Hurst Pl HA4 ....174 B2
Hurst Way LU3 ....44 F5
Hutchings Lo ⓑ WD3 ...165 E1
Hutton Cl
  Hertford SG14 ....113 A6
  Luton LU4 ....44 E1
Hutton Gdns HA3..........176 C3
Hutton La HA3...............176 D3
Hutton Wlk HA3............176 C3
Hyatt Ind Est SG1..........50 A5
Hyburn Cl
  Bricket Wood AL2 ....140 F1
  Hemel Hempstead HP3 ...125 B2
Hydean Way SG2 ....51 B3
Hyde Ave
  Potters Bar EN6 ....159 B6
  Stotfold SG5 ....11 E5
Hyde Cl
  Barnet EN5 ....171 F6
  Harpenden AL5 ....86 B4
Hyde Ct
  Cheshunt EN8 ....162 E5
  London Colney AL2 .....142 B4
Hyde Gn E SG2 ....51 B3
Hyde Gn N SG2..............51 B3
Hyde Gn S SG2 ....51 B3
Hyde Ho ⑥ LU2 ....45 A8
Hyde La
  Bedmond HP3 ....139 D5
  Bovingdon HP3 ....137 A3
Hyde La continued
  Park Street AL2...........141 D3
  Peters Green LU2 ....45 F7
Hyde Mdws HP3...........137 A4
Hyde Mead EN9 ....149 E8
Hyde Mead Ho EN9 .....149 E8
Hyde Rd
  Caddington LU1 ....62 F4
  Watford WD17............167 A7
Hyde Terr HP3 ....139 E7
Hyde The
  Stevenage SG2 ....51 C3
  Ware SG12 ....93 B2
Hyde Valley AL7 ....110 F4
Hyde View Rd AL5 ....86 B4
Hyde Way AL7 ....110 E6
Hyperion Ct HP2...........124 F6
Hyver Hill NW7 ....170 D2

I

Ibberson Way SG4........35 A7
Iceni Ct SG6...................23 B7
ICKLEFORD 21 E4
Ickleford Bury SG5 ....21 E3
Ickleford Gate SG5 ....21 D3
Ickleford Prim Sch
  SG5 ....21 E4
Ickleford Rd SG5 ....34 F8
Ickley Cl LU4 ....44 B5
Icknield Cl
  Ickleford SG5 ....21 E4
  St Albans AL3 ....126 F1
Icknield Gn
  Letchworth Garden City
  SG6...........................22 E6
  Tring HP23.................100 A6
Icknield High Sch LU3 ...45 C5
Icknield Inf Sch SG6 ....22 D6
Icknield Jun Sch LU3.....45 B5
Icknield Rd LU3 ....44 F4
Icknield Walk Fst Sch
  SG8 ....7 E7
Icknield Way
  Baldock SG7 ....12 E1
  Dagnall LU6 ....81 A8
  Letchworth Garden City
  SG6...........................22 E6
  Luton LU3 ....45 B7
  Tring HP23...................99 E4
Icknield Way E SG2 .....12 E1
Icknield Wlk SG8 ....7 F7
Idenbury Ct LU1.............63 C7
Ilex Ct HP4 ....122 B4
Ilford Cl LU2 ....46 D3
Ilkley Rd WD19 ....175 D5
Imberfield LU4 ....44 C3
Immanuel Coll WD20 ...168 E2
Imperial Pk
  Watford WD24............154 C1
  Watford WD24............167 C8
Imperial Way
  Hemel Hempstead
  HP3..........................138 E7
  Watford WD24............167 C8
Impresa Pk EN11 ....135 C7
Indells AL10 ....129 F4
Ingelheim Ct SG1.........50 D8
Ingersoll Rd EN3 ....162 C1
Ingfield EN6 ....145 A1
Ingles AL8.......................89 E2
Ingleside Dr SG1 ....36 B1
Inglewood Gdns AL2 ...141 E6
Ingram Gdns LU2...........45 D7
Inkerman Rd AL1..........127 E2
Inkerman St LU1............63 D7
Innes Ct HP3 ....138 D8
Innova Way EN3 ....162 F3
Inn's Cl SG1 ....50 D6
Inskip Cres SG1 ....50 C5
IO Ctr
  Holdbrook EN9............163 A5
  Stevenage SG1 ....50 D2
Iona Cl SG1 ....36 F2
Ionian Way ② HP2.......124 F6
Iredale View AL2 ....13 A1
Irene Stebbings Ho
  AL4............................128 C4
Ireton Ct SG1 ....50 C6
Iron Dr SG13 ....114 B7
Irving Cl CM23 ....76 D4
Irving Cres LU7..............80 A8
Isabel Ct EN11 ....135 B8
Isabel Gate EN8 ....148 F5
Isabella Ho EN8 ....163 A5
Isabelle Cl EN7 ....147 C2
Isenburg Way HP2 ....124 D8
Isherwood Ct SG8 ....7 C8
Island Centre Way
  EN3 ....163 A2
Island Ct CM23 ....77 A5
Islay Ho ④ WD18 ....166 F3
Itaska Cotts WD23 ....168 E1
Ivatt Ct SG4 ....35 C7
Iveagh Cl HA6...............174 B2
Iveagh Ct HP2 ....124 D4
Ivel Ct SG6 ....23 C4
Ivel Rd SG1 ....50 C7
Ivel Way
  Baldock SG7 ....24 A6
  Stotfold SG5 ....11 F8
Ives Rd SG14 ....113 B7
IVINGHOE 80 F5

Ivinghoe Cl
  St Albans AL4 ....128 C8
  Watford WD25............154 D4
Ivinghoe Rd
  Bushey WD23 ....168 D2
  Rickmansworth WD3 ...165 A2
Ivory Cl AL4 ....128 C1
Ivory Ct HP3.................138 E8
Ivybridge EN10 ....135 A4
Ivy Ct LU1.......................63 B8
Ivy Ho WD19 ....167 D3
Ivy House La HP4.........122 E4
Ivy Lea WD3.................165 A1
Ivy Rd LU1 ....63 C8
Ivy Terr EN11 ....135 C8
Ivy Wlk AL10 ....129 F8

J

Jackdaw Cl SG2............51 C8
Jackdaws AL7...............111 C6
Jackets La HA6.............174 B3
Jacketts Field WD5 ......153 F8
Jackman's Pl SG6 ....23 B5
Jacks Hill Pk SG4..........36 C7
Jacks La UB9................173 A2
Jacksons Ct SG9 ....40 E8
Jacksons Dr EN7 ....148 A3
Jackson's La SG8...........16 E5
Jackson Sq ⑩ CM23 .....76 F7
Jackson St SG12 ....12 E1
Jackson Wharf ㉔
  CM23...........................76 F7
Jacob Ct
  Holdbrook EN3............163 A2
  St Albans AL3 ....128 C1
Jacobs Ladder AL9 ......130 C5
Jakes View AL2.............141 C4
James Bedford Cl
  HA5 ....175 C1
James Cl WD23............167 E4
James Ct
  London Colney AL2 .....142 B4
  Luton LU4 ....44 B2
  ⓔ Luton, New Town LU1....63 F3
  Northwood HA6 ....174 F2
James Foster Ho SG5...21 E1
James Lee Sq EN3 ....163 A1
James Marshall
  Commercial Ctr AL5...86 A1
Jameson Ct AL1 ....127 F4
Jameson Rd AL5 ....86 B3
James Way
  South Oxhey WD19 .....175 D6
  Stevenage SG1 ....50 C7
Jane Cl HP2..................125 B8
Jarden SG6 ....23 C4
Jardine Ct ① SG1 ....51 A8
Jarman Cl HP3 ....124 E1
Jarman Way
  Hemel Hempstead
  HP2..........................124 F2
  Royston SG8 ....7 B7
Jarvis Cl EN5 ....171 D4
Jarvis Cleys EN7 ....147 F5
Jasmin Cl
  Bishop's Stortford
  CM23...........................76 C6
  Northwood HA6 ....174 F2
Jasmine Ct SG13 ....11 F7
Jasmine Dr SG13 ....114 A6
Jasmine Gdns AL10.......130 A7
Jasmin Hill HP5 ....136 B2
Jasons Hill HP5 ....136 B2
Jasper Ct EN3 ....162 C1
Jay Cl SG6.......................22 E8
Jays Cl AL2 ....155 A8
Jaywood LU2 ....46 C6
J Ct CM20.....................117 F1
Jeans La CM23 ....76 E7
Jeans Way LU5...............44 A1
Jeeves Yd ⑦ SG4 ....34 F6
Jeffrey Cl SG8 ....7 C8
Jeffries Rd SG12 ....93 B1
Jellicoe Gdns HA7.......176 F4
Jellicoe Rd WD18..........167 A3
Jenkins Ave AL2...........140 E1
Jenkins Ct HP22............60 C3
Jenkins La
  Bishop's Stortford
  CM22...........................77 C5
  St Leonards HP23 ....119 E3
Jenningsbury Ct
  SG13 ....114 A4
Jennings Cl SG1 ....50 E3
Jennings Rd AL1 ....128 A4
Jennings Way
  Barnet EN5 ....171 C6
  Hemel Hempstead HP2 ...124 E1
Jenning Wood AL6 ....89 F7
Jenyns Sch SG11 ....55 F7
Jephson Ct ⑩ LU1..........63 E6
Jepps Cl EN7 ....147 E4
Jepps La SG8...................7 D6
Jerome Dr AL3 ....127 A1
Jersey Cl EN11 ....135 A7
JERSEY FARM 128 E7
Jersey Ho
  Enfield EN3 ....162 D1
  ⑨ Watford WD18........166 F3
Jersey La
  St Albans AL4 ....128 B5
  St Albans, Marshalswick
  AL4...........................128 A5
Jersey Rd LU4 ....44 A3
Jervis Ave EN3 ....162 E4
Jervis Rd CM23 ....76 F6

Jessop Ct EN9...............163 F5
Jessop Rd SG1 ....37 A1
Jeve Cl SG7 ....13 A1
Jewell Ct WD25 ....154 D5
Jill Grey Pl SG4 ....34 F6
Jilliffer Rd LU4...............44 A2
Jim Desormeaux Bglws
  CM20.........................117 E2
Jinnings The AL2 ....162 D2
Joan Player Ho EN3 ....162 D2
Jocelyns CM17 ....118 C4
Jocketts Hill HP1 ....123 F3
Jocketts Rd HP1 ....123 F2
JOCKEY END 103 F8
Jodies Ct AL4 ....128 C5
Joel St HA6 ....175 A1
Johnby Ct EN3 ....162 E2
John Ct EN11...............115 A1
John Dyde Cl ② CM23 ...77 A4
John Eccles Ho AL7 .....110 F5
John Eliot Cl EN9 ....135 E2
John F Kennedy RC Sch
  HP1...........................123 F4
John Hall Ct SG5 ....33 C3
John Henry Newman RC
  Sch The SG1 ....36 B1
John Howland Ct SG16 ...10 D8
John Lamb Ct HA3........176 E2
John Rix Ho SG15 ....11 A4
John Sale Ct SG16 ....4 C4
Johns La HP5 ....121 E1
Johnson Ct HP3............124 E1
Johns Rd CM23..............59 A1
John St
  Luton LU1 ....63 E7
  ⑥ Royston SG8 ....7 D6
John Tate Rd SG13......113 F6
John Warner Sch The
  EN11.........................115 B3
Joiner's Cl HP5.............136 B1
Joint The SG8 ....16 E6
Jones Cl SG1 ....50 C7
Jones Rd EN7 ....147 B1
Jonquil Cl AL7 ....111 B4
Jordan Cl WD25 ....153 F4
Jordans AL7..................111 C7
Jordans Rd WD3 ....165 A1
Jordan's Way AL2 ....140 F1
Jocelyn's Yd ⑭ CM23 ...77 A7
Joseph Ct ② AL1 ....128 C2
Joshua Wlk EN8 ....163 A5
Joslyn Cl EN3 ....163 A1
Jowitt Ho ⑧ SG1 ....50 E6
Joyce Ct EN9 ....163 D5
Jubilee Ave
  London Colney AL2 .....142 D5
  Ware SG12 ....93 F2
Jubilee Cl
  Lower Stondon SG16 ...10 B3
  Pinner HA5 ....175 C1
Jubilee Cott ⑬ CM23 ....77 A7
Jubilee Cotts
  Aspenden SG9 ....40 D5
  Great Hormead SG9 .....42 A8
Jubilee Cres SG15 ....11 A2
Jubilee Ct
  Harpenden AL5 ....86 C3
  Hatfield AL10..............130 B8
  Waltham Abbey EN9 ...163 F6
Jubilee Meml Ave SG1...50 D8
Jubilee Rd
  Letchworth Garden City
  SG6...........................23 D7
  Stevenage SG1 ....50 B8
  Watford WD24............154 A1
Jubilee St LU2 ....45 F1
Jubilee Trad Ctr SG6 ....23 D7
Jubilee Wlk
  Kings Langley WD4 .....139 A1
  South Oxhey WD19 .....175 B6
Judge's Hill EN6...........145 F2
Judge St WD24.............154 B1
Julia Ct LU3 ....45 A6
Julia Gate SG2 ....51 C8
Julian's Cl SG1 ....50 C8
Julian's Rd SG1 ....50 B8
Julie Ho EN11 ....135 A4
Julius Gdns LU3 ....44 F7
Junction Cotts AL8 ......110 D7
Juniper Ave AL2...........155 A8
Juniper Cl
  Barnet EN5 ....171 D4
  Cheshunt EN10 ....148 E6
  Luton LU4 ....44 F2
  Rickmansworth WD3 ...173 D7
Juniper Ct HA3..............176 E4
Juniper Gate SG2 ....173 D8
Juniper Gdns
  Oaklands AL6................89 E7
  Shenley WD7..............156 E6
Juniper Gn HP1 ....123 E4
Juniper Gr WD17 ....154 A1
Juniper Ho HP10 ....148 F6
Juno Rd HP2 ....124 F6
Jupiter Dr HP2 ....124 F6
Jupiter Gate SG2 ....51 D8
Juxon Cl HA3................176 B2

K

Kaida Ho ⑥ WD3 ....165 D2
Kardwell Cl SG4 ....35 A6
Karen Ho SG16 ....10 A4
Karens Ct EN3...............162 D2
Katemon Ct SG12.........115 D4
Kates Cl EN5 ....171 A4
Katescroft AL7 ....110 E2
Katherine Cl HP3 ....138 E8
Katherine Pl WD5 ....154 A7
Kathleen Ct LU3............44 E4
Katrine Sq HP2 ....124 E2
Kay Cl HP23 ....100 A5
Kay Wlk AL4..................128 D3
Keats Cl
  Borehamwood WD6.....170 A5
  Hemel Hempstead HP2 ...105 B1
  Royston SG8 ....7 C8
  Stevenage SG2 ....51 C7
Keats Ho ⑱ AL5 ....86 B1
Keats Way SG4 ....35 C7
Keble Ct ⑤ WD6...........169 F8
Keble Terr WD5.............153 F7
Kecksy's CM21 ....97 F4
Keeble Cl LU2 ....46 E1
Keele Cl WD24 ....167 C7
Keepers Cl
  Cheddington LU7 ....80 A7
  Luton LU2 ....46 C2
Keiths Rd HP3 ....125 A2
Keiths Wood SG3 ....68 F5
Kelbys AL7 ....111 C7
Keller Cl SG2.................51 B4
Kelling Cl LU2 ....45 C8
Kelly Cl WD6 ....170 D7
Kelly Ct WD6 ....170 C7
Kelman Cl EN8 ....162 D8
Kelmscott Cl WD18 .....167 A4
Kelmscott Cres WD18 ...167 A4
KELSHALL 15 D5
Kelshall St SG8 ....15 E5
Kelvin Cl LU1 ....63 E6
Kelvin Cres HA3 ....176 E3
Kemble Cl EN6 ....159 D6
Kemble Ho HA7 ....176 F5
Kempe Cl AL1 ....141 C7
Kempe Rd EN1 ....162 C3
Kemp Pl WD23 ....168 A3
KEMPROW 155 D3
Kemprow WD25 ....155 D3
Kemps Dr HA6..............174 F3
Kempsey Cl LU2 ....46 D2
Kendal Cl LU3 ....44 D7
Kendale HP3 ....125 B2
Kendale Rd
  ⑤ Hitchin SG4 ....34 F6
  Luton LU4 ....44 B2
Kendall Cl AL7 ....110 F2
Kendall Ct WD6 ....170 C8
Kendall Manor HA6......174 C3
Kendal Rd EN9 ....163 C4
Kendals Cl WD7 ....155 E3
Ken Davies Ct AL3........127 F7
Kenerne Dr EN5 ....171 E4
Kenford Ct WD25 ....154 B7
Kenilworth Cl
  Borehamwood WD6.....170 C6
  Hemel Hempstead HP2 ...124 E7
  Stevenage SG2 ....69 C7
Kenilworth Cres EN1 ...161 E1
Kenilworth Ct WD17 ....167 A8
Kenilworth Dr
  Borehamwood WD6.....170 D6
  Croxley Green WD3 .....166 B5
Kenilworth Gdns
  WD19........................175 C5
Kenilworth Ho WD6......170 C6
Kenilworth Prim Sch
  WD6..........................170 D6
Kenilworth Rd LU1........63 C8
Kenmare Ct SG1 ....36 F3
Kennedy Ave EN11.......134 F6
Kennedy Cl
  Cheshunt EN8 ....148 E3
  London Colney AL2 .....142 D5
  Pinner HA5 ....175 C1
Kennedy Ct WD23 ....176 B8
Kennedy Rd SG12..........71 E7
Kennel La AL5 ....85 A5
Kennelwood La AL10 ...130 B6
Kennesbourne Ct AL5...85 D4
Kenneth Gdns ⑥ HA7...176 F4
Kenneth Rd LU2 ....46 A1
Kennett Way SG1..........36 F3
Kenning Rd EN11 ....135 B8
Kensington Rd LU3........45 B3
Kensington Ave
  WD18........................166 F5
Kensington Cl AL1 ....128 A1
Kensington Ct EN1 ......161 E1
Kensington Mews
  WD18........................167 A5
Kensington Way WD6...170 D6
KENSINGTON COMMON
  ....82 F8
Kensworth Lower Sch
  LU6............................82 F8
KENSWORTH LYNCH ...82 F8
Kensworth Rd LU6.........82 D4
Kent Cl WD6 ....157 D1
Kent Cres CM23.............76 E4
Kentish La AL9 ....145 C7
Kenton Gdns AL1..........127 F2
Kenton La HA3 ....176 F3
Kent Pl SG5 ....34 D8

Kent Rd LU1.............62 F8
Kents Ave HP3............138 D7
Kents La SL1..............55 E2
Kenwood Dr WD3.........172 F8
Kenworth Cl EN6........162 D6
Kenyon Pl AL7.............110 E3
Kerdistone Cl EN6......145 B1
Kernow Ct LU2............46 A1
Kerr Cl SG3................68 F5
Kerri Ct EN5..............171 C5
Kerril Croft CM20.......117 A1
Kershaw Cl LU3...........45 A8
Kershaw's Hill SG4.......34 F6
Kessingland Ave SG1.....36 A1
Keston Mews WD17......167 B7

Kestrel Cl
  Berkhamsted HP4.......122 D3
  Stevenage SG2..........51 D2
  Watford WD25...........154 E5
Kestrel Ct 4 SL2..........93 C3
Kestrel Gdns CM23.......76 F2
Kestrels The AL2.........154 F8
Kestrel Way
  Luton LU4................44 A5
  Royston SG8..............7 E8
  Welwyn Garden City
    AL7.....................110 F8
Keswick Cl AL1...........128 B1
Keswick Dr EN3...........162 C1
Kettering Rd SG1.........162 D2
KETTLE GREEN............74 D1
Kettle Green Rd SG10....74 E2
Ketton Cl LU2..............64 A7
Kevere Ct HA6............174 B5
Kewferry Dr HA6.........174 C5
Kewferry Rd HA6.........174 C5
Keyfield Terr AL1........127 D2
Keymer Cl LU2.............46 C3
Keynton Ct SG14..........112 F7
KEYSERS ESTATE.........135 B1
Keysers Ct EN10..........135 B1
Keys Ho 6 EN3............162 D2
Kibes La SG12..............93 E1
Kidner Cl LU2.............45 E5
Kilbride Ct HP2..........124 F7
Kilby Cl WD25............154 D4
Kilby Rd SG1..............50 C5
Kildonan Cl WD17........166 F8
Kilfillan Gdns HP4.......122 A4
Kilfillan Pk HP4...........122 A4
Killigrew Inf Sch AL2....141 B6
Killigrew Jun Sch
  AL2.......................141 B6
Kilmarnock Ct LU2........45 E5
Kilmarnock Rd WD19.....175 D6
Kiln Ave HP6..............150 C1
Kiln Cl HP4................123 B6
Kiln Cotts HP5............123 B6
Kilncroft HP3.............125 B1
Kilnfield AL7................89 F1
Kiln Ground HP3..........125 A1
Kiln House Ct SG12........93 E2
Kiln House Yd SG8........77 F7
Kiln La HP5................150 B8
Kiln Rd HP23..............120 B6

Kiln Way
  Dunstable LU5...........44 A1
  Northwood HA6.........174 E4
Kilsmore La EN8..........148 D2
Kilverton Dr EN2.........161 D1
Kilworth Cl AL7...........111 B4
Kimberley Cl.............11 F2
Kimberley Ct CM23.......77 A5
Kimberley Rd AL3........127 D4
Kimble Cl WD18..........168 C2
Kimble Cres WD23........45 D5
Kimblewick WD19........167 E1
Kimbolton Cres SG2......69 A7
Kimbolton Gn WD6.......170 C5
Kimps Way HP3...........139 A8
KIMPTON...................66 C1

Kimpton Cl
  Hemel Hempstead
    HP2....................125 B8
  Woolmer Green SG3.....69 A2
Kimpton Pl WD5..........154 D5
Kimpton Prim Sch SG4...66 C1

Kimpton Rd
  Ayot St P AL6............89 A6
  Blackmore End SG4, AL4..87 C7
  Codicote SG4.............67 B3
  Luton LU1, LU2...........64 A6
  Peters Green LU2, SG4...65 E2
Kimptons Ct EN6.........158 D7
Kimptons Mead EN6......158 D7
Kinderscout HP3.........125 A1
Kindersley Cl AL6.........89 C6
Kindersley Way WD5.....153 D8
Kinetic Bsns Ctr WD6....150 B4
Kinetic Cres EN3.........162 F3
King Arthur Ct EN8.......162 E8
King Charles Rd WD7.....156 E7
King Edward Pl AL4.......87 D1

King Edward Rd
  Cheshunt EN8............162 E6
  Shenley WD7............156 F6
  Watford WD19...........167 E3
King Edward's Rd
  SG12.....................93 E2
King Edward St HP3......138 D7

Kingfisher Cl
  Harrow HA3.............176 F3

Kingfisher Cl continued
  Northwood HA6.........174 B2
Stansted Abbotts
  SG12.....................115 C3
Wheathampstead AL4....87 D1

Kingfisher Ct
  Enfield EN2..............160 F1
  Hitchin SG4..............35 A6
Letchworth Garden City
  SG6.......................22 E8
Kingfisher Dr HP3........138 F6
Kingfisher Lure
  Kings Langley WD4......139 B2
  Rickmansworth WD3.....165 B5
Kingfisher Rise SG2.......51 D2
Kingfisher Way
  Bishop's Stortford
    CM23...................77 A7
  Royston CM19...........116 A1
King George Ave
  WD23.....................168 B3
King George Cl SG1........50 E6
King George Rd
  Waltham Abbey EN9.....163 C5
  Ware SG12...............93 E2
King Georges Ave
  WD18.....................166 E5
King George's Cl SG5.....21 D1
King George's Way
  SG4.......................66 E6
Kingham Rd SG12.........94 E5
Kingham Way LU4........45 E1
King Harold Ct EN9.......163 C6
King Harold Sch EN9.....163 C6
King Harry La AL3........127 B1
King Harry St HP2........124 D2
King Henry Ct LU3........45 B2
King Henrys Ct EN9......163 C3
King Henry's Mews
  EN3.......................163 A2
King James Ave EN6......146 E2
King James Way SG8.......7 C8
Kingley Pk WD4..........139 B2

Kings Ave
  Hemel Hempstead
    HP3....................138 F7
  Watford WD18..........167 A5
Kingsbridge Rd CM23....77 A8
Kingsbury Ave AL3.......127 C4
Kingsbury Watermill*
  AL3.......................127 B4

Kings Cl
  Chipperfield WD4........152 B8
  Northwood HA6.........174 F4
  6 Watford WD18.......167 C5
Kingscroft AL7.............111 B7

Kings Ct
  Berkhamsted HP4.......122 C5
  Bishop's Stortford CM23..77 A8
  8 Borehamwood WD6..169 F8
  Harpenden AL5..........107 B8
Kingsdale Ho AL6..........89 B3
Kingsdale Rd HP4........122 A3
Kingsdown SG4............35 A6
Kingsdown Rd LU2........45 D5
Kings Farm Rd WD3......164 D3
Kingsfield EN11...........135 A8
Kings Field Cotts
  WD5......................153 F8
Kingsfield Ho WD19......167 D2
Kingsfield Dr EN3.........162 D4
Kingsfield Rd
  Dane End SG12...........71 D2
  Watford WD18..........167 D3
Kingsfield Way EN3.......162 D4
Kingsgate AL3.............127 B1
Kings Head Ct CM21......97 E2
Kings Heath Pk AL5.......86 C6
Kings Hedges SG5........34 C8
Kingshill Ave AL4.........128 B6
Kingshill Ct 8 EN5.......171 C5
Kingshill Inf Sch SG3.....69 D3
Kingshill Way HP4........122 B2
Kingshott Sch SG4........35 B5
King's La WD4.............152 B8
Kingsland Ct EN6.........158 F6
Kingsland Ct 7 LU1......63 F6
Kingsland Rd
  Hemel Hempstead
    HP1....................124 A1
  Luton LU1................63 F6
Kingsland Way SG7.......4 D4
KINGS LANGLEY..........139 A1
Kings Langley Prim Sch
  WD4......................138 F3
Kings Langley Sch
  WD4......................138 E3
Kings Langley Sta
  WD4......................139 C1
Kingsley Ave
  Borehamwood WD6.....169 F7
  Cheshunt EN8...........148 C2
Kingsley Cl AL7..........110 F2
Kingsley High Sch
  HA3......................176 C3
Kingsley Rd LU3..........45 B5
Kingsley Wlk HP23.......100 A4
Kings Mdw WD4..........139 A3
Kingsmead
  Cheshunt EN8...........148 D3
  Cuffley EN6.............146 E3
Lower Nazeing EN9,
  EN10......................135 C1
  Sawbridgeworth CM21..97 E1
  St Albans AL4............128 D6
Kingsmead Rd CM23.....77 A8
Kings Mews CM21.........97 E2

King's Mews 7 HP2.....124 D4
Kingsmill Ct 1 AL10....130 B3
Kings Oak WD3...........166 A5
Kings Oak Private Hospl
  The EN2.................161 A1
Kings Park Ind Est
  WD4......................139 B2
Kings Pl AL9..............130 C7

Kings Rd
  Barnet EN5..............171 C6
  Berkhamsted HP4.......122 B3
  Stevenage SG1...........50 D4
King's Rd
  Cheshunt EN8............162 E5
  Hertford SG13...........114 A7
  Hitchin SG5.............34 F8
  London Colney AL2.....142 C5
  St Albans AL3...........127 C3
Kings Sch The AL5........85 F4

King St
  Bishop's Stortford
    CM23...................76 F7
  Luton LU1................63 E7
  Markyate AL3............37 D6
  2 Royston SG8..........7 C8
  Tring HP23..............100 A3
  Watford WD18..........167 C5
King Street Mews 1
  CM23.....................76 F7
KING'S WALDEN..........48 A3
King's Walden Rd SG5....33 D2
Kings Walden Rise
  SG2.......................51 C8

Kingsway
  Cuffley EN6.............146 E1
  Luton LU4................45 A1
  Royston SG8.............7 C8
  Stotfold SG5.............11 F7
  Ware SG12...............93 D3
Kingsway Gdns SG5......11 F7
Kingsway Inf Est LU1....63 A8
Kingsway Inf Sch
  WD25.....................154 A5
Kingsway Jun Sch
  WD25.....................154 A5
Kingsway North Orbital Rd
  WD25...................154 B5
Kingswell Ride EN6.....146 E1
King's Wlk SG8.............7 D5
KINGSWOOD.............154 A5
Kingswood Ave SL4......35 D8
Kingswood Rd WD25....154 B5
Kingwell Rd EN4.........159 D1
King Williams Ct EN9....159 C3
Kinloch Ct 8 AL5..........86 B1
Kinross Cres LU3.........44 D8
Kinsbourne Cl AL5........85 C4
Kinsbourne Cres AL5.....85 D4
Kinsbourne Ct AL5........85 F3
KINSBOURNE GREEN....85 C5
Kinsbourne Green La
  AL5......................85 B3
Kintyre Ho 2 WD18.....166 F3
Kipling Cl SG4............35 C7
Kipling Gr HP2............105 B1
Kipling Pl HA7............176 F4
Kipling Rd LU3.............2 E1
Kipling The LU3...........45 B6
Kirby Cl HA6.............174 F4
Kirby Dr LU3..............44 A8
Kirkcaldy Gn 1
  WD19.....................175 C7
Kirkdale Ct 8 LU1........63 E6
Kirkdale Rd AL5..........86 A2
Kirklands AL3.............89 D2
Kirkwick Ave AL5........86 A1
Kitchener Cl AL1........128 B2
Kitcheners La SG2........38 B1
Kitchen Garden Cl SG3...34 E6
Kitching La
  Stevenage SG1...........50 A5
  St Ippolyts SG4.........49 F5
Kite Field HP4............121 E7
Kite Way SG6.............22 E8
Kitsbury Rd HP4.........122 B4
Kitsbury Rd HP4.........122 B4
Kitsbury Terr HP4........122 B4
Kitt's La SG7..............25 C8
Kitson Way CM20........117 C1
Kitswell Way WD7.......156 A6
KITT'S END...............158 E1
KITT'S END Rd EN5.....158 E2
Kiwi Ct SG5...............21 F1
Klondyke AL5.............85 D4
Knap Cl SG6..............23 D8
KNEBWORTH..............69 A5
Knebworth Ct CM23.....76 D6
Knebworth Ctry Pk*
  SG3......................68 C7
Knebworth Gate SG3.....68 B8
Knebworth Ho* SG3.....68 B8
Knebworth Path WD6...170 D5
Knebworth Prim Sch
  SG3......................68 F5
Knebworth Sta SG3......68 F5
KNEESWORTH..............2 A5
Kneesworth House Hospl
  SG8.......................2 C5
Kneesworth Rd SG8.......2 F8
Knella Gn AL7.............111 A6
Knella Rd AL7.............111 A6
Knifton Ct EN6...........158 D8

Knightsbridge Ct 8
  WD18.....................166 F5
Knightsbridge Way
  HP2......................124 E4

Knights Cl
  Bishop's Stortford
    CM23...................76 C8
  Buntingford SG9........40 E6
Knightscote Cl UB9......173 D1

Knights Ct
  Bushey WD23...........168 D1
  Standon SG11...........55 F1
Knight's Ct CM21........97 E2
Knightsfield AL8..........89 D2
Knights Field LU2........45 D1
Knightsfield Sch AL8.....89 D3

Knights Orch
  Hemel Hempstead
    HP1....................123 F5
  St Albans AL3...........127 C3
Knights Properties
  EN11.....................135 B6
Knights Row CM23.......78 E6
Knight St CM01............97 E2
Knights Templar Sch The
  SG7......................23 E8
Knights Templars Gn
  SG2.......................51 C8
Knocking Hoe National
  Nature Reserve*
  SG5........................20 A2
Knoll Cres HA6...........174 F2
Knolles Cres Al A9.......144 B7
Knoll Gn HP2.............124 E7
Knoll Rise LU2............45 E4
Knolls The SG13.........114 B7
Knoll Cl SG1...............37 B3
Knowle Cl SG1............36 B1
Knowle Dr AL5...........107 D7
Knowle Ho EN11.........135 A5
Knowle The EN11........135 A5
Knowl Piece SG4..........22 A3
Knowl Pk WD6...........169 E4
Knowl Way WD6.........169 F4
Knutsford Ave WD24....154 D1
Knutsford Sch WD24....154 D1
Koh-I-Noor Ave
  WD3......................168 A3
Kristiansand Way SG6...23 C8
Kymswell Rd SG2........51 C3
Kynance Ct LU2...........46 A2
Kynaston Cl HA3.........176 D3
Kynaston Wood HA3....176 D3
Kyrkeby SG6..............23 C4
Kytes Dr WD25..........154 D6

L

LABBY GREEN.............112 A3
Laburnham Cotts SG12..94 F4
Laburnum Cl
  Cheshunt EN8...........162 D8
  Luton LU3...............45 C7
Laburnum Gr
  Chiswell Green AL2.....141 B6
  Luton LU3...............45 B7
Laburnum Rd EN11.......135 B8
Laburnum Way EN7.....147 B3
Lachbury Cl LU1..........63 A6
Lackmore Rd EN1........162 C4
Lacre Way SG6............23 C7
Ladbrooke Cl WD3.......165 C4
Ladbrooke Dr EN6.......159 A7
Ladbrooke JMI Sch
  EN6......................159 B7
Ladies Gr AL3.............127 C5
Lady Cooper Ct HP4.....122 E6
Lady Gr AL7...............110 E2
Ladygrove Cotts SG4.....48 F5
Ladygrove Ct SG4........48 F5
Ladyhill AL4...............86 F3
Lady Mdw HP3...........138 D4
Lady St John Sq SG14...92 A1
Lady's Cl WD18..........167 C5
Ladyshot CM20...........118 B1
Ladysmith Rd
  Harrow HA3.............176 E1
  Ivinghoe LU7............80 E5
  St Albans AL3...........127 D4
Lady Spencer's Gr
  AL1......................127 C2
Ladywalk WD3...........172 E6
Ladywell Prospect
  CM21.....................98 A1
Ladywood Cl WD3.......165 C4
Ladywood Rd SG14......112 F6
Lady Zia Wernher Sch
  LU2......................46 B3
Laelia Ho AL1............128 A2
Lagley Ho HP4...........122 A5
Laguna Ct 4 AL1.........127 E3
Laidon Sq HP2............124 D7
Lake Dr WD23...........176 D8
Lakeland Cl HA3.........176 D4
Lake Rd EN1..............135 E2
Lakes Ct SG12............115 B4
Lakeside
  Borehamwood WD6.....170 A4
  Tring HP23..............100 A5
Lakeside Pl AL2..........142 D4
Lakeside Rd EN8.........148 C3
Lakeside Sch AL8........110 B4
Lake The WD23..........168 D1
Lakeview LU3.............45 D2

Lake View
  Bishop's Stortford
    CM23...................76 C3
  Potters Bar EN6........159 C6
Lake Villas SG9...........43 B4
Lalleford Rd LU2..........46 D1
Lalsham Ho 4 WD19...175 C7

Lamb Cl
  Hatfield AL10...........130 B4
  Watford WD25...........154 C5
Lamb Ct AL4..............108 E7
Lambert Ct WD23........167 D5
Lamberton Cl WD6.......170 A8
Lamb La AL3..............106 B5
Lamb Mdw SG15..........11 A3
Lambourn Chase
  WD7......................155 F3
Lambourn Dr LU2.........45 E6
Lambourn Gdns AL5.....85 F3
Lambs Cl
  Cuffley EN6.............146 F2
  Dunstable LU5...........44 A1
Lambs Gdns SG12........95 D4
Lambton Ave EN8........162 D6
Lamer La AL4.............87 D3
Lamers Rd LU2............46 B2
Lammasmead EN10......148 F8
Lammas Med SG5.........21 E2
Lammas Path SG2.........51 B4
Lammas Rd
  Cheddington LU7.........80 A7
  Watford WD18..........167 C4
  Watton at S SG14........70 D4
Lammas Way SG6.........22 F8
Lamorna Cl
  Luton LU3................44 F6
  Radlett WD7.............156 B5
Lamorna Ct 2 HA3.....176 E1
Lampits EN11.............135 B6
Lamsey Rd HP3...........124 D3
Lancaster Ave
  Hadley Wood EN4.......159 D1
  Hitchin SG5.............34 E8
  Luton LU2................45 C8
Lancaster Ct SG1.........36 E2
Lancaster Dr HP3........136 F4
Lancaster Rd
  Hitchin SG5.............34 E8
  St Albans AL1...........127 F5
Lancaster Way
  Abbots Langley WD5....153 F8
  Bishop's Stortford CM23..76 C3
  Welwyn AL6.............89 C3
Lance Ho SG13..........114 B8
Lancelot Ct WD23......168 A7
Lancing Ho 5 AL5.......86 B1
Lancing Rd LU2...........46 D3
Lancing Way WD3........166 B4
Landau Way EN10........148 F5
Landford Cl WD3.........173 E8
Landing The WD7........156 A6
Landmead Rd EN8.......148 E2
Landridge Dr EN1........162 B1
Lands' End WD6..........169 D3
Lane End
  Berkhamsted HP4.......121 F4
  Hatfield AL10...........129 F7
Lanefield Wlk AL8........110 C6
Lane Gdns WD23.........168 E2
Lanercost Cl AL4.........90 A7
LANES END................119 C4
Langbridge Cl SG4.......35 A4
Langdale Ave AL5........86 E2
Langdale Ct 2 HP2.....124 E6
Langdale Gdns EN3......162 D4
Langdale Terr WD6......170 C6
Langdon St HP23........100 A3
Langfield Ct EN9..........135 E1
Langford Cl AL4..........128 C5
Langford Dr LU2..........46 A3
Langham Cl
  Luton LU2................45 D7
  St Albans AL4...........128 D8
Langham Ho 9 LU1.....63 D8
Langholme SG8...........168 C1
Langland Ct HA4.........174 D3
Langland Dr HA5.........175 E3
Langleigh SG6............11 F1
LANGLEY..................49 F1
Langley Ave HP3.........138 F8
LANGLEYBURY............153 B4
Langleybury La WD4....153 B4
Langley Cres
  Kings Langley WD4.....139 A1
  St Albans AL4............127 C5
Langley Gn EN7..........147 C3
Langley Gn LU3............135 D1
Langley Gr AL4...........108 C2
Langley Hill WD4........138 F2
Langley Hill Cl WD4.....139 A2
Langley La
  Abbots Langley WD5....153 A8
  Langley SG4.............49 F2
Langley Lodge La
  WD4......................153 A8
Langley Par WD5........153 F8
Langley Rd
  Abbots Langley WD5....153 F8
  Chipperfield WD4.......138 B1
  Watford WD17..........167 A8
Langley Row EN5........171 F8
Langley Sidings SG1.....50 D2
Langley St LU1............63 E6
Langley Terrace Ind Pk 17
  LU1......................63 E6

Langley Way WD17 . . . . . . .166 F8
Langley Wharf WD4 . . . . . .139 A4
Langmead Dr WD23 . . . . . .168 D1
Langstone Ley AL7 . . . . . . .111 B5
Langthorne Ave SG1 . . . . . . .50 E6
Langton Gr HA6 . . . . .174 C5
Langton Ho EN11 . . . . .134 F6
Langton Rd
 Harrow HA3 . . . . .176 C3
 Hoddesdon EN11 . . . . . . .134 F6
Langwood 5 WD17 . . . . . . .167 A8
Langwood Gdns
 WD17 . . . . .167 A8
Langwood Ho 4
 WD3 . . . . .165 E1
Langworthy HA5 . . . . .176 A4
Lankester Rd SG8 . . . . .7 C5
Lannock SG6 . . . . .23 D4
Lannock Hill SG4 . . . . .23 E1
Lannock Prim Sch SG6 . . . . .23 C4
Lanrick Copse HP4 . . . . . . .122 C5
Lansdowne Ct EN10 . . . . . . .135 A3
Lansdowne Pl AL1 . . . . .142 A8
Lansdowne Rd LU3 . . . . .45 D1
Lanterns La SG2 . . . . .51 D5
Lanthony Ct SG15 . . . . .11 A4
Lanthorn Cl EN10 . . . . .134 E4
Laporte Way LU4 . . . . .44 F1
Lapwing Cl HP2 . . . . .124 E6
Lapwing Dell SG6 . . . . .23 B3
Lapwing Rd LU4 . . . . .44 A4
Lapwing Rise SG2 . . . . .51 D3
Lapwing Way WD5 . . . . . . .154 A8
Larch Ave
 Bricket Wood AL2 . . . . . . .140 E1
 Hitchin SG4 . . . . .35 A4
Larch Cl EN7 . . . . .147 E4
Larches Ave EN1 . . . . .162 C4
Larches The
 Berkhamsted HP4 . . . . . . .121 D5
 Little Chalfont HP6 . . . . . .150 E3
 Luton LU2 . . . . .45 D1
 Northwood HA6 . . . . .174 C4
 St Albans AL4 . . . . .128 D7
 Ware SG12 . . . . .93 C4
 Watford WD17 . . . . .167 A4
Larch La AL6 . . . . .89 F8
Larch Rise HP4 . . . . .122 A5
Larch View HP1 . . . . .124 B2
Larchwood CM23 . . . . .76 D5
Larchwood Rd HP2 . . . . . . .124 E5
Larken Cl WD23 . . . . .168 C1
Larken Dr WD23 . . . . .168 C1
Larkens Cl SG11 . . . . .55 D3
Larkin Cl SG2 . . . . .2 D1
Larkins Cl SG7 . . . . .12 F1
Larkins La SG10 . . . . .74 F1
Larkinson SG1 . . . . .50 C7
Lark Rise AL10 . . . . .130 A3
Larkspur Cl
 Bishop's Stortford
 CM23 . . . . .76 D6
 Hemel Hempstead HP1 . . .123 E4
Larkspur Gdns LU4 . . . . .44 F2
Larks Ridge AL2 . . . . .141 A4
Larkway CM23 . . . . .76 C6
Larkswood Rise AL4 . . . . . .128 C8
Larmans Rd EN3 . . . . .162 D3
Larsen Dr EN9 . . . . .163 D5
Larwood Gr SG1 . . . . .51 A8
Larwood Sch SG1 . . . . .50 F7
LATCHFORD 73 F5
Latchford Mews 8
 AL4 . . . . .87 D1
Latchford Pl HP1 . . . . .124 A2
LATCHMORE BANK 77 B2
Latchmore End
 Bishop's Stortford
 CM22 . . . . .77 B2
 Little Hallingbury CM22 . . .98 B8
Latchmore Cl SG4 . . . . .34 F5
Lathwell Ct LU2 . . . . .45 E1
LATIMER 150 E3
Latimer Cl
 Hemel Hempstead
 HP2 . . . . .125 B8
 Pinner HA5 . . . . .175 C2
 Watford WD18 . . . . .166 E2
Latimer Ct EN8 . . . . .162 F5
Latimer Gdns
 Pinner HA5 . . . . .175 C2
 Welwyn Garden City
 AL7 . . . . .111 B6
Latimer Pl HA6 . . . . .174 F5
Latimer Rd
 Little Chalfont HP6,
 HP5 . . . . .150 C2
 Luton LU1 . . . . .63 E6
Latium Cl AL1 . . . . .127 D2
Lattimore Ho 9
 AL1 . . . . .127 E3
Lattimore Rd
 St Albans AL1 . . . . .127 E3
 Wheathampstead AL4 . . . .108 C8
Latton Hall Cl CM20 . . . . . .118 A1
Lauderdale Rd WD4 . . . . . .153 C6
Laughton Ct WD6 . . . . .170 D7
Launceston WD3 . . . . .164 B3
Laundry La EN9 . . . . .149 E6
Launton Cl LU3 . . . . .31 B1
Laura Ct HA2 . . . . .176 C1
Laural Ct EN6 . . . . .146 F2
Laurance Haines Prim Sch
 The WD18 . . . . .167 A3

Laureate Way HP1 . . . . . . .124 B5
Laurel Ave EN6 . . . . .158 F7
Laurel Bank HP3 . . . . .137 F8
Laurel Cl
 Hemel Hempstead
 HP2 . . . . .124 F4
 Watford WD19 . . . . .167 D2
Laurel Ct EN6 . . . . .146 F1
Laureldene SG10 . . . . .74 F1
Laurel Fields EN6 . . . . .158 F8
Laurel Mews SG7 . . . . .12 F1
Laurel Pk HA3 . . . . .176 F3
Laurel Rd AL1 . . . . .127 F3
Laurelsfield AL3 . . . . .141 B8
Laurelside Wlk LU5 . . . . .44 A2
Laurels The
 Bushey WD23 . . . . .176 E8
 Chiswell Green AL2 . . . . . .141 A3
 Hammond Street EN7 . . . .147 E5
 Potten End HP4 . . . . .123 C6
 Welwyn SG5 . . . . .21 E3
Lauries Cl HP1 . . . . .123 C1
Laurino Pl WD23 . . . . .176 C8
Lavender Cl
 Bishop's Stortford
 CM23 . . . . .76 D6
 Hammond Street EN7 . . . .147 F4
 Harlow CM20 . . . . .117 E1
 Hatfield AL10 . . . . .129 F8
 Luton LU2 . . . . .45 F7
Lavender Cres AL3 . . . . .127 C5
Lavender Croft SG5 . . . . .35 B6
Lavender Ct SG7 . . . . .12 C1
Lavender Gdns
 Enfield EN2 . . . . .161 B1
 Harrow HA3 . . . . .176 E4
Lavender Prim Sch
 EN2 . . . . .161 B1
Lavender Rd EN2 . . . . .161 D1
Lavender Way SG5 . . . . .34 D7
Lavender Wlk HP2 . . . . .124 D5
Lavinia Ave WD25 . . . . .154 D5
Lavrock La AL5 . . . . .165 F2
Lawford Ave WD3 . . . . .164 C3
Lawford Cl
 Chorleywood WD3 . . . . . .164 C3
 Luton LU3 . . . . .63 C7
Law Hall La AL4 . . . . .66 A8
Law Hall Lane Cotts
 SG4 . . . . .66 A8
Lawn Ave SG4 . . . . .66 C1
Lawn Gdns LU1 . . . . .63 D5
Lawn La HP3 . . . . .138 D8
Lawn Mans 8 EN5 . . . . . . .171 F5
Lawns Cl SG5 . . . . .33 C2
Lawns Ct SG8 . . . . .7 D5
Lawns Dr The EN10 . . . . . . .134 F2
Lawns The
 Harrow HA5 . . . . .176 B3
 Hemel Hempstead HP1 . . .123 F4
 Shenley WD7 . . . . .156 E6
 St Albans AL3 . . . . .127 C4
 Stevenage SG2 . . . . .51 B4
 Welwyn Garden City AL8 . .89 D1
Lawnswood EN5 . . . . .171 E4
Lawn The CM20 . . . . .118 B3
Lawn Vale HA5 . . . . .175 E1
Lawrance Gdns EN8 . . . . . .148 D3
Lawrance Rd AL3 . . . . .127 C7
Lawrence Ave
 Letchworth Garden City
 SG6 . . . . .23 A4
 Sawbridgeworth CM21 . . . .97 E4
 Stansted Abbotts
 SG12 . . . . .115 C4
 Stevenage SG1 . . . . .50 E3
Lawrence Cl SG14 . . . . .112 E7
Lawrence Ct 4
 WD19 . . . . .175 D7
Lawrence End Rd LU2 . . . . .65 D4
Lawrence Hall 11 LU1 . . . . .63 F7
Lawrence Moorings
 CM21 . . . . .97 F2
Lawrie Ct HA3 . . . . .176 F3
Laxton Cl LU2 . . . . .46 E1
Laxton Gdns
 Baldock SG7 . . . . .24 A7
 Welwyn SG3 . . . . .57 A4
Layard Rd EN1 . . . . .161 F1
Lay Brook AL4 . . . . .128 A2
Layham Dr LU2 . . . . .46 E1
Layhill HP2 . . . . .124 D5
Layston CE Fst Sch
 SG9 . . . . .40 F8
Layston Mdw SG9 . . . . .40 F6
Layston Pk SG8 . . . . .7 D5
Layton St AL7 . . . . .110 E3
Lea Bank LU3 . . . . .44 E6
Lea Bank Ct LU3 . . . . .44 E6
Lea Bushes WD25 . . . . .154 E4

LEAGRAVE 44 D5
Leagrave High St LU4 . . . . . . .44 B3
Leagrave Prim Sch
 LU4 . . . . .44 C4
Leagrave Rd LU4 . . . . .45 B2
Leagrave Sta LU4 . . . . .44 E5
Leahoe Gdns SG13 . . . . . . .113 C5
Lea Ind Est AL5 . . . . .86 C4
Lealands High Sch
 LU3 . . . . .44 C8
Lea Manor High Sch
 LU3 . . . . .44 F8
Leamington Rd LU3 . . . . .45 A7
Lea Mount EN7 . . . . .147 E3
Leander Gdns WD25 . . . . . .154 E2
Lea Prim Sch The AL5 . . . . . .86 B4
Lea Rd
 Harpenden AL5 . . . . .86 B3
 Hoddesdon EN11 . . . . . . .135 C8
 Broxbourne EN9 . . . . .163 A5
 Luton LU1 . . . . .63 F7
 Watford WD24 . . . . .154 B1
Lea Road Ind Pk EN9 . . . . . .163 A5
Leasey Bridge La AL4 . . . . . .87 A1
Leasey Dell Dr AL4 . . . . .87 A2
Leaside HP2 . . . . .125 C2
Leaside Cl AL5 . . . . .86 C3
Leaside Lo 6 EN11 . . . . . . .135 D8
Leaside Wlk 6 SG12 . . . . . . .93 D1
Leas The
 Baldock SG7 . . . . .23 E7
 Hemel Hempstead HP3 . . .139 A7
 Watford WD23 . . . . .167 F7
Leat Cl CM21 . . . . .97 F3
Leathersellers Cl 7
 EN5 . . . . .171 E6
Leathwaite Cl LU3 . . . . .45 A6
LEA VALLEY 86 F2
Lea Valley Education
 Support Unit EN6 . . . . . .162 D5
Lea Valley High Sch
 EN3 . . . . .162 C4
Leavesden CE Prim
 Sch WD5 . . . . .154 A8
Leaves Spring SG2 . . . . .51 A2
Leaview EN9 . . . . .163 B6
Lea Wlk AL5 . . . . .86 C4
Lebanon Cl WD17 . . . . .153 D2
Le Corte Cl WD4 . . . . .138 F2
Lectern La AL1 . . . . .141 E7
Leda Ave EN3 . . . . .162 D1
LEDBURN 61 C8
Ledgemore La HP1,
 EN9 . . . . .103 F5
Ledwell Rd LU1 . . . . .62 F3
Lee Bridge Cnr LU2 . . . . .85 F7
Leeches Way LU7 . . . . .80 A7
Lee Cl
 Hertford SG13 . . . . .113 C4
 Stansted Abbotts
 SG12 . . . . .115 C4
Leecroft Rd EN5 . . . . .171 E5
Lee Farm Cl HP5 . . . . .136 A1
Leefe Way EN6 . . . . .146 D3
Leeming Rd WD6 . . . . .169 F8
Lees Ave HA6 . . . . .174 F2
Leeside
 Barnet EN5 . . . . .171 E3
 Potters Bar EN6 . . . . .159 D7
Leeside Works SG12 . . . . . .115 C4
Leeswood Ct SG14 . . . . . . .112 F7
Leete Pl SG8 . . . . .7 D7
Lee The HA6 . . . . .174 F5
Lee Valley Cty Pk*
 EN10 . . . . .135 B3
Lee Valley Park Farms
 Visitor Ctr* EN9 . . . . . . .149 C3
Lee Valley Park Vst Ctr*
 EN9 . . . . .163 C6
Leeway Cl HA5 . . . . .175 F3
Leggatts Cl WD24 . . . . .153 F3
Leggatts Rise WD25 . . . . . . .154 A4
Leggatts Way WD24 . . . . . . .154 A3
Leggatts Wood Ave
 WD24 . . . . .154 A3
Leggett Gr SG1 . . . . .50 E8
Leghorn Cres LU4 . . . . .44 A3
Legions Way CM23 . . . . .77 A8
Legra Ave EN11 . . . . .135 A6
Leicester Cl LU4 . . . . .44 E1
Leicester Rd LU4 . . . . .44 E1
Leigh Comm AL7 . . . . .110 F4
Leigh Ct LU6 . . . . .82 C2
Leigh Rodd WD19 . . . . .175 F7

Lemsford Springs (Nature
 Reserve)* AL8 . . . . .110 A5
Lemsford Village AL8 . . . . . .109 F5
Lennon Cl LU3 . . . . .63 D7
Lennox Ct LU3 . . . . .45 A7
Lennox Gn LU2 . . . . .46 F2
Lensbury Cl EN8 . . . . .148 E3
Leonard Ct HA3 . . . . .176 E3
Leonard's Cl AL6 . . . . .89 E8
Lesbury Cl LU2 . . . . .46 E1
Leslie Cl SG2 . . . . .51 C2
Letchfield HP5 . . . . .150 B8
LETCHFORD GARDEN CITY
 .22 C5
Letchmore Cl SG1 . . . . .50 D6
LETCHMORE HEATH 168 E8
Letchmore Inf Sch
 SG1 . . . . .50 D7
Letchmore Rd
 Radlett WD7 . . . . .156 A3
 Stevenage SG1 . . . . .50 D6
Letchworth Bsns & Ret Pk
 SG6 . . . . .23 C6
Letchworth Cl WD19 . . . . . .175 D5
Letchworth Gate SG6 . . . . . .23 B4
Letchworth La SG6 . . . . .22 F3
Letchworth Mus & Art
 Gall* SG6 . . . . .22 F5
Letchworth Rd
 Baldock SG7 . . . . .23 D7
 Luton LU3 . . . . .45 A4
Letchworth Sta SG6 . . . . . . .22 F6
Letter Box Row SG4 . . . . .34 F3
LETTY GREEN 112 A2
Level's Gn CM23 . . . . .58 C5
LEVEL'S GREEN 58 C5
Levenage La SG12 . . . . .95 E3
Leven Cl
 Cheshunt EN8 . . . . .162 D6
 South Oxhey WD19 . . . . .175 D5
Levendale LU4 . . . . .44 C5
Leven Dr EN8 . . . . .162 D6
LEVENS GREEN 54 C1
Leventhorpe Sch The
 CM21 . . . . .97 E4
Leven Way HP2 . . . . .124 D7
Leveret Cl WD25 . . . . .154 A5
LEVERSTOCK GREEN
 . . . . .125 E5
Leverstock Green CE Prim
 Sch HP2 . . . . .125 D2
Leverstock Green Rd
 Hemel Hempstead
 HP2 . . . . .125 B3
 Hemel Hempstead HP2,
 HP3 . . . . .125 C2
Leverstock Green Way HP2,
 HP3 . . . . .125 D2
Leverton Inf Sch The
 EN9 . . . . .163 F5
Leverton Jun Sch The
 EN9 . . . . .163 F5
Leverton Way EN9 . . . . .163 C6
Lewes Way WD3 . . . . .166 D4
Lewington Ct EN3 . . . . .162 D2
Lewis Cl UB9 . . . . .173 C1
Lewisham Ct 9 WD18 . . . . .163 A1
Lewis Ho 3 WD18 . . . . .166 F3
Lewis La SG15 . . . . .11 A6
Lewsey Park Ct LU4 . . . . .44 A4
Lewsey Rd LU4 . . . . .44 B2
Lexington Cl WD6 . . . . .169 F6
Lexington Ct EN6 . . . . .158 D8
Lexington Way EN5 . . . . . . .171 D5
Leyburne Cl LU7 . . . . .61 C8
Leyburne Rd LU3 . . . . .45 B6
Leycroft Way AL5 . . . . .107 E7
Leyden Rd SG1 . . . . .50 D2
LEY GREEN 47 F5
Leygreen Cl LU2 . . . . .64 A8
LEY HILL 136 B1
Leyhill Dr LU1 . . . . .63 B4
Ley Hill Sch HP5 . . . . .136 B1
Ley Ho AL7 . . . . .111 C6
Leyland Ave AL1 . . . . .127 D1
Leyland Cl EN8 . . . . .148 C2
Ley Park Prim Sch
 EN10 . . . . .134 F1
Leys Ave SG6 . . . . .22 F6
Leys Cl UB9 . . . . .173 D2
Leysdown AL7 . . . . .111 D6
Leys Prim Sch The
 SG1 . . . . .37 A2
Leys Rd WD3 . . . . .124 F1
Leys The
 Radlett WD7 . . . . .156 A2
 St Albans AL4 . . . . .128 D6
 Tring HP23 . . . . .100 B4

Lilac Way AL5 . . . . .107 D6
Lilbourne Dr SG13 . . . . .114 A7
LILLEY 47 C5
Lilley Bottom LU2, SG4 . . . . .47 C5
Lilley Bottom Rd SG4 . . . . . .48 B1
Lilleyhoo La LU2, SG5 . . . . . .32 F2
Lilley Old School Ct
 LU2 . . . . .32 D2
Lilliard Cl EN11 . . . . .115 B2
Lilly La HP2 . . . . .125 D7
Lily Wlk SG16 . . . . .10 A3
Limberlost The AL6 . . . . .89 E7
Limbrick Rd AL5 . . . . .107 C6
LIMBURY 44 F5
Limbury Rd LU3 . . . . .44 F4
Lime Ave
 Blackmore End AL4 . . . . . .87 B7
 Luton LU4 . . . . .44 C3
Lime Cl
 Aston SG2 . . . . .51 D4
 Harrow HA3 . . . . .176 F1
 Ware SG12 . . . . .93 E2
 Watford WD19 . . . . .167 D2
Limedene Cl HA5 . . . . .175 D2
Lime Gr
 Royston SG8 . . . . .7 E8
 Totteridge N20 . . . . .171 F1
Limekiln Cl SG8 . . . . .7 E5
Limekiln La
 Baldock SG7 . . . . .23 F7
 Stansted Mountfitchet
 CM24 . . . . .59 C5
Lime Pk CM23 . . . . .77 A6
Limes Cres 4 CM23 . . . . . . .77 A7
Limes Ct
 Cheshunt EN8 . . . . .162 D7
 7 Hoddesdon EN11 . . . . .135 A6
 Redbourn AL3 . . . . .106 A6
Limes The
 Buckland SG9 . . . . .27 D8
 Cheshunt EN10 . . . . .148 F7
 Hertford SG14 . . . . .113 C6
 Hitchin SG5 . . . . .34 D6
 5 Luton LU1 . . . . .63 E5
 2 Northwood HA6 . . . . . .174 E5
 St Albans AL4 . . . . .127 E5
 Welwyn Garden City
 AL7 . . . . .111 A4
Limetree Ave LU1 . . . . .85 A7
Limetree Ct HA5 . . . . .176 A3
Lime Tree Cl AL2 . . . . .142 B5
Lime Tree Pl AL1 . . . . .127 E2
Lime Tree Wlk
 Bushey WD23 . . . . .176 E8
 Enfield EN2 . . . . .161 C5
 Rickmansworth WD3 . . . .165 B4
Lime Walk Prim Sch
 HP3 . . . . .124 F1
Lime Way WD7 . . . . .156 C8
Lime Wlk HP3 . . . . .124 F1
Limit Home Pk HP4 . . . . . . .121 D7
Linacres LU4 . . . . .44 D4
Linbridge Way LU2 . . . . .46 E2
Linces Way AL7 . . . . .111 B4
Lincoln Cl
 Bishop's Stortford
 CM23 . . . . .76 D5
 Welwyn Garden City
 AL7 . . . . .111 D6
Lincoln Ct
 Berkhamsted HP4 . . . . . . .122 B4
 Borehamwood WD6 . . . . .170 D4
Lincoln Dr
 Croxley Green WD3 . . . . .166 B6
 South Oxhey WD19 . . . . .175 C7
Lincoln Field WD23 . . . . . . .167 D7
Lincoln Hill SG9 . . . . .29 A5
Lincoln Mews AL3 . . . . .127 C2
Lincoln Rd
 Luton LU4 . . . . .45 B1
 Stevenage SG1 . . . . .37 B2
Lincoln's Cl AL4 . . . . .128 D8
Lincoln Way WD3 . . . . .166 B5
Lindbergh AL7 . . . . .111 C6
Linden Ave WD18 . . . . .166 F5
Linden Cl EN7 . . . . .148 B1
Linden Cres LU1 . . . . .128 C3
Lindencroft SG6 . . . . .12 A1
Linden Ct
 Harpenden AL5 . . . . .107 B8
 4 Luton LU2 . . . . .63 F8
Linden Glade HP1 . . . . .124 A2
Linden Gn SG6 . . . . .23 A8
Linden Lea WD25 . . . . .154 A6
Linden Rd
 Luton LU4 . . . . .44 E4
 Redbourn AL3 . . . . .106 A6
Linden Sq UB9 . . . . .173 A4
Lindens The
 Bishop's Stortford
 CM23 . . . . .76 F6
 Hatfield AL10 . . . . .129 F6
 Hemel Hempstead HP3 . . .137 F8
 Stevenage SG2 . . . . .50 E4
Lindley Cl AL5 . . . . .86 A4
Lindlings HP1 . . . . .123 E2
Lindrick Ho 11 WD19 . . . . .175 C7
Lindsay Cl SG8 . . . . .35 B5
Lindsay Ct SG8 . . . . .2 C1
Lindsay Pl EN7 . . . . .148 B1
Lindsey Ct CM23 . . . . .58 F1
Lindsey Rd
 Bishop's Stortford
 CM23 . . . . .58 F1
 Luton LU2 . . . . .46 D1
Lindum Pl AL3 . . . . .127 A1
Linfield Ct SG14 . . . . .112 F7
Lingfield Cl HA6 . . . . .174 E3

Lingfield Rd
Royston SG8 . . . . 7 F6
Stevenage SG1 . . . . 37 C1
Lingfield Way WD17 . . . 153 F1
Lingholm Way EN5 . . . 171 D4
Lingmoor Dr WD25 . . . 154 C6
Lington Ave HP5 . . . . . 136 A1
Link Cl AL10 . . . . 130 B5
Link Dr AL10 . . . . 130 B5
Linkfield AL7 . . . . 110 E2
Link Rd
Bishop's Stortford
CM23 . . . . 76 F8
Hemel Hempstead HP1 . 124 C6
Oaklands AL6 . . . . 89 F8
Watford WD24 . . . . 167 D7
Links Ave SG13 . . . . . . 114 B7
Links Bsns Ctr The
CM23 . . . . 77 C7
Links Dr
Borehamwood WD6 . . . 169 F5
Radlett WD7 . . . . 155 F6
Linkside Rd CM23 . . . . . 77 C6
Links The
Cheshunt EN8 . . . . 148 D5
Welwyn Garden City
AL8 . . . . 110 B6
Links View AL3 . . . . . . 127 C5
Linksway HA6 . . . . 174 C2
Links Way
Croxley Green WD3 . . . 166 C5
Radlett WD7 . . . . 45 D8
Link The SG6 . . . . 12 A1
Linkway HA5 . . . . 175 D2
Link Way CM23 . . . . 76 E6
Linkways Ct 1 SG1 . . . . 50 F5
Linkways E SG1 . . . . 50 F5
Linkways W SG1 . . . . 50 F5
Link Wlk AL10 . . . . 130 B6
Linley Ct AL1 . . . . 127 F6
Linley Dell LU2 . . . . 46 D2
Linnet Cl
Bushey WD23 . . . . 168 C1
Letchworth Garden City
SG6 . . . . 22 E8
Luton LU4 . . . . 44 A4
Linnet Rd WD5 . . . . . . 154 A8
Linnet Wlk 8 AL10 . . . . 130 A3
Linnins Pond AL5 . . . . . . 84 B1
Linsey Cl HP3 . . . . 139 A7
Linster Gr WD6 . . . . . . 170 C4
Linten Cl SG4 . . . . 35 C6
Linton Ave WD6 . . . . . 169 F7
Lintons EN11 . . . . 135 B7
Lintott Cl SG1 . . . . 50 D6
Linwood CM21 . . . . 97 E2
Linwood Rd
Harpenden AL5 . . . . . . 107 C5
Ware SG12 . . . . 93 F3
Lion Ct WD6 . . . . 170 C4
Lion Yd SG4 . . . . 66 D1
Liphook Rd WD19 . . . . 175 D6
Lippitts Hill LU2 . . . . . . 45 E5
Lismirrane Ind Pk
WD6 . . . . 169 B3
Lismore
Hemel Hempstead
HP3 . . . . 125 C1
Stevenage SG2 . . . . 51 C1
Lister Ave SG4 . . . . 34 F5
Lister Cl SG1 . . . . 36 C2
Lister Cotts WD6 . . . . . 169 A4
Lister Hospl AL1 . . . . . . 36 B2
Liston Cl LU4 . . . . 44 B5
Little Acre AL2 . . . . 127 D6
Little Acres SG12 . . . . . 114 D8
LITTLE ALMSHOE 49 B8
Little Almshoe La
St Ippolyts SG4 . . . . 35 C1
St Ippolyts SG4 . . . . 49 A8
Little Almshoe Rd SG4 . . 49 A8
Little Beechill EN2 . . . . 160 D5
LITTLE BERKHAMSTED 132 C4
Little Berkhamsted La AL9,
SG13 . . . . 132 B3
Little Berries LU3 . . . . . . 44 E7
Little Bridge Rd 17
HP4 . . . . 122 D4
Littlebrook Gdns EN8 . . 148 D1
Little Burrow AL7 . . . . 110 D4
Littlebury Cl SG5 . . . . . . 12 A5
Little Bushey La
WD23 . . . . 168 C5
Little Catherells HP1 . . 123 F5
LITTLE CHALFONT 150 D7
LITTLE CHISHILL 18 E7
Little Chishill Rd SG8 . . 18 C8
Little Church Rd LU2 . . . 46 B3
Littlecote PI HA5 . . . . . 175 E2
Little Croft Ct SA2 . . . . 142 A4
Little Dell AL8 . . . . 110 D8
Littlefield Rd LU2 . . . . . 46 B2
LITTLE GADDESDEN . . . 102 D7
Little Gaddesden CE Prim
Sch HP4 . . . . 102 D7
Little Gaddesden Ho
HP4 . . . . 102 E6
Little Ganett AL7 . . . . . 111 C4
Little Gr WD23 . . . . . . 168 B5
Little Graylings WD5 . . 153 E6
Little Green Jun Sch
WD3 . . . . 166 B6
Littlegreen La LU1 . . . . . 62 E3
Little Green La WD3 . . . 166 B6
Little Grove Ave EN7 . . 147 E4
LITTLE HADHAM 57 C2

Little Hadham Prim Sch
SG11 . . . . 57 C2
Little Hallingbury CE Prim
Sch CM22 . . . . 98 C7
LITTLE HALLINGBURY 98 D8
Little Hardings AL7 . . . 111 C7
Little Hayes WD4 . . . . 139 A2
Little Heath CM22 . . . . . 98 F3
LITTLE HEATH
Potten End 123 B5
Potters Bar 145 B2
Little Heath Cotts
HP4 . . . . 123 B4
Little Heath La HP4 . . . 123 B4
Little Heath Prim Sch
EN6 . . . . 145 C1
Little Heath Spinney
AL3 . . . . 127 C5
Little Henleys SG12 . . . . 95 D1
Little Hill WD3 . . . . . . 164 C3
Little Hoo HP23 . . . . 99 F4
LITTLE HORMEAD 42 A6
Little How Croft WD5 . . 153 C8
Little Hyde SG1 . . . . 51 B4
Little La
Harpenden AL5 . . . . . . 107 C6
Pirton SG5 . . . . 20 D5
Little Lake AL7 . . . . . . 111 B3
Little Larkins EN5 . . . . 171 E3
Little Ley AL7 . . . . 110 E3
Little Martins WD23 . . 168 B4
Little Mdw AL7 . . . . 63 B3
Little Mead AL10 . . . . . 130 B8
Little Mimms 2 HP2 . . . 124 E4
Little Mollards HP2 . . . . 60 A3
Little Moss La HA5 . . . . 175 E1
Little Mundells AL7 . . . 110 F8
Little Munden CE Prim
Sch SG12 . . . . 71 E8
Little Orch 7 HP4 . . . . 125 A5
Little Orchard Cl
Abbots Langley WD5 . . 153 D7
Pinner HA5 . . . . 175 E1
Little Oxhey La WD19 . . 175 E6
Little Parndon Sch
CM20 . . . . 117 B1
Little Piper's Cl EN7 . . . 147 B2
Little Pk HP3 . . . . 137 A3
Little Potters WD23 . . . 168 E2
Little Reddings Prim Sch
WD23 . . . . 168 B4
Little Ridge AL7 . . . . . 111 A6
Little Rivers AL7 . . . . . 111 A7
Little St EN9 . . . . 163 C3
Little Stock Rd EN7 . . . 147 D5
Little Stream CM HA4 . . 174 C5
Little Thistle AL7 . . . . . 111 C4
LITTLE TRING 99 F6
Little Tring Rd HP23 . . . 99 F6
Little Twye HP23 . . . . . 119 F3
Little Twye Rd HP23 . . 119 F3
Little Wade AL7 . . . . . 110 F3
Little Widbury SG12 . . . 93 F1
Little Widbury La SG12 . 93 F1
Little Windmill Hill
WD4 . . . . 151 F7
Little Wlk 7 EN11 . . . . 135 B7
Little Wood Croft LU3 . . 44 E7
LITTLE WYMONDLEY . . . 35 E3
Little Youngs AL8 . . . . 110 D6
Liverpool Rd
Luton LU1 . . . . 63 D7
St Albans AL1 . . . . 127 E3
Watford WD18 . . . . . . 167 B4
Livingstone Ct EN5 . . . 171 E7
Livingstone Link SG2 . . . 51 B8
Livingstone Wlk HP2 . . 124 F7
Lloyd Mews SG1 . . . . . . 36 A1
Lloyd Taylor Cl SG11 . . . 57 B2
Lloyd Way SG4 . . . . 66 C1
Loates La WD17 . . . . . 167 C6
Loates Pasture CM24 . . . 59 D8
Local Board Rd
WD17 . . . . 167 D4
Locarno Ave LU4 . . . . . . 44 C6
Lochinver House Sch
EN6 . . . . 145 B1
Lochnell Rd HP4 . . . . . 121 F6
Lockers Park La HP1 . . 124 B3
Lockers Park Sch
HP1 . . . . 124 B3
Locket Rd HA3 . . . . . . 176 F1
Locket Road Mews 4
HA3 . . . . 176 F1
Lock Ho HP3 . . . . 138 E7
Lockley Cres AL10 . . . . 130 B7
Lockleys Dr AL6 . . . . . . 89 C5
Lock View CM21 . . . . . . 97 F2
Lockyer Mews EN1 . . . 163 B1
Lodge Ave WD6 . . . . . 169 F4
Lodge Cl
Cheddington LU7 . . . . . 80 A7
Hertford SG13 . . . . . . 113 C8
Lodge Cres EN8 . . . . . 162 D5
Lodge Ct
Abbots Langley
WD25 . . . . 154 A7
Ickleford SG5 . . . . 21 E3
Lodge Dr
Hatfield AL9 . . . . 130 D8
Rickmansworth WD3 . . 165 C5
Lodge End
Croxley Green WD3 . . . 166 D5
Radlett WD7 . . . . 156 B5
Lodge Farm SG4 . . . . . . 67 E1

Lodge Farm Prim Sch
SG2 . . . . 51 C7
Lodge Field AL7 . . . . . . 89 E1
Lodge Gdns AL5 . . . . . . 86 A2
Lodge La EN9 . . . . 163 D4
Lodge The
Harefield UB9 . . . . 173 C3
Watford WD24 . . . . . . 167 C7
Lodge Way SG2 . . . . 51 A1
Loftus Cl LU4 . . . . 44 B3
Logan Cl AL2 . . . . 142 B4
Logans EN5 . . . . 171 D6
Loire Mews AL5 . . . . . . 107 C7
Lombardy Cl HP2 . . . . . 125 D2
Lombardy Dr HP4 . . . . 122 D3
Lombardy Way WD6 . . 169 E7
Lomond Cl HP2 . . . . . . 124 D7
Lomond Way SG1 . . . . . 37 C3
London Coll of
Professional Studies
LU2 . . . . 63 D7
LONDON COLNEY 142 E5
London Colney Jun Mix Inf
Sch AL2 . . . . 142 D6
London Luton Airport
LU2 . . . . 64 D7
London Rd
Aston Clinton HP22 . . . 99 A4
Baldock SG7 . . . . 23 F6
Barkway SG8 . . . . 17 D1
Barley SG8 . . . . 8 F1
Berkhamsted HP4 . . . . 122 E3
Bishop's Stortford CM23 . 77 A5
Buntingford SG9 . . . . . . 40 F6
Bushey WD23 . . . . 167 F3
Hemel Hempstead HP1,
HP3 . . . . 124 A1
Hertford Heath SG13 . . 114 B3
Hertford SG13 . . . . . . 113 C5
Hitchin SG4 . . . . 34 F5
Knebworth SG3 . . . . . . 69 A3
Langley SG4 . . . . 49 D5
Luton LU1 . . . . 84 F7
Luton, New Town LU1 . . 63 E4
Markyate AL3 . . . . 83 F5
Royston SG8 . . . . 7 D6
Sawbridgeworth CM21 . 97 E2
Shenley WD7 . . . . 157 A5
Spellbrook CM23 . . . . . . 97 F7
St Albans AL1 . . . . 142 C7
Stevenage SG1, SG2 . . . 50 D3
Stotfold SG5 . . . . 3 A2
Tring HP23 . . . . 100 C3
Ware SG12 . . . . 114 D1
Welwyn AL6 . . . . 89 C4
London Rd/ Moor La Rdbt
WD3 . . . . 173 E8
London Row SG15 . . . . . 11 A3
London School of
Theology HA6 . . . . . . 174 D4
Londrina Ct 16 HP4 . . . 122 D4
Londrina Terr 15 HP4 . . 122 D4
Long Acre CM17 . . . . . 118 B4
Longacres AL4 . . . . 128 D3
Long Arrotts HP1 . . . . . 124 B5
Long Barn Cl WD25 . . . 154 A7
Long Buftlers AL5 . . . . 107 F8
Long Chauldern HP1 . . 123 E3
Long Cl LU2 . . . . 46 C3
Longcliffe Path
WD19 . . . . 175 A7
Longcroft WD19 . . . . . 167 B2
Long Croft CM24 . . . . . 59 D8
Longcroft Ave AL5 . . . . 85 F1
Long Croft Dr EN8 . . . 163 A5
Longcroft Gdns AL8 . . 110 D5
Longcroft La
Bovingdon HP3 . . . . . 137 D5
Welwyn Garden City
AL8 . . . . 110 D5
Longcroft Rd
Luton LU1 . . . . 63 A7
Maple Cross WD3 . . . . 172 D5
Stevenage SG1 . . . . 50 E7
Longcrofts EN9 . . . . . . 163 E5
Long Cutt AL3 . . . . 106 A6
Longdean Pk HP3 . . . . 139 A7
Longdean Sch HP3 . . . 139 B8
Longcroft La
Welwyn Garden City
AL8 . . . . 110 D5
Long Elmes HA3 . . . . . 176 C2
Long Elms WD5 . . . . . . 153 D6
Long Elms Cl WD5 . . . . 153 D6
Long Fallow AL2 . . . . . 141 A4
Long Field 3 HP3 . . . . . 125 B1
Longfield Ave HA3 . . . . 176 E1
Longfield Cl WD24 . . . . 154 A1
Longfield Dr LU4 . . . . . . 44 D1
Longfield Gdns HP23 . . . 99 E3
Longfield La EN7 . . . . . 148 A4
Longfield Rd
Harpenden AL5 . . . . . . 107 C7
Tring HP23 . . . . 99 F3
Longfields SG1 . . . . 51 C1
Long Gr LU7 . . . . 80 C3
Long Hale LU7 . . . . 80 C4
Long Hedge LU7 . . . . . . 80 C4
Long Hyde SG2 . . . . 51 B4
Long John HP3 . . . . . . 124 F1
Long La
Aston SG2 . . . . 51 E5
Bendish SG4 . . . . 66 A7
Bovingdon HP3 . . . . . . 150 F8
Chorleywood WD3 . . . . 164 D2
Rickmansworth WD3 . . 172 F8

Longlands HP2 . . . . 125 A3
Longlands Cl EN8 . . . . 162 D7
Longlands Prim Sch
EN10 . . . . 148 F6
Longlands Rd AL7 . . . . 110 F5
Long Leaves SG1 . . . . . . 51 A2
Longlees WD3 . . . . 172 D5
Long Ley
Cheddington LU7 . . . . . 80 A7
Harlow CM20 . . . . 117 F1
Welwyn Garden City
AL7 . . . . 111 C6
Longman Ct HP3 . . . . . 138 E6
Longmans SG11 . . . . . . 55 F7
Longmans Cl WD18 . . . 166 C3
LONG MARSTON 79 B4
Long Marston CE Prim
Sch HP23 . . . . 79 B4
Long Marston Rd
Cheddington HP23, LU7 . 79 F2
Marsworth HP23 . . . . . . 79 F2
Long Mdw
Bishop's Stortford
CM23 . . . . 76 D6
Markyate AL3 . . . . 83 F5
Watton at St St SG14 . . . 70 D4
Longmead
Buntingford SG9 . . . . . . 40 D7
Hatfield AL10 . . . . 130 B8
Letchworth Garden City
SG6 . . . . 22 E2
Woolmer Green SG3 . . . 69 A2
Longmeadow Dr SG5 . . . 21 F5
Longmeadow Rd SG2 . . . 51 C1
Longmeadow Prim Sch
SG2 . . . . 51 B1
Long Moor EN8 . . . . . . 148 E2
Longmore Gdns AL7 . . 110 F5
Long Pightle Mobile Home
Pk WD3 . . . . 152 F2
Longridge WD7 . . . . . 156 B5
Long Ridge SG2 . . . . . . 51 D1
Long Room SG9 . . . . . . 173 A3
Long Row SG5 . . . . 19 D1
Long Spring AL3 . . . . . 127 F7
Longstanton Ct HP2 . . 105 B1
Long View HP4 . . . . . . 122 A6
Long Wlk EN8 . . . . 149 A1
Longwood Rd SG14 . . . 112 F8
Longwood Sch HP23 . . 167 F5
Loning The EN3 . . . . . 162 C1
Lonsdale EN2 . . . . 124 E6
Lonsdale Cl
Luton LU5 . . . . 45 B5
Pinner HA5 . . . . 175 F1
Lonsdale Ct SG1 . . . . . . 50 F7
Lonsdale Rd SG1 . . . . . . 50 F7
Lonsdale Sch SG1 . . . . . 50 F7
Loom La WD7 . . . . 156 A2
Loom Pl WD7 . . . . 156 A3
Loop Rd EN9 . . . . 163 B7
Loppys Hill CM24 . . . . . 59 E6
Lorane Ct WD17 . . . . . 167 A7
Lord Mead La AL6, SG4 . 88 C7
Lords Ave CM23 . . . . . . 76 B7
Lords Cl SG11 . . . . 156 F7
Lordship Ctr SG6 . . . . . . 23 A3
Lordship Rd EN7 . . . . . 148 B1
Lords Mdw AL3 . . . . . 106 A5
Lords Rd 15 LU2 . . . . . . 45 D1
Lord St
Hoddesdon EN11 . . . . . 134 D6
Watford WD17 . . . . . . 167 C6
Lords Wood AL7 . . . . . 111 C6
Loreto Coll AL1 . . . . . 127 E3
Lorimer Cl LU2 . . . . 45 E6
Loring Rd AL6 . . . . 89 D7
Lorne Rd HA3 . . . . 176 F1
Lorraine Pk HA3 . . . . . 176 E3
Lothair Ct 3 AL10 . . . . 130 A6
Lothair Rd LU2 . . . . 46 A4
LOUDWATER 165 D6
Loudwater Dr WD3 . . . 165 C5
Loudwater Hts WD3 . . 165 C5
Loudwater La WD3 . . . 165 C5
Loudwater Ridge
WD3 . . . . 165 C5
Louisa Cotts HP23 . . . . 100 A3
Louise Wlk HP3 . . . . . 137 A3
Louisville Cl SG12 . . . . 115 C4
Louvain Way WD25 . . . 153 E7
Lovatts AL1 . . . . 166 A5
Love La
Abbots Langley WD5 . . 139 F1
Ashwell SG7 . . . . 4 A4
Kings Langley WD4 . . . 138 E3
Pinner HA5 . . . . 175 E1
Lovell Cl HP1 . . . . 124 A3
Lovell Cl SG4 . . . . 35 A6
Lovell Rd EN1 . . . . 162 B3
Lovering Rd EN7 . . . . . 147 E5
Lovett Rd AL2 . . . . 142 A5
Lovett La AL2 . . . . 142 A5
Lowbell La AL2 . . . . . . 142 E4
Lower Adeyfield Rd
HP2 . . . . 124 D4
Lower Barn HP3 . . . . . 138 F8
Lower Bourne Cl 5
SG12 . . . . 93 C3
Lower Bourne Gdns
SG12 . . . . 93 C3

Lower Clabdens SG12 . . 93 F1
Lower Cotts SG9 . . . . . . 30 B2
Lower Dagnall St AL3 . . 127 C3
Lower Derby Rd 4
WD17 . . . . 167 C5
Lower Emms HP2 . . . . 125 C8
Lower End HP22 . . . . . . 79 F3
Lower End HP22 . . . . . . 60 B2
Lower Farm Cotts SG18 . 3 B7
Lowerfield AL7 . . . . . . 111 A5
Lower Gn AL6 . . . . 90 E2
Lower Gower Rd SG8 . . . 7 D8
LOWER GREEN
Ickleford 21 E5
Meesden 29 E6
Lower Harpenden Rd LU1,
LU2 . . . . 64 C3
Lower Hatfield Rd
SG13 . . . . 112 F1
Lower High St WD17 . . 167 D4
Lower Icknield Way
Marsworth HP23 . . . . . 80 A1
Wilstone HP22, HP23 . . 99 C7
Lower Innings SG5 . . . . . 34 D8
Lower Kings Rd HP4 . . 122 C5
Lower King St SG8 . . . . . 7 D6
Lower Luton Rd AL4,
AL5 . . . . 86 C3
Lower Mardley Hill
AL6 . . . . 89 F8
Lower Margaret Gdns
SG12 . . . . 93 F3
Lower Mdw EN8 . . . . . 148 D4
LOWER NAZEING 149 E8
Lower Paddock Rd
WD19 . . . . 167 F3
Lower Park Cres CM23 . . 76 F5
Lower Paxton Rd AL1 . . 127 E2
Lower Plantation
WD3 . . . . 165 C6
Lower Rd
Breachwood Green
SG4 . . . . 47 F1
Chorleywood WD3 . . . 164 D5
Great Amwell SG12 . . . 114 F6
Hemel Hempstead HP3 . 139 A5
Little Hallingbury CM22 . 98 C7
Lower Sales HP1 . . . . . 123 F4
Lower Sean SG2 . . . . . . 51 A3
LOWER SHEERING 98 A1
Lower Sheering CM21 . . 98 A3
Lower Shott EN7 . . . . . 147 F5
Lower St CM24 . . . . 59 F7
LOWER STONDON 10 A3
Lower Tail WD19 . . . . . 175 E7
Lower Titmore Gn SG4 . . 35 C1
LOWER TITMORE GREEN
. . . . 35 F1
Lower Tub WD23 . . . . . 168 D2
Lower Yott HP2 . . . . . . 124 F2
Lowes Cl SG1 . . . . 37 C2
Lowestoft Rd WD24 . . . 167 B8
Loweswater Cl WD25 . . 154 C1
Lowewood Mus*
EN11 . . . . 135 A5
Lowfield CM21 . . . . 97 E1
Lowfield Ct 14 EN11 . . . 135 A6
Lowfield La EN11 . . . . . 135 A6
Lowgate La
Dane End SG12 . . . . . . 72 A4
Thundridge SG12 . . . . . 72 C5
Low Hill Rd CM19 . . . . 135 F6
Lowlands AL9 . . . . 130 C8
Low Rd AL9 . . . . 131 F8
Lowson Gr WD19 . . . . 167 F2
Lowswood Cl HA6 . . . . 174 C2
Lowther Cl WD6 . . . . . 169 F4
Loxley Cl SG12 . . . . 93 E1
Loxley Rd HP4 . . . . . . 121 F6
Loxwood Cl HP3 . . . . . 137 F8
Loyd Ct AL4 . . . . 128 C1
Lucan Rd EN5 . . . . 171 E6
Lucas Ct EN9 . . . . 163 F6
Lucas Gdns LU3 . . . . . . 45 B8
Lucas La
Ashwell SG7 . . . . 4 E4
Hitchin SG5 . . . . 34 D7
Lucern Ct EN7 . . . . 147 E4
Lucerne Way LU3 . . . . . 45 C4
Lucida Ct 2 WD18 . . . . 166 E4
Lucks Hill HP1 . . . . 123 E3
Ludgate HP2 . . . . 99 F4
Ludlow Ave LU1 . . . . . . 63 E4
Ludlow Mead WD19 . . 175 B7
Ludlow Way AL7 . . . . . 110 F4
Ludwick Cl AL7 . . . . . . 110 F4
Ludwick Gn AL7 . . . . . 110 F5
Ludwick Way AL7 . . . . 110 F5
LUFFENHALL 38 C7
Luffenham Ho 1
WD19 . . . . 175 D7
Lukes La HP23 . . . . 79 D3
Lukes Lea HP23 . . . . 80 A1
Lullington Ct LU2 . . . . . 46 C3
Lullington Garth WD6 . 170 B4
Lulworth Ave EN7 . . . . 147 B2
Lumbards AL7 . . . . 90 A1
Lumen Rd SG8 . . . . 7 D7
Luna PI AL1 . . . . 128 A3
Lunardi Ct SG11 . . . . . . 55 C3
Lundin Wlk WD19 . . . . 175 D6
Lundy Ho WD18 . . . . . 166 F4
LUTON 63 F7
Luton Airport Parkway Sta
LU1 . . . . 64 B5

Luton Dr The LU1 . . . .**64** B3
Luton & Dunstable Hospl
LU4 . . . .**44** C2
Luton Ent Pk LU3 . . . .**44** B8
Luton La
Harpenden AL5 . . . .**85** B1
Redbourn AL3 . . . . **106** A8
Luton Maternity Hospl
LU4 . . . .**44** C2
Luton Rd
Caddington LU1 . . . .**63** A4
Cockernhoe LU2 . . . .**46** E3
Dunstable LU5 . . . .**44** A1
Great Offley SG5 . . . .**33** B2
Harpenden AL5 . . . .**85** D4
Kimpton SG4 . . . .**66** B2
Luton LU4 . . . .**44** A7
Markyate AL3 . . . .**83** F7
Streatley LU3 . . . .**31** A6
Luton Ret Pk LU1 . . . .**64** A6
Luton Sixth Form Coll
LU2 . . . .**45** E4
Luton Sta LU2 . . . .**63** E8
Luton Town FC LU1 . . . .**63** C8
Luton Univ, Putteridge
Bury LU2 . . . .**46** D6
Luton White Hill SG5 . . . . .**33** B2
Luxembourg Cl LU3 . . . .**44** D8
Luxford Pl CM21 . . . .**97** F1
Luynes Rise SG12 . . . .**69** E6
Lybury La AL3 . . . . **105** F7
Lycaste Cl AL1 . . . . **128** A2
Lych Gate WD25 . . . . **154** D6
Lychgate Cotts HP3 . . . . . . **137** B4
Lydekker Mews ❶ AL5 . . . . .**86** A2
Lydia Ct AL6 . . . . **144** C7
Lydia Mews AL6 . . . . **144** C7
Lye Hill SG4 . . . .**65** D7
Lye La AL2 . . . . **141** A2
Lye The HP4 . . . . **102** D6
Lygean Ave SG12 . . . .**93** E1
Lygetun Dr LU3 . . . .**44** F7
Lygrave SG2 . . . .**69** C8
Lyles La AL8 . . . . **110** E8
Lyle's Row SG4 . . . .**34** F6
Lymans Rd SG15 . . . .**11** A6
Lyme Ave HP4 . . . . **121** D7
Lymington Ct WD25 . . . . . . **154** A5
Lymington Rd SG1 . . . .**50** B8
Lynbury Ct WD18 . . . . **167** A6
Lynch Cl AL4 . . . . **128** D2
Lynch Hill LU6 . . . .**83** A8
Lynch The EN11 . . . . **135** B8
Lyndale SG1 . . . .**50** E4
Lyndhurst Ave HA5 . . . . . . **175** B4
Lyndhurst Cl AL5 . . . .**86** C2
Lyndhurst Dr AL5 . . . .**86** C2
Lyndhurst Gdns HA5 . . . . . **175** B2
Lyndhurst Rd LU1 . . . .**63** C7
Lyndhurst Wlk ❶₃
WD6 . . . . **169** F8
Lyne Ave HA5 . . . . **175** E4
Lyndon Mead AL4 . . . . **108** C2
Lyneham Rd LU2 . . . .**46** C1
Lyne Way HP1 . . . . **123** F5
Lynford Cl EN5 . . . . **170** F4
Lynmouth Rd AL7 . . . . **110** F6
Lynn Cl HA3 . . . . **176** D1
Lynsey Cl AL3 . . . . **106** A6
Lynton Ave
Arlesey SG15 . . . .**11** A5
St Albans AL1 . . . . **128** C2
Lynton Crest EN6 . . . . **159** A7
Lynton Ct CM23 . . . .**76** E4
Lynton Par EN8 . . . . **148** D1
Lynwood Ave LU2 . . . .**46** A3
Lynwood Dr HA6 . . . . **174** F2
Lynwood Hts WD3 . . . . **165** C4
Lynwood Rd HA6 . . . . **129** A3
Lyrical Way HP1 . . . . **124** B5
Lysander Cl HP3 . . . . **137** A4
Lysander Way
Abbots Langley WD5 . . . . . **154** A7
Welwyn Garden City
AL7 . . . . **111** D7
Lys Hill Gdns SG14 . . . . . . **113** B8
Lysley Pl AL9 . . . . **145** C4
Lytham Ave WD19 . . . . **175** D5
Lytton Almshouses
SG3 . . . .**68** B5
Lytton Ave
Enfield EN3 . . . . **162** E1
Letchworth Garden City
SG6 . . . .**22** F5
Lytton Fields SG3 . . . .**68** F5
Lytton Gdns AL8 . . . . **110** D6
Lytton Rd HA5 . . . . **175** E3
Lyttons Way EN11 . . . . **115** A1
Lytton Way SG1 . . . .**50** C6

M

Mabbutt Cl AL2 . . . . **140** E1
Mabey's Wlk CM21 . . . .**97** B1
McAdam Cl EN11 . . . . **135** A8
Macaulay Rd LU4 . . . .**44** A2
McClintock Pl EN3 . . . . **163** B2
McDonald Ct AL10 . . . . **130** A3
Macdonald Gdns
WD25 . . . . **153** F4
McDougall Rd ❶₃
HP4 . . . . **122** D4
Macers Ct EN10 . . . . **148** F7
Macer's La EN10 . . . . **148** F7

Macfadyen Webb Ho
SG6 . . . .**23** A7
McGredy EN7 . . . . **148** B2
Macintosh Cl EN7 . . . . **147** D5
MacIntyre Sch HP22 . . . .**60** C3
McKellar Cl WD23 . . . . **176** C8
McKenzie Rd EN10 . . . . **135** A3
Mackenzie Sq SG2 . . . .**51** B3
Mackerel Hall SG8 . . . .**7** B6
MACKERYE END **86** F4
Maddison Hts ❼
WD18 . . . . **166** F5
Maddocks Ho SG6 . . . .**23** D4
Maddox Rd
Harlow CM20 . . . . **117** E1
Hemel Hempstead HP2 . . . **125** B3
Made Feld SG1 . . . .**50** F5
Madford Ret Pk LU4 . . . .**44** F2
Madgeways Cl SG12 . . . . . . **114** F5
Madgeways La SG12 . . . . . . **114** F5
Madrasa Islamia Sch
AL3 . . . .**45** C2
Madresfield Ct WD7 . . . . . . **156** E6
Magdalene Ct SG7 . . . .**12** F1
Magellan Cl SG2 . . . .**51** D5
Magisters Lo WD3 . . . . **166** A3
Magna Cl AL5 . . . . **107** D6
Magnaville Rd
Bishop's Stortford
CM23 . . . .**76** E4
Bushey WD23 . . . . **168** F2
Magnolia Ave WD5 . . . . . . **154** A7
Magnolia Cl
Hertford SG13 . . . . **114** A6
Park Street AL2 . . . . **141** A5
Magpie Cl EN1 . . . . **162** A1
Magpie Cres SG2 . . . .**51** D4
Magpie Hall Rd WD23 . . . . **176** E8
Magpie La LU2 . . . .**45** E6
Magpie Wlk ❽ AL10 . . . . . **130** A3
Maidenhall Prim Sch
LU4 . . . .**45** A2
Maidenhead St ❸
SG14 . . . . **113** D6
Maidenhead Yd SG14 . . . . **113** D6
Maidensfield AL8 . . . .**89** D1
Maiden St SG4 . . . .**24** C1
Main Ave HA6 . . . . **174** C7
Main Par WD3 . . . . **164** C5
Main Rd SG14 . . . .**91** D3
Main Rd N HP4 . . . .**81** A6
Main Rd S HP4 . . . .**81** D4
Maison Alfont HA3 . . . . **176** F8
Maitland Ho ❶ HP1 . . . . . . **124** D2
Maitland Rd CM24 . . . .**59** E6
Major Haddock Cl SG8 . . . . . .**7** C7
Malden Fields SG7 . . . . **167** D4
Malden Ho ❶❺ WD19 . . . . **175** C7
Malden Lodge ❷
WD17 . . . . **167** A7
Malden Rd
Borehamwood WD6 . . . . . . **170** A6
Watford WD17 . . . . **167** B7
Maldon Ct LU4 . . . .**44** E2
Malham Cl LU4 . . . .**44** E2
Malin Ct HP3 . . . . **138** C8
Malins Cl EN5 . . . . **171** C4
Malkin Way ❶ WD18 . . . . . **166** F5
Mallard Ct
❸ Bishop's Stortford
CM23 . . . .**77** A6
❼ Rickmansworth
WD3 . . . . **165** D2
Mallard Gdns LU3 . . . .**45** A5
Mallard Mews AL5 . . . .**86** C3
Mallard Rd
Royston SG8 . . . .**7** C6
Stevenage SG2 . . . .**51** D2
Watford WD5 . . . . **154** A8
Mallards Ct WD19 . . . . **175** F7
Mallards The HP3 . . . . **138** F6
Mallard Way
Northwood HA6 . . . . **174** C3
Roydon CM19 . . . . **116** A1
Watford WD25 . . . . **154** E3
Mallion Ct EN9 . . . . **163** F6
Mallories CM20 . . . . **117** F2
Mallow The LU3 . . . .**44** F3
Mallow Wlk
Goff's Oak EN7 . . . . **147** D3
Royston SG8 . . . .**7** E5
Mall The AL2 . . . . **141** C4
Malm Cl WD3 . . . . **173** D8
Malmes Croft HP3 . . . . **125** C1
Malmsdale AL8 . . . .**89** D2
Maltby Dr EN1 . . . . **162** B1
Malthouse Ct ❺ AL1 . . . . . **127** D2
Malthouse Gn LU2 . . . .**46** F1
Malthouse La SG5 . . . .**12** A7
Malthouse Pl WD7 . . . . **156** A5
Malthouse The ❶₆
SG14 . . . . **113** D6
Malting Cotts SG9 . . . .**40** D5
Malting La
Aldbury HP23 . . . . **101** D5
Braughing SG11 . . . .**55** E7
Dagnall HP4 . . . .**81** C5
Much Hadham SG10 . . . .**74** F2
Malting Mead AL10 . . . . . . **130** C6
Maltings Cl
Baldock SG7 . . . .**13** B1
Royston SG8 . . . .**7** C7
Maltings Ct ❷ SG7 . . . .**23** F8
Maltings Dr AL4 . . . . **108** C8
Maltings Ind Est The
SG12 . . . . **114** D8
Maltings La SG8 . . . .**9** E2

Maltings Mews SG13 . . . . **113** C5
Maltings Orch SG8 . . . .**20** D3
Maltings The
Abbots Langley WD4 . . . . . **153** C5
Ashwell SG7 . . . .**4** E4
Hemel Hempstead HP2 . . . **124** D4
Letchworth Garden City
SG6 . . . .**12** C1
Pitstone LU7 . . . .**80** D2
Royston SG8 . . . .**7** C7
St Albans AL1 . . . . **127** D3
Walkern SG2 . . . .**52** B8
Maltsters Lo ❾ EN11 . . . . . **135** D8
Malus Cl HP7 . . . . **125** A4
Malvern Cl
Bushey WD23 . . . . **168** C3
Hatfield AL10 . . . . **129** F6
St Albans AL4 . . . . **128** C7
Malvern Rd
Enfield EN3 . . . . **162** E2
Luton LU1 . . . .**63** B7
Malvern Way
Croxley Green WD3 . . . . . . **166** B8
Hemel Hempstead HP2 . . . **124** F6
Malvern Way Inf Sch
WD3 . . . . **166** C4
Malzeard Ct ❷₀ LU3 . . . .**45** D1
Malzeard Rd LU3 . . . .**45** D1
Manan Cl HP3 . . . . **125** C1
Manchester Cl SG1 . . . .**36** F3
Manchester St LU1 . . . .**63** E7
Mancroft Rd LU1 . . . .**62** E2
Mandela Pl ❹ WD24 . . . . . **167** D7
Mandelyns HP4 . . . . **121** F7
Mandeville Cl
Hertford SG13 . . . . **113** C3
Hoddesdon EN10 . . . . **134** F3
Watford WD17 . . . . **153** F1
Mandeville Dr AL1 . . . . **141** D8
Mandeville Prim Sch
Sawbridgeworth CM21 . . . . .**97** D3
St Albans AL1 . . . . **141** D8
Mandeville Rd
Enfield EN3 . . . . **162** E3
Hertford SG13 . . . . **113** C3
Potters Bar EN6 . . . . **159** C7
Mandeville Rise AL8 . . . . . **110** E8
Mangrove Dr SG13 . . . . **113** E4
MANGROVE GREEN **46** E4
Mangrove La SG13 . . . . **113** E2
Mangrove Rd
Cockernhoe LU2 . . . .**46** E4
Hertford SG13 . . . . **113** E5
Luton LU2 . . . .**46** C2
Manhattan Ave WD18 . . . . **166** F5
Manhattan Ho ❾
WD18 . . . . **166** E5
Manland Ave AL5 . . . .**86** C3
Manland Prim Sch AL5 . . . .**86** B3
Manland Way AL5 . . . .**86** C3
Manly Highway SG5 . . . .**34** B7
Manly Highway Cotts
SG5 . . . .**34** A7
Manly Rd HP2 . . . . **124** E4
Manly Dixon Dr EN3 . . . . . **162** E2
Mannicotts AL3 . . . . **110** B6
Manning Cl WD19 . . . . **167** D3
Manning Pl LU2 . . . .**46** C2
Manor Ave HP3 . . . . **138** D8
Manor Cl
Barnet EN5 . . . . **171** E5
Berkhamsted HP4 . . . . **122** C4
Harpenden AL5 . . . . **107** A6
Hatfield AL10 . . . . **129** F8
Hertford SG14 . . . . **113** D8
Ickleford SG5 . . . .**21** E3
Letchworth Garden City
SG6 . . . .**22** F3
Manor Cotts
Chorleywood WD3 . . . . **164** B3
Northwood HA6 . . . . **174** F2
Nuthampstead SG8 . . . .**38** D7
Manor Cres SG4 . . . .**35** B6
Manorcroft Par ❻
EN8 . . . . **148** D1
Manor Ct
Caddington LU1 . . . .**62** F4
Cheshunt EN8 . . . . **162** D8
Enfield EN1 . . . . **162** B3
Harefield UB9 . . . . **173** C1
Potters Bar EN6 . . . . **159** C2
Radlett WD7 . . . . **155** F1
Waltham Abbey EN9 . . . . . **163** D6
Manor Dr AL2 . . . . **141** A4
Manor Farm Bsns Pk
SG5 . . . .**19** A6
Manor Farm Cl LU4 . . . .**44** C3
Manor Farm La LU7 . . . .**61** C8
Manor Farm Rd EN1 . . . . . . **162** B4
Manor Farm Stables
SG5 . . . .**68** C5
Manor Fields Prim Sch
CM23 . . . .**76** D5
Manor Ho The ❷
HA6 . . . . **174** F5
Manor House Dr
Northwood HA6 . . . . **174** B3
Stevenage SG2 . . . .**51** D7
Manor House Gdns
WD5 . . . . **153** D8
Manor Links CM23 . . . .**77** C7
Manor Lodge Sch
WD7 . . . . **143** C1
Manor Par AL10 . . . . **129** F8
Manor Place Ind Est
WD6 . . . . **170** C6
Manor Pound Rd LU7 . . . . . .**80** A7

Manor Rd
Barnet EN5 . . . . **171** E5
Bishop's Stortford CM23 . . . .**77** A7
Caddington LU1 . . . .**62** F2
Cheddington LU7 . . . .**79** F7
Harlow CM17 . . . . **118** C5
Hatfield AL10 . . . . **129** F8
Hoddesdon EN11 . . . . **135** A7
Lea Valley AL4 . . . .**86** F2
London Colney AL2 . . . . . . **142** C5
Luton LU1 . . . .**63** F6
Potters Bar EN6 . . . . **159** A8
St Albans AL1 . . . . **127** E4
Stansted Mountfitchet
CM24 . . . .**59** E5
Tring HP23 . . . . **100** A4
Waltham Abbey EN9 . . . . . **163** D6
Watford WD17 . . . . **167** B8
Manorside EN5 . . . . **171** E5
Manor St HP4 . . . . **122** D4
Manor View SG2 . . . .**51** B1
Manorville Rd HP3 . . . . **138** C7
Manor Way
Borehamwood WD6 . . . . . . **170** C6
Cheshunt EN8 . . . . **148** E1
Croxley Green WD3 . . . . . . **166** B5
Letchworth Garden City
SG6 . . . .**22** F3
Potters Bar EN6 . . . . **145** A1
Mansard Cl HP23 . . . . **100** A3
Mansdale La AL1 . . . . **127** F4
Manse Ct AL3 . . . .**83** F5
Mansells La SG4 . . . .**67** F3
Mansfield CM21 . . . .**97** A1
Mansfield Cl SG14 . . . . **113** C8
Mansfield Gdns SG14 . . . . **113** C8
Mansfield Mews ❶
SG7 . . . .**23** F8
Mansfield Rd
Baldock SG7 . . . .**23** E8
Luton LU4 . . . .**45** B1
Mansion Dr HP23 . . . . **100** B3
Mansion Ho ❻ HA6 . . . . . . **174** E3
Mansion The HP4 . . . . **122** E6
Manston Cl EN8 . . . . **148** C1
Manston Dr CM23 . . . .**59** B1
Manston Way LU4 . . . . **128** C2
Manton Dr LU2 . . . .**45** D3
Manton Rd
Hitchin SG4 . . . .**35** B6
Holdbrook EN3 . . . . **163** A1
Manx Cl LU4 . . . .**45** A2
Maple Ave
Bishop's Stortford
CM23 . . . .**76** D8
St Albans AL3 . . . . **127** C7
Maple Cl
Bishop's Stortford
CM23 . . . .**76** D8
Hatfield AL10 . . . . **130** A4
Watford WD23 . . . . **167** E7
Maple Cotts AL5 . . . . **107** B5
Maplecroft La EN9 . . . . **135** E2
MAPLE CROSS **172** D6
Maple Cross Jun Mix Inf
Sch WD3 . . . . **172** E5
Maple Ct
❺ Borehamwood
WD6 . . . . **170** A5
❶ Enfield EN3 . . . .**63** D6
❽ Pinner HA5 . . . . **175** C1
Stansted Abbotts
SG12 . . . . **115** D3
Watford WD25 . . . . **154** D3
Maplefield AL2 . . . . **141** C2
Maple Flats AL5 . . . .**86** A3
Maple Gn HP1 . . . . **123** E5
Maple Gr
Bishop's Stortford
CM23 . . . .**76** D8
Watford WD17 . . . . **167** A8
Welwyn Garden City AL7 . . .**89** F1
Maple Grove Prim Sch
HP2 . . . . **125** A8
Maple Leaf Cl
Abbots Langley WD5 . . . . . **154** A7
Stansted Abbotts
SG12 . . . . **115** D4
Mapleleaf Villas EN8 . . . . . **148** D4
Maple La SG4 . . . . **113** C5
Maple Lodge Cl WD3 . . . . . **172** E6
Maple Pk EN11 . . . . **135** C6
Maple Pk AL7 . . . . **111** A6
Maple Prim Sch AL1 . . . . . **127** E4
Maple Rd AL5 . . . .**85** F1
Maple Rd E LU4 . . . .**63** B8
Maple Rd W LU4 . . . .**63** B8
Maple River Ind Est
CM20 . . . . **118** B6
Maples Ct ❶ SG5 . . . .**34** E7
Maple Spring CM23 . . . .**76** D8
Maples The
Goff's Oak EN7 . . . . **147** E3
Hitchin SG4 . . . .**34** F5
St Albans AL3 . . . . **127** F3
Maplethorpe Ct SG12 . . . . .**93** C1
Mapleton Cres EN3 . . . . . . **162** C1
Maple Way
Kensworth Common
LU6 . . . .**82** E8
Royston SG8 . . . .**7** E8
Maplewood SG12 . . . .**93** C3
Maplewood Ct ❻
HA6 . . . . **174** F5

Maran Ave AL6 . . . .**89** C4
Marbury Pl AL3 . . . . **144** F4
Marchbank Ho HA6 . . . . . . **174** C3
Marchmont Gn HP2 . . . . . . **124** D5
Marconi Way AL4 . . . . **128** D3
Marcus Cl ❸ SG1 . . . .**51** C8
Marden Hill Ho AL6 . . . . . . **111** F8
Mardle Cl AL1 . . . .**62** E2
Mardley Ave AL6 . . . .**90** A8
MARDLEYBURY **69** C2
Mardleybury Ct SG3 . . . .**69** A1
Mardleybury Rd SG3 . . . .**69** B1
Mardley Dell AL6 . . . .**68** F1
Mardley Hill AL6 . . . .**69** A1
Mardley Hts AL6 . . . .**69** A1
Mardley Wood AL6 . . . .**68** F1
Mardon HA5 . . . . **175** F3
Mardyke Rd CM20 . . . . **118** A2
Marford Rd
Hatfield AL4, AL6 . . . . **109** C7
Wheathampstead AL4 . . . . **108** C3
Margaret Ave AL3 . . . . **127** D5
Margaret Cl
Abbots Langley WD5 . . . . . **153** F7
Potters Bar EN6 . . . . **159** C6
Waltham Abbey EN9 . . . . . **163** D6
Margaret Cotts WD7 . . . . . **156** C8
Margaret Wix Prim Sch
AL3 . . . . **127** C7
Margeholes WD19 . . . . **175** C7
Margery Wood AL7 . . . .**90** A1
Margherita Pl EN9 . . . . **163** F5
Margrave Gdns
CM23 . . . .**76** E5
Marguerite Way CM23 . . . . .**76** C6
Marian Gdns WD25 . . . . . . **154** B6
Maricas Ave HA3 . . . . **176** D3
Marigold Pl CM17 . . . . **118** B4
Marina Gdns EN8 . . . . **148** C1
Mariner Way ❷ HP2 . . . . . **125** A2
Marion Cl WD23 . . . . **167** F8
Marion Wlk ❽ HP2 . . . . . . **124** F8
Markab Rd HA6 . . . . **175** A5
Markeston Gn WD19 . . . . . **175** D6
Market Hill
Buntingford SG9 . . . .**40** E7
Royston SG8 . . . .**7** D5
❻ Royston SG8 . . . .**7** C6
Market Ho ❷ CM20 . . . . . . **117** D1
Market Oak La HP3 . . . . . . **139** A7
Market Pl
Hatfield AL10 . . . . **130** B6
❻ Hertford SG14 . . . . **113** D6
Hitchin SG5 . . . .**34** C7
St Albans AL3 . . . . **127** D4
Stevenage SG1 . . . .**50** D5
Watford WD17 . . . . **167** C5
Market Sq
Biggleswade SG18
❽ Bishop's Stortford
CM23 . . . .**76** F7
Luton LU1 . . . .**63** B6
Stevenage SG1 . . . .**50** D5
Waltham Abbey EN9 . . . . . **163** D6
Market St
❼ Bishop's Stortford
CM23 . . . .**76** F7
Harlow CM17 . . . . **118** C4
Hertford SG14 . . . . **113** D6
Watford WD18 . . . . **167** B5
Markfield Cl LU3 . . . .**45** C7
Mark Hall Moors
CM20 . . . . **118** B3
MARK HALL NORTH **118** A1
Mark Hall Sch CM17 . . . . . **118** C3
MARK HALL SOUTH **118** A1
Markham Cl WD6 . . . . **169** F6
Markham Rd
Hammond Street EN7 . . . . **147** C6
Luton LU3 . . . .**45** C8
Mark Rd HP2 . . . . **125** B5
MARKYATE **83** E6
Markyate Rd LU1 . . . .**63** B1
Markyate Village Sch
AL3 . . . .**83** D6
Marlands CM21 . . . .**97** E4
Marlborough Bldgs ❷
AL1 . . . . **127** E3
Marlborough Cl
Bishop's Stortford
CM23 . . . .**76** F5
Oaklands AL6 . . . .**89** F8
Weston SG4 . . . .**37** B8
Marlborough Ct
❽ Luton LU1 . . . .**63** D7
Northwood HA6 . . . . **174** F3
Marlborough Gate
AL1 . . . . **127** E3
Marlborough Ho HP4 . . . . . **122** B3
Marlborough Pk AL5 . . . . . **107** C7
Marlborough Rd
Luton LU3 . . . .**45** D1
St Albans AL1 . . . . **127** E3
Stevenage SG2 . . . .**51** C5
Watford WD18 . . . . **167** B5
Marlborough Rise
HP2 . . . . **124** E6
Marlborough Sch
AL1 . . . . **141** E8
Marlborough Wks LU3 . . . . .**44** F4
Marle Gdns EN9 . . . . **163** C7
Marley Ct EN10
Marley Rd AL7 . . . . **111** A4
Marlin Cl HP4 . . . . **121** F5
Marlin Copse HP4 . . . . **122** A3
Marlin Hill HP23 . . . . **120** A8
Marlins Cl WD3 . . . . **164** E7
Marlins End HP4 . . . . **121** F3
Marlins Mdw WD18 . . . . . . **166** D3

Marlin Sq WD5 ....153 F8
Marlins The HA6 ....174 F5
Marlins Turn HP1 ......124 B6
Marlow Ave LU1 ....63 A8
Marlowe Cl SG2 ....51 C8
Marlowes HP1 ....124 D3
Marlow Ho LU1 ....63 A8
Marmet Ave SG6 ....22 E6
Marnham Rise HP1 ......124 A5
Marquis Ctr SG7 ....13 A1
Marquis Cl
  Bishop's Stortford
  CM23 ....76 B7
  Harpenden AL5 ....86 D2
Marquis Ct
  Hoddesdon EN11 ......135 C8
  12 Luton LU2 ....45 D1
Marquis La AL5 ....86 D2
Marrilyne Ave EN3 .....162 F1
Marriott Rd
  Barnet EN5 ....171 D6
  Luton LU3 ....45 B6
Marriotts CM17 ....118 C5
Marriotts Sch SG2 .....51 A6
Marriotts Way HP3 .....124 D1
Marriott Terr WD3 .....164 F5
Marryat Rd EN1 ....162 B4
Marscefield SG5 ....11 E6
Marsden Cl AL8 ....110 B4
Marsden Gn AL8 ....110 B4
Marsden Rd AL8 ....110 C5
Marshall Ave AL3 ......127 F6
Marshall Rd LU2 ....46 C2
Marshalls Heath La AL4, AL5 ....87 A4
Marshall's La SG12, SG11 ....72 C2
Marshalls Way AL4 .....86 F2
Marshals Ct AL1 ....128 B5
Marshal's Dr AL1 ......128 A6
MARSHALSWICK 128 B6
Marshalswick La AL1 ...128 B6
Marshorn CM23 ....76 C8
Marsh Cl EN8 ....162 F6
Marshcroft Dr EN8 .....148 F1
Marshcroft La HP23 ....100 D6
Marshe Cl EN6 ....159 D7
MARSH FARM 44 E7
Marshgate SG1 ....50 D5
Marshgate Dr SG13 .....113 E2
Marshgate Trad Est SG13 ....113 E2
Marsh Hill HP1 ....149 E4
Marsh Ho LU3 ....44 F4
Marsh La
  Harlow CM17 ....118 E5
  Stansted Abbotts SG12 ....115 D4
  Ware SG12 ....114 E4
MARSHMOOR 130 D1
Marshmoor Cres AL9 ....130 D1
Marshmoor La AL9 ......144 D8
Marsh Rd LU3 ....44 F4
Marsom Gr LU3 ....45 B8
Marston Cl HP3 ....125 A2
Marston Ct HP23 ....79 B4
Marston Gdns LU2 ......45 D4
Marston Rd EN11 ....135 B7
MARSWORTH 80 A1
Marsworth Ave HA5 .....175 D2
Marsworth CE Inf Sch HP23 ....80 A2
Marsworth Cl WD18 .....166 E2
Marsworth Rd LU7 ......80 D4
Marsworth Resr Nature Reserve* HP23 ....100 A8
Marten Gate AL4 ....128 A7
Martham Ct AL5 ....86 C3
Marthorne Cres HA3 ....176 D1
Martian Ave HP2 ....124 F8
Martin Cl LU3 ....130 A3
Martindale Ct SG7 .....23 F6
Martindale Prim Sch HP1 ....123 F4
Martindale Rd HP1 .....123 F4
Martindales The LU2 ...63 F7
Martinfield Bsns Ctr AL7 ....110 F7
Martingale Rd SG8 .....7 E6
Martini Dr EN3 ....163 A4
Martins Cl WD7 ....155 E3
Martins Dr
  Cheshunt EN8 ....148 E3
  Hertford SG13 ....114 B6
Martins Way SG6 ....36 C1
Martins Wlk WD6 ....170 A5
Martlesham AL7 ....111 E6
Martyr Cl AL1 ....141 D7
Marwood Cl WD4 ....138 F2
Mary Barfield Ho SG8 ....7 D8
Mary Brash Ct LU2 ....46 C3
Mary Cross Cl HP23 ....100 D1
Mary Exton Jun Mix Inf Sch SG4 ....35 C7
Maryland AL10 ....129 F6
Mary McArthur Pl CM24 ....59 E8
Marymead Cl SG2 ......69 A8
Marymead Dr SG2 ......69 A8
Marymead Jun Inf Est SG2 ....69 B8
Mary Park Gdns CM23 ....76 F4
Maryport Rd LU4 ......45 A2
Mary Proud Ct AL6 ....89 E7

Mary Way WD19 ....175 C6
Masefield SG4 ....35 C7
Masefield Ave
  Borehamwood WD6 ....170 B4
  Stanmore HA7 ....176 F5
Masefield Cl AL5 .....86 B4
Masefield Rd AL5 .....86 B4
Masefield Way SG8 ....2 D1
Maslen Rd AL4 ....128 C1
Mason Cl WD6 ....170 D7
Masons Ct CM23 ....76 E7
Masons Rd
  Enfield EN1 ....162 C3
  Hemel Hempstead HP2 ....125 B4
Mason's Yd 2 HP4 .....122 D4
Mason Way EN9 ....163 F6
Massey Ho HP23 ....100 B5
Masterman Wharf 12 CM23 ....76 D3
Masters Ct LU1 ....63 B5
Matching La CM23 .....76 D8
Mathams Dr CM23 ......76 D5
Mathews Cl SG1 ....36 D1
Matisse Ho 5 WD18 ....166 E5
Matlock Cl EN5 ....171 D4
Matlock Cres
  Luton LU4 ....44 C1
  South Oxhey WD19 ....175 C7
Matthew Gate SG4 .....35 A5
Mattocke Rd SG5 ......21 C1
Maude Cres WD24 ......154 B1
Maud Jane's Cl LU7 ....80 E5
Maulden Ct LU2 ....46 C1
Maxted Cl HP2 ....125 C5
Maxted Cnr HP2 ....125 C5
Maxwell Cl WD3 ....173 A8
Maxwell Rd
  Borehamwood WD6 ....170 B6
  Northwood HA6 ......174 E3
  St Albans AL1 ....128 B2
  Stevenage SG1 ....50 B5
Maxwell Rise WD19 ....167 E2
Maxwell's Path SG5 ....34 D8
Maybell Cl LU3 ....163 A1
Maybury Ave EN8 ......148 B3
Maybury Cl EN1 ....162 B1
May Cl AL3 ....127 D5
Maycock Gr HA6 ....174 F4
May Cotts WD18 ....167 C4
Maycroft
  Letchworth Garden City SG6 ....12 A1
  Pinner HA5 ....175 B1
Maycroft Rd EN7 .....147 E5
Maydencroft La SG4 ....34 E3
Maydwell Lo WD6 ......169 F7
Mayer Rd EN9 ....163 B3
Mayes Cl CM23 ....77 D8
Mayfair Cl AL4 ....128 C8
Mayfair Ct WD18 ......166 E5
Mayfare WD3 ....166 D4
Mayfield
  Waltham Abbey EN9 ....163 E5
  Welwyn Garden City AL8 ....89 C2
Mayfield Cl
  Harlow CM17 ....118 F4
  Harpenden AL5 ....85 E3
Mayfield Cl WD23 .....167 F3
Mayfield Inf Sch EN8 ....148 E4
Mayfield Pk CM23 .....76 D3
Mayfield Rd LU2 ......46 B4
Mayflower Ave HP2 ....124 D3
Mayflower Cl
  Codicote SG4 ....67 F1
  Hertingfordbury SG14 ....112 C4
  Lower Nazeing EN9 ....149 E8
Mayflower Gdns CM23 ....76 B8
Mayflower Rd AL2 .....141 B4
May Gdns WD6 ....169 D3
Mayhill Rd EN5 ....171 E3
Maylands Ave HP2 .....125 B5
Maylands Ct HP2 ......125 B4
Maylands Rd WD19 .....175 C6
Maylins Cl SG1 ....50 B7
Maylin Cl LU2 ....46 B4
Maylins Dr CM21 ......97 D2
Maynard Ct
  2 Holdbrook EN3 ....163 A1
  Waltham Abbey EN9 ....163 F5
Maynard Dr AL1 ....141 D8
Maynard Pl EN6 ....146 E2
Maynard Rd HP2 ....124 D2
Mayne Ave
  Luton LU4 ....44 C4
  St Albans AL3 ....127 A2
Mayo Cl EN8 ....148 C3
Mayo Gdns HP1 ....124 B2
Maypole St CM17 .....118 C1
Mayshades Cl SG3 ....69 A2
Maytree La EN5 ......171 D3
May St
  Great Chishill SG8 ....9 E2
  Luton LU1 ....63 D8
Maythorne Cl WD18 ....166 E5
Mayne Cres WD24 .....153 F4
Maytree La HA7 ......176 F3
Maytrees
  Hitchin SG4 ....35 A6
  Radlett WD7 ....156 A2
Maze Green Hts CM23 ....76 D7
Maze Green Rd CM23 ....76 D7
Mazoe Rd CM23 ....76 F5
Mead Bsns Ctr SG13 ....113 E7
Mead Cl
  Harrow HA3 ....176 D2
  Stevenage SG1 ....50 F6

Mead Ct
  Stansted Mountfitchet CM24 ....59 D7
  Waltham Abbey EN9 ....163 B5
Meadgate Rd EN9 .....135 C3
Mead Ho AL10 ....130 B8
Mead La SG13 ....113 E7
Mead Lo 3 EN11 ......135 D8
Meadow Ave WD7 ......156 C8
Meadowbank
  Hitchin SG4 ....22 B1
  Kings Langley WD4 ....139 A1
  Watford WD19 ....167 C2
Meadowbank Ct HP3 ....137 B3
Meadowbanks EN5 .....171 A4
Meadowbrook HP23 ....100 B6
Meadow Cl
  Barnet EN5 ....171 F3
  Bricket Wood AL2 ....141 A2
  Datchworth SG3 .....69 D1
  Enfield EN3 ....162 E1
  Hertford SG13 ....113 F7
  London Colney AL2 ....142 D4
  Radlett WD7 ....142 C1
  St Albans AL4 ....128 C6
  Tring HP23 ....100 A4
  Welwyn Garden City AL7 ....111 C6
Meadowcroft
  Berkhamsted HP4 .....121 D7
  Bushey WD23 ....168 B3
  St Albans AL1 ....142 A8
  Stansted Mountfitchet CM24 ....59 E7
Meadow Croft
  Caddington LU1 ......62 F4
  Hatfield AL10 ....129 F5
Meadow Cross EN9 ....163 E5
Meadow Dell AL10 ....129 F5
Meadow Gn AL8 ....110 C6
Meadow La LU7 ....80 E3
Meadowlands CM23 ....59 A2
Meadow Rd
  Berkhamsted HP4 .....122 B6
  Borehamwood WD6 ....170 B7
  Bushey WD23 ....168 B4
  Hemel Hempstead HP3 ....139 A7
  Luton LU3 ....45 B4
  Watford WD25 ....154 B5
Meadowside WD25 .....154 B8
Meadows The
  Bishop's Stortford
  Breachwood Green SG4 ....47 C1
  Hemel Hempstead HP1 ....123 E4
  Sawbridgeworth CM21 ....98 A2
Meadows View Cotts SG12 ....94 C7
Meadowsweet Cl
  Hemel Hempstead HP2 ....124 E6
  Luton LU4 ....44 C8
  Stevenage SG1 ....37 B4
Meadow The
  Hertford Heath SG13 ....114 E2
  Welwyn Garden City AL7 ....111 C6
Meadow View
  Buntingford SG9 .....40 D6
  Redbourn AL3 ....106 A8
Meadow Way
  Bedmond WD5 ....139 F4
  Caddington LU1 ......62 F4
  Codicote SG4 ....67 E1
  Great Offley SG5 ....33 C3
  Hitchin SG4 ....34 D6
  Kings Langley WD4 ....139 A1
  Letchworth Garden City SG6 ....12 B6
  Potters Bar EN6 .....159 A5
  Rickmansworth WD3 ....165 C2
  Sawbridgeworth CM21 ....98 A1
  Stotfold SG5 ....11 F6
  Therfield SG8 ....16 A6
Meadow Way The HA3 ....176 E2
Meadow Wlk
  Harpenden AL5 ....107 C8
  Standon SG11 ....55 E2
Meadow Wood Sch WD23 ....168 C4
Mead Park Ind Est CM20 ....117 F4
Mead Pl WD3 ....165 B1
Mead Rd WD7 ....157 A6
Meads Ind Est AL4 ....87 D1
Meads AL4 ....87 D1
Meads Prim Sch The AL5 ....85 A6
Meads The
  Berkhamsted HP4 .....121 F6
  Bricket Wood AL2 ....140 F2
  Letchworth Garden City SG6 ....22 E6
  Luton LU3 ....45 A3
  Stansted Mountfitchet CM24 ....59 F6
  Tring HP23 ....100 B4
Mead The
  Cheshunt EN8 ....148 C2
  Hitchin SG5 ....21 F7
  Hoddesdon EN10 ......135 B2
  South Oxhey WD19 ....175 E7
Mead View SG9 ....43 E6
Meadview Rd SG12 ....114 D8
Meadway
  Barnet EN5 ....171 F5
  Berkhamsted HP4 .....122 E5
  Colney Heath AL4 ....143 D8
  Enfield EN3 ....162 D3
  Harpenden AL5 ....107 E8

Meadway continued
  Hoddesdon EN11 ......135 A4
  Knebworth SG3 ....68 F4
  Stevenage SG1 ....50 A6
  Stevenage SG1 ....50 B7
  Welwyn Garden City AL7 ....110 F4
Meadway WD23 ....167 E7
Meadway Ct SG1 ......50 B6
Meadway The EN6 .....146 F2
Meautys AL1 ....127 A1
Medalls Link SG2 ....51 A3
Medalls Path SG2 ....51 A3
Medcalf Rd EN3 ......162 F2
Medina Rd LU4 ....45 A1
Medlows AL5 ....85 E2
Medow Mead WD7 ......155 F6
Medway Cl WD25 ......154 C5
Medway Rd HP2 ....124 F8
Medwick Mews HP2 ....125 B8
Mees Cl LU3 ....31 A1
MEESDEN 27 D7
Meeting Alley WD17 ....167 C5
Meeting House La
  Baldock SG7 ....12 E1
  Stevenage SG1 ....40 E7
Megg La WD4 ....138 B1
Melbourne Cl
  St Albans AL3 ....127 F7
  Stotfold SG5 ....11 F6
Melbourne Ct
  Cheshunt EN8 ....162 F5
  Welwyn Garden City AL8 ....110 B5
Melbourne Rd WD23 ....168 B3
Melbourn Rd SG8 .....7 D7
Melbourn St SG8 .....7 D6
Melford Cl 3 LU2 ....46 D1
Melia Cl WD25 ....154 C4
Melings The HP2 .....125 B8
Melne Rd SG2 ....69 B8
Melrose Ave
  Borehamwood WD6 ....170 B4
  Potters Bar EN6 .....159 B7
Melrose Cl EN8 ......148 C6
Melrose Pl WD17 .....153 F1
Melson Sq 8 LU2 .....63 E7
Melson St LU1 ....63 E7
Melsted Rd HP1 ......124 B3
Melvern Cl SG2 ......69 B7
Melvyn Cl EN7 ....147 B3
Memorial Ct LU3 .....44 F4
Memorial Rd LU3 .....44 F4
Mendip Cl AL4 ....128 C8
Mendip Rd WD23 .....168 C3
Mendip Way
  Hemel Hempstead HP2 ....124 E6
  Luton LU3 ....44 C8
  Stevenage SG1 ....37 B4
Mendlesham AL7 ......111 E6
Mentley La SG11 .....54 E4
Mentley La E SG11 ....55 D4
Mentley La W SG11 ....55 C4
MENTMORE 61 C4
Mentmore* LU7 ....61 C4
Mentmore Cross Rds LU7 ....60 F6
Mentmore Rd
  Cheddington LU7 .....79 F8
  St Albans AL1 ....127 F5
Mentmore View HP23 ....99 F5
Mepham Cres HA3 .....176 C3
Mepham Gdns HA3 .....176 C3
Mercer Pl HA5 ....175 C1
Mercers HP2 ....124 E5
Mercers Ave CM23 ....76 C4
Mercers Row AL1 .....127 C1
Merchant Dr SG13 ....113 F7
Merchants Wlk SG1 ....13 B1
Merchant Taylors' Sch HA6 ....166 C1
Mercia Rd SG7 ....24 A8
Mercury Ct AL10 .....129 C6
Mercury Ho SG13 .....113 A6
Mercury Ho 8 WD18 ....166 E5
Mercury Wlk 1 HP2 ....124 F6
Mereden Ct AL1 ......141 C8
Meredew Ct SG6 .....23 B7
Meredith Cl HA5 .....175 D3
Meredith Rd SG1 .....51 A8
Merefield CM21 ......97 E1
MERIDEN 154 E3
Meriden Ho 4 WD25 ....154 C2
Meridian Bsns Pk EN9 ....163 B4
Meridian Ho EN10 ....135 C2
Meridian Sch SG8 ....7 E7
Meridian Way
  Stansted Abbotts SG12 ....115 B5
Merle Ave UB9 ....173 C1
Merlin Ctr The AL4 ....128 F3
Merling Croft HP4 ....121 E7
Merlin Way WD25 .....153 F5
Mermaid Cl SG4 ......35 B7
Merrick Cl SG1 ......37 B4
Merrifield Ct AL7 ....110 D3
Merrill Pl 2 CM23 ....76 E5
Merritt Wlk AL9 .....144 B8
Merrow Dr HP1 ....123 E4
Merrows Cl HA6 ......174 C4
Merryfield WD17 .....154 A1
Merryfields AL4 .....128 C4
MERRY HILL 168 B1

Merry Hill Inf Sch WD23 ....168 B2
Merry Hill Mount WD23 ....168 B1
Merry Hill Rd WD23 ....168 B1
Mersey Pl
  Hemel Hempstead HP2 ....124 F8
  1 Luton LU1 ....63 D7
Merton Ct 6 WD6 .....169 F8
Merton Rd
  Enfield EN2 ....161 D1
  Watford WD18 ....167 B5
Meryfield Cl WD6 ....169 F7
Meryfield Prim Sch WD6 ....169 F8
Metford Cres EN3 ....163 A1
Metro Ctr
  St Albans AL4 ....127 F7
Metro Ind Est AL10 ....166 D2
Metropolitan Mews 10 WD18 ....166 E5
Metropolitan Pl WD18 ....166 F5
Metropolitan Station App WD18 ....166 F5
Mews The
  Bishop's Stortford CM22 ....77 A3
  3 Harpenden AL5 ....86 B1
  Letchworth Garden City SG6 ....12 C1
  Sawbridgeworth CM21 ....97 E3
  St Albans AL1 ....127 E5
  Stansted Mountfitchet CM24 ....59 F7
Meyer Gn EN1 ....162 A1
Meyrick Ave LU1 .....63 C6
Meyrick Ct
  Luton LU1 ....63 D6
  St Albans AL1 ....128 B3
Mezen Cl HA4 ....174 D5
Michael Muir Ho SG5 ....21 D1
Michaels Rd CM23 ....59 A2
Michigan Cl EN10 ....148 E5
MICKLEFIELD GREEN 152 B1
Micklefield Green Cotts WD3 ....152 B2
Micklefield Rd HP2 ....125 C3
Micklefield Way WD6 ....156 E1
Micklem Dr HP1 ......123 F4
Micklem Prim Sch HP1 ....124 A4
Midcot Way HP4 ......121 F6
Midcroft Ho HP23 ....100 A3
Middle Down WD25 ....155 B3
Middle Drift SG8 ....7 C6
Middlefield
  Hatfield AL10 ....130 A6
  Welwyn Garden City AL7 ....110 E3
Middlefield Ave EN11 ....135 A8
Middlefield Cl
  Hoddesdon EN11 ......135 A8
  St Albans AL4 ....128 C6
Middlefield La SG6 ....10 C7
Middlefield Rd EN11 ....135 A8
Middlefields SG6 .....11 F1
Middlefields Ct SG6 ....11 F1
Middle Furlong WD23 ....168 B5
Middle Hill HP1 .....123 F3
Middleknights Hill HP1 ....124 A6
Middle La HP3 ....137 A1
Middlemarch SG5 ....11 C3
Middle Ope WD24 .....154 B2
Middle Rd
  Berkhamsted HP4 .....122 B4
  Waltham Abbey EN9 ....163 B7
Middle Row
  5 Bishop's Stortford CM23 ....76 D7
  1 Stevenage SG1 ....50 C7
Middlesborough Cl SG1 ....36 F2
Middle St EN9 ....149 F8
Middleton Rd
  Luton LU2 ....46 D4
  Rickmansworth WD3 ....165 A1
Middle Way WD24 .....154 B2
Middle Way The HA3 ....176 F1
Midhurst SG6 ....22 F8
Midhurst Gdns LU3 ....45 C4
Midland Cotts SG5 ....22 A1
Midland Rd
  Hemel Hempstead HP2 ....124 D3
  Luton LU2 ....63 E8
Midland Way SG16 ....10 B3
Midway AL3 ....141 B8
Mike Mably Ho AL10 ....129 F7
Milbourne Ct 1 WD17 ....167 A7
Milburn Cl LU3 ......31 B1
Milby Ct 4 WD6 .....169 F8
Mildmay Rd SG1 .....37 B1
Mildred Ave
  Borehamwood WD6 ....170 B5
  Watford WD18 ....167 A5
Mile Cl EN9 ....163 C6
Mile House Cl AL1 ....142 A8

Mile House La AL1 . . . . **142** A8
Milestone Cl SG2 . . . . **51** D4
Milestone Rd
Harlow CM17 . . . . **118** C2
Hitchin SG5 . . . . **21** D2
Knebworth SG3 . . . . **69** A5
Milford Cl AL4 . . . . **128** D7
Milford Hill AL5 . . . . **86** D4
Milksey La SG4 . . . . **36** C5
Millacres SG12 . . . . **93** E1
Milland Dr WD6 . . . . **170** D8
Millard Way SG4 . . . . **22** C1
Millbank HP3 . . . . **138** D7
Mill Bridge
Barnet EN5 . . . . **171** F3
Hertford SG14 . . . . **113** C6
Millbridge Mews 2
SG14 . . . . **113** C6
Millbrook Ct SG12 . . . . **93** D2
Millbrook Rd WD23 . . . . **167** F8
Millbrook Sch EN8 . . . . **148** D2
Mill Cl
Buntingford SG9 . . . . **40** E7
Hatfield AL8 . . . . **110** A5
Hemel Hempstead, Nash Mills
HP3 . . . . **139** A6
Hemel Hempstead, Piccotts
End HP1 . . . . **124** B7
Hitchin SG4 . . . . **35** C8
Stotfold SG5 . . . . **12** A6
Ware SG12 . . . . **93** D1
Wingrave HP22 . . . . **60** A3
Mill Cnr
Barnet EN5 . . . . **171** F8
Roydon CM19 . . . . **116** A1
Mill Cotts
Barkway SG8 . . . . **17** C5
Wingrave LU7 . . . . **60** D8
Millcrest Rd EN7 . . . . **147** B3
Millcroft CM23 . . . . **59** A1
Mill Ct CM20 . . . . **117** D3
MILL END
Rickmansworth **173** A8
Rushden **25** E4
Sandon **26** E6
Mill End SG11 . . . . **55** F2
Millennium Ct WD3 . . . . **165** E2
Millennium Wharf 1
WD3 . . . . **165** E1
Miller Ave EN3 . . . . **163** A1
Miller Cl
Pinner HA5 . . . . **175** C1
Redbourn AL3 . . . . **106** B5
Millers Cl CM23 . . . . **76** C5
Millers Cl SG14 . . . . **113** D5
Millers Ho The SG12 . . . . **115** D4
Millers La SG12 . . . . **115** C4
Millers Rise AL1 . . . . **127** E3
Millers View SG10 . . . . **74** E1
Miller Way SG1 . . . . **50** E6
Mill Farm Cl HA5 . . . . **175** C1
Millfield
Berkhamsted HP4 . . . . **122** D5
Thundridge SG12 . . . . **93** E8
Welwyn Garden City
AL7 . . . . **111** C7
Millfield CM17 . . . . **118** C4
Millfield Cl AL2 . . . . **142** D5
Mill Gdns HP23 . . . . **100** A4
MILL GREEN **130** E8
Millgreen Cotts AL9 . . . . **131** F8
Mill Green La AL4 . . . . **110** F1
Mill Green Rd AL4 . . . . **110** E5
Mill Green Watermill &
Mus★ AL9 . . . . **130** D8
Mill Ground Cotts SG4 . . . . . . **24** C1
Mill Hatch CM20 . . . . **118** A4
Mill Hill
Farnham CM23 . . . . **58** E5
Royston SG8 . . . . **7** E4
Stansted Mountfitchet
CM24 . . . . **59** E6
Millhoo Ct EN9 . . . . **163** F5
Millhouse La WD5 . . . . **140** A4
Millhurst Mews CM17 . . . . . . **118** E4
Milligan Cl LU4 . . . . **44** D4
Milliners Ct
Luton LU3 . . . . **45** C1
St Albans AL1 . . . . **127** E3
Milliners Way
Bishop's Stortford
CM23 . . . . **76** C4
Luton LU3 . . . . **45** C1
Mill La
Albury SG11 . . . . **57** C6
Arlesey SG15 . . . . **10** F4
Cheshunt EN8 . . . . **148** F5
Flamstead AL3 . . . . **84** A1
Harlow CM17 . . . . **118** E4
Hatfield Heath CM22 . . . . . . **98** F3
Hexton SG5 . . . . **19** C3
Hitchin SG4 . . . . **34** F3

Mill La continued
Hoddesdon EN10 . . . . **135** A2
Kings Langley WD4 . . . . **139** A2
Meesden SG9 . . . . **30** A5
Sawbridgeworth CM21 . . . . . **97** F3
Stotfold SG5 . . . . **12** A6
Therfield SG8 . . . . **15** F8
Watton at S SG12 . . . . **71** A6
Welwyn AL6 . . . . **89** C5
Weston SG4 . . . . **24** C1
Wingrave HP22 . . . . **60** C2
Mill Lane EL EN10 . . . . **134** F2
Mill Mead Prim Sch
SG14 . . . . **113** C6
Millmead Way SG14 . . . . **113** B6
Mill Race SG12 . . . . **115** D4
Mill Rd
Hertford SG14 . . . . **113** D6
Royston SG8 . . . . **7** D7
St Ippolyts SG4 . . . . **35** A3
Millside CM23 . . . . **77** A5
Mill Side CM24 . . . . **59** E6
Mill St
Ashwell SG7 . . . . **4** D1
Berkhamsted HP4 . . . . **122** C4
Bishop's Stortford CM23 . . . . **77** A5
Hemel Hempstead HP1 . . . . **138** D8
Luton LU1 . . . . **63** D8
Millstream Cl
Hertford SG14 . . . . **113** B6
Hitchin SG4 . . . . **22** A1
Mill Stream Lo WD3 . . . . **173** A8
Mill Studio Bsns Ctr 6
SG12 . . . . **79** C1
Mill The HP23 . . . . **119** D5
Millthorne Cl WD3 . . . . **165** F4
Mill View AL2 . . . . **141** D4
Mill View Rd HP23 . . . . **99** F4
Millwards AL10 . . . . **130** B2
Mill Way
Breachwood Green
SG4 . . . . **47** D2
Rickmansworth WD3 . . . . . . **164** F1
Watford WD23 . . . . **167** E8
Mill Wlk 11 AL4 . . . . **87** D1
Millwood Ct SG5 . . . . **11** F6
Millwright Wlk HP3 . . . . **138** F6
Milne CE SG6 . . . . **23** B3
Milne Field HA5 . . . . **176** A3
Milner Ct WD25 . . . . **154** B6
Milner Ct
Bushey WD23 . . . . **168** B3
Luton LU2 . . . . **63** E8
Mileway WD6 . . . . **173** B2
Milton Ave EN5 . . . . **171** F4
Milton Cl LU3 . . . . **2** C1
Milton Ct
Hammond Street EN7 . . . . . **147** F5
Milton EE Harpenden AL5 . . . . . **86** B1
Hemel Hempstead HP2 . . . . **105** B1
Waltham Abbey EN9 . . . . . . **163** C5
Milton Dene HP2 . . . . **125** B8
Milton Dr WD6 . . . . **170** B4
Milton Rd
Harpenden AL5 . . . . **86** B1
Luton LU1 . . . . **63** C6
Ware SG12 . . . . **93** D2
Milton St
Waltham Abbey EN9 . . . . . . **163** C5
Watford WD24 . . . . **167** B8
Milton View SG4 . . . . **35** C7
Milverton Gn LU3 . . . . **45** A7
Mimms Hall Rd EN6 . . . . **158** F7
Mimms La EN6, WD7 . . . . **157** C6
Mimram Cl SG14 . . . . **66** E2
Mimram Pl AL6 . . . . **89** C5
Mimram Rd
Hertford SG14 . . . . **113** B5
Welwyn AL6 . . . . **89** C5
Mimram Wlk AL6 . . . . **89** C5
Minall Cl HP23 . . . . **99** F4
Minchen Rd CM20 . . . . **118** A1
Minderhall Ct SG1 . . . . **50** C7
Minehead Way SG1 . . . . **50** A7
Mineral Cl EN5 . . . . **171** C4
Minerva Cl SG1 . . . . **51** C8
Minerva Dr WD24 . . . . **153** E3
Minims The AL10 . . . . **130** A7
Minister Cl AL2 . . . . **141** E3
Minoan Dr HP3 . . . . **138** E7
Minorca Way LU4 . . . . **44** A3
Minsden Rd SG2 . . . . **51** D3
Minster Cl AL10 . . . . **130** A3
Minster Ho AL10 . . . . **130** A3
Minster Rd SG6 . . . . **7** C8
Minstrel Cl HP1 . . . . **124** B4
Minstrel Ct HA3 . . . . **176** E1
Minsden Dr HP3 . . . . **125** C1
Missenden Ho WD18 . . . . **166** E2
Miss Joans Ride HP4,
LU6 . . . . **81** E7
Mistletoe Cl LU2 . . . . **64** C8
Mistletoe Hill LU2 . . . . **64** C8
Mistley Rd CM20 . . . . **118** A2
Mitchell Cl
Abbots Langley WD5 . . . . . . **154** A7
Bovingdon HP3 . . . . **136** F4
St Albans AL1 . . . . **141** D7
Welwyn Garden City
AL7 . . . . **111** C6
Mitre Bldgs 6 CM20 . . . . **117** C1
Mitre Cl SG14 . . . . **113** D6
Mitre Gdns CM23 . . . . **77** A4
Mixes Hill Cl LU2 . . . . **46** A4
Mixes Hill Rd LU2 . . . . **45** F4
Mixies The SG5 . . . . **11** E6

Moakes The LU3 . . . . **44** E7
Moat Cl WD23 . . . . **168** B4
Moatfield Rd WD23 . . . . **168** B4
Moat La
Luton LU3 . . . . **45** B4
Wingrave HP22 . . . . **60** B2
Moatside SG9 . . . . **29** B7
Moat The SG11 . . . . **55** D3
Moatview Ct WD3 . . . . **168** B4
Moatwood Gn AL7 . . . . **110** E5
Mobbsbury Way SG2 . . . . **51** C7
Mobley Gn LU2 . . . . **46** B3
Modena Mews 13
WD18 . . . . **166** E5
Moffats Cl AL9 . . . . **145** A5
Moffats La AL9 . . . . **144** F5
Moira Cl LU3 . . . . **44** D7
Molescroft AL5 . . . . **85** D4
Moles La SG9 . . . . **28** A3
Molesworth EN11 . . . . **115** A2
Molewood Rd SG14 . . . . **113** B7
Mollison Ave EN3 . . . . **163** A3
Molteno Rd WD17 . . . . **167** A8
Molyneaux Ave HP3 . . . . **136** F4
Momples Rd CM20 . . . . **118** B1
Monarch Hall LU2 . . . . **64** C8
Monarch's Way EN8 . . . . **162** E6
Monarch Wlk WD7 . . . . **156** F6
Monastery Cl AL3 . . . . **127** C3
Monet Ho 2 WD18 . . . . **166** E5
MONEYHILL **165** B1
Moneyhill Ct WD3 . . . . **165** B1
Money Hill Par WD3 . . . . **165** C1
Money Hill Rd WD3 . . . . **165** C1
Money Hole La AL6 . . . . **111** E7
Monica Cl WD24 . . . . **167** D7
MONKEN HADLEY **171** E7
Monkhams Hall EN9 . . . . **149** C2
Monklands SG6 . . . . **22** D6
Monks Cl
Hoddesdon EN10 . . . . **135** A3
Letchworth Garden City
SG6 . . . . **22** C6
Redbourn AL3 . . . . **106** B5
St Albans AL1 . . . . **127** E1
Monks Gate AL1 . . . . **127** E1
Monks Horton Way
AL1 . . . . **128** A4
Monksmead WD6 . . . . **170** C5
Monksmead Sch
WD6 . . . . **170** C6
Monks Rise AL8 . . . . **89** D2
Monks Row 6 SG12 . . . . **93** D2
Monks View SG2 . . . . **50** F2
Monks Walk Sch AL8 . . . . **89** C3
Monkswick Rd CM20 . . . . **117** F1
Monks Wlk SG9 . . . . **40** E7
Monkswood Ave EN9 . . . . **163** D6
Monkswood Dr CM23 . . . . **76** D6
Monkswood Gdns
WD6 . . . . **170** D5
Monkswood Ret Pk
SG1 . . . . **50** E2
Monkswood Way SG1 . . . . **50** E3
Monmouth Rd WD17 . . . . **167** B6
Monro Gdns HA3 . . . . **176** E3
Monro Ind Est EN8 . . . . **162** E5
Mons Ave SG7 . . . . **23** F6
Mons Cl AL5 . . . . **107** D6
Monson Rd EN10 . . . . **134** F3
Montacute Rd WD23 . . . . **168** E2
Montague Ave LU4 . . . . **44** C6
Montague 6 EN5 . . . . **171** F5
Montague Hall Pl
WD23 . . . . **168** A3
Montague Rd HP4 . . . . **122** B4
Montayne Rd EN8 . . . . **162** D7
Monterey Lo HA6 . . . . **174** E4
Montesole Ct EE HA5 . . . . . . **175** C1
Montessori At Little
Cheverells AL3 . . . . **83** D4
Montfitchet Wlk SG2 . . . . **51** D7
Montgomerie Cl HP4 . . . . **122** A6
Montgomery Ave
HP2 . . . . **125** A4
Montgomery Dr EN8 . . . . **148** E3
Monton Cl LU3 . . . . **44** F6
Montrose Ave LU3 . . . . **45** C3
Montrose Rd HA3 . . . . **176** F1
Monument Pl AL3 . . . . **127** D4
Moon La EN5 . . . . **171** F5
Moorend AL7 . . . . **111** A3
Moor End Rd HP1 . . . . **124** C2
Moorfield Rd HA6 . . . . **174** F6
Moorfields SG9 . . . . **41** B8
MOOR GREEN **39** D2
Moor Hall La CM23 . . . . **76** B3
Moor Hall Rd CM17 . . . . **118** F4
Moorhen Way SG19 . . . . **116** A1
Moorhurst Ave EN7 . . . . **147** B2
Moorings The
Bishop's Stortford
CM23 . . . . **77** A5
Radlett WD7 . . . . **156** A6
St Albans AL1 . . . . **127** C4
Watford WD23 . . . . **167** E5
Moor La
Moor Park WD3 . . . . **174** A8
Sarratt WD3 . . . . **151** E3
Moorland Gdns LU2 . . . . **63** D8
Moorland Rd
Harpenden AL5 . . . . **86** B4
Hemel Hempstead HP1 . . . . **124** A1
Moorlands
Park Street AL2 . . . . **141** E3
Welwyn Garden City
AL7 . . . . **111** A3

Moorlands Reach
CM21 . . . . **98** A1
Moorlands Cl SG14 . . . . **44** C3
Moor Lane Crossing
WD18 . . . . **166** C2
Moormead Cl SG5 . . . . **34** D6
Moormead Rd WD5 . . . . **34** D6
Moor Mill La AL2 . . . . **141** E2
MOOR PARK **174** D6
Moor Park Rd HA6 . . . . **174** D4
Moor Park Sta HA6 . . . . **174** D4
Moor Pk Ind Ctr
WD18 . . . . **166** C2
Moor's Farm Cotts
HP5 . . . . **136** B4
Moorside
Hemel Hempstead
HP3 . . . . **138** B8
Welwyn Garden City
AL7 . . . . **111** A3
Moors Ley SG2 . . . . **38** B1
Moor St LU1 . . . . **63** C8
Moors The AL7 . . . . **111** A7
Moors Wlk AL7 . . . . **111** C6
Moortown Rd WD19 . . . . **175** C6
Moor View WD18 . . . . **167** A3
Moorview Ho HP2 . . . . **124** E5
Moormead Cl SG14 . . . . **70** D3
Moran Cl AL2 . . . . **154** F8
Moray Ho HA6 . . . . **174** D3
Morecambe Cl
Luton LU4 . . . . **44** B3
Stevenage SG1 . . . . **50** B7
Morefields HP23 . . . . **100** A6
Moremead EN9 . . . . **163** D6
Moreton Ave AL5 . . . . **85** F2
Moreton Cl EN7 . . . . **148** B4
Moreton End Cl AL5 . . . . **85** F2
Moreton End La AL5 . . . . **85** F2
Moreton Pk Ind Est
LU2 . . . . **46** A2
Moreton Pl AL5 . . . . **85** F3
Moreton Rd N LU2 . . . . **46** A2
Moreton Rd S LU2 . . . . **46** A2
Morgan Cl
Luton LU4 . . . . **44** B3
Northwood HA6 . . . . **174** F4
Stevenage SG1 . . . . **36** D1
Morgan Gdns WD25 . . . . **155** B2
Morgans Cl SG13 . . . . **113** D6
Morgans Cl AL3 . . . . **113** C4
Morgan's Rd SG13 . . . . **113** D4
Morgan's Wlk SG13 . . . . **113** D3
Morice Rd EN11 . . . . **134** F8
Morland Way EN8 . . . . **148** E3
Morley Gr CM20 . . . . **117** C2
Morley Hill EN2 . . . . **161** D1
Morningside WD3 . . . . **165** C1
Mornington AL6 . . . . **90** A4
Mornington Rd WD7 . . . . **156** B5
Morpeth Ave WD6 . . . . **156** F1
Morpeth Cl 8 HP2 . . . . **124** E2
Morrell Cl LU3 . . . . **45** A7
Morrell Cl AL7 . . . . **110** F7
Morrello Gdns SG4 . . . . **35** A5
Morris Cl
Lower Stondon SG16 . . . . . . **10** C5
Luton LU3 . . . . **44** E8
Morris Ct
Holdbrook EN3 . . . . **163** A2
Waltham Abbey EN9 . . . . . . **163** F5
Morrison Ct 7 EN5 . . . . **171** E5
Morriston Cl WD19 . . . . **175** C5
Morris Way AL2 . . . . **142** D5
Morse Cl UB9 . . . . **173** C1
Mortain Dr HP4 . . . . **121** F6
Mortimer Cl
Bushey WD23 . . . . **168** B3
Luton LU1 . . . . **63** A7
Mortimer Gate EN8 . . . . **148** F4
Mortimer Hill HP23 . . . . **100** B4
Mortimer Rd SG8 . . . . **7** E7
Mortimer Rise HP23 . . . . **100** B4
Morton Cl LU7 . . . . **80** C4
Morton St SG8 . . . . **7** D7
Morven Cl EN6 . . . . **159** C8
Mosquito Way AL10 . . . . **129** E7
Mossbank Ave LU2 . . . . **64** C8
Moss Bury Prim Sch
SG1 . . . . **51** A7
Moss Cl
Pinner HA5 . . . . **175** F1
Rickmansworth WD3 . . . . . . **173** D8
Mossdale Ct 3 LU4 . . . . **44** C5
Mossendew Cl UB9 . . . . **173** D2
Moss Gn AL7 . . . . **110** E4
Moss La HA5 . . . . **175** E1
Mossman Dr LU1 . . . . **62** E4
Moss Rd WD25 . . . . **154** B5
Moss Side AL2 . . . . **140** F1
Moss Way SG5 . . . . **21** C1
Mostyn Rd
Bushey WD23 . . . . **168** C4
Luton LU3 . . . . **44** E4
Motts Cl SG14 . . . . **70** D4
MOTT'S GREEN **98** D6
Mott St EN9 . . . . **163** D1
Moules Yd SG7 . . . . **4** D3
Moulton Cl 3 LU2 . . . . **63** F8
Moulton Rise LU2 . . . . **63** F8
Mountbatten Cl AL1 . . . . **142** B8
Mount Cl HP1 . . . . **123** F3
Mount Dr
Park Street AL2 . . . . **141** D6
Stansted Mountfitchet
CM24 . . . . **59** E5
Mounteagle SG8 . . . . **7** D5

Mountfield Rd
Hemel Hempstead
HP2 . . . . **124** E3
Luton LU2 . . . . **45** E2
Mountfitchet Castle &
Norman Village★
CM24 . . . . **59** F6
Mountfitchet Maths &
Computing Coll The
CM24 . . . . **59** F4
Mountfitchet Rd CM24 . . . . **59** E5
Mount Garrison SG4 . . . . **34** F7
Mountgrace Rd LU2 . . . . **46** C6
Mount Grace Rd EN6 . . . . **159** B8
Mount Grace Sch
EN6 . . . . **159** B8
Mountjoy SG4 . . . . **22** C1
Mount Keen SG1 . . . . **37** C3
MOUNT PLEASANT **173** A2
Mount Pleasant
Harefield UB9 . . . . **173** A2
Hertford Heath SG13 . . . . . **114** C4
Hitchin SG5 . . . . **34** D6
St Albans AL3 . . . . **127** C3
Mount Pleasant Cl
AL9 . . . . **130** D8
Mount Pleasant Flats
SG1 . . . . **50** E8
Mount Pleasant La
Bricket Wood AL2 . . . . **140** E1
Hatfield AL9 . . . . **130** C8
Mount Pleasant Lane Jun
Mix & Inf Sch AL2 . . . . . . **140** E1
Mount Pleasant Rd
LU3 . . . . **44** E5
Mount Rd
Hertford SG14 . . . . **113** A5
Wheathampstead AL4 . . . . . . **87** D1
Mountside HA7 . . . . **176** F2
Mount Sorrel SG13 . . . . **113** F6
Mount The
Barley SG8 . . . . **8** F1
Hammond Street EN7 . . . . . **147** D5
Mount 5 Luton LU3 . . . . **63** D8
Potters Bar EN6 . . . . **159** C1
Rickmansworth WD3 . . . . . . **165** C3
Mount Vernon Hospl
HA6 . . . . **174** B4
Mountview HA6 . . . . **174** F4
Mount View
Enfield EN2 . . . . **160** F1
London Colney AL2 . . . . **142** F4
Rickmansworth WD3 . . . . . . **165** B1
Mountview Cotts EN5 . . . . **170** F3
Mountview Rd EN7 . . . . **147** E5
Mountway EN6 . . . . **145** A1
Mount Way AL7 . . . . **110** F3
Mountway Cl AL7 . . . . **110** F3
Mowat Ind Est WD24 . . . . **154** C1
Mowbray Cres SG5 . . . . **11** F7
Mowbray Gdns SG4 . . . . **35** A5
Mowbray Rd CM20 . . . . **118** A3
Mowbrays The SG5 . . . . **11** F7
Moxes Wood LU3 . . . . **44** E4
Moxom Ave EN8 . . . . **148** E1
Moxon St EN5 . . . . **171** F6
Mozart Ct SG1 . . . . **50** C5
MUCH HADHAM **74** F3
Muddy La SG6 . . . . **22** F3
Muirfield LU2 . . . . **45** E6
Muirfield Cl WD19 . . . . **175** C6
Muirfield Gn WD19 . . . . **175** C6
Muirfield Rd WD19 . . . . **175** C6
Muirhead Way SG3 . . . . **68** F5
Mulberry Cl
Cheshunt EN10 . . . . **148** F7
Chiswell Green AL2 . . . . **141** B3
Luton LU1 . . . . **63** B7
Stotfold SG5 . . . . **11** F5
Tring HP23 . . . . **100** A5
Watford WD17 . . . . **153** C3
Mulberry Ct
Bishop's Stortford
CM23 . . . . **77** A5
Mulberry 5 Hemel Hempstead
HP1 . . . . **124** D4
Royston SG8 . . . . **7** D5
Mulberry Gdns WD7 . . . . **156** E6
Mulberry Gn CM17 . . . . **118** E4
Mulberry Lo WD19 . . . . **167** D3
Mulberry Mead AL10 . . . . **109** F1
Mulberry Pl AL3 . . . . **106** B4
Mulberry Terr CM17 . . . . **118** B4
Mulberry Way SG5 . . . . **21** D2
Mull Ho WD18 . . . . **166** F4
Mullion Cl
Harrow HA3 . . . . **176** B2
Luton LU2 . . . . **46** B5
Mullion Wlk WD19 . . . . **175** D6
Mullway SG6 . . . . **22** C6
Mulready Wlk HP3 . . . . **138** F7
Mundells
Hammond Street EN7 . . . . . **148** A4
Welwyn Garden City
AL7 . . . . **111** A8
Mundells Cl AL7 . . . . **110** F8
Munden Gr WD24 . . . . **154** D1
Munden Rd SG12 . . . . **71** E7
Munden View WD25 . . . . **154** D3
Mundesley Cl
South Oxhey WD19 . . . . **175** C6
Stevenage SG1 . . . . **36** B1
Mungo-Park Cl
WD23 . . . . **176** C8
Munro Rd WD23 . . . . **168** C4
Muntings The SG2 . . . . **51** A3
Munts Mdw SG4 . . . . **24** C1
Murchison Rd EN11 . . . . **115** B1

Muriel Ave WD18 . . . . 167 C4
Murray Cres HA5 . . . . . 175 D2
Murray Rd
 Berkhamsted HP4 . . . . . . 122 C6
 Northwood HA6 . . . . 174 E3
Murrell La SG5 . . . . .12 A5
Murton Ct AL1 . . . . .127 E4
Museum Ct HP23 . . . . . . 100 A3
Museum of St Albans★
 AL1 . . . . 127 E3
Musgrave Ct HP4 . . . . . . 147 F4
Muskalls Cl EN7 . . . . 148 A4
Muskham Rd CM20 . . . . .118 B3
Musk Hill HP1 . . . . .123 E2
Musleigh Manor SG12 . . .93 F1
Musley Cl SG4 . . . . .93 E2
Musley La SG12 . . . . .93 E2
Mus of Harlow★
 CM20 . . . . .118 B3
Mussons Path LU2 . . . . . . 45 E1
Muswell Cl LU2 . . . . 46 C3
Mutchetts Cl WD25 . . . . .154 E6
Mutford Croft ☑ LU2 . . . 46 D1
Mutton La EN6 . . . . .158 E8
Myddelton Ave EN1 . . . .161 E1
Myddelton House Gdns★
 EN2 . . . . .162 A3
Myddelton Path EN7 . . . .162 B8
Myddleton Rd LU2 . . . . . .114 D8
Myers Cl WD7 . . . . .156 E7
Myles Ct EN7 . . . . .147 C2
Mylne Cl EN8 . . . . 148 C4
Mylne Ct EN11 . . . . 135 A8
Mymms Dr AL9 . . . . .145 B4
Mymms Ho AL9 . . . . 46 C8
Mymwood Cl AL9 . . . . . .145 C4
Myrtle Cotts
 Sarratt WD3 . . . . 152 A3
 Tring HP23 . . . . .100 C8
Myrtle Gdns SG16 . . . . . . .10 A6
Myrtle Gn HP1 . . . . .123 E4
Myrtle Gr EN2 . . . . 161 D1
Myrtleside Cl HA6 . . . . . .174 D3
Myson Way CM23 . . . . . . .77 B7

N

Nags Head Cl SG13 . . . . .114 C2
Nails La ☑ CM23 . . . . . . .76 F7
Nairn Cl AL5 . . . . .107 D6
Nairn Gn WD19 . . . . .175 A7
Nan Aires HP22 . . . . .60 A3
Nancy Downs WD19 . . . .167 C3
Napier Cl AL2 . . . . .142 D6
Napier Ct
 Cheshunt EN8 . . . . .148 B3
 Luton LU1 . . . . .63 D7
Napier Dr WD23 . . . . . . .167 E5
Napier Hall LU2 . . . . .64 C8
Napier Rd LU1 . . . . 63 D7
Nappsbury Rd LU4 . . . . . .44 D5
Napsbury Ave AL2 . . . . . .142 C5
Napsbury La AL1 . . . . . . .142 A7
NAPSBURY PARK 142 B5
Nap The WD4 . . . . .139 A2
Nascot Pl WD17 . . . . .167 B7
Nascot Rd WD17 . . . . . . .167 B7
Nascot St WD17 . . . . .167 B7
Nascot Wood Inf Sch
 WD17 . . . . .154 A1
Nascot Wood Jun Sch
 WD17 . . . . .154 A1
Nascot Wood Rd
 WD17 . . . . .153 F1
Naseby Rd LU1 . . . . .63 D7
Nash Cl
 Borehamwood WD6 . . . . 169 F5
 Datchworth SG3 . . . . 69 E2
 Stevenage SG2 . . . . .51 B6
 Welham Green AL9 . . . . .144 D8
Nashe's Farm La AL4 . . . .128 E8
Nash Gn HP3 . . . . .138 F6
NASH MILLS 139 A6
Nash Mills La HP3 . . . . . .138 F5
Nash Rd SG8 . . . . 7 D5
NASTY 54 D6
Nathaniel Wlk HP23 . . . .100 A3
Nathans Cl AL6 . . . . .89 E8
Navigation Ho ☒ CM23 . .76 F7
Nayland Cl LU2 . . . . .46 E1
Nazeingbury Cl EN9 . . . .135 D1
Nazeingbury Par EN9 . . .135 D1
Nazeing Glass Works
 EN10 . . . . 135 C1
NAZEING MEAD 135 D3
Nazeing New Rd
 EN10 . . . . .135 B2
Nazeing Prim Sch
 EN9 . . . . .149 E8
Nazeing Rd EN9 . . . . 135 D1
Neagh Cl SG1 . . . . .37 C3
Neagle Cl WD6 . . . . .170 C8
Neal Cl HA6 . . . . 175 A2
Neal Ct
 Hertford SG14 . . . . .113 C6
 Waltham Abbey EN9 . . . 163 F6
Neal St WD18 . . . . .167 C4
Nectar Ct ☑ EN11 . . . . . .135 D8
Necton Rd AL4 . . . . .108 E8
Needham Rd LU4 . . . . 44 B6
Neighbourhood Ctr The
 SG1 . . . . .37 B3
Neild Way WD3 . . . . .164 F2
Nell Gwynn Ct WD7 . . . . 156 F4
Nelson Ave AL1 . . . . .142 B8

Nelson Rd
 Bishop's Stortford
  CM23 . . . . .77 A5
 Dagnall HP4 . . . . .81 C5
Nelson St SG14 . . . . .113 B7
Nene Rd SG16 . . . . .10 B4
Neptune Ct WD6 . . . . . . .170 A6
Neptune Dr LU3 . . . . . . .124 E5
Neptune Gate SG2 . . . . . .51 D8
Neston Rd WD24 . . . . . . 154 C2
Netherby Cl HP23 . . . . . .100 C6
Nethercott Cl LU2 . . . . . . .46 C1
Netherfield Ct SG12 . . . . 115 D3
Netherfield La SG12 . . . . .115 E3
Netherfield Rd AL5 . . . . .107 B4
Netherhall Rd CM19 . . . .135 F5
Nether St SG12 . . . . 95 E4
Netherstones SG5 . . . . . . .11 F7
NETHER STREET 95 E5
Netherway AL3 . . . . .141 A8
Netley Dell SG6 . . . . 23 B3
NETTESWELL 117 F1
Netteswell Cross
 CM20 . . . . .117 E2
Netteswell Orch
 CM20 . . . . .117 D1
Netteswell Rd CM20 . . . .117 F3
Netteswell Twr ◘
 CM20 . . . . .117 D1
Nettlecroft
 Hemel Hempstead
  HP1 . . . . .124 B2
 Welwyn Garden City
  AL7 . . . . .111 B7
NETTLEDEN 103 B1
Nettleden Rd
 Little Gaddesden HP4 . . .102 E4
 Nettleden HP1 . . . . .103 C1
 Potten End HP4 . . . . . . .123 B8
Nevell's Gn SG6 . . . . .22 F6
Nevells Rd SG6 . . . . .22 F6
Nevil Cl HA6 . . . . .174 D5
Neville Cl EN6 . . . . .158 F8
Neville Rd LU3 . . . . 45 A5
Neville Road Pas LU3 . . . . 45 A5
Neville's Ct SG6 . . . . 23 B7
Nevill Gr WD24 . . . . .167 B8
Nevis Rd SG1 . . . . .37 A4
Newark Cl SG8 . . . . .7 C8
Newark Gn WD6 . . . . . . .170 D6
Newark Rd LU4 . . . . .45 D2
New Barnes Ave AL1 . . . .142 A8
New Barns La CM22 . . . . . 77 D3
New Barns La SG10 . . . . . .74 C4
New Bedford Rd
 Luton, High Town LU1 . . .63 D8
 Luton LU3 . . . . .45 D3
Newberries Ave WD7 . . . 156 B4
Newberries Prim Sch
 WD7 . . . . .156 C4
Newbiggin Path
 WD19 . . . . 175 C6
Newbold Rd LU3 . . . . .45 B7
Newbolt Rd HA7 . . . . . . .176 F5
Newbury Ave EN3 . . . . . .162 F2
Newbury Cl
 Bishop's Stortford
  CM23 . . . . .76 E8
 Luton LU4 . . . . .44 E2
 Stevenage SG1 . . . . .36 D1
Newcastle Cl SG1 . . . . . . .36 F3
Newcombe Path
 WD19 . . . . 175 C6
Newcome Path WD7 . . . .157 A5
Newcome Rd WD7 . . . . . .157 A5
New Cotts
 Bendish SG4 . . . . .66 A7
 Brookmans Park AL9 . . . 144 D3
 Cheshunt EN8 . . . . .162 C5
 Markyate AL3 . . . . .83 E6
New Ct SG3 . . . . .69 A2
Newdigate Gn UB9 . . . . .173 C2
Newdigate Rd UB9 . . . . . 173 C2
Newdigate Rd E UB9 . . . .173 D2
Newell Cl SG2 . . . . .38 D7
Newell Rd HP3 . . . . .138 E8
Newell Rise HP3 . . . . . . .138 E8
Newells SG6 . . . . .23 D4
Newells Hedge LU7 . . . . . .80 D5
New England Cl
 EN11 . . . . .135 C7
New England St AL3 . . . .127 C3
New Farm SG2 . . . . .2 A8
New Farm La HA6 . . . . . .174 E2
Newfield La HP2 . . . . . . .124 F3
Newfields AL4 . . . . .128 C1
Newfield Way AL4 . . . . . .128 C1
New Ford
 EN10 . . . . .162 F5
Newford Cl HP2 . . . . .125 B4
New Ford Rd EN8 . . . . . . .162 E7
New Forge Pl AL3 . . . . . .106 B5
Newgate SG2 . . . . .51 A4
Newgate Cl AL4 . . . . .128 D6
NEWGATE STREET 146 E7
Newgatestreet Rd
 SG13 . . . . .146 E6
NEW GREENS 127 D7
New Greens Ave AL3 . . . .127 D7
NEW GROUND 101 A2
Newground Rd HP23 . . . .101 B3
New Hall Cl HP3 . . . . . . .137 A4
Newhall Ct CM17 . . . . . . .163 F6

Newhouse Cres
 WD25 . . . . .154 B6
New House Pk AL1 . . . . . .142 B7
Newhouse Rd HP3 . . . . . .137 A4
New Inn Rd SG2 . . . . .3 D5
New Kent Rd AL1 . . . . . . .127 D3
Newland Cl
 Pinner HA5 . . . . .175 F4
 St Albans AL1 . . . . 142 A8
Newland Gdns SG13 . . . .113 E6
Newlands
 Hatfield AL9 . . . . .130 C7
 Letchworth Garden City
  SG6 . . . . .23 A3
Newlands Ave WD7 . . . . .155 F5
Newlands Cl E SG4 . . . . . .34 F4
Newlands Cl W SG4 . . . . . 34 F4
Newlands Cvn Site
 WD5 . . . . .139 F5
Newlands La SG4 . . . . 34 F4
Newlands Pl EN5 . . . . . . .171 D4
Newlands Rd
 Hemel Hempstead
  HP1 . . . . .123 E3
 Luton LU1 . . . . .63 C3
Newlands Way WD26 . . .145 B1
Newlands Wlk WD25 . . . 154 D6
Newlyn Cl
 Bricket Wood AL2 . . . . .140 E1
 Stevenage SG1 . . . . 50 A6
Newlyn Ho ☑ HA5 . . . . . .175 F3
Newlyn Rd EN5 . . . . .171 F5
Newman Ave SG8 . . . . . . .7 F6
Newmans Ct SG14 . . . . . . .70 D3
Newmans Dr AL5 . . . . 85 F2
Newmarket Cl AL3 . . . . . .127 C4
Newmarket Rd SG8 . . . . . . .7 E6
NEW MILL 100 A6
NEW MILL END 64 D1
New Mill Terr HP23 . . . . .100 B6
NEWNHAM 12 E8
Newnham Cl LU2 . . . . 46 D1
Newnham Par ☑ EN8 . . .148 D1
Newnham Pl ☑ SG7 . . . . .12 E6
New Par AL3 . . . . .164 C5
New Park Dr HP2 . . . . . . .125 B3
New Park Rd
 Harefield UB9 . . . . .173 C2
 Newgate Street SG13 . . .146 D7
New Path CM23 . . . . .76 F6
New Pl AL6 . . . . .89 B4
Newport Cl EN3 . . . . .162 E2
Newport Mead WD19 . . .175 D6
Newports CM21 . . . . .97 C1
New Providence Pl ☑
 HP4 . . . . .122 D4
Newquay Gdns WD19 . . .175 B8
New Rd
 Berkhamsted HP4 . . . . . 122 D6
 Berkhamsted, Northchurch
  HP4 . . . . .121 F7
 Chipperfield WD4 . . . . . .137 F1
 Croxley Green WD3 . . . . 166 A4
 Elstree WD6 . . . . .169 D3
 Great Chishill SG8 . . . . . . .9 D6
 Harlow CM17 . . . . .118 D4
 Hatfield AL9 . . . . .110 A3
 Hertford SG14 . . . . 113 D8
 Hoddesdon EN10 . . . . . .135 A4
 Little Hadham SG11 . . . . .75 A7
 Lower Stondon SG17 . . . . 10 A8
 Radlett, Letchmore Heath
  WD25 . . . . .168 E8
 Radlett WD7 . . . . .156 A6
 Shenley WD7 . . . . .157 A5
 South Mimms EN6 . . . . .158 A6
 Tring HP23 . . . . .100 B6
 Ware SG12 . . . . 93 D1
 Watford WD17 . . . . .167 C5
 Welwyn AL6 . . . . .89 F3
 Woolmer Green SG3 . . . .69 B3
New River Ave SG12 . . . . 115 B4
New River Cl EN11 . . . . . .135 B7
New River Ct EN7 . . . . . .162 B8
New River Trad Est
 EN8 . . . . .148 D5
NEWSELLS 17 D7
New St
 Berkhamsted HP4 . . . . . 122 D4
 Cheddington LU7 . . . . . . .79 F7
 ☐ Luton LU1 . . . . .63 E1
 Sawbridgeworth CM21 . . 97 E3
 Slip End LU1 . . . . .63 C1
 Watford WD18 . . . . .167 C5
New Station Cotts
 EN10 . . . . .135 A3
Newstead Cl AL10 . . . . . .129 F2
Newstead Ho UB9 . . . . . .173 C1
Newteswell Dr EN9 . . . . .163 D7
Newton Cl
 Harpenden AL5 . . . . .107 D6
 Hoddesdon EN11 . . . . . .115 B2
Newton Cres WD6 . . . . . .170 C5
Newtondale LU4 . . . . 44 C5
Newton Dr CM21 . . . . . . .97 D1
Newton Rd
 Harrow HA3 . . . . .176 E1
 Stevenage SG2 . . . . 51 B6
Newtons Way SG4 . . . . . . .34 F8
NEWTOWN 40 F8
NEW TOWN 76 F5
New Town CM23 . . . . .76 F6
New Town Rd ☑ LU1 . . . .63 E6

New Town St LU1 . . . . . . .63 E6
New Wood AL7 . . . . 111 C7
Nexus Ct AL1 . . . . .127 D2
Niagara Cl EN8 . . . . 148 D2
Nicholas Breakspear RC
 Sch AL4 . . . . .128 E2
Nicholas Cl
 St Albans AL3 . . . . 127 D6
 Watford WD24 . . . . .154 B2
Nicholas La ☒ SG14 . . . .113 B8
Nicholas Pl SG1 . . . . .36 D1
Nicholas Rd WD6 . . . . . . .169 F4
Nicholas Way
 Hemel Hempstead
  HP2 . . . . .124 F5
Nicholls Cl AL3 . . . . .105 F5
Nicholls Yd SG8 . . . . .16 F5
Nichols Cl LU2 . . . . 46 C2
Nicholson Ct EN11 . . . . . .135 B6
Nickelby Way SG5 . . . . . . .11 C2
Nickmar Ct LU3 . . . . 45 D2
Nicola Cl HA3 . . . . .176 D1
Nicoll Way WD6 . . . . . . .170 D5
Nicolson Dr WD23 . . . . . .176 C8
Niedderdale HP2 . . . . . . .124 F6
Nightingale Ave SG8 . . . . . .2 A5
Nightingale Cl
 Kneesworth SG8 . . . . .2 A6
 Luton LU2 . . . . 46 C6
 Radlett WD7 . . . . .155 F3
 Watford WD5 . . . . .154 A8
Nightingale Ct
 Hertford SG14 . . . . 113 C6
 Hitchin SG5 . . . . 35 A8
 ◘ Luton LU3 . . . . .63 C8
 Radlett WD7 . . . . .156 A4
 Rickmansworth WD3 . . .165 C3
Nightingale La AL1,
 AL4 . . . . .142 C7
Nightingale Lo HP4 . . . . .122 B4
Nightingale Pl WD3 . . . . .165 D2
Nightingale Rd
 Bushey WD23 . . . . .168 A4
 Hammond Street EN7 . . .147 C4
 Hitchin SG5 . . . . 34 F8
 Rickmansworth WD3 . . .165 C2
Nightingales
 Bishop's Stortford
  CM23 . . . . .77 B7
 Waltham Abbey EN9 . . .163 E6
Nightingale Terr SG15 . . .11 A3
Nightingale Way
 Baldock SG7 . . . . 23 F6
 Royston SG8 . . . . .7 E8
Nightingale Wlk
 Hemel Hempstead
  HP2 . . . . .105 C1
 Stevenage SG2 . . . . 51 C5
Nimbus Way SG4 . . . . 35 C7
Nimmo Dr WD23 . . . . . . .168 D2
Nimrod Cl AL4 . . . . .128 C5
Nimrod Dr AL10 . . . . .129 D6
Nine Acre La AL10 . . . . . .129 F4
Nine Ashes SG12 . . . . . . .116 D7
Ninefields EN9 . . . . .163 F6
Ninesprings Way SG4 . . . .35 B6
Ninfield Cl LU2 . . . . .46 D1
Ninian Rd HP2 . . . . .124 E8
Ninnings Cotts AL5 . . . . .107 A8
Ninning's La AL6 . . . . .68 D2
Ninth Ave LU3 . . . . 44 D7
Niton Cl EN5 . . . . .171 D3
Niven Cl WD6 . . . . .170 C8
Noahs Court Gdns
 SG13 . . . . .113 E6
Noake Mill La HP1 . . . . . .124 A8
Nobel Sch The SG2 . . . . . .51 C7
Nobel Villas EN9 . . . . . . .163 D5
NOBLAND GREEN 95 A8
Nobles The CM23 . . . . . . .76 D6
Nodes Dr SG2 . . . . .51 A1
Node Way Gdns AL6 . . . . . 89 C3
Noke La AL2 . . . . .140 E4
Noke Lane Bsns Ctr
 AL2 . . . . .140 E4
Noke Shot AL5 . . . . .107 A4
Nokeside SG2 . . . . .69 B8
Noke Side AL2 . . . . .141 A4
Nokes The HP1 . . . . .124 A5
Noke The SG2 . . . . .69 B8
Nolan Path ◘ WD6 . . . . .169 F8
Nook The SG2 . . . . .115 B4
Norbury Ave WD24 . . . . .167 C7
NORCOTT HILL 101 D2
Norfolk Ave WD24 . . . . . .154 C1
Norfolk Ct
 ◘ Barnet EN5 . . . . .171 E5
 ☑ Rickmansworth
  WD3 . . . . .165 E1
Norfolk Gdns WD6 . . . . . .170 D5
Norfolk Rd
 Buntingford SG9 . . . . . . .40 E8
 Luton LU2 . . . . 46 A7
 Rickmansworth WD3 . . .165 E1
Norfolk Way CM23 . . . . . .76 F5
Norman Ave CM23 . . . . . .76 D6
Norman Cl
 St Albans AL1 . . . . .141 E8
 Waltham Abbey EN9 . . . 163 D6
Norman Cres HA5 . . . . . .175 C2
Norman Ct
 Potters Bar EN6 . . . . . . .145 C1
 Stansted Mountfitchet
  CM24 . . . . .59 E7
 Stevenage SG1 . . . . .36 F1
Normandy Ave EN5 . . . . .171 C5
Normandy Ct HP1 . . . . . .124 D4

Normandy Dr HP4 . . . . . .122 B6
Normandy Ho EN2 . . . . . .161 C1
Normandy Rd AL3 . . . . . .127 D4
Normandy Way EN11 . . .135 D8
Norman Rd
 Luton LU3 . . . . .45 B2
 Welwyn AL6 . . . . .89 B3
Normans Cl SG6 . . . . .11 F1
Normansfield Cl
 WD23 . . . . .168 B2
Normans La AL6 . . . . 68 C2
Norman's La ★ 7 D5
Norman Way CM23 . . . . . .59 E7
Norrington End AL3 . . . . . 84 E1
Norris Cl
 Bishop's Stortford
  CM23 . . . . .77 C7
 London Colney AL2 . . . . 142 E5
Norris Gr EN10 . . . . .134 E3
Norris La EN11 . . . . .135 A7
Norris Rd EN11 . . . . .135 A6
Norris Rise EN11 . . . . . . .134 F7
Norris Works ☒
 SG14 . . . . .113 D6
North App
 Moor Park HA6 . . . . .174 C8
 Watford WD25 . . . . .154 A5
North Ave
 Letchworth Garden City
  SG6 . . . . .23 B8
 Shenley WD7 . . . . .156 E7
NORTHAW 146 A1
Northaw CE Prim Sch
 EN6 . . . . .146 A1
Northaw Cl HP2 . . . . .125 B8
Northaw Pk EN6 . . . . . . .159 F7
Northaw Rd E EN6 . . . . . .146 B1
Northaw Rd W EN6 . . . . .160 C8
North Barn EN10 . . . . . . .135 B1
Northbridge Rd HP4 . . . .122 A6
Northbrook Dr HA6 . . . . .174 E3
Northbrook Rd EN5 . . . . .171 E3
NORTHCHURCH 121 D6
Northchurch La HP4,
 HP5 . . . . .121 D2
Northchurch St Mary's CE
 Fst Sch HP4 . . . . .121 E6
North Cl
 Barnet EN5 . . . . .171 C4
 Chiswell Green AL2 . . . .141 B6
 Royston SG8 . . . . 7 C7
Northcliffe Dr N20 . . . . . .171 F1
North Comm AL3 . . . . . . .106 A5
North Common Rd
 AL3 . . . . .106 A4
Northcote ◘ HA5 . . . . . . .175 C1
Northcotts AL9 . . . . .130 C6
North Cotts AL2 . . . . .142 A6
Northcourt WD3 . . . . . . .165 A1
North Ct AL1 . . . . .83 E5
Northdown Rd AL10 . . . . .130 A2
North Dr
 Hatfield AL10 . . . . .130 C7
 High Cross SG11 . . . . .72 E1
Letchford Garden City
 SG5 . . . . .11 C3
 St Albans AL4 . . . . .128 C1
North Drift Way LU1 . . . . .63 B6
North Hts HP23 . . . . .125 C1
NORTH END 15 D6
North End SG16 . . . . .10 C3
Northern Ave SG16 . . . . . .10 C3
Northern Ho
 Hitchin SG4 . . . . 35 B7
 Hitchin SG4 . . . . 35 B7
Northfield
 Braughing SG11 . . . . .55 F7
 Hatfield AL10 . . . . .130 B8
 Standon SG11 . . . . 55 E2
Northfield Gdns
 WD24 . . . . .154 C2
Northfield Rd
 Aldbury HP23 . . . . .100 F3
 Borehamwood WD6 . . . . 170 B8
 Cheshunt EN8 . . . . .162 E7
 Guilden Morden SG7 . . . . .1 C2
 Harpenden AL5 . . . . .86 C4
 Sawbridgeworth CM21 . . 97 E4
Northfields
 Letchford Garden City
  SG6 . . . . .11 F1
 Stansted Mountfitchet
  CM24 . . . . .59 E7
Northfields Inf Sch
 SG6 . . . . .11 F1
Northgate HA6 . . . . 174 C3
North Gate CM20 . . . . . . .117 C1
Northgate End CM23 . . . . .76 F8
Northgate Ho EN8 . . . . . .148 D2
Northgate Path ☐
 WD6 . . . . .169 F8
Northgate Prim Sch
 CM23 . . . . .76 E8
North Gn SG2 . . . . .91 F1
North Hertfordshire Coll
 SG1 . . . . .50 D4
North Hertfordshire Coll
 (Goldsmith Ctr) SG6 . . . . 22 F1
North Hertfordshire Coll
 (Hitchin Ctr) SG4 . . . . . .35 B8
North Hill 164 E8
Northlands EN6 . . . . .159 D8

North Luton Ind Est
LU4. . . . . .44 B7
NORTH MYMMS 144 A5
Northolt Ave CM23. . . . . . .59 B1
North Orbital Commercial
Pk AL1. . . . . 142 A7
North Orbital Rd
Bricket Wood AL2. . . . . . . .140 E2
Chiswell Green AL2 . . . . . . .141 B5
Colney Heath AL4 . . . . 129 C2
London Colney AL1, AL2,
AL4. . . . . .142 D6
Park Street AL2 . . . . .141 E6
Watford WD25 . . . . .154 D7
North Pl
Harlow CM20. . . . . .118 B5
Hitchin SG5 . . . . .21 D1
4 Waltham Abbey
EN9. . . . . .163 B6
North Rd
Baldock SG7 . . . . .12 E2
Berkhamsted HP4 . . . . . . .122 B4
Cheshunt EN8 . . . . .162 E6
Chorleywood WD3 . . . . . . .164 D4
Hertford, Broadoak End
SG14 . . . . .113 A7
Hertford SG14 . . . . .113 C6
Hoddesdon EN11. . . . . . . .135 A7
Stevenage SG1 . . . . .36 C2
North Ride AL6. . . . . .89 C6
Northridge Way HP1. . . . .124 A3
North Riding AL2. . . . . . . .141 A1
North Road Ave SG14 . . . .113 A7
North Road Gdns
SG14 . . . . .113 B6
Northside AL4 . . . . .108 B1
North St
4 Bishop's Stortford
CM23 . . . . .76 F7
Lower Nazeing EN9 . . . . . .135 E1
Luton, Hart Hill LU2. . . . . . .45 E1
Luton, High Town LU2 . . . . .63 E8
North Terr 2 CM23 . . . . . .76 F8
Northumberland Ave
EN1 . . . . .162 B1
North View Cotts SG12 . . . .95 D4
Northview Rd LU2. . . . . . . .45 F2
NORTH WATFORD 154 B2
Northway
Rickmansworth WD3 . . . . .165 D2
1 Welwyn Garden City
AL7 . . . . .89 F1
Northwell Dr LU3. . . . . . . .44 F7
North Western Ave
Bushey WD23, W25. . . . . .168 C6
Stanmore WD6 . . . . .169 A2
Watford, Garston
WD24 . . . . .154 C3
Watford, Leavesden Green
WD2. . . . . .153 D4
Northwick Rd WD19 . . . . .175 C6
NORTHWOOD 174 D2
Northwood AL7. . . . . .111 D6
Northwood Cl EN7. . . . . . .147 F4
Northwood Coll HA6 . . . . .174 D3
NORTHWOOD HILLS 174 F1
Northwood Hills Cir
HA6 . . . . .175 A2
Northwood Hills Sta
HA6 . . . . .175 A1
Northwood & Pinner
Hospl HA6 . . . . .175 A2
Northwood Prep Sch
WD3. . . . . .174 C8
Northwood Rd UB9 . . . . . .173 E3
Northwood Sch HA6 . . . . .175 B2
Northwood Sta HA6 . . . . . .174 E3
Northwood Way
Harefield UB9 . . . . .173 D2
Northwood HA6 . . . . .175 A3
NORTON 12 C1
NORTON BURY 12 C2
Norton Bury La SG6 . . . . . .12 D3
Norton Cl WD6. . . . . .170 A5
Norton Cres SG2 . . . . .23 E8
NORTON GREEN 50 B3
Norton Green Rd SG1. . . . .50 C4
Norton Rd
Letchworth Garden City SG5,
SG6, SG7. . . . . .12 C2
Luton LU3 . . . . .44 F4
Stevenage SG1 . . . . .50 D4
Norton Road Prim Sch
LU3. . . . . .44 F4
Norton St Nicholas CE
Prim Sch SG6. . . . . .12 C1
Norton Street La SG4. . . . .67 B7
Norton Way N SG6. . . . . . .23 A7
Norton Way S SG6 . . . . . . .23 A5
Norvic Rd HP23. . . . . .80 A1
Norwich Cl SG1 . . . . .37 B1
Norwich Ho 3 WD6 . . . . .170 F7
Norwich Way WD3. . . . . . .166 B5
Norwood Cl SG14 . . . . . . .112 F7
Norwood Rd EN8 . . . . . . .148 E1
Nottingham Cl WD25 . . . .154 A6
Nottingham Rd WD3. . . . .164 C1
Novello Way WD6 . . . . . . .170 D8
Nugents Ct HA5 . . . . .175 E2
Nugent's Pk HA5 . . . . . . .175 F2
Numbers Farm WD4 . . . . .139 C2
Nunfield WD4 . . . . .152 B8
Nunnery Cl AL1. . . . . .127 E1
Nunnery La LU3. . . . . .45 B5
Nunnery Stables AL1 . . . . .127 D1

Nunsbury Dr EN10 . . . . . .148 E6
Nunsbury Drive Cotts
EN10 . . . . .148 E6
Nun's Cl SG5. . . . . .34 E7
Nuns La AL1. . . . . .141 E8
NUP END. 60 B1
Nup End Bsns Pk SG3. . . . .68 B4
Nup End Cl HP22 . . . . .60 B3
Nup End La HP22. . . . . . . .60 B3
Nupton Dr EN5 . . . . .171 C3
Nurseries Rd AL4. . . . . . . .108 E7
Nursery Cl
Bishop's Stortford
CM23 . . . . .76 F6
Stevenage SG2 . . . . .69 A8
Watford WD19. . . . . .167 B1
Nursery Cotts SG1 . . . . . . .50 A6
Nursery Ct SG6 . . . . .22 F6
Nursery Fields SG21. . . . . .97 D2
Nursery Gdns
Goff's Oak EN7 . . . . .147 D3
Tring HP23. . . . . .100 B4
Ware SG12 . . . . .93 E1
Welwyn Garden City AL7 . . .89 E1
Nursery Hill
Hitchin SG4 . . . . .34 F6
Welwyn Garden City AL7 . . .89 E1
Nursery Par LU3 . . . . .44 E5
Nursery Rd
Bishop's Stortford
CM23 . . . . .76 F6
4 Cheshunt EN8 . . . . . . .148 F6
Hoddesdon EN11 . . . . . . .115 B1
Lower Nazeing EN9 . . . . . .135 D2
Luton LU3 . . . . .44 F5
Nursery Row 3 EN5. . . . . .171 E6
Nursery Terr AL4 . . . . .108 E7
Nutcroft SG3 . . . . .69 D2
Nut Gr AL8 . . . . .89 D1
NUTHAMPSTEAD 18 E2
Nuthampstead Rd SG8. . . .17 E2
Nutleigh Gr SG5. . . . . .21 D1
Nut Slip SG9 . . . . .40 E6
Nuttfield Cl WD3 . . . . . . .166 B3
Nutwood Gdns 5
EN7 . . . . .147 E5
Nye Way HP3. . . . . .137 A3
Nymans Cl LU2. . . . . .46 D3

O

Oak Ave
Bricket Wood AL2 . . . . . . .141 A1
Enfield EN2 . . . . .160 F1
Oakbank WD7 . . . . .156 B3
Oak Cl
Hemel Hempstead
HP3. . . . . .138 F7
Waltham Abbey EN9 . . . . .163 D5
Oak Court Bsns Ctr
AL3. . . . . .127 E8
Oakcroft Cl HA5 . . . . .175 B1
Oak Ct HA6. . . . . .174 D4
Oakdale AL8. . . . . .89 D1
Oakdale Ave HA5 . . . . . . .175 A1
Oakdale Cl WD19 . . . . . . .175 C6
Oakdale Rd WD19 . . . . . . .175 C6
Oakdene EN8. . . . . .148 E1
Oakdene Ct HA5 . . . . .175 F3
Oakdene Rd
Hemel Hempstead
HP3. . . . . .138 F7
Watford WD19. . . . . .154 B3
Oakdene Way AL1 . . . . . . .128 C3
Oak Dr
Berkhamsted HP4 . . . . . . .122 C8
Sawbridgeworth CM21 . . .118 C8
Oak End SG9 . . . . .40 D7
Oak Farm WD6 . . . . .170 C4
OAKFIELD 35 B6
Oakfield WD3 . . . . .165 A2
Oakfield Ave AL5 . . . . .35 B5
Oakfield Cl EN6 . . . . .158 F8
Oakfield Rd AL5 . . . . .107 A5
Oakfields SG2 . . . . .51 C1
Oakfields Ave SG3 . . . . . . .69 A6
Oakfields Cl SG2 . . . . .51 C1
Oakfields Rd SG3 . . . . .69 A6
Oak Glade HA6 . . . . .174 B2
Oak Gn WD5 . . . . .153 E7
Oak Gr
Hatfield AL10 . . . . .129 F5
Hertford SG13. . . . . .113 E4
Oak Green Way WD5. . . . .153 E7
Oak Hall CM23. . . . . .76 E8
Oakhill SG6 . . . . .23 D4
Oakhill Ave HA5 . . . . .175 E1
Oakhill Cl WD3 . . . . .172 E6
Oakhill Ct EN5. . . . . .171 D5
Oakhill Dr AL6. . . . . .89 A6
Oakhill Rd WD3 . . . . .172 D6
Oak Ho HA6. . . . . .174 B2
Oakhurst HP22. . . . . .125 B8
Oakhurst Ave AL5. . . . . . .107 A5
Oakhurst Pl WD18 . . . . . . .166 F5
Oakhurst Rd EN3 . . . . .162 D3
Oakington AL7 . . . . .111 D6
Oak La
Cholesbury HP23. . . . . . . .120 B2
Cuffley EN6 . . . . .146 F3
Graveley SG4. . . . . .36 C4
OAKLANDS 89 F7
Oaklands HP4 . . . . .122 A4
Oaklands Ave
Brookmans Park AL9 . . . . .144 E4

Oaklands Ave continued
Watford WD19. . . . . .167 B1
Oaklands Cl CM23 . . . . . . .59 B2
Oaklands Coll AL1 . . . . . . .127 E3
Oaklands Coll
(Borehamwood Campus)
WD6. . . . . .170 C7
Oaklands Coll Smallford
Campus AL4 . . . . .128 E4
Oaklands Coll (Welwyn
Garden City Campus)
AL8. . . . . .110 D7
Oaklands Ct
Oaklands AL6. . . . . .89 E7
Watford WD17. . . . . .167 A8
Oaklands Dr CM23 . . . . . . .59 B2
Oaklands Gate HA6 . . . . . .174 E4
Oaklands Gr EN10 . . . . . . .148 E7
Oaklands La
Arkley EN5. . . . . .171 B5
St Albans AL4 . . . . .128 F5
Oaklands Pk CM23. . . . . . .59 B2
Oaklands Prim Sch
AL6. . . . . .89 E7
Oaklands Rd
Hammond Street EN7 . . . .147 E5
Totteridge N20. . . . . .171 F2
Oaklands Rise AL6. . . . . . .89 F7
Oaklands Wood AL10 . . . .130 A5
Oakland View AL6 . . . . . . .89 F7
Oaklawn HP23. . . . . .100 A3
Oaklea AL6. . . . . .89 E7
Oaklea Cl AL6. . . . . .89 E8
Oaklea Wood AL6. . . . . . . .89 E7
Oakleigh Cl CM23 . . . . . . .76 D8
Oakleigh Dr WD3 . . . . . . .166 C3
Oakleigh Rd HA5 . . . . . . .175 F4
Oakley Cl LU4 . . . . .44 D4
Oakley Ct SG8 . . . . .7 D7
Oakley Rd
Harpenden AL5 . . . . .107 D7
Luton LU4 . . . . .44 E3
Oakmeade HA5. . . . . .176 A4
Oakmede 6 EN5 . . . . .171 D5
Oakmere Ave EN6 . . . . . . .159 C6
Oakmere Cl EN6. . . . . . . .159 D8
Oakmere La EN6. . . . . . . .159 C7
Oakmere Prim Sch
EN6. . . . . .159 D7
Oak Path WD23. . . . . .168 B3
Oak Piece AL6. . . . . .89 E7
Oak Piece Ct AL6. . . . . . . .89 E7
Oak Pk SG12 . . . . .95 B1
Oak Rd
Luton LU4 . . . . .63 C8
Woolmer Green SG3 . . . . . .69 B1
Oakridge AL2. . . . . .140 F2
Oakridge Ave WD7. . . . . . .155 F6
Oakridge Ct WD7. . . . . . . .155 E5
Oakroyd Ave EN6. . . . . . . .158 F6
Oakroyd Cl EN6. . . . . .158 F6
Oaks Cl
Hitchin SG4 . . . . .34 F5
Radlett WD7 . . . . .155 F4
Oaks Cross SG2 . . . . .51 B1
Oaks Ret Pk CM20 . . . . . .117 F3
Oak St
Bishop's Stortford
CM23 . . . . .76 F6
Hemel Hempstead HP3 . . .138 F7
Oaks The
Berkhamsted HP4 . . . . . . .122 A4
Slip End LU1 . . . . .63 C1
Watford WD19. . . . . .167 C1
Oaktree Cl
14 Bishop's Stortford
CM23 . . . . .76 F7
Goff's Oak EN7 . . . . .147 B3
Oaktree Cotts SG12. . . . . .114 F6
Oak Tree Ct
Elstree WD6. . . . . .169 D3
Oaklands AL6. . . . . .89 E8
Oaktree Garth AL7. . . . . . .110 E5
Oak Tree Row SG13. . . . . . .46 A2
Oak View WD18 . . . . .166 E6
Oakview Cl
Cheshunt EN7 . . . . .148 B3
Harpenden AL5 . . . . .106 F5
Watford WD19. . . . . .167 C3
Oak View Prim Sch
LU1. . . . . .130 B4
Oakway LU6. . . . . .82 B7
Oak Way AL5. . . . . .107 A5
Oakway Pl WD7 . . . . .156 A5
Oakwell Cl SG2 . . . . .69 D7
Oakwell Dr EN6 . . . . .160 B7
Oakwood
Berkhamsted HP4 . . . . . . .121 F3
Waltham Abbey EN9 . . . . .163 E5
Oakwood Ave WD6. . . . . .170 B5
Oakwood Dr
Harpenden AL5 . . . . .106 F5
St Albans AL4 . . . . .128 C4
Oakwood Est CM20 . . . . .118 B4
Oakwood Mews 5
CM17 . . . . .118 C4
Oakwood Prim Sch
AL4. . . . . .128 C4

Oakwood Rd
Bricket Wood AL2 . . . . . . .140 F2
Pinner HA5 . . . . .175 B1
Oban Terr LU1 . . . . .63 B8
Oberon Cl WD6. . . . . .170 C8
Obrey Way CM23. . . . . . . .76 E3
Observer Dr WD18. . . . . . .166 E5
Occupation Rd WD18 . . . .167 B4
Octagon The SG12 . . . . . . .93 D2
Octavia Ct WD24. . . . . . . .167 C7
Oddfellows Ct 10
SG14 . . . . .113 D6
Oddy Hill
Tring HP23. . . . . .100 C3
Wigginton HP23. . . . . .100 C2
Odeon Par WD24 . . . . . . .154 B3
Odessey Rd WD6 . . . . .170 B8
Offa Rd AL3 . . . . .127 C3
Offas Way AL4. . . . . .108 D8
Offerton Ho 6 WD19 . . . .175 C7
Offley Cross SG5 . . . . .34 B5
Offley Endowed Prim Sch
SG5. . . . . .33 C3
Offley Hill SG5 . . . . .33 C3
Offley Rd SG5 . . . . .34 D6
Ogard Rd EN11. . . . . .135 C8
Okeford Cl HP23. . . . . .99 F4
Okeford Dr HP23. . . . . . . .127 C3
Okeley La HP23. . . . . .99 E3
Old Airfield Ind Est
HP23. . . . . .79 E5
Old Bakery SG5. . . . . .34 E7
Old Barn La WD3 . . . . . . .165 F4
Old Barn Mews WD3. . . . .165 F4
Old Bedford Rd
Luton LU2 . . . . .45 E4
Luton, Warden Hill LU2. . . .45 D6
Old Bell Cl CM24 . . . . .59 D6
Old Bourne Way SG14 . . . .37 A3
Old Brewery Cl SG5. . . . . .11 F7
Old Brewery Pl SG4. . . . . .66 D1
Old Chantry La SG4. . . . . .35 F2
Old Chapel Mews SG4 . . . .67 F1
Old Charlton Rd SG5. . . . .34 E6
Old Chorleywood Rd
WD3. . . . . .165 D3
Old Church La SG12 . . . . . .93 E7
Old Coach Rd The
SG14 . . . . .112 C4
Old Common Rd
WD3. . . . . .164 D5
Old Common The SG9. . . . .43 B4
Old Crabtree La HP2 . . . . .124 E2
Old Cross SG14 . . . . .113 C6
Old Cross Wharf 25
SG14 . . . . .113 D6
Old Dairy Mews The
AL1. . . . . .128 B3
Old Dean HP3 . . . . .137 A4
Old Dr The AL8 . . . . .110 B5
Olde Ct HA6. . . . . .174 E4
Olden Mead SG6 . . . . .23 B3
Olde Swann Ct SG1. . . . . . .50 C8
Old Farm LU7 . . . . .80 D4
Oldfield Cl EN8 . . . . .148 E3
Oldfield Ct AL1. . . . . .127 E3
Oldfield Dr EN8. . . . . .148 E3
Oldfield Farm Rd
Lower Stondon SG16. . . . . .10 B4
Lower Stondon SG16. . . . . .10 C4
Oldfield Rd
Hemel Hempstead
HP1. . . . . .123 E2
London Colney AL2 . . . . . .142 D6
Oldfield Rise SG4. . . . . . . .66 E7
Old Fishery La
Hemel Hempstead HP1. . . .137 F8
Old Fold Cl EN5. . . . . .171 E8
Old Fold La EN5. . . . . .171 F8
Old Fold View EN5. . . . . . .171 C6
Old Forge Cl
Abbots Langley
WD25 . . . . .154 A6
Welwyn Garden City AL7 . . .89 F2
Old Forge End SG13. . . . . .114 B3
Old Forge Row SG13. . . . .114 B3
Old Forge The HP23. . . . . .79 B4
Old French Horn La
AL10 . . . . .130 B6
Old Gannon Cl HA6. . . . . .174 C5
Old Garden Ct AL3. . . . . . .127 C3
Old Gorhambury Ho*
AL3 . . . . .126 C4
Old Granary The SG7. . . . . .4 D4
Old Grove Ct EN7. . . . . . . .147 D5
Old Hale Way SG5 . . . . . . .21 E2
Old Hall Cl HA5 . . . . .175 E2
Old Hall Dr HA5 . . . . .175 E2
Oldhall Ct SG4 . . . . .66 E7
Oldhall St SG14. . . . . .113 D6
OLD HALL GREEN 54 F1
Oldhall St SG14. . . . . .113 D6
Oldhams Trad Est
WD24. . . . . .154 C2
OLD HARLOW 118 C4
Old Harpenden Rd
AL3. . . . . .127 E6
Old Hat Factory The 2
LU2. . . . . .45 D1
OLD HATFIELD 130 D6
Old Herns La LU2 . . . . .46 F4
Old Hertford Rd AL9 . . . . .130 C8
Old Highway EN11. . . . . . .135 C8
Oldhill Wood LU6. . . . . . . .82 D6
Oldhouse Croft CM20 . . . .117 E2

Old House Ct HP2 . . . . . . .124 F3
Old House La
Lower Nazeing EN9 . . . . . .149 F8
Sarratt WD4. . . . . .152 F4
Old House Rd HP2 . . . . . . .124 F3
Oldings Cnr AL9 . . . . .110 B1
OLD KNEBWORTH 68 C6
Old Knebworth La SG3,
SG2 . . . . .68 D8
Old La SG3 . . . . .69 B5
Old Lays AL10 . . . . .130 A2
Old Library La 27
SG14 . . . . .113 D6
Old London Rd
Hertford SG13. . . . . .113 E6
St Albans AL1 . . . . .127 E1
Old Lyndale Sch 11
AL1. . . . . .127 C4
Old Maltings Ct The 3
AL1. . . . . .135 A6
Old Maltings The 2
CM23 . . . . .77 A7
Old Maple HP2 . . . . .104 F1
Old Meadow Cl HP4 . . . . .122 A2
Old Mile House Ct
AL1. . . . . .142 A8
Old Mill Gdns HP4 . . . . . .122 D4
Old Mill La CM27 . . . . .98 B6
Old Mill Rd WD4. . . . . . . .153 C5
Old Nazeing Rd EN10 . . . .135 C1
Old North Rd
Kneesworth SG8 . . . . .2 B4
Royston SG8 . . . . .7 C8
Old Nursery Way AL6 . . . . .89 A7
Old Oak AL1. . . . . .141 E8
Old Oak Cl SG15. . . . . .11 A8
Old Oak Mews HP4 . . . . . .121 E7
Old Oak Ind Est SG15 . . . .11 A8
Old Oaks EN9 . . . . .163 E7
Old Orch
Luton LU1 . . . . .63 D5
Park Street AL2. . . . . .141 D5
Old Orchard Cl EN4. . . . . .159 F1
Old Orchard Mews
HP4 . . . . .122 C3
Old Parkbury La AL2. . . . .141 F1
Old Park Rd SG5 . . . . .34 E7
Oldpark Ride EN7 . . . . . . .161 D7
Old Priory Pk AL1 . . . . . . .127 E2
Old Rd CM17 . . . . .118 D5
Old Rectory Cl AL5. . . . . . .86 A2
Old Rectory Ct EN5. . . . . .171 E5
Old Rectory Dr AL10. . . . .130 B5
Old Rectory Gdns
AL4. . . . . .108 D8
Old Redding HA3 . . . . . . .176 C6
Old River La CM23 . . . . . . .76 F7
Old School Cl AL3. . . . . . . .142 A4
Old School Cl SG1 . . . . . . .50 F1
Old School Cotts HP5. . . . .136 D5
Old School Flats The
HP23. . . . . .99 D8
Old School Gn SG2 . . . . . .52 E5
Old School Orch SG14 . . . .70 E3
Old School The
Hertford Heath SG13. . . . .114 C4
Shillington SG5 . . . . .19 E8
Old School Wlk
Arlesey SG15. . . . . .11 A4
Slip End LU1 . . . . .63 C1
Old's Cl WD18. . . . . .166 B1
Old Shire La WD3 . . . . . . .164 A2
Old Solesbridge La
WD3. . . . . .165 A3
Old Sopwell Gdns
AL1. . . . . .127 E1
Old South Cl HA5. . . . . . . .175 D2
OLD TOWN 50 C8
Old Uxbridge Rd WD3 . . . .172 E3
Old Vicarage Gdns
AL3. . . . . .83 D6
Old Waddling La 5
AL4. . . . . .87 D1
Old Walled Gdn The
SG1. . . . . .36 C1
Old Watford Rd AL2 . . . . .140 E2
Old Watling St AL3. . . . . . .84 B3
Oldwood AL6. . . . . .89 D7
Old Works The 4
AL1. . . . . .127 E2
Olive Cl AL1. . . . . .128 B1
Oliver Cl
Hemel Hempstead
HP3. . . . . .138 E7
Hoddesdon EN11. . . . . . . .135 B8
Park Street AL2. . . . . .141 D4
Oliver Ct SG12 . . . . .92 E4
Oliver Rd HP3. . . . . .138 E7
Olivers Cl HP4 . . . . .123 C7
Oliver's La SG5 . . . . .11 F7
Olive Taylor Ct HP4 . . . . . .124 F7
Olivia Ct 1 EN5. . . . . .171 F5
Olivia Gdns UB9 . . . . .173 C2
Olivia Mews HA3 . . . . .176 E3
Olleberrie La HP3,
WD3. . . . . .151 D7
Olwen Mews HA5 . . . . . . .175 D1
Olyard Ct LU1 . . . . .63 B6
Olympus Rd SG16. . . . . . . .10 A7
Omega Ct
4 Ware SG12. . . . . .93 D1
5 Watford WD18 . . . . . .166 E4
Omega Maltings 2
SG12 . . . . .93 E1
Onslow Cl AL10. . . . . .130 D5
Onslow Rd LU4 . . . . .44 D5

Onslow St Audrey's Sch AL10 . . . 130 B5
Ontario Cl EN10 . . . 148 E6
On The Hill WD19 . . . 175 E8
Opening The SG4 . . . 88 F8
Openshaw Way SG6 . . . 23 A6
Optima Bsns Pk EN11 . . . 135 C7
Opulens Pl HA6. . . 174 C3
Opus Ct WD6 . . . 170 A6
Oram Pl HP3 . . . 138 D8
Orbital 25 Bsns Pk WD18. . . 166 D2
Orbital Cres WD5 . . . 153 F4
Orbital Ctr The SG1 . . . 50 B6

Orchard Ave
Berkhamsted HP4 . . . 122 A4
Harpenden AL5 . . . 85 F1
Watford WD25. . . 154 B8
Orchard Cl
Borehamwood WD6 . . . 169 F6
Bushey WD23 . . . 168 D1
Caddington LU1. . . 62 E4
Chorleywood WD3 . . . 164 D5
Cuffley EN6 . . . 146 E3
Hemel Hempstead HP2 . . . 124 F4
Kneesworth SG8 . . . 2 A5
Letchworth Garden City SG6. . . 22 F8
Little Berkhamsted SG13. . . 132 C4
Radlett WD7 . . . 155 E3
St Albans AL1 . . . 127 F2
Stansted Abbotts SG12. . . 115 C4
St Ippolyts SG4 . . . 34 F3
Ware SG12 . . . 93 D2
Wingrave HP22 . . . 60 B3
Orchard Cres SG1 . . . 50 C7
Orchard Croft CM20. . . 118 A2

Orchard Ct
Bovingdon HP9 . . . 137 A4
Potters Bar EN6 . . . 158 D8
Potters Bar EN6 . . . 159 A8
Orchard Ctr The LU4 . . . 44 C4
Orchard Dr
Chiswell Green AL2 . . . 141 B5
Chorleywood WD3 . . . 164 D5
Standon SG11 . . . 55 E2
Watford WD17. . . 166 F8
Orchard Gdns EN9 . . . 163 C6

Orchard Ho
Braughing SG11. . . 55 F7
London Colney AL2 . . . 142 B5
Orchard House La AL1. . . 127 C2
Orchard Lea CM21. . . 97 C1
ORCHARD LEIGH . . . 136 A3
Orchard Leigh HP5 . . . 136 A3
Orchard Leigh Villas HP5 . . . 136 A3
Orchard Mead AL10. . . 129 F5
Orchard On The Green The WD3 . . . 165 F4
Orchard Pl EN8. . . 148 D1
Orchard Prim Sch The WD24. . . 153 F2

Orchard Rd
Baldock SG7 . . . 12 E1
Barnet EN5 . . . 171 F5
Bishop's Stortford CM23. . . 59 B1
Burnham Green AL6 . . . 90 C8
Hitchin SG4 . . . 22 B1
Royston SG8 . . . 7 B7
Stevenage SG1 . . . 50 C7
Welwyn AL6 . . . 89 C5

Orchard St
Hemel Hempstead HP3 . . . 138 D8
St Albans AL3 . . . 127 C2
Orchards The
Sawbridgeworth CM21 . . . 97 E3
Slip End LU1 . . . 63 C2
Tring HP23 . . . 99 F3

Orchard The
Baldock SG7 . . . 23 E8
Codicote SG4 . . . 67 F1
Kings Langley WD4 . . . 139 B2
Radlett WD6 . . . 168 F7
Tonwell SG12 . . . 92 E7
Welwyn Garden City AL8. . . 110 D8
Orchard View SG7 . . . 5 A3

Orchard Way
Bovingdon HP3 . . . 137 A3
Breachwood Green SG4 . . . 47 E1
Golf's Oak EN7 . . . 147 B3
Ivinghoe LU7 . . . 80 E5
Knebworth SG3 . . . 68 E5
Letchworth Garden City SG6. . . 22 F8
Lower Stondon SG16. . . 10 B3
Luton LU4 . . . 44 C4
Potters Bar EN6 . . . 145 B2
Rickmansworth WD3 . . . 165 A2
Royston SG8 . . . 7 C8
Orchid Cl
Goff's Oak EN7 . . . 147 C1
Hatfield AL10. . . 109 F1
Luton LU1 . . . 44 C6
Orchid Ct HA3. . . 176 E2
Orchid Ho AL1. . . 127 F3
Ordelmere SG6. . . 11 F1
Ordnance Rd EN3 . . . 162 E2
Oregon Way LU3. . . 45 A8

Organ Hall Rd WD6 . . . 169 E8
Orient All . . . 127 E1
Orient Ctr The WD24. . . 154 D2
Orient Lo 1 SG4 . . . 35 A8
Oriole Cl WD5 . . . 154 A8
Oriole Way CM23 . . . 76 C6
Orion Gate SG1. . . 50 F5
Orion Way HA6 . . . 175 A6
Orkney Ho WD18 . . . 166 F4
Orlando Cl SG4. . . 35 A6
Ormesby Dr EN6. . . 158 D7
Ormonde Rd HA6 . . . 174 D6
Ormsby Cl LU1 . . . 63 E5
Ormskirk Rd WD19 . . . 175 D5
Oronsay HP3 . . . 124 D1
Orphanage Rd WD17, WD24. . . 167 C7
Orpington Cl LU4 . . . 44 A3
Orton Cl AL4 . . . 128 A2
Orwell Ave SG1 . . . 36 F3
Orwell Ct 5 WD24. . . 167 D7
Orwell View SG7 . . . 13 B1
Osborne Ct
9 Luton LU1 . . . 63 F6
Potters Bar EN6 . . . 145 B1
Osborne Gdns EN6 . . . 145 B1
Osborne Rd
Cheshunt EN8 . . . 148 E4
Hoddesdon EN10 . . . 135 A4
Luton LU1 . . . 63 F6
Watford WD24. . . 154 C1
Osborne Terr WD23. . . 168 B1
Osborne Way WD23 . . . 100 D1
Osborn Way AL8 . . . 110 D6
Osbourne Ave WD4 . . . 138 F3
Osbourne Gdns 5 CM23 . . . 76 E5
Osier Ct 9 SG5. . . 34 F8
Osiers The WD3 . . . 165 A2
Osmington Pl HP23 . . . 99 F4
Osprey Cl WD25 . . . 154 E5
Osprey Ct SG6. . . 22 E8
Osprey Gdns SG2 . . . 51 D2
Osprey Ho 3 SG12 . . . 93 C3
Osprey Wlk LU4 . . . 44 A5
Ostell Cres EN3. . . 163 A1
Oster Ho E AL3 . . . 127 C1
Osterley Cl SG2 . . . 69 C7
Oster St AL3. . . 127 C4
Oswald Rd AL1 . . . 127 E2
Otley Way WD19 . . . 175 C7
Ottawa Cl LU3. . . 148 E6
Otter Gdns AL10 . . . 130 B4
Otterpool La WD25 . . . 154 E1
Otterspool La WD25 . . . 154 F1
Otterton Cl AL5 . . . 85 D2
Ottoman Terr 1 WD17 . . . 167 C6
Ottway Wlk AL6 . . . 89 C4
Otway Gdns WD23 . . . 168 E2
Otways Ct The EN6. . . 159 B6
Oudle La SG10. . . 74 F2
Oughton Cl SG5 . . . 34 C8
Oughton Head Way SG5 . . . 34 D8
Oughton Prim Sch SG5 . . . 21 C1
Oulton Cres EN6 . . . 158 D7
Oulton Rise AL5. . . 86 C3
Oulton Way WD19 . . . 175 F6
Our Lady RC Prim Sch
Welwyn Garden City AL7. . . 110 E4
Ousden Cl EN8 . . . 148 E1
Ousden Dr EN8. . . 148 E1
Ouseley Cl LU4 . . . 44 D3
Outlook Ho EN3 . . . 162 F3
Oval The
Cheshunt EN10 . . . 148 E7
Lower Stondon SG16 . . . 10 C3
Stevenage SG1 . . . 37 A1
Ovaltine Ct WD4 . . . 139 B2
Ovaltine Dr WD4 . . . 139 B2
Overfield Rd LU2 . . . 46 C1
Overlord Cl LU2. . . 134 C3
Overstone Rd
Harpenden AL5 . . . 86 C1
Luton LU4 . . . 44 D1
Overstream AL5 . . . 85 F3
Overtrees AL5 . . . 85 F3
Oving Cl LU2 . . . 46 D2
Owen Dr SG8 . . . 2 D1
Owen Jones Cl SG16. . . 10 C5
Owens Way WD3 . . . 166 A5
Owles La SG9. . . 41 A6
Oxcroft CM23. . . 76 F3
Oxendon Dr EN11 . . . 135 A5
Oxen Ind Est LU2 . . . 45 F1
Oxen Rd LU2 . . . 45 F1
Oxfield Cl HP4 . . . 122 A3
Oxford Ave AL1 . . . 128 C2
Oxford Cl
Cheshunt EN8 . . . 148 D2
Kneesworth SG8 . . . 2 A7
Moor Park HA6 . . . 174 D6
Oxford Ho 8 WD6 . . . 170 A7
Oxford Pl AL10 . . . 129 E7
Oxford Rd
Breachwood Green SG4. . . 47 E1

Oxford Rd continued
2 Luton LU1 . . . 63 C6
Oxford St WD18 . . . 167 B4
Oxhey Ave WD19. . . 167 D2
Oxhey La
Pinner HA5 . . . 176 A5
South Oxhey WD19 . . . 175 F7
Watford WD19. . . 167 D2
Oxhey Rd WD19 . . . 167 D2
Oxhey Ridge Cl HA6 . . . 175 B5
Oxhey Wood Prim Sch WD19. . . 175 C7
Ox La AL5 . . . 86 B3
Ox La AL5 . . . 86 B3
OXLEASE . . . 130 B5
Oxlease Dr AL10 . . . 130 B4
Oxleys Rd SG2 . . . 51 B3
Oxleys The CM17 . . . 118 E4
Oysterfields AL3. . . 127 C4

P

Pacatian Way SG1 . . . 51 C8
Pacific Lo 3 SG4. . . 35 A8
Packhorse Cl AL4. . . 128 C6
Packhorse La SG16 . . . 157 D8
Paddick Cl EN11 . . . 134 F7
Paddock
Hunsdon SG12. . . 95 D1
Letchworth Garden City SG6. . . 23 A5
Watford WD19. . . 167 E3
Paddock Cl AL7 . . . 111 B6
Paddock Ho SG9. . . 40 E8
Paddocks Cl SG2 . . . 51 B4
Paddocks The
Blackmore End AL4 . . . 87 B6
Chorleywood WD3 . . . 164 F5
Codicote SG4 . . . 68 A1
Hertford Heath SG13. . . 114 B7
Stevenage SG2 . . . 51 B3
Welwyn Garden City AL7. . . 111 B7
Paddock The
Bishop's Stortford CM23 . . . 76 D3
Hatfield AL10. . . 130 A6
Hitchin SG4 . . . 35 A5
Hoddesdon EN10 . . . 135 A3
Paddock Way HP1 . . . 123 E3
Stanmore HA3. . . 176 E4
Paddox Ave SG14 . . . 113 D8
Padgate Ho 12 WD19 . . . 175 C7
Padgets The EN9 . . . 163 B6
Pageant Rd AL1 . . . 127 D2
Page Cl SG7 . . . 23 F6
Page Hill SG12 . . . 93 C2
Page Rd SG13 . . . 114 A6
Pages Cl CM23 . . . 76 D5
Pages Croft HP4 . . . 122 A6
Paget Cotts SG12 . . . 71 F7
Paignton Cl LU2 . . . 45 D4
Paine's La HA5 . . . 175 D8
Paines Orch LU7 . . . 80 A8
PAINTER'S GREEN . . . 69 D8
Paisley Cl LU4 . . . 44 D3
Palace Cl WD4 . . . 139 A1
Palace Gdns
Bishop's Stortford CM23 . . . 76 E5
Royston SG8 . . . 7 C6
Palfrey Cl AL3 . . . 127 D5
Pallas Rd HP2 . . . 124 D5
Pallett Ct EN11 . . . 135 B4
Palmer Ave SG14 . . . 113 C8
Palmer Cl SG12 . . . 92 E4
Palmer Gdns EN5 . . . 171 C5
Palmer Rd SG14 . . . 113 D8
Palmers 8 CM23 . . . 76 E5
Palmers Gr EN9 . . . 135 F1
Palmers Rd WD6 . . . 170 B8
Palmerston Cl AL8 . . . 110 C6
Palmerston Ct EN8 . . . 148 E1
Palmerston Dr 7 AL4 . . . 87 D1
Palmers Way SG5 . . . 11 C2
Palmers Way EN8. . . 148 E8
Pamela Ave HP3 . . . 138 F8
Pamela Gdns CM23 . . . 76 D3
Pams La SG12 . . . 66 D1
Pancake La HP2 . . . 125 D2
Pankhurst Cres SG2 . . . 51 C5
Pankhurst Pl WD24 . . . 167 C6
Pankridge WD19 . . . 175 D8
PANSHANGER . . . 111 D7
Panshanger Aerodrome AL7. . . 111 D7
Panshanger Dr AL7 . . . 111 C6
Panshanger Prim Sch AL7 . . . 111 A7
Pantiles The WD23 . . . 168 D1
Panxworth Rd 1 HP3 . . . 124 D1
Paper Mill La SG11 . . . 55 E1
Parade
Hatfield AL10 . . . 130 C7
Letchworth Garden City SG6 . . . 11 F1
Parade The LU2 . . . 45 E6
Parade The
South Oxhey WD19 . . . 175 D7
South Oxhey WD19 . . . 175 E7
Watford WD17. . . 167 B6
PARADISE . . . 124 C1
Paradise HP2 . . . 124 D2
Paradise Cl EN7 . . . 148 B3
Paradise Ind Est HP2 . . . 124 D2
Paradise Rd EN9 . . . 163 C5

Paradise Wildlife Pk* EN10. . . 133 F2
Paramount Ind Est WD24. . . 154 C1
Par Cl SG13 . . . 114 B7
Parish Cl WD25. . . 154 C5
Parishes Mead SG2. . . 51 D4
Park Ave
Bishop's Stortford CM23 . . . 76 F3
Luton LU1 . . . 44 C7
Potters Bar EN6 . . . 159 D6
Radlett WD7 . . . 156 B6
Rickmansworth WD3 . . . 165 A5
St Albans AL1 . . . 128 A4
Watford WD23. . . 167 E7
Watford, West Watford WD18 . . . 167 A5
Park Ave N AL5. . . 85 F1
Park Avenue Maisonettes WD23. . . 167 F7
Park Avenue Trad Est LU3. . . 44 C7
Park Ave S AL5. . . 85 F1
Park Cl
Baldock SG7 . . . 23 F7
Brookmans Park AL9 . . . 145 A5
Harrow HA3. . . 176 E2
Hatfield AL9. . . 130 C6
Hitchin SG5 . . . 34 E6
Markyate AL3 . . . 83 D5
Rickmansworth WD3 . . . 174 B6
Stevenage SG2 . . . 51 B1
Watford WD17. . . 167 D6
Park Cnr AL4 . . . 143 B8
Park Cres
Baldock SG7 . . . 23 E7
Borehamwood WD6 . . . 169 F6
Harrow HA3. . . 176 E2
Park Dr
Baldock SG7 . . . 23 E7
Potters Bar EN6 . . . 159 B8
Harlow CM20. . . 117 D2
Stanmore HA3. . . 176 E4
Parker Ave SG14 . . . 113 D8
Parker Cl SG6. . . 22 E4
Parker's Field SG2. . . 51 C4
PARKER'S GREEN . . . 53 B7
Parkers La SG2 . . . 3 D5
Parker St WD24 . . . 167 B8
Park Farm Cl SG16 . . . 10 D8
Park Farm Ind Est
Buntingford SG9 . . . 40 D8
Nuthampstead SG8 . . . 18 C2
Park Farm La SG8 . . . 18 C2
Parkfield
Chorleywood WD3 . . . 164 F5
Letchworth Garden City SG6. . . 23 D4
Markyate AL3 . . . 83 D5
Parkfield Ave HA4 . . . 176 C1
Parkfield Cres
Harrow HA4 . . . 176 C1
Kimpton SG4 . . . 66 D1
Parkfield Ho HA2 . . . 176 B2
Parkfields AL8. . . 110 D6
Parkfield View EN6 . . . 159 B7
Park Gate SG4. . . 34 F6
Parkgate Inf Sch WD24. . . 154 C2
Parkgate Jun Sch WD24. . . 154 C2
Parkgate Rd WD24. . . 154 C2
Park Gdns SG7 . . . 23 E7
Park Hill
Harlow CM17. . . 118 B4
Harpenden AL5 . . . 85 F2
Park Hill Rd HP1 . . . 124 B3
Park Ho
Berkhamsted HP4 . . . 122 B5
Watford WD18 . . . 166 F3
Welwyn Garden City AL8 . . . 110 D7
Park Homes AL2 . . . 142 C6
Parkhurst Rd SG14 . . . 113 C7
Park Ind Est AL2. . . 141 E4
Parkins Cl SG11 . . . 73 A6
Parkinson Cl AL4 . . . 108 D8
Park La
Bishop's Stortford CM23 . . . 76 F4
Cheshunt EN7 . . . 162 D6
Colney Heath AL4 . . . 129 C1
Hammond Street EN7 . . . 148 A4
Harefield UB9. . . 173 B2
Harlow CM20 . . . 117 D2
Hemel Hempstead HP2 . . . 124 D2
Hoddesdon EN10 . . . 134 F3
Kimpton SG4 . . . 66 C1
Old Hammond Street SG3 . . . 68 D5
Standon SG11 . . . 55 D3
Waltham Abbey EN9 . . . 163 D7
Park Lane Paradise EN7 . . . 148 A6

Park Lo
6 Harpenden AL5 . . . 86 A1
Watford WD25 . . . 154 D5
Park Mans HA6 . . . 174 C7
Park Mdw AL9 . . . 130 C6
Parkmead 6 LU1 . . . 63 F6
Park Mead CM20 . . . 117 B1
Park Mews AL9 . . . 130 C6
Park Mount AL5 . . . 85 F3
Park Nook Gdns EN2 . . . 161 D2
Park Pl
Park Street AL2 . . . 141 D4
Stevenage SG1 . . . 50 D5
Park Place Chambers SG1 . . . 50 D5
Park Rd
Barnet EN5 . . . 171 F5
Bushey WD23 . . . 168 A3
Cheshunt EN8 . . . 162 D6
Enfield EN3 . . . 162 E3
Hemel Hempstead HP1 . . . 124 C1
Hertford SG13 . . . 113 E6
Hoddesdon EN11 . . . 135 A6
Northaw EN6 . . . 146 A1
Radlett WD7 . . . 156 A4
Rickmansworth WD3 . . . 165 E2
Stansted Mountfitchet CM24 . . . 59 E6
Tring HP23 . . . 100 A3
Ware SG12 . . . 93 B2
Watford WD17. . . 167 B8
Park Rise
Berkhamsted HP4 . . . 121 E6
Harpenden AL5 . . . 85 E3
Harrow HA3 . . . 176 E2
Park Rise Cl AL5 . . . 85 E3
Park St W LU1 . . . 63 E7
Parkside
Cheshunt EN8 . . . 162 D7
Cheshunt, Waltham Cross EN8 . . . 162 E5
Potters Bar EN6 . . . 159 C7
Watford WD19 . . . 167 C3
Welwyn AL6 . . . 89 C5
Wyddial SG9 . . . 27 D2
Parkside Bsns Ctr EN11 . . . 135 C8
Parkside Com Prim Sch WD6 . . . 156 F1
Parkside Ct EN7 . . . 148 B3
Parkside Dr WD7 . . . 166 F7
Parkside Rd HA6 . . . 174 F5
Park Sq LU1 . . . 63 E7
Park St
Baldock SG7 . . . 23 E8
Berkhamsted HP4 . . . 122 B5
Hatfield AL9. . . 130 C6
Hitchin SG4 . . . 34 E6
Luton LU1 . . . 63 F6
Park Street AL2 . . . 141 D5
Tring HP23 . . . 100 A3
PARK STREET . . . 141 D5
Park Street CE Prim Sch AL2. . . 141 D4
Park Street La AL2 . . . 141 C3
Park Street Sta AL2 . . . 141 D5
Park Terr
Enfield EN3 . . . 162 E1
2 Luton LU1 . . . 63 F6
Much Hadham SG10 . . . 74 F3
Park The
Redbourn AL3 . . . 106 B5
St Albans AL3 . . . 128 A5
PARK TOWN . . . 63 F6
Park Viaduct LU1 . . . 63 F6
Park View
22 Bishop's Stortford CM23 . . . 76 F7
Great Hormead SG9 . . . 42 A7
Hatfield AL9 . . . 130 C7
Hemel Hempstead HP1 . . . 124 B5
Hoddesdon EN11 . . . 135 A5
Pinner HA5 . . . 175 F2
Potters Bar EN6 . . . 159 C6
Stevenage SG2 . . . 51 B1
Park View Cl
Luton LU1 . . . 44 D6
St Albans AL1 . . . 128 A2
Park View Cotts CM23 . . . 76 F3
Parkview Ct HA3 . . . 176 E3
Park View Ct HP4 . . . 122 B4
Park View Dr AL3 . . . 83 D6
Parkview Ho WD19 . . . 167 D3
Park View Rd
Berkhamsted HP4 . . . 122 B4
Pinner HA5 . . . 175 B3
Parkway
Sawbridgeworth CM21 . . . 97 F1
St Albans AL3 . . . 127 F2
Stevenage SG2 . . . 51 A1
Welwyn Garden City AL8 . . . 110 A6
Park Way
Hitchin SG4 . . . 34 E6
Rickmansworth WD3 . . . 165 C1
Parkway Cl AL8 . . . 110 C6
Parkway Cl AL1 . . . 142 B8
Parkway Gdns AL8 . . . 110 D5
Parkway Rd LU1 . . . 64 B5
Parkwood Cl EN10 . . . 134 F4
Parkwood Dr HP1 . . . 123 F3
Parliament Sq SG14 . . . 113 D6
Parmiter's Sch WD25 . . . 154 C8
Parndon Mill La CM20 . . . 117 B3

Parnell Cl WD5............139 F1
Parnel Rd SG12.............93 F2
Parr Cres HP2.............125 B8
Parrotts Cl WD3..........166 A4
Parrotts Field EN11......135 B7
Parrott's La HP23........120 A4
Parsonage Ct
  Abbots Langley WD5.....139 E1
  Tring HP23.............100 A4
Parsonage Ct
  Borehamwood WD6.......170 C4
  Tring HP23.............100 C4
Parsonage Farm
  Rickmansworth WD3......165 C2
  Wingrave HP22..........60 B3
Parsonage Farm Trad Est
  CM24....................59 F3
Parsonage La
  Albury SG11.............57 A6
  Bishop's Stortford CM23..77 C8
  King's Walden SG4......48 A5
  Stansted Mountfitchet
    CM24..................59 F4
  Welham Green AL9......144 B8
Parsonage Pl HP23.......100 A3
Parsonage Rd
  Rickmansworth WD3......165 D2
  Welham Green AL9......144 B8
Parson's Cl AL3.........84 B1
Parsons Ct 12 WD6......170 A5
Parsons Green Est
  SG1....................37 C2
Parthia Cl SG8...........7 E6
Partridge Cl
  Barnet EN5............171 C3
  Bushey WD23...........168 C1
  Luton LU4.............44 A5
Partridge Hill SG7.......4 C3
Partridge Rd AL3........127 D7
Partridges The HP3.....125 A1
Parva Cl AL5...........107 D6
Parvills SG9...........163 D7
Parys Rd LU3...........45 B6
Pascal Way SG6.........23 B8
Pasfield SG6...........163 D6
Passfield Cotts SG11....72 F1
Passingham Ave SG4......35 A6
Paston Rd HP2..........124 E5
Pasture Cl WD23........168 C2
Pasture La SG4.........65 E8
Pasture Rd SG6.........22 E3
Pastures LU4...........44 A3
Pastures The
  Chiswell Green AL2....141 A7
  Hatfield AL10.........130 B4
  Hemel Hempstead HP1...123 E4
  Stevenage SG2.........51 D8
  Totteridge N20........171 F1
  Ware SG12.............93 C3
  Watford WD19..........167 C2
  Welwyn Garden City
    AL7.................111 B4
Pastures Way LU4.......44 A4
PATCHETTS GREEN........168 D8
Paternoster Ct EN9....163 F6
Paternoster Hill EN9..163 F7
Pathway The
  Radlett WD7...........155 F3
  Watford WD19..........167 D1
PATIENT END............42 F3
Pat Larner Ho 9 AL1...127 D2
Patmore Cl CM23........76 C8
Patmore Heath (Nature
  Reserve)* SG11........57 D8
Patmore Link Rd HP2....125 C2
Patmore Rd EN9........163 E5
Patricia Gdns CM23.....76 E5
Patrick Gr EN9........163 B6
Paul Cl EN7...........147 C6
Paul's Gn EN8.........162 E6
Pauls La EN11.........135 A6
Paxton Dr SG5..........11 C2
Paxton Rd
  Berkhamsted HP4.......122 D4
  St Albans AL1.........127 E2
Payne End SG9..........15 B1
Paynes Cl SG6..........12 A1
Paynes Field Cl HP4...121 D7
Paynesfield Rd WD23...168 F2
Paynes La EN9.........149 C7
Payne's Pk SG5.........34 A7
Peabody Cl EN3.........163 A2
Peace Cl EN7..........148 B2
Peace Dr WD17.........167 A6
Peace Gr AL6..........90 A7
Peace Mews LU4........44 B2
Peace Prospect
  WD17.................167 A6
Peach Ct LU1..........63 F6
Peacocks Cl HP4.......121 F6
Peacock Wlk WD5.......154 A8
Peakes La EN7.........147 F4
Peakes Pl AL1.........127 F3
Peakes Way EN7........147 F4
Pea La HP4............121 D7
Pearces Wlk 4 AL1.....127 D2
Pearl Ct
  Baldock SG7...........12 F1
  16 Hoddesdon EN11...135 A6
Pearman Dr SG12........71 E7
Pearsall Cl SG6.........23 B5
Pearson Ave SG13.......113 C4
Pearsons Cl SG13.......113 C4
PEARTREE..............110 F5

Peartree Cl
  Hemel Hempstead
    HP1.................124 A4
  Welwyn Garden City
    AL7.................110 E6
Pear Tree Cl SG6.......10 B3
Peartree Ct
  Watford WD24..........154 D3
  Welwyn Garden City
    AL7.................110 E5
Pear Tree Dell SG6.....23 B3
Peartree Farm AL7......110 E6
Peartree La AL7........110 E6
Peartree Prim Sch
  AL7..................110 E6
Peartree Rd
  Hemel Hempstead
    HP1.................124 A4
  Luton LU2.............46 C4
Peartree Spring Inf Sch
  SG2...................51 B3
Peartree Spring Jun Sch
  SG2...................51 B3
Peartree Way SG2.......51 A3
Pear Tree Wlk EN7.....147 E5
Peascroft Rd HP3......125 B1
Peascroft SG9..........39 C7
Peasleys Yd CM23.......77 B7
Peasmead SG9..........40 E6
Pebbles The SG7........12 C4
Peck's Hill EN9.......135 E2
Peckworth Ind Est
  SG16.................10 A4
Pedlars La SG8.........15 E7
Pedley Hill HP4, LU6...82 C1
Peel Cres SG14........113 C8
Peel Pl 6 LU1..........63 D7
Peel St LU1............63 D7
Peerglow Ctr SG12.....114 E8
Peerglow Ind Est
  WD18.................166 B1
Pegasus Cl WD5........153 F7
Pegasus Ho EN6........162 D8
Pegasus Pl AL3........127 D5
Pegmire La WD23.......168 C8
Pegrum Dr AL2.........142 B5
PEGSDON...............19 D1
Pegsdon Cl LU3........45 B7
Pegsdon Way SG5.......19 E1
Pegs La SG12...........95 D5
Peg's La SG13.........113 D5
Peitley Cotts AL3......84 A1
Pelham Ct
  Hemel Hempstead
    HP2.................125 C3
  Welwyn Garden City
    AL7.................111 C3
Pelham La WD25........155 B3
Pelham Rd SG11.........55 F7
Pelhams The WD25......154 D4
Pelican Way SG6........11 F1
Pemberton Almshouses 6
  AL3..................127 D4
Pemberton Cl AL1......141 D8
Pembridge Chase
  HP3..................137 A3
Pembridge Cl HP3......136 F3
Pembridge La EN10.....133 E2
Pembridge Rd HP3......137 A3
Pembroke Ave
  Enfield EN1...........162 B1
  Luton LU4.............44 F3
Pembroke Cl EN10......148 E8
Pembroke Dr EN7.......147 B2
Pembroke Ho 8
  WD6..................170 A5
Pembroke Rd
  Baldock SG7...........23 F8
  Moor Park HA6........174 C7
Pemsel Ct HP3.........124 E7
Penda Cl LU3...........44 F7
Pendennis Cl AL5......107 C3
Penfold Cl SG2.........24 A7
Penfold Trad Est
  WD24.................167 C8
Pengelly Ct EN7.......148 B1
Pengelly Ct 8 HA3.....176 E1
Penhill LU3............44 E6
Penhill Cl LU3........44 E6
Penman Cl AL2.........141 A4
Pennard Ho 3 WD19....175 D7
Penn Cl WD3...........164 D3
Penne Cl WD7..........156 A5
Penn Ho
  Moor Park HA6........174 C7
  11 South Oxhey WD19..175 C7
Pennine Ave LU3.......44 D8
Pennine Way HP2.......125 A2
Pennington La CM24....59 D8
Penningtons CM23......76 C5
Penn Pl 3 WD3.........165 D2
Penn Rd
  Chiswell Green AL2...141 C4
  Rickmansworth WD3....165 A1
  Stevenage SG1........50 E4
Penns The SG8.........17 E6
Penn Way
  Chorleywood WD3......164 D3
  Letchworth Garden City
    SG6.................23 B3
Penny Croft AL5.......107 A4
Penny Ct WD17.........167 B7
Pennyfather Cl SG3....69 E2
Pennyfathers La AL6...90 B4
Pennymead CM20........118 A1
Penray EN5............171 C6
Penrose Ave WD19.....175 E8
Penrose Cl HP2........124 E7

Pear Tree Ct SG6......10 B3

Penscroft Gdns WD6....170 D5
Penshurst CM17........118 C3
Penshurst Rd EN6......159 D7
Penta Ct WD6..........170 A5
Pentagon HP2..........124 F6
Pentland Rd WD3......168 C3
Pentland Rise SG1.....37 C3
Pentley Cl AL8........89 D1
Pentley Pk AL8........89 D1
Penton Dr EN8.........148 D2
Pentrich Ave EN1......162 A1
Penzance Cl UB9.......173 D1
Peplins Cl AL9........144 E5
Peplins Way AL9......144 E5
Peppard Cl AL3........105 A6
Peppercorn Wlk SG4....35 B7
Pepper Ct SG7.........23 F8
Pepper Hall SG12.....114 F4
Peppermint Rd SG5.....34 F7
PEPPERSTOCK..........63 C1
Peppett's Gn HP5......120 D1
Pepsal End SG2........69 B8
Pepsal End Rd LU1.....64 B7
Pepys Cres AL5........171 C4
Pepys Ct 4 EN11......135 D8
Pepys Way SG2.........23 E8
Percheron Dr LU4......44 A3
Percheron Rd WD6.....170 D3
Percival Ct EN8.......148 E1
Percival Way LU2......64 C7
Percy Rd WD18........167 B5
Peregrine Cl
  Bishop's Stortford
    CM23...............76 D6
  Watford WD25........154 C5
Peregrine Rd LU4.....44 A4
Perham Way AL2.......142 D6
Perivale Gdns WD25...154 B5
Periwinkle Cl SG6.....17 C5
Periwinkle La SG5.....21 F1
Permain Cl WD7.......156 E6
Perowne Way SG11......55 E3
Perram Cl EN10.......148 E5
Perrett Gdns SG14.....112 E7
Perriors Cl EN7.......148 A4
Perrott Ct AL4........128 A8
Perry Dr SG8...........7 E7
Perry Gn HP2..........105 A1
PERRY GREEN
  Much Hadham...........96 B8
  Peters Green.........65 C3
Perry Hill EN9........149 F8
Perrymead LU2.........46 F2
Perry Mead WD23......168 C3
Perrysfield Rd EN8....148 E5
Perrywood AL10.......148 C6
Pescot Hall HP1......124 B5
Petard Cl LU4.........44 A2
Peterborough Ho 9
  WD6.................170 A7
Peterlee Ct 2 HP2....124 F7
Peters Ave AL2........142 C5
Petersfield AL3......127 C7
PETERS GREEN.........65 C2
Peterslea WD4........139 B2
Peter's Pl AL7.......121 E6
Peters Way SG3........68 F6
Peters Wood Hill
  SG12................114 E7
Pettys Ct EN8........148 D3
Petunia Ct LU3........45 C1
Petworth Cl SG2......69 C7
Pevensey Cl LU2.......46 D4
Pewterers Ave CM23...76 C4
Pheasant Cl
  Berkhamsted HP4......122 C3
  Tring HP23..........100 B6
Pheasants La EN2.....161 C1
Philipshill Wood (Nature
  Reserve)* WD3.......164 A2
Phillimore Cl WD7....155 E3
Phillimore Rd WD7....155 E3
Phillipers WD25.....154 E4
Phillips Ave SG8......7 E8
Phipps Hatch La EN2...161 C1
Phoebe Rd 8 HP2......124 F6
Phoenix Cl HA6.......174 F6
Phoenix Ct EN3.......162 C1
Phoenix Ho 4 AL1.....128 B2
Phyllis Courtnage Ho 4
  HP2.................124 D5
Picardy Ho EN2.......161 C1
PICCOTTS END.........124 C7
Piccotts End La HP2...124 D7
Piccotts End Rd HP1...124 C7
Pickets Cl WD23......168 E1
Picketts AL8..........89 D1
Pickford Hill AL5.....86 D4
Pickford Rd
  Markyate AL3.........83 D5
  St Albans AL1.......128 B2
Pick Hill EN9........163 F7
Picknage Cnr SG8......9 A2
Picknage Rd SG8......9 A2
Pie Cnr AL3...........84 C1
Pie Gdn AL3...........84 C2
Pieman Spring HP1....124 B5
Pietley Hill AL3......84 A1
Pigeonwick AL5........86 B3
Piggottshill La AL5...107 D8
Piggotts La LU4.......44 D4
Piggotts Way CM23....76 E5
Piggy La WD3........164 B3

Pightle Cl SG8.........7 D7
Pightle The LU7.......80 D3
Pig La CM22...........77 A3
Pike End SG1..........50 D6
Pikes Cotts EN5......171 C5
Pikes Leap 6 AL4......87 D1
Pilgrim Cl
  Chiswell Green AL2...141 C4
  Watford WD25........154 D6
Pilgrims Row SG9......40 F3
Pilgrims Way SG1......37 B2
Pilkington Manor 12
  HP4.................122 C4
Piltdown Rd WD19.....175 D6
PIMLICO..............139 E7
Pimlico Ct 2 SG13....113 C5
Pinchfield WD3......172 D5
Pindar Rd EN11.......135 C7
Pine Cl
  Berkhamsted HP4......122 B4
  Cheshunt EN8........148 D3
Pine Crest AL6........89 E8
Pinecroft HP3.........138 F7
Pinecroft Cres EN5...171 E5
Pinecroft Ct HP3.....138 F7
Pine Gr
  Bishop's Stortford
    CM23...............77 B6
  Bricket Wood AL2.....140 F1
  Brookmans Park AL9...145 B6
  Totteridge N20......171 F1
  Watford WD23........167 F8
Pinehill Hospl SG4....35 A7
Pinehill Rd SG4.......35 A7
Pinehurst Cl WD5.....153 E7
Pinelands CM23........58 F1
Pine Ridge AL1.......142 A8
Pineridge Ct 4 EN5...171 D5
Pines Ave SG1.........162 B3
Pines Cl HA6.........174 E4
Pines Hill CM23.......59 D5
Pines The
  Borehamwood WD6.....169 F7
  Hemel Hempstead HP3..137 F2
Pine Tree Cl HP2.....124 D4
Pinetree Ct SG1......50 D4
Pinetree Gdns 5
  HP2.................124 E2
Pinetree Ho WD25.....154 E3
Pine Wlk HP4.........121 E7
Pinewood AL7.........110 E4
Pinewood Ho HA5.....176 B4
Pinewood Cl
  Borehamwood WD6.....170 D7
  Pinner HA5..........176 B4
  South Oxhey WD19....175 B5
  St Albans AL4.......128 C3
  Watford WD17........167 A8
Pinewood Dr EN6......158 F8
Pinewood Gdns HP1....124 B3
Pinewood Lo 11
  WD23...............168 D1
Pinewoods 4 SG2......50 F1
Pinewood Sch SG12....114 D7
Pinfold Rd WD23......167 F7
Pinford Dell 4 LU2...46 D1
PIN GREEN............37 C2
Pin Green Ind Est SG1..37 C2
Pinks Farm WD7......157 C8
Pinnacles EN1........163 E5
Pinnate Pl AL7.......110 E4
PINNER...............175 E1
PINNER GREEN.........175 C1
Pinner Hill HA5......175 B3
Pinner Hill Rd HA5...175 C1
Pinner Park Ave HA2...176 C1
Pinner Park Gdns
  HA2.................176 C1
Pinner Rd
  Northwood HA6........175 A1
  Watford WD19........167 E2
Pinner Wood Sch
  HA5.................175 C2
Pinnocks Cl SG7......23 F7
Pinnocks La SG7......23 F8
Pinto Cl WD6........170 D3
Pioneer Way WD18....166 F3
Pipers Ave AL5.......107 D7
Pipers Cl AL3........106 A6
PIPER'S END..........112 B1
Pipers Hill HP1......103 D3
Pipers La
  Caddington AL3, LU1..62 F1
  Wheathampstead AL5...107 F7
Pipit Cl SG8..........7 E8
Pipit Ct EN3.........162 C2
Pippens AL8..........89 E1
Pippin Cl WD7........156 E6
Pippin Gr SG8.........7 C7
Pippins The WD25.....154 C5
PIRTON..............20 E4
Pirton Cl
  Hitchin SG5.........34 C6
  St Albans AL4.......128 C8
Pirton Cross SG5.....34 A7
Pirton Ct HP2........124 F4
Pirton Hill Inf Sch LU4..44 B6
Pirton Hill Jun Sch
  LU4................44 B6
Pirton Rd
  Hitchin SG5.........34 C6
  Holwell SG5.........21 A7
  Luton LU4...........44 D5
Pirton Sch SG5.......20 D4
Pisa Ho 17 WD18......166 E5
Pishiobury Dr CM21...118 D8
Pitsfield AL8.........89 D1

Pitsford Terr LU2.....46 A1
PITSTONE.............80 D4
Pitstone Cl AL4......128 C8
Pitstone Common Forest
  Trails* HP4........101 E7
Pitstone Green Bsns Pk
  LU7................80 D2
Pitstone Green Mus*
  LU7................80 D2
Pitstone Windmill*
  LU7................80 F4
Pitt Cl SG2..........51 B3
Pitt Dr AL4..........142 C8
Pitteway Wlk SG14....113 C6
Pittman's Field CM20..117 F1
Pix Ct SG15..........11 A8
Pixies Hill Cres HP1..123 F2
Pixies Hill Prim Sch
  HP1................123 F2
Pixies Hill Rd HP1....123 F2
Pixmore Ave SG6......23 B6
Pixmore Ind Est SG6...23 A5
Pixmore Jun Sch SG6...23 A5
Pixmore Way SG6......23 A5
Pix Rd
  Letchworth Garden City
    SG6...............23 A6
  Stotfold SG5........11 E5
Place Farm 10 AL4.....87 D1
Plaistow Way AL4......9 E2
Plaiters Cl HP23......100 B4
Plaitford Cl WD3.....173 E8
Plantagenet Pl 4
  EN9................163 B6
Plantation Rd LU3....44 D7
Plantation Wlk HP4...124 A6
Plash Dr SG1.........50 E5
Plashes Cl SG11......55 D2
Plashes Dr SG9.......40 F6
Plashets CM22........98 C1
Platt Cl LU4.........44 D4
Plaw Hatch Cl CM23...77 B8
Plaw Hatch Cnr CM23..77 D8
Playford Sq LU4......44 A5
Pleasance The AL4....85 D4
Pleasant Pl WD3......172 E3
Pleasant Rd CM23.....76 E8
Pleasant Rise AL9...130 C8
Plewes Cl LU6........82 E8
Plomer Ave EN11......114 F1
Plotters Ct 7 EN11...135 D8
Plough Cl SG8.........5 B8
Plough Hill EN6......146 E2
Plough La
  Harefield UB9.......173 C4
  King's Walden SG4...48 A3
  Potten End HP4......123 B7
  Sarratt WD3.........151 F6
Ploughmans Cl CM23...76 C5
Ploughmans End AL7...111 C5
Plover Cl HP4.........122 C3
Plover Ct SG13.......162 C3
Plummers La LU2......65 C2
Plumpton Cl LU2......46 D3
Plumpton Rd EN11.....135 C8
Plum Tree Rd SG16....10 B2
Pluto Rise HP2.......124 F5
Plymouth Cl LU2......46 B1
Poets Chase HP1......124 B4
Poets Cl HP1.........124 B4
Poets Ct AL5.........86 B1
Poets Gate
  Goff's Oak EN7.......147 E3
  Widford SG12........95 D4
Polayn Garth AL8......110 C7
Polegate LU2..........46 D2
Polehanger La HP1....123 E5
Poles Hill WD3.......151 E6
Poles La
  Thundridge SG12.....93 C3
  Ware SG12...........93 C3
Poles Pk SG12........93 C6
Police Row SG8.......15 F7
Police Station La
  WD23...............168 B3
Pollard Gdns SG1.....50 F8
Pollards WD3.........172 D5
Pollards Ct EN7......147 C2
Pollards Way
  Lower Stondon SG16...10 A3
  Pirton SG5..........20 D4
Pollicott Cl AL4.....128 C8
Pollywick Rd HP23....100 D1
Polsten Mews EN5.....163 A2
Polzeath Cl LU2......46 C4
Pomeroy Cres WD24....154 B3
Pomeroy Gr LU2.......45 C4
Pomfret Ave LU2......45 F1
Pond Cl
  Harefield UB9.......173 C1
  Luton LU4...........44 B5
  Stevenage SG1.......50 A4
  Tring HP23..........100 A4
Pond Croft
  Hatfield AL10.......129 F5
  Welwyn Garden City
    AL7...............110 E5
Pondcroft Rd SG3.....69 A4
Pond Field AL7.......90 A1
Pondfield Cres AL4...128 B7
Pond Gdns SG4........67 F1
Pond La
  Baldock SG7.........23 E7
  Little Gaddesden HP4..102 E7
  Stansted Mountfitchet
    CM24..............59 D7

Pond Rd HP3 . . . . 139 A6
Pondside SG4 . . . . 36 C4
Pondsmeade AL2 . . . . . . 106 B5
Pondwick Rd AL5 . . . . 85 E2
Pondwicks Cl AL1 . . . . . . 127 C2
Pondwicks Rd LU1 . . . . 63 F7
Ponsbourne St Mary's CE
  Prim Sch SG13 . . . . . . .146 E7
Pooleys La AL9 . . . . .144 C8
Pope Ct HP23 . . . . 99 F3
Pope Paul RC Prim Sch
  EN6 . . . . .158 F6
Popes Cl LU2 . . . . 45 D1
Popes La WD24 . . . . .154 B1
Pope's Rd WD5 . . . . .153 E8
Popes Row SG12 . . . . 93 D3
Popis Gdns SG12 . . . . 93 E2
Poplar Ave
  Hatfield AL10 . . . . .129 C6
  Luton LU3 . . . . 45 C8
Poplar Cl
  High Cross SG11 . . . . 72 F2
  Hitchin SG4 . . . . 35 B6
  Pinner HA5 . . . . .175 D2
  Royston SG8 . . . . 7 E7
Poplar Dr
  Royston SG8 . . . . 7 E7
  Stotfold SG5 . . . . 11 F8
Poplar Rd LU6 . . . . 82 E8
POPLARS 51 D3
Poplars AL7 . . . . .111 B7
Poplars Cl
  Hatfield AL10 . . . . .129 D5
  Luton LU3 . . . . 46 B3
  Watford WD25 . . . . .154 B7
Poplar Shaw EN9 . . . . . . .163 F6
Poplars The
  Arlesey SG15 . . . . 11 A8
  Borehamwood WD6 . . . . .170 A8
  Great Hallingbury CM22 . . 77 F4
  2 Hammond Street
  EN7 . . . . .147 E5
  Harefield UB9 . . . . .173 C2
  Hemel Hempstead HP1 . . .124 B2
  Ickleford SG5 . . . . 21 F5
  St Albans AL1 . . . . .142 B7
Poplar View SG12 . . . . 92 E4
Popple Way SG1 . . . . 50 E6
Poppy Cl
  Hemel Hempstead
  HP1 . . . . .123 D4
  Luton LU3 . . . . 45 D2
Poppy Ct 8 AL5 . . . . 86 A1
Poppyfields AL7 . . . . .111 C5
Poppy Mead SG1 . . . . 50 F4
Poppy Wlk
  Goff's Oak EN7 . . . . .147 D3
  Hatfield AL10 . . . . .129 F8
Porlock Ct LU2 . . . . 46 C1
Porters Cl SG9 . . . . 40 E8
PORTER'S END 87 A7
Porters Hill AL5 . . . . 86 C4
Porter's Mews SG4 . . . . . . 67 F1
Porters Park Dr WD7 . . . .156 E7
Porters Wood AL3 . . . . . .127 F7
Port Hill SG14 . . . . .113 C7
Port La CM22 . . . . 77 B2
Portland Ct 18 EN11 . . . .135 A6
Portland Ct LU4 . . . . 45 A1
Portland Dr
  Cheshunt EN7 . . . . .162 A8
  Enfield EN2 . . . . .161 E1
Portland Hts HA6 . . . . . . .174 F6
Portland Ind Est SG15 . . . 11 A3
Portland Pl
  17 Bishop's Stortford
  CM23 . . . . 76 F7
  Hertford Heath SG13 . . . .114 C4
Portland Rd
  Bishop's Stortford
  CM23 . . . . 76 F7
  Luton LU1 . . . . 45 A1
Portland St AL3 . . . . .127 C4
Portman Cl
  Hitchin SG5 . . . . 21 C2
  St Albans AL4 . . . . .128 C7
Portman Hall HA3 . . . . . .176 D5
Portman Ho AL3 . . . . .127 D6
Portmill La SG5 . . . . 34 F7
Port Vale SG14 . . . . .113 C6
Posthouse La AL6 . . . . 90 A1
Postfield AL7 . . . . .111 C6
Posting Ho HP23 . . . . . . .101 A3
Post Office Cotts
  CM22 . . . . 98 C8
Post Office Rd CM20 . . . . .117 F1
Post Office Row SG4 . . . . . 24 B1
Post Office Wlk 8
  SG14 . . . . .113 C6
Postwood Gn SG13 . . . . . .114 C3
Post Wood Rd SG12 . . . . .114 E7
Potash La HP23 . . . . 79 A5
POTTEN END 123 C2
Potten End CE Fst Sch
  HP4 . . . . .123 B6
Potten End Hill HP23 . . . .123 E8
POTTERS BAR 159 D6
Potters Bar Com Hospl
  EN6 . . . . .159 C5
Potters Bar Mus★ 158 F7
Potters Bar Sta EN6 . . . . .158 F7
POTTERS CROUCH 140 D7
Potterscrouch La AL2,
  AL3 . . . . .140 E7
Potters Ct EN6 . . . . .159 A7
Potters Field AL3 . . . . . . .127 E7
POTTER'S GREEN 89 D7
POTTERSHEATH 89 D7

Pottersheath Rd AL6 . . . . . 68 D1
Potters Heights Cl
  HA5 . . . . .175 B3
Potters La
  Borehamwood WD6 . . . . .170 C8
  Stevenage SG1 . . . . 50 B4
Potters Mews WD6 . . . . . .169 D3
Potter St
  Bishop's Stortford
  CM23 . . . . 76 F7
  Pinner HA5 . . . . .175 B2
Potter Street Hill
  HA5 . . . . .175 B3
Potters Wood Cl SG12 . . . . 72 C6
Pottery Cl LU3 . . . . 44 F7
Potton Rd SG8 . . . . 1 F6
POUCHEN END 123 D2
Pouchen End La HP1 . . . .123 D3
Poultney Cl WD7 . . . . . . .156 F7
Poultney Rd CM24 . . . . . . 59 E8
Pound Ave SG1 . . . . 50 D6
Pound Cl
  Lower Nazeing EN9 . . . . .149 E8
  Sandridge AL4 . . . . .108 C2
Poundfield WD25 . . . . . . .153 F4
Pound Gn SG8 . . . . 1 F5
Pound La
  Heath End HP5 . . . . .121 A1
  Hemel Hempstead HP1 . . .124 A2
Poundwell AL7 . . . . .111 A5
Powdermill La EN9 . . . . . .163 B6
Powdermill Mews 2
  EN9 . . . . .163 B6
Powdermill Way EN9 . . . .163 B6
Power Ct LU1 . . . . 63 F7
Power Dr EN3 . . . . .162 F3
Powis Ct
  Bushey WD23 . . . . .168 D1
  Potters Bar EN6 . . . . . . .159 C5
Powys Ct WD6 . . . . .170 D6
Poynders Hill HP2 . . . . . .125 C3
Poynders Mdw SG4 . . . . . . 88 F8
Poynings Cl AL5 . . . . .107 F8
Poynters Cl LU5 . . . . 44 A2
Prae Cl AL3 . . . . .127 B3
Praetorian Ct AL1 . . . . . .141 C8
Prae Wood Prim Sch
  AL3 . . . . .127 A1
Prebendal Dr LU6 . . . . 63 B2
Precinct The EN10 . . . . . .134 F3
Premier Bsns Pk LU3 . . . . 44 B8
Premier Ct EN3 . . . . .162 D1
Premier Ho SG1 . . . . 50 C5
Premier Pl WD18 . . . . . . .166 F4
Prentice Way LU2 . . . . 64 D7
Prescott Rd EN8 . . . . .148 E4
PRESDALES 114 C7
Presdales Ct SG12 . . . . . .114 D8
Presdales Dr SG12 . . . . . .114 E8
Presdales Sch SG12 . . . . .114 D7
Presentation Ct LU1 . . . . . 63 F6
President Way LU2 . . . . . . 64 D8
Prestatyn Cl SG1 . . . . 50 B8
PRESTON 48 D6
Preston Ct HA6 . . . . .175 A1
Preston Gdns
  Enfield EN3 . . . . .162 E2
  Luton LU2 . . . . 45 F2
Preston Path LU2 . . . . 45 F2
Preston Prim Sch SG4 . . . . 48 D6
Preston Rd
  Preston SG4 . . . . 48 E8
  St Ippolyts SG4 . . . . 34 F1
Prestwick Cl LU2 . . . . 45 E5
Prestwick Dr CM23 . . . . . . 59 B1
Prestwick Rd WD19 . . . . .175 D6
Prestwood 2 WD7 . . . . . .175 E8
Prestwood Rd WD18 . . . . .167 A5
Pretoria Rd WD18 . . . . . .167 A5
Pretty Cnr HA6 . . . . .175 A5
Priestland Gdns HP4 . . . . .122 E6
Priestleys LU1 . . . . 63 D5
Priestly Rd SG2 . . . . 51 B5
Primary Way SG15 . . . . . . 11 A4
Primett Rd SG1 . . . . 50 C7
Primley La CM22 . . . . 98 C1
Primrose Cl
  Arlesey SG15 . . . . 11 A4
  Bishop's Stortford CM23 . . 76 C6
  Hatfield AL10 . . . . .130 B4
  Hemel Hempstead HP1 . . .123 E2
  Luton LU3 . . . . 45 D2
Primrose Cotts WD7 . . . . .156 A4
Primrose Ct SG1 . . . . 50 D7
Primrose Dr SG13 . . . . . . .114 B6
Primrose Gdns
  Bushey WD23 . . . . .168 B2
  Radlett WD7 . . . . .156 A4
Primrose Hill WD4 . . . . . .139 B3
Primrose Hill Rd SG1 . . . . 50 D7
Primrose La
  Arlesey SG15 . . . . 11 A4
  Radlett WD25 . . . . .155 D1
Primrose Path EN7 . . . . . .162 A8
Primrose View 7 F5
Prince Andrew Dr SG5 . . . 12 A6
Prince Andrew's Cl SG8 . . . 7 D5
Prince Charles Ave
  SG5 . . . . 12 A6
Prince Edward St 6
  HP4 . . . . .122 C4
Prince Edward Way
  SG5 . . . . 12 A6
Prince Eugene Pl
  AL1 . . . . .141 C8
Prince Harry Cl SG5 . . . . . 12 A6
Prince Of Wales Cl
  SG15 . . . . 11 A3

Prince of Wales Prim Sch
  EN3 . . . . .162 F2
Prince Pk HP1 . . . . .124 A2
Princes Ave
  Enfield EN3 . . . . .162 E4
  Watford WD18 . . . . .167 A5
Princes Cl HP4 . . . . .122 A6
Princes Ct
  Bishop's Stortford
  CM23 . . . . 76 C7
  Hemel Hempstead HP3 . . .138 B8
Princes Gate CM20 . . . . . .117 E3
Princes Mews SG8 . . . . 7 C6
Princes Pl 18 SG12 . . . . . . 45 D1
Princess Alexandra Hospl
  CM20 . . . . .117 C1
Princess Diana Dr
  AL4 . . . . .128 D2
Princess Helena Coll The
  SG4 . . . . 48 E6
Princess Lo 10 LU1 . . . . . . 63 D7
Princess St LU1 . . . . 63 D7
Princess St SG12 . . . . 93 D2
Prince's St SG5 . . . . 21 C4
Prince St WD17 . . . . .167 C6
Prince Way LU2 . . . . 64 D8
Prince William Cl SG5 . . . . 12 A6
Princip Way 4 WD18 . . . .166 E4
Printers Ct AL1 . . . . .127 D2
Printers Way SG12 . . . . . .118 A5
Priors 9 CM23 . . . . 77 B7
Priors Ct SG13 . . . . .114 B3
Priors Ct CM22 . . . . 98 A2
Priors Hill SG5 . . . . 20 C4
Priors Wood Prim Sch
  SG12 . . . . 94 A3
Priors Wood Rd SG13 . . . .114 C3
Priory Ave CM17 . . . . .118 C5
Priory Cl
  Cheshunt EN10 . . . . .148 E7
  Hoddesdon EN11 . . . . . . .135 A5
  Royston SG8 . . . . 7 E6
  Stanmore HA7 . . . . .176 F1
  Totteridge N20 . . . . .171 C1
Priory Ct
  6 Berkhamsted HP4 . . . .122 C4
  Bishop's Stortford CM23 . . 76 F7
  13 Hertford SG14 . . . . . .113 D6
  Hitchin SG4 . . . . 34 F5
  6 St Albans AL1 . . . . . . .127 E2
Priory Dell SG5 . . . . 50 F5
Priory Dr
  Stanmore HA7 . . . . .176 F1
  Stansted Mountfitchet
  CM24 . . . . 59 E5
Priory End SG4 . . . . 34 F5
Priory Fields 7
  WD17 . . . . .167 A8
Priory Gdns
  Berkhamsted HP4 . . . . . .122 C4
  Luton LU2 . . . . 45 D4
Priory La
  Great Wymondley SG4 . . . 35 F4
  Royston SG8 . . . . 7 D6
Priory Lo WD3 . . . . .165 D2
Priory Orch SG4 . . . . 34 B2
Priory Row SG12 . . . . 95 E4
Priory Sch The SG5 . . . . . . 21 E2
Priory St
  Hertford SG14 . . . . .113 D6
  Ware SG12 . . . . 93 C1
Priory View
  Bushey WD23 . . . . .168 C3
  Little Wymondley SG4 . . . 35 E4
Priory Way SG4 . . . . 34 F5
Priory Wharf 12 SG14 . . .113 D6
Priory Wlk AL1 . . . . .141 E8
Pritchett Cl EN3 . . . . .163 A2
Proctors Way CM23 . . . . . . 77 A4
Proctor Way LU2 . . . . 64 C7
Progress Ho 21 LU2 . . . . . 45 D1
Progression Ctr HP2 . . . . .125 A6
Progress Way LU4 . . . . . . 44 A7
Prospect La AL5 . . . . .107 A4
Prospect Pl AL6 . . . . 89 C5
Prospect Rd
  Cheshunt EN8 . . . . .148 C2
  St Albans AL1 . . . . .127 D1
Protea Way SG4 . . . . 23 B6
Providence Gr SG7 . . . . . . 23 F7
Providence Pl 17
  SG14 . . . . .113 D6
Providence Way SG7 . . . . . 23 F7
Provost Way LU2 . . . . 64 C8
Prowse Ave WD23 . . . . . .176 C8
Pryor Cl WD5 . . . . .153 F7
Pryor Ct SG1 . . . . 50 D7
Pryor Rd SG7 . . . . 23 F6
Pryors Cl CM23 . . . . 77 A6
Pryors Ct SG7 . . . . 12 F1
Pryor Way SG6 . . . . 23 D5
PUCKERIDGE 55 D3
Puddephat's La AL3 . . . . .104 D7
Pudding La
  Barley SG8 . . . . 9 A1
  Hemel Hempstead HP1 . . .124 A5
Puddingstone Dr AL4 . . . .128 C1
PUDDS CROSS 136 E2
Pudgell The SG8 . . . . 9 E2
Pulham Ave EN10 . . . . . . .134 C3
Pullar Meml CE Prim Sch
  SG11 . . . . 72 E2
Puller Rd
  Barnet EN5 . . . . .171 E7

Puller Rd continued
  Hemel Hempstead HP1 . . .124 A2
Pulleys Cl HP1 . . . . .123 F4
Pulleys La HP1 . . . . .123 F4
Pullman Cl AL1 . . . . .127 E1
Pullman Dr SG4 . . . . 35 B7
Pulter's Way SG4 . . . . 35 A6
Pump Hill SG9 . . . . 30 A2
Pump Ho The 12 CM23 . . . 77 A7
Punchard Cres EN3 . . . . . .163 B1
Punch Bowl La AL3 . . . . . .126 B8
Purbeck Rd 3 WD18 . . . . .166 F3
Purbrook Ave WD25 . . . . .154 C3
Purcell Cl
  Burnham Green AL6 . . . . . 90 E6
  Radlett WD6 . . . . .169 D8
Purcell Ct SG1 . . . . 50 C8
Purcell Ct WD23 . . . . .168 A7
Purdom Rd AL7 . . . . .110 E3
Purkiss Rd SG13 . . . . .113 C3
Purley Ctr LU3 . . . . 44 E7
Purlings Rd WD23 . . . . . .168 B4
Pursley Gdns WD6 . . . . . .157 A1
Purway Cl LU3 . . . . 44 E7
PURWELL 35 D8
Purwell La SG4 . . . . 35 D8
Purwell Prim Sch SG4 . . . . 35 D8
Putney Rd EN3 . . . . .162 D3
PUTTENHAM 78 E2
Puttenham Cl WD19 . . . . .175 D8
Puttenham Ct HP23 . . . . . . 78 F2
Putteridge High Sch
  LU2 . . . . 46 C5
Putteridge Inf Sch LU2 . . . 46 C5
Putteridge Jun Sch
  LU2 . . . . 46 C5
Putteridge Rd LU2 . . . . . . 46 B4
Putterills The AL5 . . . . 86 A1
Putters Croft HP2 . . . . . . .124 F4
Puttocks Cl AL9 . . . . .144 C8
Puttocks Dr AL9 . . . . .144 C8
Pye Cnr CM20 . . . . .117 D5
Pye Gdns CM23 . . . . 76 E8
Pyghtle Ct LU2 . . . . 63 A7
Pyghtle The
  Buntingford SG9 . . . . 40 D7
  Luton LU1 . . . . 63 A7
Pyms Cl SG6 . . . . 23 B8
Pynchbek CM23 . . . . 76 E3
Pynchon Paddocks
  CM22 . . . . 98 D7
Pynefield Ho WD3 . . . . . . .164 F2
Pytchley Cl LU2 . . . . 45 E5

Q

Quadrangle The AL8 . . . . .110 C7
Quadrant Pk AL7 . . . . . . .110 F8
Quadrant The
  Letchworth Garden City
  SG6 . . . . 22 F6
  Rickmansworth WD3 . . . .165 E2
  Royston SG8 . . . . 7 D5
  St Albans AL4 . . . . .128 B6
  Stevenage SG1 . . . . 50 D4
Quail Wlk SG8 . . . . 7 E8
Quaker La EN9 . . . . .163 C5
Quaker St SG12 . . . . 93 E3
Quakers La EN6 . . . . .159 B8
Quantock Cl
  Luton LU3 . . . . 45 B8
  St Albans AL4 . . . . .128 C7
  Stevenage SG1 . . . . 37 D3
Quantock Rise LU3 . . . . . . 31 B1
Quantocks LU3 . . . . .124 F6
Quarry Ct LU7 . . . . 80 D2
Quarry Rd LU2 . . . . 64 C8
Quartermass Cl HP1 . . . . .124 A4
Quartermass Rd HP1 . . . .124 A4
Queen Anne's Cl SG5 . . . .11 F5
Queen Bee Ct AL10 . . . . . .129 D7
Queen Elizabeth Ct
  Barnet EN5 . . . . .171 E5
  4 Cheshunt EN10 . . . . . .148 E7
  Waltham Abbey EN9 . . . .163 C3
Queen Elizabeth II Hospl
  AL7 . . . . .111 A2
Queen Elizabeth's Girls
  Sch EN5 . . . . .171 F6
Queen Elizabeth's Sch
  EN5 . . . . .171 D6
Queen Hoo La AL6 . . . . . . 90 C6
Queen Mary's Ave
  WD18 . . . . .166 E5
Queen Marys Ct EN9 . . . .163 C4
Queens Ave WD18 . . . . . .166 F5
Queens Cl
  4 Cheshunt EN8 . . . . . . .148 D3
  Stansted Mountfitchet
  CM24 . . . . 59 E8
Queen's Cl CM21 . . . . 97 F4
Queens Cres
  Bishop's Stortford
  CM23 . . . . 76 E5
  St Albans AL3 . . . . .128 B6
Queens Ct
  6 Borehamwood
  WD6 . . . . .169 F8
  Cheshunt EN8 . . . . .162 F5
  1 Luton LU2 . . . . 45 D1
  4 Watford WD17 . . . . . .167 C6
Queen's Ct
  Aspenden SG9 . . . . 40 D5
  Hertford SG13 . . . . .113 D5

Pon–Rai 209

Queen's Ct continued
  St Albans AL1 . . . . .128 B3
Queens Dr WD5 . . . . .153 F7
Queen's Dr EN8 . . . . .163 A5
Queen's Dr The WD3 . . . .165 A3
Queensgate EN6 . . . . .162 F5
Queens Gate 7
  WD17 . . . . .167 C6
Queensgate Ctr CM20 . . . .117 F4
Queens Head Wlk
  EN10 . . . . .148 E8
Queen's Pl WD17 . . . . . . .167 C6
Queens Rd
  Barnet EN5 . . . . .171 D6
  Berkhamsted HP4 . . . . . .122 A5
  Royston SG8 . . . . 7 D7
  Ware SG12 . . . . 93 F2
Queen's Rd
  Cheshunt EN8 . . . . .162 E6
  Harpenden AL5 . . . . .107 B7
  Hertford SG13 . . . . .113 D5
  Watford WD17 . . . . .167 C6
Queens Road Est EN5 . . . .171 D6
Queens' Sch WD23 . . . . . .168 A6
Queens Silver Ct HA6 . . . .174 E2
Queen's Sq The HP2 . . . . .124 F4
Queen St
  Chipperfield WD4 . . . . . .152 A7
  Hitchin SG4, SG5 . . . . . . 34 F7
  Pitstone LU7 . . . . 80 D4
  St Albans AL3 . . . . .127 C3
  Stotfold SG5 . . . . 12 A6
  Tring HP23 . . . . .100 A3
Queens Terr HA3 . . . . . . .176 E1
Queensway
  Hatfield AL10 . . . . .130 B6
  Hemel Hempstead HP1,
  HP2 . . . . .124 E4
  Royston SG8 . . . . 7 D7
  Stevenage SG1 . . . . 50 D5
Queens Way
  Cheshunt EN8 . . . . .162 F5
  Shenley WD7 . . . . .156 E7
Queensway Ho 1
  AL10 . . . . .130 A6
Queenswood Cres
  WD25 . . . . .154 A6
Queenswood Dr SG4 . . . . . 22 C1
Queenswood Sch
  AL9 . . . . .145 D3
Queen Victoria Meml
  Hospl AL6 . . . . 89 B4
Quendell Wlk HP2 . . . . . .124 E3
Quendon Dr EN9 . . . . .163 D6
Quickbeams AL7 . . . . 90 A1
Quickley La WD3 . . . . .164 C4
Quickley Rise WD3 . . . . . .164 C3
Quickly Brow WD3 . . . . . .164 B3
Quickmoor La WD4 . . . . . .152 C6
Quickswood LU3 . . . . 45 A7
Quickwood Cl WD3 . . . . . .165 A6
Quills SG6 . . . . 23 D4
Quilter Cl LU3 . . . . 44 F4
Quinces Croft HP1 . . . . . .124 A5
Quincey Rd SG12 . . . . 93 C4
Quin Cl SG11 . . . . 55 F7
Quinn Way SG6 . . . . 23 C5
Quinta Dr EN5 . . . . .171 C4

R

Raans Rd HP6 . . . . .150 A1
Raban Cl SG2 . . . . 51 C1
Raban Ct SG7 . . . . 12 F1
Rabia Boys Sch LU4 . . . . . 45 B1
Rabia Girls Sch LU4 . . . . . 45 A1
RABLEYHEATH 68 D3
Rabley Heath Rd AL6 . . . . 68 B2
Rackham Dr LU3 . . . . 45 C5
Radburn Cre SG6 . . . . 23 C5
Radburn Prim Sch
  SG6 . . . . 23 C5
Radburn Way SG6 . . . . . . 23 C4
Radcliffe Rd SG5 . . . . 35 A8
RADLETT 156 C5
Radlett La WD7 . . . . .156 E6
Radlett Lodge Sch
  WD7 . . . . .156 B8
Radlett Park Rd WD7 . . . .156 A4
Radlett Prep Sch
  WD7 . . . . .156 C1
Radlett Rd
  London Colney AL2 . . . . .141 E4
  Watford WD24 . . . . .167 D7
Radlett Sta WD7 . . . . .156 A4
Radnor Ct HA3 . . . . .176 F2
Radstone Pl LU2 . . . . 46 F1
RADWELL 12 C4
Radwell Cotts SG7 . . . . . . 12 C5
Radwell La SG7 . . . . 12 C4
Raebarn Gdns EN5 . . . . . .171 B4
Raffin Cl SG3 . . . . 69 E3
Raffin Green La SG3 . . . . . 69 F4
Raffin Pk SG3 . . . . 69 E3
Ragged Hall La AL2 . . . . .140 E7
Raglan Ave EN7 . . . . .162 D5
Raglan Gdns WD19 . . . . . .167 B1
Raglan Ho HP4 . . . . .122 A4
Rags La EN7 . . . . .147 E4
Railway Cotts HP23 . . . . .100 F5
Railway Pl SG13 . . . . .113 D6
Railway Rd EN8 . . . . .162 F6
Railway St SG13, SG14 . . .113 D6
Railway Terr WD4 . . . . . . .139 A4

Railway The SG16 . . . . .10 B3
Rainbow Cl AL3 . . . . .105 F6
Rainbow Ct WD19 . . . . . . .167 C3
Rainer Cl EN8 . . . . .148 D2
Rainsborough Ct
  SG13 . . . . .114 A7
Rainsford Rd CM24 . . . . . . .59 E8
Raleigh Cres SG2 . . . . .51 B8
Raleigh Gr LU4 . . . . .44 D1
Rally The SG15 . . . . .11 A7
Ralph Sadleir Mid Sch
  SG11 . . . . .55 E3
Ralph Swingler Pl SG6 . . .23 A4
Ralston Way WD19 . . . . . .175 D8
Ramblers La CM17 . . . . .118 D1
Ramblers Way AL7 . . . . . . .111 C5
Rambling Way HP4 . . . . . .123 C6
Ramerick Gdns SG15 . . . . .11 A2
Ram Gorse CM20 . . . . .117 B2
Ramney Dr EN3 . . . . .162 E2
Ramney Ho EN8 . . . . .163 A5
Ramparts The AL3 . . . . . . .127 B2
Ramridge Prim Sch
  LU2 . . . . .46 B2
Ramridge Rd LU2 . . . . .46 A2
Ramryge Ct AL1 . . . . .127 D1
Ramsay Cl EN10 . . . . .134 E2
Ramsbury Rd AL1 . . . . . . .127 E2
Ramsdell SG1 . . . . .50 F5
Ramsey Cl
  Brookmans Park AL9 . . . .145 D4
  St Albans AL1 . . . . .128 A1
Ramsey Lodge Ct
  AL1 . . . . .127 E4
Ramson Rise HP1 . . . . . . .123 E2
Ram Yard (Ind Est)
  SG15 . . . . .11 A4
Randalls Ride HP2 . . . . . .124 E5
Randalls Wlk AL1 . . . . . . .140 F1
Randals Hill SG2 . . . . .51 C3
Randolph Ct HA5 . . . . .176 A3
Randon Cl HA2 . . . . .176 B1
Rand's Cl SG5 . . . . .21 B7
Rand's Cotts SG5 . . . . .21 B7
Rand's Mdw SG5 . . . . .21 B7
Ranelagh Rd HP2 . . . . . . .125 B3
Ranleigh Wlk AL5 . . . . . . .107 D6
Rannock Cl LU3 . . . . .44 D8
Ranskill Rd WD6 . . . . .170 A8
Ransom Cl
  Hitchin SG4 . . . . .34 F4
  Watford WD19 . . . . .167 C2
Ransom Yd SG5 . . . . . . .34 F7
Rant Mdw
  Hemel Hempstead
    HP3 . . . . .125 A1
  Hemel Hempstead HP3 . .125 A2
Ranulf Cl CM17 . . . . .118 C6
Ranworth Ave
  Hoddesdon EN11 . . . . . . .115 B2
  Stevenage SG2 . . . . .69 C7
Ranworth Cl HP3 . . . . .124 D1
Ranworth Gdns EN6 . . . . .158 D8
Raphael Cl WD7 . . . . .156 E7
Raphael Dr WD24 . . . . . . .167 D7
Rapper Ct LU3 . . . . .63 D8
Rasehill Cl WD3 . . . . .165 D4
Rathlyn HP3 . . . . .139 B8
Ratty's La EN11 . . . . .135 D6
Raveley Cotts WD23 . . . . .168 A3
Ravenbank Rd LU2 . . . . . . .46 C5
Raven Cl WD3 . . . . .165 D2
Raven Ct AL10 . . . . .130 A4
Ravenfield Rd AL7 . . . . . . .110 F6
Ravenhill Way LU4 . . . . . . .44 B4
Ravenscroft
  Harpenden AL5 . . . . .107 D6
  Hoddesdon EN10 . . . . . . .134 F3
  Watford WD25 . . . . .154 E4
Ravenscroft Pk EN5 . . . . .171 D5
Ravenscroft a Tech
  Coll The N20 . . . . .171 F2
Ravens Ct
  Berkhamsted HP4 . . . . . .122 E6
  Long Marston HP23 . . . . . .79 B4
Ravensdell HP1 . . . . .123 F4
Ravens La HP4 . . . . .122 D4
Ravensthorpe LU2 . . . . . . .46 B4
Ravens Wharf HP4 . . . .122 D4
Ravenswood Pk HA6 . . . . .174 A4
Rawdon Dr EN11 . . . . .135 A5
Raybarn Rd HP1 . . . . .124 A5
Raydon Rd EN8 . . . . .162 D7
Rayfield AL8 . . . . .89 D1
Rayleigh Ho WD5 . . . . . . .153 F7
Raymer Cl AL1 . . . . .127 E4
Raymer Ct AL1 . . . . . . .127 E4
Raymond Cl WD5 . . . . . . .153 D7
Raymond Cotts SG5 . . . . . .21 E4
Raymond Ct EN6 . . . . .159 C5
Raymonds Cl AL7 . . . . . . .110 E4
Raymonds Plain AL7 . . . . .110 E4
Raynham Cl CM23 . . . . . . .77 C8
Raynham Rd CM23 . . . . . . .77 B8
Raynham St SG13 . . . . . . .113 E6
Raynham Way LU2 . . . . . . .46 D1
Raynsford Rd SG12 . . . . . . .93 E1
Raynton Rd EN3 . . . . .162 D2
Ray's Hill HP5 . . . . .120 C2
Readings The WD3 . . . . . .164 F6
Recreation Ground
  Stansted Mountfitchet
    CM24 . . . . .59 E6
  Wingrave HP22 . . . . .60 B2

Rectory Cl
  Bishop's Stortford
    CM23 . . . . .76 D3
  Essendon AL9 . . . . .131 F6
  Hunsdonbury SG12 . . . . .116 D8
Rectory Croft SG11 . . . . . . .36 D1
Rectory Dr CM23 . . . . .58 D6
Rectory Gdns AL10 . . . . . .130 B5
Rectory La
  Berkhamsted HP4 . . . . . .122 C4
  Datchworth SG3 . . . . .69 C2
  Farnham CM23 . . . . .58 D6
  Kings Langley WD4 . . . . .139 A3
  Lilley LU2 . . . . .32 E4
  Rickmansworth WD3 . . . .165 D1
  Shenley WD7 . . . . .157 B7
  Stevenage SG1 . . . . .36 D1
  Watton at S SG14 . . . . . . .70 D3
Rectory Rd
  Rickmansworth WD3 . . . .165 D2
  Welwyn Garden City AL8 . .89 B1
Rectory Wood CM20 . . . . .117 C1
Redan Rd SG12 . . . . .93 E3
REDBOURN 106 B6
Redbournbury La
  AL3 . . . . .106 D2
Redbournbury Watermill
  AL3 . . . . .106 D2
Redbourn Ho AL3 . . . . . . .106 A8
Redbourn Ind Est AL3 . . .106 B5
Redbourn Inf Sch
  AL3 . . . . .106 A6
Redbourn Jun Sch
  AL3 . . . . .106 A6
Redbourn La AL3, AL5 . . . .106 E6
Redbourn Rd
  Hemel Hempstead
    HP2 . . . . .125 B8
  St Albans AL3 . . . . .128 E7
Redbourn Village Mus*
  AL3 . . . . .106 A6
Red Brick Cotts SG11 . . . . .57 B1
Red Brick Row CM22 . . . . .98 B8
Redcar Dr SG1 . . . . .50 A6
Redcote End AL5 . . . . .107 A7
Red Cottage HP23 . . . . . . .100 D1
Red Cow Cotts LU6 . . . . . . .83 C8
Redding Ho WD18 . . . . . . .166 E3
Redding La AL5 . . . . .105 F8
Reddings
  Hemel Hempstead
    HP3 . . . . .125 A1
  Welwyn Garden City
    AL8 . . . . .110 C7
Reddings Ave WD23 . . . . .168 B4
Reddings Prim Sch The
  HP3 . . . . .125 A1
Reddings The WD6 . . . . . .169 F6
Redditch Ct HP2 . . . . . .124 E7
Redfern Ct WD18 . . . . .166 D3
Redferns Cl LU1 . . . . .63 A6
Redferns Ct LU1 . . . . .63 A6
Redfield Cl AL3 . . . . .106 A5
Redgrave Gdns LU3 . . . . . . .44 F7
Redhall Cl AL10 . . . . .129 F1
Redhall Dr AL10 . . . . .129 F1
Redhall La
  Colney Heath AL4 . . . . . .129 E1
  Sarratt WD3 . . . . .165 E8
Redheath Cl WD25 . . . . . .153 F4
REDHILL 25 E7
Redhill Rd SG5 . . . . .34 D8
Redhoods Way E SG6 . . . . .22 E7
Redhoods Way W SG6 . . . .22 E6
Red House CM21 . . . . .114 E8
Redhouse The EN10 . . . . . .134 F1
Redlands Rd EN3 . . . . .162 E1
Red Lion CM25 . . . . .155 C2
Red Lion Cotts SG5 . . . . . . .33 D2
Red Lion Ct CM23 . . . . .77 A7
Red Lion La
  Hemel Hempstead
    HP3 . . . . .139 A5
  Sarratt WD3 . . . . .152 A4
Red Lion Yd SG12 . . . . .94 E4
Red Lo WD6 . . . . .169 F6
Red Lodge Gdns HP4 . . . .122 A3
Redmire Cl LU4 . . . . .44 B6
Redoubt Cl SG4 . . . . .22 A1
Redpale Ct WD3 . . . . .165 E1
Red Rails LU1 . . . . .63 C5
Red Rails Ct LU1 . . . . .63 C5
Red Rd WD6 . . . . .169 F6
Redricks La CM21 . . . . . . .118 A4
Redvers Cl CM23 . . . . .59 A2
Redwell Ct EN8 . . . . .162 F5
Redwing Cl SG2 . . . . .51 D4
Redwing Rd SG6 . . . . .154 A8
Redwing Rise SG8 . . . . .7 E8
Redwood Cl WD19 . . . . . .175 D6
Redwood Dr
  Hemel Hempstead
    HP3 . . . . .124 E1
  Luton LU3 . . . . .44 C8
Redwood Rise WD6 . . . . . .157 A2
Redwoods
  Hertford SG14 . . . . .113 C7
  Welwyn Garden City AL8 . .89 D3
Redwoods The CM23 . . . . .76 D8
Redwood Way EN5 . . . . . .171 D4
REED 16 E5
Reed Cl AL2 . . . . .142 E4
REED END 16 C5
Reed Fst Sch SG8 . . . . .16 E5
Reedham Cl AL2 . . . . .141 A2
Reedings Jun Sch
  CM21 . . . . .97 F3
Readings Way CM21 . . . . . .97 F4

Reed Pl AL5 . . . . .85 F3
Reeds Chapel
  SG14 . . . . .167 C7
Reeds Cres WD24 . . . . . . .167 C7
Reedsdale LU2 . . . . .46 F2
Reeds The AL7 . . . . .110 D5
Reeves Ave LU3 . . . . .45 B4
Reeves Pightle SG8 . . . . .9 F3
Regal Cl SG11 . . . . .55 E2
Regal Ct
  Hitchin SG5 . . . . .34 F8
  Tring HP23 . . . . .100 A3
Regal Way WD24 . . . . .154 C1
Regency Cl CM23 . . . . .76 E7
Regency Ct
  Hemel Hempstead
    HP2 . . . . .124 D3
  Hoddesdon EN10 . . . . . . .148 F8
  St Albans AL1 . . . . .128 B3
  Watford WD7 . . . . .167 A8
Regency Ho WD7 . . . . .156 A4
Regent Cl
  Kings Langley WD4 . . . . .139 A3
  St Albans AL4 . . . . .128 C7
  Welwyn Garden City
    AL7 . . . . .110 E5
Regent Ct
  Stotfold SG5 . . . . .11 F7
  Welwyn Garden City
    AL7 . . . . .110 E5
Regent Gate EN8 . . . . .162 E5
Regents Cl WD7 . . . . .156 A5
Regents Ct AL1 . . . . . . .128 B2
Regent's St HA5 . . . . .175 D1
Regent St
  Luton LU1 . . . . .63 E7
  Stotfold SG5 . . . . .11 F7
  Watford WD24 . . . . .154 B1
Regina Cl EN5 . . . . .171 D6
Reginald Mews
  CM17 . . . . .118 C3
Reginald Rd HA6 . . . . .174 F3
Reginald St LU2 . . . . .45 E1
Reiss Ho AL7 . . . . .110 F6
Remus Cl AL1 . . . . .141 D7
Rendlesham Ave
  WD7 . . . . .155 F2
Rendlesham Cl SG12 . . . . . .93 B2
Rendlesham Rd EN2 . . . . .161 B1
Rendlesham Way
  WD3 . . . . .164 C3
Rennie Ct EN3 . . . . . . .163 A1
Rennison Cl EN7 . . . . .147 F4
Renoir Ho WD18 . . . . .166 E5
Renshaw Cl LU2 . . . . .46 E2
Repton Cl LU3 . . . . .44 F6
Repton Gn AL3 . . . . .127 D6
Repton Way WD3 . . . . . . .166 A4
Reson Way HP1 . . . . .124 B2
Reston Ct WD6 . . . . .157 B1
Reston Path
  Borehamwood WD6 . . . . .157 A1
Retford Cl WD6 . . . . .157 A1
Retreat The WD5 . . . . .153 C8
Revels Cl SG14 . . . . .113 D8
Revels Rd SG14 . . . . .113 D8
Rex The HP4 . . . . .122 C4
Reynard Copse CM23 . . . . .58 F1
Reynards Rd AL6 . . . . .89 C7
Reynard's Way AL2 . . . . . .140 F2
Reynard Way SG13 . . . . . .114 B6
Reynolds SG6 . . . . .11 F1
Reynolds Cl HP1 . . . . .124 A4
Reynolds Cres AL4 . . . . . .128 B8
Rhee Spring SG7 . . . . .13 B1
Rhodes Arts Complex &
  Bishop's Stortford Mus*
  CM23 . . . . .77 A6
Rhodes Ave CM23 . . . . .76 F5
Rhodes Way WD24 . . . . . .167 D8
Rhymes HP1 . . . . .124 B5
Ribbledale AL2 . . . . .142 F4
Ribblesdale HP2 . . . . .124 E6
Rib Cl SG11 . . . . .55 E2
Ribocon Way LU4 . . . . .44 B7
Ribston Cl WD7 . . . . .156 D6
Rib Vale SG14 . . . . .92 D1
Rib Way SG9 . . . . .40 E7
Riccat La SG1 . . . . .36 F3
Rice Cl HP2 . . . . .124 F4
Richard Ct EN5 . . . . . .171 E6
Richard Hale Sch
  SG13 . . . . .113 D5
Richards Cl
  Bushey WD23 . . . . .168 D2
  Luton LU1 . . . . .63 B6
Richards Ct LU3 . . . . .63 B5
Richardson Cl AL2 . . . . . . .142 E4
Richardson Cres EN7 . . . . .147 B6
Richardson Pl AL4 . . . . . . .129 B1
Richards St AL10 . . . . .129 F7
Richard Stagg Cl AL1 . . . .128 C1
Richard Whittington Prim
  Sch CM23 . . . . .76 E4
Richfield Rd WD23 . . . . . . .168 C2
Richmond Cl
  Bishop's Stortford
    CM23 . . . . .76 C7
  Borehamwood WD6 . . . . .170 D4
  Cheshunt EN8 . . . . .148 C2
  Ware SG12 . . . . .93 B3
Richmond Ct
  Hatfield AL10 . . . . .130 B3
  Hoddesdon EN10 . . . . . . .134 F3
  Luton LU2 . . . . .45 D3
  Potters Bar EN6 . . . . .159 C8
  St Albans AL1 . . . . .128 A3

Richmond Dr WD17 . . . . . .166 E7
Richmond Gdns HA3 . . . . .176 F3
Richmond Hill AL1 . . . . . . .128 A2
Richmond Hill Sch LU2 . . .45 E2
Richmond Rd EN6 . . . . . . .159 C8
Richmond Way WD3 . . . . .166 C5
Richmond Wlk AL4 . . . . . .128 D7
Rickfield Cl AL10 . . . . .130 A3
RICKMANSWORTH 165 C1
Rickmansworth La
  SL9 . . . . .172 A5
Rickmansworth Park Jun
  Mix Inf Sch WD3 . . . . .165 E2
Rickmansworth PNEU Sch
  WD3 . . . . .165 C3
Rickmansworth Rd
  Chorleywood WD3 . . . . . .164 F6
  Harefield UB9 . . . . .173 D3
  Northwood HA6 . . . . .174 D3
  Pinner HA5 . . . . .175 C1
  Watford WD18 . . . . .166 E5
Rickmansworth Sch
  WD3 . . . . .165 F3
Rickmansworth Sta
  WD3 . . . . .165 D2
Rickyard Cl LU2 . . . . .46 B3
Rickyard Mdw AL3 . . . . . .106 A5
Rickyard The
  Ashwell SG7 . . . . .4 D3
  Letchworth Garden City
    SG6 . . . . .12 C1
Riddell Gdns SG7 . . . . .23 F8
Riddy Hill Cl SG4 . . . . .35 A6
Riddy La
  Hitchin SG4 . . . . .35 A6
  Luton LU3 . . . . .45 C5
Riddy The SG4 . . . . .88 F8
RIDGE 157 F5
Ridge Ave
  Harpenden AL5 . . . . .85 E4
  Letchworth Garden City
    SG6 . . . . .23 A6
Ridge Ct LU2 . . . . .46 A1
Ridgedown AL3 . . . . .106 A5
Ridgefield WD7 . . . . .153 E2
Ridgehurst Ave WD25 . . . .153 F5
Ridge La WD17 . . . . .153 F2
Ridge Lea HP1 . . . . .123 F3
Ridgeleigh Ct EN5 . . . .171 E6
Ridge Rd SG6 . . . . .23 A6
Ridge St WD24 . . . . .154 B1
Ridge The
  Barnet EN5 . . . . .171 F4
  Letchworth Garden City
    SG6 . . . . .23 A6
  Northwood HA6 . . . . .174 F3
Ridge View HP23 . . . . .100 C5
Ridgeview Cl EN5 . . . . . . .171 D3
Ridgeway
  Berkhamsted HP4 . . . . . .121 F4
  Harpenden AL5 . . . . .85 E4
  Kensworth Common LU6 . .82 E8
  Little Hadham SG11 . . . . .57 B1
  London Colney WD7 . . . . .156 C8
  Stevenage SG1 . . . . .50 F5
  Welwyn Garden City
    AL7 . . . . .111 B6
Ridge Way SG2 . . . . .68 D4
Ridgeway Cl HP3 . . . . .138 C5
Ridgeway Ct HA5 . . . . .176 A3
Ridgeway The
  Codicote SG4 . . . . .67 F1
  Cuffley EN6 . . . . .146 A4
  Hadley Wood EN2, EN4 . .160 D3
  Hertford SG14 . . . . .112 F7
  Hitchin SG4 . . . . .34 D6
  Radlett WD7 . . . . .155 F2
  St Albans AL4 . . . . .128 C7
  Ware SG12 . . . . .93 C3
  Watford WD3 . . . . .153 E2
Ridgeway View LU7 . . . . . .80 D4
Ridgewood Dr AL5 . . . . . . .85 E4
Ridgewood Gdns AL5 . . . . .85 E4
Ridgmont Rd AL1 . . . . . . .127 E2
Ridgway Rd LU2 . . . . .42 F1
Ridings The
  Bishop's Stortford
    CM23 . . . . .76 D4
  Hertford SG14 . . . . .113 A5
  Latimer HP5 . . . . .150 D3
  Luton LU3 . . . . .45 C1
  Markyate AL3 . . . . .83 C6
  Stevenage SG2 . . . . .51 B3
Ridler Rd EN1 . . . . .161 E1
Ridlins End SG2 . . . . .51 C2
Rigby Pl EN3 . . . . .163 A2
Rigery La SG11 . . . . .73 A7
Riley Rd EN3 . . . . .162 C1
Ringmer Ct LU2 . . . . .46 C3
RINGSHALL 81 B1
Ringshall Dr HP4 . . . . .102 C8
Ringshall Rd HP4 . . . . .81 B3
Ringtale Pl SG7 . . . . .13 B1
Ringway Rd AL2 . . . . .141 B4
Ringwood Rd LU2 . . . . .45 D7
Ripley Rd
  Enfield EN2 . . . . .161 C1
  Luton LU4 . . . . .44 C1
Ripley Way
  Cheshunt EN7 . . . . .148 B1
  Hemel Hempstead HP1 . .123 E4
Ripon Rd SG1 . . . . .37 A2
Ripon Way
  Borehamwood WD6 . . . . .170 D4
  St Albans AL4 . . . . .128 D7
Rise Cotts SG12 . . . . .95 D2
Risdale Cl HP3 . . . . .138 E8
Risdale Hill HP3 . . . . .138 E8

Risdale Rd HP3 . . . . .138 E8
Rise The
  Baldock SG7 . . . . .23 E7
  Borehamwood WD6 . . . . .169 F4
  Harrow HA3 . . . . .176 C1
  Park Street AL2 . . . . .141 D6
Rising Hill Cl HA6 . . . . . . .174 C4
River Ct
  Ickleford SG5 . . . . .21 F4
  Sacombe SG12 . . . . .92 E4
  Sawbridgeworth CM21 . . .97 F3
Riverfield La CM21 . . . . . . .97 E3
Riverford Cl AL5 . . . . .86 B4
River Gn SG9 . . . . .40 E8
River Hill AL3 . . . . .84 B2
River Lee Ctry Pk*
  EN9 . . . . .149 B1
River Mead SG5 . . . . .21 C2
River Meads SG12 . . . . . . .115 C4
Rivermill CM20 . . . . .117 C2
Rivermill Ct SG8 . . . . .7 F2
River Park Ind Est
  HP4 . . . . .122 A5
River Pk HP1 . . . . .124 A1
River Point EN8 . . . . .162 E7
Riversend Rd HP3 . . . . . . .138 C8
Rivershill SG14 . . . . .70 E3
Riverside
  Bishop's Stortford
    CM23 . . . . .76 F7
  Buntingford SG9 . . . . .40 E7
  Hemel Hempstead HP3 . .138 F6
  Hertford SG14 . . . . .113 D6
  Hoddesdon EN11 . . . . . . .135 C8
  London Colney AL2 . . . . .142 E4
  Welwyn AL6 . . . . .89 B5
Riverside Ave EN10 . . . . . .135 A1
Riverside Bsns Pk
  CM24 . . . . .59 E6
Riverside Cl
  Kings Langley WD4 . . . . .139 B2
  St Albans AL1 . . . . .127 E1
Riverside Club (Tennis
  Ctr) The HA6 . . . . .174 B3
Riverside Ct
  Harlow CM20 . . . . .118 C6
  St Albans AL1 . . . . .127 E1
Riverside Dr WD3 . . . . . . .165 D1
Riverside Est AL5 . . . . .86 C4
Riverside Gdns HP4 . . . . . .122 A5
Riverside Ind Est AL2 . . . .142 E4
Riverside Mews
  Hoddesdon EN10 . . . . . . .148 E8
  Ware SG12 . . . . .93 D1
Riverside Path EN8 . . . . . .148 C2
Riverside Rd
  Luton LU3 . . . . .45 A5
  St Albans AL1 . . . . .127 E2
  Watford WD19 . . . . .167 B3
Riverside Sh Ctr HP2 . . . . .124 C1
Riverside Wlk CM23 . . . . . .76 F7
Riversmead EN11 . . . . .135 A3
Riversmeet SG14 . . . . .113 B5
River St SG12 . . . . .93 E1
River View AL7 . . . . .89 F2
River Way
  Harlow CM20 . . . . .118 B5
  Luton LU3 . . . . .44 E5
Rivett Cl SG7 . . . . .13 A1
Roan Wlk SG8 . . . . .7 E2
Roaring Meg Ret Pk
  SG1 . . . . .50 E3
ROAST GREEN 30 F3
Robbery Bottom La
  AL6 . . . . .90 A8
Robbs Cl HP1 . . . . .124 A5
Robe End HP1 . . . . .123 F5
Robert Allen Ct LU1 . . . .63 E6
Robert Ave AL1 . . . . .141 C7
Robert Cl EN6 . . . . .158 E6
Robert Humbert Ho
  SG6 . . . . .23 A3
Robert Saunders Ct
  SG6 . . . . .22 E4
Roberts Cl EN8 . . . . .148 E1
Roberts Ct SG4 . . . . .66 F7
Roberts La SL9 . . . . .172 B5
Robertson Cl EN10 . . . . . .148 E1
Robertson Rd HP4 . . . .122 D4
Roberts Rd WD18 . . . . . . .167 C4
Roberts Way AL10 . . . . . . .129 F3
Roberts Wood Dr SL9 . . . .172 A5
Robert Tebbutt Ct SG5 . . . .34 E6
Robert Wallace Cl
  CM23 . . . . .58 F1
Robeson Way WD6 . . . . . .170 C8
Robina Cl HA6 . . . . .174 F2
Robin Cl SG12 . . . . .115 C3
Robin Ct AL5 . . . . .86 B4
Robin Hill HP4 . . . . .122 C3
Robin Hood Dr
  Harrow HA3 . . . . .176 F3
  Watford WD25 . . . . .167 F8
Robin Hood La AL10 . . . . .130 A6

Robin Hood Mdw
　HP2 . . . . .124 F8
Robin Jeffrey Ct **17**
　CM23 . . . . .76 F6
Robin Mead AL7 . . . . .90 A1
Robins Cl AL2 . . . . .142 E4
Robinsfield HP1 . . . . .124 A3
Robins Nest Hill
　SG13 . . . . .132 C6
Robinson Ave EN7 . . . . . .147 B3
Robinson Cl CM23 . . . . . . .76 F5
Robinson Cres WD23 . . . .168 C1
Robins Rd HP3 . . . . .125 A1
Robinsway EN9 . . . . .163 E5
Robins Way AL10 . . . . . . .129 F2
Robinwood LU2 . . . . .45 E5
Robin Way EN6 . . . . .146 E3
Robsons Cl EN8 . . . . .148 C2
Rochdale Ct **6** LU1 . . . . . .63 E6
Rochester Ave LU2 . . . . . .46 C4
Rochester Ct **15** EN5 . . .171 F5
Rochester Dr WD25 . . . . .154 C4
Rochester Way
　Croxley Green WD3 . . . . .166 B5
　Royston SG8 . . . . .7 D8
Rochford Ave EN9 . . . . . .163 D5
Rochford Cl
　Cheshunt EN10 . . . . .148 E5
　Stansted Mountfitchet
　CM24 . . . . .59 E5
Rochford Dr LU2 . . . . .46 E2
Rochford Ho EN9 . . . . . . .163 D6
Rochford Rd CM23 . . . . . . .59 C1
Rockfield Ave LU2 . . . . . . .93 D3
Rockingham Cl LU7 . . . . . .80 D3
Rockingham Gate
　WD23 . . . . .168 C3
Rockingham Way SG1 . . . .50 E4
Rockleigh SG1 . . . . .113 C6
Rockley Rd LU1 . . . . .63 A7
Rockliffe Ave WD4 . . . . . .139 A1
Rock Rd SG8 . . . . .7 C8
Rockways SG5 . . . . .170 F3
Rockwell Ct **6** WD18 . . .166 D4
Rodeheath LU4 . . . . .44 D3
Roden Cl CM17 . . . . .119 D4
Rodgers Ct WD6 . . . . . . .169 D3
Rodings Row EN5 . . . . . .171 E5
Rodney Ave AL1 . . . . .128 A1
Rodney Cres EN11 . . . . . .135 A8
Rodwell Yd HP23 . . . . . . .100 A3
Roebuck Cl
　Hertford SG13 . . . . .114 A6
　Luton LU1 . . . . .63 B6
Roebuck Gate SG2 . . . . . .50 F1
Roebuck Prim Sch SG2 . . .50 E2
Roebuck Ret Pk SG1 . . . . .50 E2
Roe Cl SG5 . . . . .11 E5
Roecroft Lower Sch
　SG5 . . . . .11 F6
Roedean Ave EN3 . . . . . .162 C1
Roedean Cl LU2 . . . . .46 D3
Roe End La AL3 . . . . .83 B4
Roefields Cl HP3 . . . . . . .138 A7
ROE GREEN
　Hatfield 130 A6
　Sandon 26 B8
Roe Green Cl AL10 . . . . . .129 E4
Roe Green Ctr AL10 . . . . .129 F4
Roe Green La AL10 . . . . . .129 F5
Roe Hill Cl AL10 . . . . .129 F4
Roehyde Way AL10 . . . . . .129 C2
ROESTOCK 143 E8
Roestock Gdns AL4 . . . . . .129 E1
Roestock La AL4 . . . . .129 E1
Rofant Rd HA6 . . . . .174 E4
Rogate Rd LU2 . . . . .46 C5
Roger de Clare Sch
　SG12 . . . . .55 E2
Rogers Cl EN7 . . . . .147 D4
Roger's La SG9 . . . . .29 A5
Rogers Ruff HA6 . . . . .174 C2
Rokewood Mews **3**
　SG12 . . . . .93 D2
Roland St AL1 . . . . .128 B2
Rolleston Ct SG12 . . . . . . .93 C3
Rollswood AL7 . . . . .110 E3
Rollswood Rd AL6 . . . . . . .89 B8
Rollys La SG7 . . . . .4 D4
Roman Rd LU4 . . . . .173 B2
Roman Rise CM21 . . . . . . .97 D2
Romans End AL1 . . . . . . .127 C1
Roman St **8** EN11 . . . . .135 A7
Roman Theatre of
　Verulamium The★
　AL3 . . . . .127 A3
Roman Vale CM17 . . . . . .118 C5
Roman Way
　Markyate AL3 . . . . .83 E6
　Standon SG11 . . . . .55 D3
　Waltham Abbey EN9 . . . . .163 B4
　Welwyn AL6 . . . . .89 C4
Roman Way Fst Sch
　SG8 . . . . .7 C8
Romany Cl SG6 . . . . .22 C6
Romany Rd HP2 . . . . .125 E4
Romeland
　Borehamwood WD6 . . . . .169 D3
　St Albans AL3 . . . . .127 C3
　Waltham Abbey EN9 . . . . .163 C6

Romeland Ct WD6 . . . . . .169 D3
Romeland Hill AL3 . . . . . .127 C3
Romilly Dr WD19 . . . . . . .175 F6
Ronald Ct AL2 . . . . .140 E2
Ronaldin Ave LU3 . . . . . . .45 B3
Ronsons Way AL4 . . . . . .127 F7
Rookery Dr LU2 . . . . .45 A6
ROOKERY THE 167 B2
Rookery The
　Hatfield AL9 . . . . .144 D8
　Stansted Mountfitchet
　CM24 . . . . .59 E8
　Westmill SG9 . . . . .40 F3
Rookery Yd SG1 . . . . .50 C7
Rookes Cl SG6 . . . . .23 B3
Rooks Cl AL8 . . . . .110 D5
Rooks Hill
　Rickmansworth WD3 . . . . .165 D5
　Welwyn Garden City
　AL8 . . . . .110 C5
Rook's Nest Cotts SG1 . . .36 E2
Rook's Nest Farm Barns
　SG1 . . . . .36 E2
Rooks Nest La SG8 . . . . . .16 A5
Rook Tree Cl SG5 . . . . . . .12 A6
Rook Tree La SG5 . . . . . . .12 A6
Rookwood Dr SG2 . . . . . . .51 B1
Rosary Ct EN6 . . . . .145 B1
Rosary Gdns WD23 . . . . .168 C2
Rose Acre
　Pimlico SG5 . . . . .139 E6
　Redbourn AL3 . . . . .105 F6
Roseacre Gdns AL7 . . . . .116 D6
Roseacres CM21 . . . . .97 D3
Rosebank EN9 . . . . .163 E6
Roseberry La HP23 . . . . . .79 D1
Roseberry Ct WD17 . . . . .167 A8
Rosebery CM23 . . . . .76 E7
Rosebery Ave AL5 . . . . . . .85 F1
Rosebery Mews LU7 . . . . .61 D4
Rosebery Rd WD23 . . . . .168 B2
Rosebery Way HP23 . . . . .100 B5
Rosebriar Wlk WD24 . . . .153 F3

Rose Cotts
　Arlesey SG15 . . . . .11 A6
　Bricket Wood AL2 . . . . . .141 B1
　Meesden SG9 . . . . .30 A5
　Wyddial SG9 . . . . .28 A3
Rosecroft Ct HA6 . . . . . . .174 C4
Rosecroft Dr WD17 . . . . .153 E3
Rosecroft La AL6 . . . . .90 A8
Rose Ct
　Hammond Street EN7 . . . .148 A4
　St Albans AL4 . . . . .128 C5
ROSEDALE 148 A3
Rosedale AL7 . . . . .89 F2
Rosedale Ave EN7 . . . . . .147 F2
Rosedale Cl
　Bricket Wood AL2 . . . . . .140 E1
　Luton LU3 . . . . .44 C7
Rosedale Way EN7 . . . . . .148 A3
Rose Garden Mews
　WD3 . . . . .165 B5
Rose Gdns WD18 . . . . . . .167 A4
Rosehall HP1 . . . . .123 E4
Rosehill HP4 . . . . .122 B4
Rosehill Cl EN11 . . . . . . .134 F6
Rosehill Gdns WD5 . . . . .153 C7
Rose La AL4 . . . . .87 C2
Roselands Ave EN11 . . . .114 F1
Roselands Prim Sch
　EN11 . . . . .114 F1
Rose Lawn WD23 . . . . . . .168 C1
Roseley Cotts CM20 . . . . .117 B4
Rosemary Ct **1** CM17 . .118 C4
Rosemary Ct **2** HA5 . . .176 A3
Rosemary Dr AL2 . . . . . . .142 A5
Rosemary La SG13 . . . . . . .10 A3
Rosemary Lo **5** SG5 . . . .34 F7
Rose Mdw SG11 . . . . .41 E4
Rose Mead AL6 . . . . .145 C1
Rosemont Cl SG6 . . . . .22 E6
Rosemoor Ct AL7 . . . . . . .110 F5
Rosetta Ho **3** HP1 . . . . .124 D3
Rose Vale EN11 . . . . .135 A6
Rose Wlk
　Royston SG8 . . . . .7 C7
　St Albans AL4 . . . . .128 C5
Rose Wlk The WD7 . . . . . .156 B3
Rose Wood Cl LU2 . . . . . . .45 F3
Rosewood Ct HP1 . . . . . .123 E4
Rosewood Dr EN2 . . . . . .161 A4
Roslyn Cl EN10 . . . . .134 E2
Ross Cl
　Hatfield AL10 . . . . .130 A8
　Luton LU1 . . . . .63 B6
　Stanmore HA3 . . . . .176 C3
Ross Cres WD25 . . . . .154 A4
Ross Ct SG2 . . . . .51 B7
Rossendale Cl EN2 . . . . . .161 B3
Rossetti Lo SG8 . . . . .7 D8
Rossfold Rd LU3 . . . . .44 D8
Rossgate HP1 . . . . .124 A3
Rossgate Prim Sch
　HP1 . . . . .124 A5
Ross Haven Pl HA6 . . . . . .174 F2
Rossington Ave WD6 . . . .156 E1
Rossington Cl EN1 . . . . . .162 B1
Rossiter Fields EN5 . . . . .171 F3
Rosslyn Cres LU3 . . . . .45 C5
Rosslyn Rd WD18 . . . . . .167 B6
Rossway SG14 . . . . .91 B1
Rossway La HP4 . . . . .121 A7
Roswell Ct EN8 . . . . .148 E1
Rothamsted Ave AL5 . . . . .86 A1

Rothamsted Ct **2** AL5 . . .86 A1
Rothamsted Experimental
　Sta AL5 . . . . .107 A8
Rotheram Ave LU1 . . . . . . .63 B5
Rother Cl WD25 . . . . .154 C5
Rother Field AL2 . . . . .46 D3
Rotherfield Rd EN3 . . . . . .162 D2
Rothesay Ct HP4 . . . . .122 A4
Rothesay Rd LU1 . . . . .63 D7
Roughdown Ave HP3 . . . .138 A8
Roughdown Rd HP3 . . . . .138 A8
Roughdown Villas
　HP3 . . . . .138 A8
Roughdown Villas Rd
　HP3 . . . . .138 A8
Roughs The HA6 . . . . .174 E7
Roughwood Cl WD17 . . . .153 E1
Roundabout Ho HA6 . . . . .175 A2
Roundabout La AL6 . . . . . .89 F8
Roundbush La WD25 . . . .155 C1
Roundcroft EN7 . . . . .147 F5
Round Diamond Prim Sch
　SG1 . . . . .37 B3
Roundfield AL5 . . . . .86 A3
ROUND GREEN 45 F2
Roundhay SG11 . . . . .55 D1
Roundhedge Way
　EN2 . . . . .160 F1
Roundhills EN9 . . . . .163 E4
Round House Ct **6**
　EN8 . . . . .148 D1
Roundings The SG13 . . . .114 C2
Round Mead SG2 . . . . .51 D3
Roundmoor Dr EN8 . . . . .148 E1
Roundway The WD18 . . . .166 F2
Roundwood HP3 . . . . .138 E4
Roundwood Cl
　Hitchin SG4 . . . . .22 C2
　Oaklands AL6 . . . . .89 D8
Roundwood Ct AL5 . . . . . .85 F3
Roundwood Dr AL8 . . . . . .110 C7
Roundwood Gdns AL5 . . . .85 F3
Roundwood La AL5 . . . . . .85 F3
Roundwood Park Sch
　AL5 . . . . .85 E2
Roundwood Pk AL5 . . . . . .85 F3
Roundwood Prim Sch
　AL5 . . . . .85 F3
Rounton Rd EN9 . . . . .163 E6
Rousebarn La WD3 . . . . . .166 C7
Rowan Cl
　Bricket Wood AL2 . . . . . .155 A8
　5 Harrow HA7 . . . . . . .176 A3
　Luton LU1 . . . . .63 B7
　Shenley WD7 . . . . .156 E6
　St Albans AL4 . . . . .128 C3
　Weston SG4 . . . . .37 B8
Rowan Cres
　Letchworth Garden City
　SG6 . . . . .22 C7
　Stevenage SG1 . . . . .50 E7
Rowan Dr EN10 . . . . .148 E6
Rowan Gr SG4 . . . . .35 A4
Rowans Cl AL7 . . . . .90 A1
Rowans Prim Sch AL7 . . . .90 A1
Rowans The
　Baldock SG7 . . . . .23 E7
　Hemel Hempstead HP1 . . .124 A3
　Hoddesdon EN10 . . . . . . .134 F3
Rowan Way AL5 . . . . .107 C8
Rowan Wlk
　2 Hatfield AL10 . . . . . .130 A2
　Sawbridgeworth CM21 . . . .97 E2
Rowbeech Cott LU6 . . . . . .83 C8
Rowbourne Pl EN6 . . . . . .146 D3
Rowcroft HP1 . . . . .123 E2
Rowel Field LU2 . . . . .46 C1
Rowington Cl LU2 . . . . . . .46 C1
Rowland Ct LU7 . . . . .80 D3
Rowland Pl HA6 . . . . .174 E3
Rowland Rd SG1 . . . . .50 F4
Rowlands Ave HA5 . . . . . .176 B4
Rowlands Cl EN8 . . . . . . .148 D1
Rowlands Ct **3** EN8 . . . .148 D1
Rowland Way SG6 . . . . . . .22 F6
Rowlatt Cl AL1 . . . . .127 E4
Rowlatt Dr AL3 . . . . .127 A1
Rowley Cl WD19 . . . . .167 E3
Rowley Gdns EN8 . . . . . . .148 D3
ROWLEY GREEN 170 F5
Rowley Green Rd
　EN5 . . . . .171 A4
Rowley La
　Barnet EN5 . . . . .170 F5
　Borehamwood WD6 . . . . .170 D7
Rowley's Rd **2** SG13 . . .113 F7
Rowley Wlk HP2 . . . . .125 C8
Rowney Gdns CM21 . . . . .118 C8
Rowney La SG12 . . . . .72 B5
Rowney Wood CM21 . . . . .97 C1
Rows The **1** CM20 . . . . .117 D1
Row The HP5 . . . . .120 D2
Roxley Cotts SG9 . . . . .23 B2
Roxley Manor SG6 . . . . . . .36 B8
Royal Ave EN8 . . . . .162 E6
Royal Ct
　Aldbury HP23 . . . . .101 A5
　Hemel Hempstead HP3 . . .138 C4
Royal Gunpowder Mills★
　EN9 . . . . .163 B7
Royal Masonic Sch for
　Girls WD3 . . . . .165 D4
Royal National
　Orthopaedic Hospl
　HA7 . . . . .169 B1
Royal Oak Cl SG9 . . . . .27 D5
Royal Oak Gdns **6**
　CM23 . . . . .76 F6

Royal Oak La SG5 . . . . . . .20 D4
Royal Quarter **4** SG5 . . . .34 F8
Royal Rd AL1 . . . . .128 B3
Royal Veterinary Coll
　(Univ of London)
　AL9 . . . . .144 D3
Royce Cl EN10 . . . . .134 F2
Royce Gr WD25 . . . . .153 F5
ROYDON 116 C1
Roydon Cl LU4 . . . . .44 A4
Roydon Ct HP2 . . . . .105 A1
Roydon Lodge Chalet Est
　CM19 . . . . .116 C1
Roydon Mill Leisure Pk
　CM19 . . . . .116 A1
Roydon Rd
　Harlow CM19 . . . . .116 C1
　Stanstead Abbotts
　SG12 . . . . .115 E4
Roydon Sta CM19 . . . . . .116 B2
Roy Rd HA6 . . . . .174 F3
Royse Gr SG8 . . . . .7 D4
Roysia Mid Sch SG8 . . . . . . .7 D8
ROYSTON 7 C5
Royston & Dist Hospl
　SG8 . . . . .7 D4
Royston & District Mus★
　SG8 . . . . .7 C6
Royston Gr HA5 . . . . .176 A4
Royston Park Rd HA5 . . . .176 A5
Royston Rd
　Baldock SG7 . . . . .13 D2
　Barkway SG8 . . . . .17 C5
　Barley SG8 . . . . .8 F3
　St Albans AL1 . . . . .128 B2
　Royston Sta SG8 . . . . .7 C5
Rubin Pl SG1 . . . . .163 A2
Rucklers La WD4 . . . . . . .138 C4
RUCKLERS LANE 138 E5
Ruckles Cl SG1 . . . . .50 E5
Rudd Cl SG2 . . . . .51 B3
Rudham Gr SG4 . . . . .23 C3
Rudolf Steiner Sch
　WD4 . . . . .138 E2
Rudolph Rd WD23 . . . . . .168 A3
Rudyard Cl LU4 . . . . .44 D3
Rue De St Lawrence
　EN9 . . . . .163 C5
Rueley Dell Rd LU2 . . . . . .32 D2
Rufford Ct WD17 . . . . . . .153 F2
Rugby Way WD3 . . . . .166 B4
Ruins The AL3 . . . . .106 B5
Rumballs Cl HP2 . . . . .139 A8
Rumballs Ct CM23 . . . . . . .76 C4
Rumballs Rd HP2 . . . . . . .139 A8
Rumbold Rd EN11 . . . . . .135 C8
Rumsley EN7 . . . . .148 A4
Runcie Cl AL4 . . . . .128 A7
Runcorn Cres HP2 . . . . . .124 F7
Rundells SG6 . . . . .23 D4
Runfold Ave LU3 . . . . .45 A5
Runham Cl LU4 . . . . .44 A4
Runham Rd HP3 . . . . .125 E1
Runley Rd LU1 . . . . .62 F7
Runnalow SG6 . . . . .22 E7
Runsley AL7 . . . . .90 A1
Runswick Ct SG1 . . . . .50 A7
Runway The AL10 . . . . . . .129 D7
Ruscombe Dr AL2 . . . . . . .141 C5
Ruscote HP4 . . . . .122 A3
Rush Cl SG12 . . . . .115 C4
RUSHDEN 25 F3
Rushden Rd SG9 . . . . .26 A8
Rushen Dr EN9 . . . . .163 C3
Rushen Dr SG13 . . . . .114 C3
Rushes Ct CM23 . . . . .77 A5
Rushfield
　Potters Bar EN6 . . . . .158 E6
　Sawbridgeworth CM21 . . . .97 D3
Rushfield Rd SG12 . . . . . . .93 F3
RUSH GREEN 49 E4
Rushleigh Ave EN8 . . . . . .148 D1
Rushleigh Gn CM23 . . . . . .76 D4
Rush Leys Ct AL2 . . . . . . .142 A4
Rushmere Ct **1** HP2 . . .138 E7
Rushmere La HP5 . . . . . . .136 B3
Rushmoor Cl WD3 . . . . . .173 D8
Rushmore Cl LU1 . . . . .62 E4
Rushton Ave WD25 . . . . .154 A4
Rushton Ct
　Cheshunt EN8 . . . . .148 D2
　Enfield EN1 . . . . .162 B2
Ruskin Ave EN9 . . . . .163 E5
Ruskin Cl EN7 . . . . .147 E5
Ruskin La SG4 . . . . .35 C7
RUSLING END 67 D7
Rusper Cl LU2 . . . . .46 D3
Russell Ave AL3 . . . . .127 D3
Russell Cl
　Kensworth Common
　LU6 . . . . .82 E8
　Moor Park HA6 . . . . .174 C5
　Stevenage SG2 . . . . .51 B2
Russell Cres WD25 . . . . . .153 F4
Russellcroft Rd AL8 . . . . . .110 C7
Russell Ct AL2 . . . . .141 A1
Russell La WD17 . . . . . . .153 D3
Russell Mead HA3 . . . . . .176 F2
Russell Pl HP3 . . . . .138 C4

Russell Rd
　Enfield EN1 . . . . .161 F1
　Moor Park HA6 . . . . .174 C6
Russell Rise LU1 . . . . .63 D6
Russell Sch The WD3 . . . .164 B5
Russells Nursery
　WD17 . . . . .153 D3
Russell's Ride EN8 . . . . . .162 E8
Russell's Slip SG5 . . . . . . .34 D6
Russell St
　Hertford SG14 . . . . .113 C6
　Luton LU1 . . . . .63 D6
Russell Way WD19 . . . . . .167 B2
Russet Cl EN7 . . . . .147 E5
Russet Dr
　Shenley WD7 . . . . .156 E7
　St Albans AL4 . . . . .128 C2
Russett Ho AL7 . . . . .111 D6
Russettings **3** HA5 . . . . .175 F3
Russett Wood AL7 . . . . . .111 D5
Rutherford Cl
　Borehamwood WD6 . . . . .170 C7
　Stevenage SG1 . . . . .50 A6
Rutherford Way
　WD23 . . . . .168 C1
Ruthin Cl LU1 . . . . .63 D5
Ruthven Ave EN8 . . . . . . .162 D6
Rutland Cres LU2 . . . . .64 A7
Rutland Ct LU2 . . . . .64 A7
Rutland Gdns HP2 . . . . . .124 F4
Rutland Hall LU2 . . . . .64 A7
Rutland Pl WD23 . . . . . . .168 D1
Rutts The WD23 . . . . .168 D1
Ryall Cl AL2 . . . . .140 D2
Ryans Ct LU2 . . . . .45 F1
Ryan Way WD24 . . . . .167 C8
Rydal Ct WD25 . . . . .154 B7
Rydal Mount EN6 . . . . . . .158 E6
Rydal Way LU3 . . . . .44 F5
Ryder Ave SG5 . . . . .21 D3
Ryder Cl
　Bovingdon HP3 . . . . .137 A4
　Bushey WD23 . . . . .168 B3
　Hertford SG13 . . . . .114 B7
Ryders Ave AL4 . . . . .129 E3
Ryder Seed Mews **3**
　AL1 . . . . .127 D2
Ryders Hill SG1 . . . . .37 C3
Ryder Way SG5 . . . . .21 D3
Ryde Sch The AL9 . . . . . . .130 C8
RYDE THE 130 C8
Ryde The AL9 . . . . .130 C8
Rye Cl
　Harpenden AL5 . . . . .86 B4
　Stevenage SG1 . . . . .36 F3
Ryecroft
　Hatfield AL10 . . . . .129 F3
　Stevenage SG1 . . . . .50 E7
Ryecroft Cl HP2 . . . . .125 C2
Ryecroft Cres EN5 . . . . . .171 B4
Ryecroft Ct AL4 . . . . .128 C2
Ryecroft Way LU2 . . . . . . .46 A4
Ryefeld Cl EN11 . . . . .115 B2
Ryefield LU3 . . . . .31 A1
Ryefield Cres HA6 . . . . . .175 A1
Rye Gdns SG7 . . . . .13 B1
Rye Hill
　Harpenden AL5 . . . . .86 B4
　Luton LU2 . . . . .45 C1
Rye House Gatehouse★
　EN11 . . . . .135 D8
Rye House Sta EN11 . . . .135 C8
Ryelands AL3 . . . . .110 F3
Rye Mead Cotts EN11 . . .135 C8
RYE PARK 135 B7
Rye Park Ind Est
　EN11 . . . . .135 D7
Rye St CM23 . . . . .58 F1
Rylands Heath LU2 . . . . . .46 F2
Ryley Cl SG16 . . . . .10 B5
Ryman Ct WD3 . . . . .164 C3
Rymill Cl HP3 . . . . .137 A3
Ryton Cl LU1 . . . . .63 B6

S

Saberton Cl AL3 . . . . .105 F4
Sabine Ho WD5 . . . . .153 F7
SACOMBE 71 E3
Sacombe Gn LU3 . . . . .31 B1
SACOMBE GREEN 72 A4
Sacombe Green Rd
　SG12 . . . . .71 E4
Sacombe Mews SG2 . . . . . .69 D7
Sacombe Pound SG12 . . . .71 E3
Sacombe Rd
　Hemel Hempstead
　HP1 . . . . .123 F5
　Hertford SG14 . . . . .92 C1
　Stapleford SG14 . . . . .92 B4
Sacombes Lane Cotts
　CM21 . . . . .96 F7
Sacombs Ash La CM21 . . . .96 E7
Sacred Heart Language
　Coll The HA3 . . . . .176 E1
Sacred Heart Prim Sch
　LU2 . . . . .46 A3
Sacred Heart RC Prim Sch
　Bushey WD23 . . . . .167 F3
　Ware SG12 . . . . .93 D1
Saddlers Cl
　Arkley EN5 . . . . .171 B4
　Baldock SG7 . . . . .23 E8

Saddlers Cl continued
Bishop's Stortford CM23 ....**76** C4
Borehamwood WD6.......**170** D3
Pinner HA5 ....**176** A4
Saddlers Mews AL3........**83** E5
Saddlers Path WD6 ....**170** D4
Saddlers Pl SG8 ....**7** C7
Saddlers Wlk WD4......**139** A2
Sadleir Rd AL1...........**127** E1
Sadler Cl EN7 ....**147** C6
Sadlers Way SG14 ....**113** A6
Sadlier Rd SG11..........**55** E2
Saffron Cl
Arlesey SG15 ....**11** A7
Hoddesdon EN11.........**134** F7
Luton LU2 ....**45** D7
Saffron Green Prim Sch
WD6.....................**170** E5
Saffron Hill SG6..........**22** E6
Saffron La HP1..........**124** B4
Saffron Mdw SG11........**55** E2
Saffron St SG8 ....**7** F5
Sainfoin End HP2.......**125** A5
St Adrian's RC Prim Sch
AL1.....................**141** C8
St Agnells Ct HP2 ....**125** A7
St Agnells La HP2 ....**125** A8
ST ALBANS............**127** F4
St Alban & St Stephen RC
Inf Sch AL1............**127** E4
St Alban & St Stephen RC
Jun Sch AL1............**128** A3
St Albans City Hospl
AL3.....................**127** C5
St Albans City Sta
AL3.....................**127** F3
St Albans City Walls*
AL3.....................**127** B2
St Albans Dr SG1 ....**36** E1
St Albans Girls' Sch
AL3.....................**127** E7
St Albans High Sch for
Girls AL1...............**127** E4
St Albans Highway
SG4.......................**48** F8
St Albans Hill HP3......**124** F1
St Albans La WD5 ......**140** A5
St Albans Link SG1......**36** E1
St Albans Music Sch
AL3.....................**127** D6
St Albans Organ Mus*
AL1.....................**128** B2
St Albans RC Prim Sch
CM20....................**117** F2
St Albans Rd
Barnet EN5 ....**171** E7
Codicote SG4.............**88** F7
Dancers Hill EN5 ......**158** C3
Harpenden AL5 ....**107** B6
Hemel Hempstead HP2,
HP3....................**124** D2
Redbourn AL3 ....**106** C3
Ridge EN6..............**157** F8
Sandridge AL4 ....**108** B1
St Albans AL4 ....**128** A8
St Albans Rd E AL10.....**130** B6
St Albans Rd W AL10...**129** D5
St Albans Ret Pk AL1 ....**127** D1
St Albans Sch AL3 ....**127** C3
St Albert the Great RC
Prim Sch HP3.........**125** A2
St Aldates Ct LU3.........**45** B3
St Andrew Mews ⊞
SG14 ....**113** C6
St Andrew's Ave AL5....**85** F1
St Andrew's CE Prim Sch
SG4.......................**35** A7
St Andrew's CE Prim Sch
Much Hadham SG10 .....**74** F2
Stanstead Abbotts
SG12 ....**115** D4
St Andrews Cl LU1.......**63** B1
St Andrews Dr
St Albans AL1 ....**142** B8
Stevenage SG1 ....**36** F2
St Andrews Gr AL3 ....**45** C3
St Andrew's Ho ⊞ CM20...**117** F2
St Andrews Mews AL3 ...**45** A4
St Andrews Montessori
Prep Sch WD25 ....**154** C8
St Andrew's Pl ⊞ SG4....**34** F6
St Andrews Pl ⊞
WD19...................**175** D2
St Andrew's Rd HP3 ....**138** D7
St Andrew St SG14 ....**113** C6
St Andrews Terr
WD19...................**175** C5
St Andrews Wlk LU1.....**63** C1
St Anna Rd EN5 ....**171** D4
St Annes Cl WD19 .....**175** C6
St Anne's Cl EN7 ....**148** A3
St Anne's Ct ⏆ SG5 ......**34** F8
St Anne's Pk EN10......**135** A4
St Anne's Rd
Hitchin SG5 ....**34** F8
London Colney AL2 ...**142** D4
St Ann's La LU1 ....**63** F7
St Ann's Rd LU1..........**63** F7
St Anthonys Ave HP3 ...**125** B1
St Anthonys RC Prim Sch
WD18....................**166** E4
St Audreys Cl AL10.....**130** B2
St Audreys Gn AL10 ...**110** F5
St Augusta Ct AL3 .....**127** D5

St Augustine Ave LU3.....**45** C3
St Augustine Cl ⊞ SG5 ..**34** F8
St Augustines Cl
EN10....................**134** F3
St Augustines Dr
EN10....................**134** F3
St Augustine's RC Prim
Sch EN10...............**135** B6
St Barnabas Ct
Harrow HA3............**176** C2
Hemel Hempstead HP2 ..**125** A3
St Bartholomew's CE Prim
Sch HP23 ....**100** D1
St Barts Cl AL4 ....**128** D2
St Bernadette RC Prim
Sch AL2 ....**142** D4
St Bernard's Cl LU3......**45** C3
St Bernard's Rd AL3....**127** E4
St Brelades Pl AL4......**128** D7
St Catharine's Rd
EN10....................**135** A4
St Catherine of Siena RC
Prim Sch WD25 ......**154** D6
St Catherines Ave LU3 ...**45** B3
St Catherine's CE Prim
Sch SG12 ....**93** B2
St Catherines Ct AL3....**76** E7
St Catherine's Hoddesdon
CE Prim Sch EN11.....**135** B6
St Catherine's Rd
EN10....................**135** A4
St Christopher Sch
WD3.....................**164** D5
St Christophers Ct
WD3.....................**164** D5
St Clement Danes Sch
WD3.....................**164** D7
St Clement's CE Jun Sch
EN8.....................**148** E4
St Clements Cl EN9....**163** C6
St Columba's Coll
AL3.....................**127** C1
St Cross Chambers
EN10....................**135** A4
St Cross Ct EN11 ....**135** A4
St Cross RC Prim Sch
EN11....................**135** A4
St Cuthbert Mayne RC Jun
Sch HP1...............**124** B4
St Cuthberts Gdns ⏆ **175** F3
St Cuthberts Rd EN11...**115** C1
St Davids Cl SG1 ....**36** F2
St David's Cl HP2.......**125** D2
St David's Dr EN10 ....**134** F4
St Dominic RC Prim Sch
AL5.....................**107** B8
St Dunstan's Rd SG12...**116** D8
St Edmunds HP4 ....**122** C3
St Edmund's Coll SG11 ...**55** A1
St Edmund's Way
CM17....................**118** C4
St Edmunds Wlk AL1 ...**128** C2
St Elizabeth's Sch & Coll
SG10 ....**96** C6
St Elmo Ct SG4...........**34** F5
St Ethelbert Ave LU3....**45** C4
St Etheldreda's Dr
AL10....................**130** C5
St Evroul Ct ⏆ SG12 .....**93** D2
St Faiths Cl SG4...........**22** B1
St Francis Cl
Buntingford SG9 ....**40** F6
Potters Bar EN6 ....**159** C5
Watford WD17..........**167** B1
St Francis' Coll SG6.......**22** E4
St George's Dr WD19 ....**175** E6
St Georges End SG9 ......**29** A6
St George's Rd
Enfield EN1 ....**161** F1
Hemel Hempstead HP3 ..**138** C7
Watford WD24..........**154** B1
St George's Sch AL5....**86** B2
St George's Way SG1 ....**50** D5
St Georges Works
EN8.....................**148** F1
St Giles' Ave EN6 ......**158** B7
St Giles' CE Prim Sch
EN6.....................**158** A7
St Giles Ct EN8 ....**162** C4
St Giles Rd SG4 ....**67** F2
St Helena Ct ⏆ AL5 ......**86** A2
St Helen's CE Prim Sch
AL4.....................**108** D8
St Helen's Cl AL4.......**108** D8
St Helen's Sch HA6....**174** E4
St Heliers Rd AL4......**128** B8
St Hilda's Ave
Bushey WD23 ....**168** B2
Harpenden AL5...........**85** F2
St Hugh's Ct SG11.......**73** A8
ST IBBS.................**35** B2
St Ignatius Coll EN1 ...**162** B4
ST IPPOLYTS...........**35** B3
St Ippolyts CE Prim Sch
SG4.......................**35** B3
St Ives Cl
Luton LU3 ....**45** B3
Welwyn AL6...............**89** F3
St James Ct ⏆ AL1 ......**128** A2
St James Ctr CM20 .....**118** A4
St James Rd
Harpenden AL5 ....**86** B4
Watford WD18.........**167** B4
St James' Rd LU3.........**45** B3
St James's Ct AL5........**86** B3
St James's Rd EN7 .....**147** D3
St James Way CM23 ....**76** C3

St Joan of Arc RC Sch
WD3.....................**165** E2
St John Cl LU1 ....**63** B5
St John Fisher RC Prim
Sch AL4 ....**128** C6
St John RC Prim Sch
SG7.......................**23** F7
St Johns SG11...........**55** E3
St John's Ave CM17.....**118** C4
St John's CE Inf Sch
WD7.....................**155** F4
St John's CE Prim Sch
Crews Hill EN2........**161** B2
Welwyn Garden City AL6...**89** F2
St John's CE Prim Sch
AL8.....................**109** F5
St Johns Cl
⏆ Hemel Hempstead
HP1.....................**124** B1
Welwyn AL6...............**89** C6
St John's Cres EN6 .....**159** C6
St John's Cres CM24....**59** E7
St Johns Ct
Luton LU1 ....**63** B5
Rickmansworth WD3...**165** B1
St Albans AL3 ....**128** B5
Ware SG12 ....**93** F3
St John's Ct
Harpenden AL5 ....**107** C7
⏆ Hertford SG13 ......**113** D6
St John's Ct ⏆ HA6.....**174** E3
St Johns La AL10 ....**110** C5
St John's La CM24......**59** E7
St John's Path SG4......**34** F5
St Johns Prep Sch
EN6.....................**159** E5
St John's Rd
Arlesey SG15 ....**11** A4
Harpenden AL5 ....**107** C7
Hemel Hempstead HP1 ..**124** B1
Hitchin SG4 ....**34** F6
Stanstead Mountfitchet
CM24....................**59** E7
Watford WD17.........**167** B7
St John's Sch HA6......**175** B4
St John's St SG13 ......**113** D6
St John's Terr EN2 .....**161** D2
St John's Well Ct
HP4.....................**122** B5
St John's Well La
HP4.....................**122** B5
St John Wlk CM17......**118** C4
St John The Baptist CE
Prim Sch SG12........**115** A5
St Joseph RC Prim Sch
WD19...................**175** C7
St Joseph's Cl LU3......**45** A4
St Josephs Gn AL7 .....**110** D3
St Joseph's in the Park
Sch SG14 ....**113** A4
St Joseph's RC Inf Sch
LU3.......................**45** A4
St Joseph's RC Jun Sch
LU3.......................**45** A4
St Joseph's RC Prim Sch
Bishop's Stortford
CM23....................**76** E6
Cheshunt EN8 ....**162** E7
Hertford SG14 ....**113** A7
St Joseph's Rd EN6....**162** E6
ST JULIANS............**141** D8
St Julian's Rd AL1......**127** D1
St Katherines Cl SG5....**21** D3
St Katherine's Cotts
SG5.....................**21** E7
St Katherine's Way
HP4.....................**121** E7
St Laurence Dr EN10...**148** F8
St Lawrence Ct WD5....**139** E1
St Lawrence Ct LU3......**45** C3
St Lawrence Way AL2...**140** F1
ST LEONARDS........**119** E3
St Leonards Cl
Hertford SG14 ....**113** E8
St Leonards Cl SG1.....**51** B8
St Leonards Cor AL4 ..**108** C1
St Leonards Ct AL4 ....**108** C1
St Leonards Rd EN9 ...**149** B6
St Leonard's Rd SG14...**113** D8
St Louis Cl EN6 ....**159** C6
St Luke's Ave EN2 .....**161** D1
St Luke's Cl LU4.........**44** E2
St Lukes Cl AL10 ......**130** B6
St Lukes Pl ⏆ AL1.......**128** B2
St Luke's Sch AL3 .....**106** A6
St Magnus Ct HP3 ....**125** C1
St Margaret Clitherow RC
Prim Sch SG2............**50** F2
St Margaret of Scotland
Jun Sch LU1 ....**63** B5
St Margaret of Scotland
RC Inf Sch LU1.........**63** B5
ST MARGARETS.......**115** B4
St Margarets SG2.........**50** F2
ST MARGARET'S.......**103** C3
St Margarets Ave LU3...**45** B3
St Margarets Cl AL3.....**31** A6
St Margaret's Ct HP4 ..**122** D3
St Margaret's Rd
SG12 ....**115** B2
St Margaret's Sch
WD23...................**168** A2

St Margarets Sta
SG12 ....**115** C4
St Margarets Way
HP2.....................**125** D3
St Marks Cl AL4 ....**129** B1
St Mark's Cl SG5........**21** D1
St Martha's Convent Jun
Sch EN5 ....**171** E5
St Martin de Porres RC
Prim Sch LU4..........**44** A4
St Martins HA6 ....**174** D5
St Martin's Ave LU2.....**45** F2
St Martins Ct
Harpenden AL5 ....**86** C4
South Oxhey WD19 ...**175** C6
St Martins Rd EN11 ...**135** C6
St Martin's Rd SG3 .....**69** A5
St Martin's Sch HA6 ..**174** D5
St Mary RC Prim Sch
SG8.......................**7** D7
St Mary's Ave
Berkhamsted UB2 ....**121** D6
Moor Park HA6 ....**174** E5
Stotfold SG5 ....**11** F6
St Mary's CE High Sch
EN8.....................**148** B1
St Mary's CE Jun Sch
SG12 ....**93** D3
St Mary's CE Prim Sch
WD3.....................**173** D7
St Mary's CE Prim Sch
Stansted Mountfitchet
CM24....................**59** E7
Welham Green AL9 ....**144** B8
St Marys Church Rd
SG4.......................**35** F3
St Marys Cl
Aston SG2 ....**51** E2
Welwyn AL6...............**89** C5
St Mary's Cl
Letchworth Garden City
SG6.......................**22** F2
Pirton SG5 ....**20** D4
Redbourn AL3 ....**106** A4
St Mary's Ctyd ⏆
SG12 ....**93** D3
St Mary's Dr CM24......**59** F5
St Mary's Inf Sch SG7....**23** E6
St Mary's Jun Mix Sch
SG7.......................**23** E6
St Mary's La SG4 ....**112** F3
St Mary's Lower Sch
SG5.......................**12** A6
St Marys Pk SG8..........**7** D6
St Mary's Rd
Cheshunt EN8 ....**148** C2
Hemel Hempstead HP22 .**124** D4
Luton LU1 ....**63** F7
Standon SG11 ....**55** D2
Watford WD18.........**167** B5
St Mary's Rise SG4 .....**47** D1
St Mary's Way SG1 .....**23** E6
St Mary's Wlk AL4......**128** B7
St Matthews Cl
Luton LU2 ....**63** E8
Watford WD19.........**167** D3
St Matthew's Ct HA6...**174** E3
St Matthew's Prim Sch
LU2.....................**45** E1
St Meryl Sch WD19 ...**175** E7
St Michaels Ave HP3...**125** B1
St Michael's CE Prim Sch
Bishop's Stortford
CM23....................**76** F7
St Albans AL3 ....**127** B3
St Michaels Cl
Harlow CM20..........**117** C1
Harpenden AL5 ....**107** D7
St Michael's Cres LU3 ...**45** D3
St Michaels Ct SG1.....**51** B8
St Michael's Ct AL3....**127** B3
St Michael's Dr WD25 ...**154** B6
St Michaels Ho AL7....**110** F5
ST MICHAEL'S MEAD...**76** C5
St Michael's Mount
SG4.......................**35** A8
St Michael's RC High Sch
WD25...................**154** D7
St Michaels Rd SG4.....**35** B7
St Michael's Rd EN10...**135** A3
St Michaels St AL3.....**127** B3
St Michaels View
AL10....................**130** B7
St Michaels Way EN6 ..**145** B1
St Mildreds Ave LU3 .....**45** C3
St Monicas Ave LU3 ....**45** B3
St Neots Cl WD6........**157** A1
ST NICHOLAS...........**37** A2
St Nicholas CE Prim Sch
Harpenden AL5 ....**86** A1
Stevenage SG2 ....**50** F4
St Nicholas Cl WD6....**169** D3
St Nicholas Cl AL5......**85** F3
St Nicholas Elstree CE
Prim Sch WD6........**169** D3

St Nicholas Gn ⏆
CM17....................**118** D1
St Nicholas House Prep
Sch HP3 ....**139** B6
St Nicholas Mount
HP1.....................**123** F3
St Nicholas Sch CM17...**118** F3
St Ninian's Ct ⏆ LU2.....**63** D8
St Olam's Cl LU3........**45** B6
St Olives SG5...........**11** E6
St Pancras Ho SG8 ....**2** D1
St Paul's CE Prim Sch
WD4.....................**153** C5
St Paul's CE Prim Sch
WD4.....................**152** A8
St Pauls Cl ⏆ SG2.......**107** D8
St Paul's Cl SG2..........**50** F1
St Paul's Gdns LU1......**63** E5
St Pauls Pl AL1 ....**128** A3
St Paul's Rd
EN7.....................**148** B4
St Paul's Rd
Hemel Hempstead
HP2.....................**124** E4
Luton LU1 ....**63** E5
St Paul's Walden SG4....**49** A1
St Paul's Walden Prim Sch
SG4.......................**66** D7
St Pauls Way
Waltham Abbey EN9 ...**163** D6
Watford WD25.........**167** C7
St Peter's CE Prim Sch
WD3.....................**165** B1
St Peters Cl AL10 ......**130** A6
St Peter's Cl
Barnet EN5 ....**171** B4
Bushey WD23 ....**168** D1
Rickmansworth WD3...**165** B1
St Albans AL1 ....**127** D4
St Peters Hill HP23 ...**100** A4
St Peters Mews ⏆
AL1.....................**127** D4
St Peters Rd LU1.........**63** B7
St Peter's Rd AL1......**127** E4
St Peter's Sch AL1.....**127** E2
St Peter's St AL1.......**127** E2
St Peters Way WD3 ...**164** B5
St Philip Howard RC Prim
Sch AL10 ....**130** B4
St Raphaels Ct ⏆
AL1.....................**127** D4
St Ronans Cl EN4......**159** D1
St Rose's RC Inf Sch
HP1.....................**124** A1
St Saviours View AL1....**127** F4
St Saviours's Cres LU1....**63** D6
ST STEPHENS..........**127** D1
St Stephen's Ave AL3 ...**141** B8
St Stephen's Cl AL3....**141** B8
St Stephens Ct CM24 ...**59** D7
St Stephen's Hill AL3 ...**127** C1
St Stephens Rd EN3....**171** D4
St Stephen's Rd EN3...**162** D2
St Teresa's RC Fst & Mid
Sch HA3 ....**176** C2
St Thomas' Dr HA5 ...**175** E2
St Thomas' Dr HA5 ...**175** E2
St Thomas More RC Prim
Sch
Berkhamsted HP4 ....**122** A4
Letchworth Garden City
SG6.......................**22** D4
St Thomas of Canterbury
RC Prim Sch SG11......**55** C3
St Thomas Pl AL4......**108** D8
St Thomas's Cl LU2.....**46** A4
St Thomas's Rd LU2....**46** A4
St Vincent de Paul RC
Prim Sch SG1...........**51** A6
St Vincent Dr AL1 .....**128** A1
St Vincent Gdns LU4....**44** D3
St Vincent's Way EN6 ..**159** C6
St Winifreds Ave LU3 ...**45** C3
St Yon Ct AL4...........**128** E3
Salamander Quay
UB9.....................**173** A3
Salar Ho ⏆ AL1 ....**128** A2
Sale Dr SG7 ....**12** F1
Salisbury Ave
⏆ Harpenden AL5 .....**86** A1
St Albans AL1 ....**128** B4
Salisbury Cl
Bishop's Stortford
CM23....................**76** F5
Letchford Garden City
SG5.......................**11** D2
Potters Bar EN6 ....**159** C7
Salisbury Cres EN8 ....**162** D7
Salisbury Gdns AL7...**110** F5
Salisbury Hall Dr
AL10....................**129** E7
Salisbury Ho AL3 ......**127** C2
Salisbury Rd
Baldock SG7 ....**12** F1
Barnet EN5 ....**171** E6
Enfield EN3 ....**162** F2
Harpenden AL5 ....**86** D3
Hoddesdon EN11.....**135** C8
Luton LU1 ....**63** D6
Stevenage SG1 ....**37** A2
Watford WD24.........**154** C1
Welwyn Garden City
AL7.....................**111** A3
Salisbury Sq
Hatfield AL9..............**130** C6

Salisbury Sq continued
7 Hertford SG14 . . . . 113 D6
Sally Deards La AL6 . . . . . . 68 B3
Salmon Cl AL7 . . . . 90 A1
Salmons Cl SG12 . . . . 93 D4
Saltdean Cl LU2 . . . . 46 D4
Salters CM23 . . . . 76 C4
Salters Cl WD3 . . . . 165 E1
Salter's Cl HP4 . . . . 121 F6
Salters Gdns WD17 . . . . . 167 A8
Salusbury La SG5 . . . . 33 C2
Salvatorian RC Coll
    HA3 . . . . 176 E1
Salwey Cres EN10 . . . . . . 134 F3
Sambrook Ct HA5 . . . . . . 175 F3
Samian Gate AL3 . . . . . . 126 F1
Sampson Ave EN5 . . . . . . 171 F4
Samuel Lucas Jun Mix Inf
    Sch SG5 . . . . 34 D7
Samuel Sq AL1 . . . . 127 D2
Sancroft Rd HA3 . . . . 176 F1
Sanctuary Cl HA8 . . . . . . 173 C3
Sandalls Spring HP1 . . . . 123 F5
Sandalwood Cl LU3 . . . . . . 45 B7
Sanday Cl HP3 . . . . 125 B1
Sandbrook La HP23 . . . . . . 79 C1
Sandell Cl LU2 . . . . 45 F2
Sandeman Gdns SG12 . . . . 93 E2
Sanderling Cl SG6 . . . . 22 E8
Sanders Cl
    Hemel Hempstead
    HP3 . . . . 138 F7
    London Colney AL2 . . . . 142 D4
    Stansted Mountfitchet
    CM24 . . . . 59 D6
Sander's Cnr EN2 . . . . . . 161 B5
Sanders Pl SG4 . . . . 35 A4
Sanders Rd HP3 . . . . 139 A7
Sandfield Rd AL1 . . . . 128 A3
Sandgate Rd LU4 . . . . 44 D2
Sandhurst Ct AL5 . . . . . . 107 D6
Sandifield AL10 . . . . 130 B2
Sandle Rd CM23 . . . . 77 A7
Sandmere Cl HP2 . . . . . . 125 A2
Sandmoor Ho HA6 . . . . . 174 E4
SANDON 15 B1
Sandon Cl HP23 . . . . 99 F4
Sandon Jun Mix & Inf Sch
    SG9 . . . . 15 C1
Sandon Rd EN8 . . . . 148 C1
Sandover Cl SG4 . . . . 35 B6
Sandown Rd
    Stevenage SG1 . . . . 37 C1
    Watford WD24 . . . . 154 C1
Sandown Road Ind Est
    WD24 . . . . 154 C1
Sandpiper Ct 15 CM23 . . . . 76 F6
Sandpit Hill Cotts
    HP23 . . . . 120 B3
Sandpit La AL1, AL4 . . . . . 128 C5
Sandpit Rd AL7 . . . . 110 E4
SANDRIDGE 108 C1
Sandridgebury La
    Sandridge AL3, AL4 . . . . 108 A2
    St Albans AL3 . . . . 127 E8
Sandridge Cl
    Hadley Wood EN4 . . . . . 159 E2
    Hemel Hempstead HP2 . . 105 A1
Sandridge Ct AL4 . . . . 127 F7
Sandridge Gate Bsns Ctr
    AL1 . . . . 127 F7
Sandridge Pk AL3 . . . . . . 127 F8
Sandridge Rd AL1 . . . . . . 127 F5
Sandridge Sch AL4 . . . . . 108 D1
Sandringham Cres
    AL4 . . . . 128 B7
Sandringham Gdns 6
    CM23 . . . . 76 E5
Sandringham Lo 7
    EN11 . . . . 135 A6
Sandringham Rd
    Potters Bar EN6 . . . . . . 145 B1
    Watford WD24 . . . . 154 C2
Sandringham Sch
    AL4 . . . . 128 B7
Sandringham Way
    EN8 . . . . 162 D5
Sandy Cl SG14 . . . . 113 B6
Sandycroft Rd HP6 . . . . . 150 C1
Sandy Gr
    Borehamwood WD6 . . . . 169 F7
    Hitchin SG4 . . . . 34 F6
Sandy La
    Bushey WD25 . . . . 168 C6
    Moor Park HA6 . . . . 175 A5
Sandy Lane Cvn Site
    WD25 . . . . 168 C6
Sandy Lodge Ct HA6 . . . . 174 E5
Sandy Lodge La HA6 . . . . 174 E6
Sandy Lodge Rd WD3 . . . . 174 C8
Sandy Lodge Way
    HA6 . . . . 174 E4
Sanfoine Cl SG4 . . . . 35 C8
Sanfoin Rd AL4 . . . . 44 A4
Santers La EN6 . . . . 158 E6
Santingfield N LU1 . . . . . . 63 B6
Santingfield S LU1 . . . . . . 63 B6
Sappers Cl CM21 . . . . 97 F2
Saracen Est HP2 . . . . 125 B5
Saracens Head HP2 . . . . . 125 A4
Saracens Head Yd 1
    AL1 . . . . 127 D2
Saracens Mews AL3 . . . . . 106 B5
Sarbir Ind Pk CM17 . . . . . 118 C5
Sargents SG11 . . . . 55 F1
Sarita Cl HA3 . . . . 176 D1

Sark Ho
    Enfield EN3 . . . . 162 D1
    8 Watford WD18 . . . . . 166 F3
SARRATT 152 A4
Sarratt Ave HP2 . . . . 125 A8
Sarratt CE Prim Sch
    WD3 . . . . 152 A3
Sarratt La
    Rickmansworth WD3 . . . 165 C6
    Sarratt WD3 . . . . 165 D8
Sarratt Rd WD3 . . . . 165 C8
Sarum Pl HP2 . . . . 124 E7
Sarum Rd LU4 . . . . 44 F4
Satinwood Cl 1 HP3 . . . . 124 E1
Saturn Way HP2 . . . . 124 F6
Sauncey Ave AL5 . . . . 86 B3
Sauncey Wood AL5 . . . . . . 86 E4
Sauncey Wood La AL5 . . . . 86 E6
Sauncey Wood Prim Sch
    AL5 . . . . 86 D4
Saunders Cl
    Cheshunt EN8 . . . . 148 D4
    Letchworth Garden City
    SG6 . . . . 23 C7
Savanna Cl WD18 . . . . . . 166 F5
Savill Cl AL4 . . . . 147 C6
Savoy Cl UB9 . . . . 173 D1
Savoy Mews AL3 . . . . 141 B8
SAWBRIDGEWORTH 97 C3
Sawbridgeworth Rd
    Hatfield Heath CM22 . . . 98 D3
    Little Hallingbury CM22 . 98 B6
Sawbridgeworth Sta
    CM21 . . . . 98 A3
Sawells EN10 . . . . 134 F2
Sawtry Cl LU3 . . . . 45 A6
Sawtry Way WD6 . . . . . . 157 A1
Sawyers Ct EN3 . . . . 162 E6
Sawyers La EN6 . . . . 158 D5
Sawyers Way HP2 . . . . . . 124 F3
Sax Ho SG5 . . . . 11 E1
Saxon Ave SG5 . . . . 11 F8
Saxon Cl
    Harpenden AL5 . . . . 86 C4
    Letchford Garden City
    SG6 . . . . 11 F1
Saxon Ct
    Borehamwood WD6 . . . . 169 E8
    Hitchin SG4 . . . . 34 F6
Saxon Rd
    Luton LU3 . . . . 45 C2
    Welwyn AL6 . . . . 89 B3
    Wheathampstead AL4 . . 108 D7
Saxon Way EN9 . . . . 163 C6
Saxtead Cl LU2 . . . . 46 D1
Saxton Mews WD17 . . . . . 167 A7
Sayers Gdns HP4 . . . . . . 122 A6
Sayer Way SG3 . . . . 68 F4
Sayesbury Ave CM21 . . . . 97 E3
Sayesbury Rd CM21 . . . . . 97 E2
Sayes Gdns CM21 . . . . 97 F2
Sayfield Cotts SG8 . . . . . . 26 B8
Saywell Rd LU2 . . . . 46 B1
Scammell Way WD18 . . . . 166 F3
Scarborough Ave SG1 . . . . 50 B7
Scatterdells La WD4 . . . . 138 A2
Scholars Cl EN5 . . . . 171 E5
Scholars Ct AL4 . . . . 143 C8
Scholar's Hill SG12 . . . . . . 93 A4
Scholars Mews AL8 . . . . . 110 D8
Scholars The WD18 . . . . . 167 C4
Scholars Wlk 4 AL10 . . . . 130 A2
School Cl
    Essendon AL9 . . . . 131 F6
    Stevenage SG2 . . . . 51 B3
School Cotts SG4 . . . . 47 F6
Schoolfields SG6 . . . . 23 C5
School Gdns HP4 . . . . . . 123 B6
School Ho 1 SG7 . . . . 23 F7
School La
    Ardeley SG2 . . . . 38 F3
    Aston SG2 . . . . 51 E2
    Barley SG8 . . . . 9 A1
    Bricket Wood AL2 . . . . 157 A7
    Bushey WD23 . . . . 168 B2
    Harlow CM20 . . . . 117 B3
    Harpenden AL5 . . . . . . 107 B2
    Hatfield AL10 . . . . 130 C6
    Preston SG4 . . . . 48 E5
    Tewin AL6 . . . . 90 E2
    Watton at S SG14 . . . . . 70 E3
    Welwyn AL6 . . . . 89 B4
    Weston SG4 . . . . 24 C1
School Mead WD5 . . . . . . 153 D7
School Par UB9 . . . . 173 C1
School Rd EN6 . . . . 145 C1
School Row HP1 . . . . 123 F2
School Wlk SG4 . . . . 50 C5
Schubert Rd WD6 . . . . . . 169 D3
Scimitar Pk CM19 . . . . . . 116 F1
Scotfield Ct LU2 . . . . 46 D3
Scot Gr HA5 . . . . 175 D3
Scotscraig WD7 . . . . 155 F4
Scots Hill WD3 . . . . 165 F3
Scots Hill Cl WD3 . . . . . . 165 F3
Scots Mill La WD3 . . . . . . 165 F3
Scotswood EN5 . . . . 171 B4
Scott Ave SG12 . . . . 115 B4
Scott Cl
    Hoddesdon EN11 . . . . . 135 C6
    Royston SG8 . . . . 2 D1
Scott Rd
    Bishop's Stortford
    CM23 . . . . 76 E6

Scott Rd continued
    Luton LU2 . . . . 44 C7
Scotts Sq LU4 . . . . 51 B6
Scotts Cl SG12 . . . . 114 D8
Scott's Grotto* SG12 . . . . 114 D8
Scott's Rd SG12 . . . . 114 D8
Scotts View AL8 . . . . 110 C5
Scottswood Cl WD23 . . . . 167 E7
Scottswood Rd WD23 . . . . 167 E7
Scratchwood Nature
    Trail* NW7 . . . . 170 D2
Scriveners Cl HP2 . . . . . . 124 E3
Scrubbits Sq WD7 . . . . . . 156 A4
Scrubbits Park Rd
    WD7 . . . . 156 A4
Scrubbits Sq WD7 . . . . . . 156 A4
Seabrook LU4 . . . . 44 B3
Seabrook Rd WD4 . . . . . . 139 C8
Seacroft Gdns WD19 . . . . 175 D7
Seaford Cl LU2 . . . . 46 C3
Seaforth Ct EN8 . . . . 148 A6
Seaforth Dr EN8 . . . . 162 C8
Seal Cl LU4 . . . . 44 D3
Seaman Cl AL2 . . . . 141 D6
Seamarks Cl LU4 . . . . 45 A1
Searches La WD5 . . . . . . 140 C4
Seaton Rd
    Hemel Hempstead
    HP3 . . . . 124 E1
    London Colney AL2 . . . . 142 D5
    Luton LU4 . . . . 44 F3
Sebright Rd
    Barnet EN5 . . . . 171 D6
    Hemel Hempstead HP1 . . 124 A4
    Markyate AL3 . . . . 83 E5
Secker Cres HA3 . . . . 176 C2
Second Ave
    Letchworth Garden City
    SG6 . . . . 23 C6
    Watford WD25 . . . . 154 D4
Sedbury Cl AL3 . . . . 45 A6
Sedge Gn EN9 . . . . 135 D3
Sedgewick Cl HP4 . . . . . . 105 B1
Sedgwick Rd LU4 . . . . 44 B7
Sedley Cl EN1 . . . . 162 B1
Seebohm Cl SG5 . . . . 21 C1
Seeleys CM17 . . . . 118 C4
Sefton Cl SG5 . . . . 21 C1
Sefton Ct HA3 . . . . 176 D2
Sefton Cl AL1 . . . . 127 F4
Sefton Cl AL8 . . . . 110 B4
Selbourne Rd LU4 . . . . 45 A2
Selby Ave AL1 . . . . 127 D3
Selden Hill HP2 . . . . 124 D2
Sele Mill HP1 SG14 . . . . . 113 B6
Sele Rd SG14 . . . . 113 B6
Sele Sch The SG14 . . . . . 112 F6
Selina Cl LU4 . . . . 44 C7
Sell Ct EN7 . . . . 147 B5
Sellers Cl WD6 . . . . 170 C5
Sells Rd SG12 . . . . 93 F2
Sellwood Dr EN5 . . . . 171 D4
Selsey Dr LU2 . . . . 46 D4
Selwyn Ave AL10 . . . . . . 129 E4
Selwyn Cres AL10 . . . . . . 129 E4
Selwyn Ct SG2 . . . . 51 A3
Selwyn Dr AL10 . . . . 129 E5
Sempill Rd HP3 . . . . 124 E1
Senate Pl SG7 . . . . 37 B3
Sentis Ct HA6 . . . . 174 F4
Sequoia Cl WD23 . . . . . . 168 D1
Sequoia Pk HA5 . . . . 176 B4
Serby Ave SG8 . . . . 7 D8
SERGEHILL 140 B5
Sergehill La AL3 . . . . 140 A5
Serpentine Cl SG1 . . . . . . 37 C2
Service Industry Bays
    CM20 . . . . 117 F2
Service Rd The EN6 . . . . . 159 A7
Seven Acres HA4 . . . . . . 175 A4
Sevenoaks Cl HA6 . . . . . 174 C3
Seven Roe's Malting 5
    SG7 . . . . 23 E8
Sevens Cl HP4 . . . . 122 D4
Severalls The LU2 . . . . . . 46 B3
Severn Dr EN1 . . . . 162 A1
Severnmead HP2 . . . . . . 124 E6
Severnvale AL2 . . . . 142 F4
Severn Way
    Stevenage SG1 . . . . 36 F3
    Watford WD25 . . . . 154 C5
Sewardstone Rd
    Sewardstone E4, EN9 . . . 163 D3
    Waltham Abbey EN9 . . . 163 D3
Sewardstone St EN9 . . . . 163 C6
Sewell Cl AL4 . . . . 128 C3
Sewell Harris Cl
    CM20 . . . . 117 F1
Sewells AL8 . . . . 89 C2
Sexton Cl EN7 . . . . 147 B6
Seymour Ave LU1 . . . . 63 C1
Seymour Cl HA5 . . . . 175 F2
Seymour Cres HP2 . . . . . 124 E3
Seymour Ct
    Berkhamsted HP4 . . . . . 121 E6
    Tring HP23 . . . . 100 A4
Seymour Mews CM17 . . . . 118 C2
Seymour Rd
    Berkhamsted HP4 . . . . . 121 E6
    Luton LU1 . . . . 63 E1
    St Albans AL3 . . . . 127 C6
Shackledell SG2 . . . . 50 F2
Shacklegate La SG4 . . . . . 66 E5
Shackleton Gdns CM23 . . . 76 E6
Shackleton Spring
    SG2 . . . . 51 A3
Shackleton Way
    Abbots Langley WD5 . . . 154 A7

Shackleton Way continued
    Welwyn Garden City
    AL7 . . . . 111 D6
Shady Bush Cl WD23 . . . . 168 C2
Shady La WD17 . . . . 167 B7
Shafford Cotts
    Hemel Hempstead
    HP3 . . . . 139 A5
Shafford La AL3 . . . . 126 F6
SHAFTENHOE END 18 B8
Shaftenhoe End Rd
    Barley SG8 . . . . 9 A1
    Nuthampstead SG8 . . . . . 18 A8
Shaftesbury Ct
    Croxley Green WD3 . . . . 166 C4
    Stevenage SG1 . . . . 50 E4
Shaftesbury Dr SG5 . . . . . 11 C3
Shaftesbury High Sch
    HA3 . . . . 176 B2
Shaftesbury Ind Ctr
    SG6 . . . . 23 B7
Shaftesbury Quay 11
    SG14 . . . . 113 D6
Shaftesbury Rd
    Luton LU4 . . . . 45 B1
    Watford WD17 . . . . 167 C6
Shaftesbury Way WD4 . . . 139 C3
Shaftsbury Way WD4 . . . . 139 C3
Shakespeare Cl EN11 . . . . 115 A2
Shakespeare Ct EN11 . . . . 115 A2
Shakespeare Dr WD6 . . . . 170 A5
Shakespeare Ind Est
    WD24 . . . . 154 A1
Shakespeare Rd
    Harpenden AL5 . . . . 86 C1
    Luton LU4 . . . . 44 B2
Shakespeare St
    WD24 . . . . 154 B1
Shalcross Dr EN8 . . . . . . 148 F1
Shallcross Cres 6
    AL10 . . . . 130 A2
Shambrook Rd EN7 . . . . . 147 B6
Shangani Rd CM23 . . . . . . 76 F5
Shanklin Cl
    Goff's Oak EN7 . . . . 147 F2
    Luton LU3 . . . . 45 A4
Shanklin Gdns WD19 . . . . 175 C6
Shantock Hall La HP3 . . . . 136 E1
Shantock La HP3 . . . . 136 E1
Sharmans Cl AL6 . . . . 89 F4
Sharose Ct AL3 . . . . 83 E5
Sharpcroft 2 HP2 . . . . . . 124 D5
Sharp Ct 2 SG1 . . . . 50 E6
Sharpenhoe Rd LU3 . . . . . 31 A5
Sharpes La HP1 . . . . 123 B1
Sharples Gn LU3 . . . . 45 B8
Shaw Cl
    Bushey WD23 . . . . 176 E8
    Cheshunt EN8 . . . . 148 C3
SHAW GREEN 25 D5
Shaw's Cnr* AL6 . . . . 88 A6
Shaws The AL7 . . . . 111 C5
Shearers The 2 CM23 . . . . 76 B4
Sheares Hoppit SG12 . . . . . 95 D2
Shearwater Cl SG2 . . . . . . 51 D4
Sheepcot Dr WD25 . . . . . 154 C5
Sheepcote AL7 . . . . 111 A3
SHEEPCOTE GREEN 30 F6
Sheepcote La AL4 . . . . 87 F1
Sheepcote Rd HP2 . . . . . . 124 F3
Sheepcot La WD25 . . . . . 154 B6
Sheepcote Villas
    WD25 . . . . 154 C5
Sheepcroft Hill SG2 . . . . . 51 D3
Sheephouse Rd HP3 . . . . . 124 F1
SHEERING 98 C1
Sheering CE Prim Sch
    CM22 . . . . 98 D1
Sheering Dr CM17 . . . . . . 118 E4
Sheering Lower Rd
    Harlow CM17, CM22 . . . 118 F7
    Sheering CM22 . . . . 98 A2
Sheering Mill La CM21 . . . 97 F2
Sheering Rd
    Harlow, Churchgate Street
    CM17 . . . . 118 F4
    Harlow CM17 . . . . 118 F5
Sheethanger La HP3 . . . . 138 A7
Shefton Rise HA6 . . . . . . 175 A3
Sheldon Cl EN7 . . . . 147 E5
Shelford Rd EN5 . . . . 171 C3
Shelley Cl
    Borehamwood WD6 . . . . 170 A5
    Hitchin SG4 . . . . 35 C7
    Moor Park HA6 . . . . 174 F5
    Royston SG8 . . . . 2 D1
Shelley Ct
    Cheshunt EN7 . . . . 148 A3
    16 Harpenden AL5 . . . . . 86 B1
    Waltham Abbey EN9 . . . 163 F6
Shelley La UB9 . . . . 173 A3
Shelley Rd LU4 . . . . 44 B2
Shelton Way LU2 . . . . 46 A3
Shendish Edge HP3 . . . . . 138 F6
SHENLEY 157 A5
SHENLEYBURY 156 E8
Shenleybury WD7 . . . . . . 156 E8
Shenleybury Cotts
    WD7 . . . . 156 E8
Shenleybury Farm Cotts
    WD7 . . . . 142 E1
Shenleybury Villas
    WD7 . . . . 156 F5
Shenley Ct HP2 . . . . 125 B8
Shenley Hill WD7 . . . . . . 156 B4
Shenley La AL2 . . . . 142 C4
Shenley Prim Sch
    WD7 . . . . 156 F5

Shenley Rd
    Borehamwood WD6 . . . . 170 B6
    Hemel Hempstead HP2 . . 105 B1
    Radlett WD7 . . . . 156 C4
Shenstone Hill HP4 . . . . . 122 E5
Shenval Ho CM20 . . . . . . 118 A4
Shenval Ind Est CM20 . . . 118 B4
Shephalbury Park Prim
    Sch SG2 . . . . 51 B1
Shephall Gn SG2 . . . . 51 B2
Shephall La SG2 . . . . 51 B3
Shephall La SG2 . . . . 50 F1
Shephall View SG1 . . . . . . 51 A5
Shephall Way SG2 . . . . . . 51 C3
Shepherd Cl
    Abbots Langley WD5 . . . 153 F8
    Royston SG8 . . . . 7 E5
Shepherd Prim Sch
    WD3 . . . . 165 A1
Shepherds Cl CM23 . . . . . 76 C4
Shepherds Cl SG14 . . . . . 92 C1
Shepherds Farm
    WD3 . . . . 165 A1
Shepherds Gn HP1 . . . . . 123 E2
Shepherds La SG1 . . . . . . 50 A6
Shepherd's La WD3 . . . . . 164 E2
Shepherds Mead SG5 . . . . 21 F2
Shepherds Rd WD18 . . . . 166 F5
Shepherd's Row AL3 . . . . 106 B5
Shepherds Wlk
    Brookmans Park AL9 . . . 145 D4
    Harpenden AL5 . . . . 85 D4
    Rickmansworth WD3 . . . 165 B2
Shepherds Wlk WD23 . . . 176 D8
Shepley Mews EN3 . . . . . 163 A2
Sheppard Cl EN1 . . . . 162 B1
Sheppards Cl AL3 . . . . . . 127 E6
Sheppards Yd 4 HP1 . . . . 124 D4
Shepperton Cl WD6 . . . . . 170 D8
Sheppey's La WD5 . . . . . . 139 E3
Sheraton Cl WD6 . . . . . . 169 F4
Sheraton Ho WD3 . . . . . . 164 C5
Sheraton Mews
    WD18 . . . . 166 E5
Sherborne Ave LU2 . . . . . . 45 D6
Sherborne Cotts
    WD18 . . . . 167 C4
Sherborne Pl HA6 . . . . . . 174 D4
Sherborne Way WD3 . . . . 166 B5
Sherbourne Cl HP2 . . . . . 124 E2
Sherbourne Ct AL1 . . . . . 127 F3
Sherd Cl LU3 . . . . 44 F7
Sheredes Dr EN11 . . . . . . 134 F4
Sheredes Prim Sch
    EN11 . . . . 134 F4
Sheredes Sch EN11 . . . . . 134 F5
Sherfield Ave WD3 . . . . . 173 E8
Sheridan Cl HP1 . . . . 124 B2
Sheridan Rd
    Luton LU3 . . . . 45 C2
    Watford WD19 . . . . 167 D2
Sheridan Wlk EN10 . . . . . 134 E3
Sheriff Way WD25 . . . . . . 154 A5
Sheringham Ave SG1 . . . . 36 B1
Sheringham Cl LU2 . . . . . . 45 C7
Sherington Ave HA5 . . . . 176 A3
Sherland Ct WD7 . . . . . . 156 A4
Shernbroke Rd EN9 . . . . . 163 F5
Sherrards Mans AL8 . . . . . 89 B1
Sherrards Mews AL8 . . . . . 89 B1
Sherrardspark Rd
    AL8 . . . . 110 C8
Sherrardswood Sch
    AL6 . . . . 89 D4
Shervington Gr LU3 . . . . . . 45 C3
Sherwood Cl SG6 . . . . 22 F8
Sherwood Ave
    Potters Bar EN6 . . . . . . 158 E7
    St Albans AL4 . . . . 128 B6
Sherwood Cl
    20 Bishop's Stortford
    CM23 . . . . 76 F7
    Watford WD25 . . . . 154 A5
Sherwood Ho WD5 . . . . . 153 F8
Sherwood Pl 8 HP2 . . . . . 124 F6
Sherwood Rd LU4 . . . . 45 A2
Sherwoods Rd WD19 . . . . 167 E2
Sherwoods Rise AL5 . . . . 107 D8
Shetland Cl WD6 . . . . . . 170 D3
Shetland Ho 13 WD18 . . . 166 F3
SHILLINGTON 19 F8
Shillington Rd SG5 . . . . . . 20 B5
Shillitoe Ave EN6 . . . . . . 158 E7
Shingle Cl LU3 . . . . 45 A8
Ship La LU2 . . . . 80 D3
Shire Cl EN10 . . . . 148 F5
Shire Ct
    Hemel Hempstead
    HP2 . . . . 125 A4
    Stevenage SG1 . . . . 50 C7
Shire La
    Chalfont St P, Horn Hill
    WD3 . . . . 172 B6
    Chalfont St P, West Hyde
    WD3 . . . . 172 C4
    Chorleywood WD3 . . . . 164 C4
    Tring HP23 . . . . 120 B4
Shiremeade WD6 . . . . . . 169 F4
Shire Pk AL7 . . . . 110 E8
Shires The
    Luton LU2 . . . . 45 D1
    Royston SG8 . . . . 7 E6
    Watford WD25 . . . . 154 C8

Shirley Cl
Cheshunt EN8 .... 148 C2
Cheshunt, Wormley
  EN10..................... 148 F7
Stevenage SG2 .... 51 C8
Shirley Rd
Abbots Langley WD5 .... 153 F7
Luton LU1 .... 63 C8
St Albans AL1 .... 127 F2
Shooters Dr EN9 .... 135 E1
SHOOTERSWAY 121 C4
Shootersway HP4 ...... 121 E4
Shootersway La HP4 ... 121 F4
Shootersway Pk HP4.... 121 F3
Shoplands AL8 .... 89 D2
Shoreham Cl SG1....... 50 A8
Shortcroft CM23........ 77 D7
Short Hale LU7........ 80 D3
Short La
Aston SG2 .... 51 E4
Bricket Wood AL2 .... 140 E2
Shortlands Gn AL7 ..... 110 F5
Shortlands Pl CM23..... 76 F8
Shortmead Dr EN8...... 162 E8
Shothanger Way HP3 ... 137 D6
Shottfield Cl AL4 .... 108 D2
Shott La SG6............ 23 A5
Shrubbery Gr SG8 ...... 7 D4
Shrubbery The HP1..... 123 E4
Shrubhill Rd HP1........ 123 F2
Shrublands AL3 .... 145 B5
Shrublands Ave HP4 ... 122 A4
Shrublands Rd HP4..... 122 A5
Shrublands The EN6 ... 158 E6
Shrubs UB9............. 173 F4
Shrubs Rd UB9 .... 173 F4
Shugars Gn HP23 ...... 100 B5
Sibley Ave AL5 .... 107 E7
Sibley Cl LU2............ 46 B3
Sibthorpe Rd AL9....... 144 D7
Siccut Rd SG4 .... 35 E4
Sicklefield Cl EN7 ...... 147 F5
Siddons Rd SG2 .... 51 C6
Sidford Cl HP1.......... 123 F3
Sidford Cl SG14 .... 113 C7
Sidings The
Hatfield AL10 .... 129 E4
Hemel Hempstead HP2 .... 124 D3
Hoddesdon EN10 .... 135 A1
Lower Stondon SG16...... 10 B3
Siding Way AL2.......... 142 B5
Sidmouth Cl WD19...... 175 B8
Sidney Cl EN6 .... 162 F5
Sidney Terr CM23 .... 76 F6
Siena Pl 1 WD18........ 166 F5
Signal Cl SG16 .... 10 B3
Silam Rd SG1 .... 50 E5
Silecroft Rd LU2......... 64 B8
Silkin Ct SG2 .... 51 D3
Silk Mill Ct WD19........ 167 B2
Silk Mill Rd
Redbourn AL3 .... 106 B4
Watford WD19............ 167 B2
Silk Mill Way HP23 ..... 100 A5
Silverbirch Ave SG5..... 11 F8
Silver Birch Ct EN8 ..... 162 D8
Silver Birch Lo WD24 ... 154 B1
Silver Cl HA3 .... 176 D3
Silver Ct
Ashwell SG7............... 4 D4
Hitchin SG5 .... 34 F8
Silverdale Ho HA4 ...... 174 F4
Silverdale Rd WD23..... 167 E4
Silver Dell WD24 .... 153 F4
Silver Hill WD6, WD7 ... 157 B3
Silver Pl 12 WD18....... 166 E5
Silver St
Anstey SG9 .... 29 A5
Ashwell SG7............... 4 D4
Goff's Oak EN7 .... 147 D1
Guilden Morden SG8...... 1 F4
Luton LU1 .... 63 E7
Stansted Mountfitchet
  CM24 .... 59 D6
Waltham Abbey EN9 ...... 163 C6
Silverthorn Dr HP3 ..... 139 B7
Silver Trees AL2 .... 140 F1
Silverwood Cl HA6 ...... 174 C2
Simmonds Rise HP4 .... 124 D1
Simon Balle Sch
  SG13 .... 113 E5
Simon Dean HP3 .... 137 A4
Simplicity La 6
  CM17 .... 118 D1
Simpson Cl LU4 .... 44 D2
Simpson Dr SG2 .... 23 F8
Simpsons Cl 3 SG7 ..... 23 F8
Sinclair Ho 4 LU4 ...... 176 F4
Sinderby Cl WD6 .... 169 E8
Sinfield Cl SG1 .... 51 A5
Singlets La AL3.......... 84 C2
Sir Frederic Osborn Sch
  AL7...................... 111 B7
Sir Herbert Janes Village
  LU4 .... 44 D4
Sir John Lawes Sch
  AL5...................... 86 C3
Sir John Newsom Way
  AL7...................... 110 C3
Sir Joseph's Wlk AL5 ... 107 A8
Sir Peter's Way HP4 .... 81 E6
Sirus Rd HA6 .... 175 A5
Sish Cl SG1 .... 50 D6
Sish La SG1 .... 50 D6

Siskin Cl
Borehamwood WD6....... 170 A5
Royston SG8 .... 7 E8
Watford WD23............ 167 E5
Sisson Cl SG2 .... 51 C2
Sitwell Gr HA7 .... 176 F5
Six Acres HP3 .... 139 A8
Six Cotts SG11 .... 57 C6
Six Hills Rdbt SG1 ...... 50 D4
Six Hills Way
Stevenage SG1, SG2 ...... 50 C4
Stevenage SG2 .... 51 B4
Sixth Ave
Letchworth Garden City
  SG6...................... 23 C6
Watford WD25............ 154 D4
Skegness Rd SG1 .... 50 A8
Skegsbury La SG4 .... 65 F1
Skelton Cl LU3 .... 31 B1
Skidmore Way WD3...... 165 E1
Skillen Lo HA5 .... 175 D2
Skimpans Cl AL9 .... 144 D7
Skimpot La LU1, LU4 .... 44 B1
Skimpot Rd LU4, LU5 ... 44 A1
Skinners St CM23........ 76 C4
Skipton Cl SG2 .... 68 F8
Skua Cl LU4 .... 44 A5
Skye Rd 11 WD18........ 166 F3
Skylark Cnr SG2......... 51 D3
Skylark Pl SG8 .... 7 E8
Skyswood Prim Sch
  AL4 .... 128 C6
Skys Wood Rd AL4....... 128 B7
Slade CT WD7 .... 156 A4
Sleaford Gn WD19 ...... 175 D7
Sleapcross Gdns AL4 ... 129 C2
SLEAPSHYDE 129 C2
Sleaps Hyde SG2 .... 51 C1
Sleapshyde La AL4....... 129 C2
Sleddale HP2............ 124 F4
Sleets End HP1.......... 124 B5
Slimmons Dr AL4........ 128 A7
Slipe La EN10 .... 148 F7
SLIP END 63 C2
Slip End SG7 .... 14 B6
Slipe The LU7 .... 80 A7
Slip La SG3, AL6......... 68 C4
Slippers Hill HP2 .... 124 D4
Sloan Cl SG1 .... 50 F6
Sloansway AL7.......... 90 A1
Slowmans Cl AL2 .... 141 C3
Slype The AL4 .... 87 B5
Small Acre HP1.......... 123 F3
Smallcroft AL7 .... 111 B7
SMALLFORD 129 B4
Smallford La AL4 .... 129 B2
Smallford Works AL4 .... 129 B2
Smallwood Cl AL4 .... 108 E7
Smarts Gn EN7 .... 147 F5
Smeathman Ct HP1...... 124 C2
Smeaton Cl EN9 .... 163 E7
Smeaton Rd EN3 .... 163 A2
Smithfield HP2 .... 124 D5
Smiths Cres AL4 .... 129 C2
SMITH'S END 18 A8
Smith's End La
Barley SG8................ 17 F8
Nuthampstead SG8 .... 18 A8
Smiths La EN7 .... 147 D5
Smiths Lane Mall 5
  LU1 .... 63 E7
Smiths Sq 9 LU1......... 63 E7
Smith St WD18 .... 167 C5
Smithy The
Little Hadham SG11....... 57 B2
Sawbridgeworth CM21 .... 97 E3
SMUG OAK 141 B1
Smug Oak Bsns Ctr
  AL2...................... 141 B1
Smug Oak La AL2 .... 141 D1
SNAILSWELL 21 E6
Snailswell La SG5 .... 21 E5
Snatchup AL3 .... 106 A5
Snells Mead SG9 .... 40 F7
Snipe The SG4........... 24 B1
Snowdonia Way SG1..... 37 A4
Snowdrop Cl CM23 ...... 76 C6
SNOW END 29 A6
Snowford Cl 11 LU3..... 45 A7
Snowley Par CM23....... 59 B1
Soham Rd EN3 .... 162 F2
Solar Ct WD18........... 166 F4
Solar Way EN3 .... 162 F3
Solesbridge Cl WD3 ..... 164 F6
Solesbridge La WD3..... 165 B7
Sollershott E SG6........ 22 F4
Sollershott Hall SG6...... 22 F4
Sollershott W SG6....... 22 F4
Solomon's Hill WD3 ..... 165 D2
Solway HP2.............. 124 F5
Solway Rd N LU3........ 45 A4
Solway Rd S LU3 .... 45 A3
Somerby Cl EN10 .... 135 A2
Someries Inf Sch LU2.... 46 C3
Someries Jun Sch LU2... 46 C3
Someries Rd
Harpenden AL5 .... 86 C4
Hemel Hempstead HP1.... 123 F5
Somersby Cl LU1 .... 63 E5
Somerset Ave LU2....... 46 A1
Somerset Rd EN3 .... 163 A1
Somersham AL7......... 111 D6
Somers Rd AL9.......... 144 C7
Somers Sq AL9 .... 144 C8
Somers Way WD23...... 168 C2
Sommer's Ct SG12....... 114 E8

Sommerville Ct 12
  WD6..................... 169 F8
Sonia Cl WD19 .... 167 C2
Soothouse Spring
  AL3 .... 127 F7
Soper Mews 6 EN3 ..... 163 A1
Soper Sq 2 CM17 .... 118 C1
Sopers Rd EN6 .... 146 F2
SOPWELL 141 F8
Sopwell La AL1.......... 127 D3
Sorrel Cl
Luton LU3................. 45 B8
Royston SG8 .... 7 F5
Sorrel Garth SG4 .... 35 A6
Sotheron Rd WD17...... 167 C6
Souberie Ave SG6....... 22 F5
Souldern St WD18 ...... 167 B4
Southacre Way HA5 .... 175 C2
Southall Cl SG12........ 93 D2
South App HA6 .... 174 D7
South Bank Rd HP4..... 121 F6
South Block CM21 ...... 97 F2
Southbrook CM21....... 97 E1
Southbrook Dr 2
  EN8 .... 148 D3
South Charlton Mead La
  EN11 .... 135 D5
South Cl
Baldock SG7 .... 23 F7
Barnet EN5 .... 171 F6
Royston SG8 .... 7 B7
South Comm AL3 .... 106 B5
South Cottage Dr
  WD3..................... 164 F4
South Cottage Gdns
  WD3..................... 164 F4
South Dene HP2 .... 104 A8
Southdown Cl AL10 ..... 130 A2
Southdown Ho AL5 ..... 107 C8
Southdown Ind Est
  AL5...................... 107 C8
Southdown Rd
Harpenden AL5 .... 107 B8
Hatfield AL10.............. 130 A2
South Dr
Cuffley EN6 .... 146 E1
St Albans AL4 .... 128 E4
South Drift Way LU1..... 63 B5
SOUTH-END 96 B6
South End SG1 .... 50 D7
Southern Ave SG16 ..... 10 C3
SOUTHERN GREEN 26 A4
Southern Rise LU2....... 85 F7
Southern Terr 2
  EN11 .... 115 B1
Southern Way
Letchworth Garden City
  SG6...................... 22 E8
Studham LU6.............. 82 C4
Southernwood Cl
  HP2 .... 125 A4
Southerton Way WD7 ... 156 E6
South Farm Cotts
  AL2...................... 142 C3
Southfield
Barnet EN5 .... 171 D3
Braughing SG11........... 55 F7
Welwyn Garden City
  AL7...................... 110 D4
Southfield Ave WD23 ... 154 C1
Southfield Rd
Cheshunt EN8 .... 162 E7
Hoddesdon EN11......... 135 A7
Southfields
Letchworth Garden City
  SG6...................... 11 F1
Standon SG11 .... 55 E2
Southfield Sch AL10 .... 130 B1
Southgate SG1 .... 50 D4
Southgate Cotts WD3 ... 165 E2
Southgate Cl 5 AL5..... 86 A2
Southgate Ho EN8 ...... 148 D1
Southgate Rd EN6 ...... 159 C6
SOUTH HATFIELD 130 B2
Southhill HA6 .... 174 E2
South Hill Cl SG4........ 35 A6
South Hill Prim Sch
  HP1 .... 124 C2
South Hill Rd HP1 ...... 124 C3
South Lawns WD25 ..... 155 B3
South Ley AL7 .... 110 E3
South Ley Ct AL7........ 110 E3
South Lodge Mews 2
  SG7..................... 23 F7
Southlynn Ho 2 LU2 .... 63 F8
Southmead Cres EN8 ... 148 F1
Southmill Ct CM23....... 77 A6
Southmill Rd CM23 ..... 77 A5
Southmill Trad Ctr
  CM23 .... 77 A6
SOUTH MIMMS 158 A8
South Mundells AL7..... 110 F7
South Ordnance Rd
  EN3 .... 163 A2
SOUTH OXHEY 175 B7
South Park Ave HA4 .... 154 F4
South Park Gdns HP4... 122 B5
South Pri
Harlow CM20.............. 118 A4
Hitchin SG5 .... 34 D8
Waltham Abbey EN9 ...... 163 C6
South Rd
Baldock SG7 .... 22 A4
Bishop's Stortford CM23... 77 A5
Chorleywood WD3 .... 164 C4
Harlow CM20.............. 118 A4

South Rd continued
Luton LU1................. 63 D6
Standon SG11 .... 55 D2
South Riding AL2........ 141 A1
Southsea Ave WD18 .... 167 A5
Southsea Rd SG1........ 50 B8
Southside SG9............ 28 A3
South St
Bishop's Stortford
  CM23.................... 76 F6
Hertford SG14 .... 113 D6
Stanstead Abbotts
  SG12.................... 115 C4
South Street Commercial
Ctr 8 CM23.............. 76 F6
South View SG6 .... 22 F5
Southview Cl 1 EN7..... 147 E5
Southview Rd AL5 .... 86 D3
South View Rd HA5...... 175 B4
Southwark Cl SG1....... 37 B2
Southwark Ho 11
  WD6..................... 170 A7
South Way
Abbots Langley WD5,
  WD25.................... 153 E6
Hatfield AL10.............. 130 B2
South Weald Dr EN9 .... 163 D6
Southwold Cl SG1 .... 50 A6
Southwold Rd WD24 .... 154 C2
Soval Ct HA6 .... 174 D3
Sovereign Ct
Northwood HA6............ 175 A2
Watford WD18............ 167 A5
Sovereign Pk
Hemel Hempstead
  HP2..................... 125 B5
Luton LU4................. 44 F1
Sovereign Pk AL4........ 128 D2
Sowerby Ave LU2........ 46 C3
Spandove Ct 7 LU1 ..... 63 D6
Sparhawke SG6.......... 12 A1
Sparrow Cl LU4.......... 44 A4
Sparrow Dr SG2 .... 51 D4
Sparrows Herne
  WD23................... 168 C2
Sparrows Herne Mansion
  WD23................... 168 D2
Sparrows Way WD23 ... 168 C1
Sparrowswick Ride
  AL3 .... 127 C8
Sparrow Wlk SG5 .... 154 A4
Spayne Cl LU3........... 45 B8
Spear Cl LU3 .... 44 E6
Spectrum Ho EN3 .... 162 E3
Speedwell Cl
Hemel Hempstead
  HP1..................... 123 E2
Luton LU3................. 45 A8
Speke Cl SG2............ 51 D5
SPELLBROOK 97 F8
Spellbrook 5 SG5........ 34 D8
Spellbrook La E CM22... 97 F8
Spellbrook La W CM23... 97 F7
Spellbrook Prim Sch
  CM23 .... 97 F7
Spencer Ave EN7........ 147 E5
Spencer Cl CM24 .... 59 E6
Spencer Gate AL1....... 127 E5
Spencer Ho SG5......... 11 F6
Spencer Pl AL4 .... 108 C2
Spencer Rd
Harrow HA3............... 176 E1
Luton LU3................. 45 C2
SPENCERSGREEN 119 C7
Spencer St
Hertford SG13 .... 113 E7
St Albans AL3 .... 127 D3
Spencer Way
Hemel Hempstead
  HP1..................... 124 A6
Letchworth Garden City
  SG6...................... 22 F8
Sperberry Hill SG4....... 35 B2
Spencer Rd AL5.......... 86 C1
Speyhawk Pl EN6........ 145 B1
Sphere Ind Est AL1...... 128 A2
Spicersfield EN7......... 148 A4
Spicer St AL3............ 127 C3
Spielplatz AL2........... 141 A3
Spindle Berry Cl AL6..... 90 A7
Spinney Cl SG4.......... 35 B6
Spinney Ct AL7 .... 97 E2
Spinney Inf Sch
  CM20.................... 118 A1
Spinney Jun Sch
  CM20.................... 118 A1
Spinney La AL6 .... 68 E3
Spinney Rd LU3.......... 44 D7
Spinney Row AL2........ 142 A4
Spinneys Dr AL3......... 127 B1
Spinney St SG13 .... 114 A6
Spinney The
Baldock SG7 .... 23 E7
Berkhamsted HP4 .... 121 F3
Cheshunt EN7 .... 148 B1
1 Cheshunt EN7 .... 148 A1
Harpenden AL5 .... 85 E3
Hertford SG13 .... 113 F6
Hoddesdon EN10......... 134 F4
Potters Bar EN6 .... 159 D8
Radlett WD25 .... 155 D1

Spinney The continued
Welwyn Garden City
  AL7...................... 110 E5
Spires Sh Ctr The
EN5 .... 171 E6
Spires The
Bishop's Stortford
  CM23.................... 76 D7
Hemel Hempstead HP2 ... 124 D2
SPITALBROOK 135 B4
Spittlesea Rd LU2 .... 64 C7
Spooners Rd AL2........ 141 C4
Spratts La LU6 .... 82 F8
Spreckley Cl SG16....... 10 B5
Spring Cl
Barnet EN5 .... 171 D4
Borehamwood WD6....... 170 A8
Harefield UB9 .... 173 D2
Latimer HP5 .... 150 D3
Spring Court Rd EN2 .... 161 A1
Spring Crofts WD23..... 168 A4
Spring Dr SG2 .... 69 B8
Springfield WD23........ 168 D1
Springfield Cl
Croxley Green WD3 .... 166 B4
Potters Bar EN6 .... 159 E8
Springfield Cres AL5..... 86 B5
Springfield Ct
Bishop's Stortford
  CM23.................... 76 E8
Rickmansworth WD3 ..... 165 B1
Springfield Lo SG13 ..... 113 C5
Springfield Rd
Cheshunt EN8 .... 162 E7
Hemel Hempstead HP2.... 124 F4
Luton LU3................. 45 C6
St Albans AL4 .... 129 B3
St Albans, The Camp
  AL1...................... 128 A2
Watford WD25............ 154 B6
Spring Field Rd HP4 ..... 122 A6
Springfields
Hoddesdon EN10......... 134 F4
Waltham Abbey EN9 ...... 163 E5
Welwyn Garden City
  AL8...................... 110 B4
Springfields Ho AL8 ..... 110 C4
Spring Gdns WD25...... 154 C3
Spring Glen AL10 .... 129 F4
Springhall Cl CM21...... 97 E2
Springhall La CM21...... 97 E1
Springhall Rd CM21..... 97 E2
Springhead SG7......... 4 D4
Spring Hills CM20 .... 117 B1
Spring Hills Twr
  CM20.................... 117 A1
Spring La
Cottered SG9.............. 39 C5
Hemel Hempstead HP1.... 124 A4
Springle La SG13 .... 114 F2
Springmead Jun Mix Inf
Sch AL7.................. 111 C7
Spring Mews CM21 ..... 97 E2
Spring Pl 6 LU1.......... 63 D6
Spring Rd
Harpenden AL5 .... 85 A4
Letchworth Garden City
  SG6...................... 22 E6
Springs Cotts EN10 ..... 148 E7
Springshott SG6......... 22 E5
Springs The
Cheshunt EN10 .... 148 E6
Hertford SG13 .... 113 F7
Spring Valley Ent Ctr
AL3 .... 127 E7
Spring View Rd SG12.... 114 C8
Spring Way HP2......... 125 C5
Springwell Ave WD3 .... 173 A8
Springwell Ct
Rickmansworth WD3 ..... 173 A8
Stanstead Abbotts
  SG12.................... 115 C3
Springwell La WD3 ...... 173 A6
Spring Wlk EN10 .... 134 C2
Springwood EN7......... 148 A5
Springwood Cl UB9...... 173 D2
Springwood Wlk AL4 ... 128 D6
Spruce Way AL2......... 141 B4
Spur Cl WD5 .... 153 D6
Spurcroft LU3 .... 31 C1
Spurling Wks EN11 ...... 135 C7
Spurrs Cl SG4 .... 35 B7
Spur The
8 Cheshunt EN8........... 148 D3
Stevenage SG1 .... 50 E4
Square St 3 CM17 ...... 118 C1
Square The
Braughing SG11........... 55 F7
Buckland SG8............. 27 D5
Hemel Hempstead HP1.... 124 C3
Hoddesdon EN10......... 148 E8
Much Hadham SG10 ..... 74 F3
Potten End HP4 .... 123 B7
Redbourn AL3 .... 105 F6
Sawbridgeworth CM21 ... 97 E2
Watford WD24............ 154 B2
Squires Ct CM23 .... 76 D8
Squires Cl EN11 .... 135 A5
Squires Ride HP2........ 104 F1
Squirrel Chase HP1...... 123 E4
Squirrels Cl 2 CM23..... 76 F8
Squirrels The
Bushey WD23 .... 168 D3
Hertford SG13 .... 114 B6
Welwyn Garden City
  AL7...................... 111 C5

Sta–Sun 215

table Block The AL6 90 B2
table Cotts SG11 57 E2
table Ct AL1 127 E5
table Mews
Northaw AL9 145 E3
St Albans AL1 127 E4
tables The
Radlett WD25 155 B3
Sawbridgeworth CM21 98 B3
tacey Ct 9 CM23 76 F6
tackfield CM20 118 A3
tacklands AL8 110 B4
taddles CM22 98 B8
tadium Est The LU4 44 B1
tadium Way CM19 116 F1
taff Cotts
Harefield UB9 173 B2
London Colney WD7 142 C1
tafford Cl EN8 148 B2
tafford Ct EN10 135 A3
tafford Dr EN10 135 A3
tafford Ho
Bishop's Stortford
CM23 76 F5
Hoddesdon EN10 135 A3
tafford Rd HA3 176 C3
taffords CM17 118 E4
tag Ct WD3 164 C5
tagg Hill EN4 159 E3
tag Green Ave AL9 130 C7
tagg Ridge EN6 159 D5
tag La
Berkhamsted HP4 122 B5
Chorleywood WD3 164 C3
tainer Rd
Borehamwood WD6 156 D1
Radlett WD6 169 D8
tainers CM23 76 C5
TAINES GREEN 112 D4
tains Cl EN8 148 F3
take Piece Rd SG8 7 C5
takers Ct AL5 86 B1
tamford Ave SG8 7 D7
tamford Cl
Harrow HA3 176 E3
Potters Bar EN6 159 D7
tamford Ct SG8 7 D7
tamford Rd WD17 167 B7
tamford Yd SG8 7 C6
TANBOROUGH 110 A3
tanborough Ave
WD6 157 B1
tanborough Cl
Borehamwood WD6 157 A1
Welwyn Garden City
AL8 110 C5
tanborough Gn AL8 110 C4
tanborough La AL8 110 C4
tanborough Mews
AL8 110 D4
tanborough Prim Sch
WD25 154 C4
tanborough Rd AL8 110 C4
tanborough Sch AL8 110 B4
tanborough Sec Sch
WD25 154 B4
tanbury Ave WD17 153 E2
tandalone Farm*
SG6 22 D8
tandard Rd EN3 162 E2
tandfield WD5 139 E1
tandhill Cl SG4 34 F6
tandhill Rd SG4 34 F6
TANDON 55 E1
tandon Bsns Pk SG11 55 E1
tandon Ct SG11 55 F1
TANDON GREEN END
72 E4
tandon Hill SG11 55 D2
tandon Mill SG11 55 F2
tandon Rd SG11 56 E3
tandring Rise HP3 138 B8
tane Cl CM23 58 F1
tane Field SG6 23 B3
tanelow Cres SG11 55 D2
tane St SG7 13 A1
tanford Rd LU2 46 A1
tangate Cres WD6 170 E4
tanhope 3 HA6 174 F5
tanhope Ave HA3 176 D2
tanhope Rd
Barnet EN5 171 D3
Cheshunt EN8 162 E6
St Albans AL1 127 F3
Stanier Rise HP4 121 F7
Stanley Ave AL2 141 A6
Stanley Dr AL10 130 B3
Stanley Gdns
Borehamwood WD6 169 E8
Tring HP23 99 F3
Stanley Livingstone Ct 2
LU1 63 D6
Stanley Lodge 12 AL1 127 E4
Stanley Rd
Hertford SG13 113 E5
Northwood HA6 175 A2
Stevenage SG2 51 B7
Streatley LU3 31 A5
Watford WD18 167 C5
Stanley St LU1 63 D6
STANMORE 176 F5
Stanmore Chase AL4 128 D2
Stanmore Cres LU3 44 F4
Stanmore Rd
Stevenage SG1 50 D7
Watford WD24 167 B8
Stanmount Rd AL2 141 A6
Stannington Path
WD6 170 A8
STANSTEAD ABBOTTS
115 E4
Stanstead Dr EN11 135 B8
Stanstead Rd
Hertford Heath SG13 114 D5
Hertford SG13 114 A6
Hoddesdon EN11 115 B1
Stansted Hill SG10 75 A1
STANSTED
MOUNTFITCHET 59 D6
Stansted Mountfitchet Sta
CM24 59 E6
Stansted Mountfitchet
Windmill* CM24 59 D6
Stansted Rd
Birchanger CM23,
CM24 59 C4
Bishop's Stortford CM23 59 B2
Stanta Bsns Ctr 3
AL3 127 F7
Stanton Cl AL4 128 D7
Stanton Rd LU4 44 C1
Stantons CM20 117 B1
Stants View 1 SG13 113 F7
Staplefield Cl HA5 175 E3
STAPLEFORD 92 A7
Stapleford AL7 111 D6
Stapleford Prim Sch
SG14 92 A6
Stapleford Rd LU2 46 C4
Stapleton Cl EN6 159 D8
Stapleton Rd WD6 157 A2
Stapley Rd AL3 127 D4
Stapylton Rd EN5 171 E6
Star Holme Ct SG12 93 E1
Starkey Cl EN7 147 C6
Starlight Way AL4 128 C1
Starling Ct 16 CM23 76 F6
Starling La EN6 146 F3
Starling's Bridge SG5 34 F8
STARLING'S GREEN 30 F3
Star St SG12 93 E1
STARTOP'S END 79 F1
Startpoint LU1 63 C7
Stately Ct 22 LU3 45 D1
Statham Cl LU3 31 B1
Stathams Ct AL3 106 A3
Station App
Cheshunt EN8 162 E5
Chorleywood WD3 164 D5
Harlow CM20 118 C5
Harpenden AL5 86 B1
Hitchin SG4 35 A8
Kings Langley WD4 139 B1
Knebworth SG3 68 F5
Northwood HA6 174 E3
Radlett WD7 156 A4
South Oxhey WD19 175 D7
Station Cl
Brookmans Park AL9 144 E5
Lower Stondon SG16 10 B3
Potters Bar EN6 158 F8
Station Ct 15 SG12 93 D1
Stationers Pl HP3 138 E6
Station Footpath
WD4 139 B1
Station Par SG6 22 F6
Station Pl SG6 22 F6
Station Rd
Aldbury HP23 101 B5
Arlesey SG15 11 A4
Ashwell SG7 4 F4
Baldock SG7 12 F1
Berkhamsted HP4 122 D4
Bishop's Stortford CM23 77 A7
Borehamwood WD6 170 A5
Braughing SG11 55 E5
Bricket Wood AL2 155 A8
Brookmans Park AL9 144 D6
Buntingford SG9 40 E7
Cheddington LU7 79 F8
Cuffley EN6 146 F2
Harlow CM17 118 C4
Harpenden AL5 86 C2
Hemel Hempstead HP1 124 C1
Hoddesdon EN10 135 A3
Holdbrook EN9 163 A5
Ivinghoe LU7 80 E5
Kings Langley WD4 139 B1
Knebworth SG3 69 A5
Letchworth Garden City
SG6 22 F6
Letty Green SG14 112 B3
Long Marston HP23 79 B4
Lower Stondon SG16 10 A4
Luton, High Town LU1 63 E8
Luton, Leagrave LU4 44 E5
Much Hadham SG10 74 E1
Radlett WD7 156 A4
Rickmansworth WD3 165 D2
Sawbridgeworth CM21 97 F3
St Albans AL4 129 B3
Standon SG11 55 E2
Stanstead Abbotts
SG12 115 C4
Stansted Mountfitchet
CM24 59 E6
Steeple Morden SG7, SG8 5 C5
Tring HP23 100 D4
Ware SG12 93 E1
Watford WD17 167 B7
Watton at S SG14 70 D3
Welwyn AL6 89 E3
Wheathampstead AL4 87 D1
Station Rdbt WD3 165 D2
Station Terr
Hitchin SG4 35 A8
Park Street AL2 141 D5
Station Way
Letchworth Garden City
SG6 22 E6
St Albans AL1 127 F3
Staveley Rd LU4 44 C1
Steed Yd 6 SG7 23 E8
Steeplands WD23 168 B2
Steeple View CM23 76 F8
Sten Cl EN3 163 A2
Stephens Cl LU2 46 A3
Stephens Gdns LU2 46 A2
Stephenson Cl
Hoddesdon EN11 135 C6
Hoddesdon EN11 135 D6
Royston SG8 7 B7
Stephenson Mews SG2 51 B4
Stephenson Way WD23,
WD24 167 D7
Stephenson Wharf
HP3 138 F6
Stephenson Wk SG5 11 C2
Stephens Way AL3 105 F5
Stephyns Chambers
HP1 124 C2
Stepnells HP23 80 A1
Stepping Stones The
LU3 44 E5
Sterling Ave EN8 162 D5
Sterling Rd EN2 161 D1
STEVENAGE 50 D8
Stevenage Bsns Pk
SG1 37 C2
Stevenage Cres WD6 169 E8
Stevenage Enterprise Ctr
SG1 50 B7
Stevenage L Pk SG1 50 C4
Stevenage Mus* SG1 50 E5
Stevenage Rd
Hitchin SG4 34 F5
Knebworth SG2, SG3 68 F7
Little Wymondley SG4 35 E3
Little Wymondley, Titmore
Green SG4 35 E2
St Ippolyts SG4 35 C2
Walkern SG2 51 E8
Stevenage Rise HP2 124 F7
Stevenage Sta SG1 50 C5
Stevens Cl EN6 158 D6
Stevens Gn WD23 168 C1
Steward Cl EN8 148 E1
Stewart Cl WD5 154 A7
Stewart Pl 4 SG12 93 E1
Stewart Rd AL5 86 B2
Stewarts The CM23 76 E6
Stile Plantation SG8 7 E6
Stilton Path WD6 157 A1
Stirling Bsns Pk EN8 162 F5
Stirling Cl
Hitchin SG4 35 C7
Stevenage SG2 69 D7
Stirling Cnr EN5 170 D3
Stirling Ho WD6 170 C5
Stirling Ind Ctr WD6 170 D4
Stirling Ret Pk WD6 170 D3
Stirling Way
Borehamwood WD6 170 D4
Watford WD5 154 A7
Welwyn Garden City
AL7 111 E6
Stoat Cl SG13 114 A6
Stobarts Cl SG3 68 F6
Stock Bank SG8 8 D1
Stockbreach Cl AL10 130 A6
Stockbreach Rd AL10 130 A6
Stockbridge Cl EN7 147 E5
Stockens Dell SG3 68 F4
Stockens Gn SG3 68 F4
Stockers Farm Rd
WD3 173 D8
Stockfield Ave EN11 135 B8
Stockholm Way LU3 44 E8
Stocking Hill SG9 39 B8
Stocking La SG8 18 C1
STOCKING PELHAM 43 E7
Stockings La SG13 132 D6
Stockingstone Rd LU2 45 E3
Stockmen Field CM23 76 C5
Stockport Rd WD3 164 C2
Stocks Farm Barns
HP23 101 C7
Stocks Mdw HP2 125 A4
Stocks Rd HP23 101 D7
Stockwell Cl EN7 148 E3
Stockwell La EN7 148 B3
Stockwood Craft Mus &
Gdns* LU1 63 D4
Stockwood Cres LU1 63 D6
Stockwood Ct 18 LU1 63 D6
Stockwood Pk* LU1 63 D3
Stonecroft SG3 68 F5
Stonecroft Cl EN5 171 B5
Stonecross AL1 127 E4
Stone Cross 3 CM20 117 D1
Stonecross Cl 1 AL1 127 E4
Stonecross Rd AL10 130 B7
Stonehill Jun Mix Inf Sch
SG6 11 E1
Stonehills AL8 110 D7
Stonelea Rd HP3 138 F8
Stoneleigh CM21 97 D3
Stoneleigh Ave EN1 162 B1
Stoneleigh Cl
Cheshunt EN8 162 D6
Luton LU3 45 B7
Stoneleigh Dr EN11 115 B1
Stoneley SG6 11 F1
Stonemason Cl AL5 86 A3
Stonemead AL8 89 D3
Stonesdale LU4 44 C4
Stoneways Cl LU4 44 C6
Stoney Cl HP4 121 F6
Stoney Comm CM24 59 E5
Stoney Common Rd
CM24 59 D5
Stoneycroft
Aldbury HP23 101 C5
Hemel Hempstead HP1 124 A3
Welwyn Garden City
AL7 111 A7
Stoneyfield Dr CM24 59 E6
Stoneygate Rd LU4 44 D3
Stoney La
Bovingdon HP3 137 C5
Chipperfield WD4 137 E1
Cholesbury HP5 120 F1
Hemel Hempstead HP1 137 B8
Stoney Pl CM24 59 E5
Stonnells Cl SG6 22 F8
Stony Croft SG1 50 E6
Stony Hills SG12 92 C7
Stony La
Chenies HP5, HP6 150 E1
Great Offley LU2, SG4 47 C4
Stonyshotts EN9 163 E6
Stookslade HP22 60 A3
STOPSLEY 46 B4
STOPSLEY COMMON 45 F6
Stopsley Com Prim Sch
LU2 46 A4
Stopsley High Sch LU2 45 F4
Stopsley Mobile Home Pk
LU2 45 F4
Stopsley Way LU2 46 A3
Storehouse La SG4 34 F6
Storey Ct WD23 168 B4
Storey St HP3 138 D7
Stormont Rd SG5 21 F1
Stormont Sch EN6 159 D8
Stornoway HP3 125 B1
Stortford Hall Ind Pk
CM23 77 B7
Stortford Hall Pk CM23 77 B8
Stortford Hall Rd 3
CM23 77 B8
STORTFORD PARK 76 C8
Stortford Rd
Hatfield Heath CM22 98 E4
Hoddesdon EN11 135 C7
Little Hadham SG11 57 C2
Standon SG11 55 F2
Stort Lo CM23 76 D8
Stort Mill CM20 118 B6
Stort Rd CM23 76 F6
Stort Valley Ind Pk
CM23 59 B2
STOTFOLD 11 E7
Stotfold Ho SG5 11 F6
Stotfold Rd
Arlesey SG15 11 C7
Hinxworth SG7 3 C1
Hitchin SG4, SG6 22 C4
Letchford Garden City
SG6 11 D1
Stow The CM20 117 F2
Stox Mead HA3 176 D2
Straffan Ct LU3 44 F4
Strafford Cl EN6 159 A7
Strafford Ct SG3 69 A5
Strafford Gate EN6 159 A7
Strafford Rd EN5 171 E6
Straits The EN9 163 B7
Strandburgh Pl HP3 125 B1
Strangers Way LU4 44 C4
Strangeways WD17 153 E3
Stratfield Dr EN10 134 E4
Stratfield Rd WD6 170 A7
Stratford Lo WD17 167 B8
Stratford Rd
Luton LU4 45 B1
Watford WD17 167 A7
Stratford Way
Bricket Wood AL2 140 F2
Hemel Hempstead HP3 138 B8
Watford WD17 167 A7
Strathmore Ave
Hitchin SG5 21 F1
Luton LU1 63 F5
Strathmore Ct SG5 21 F1
Strathmore Inf Sch
SG5 21 E2
Strathmore Rd SG4 66 E6
Strathmore Wlk LU1 63 F6
Stratton Ave EN2 161 D2
Stratton Ct 13 HA5 175 F3
Stratton Gdns LU2 45 D4
Strawberry Cres AL2 142 B5
Strawberry Field
8 Hatfield AL10 130 A2
Luton LU3 44 E7
Strawberry Fields
SG12 93 B2
Strawfields AL7 111 B7
Strawmead AL10 130 B7
Strawplaiters Cl SG3 69 A2
Straw Plait Way SG15 10 F4
Straws Hadley Ct HP22 60 B2
Strayfield Rd EN2 161 B2
STREATLEY 31 A5
Street The
Braughing SG11 55 F7
Chipperfield WD4 152 A8
Dane End SG11 53 F3
Furneux Pelham SG9 43 A4
Street The *continued*
Sheering CM22 98 E1
Wallington SG7 25 C8
Stretton Way WD6 156 E1
Stringers La SG2 51 E2
Stripling Way WD18 167 A3
Stroma Cl HP3 125 C1
Stronnell Cl LU2 46 B3
Stronsay Cl HP3 125 C1
Stroud Wood Bsns Ctr
AL2 141 E4
Stuart Ct WD6 169 D3
Stuart Dr
Hitchin SG4 35 B7
Royston SG8 7 D8
Stuart Ho EN9 163 F6
Stuart Pl 8 LU1 63 D7
Stuart Rd AL6 89 B3
Stuart St Pas 7 LU1 63 D7
Stuarts Cl 3 HP3 124 D1
Stuart St LU1 63 D7
Stuart Way EN7 162 B8
Stud Gn WD25 154 B7
STUDHAM 82 C4
Studham CE Lower Sch
LU6 82 B4
Studham La
Dagnall HP4 81 D4
Whipsnade LU6 82 A7
Studios The WD23 168 A3
Studio Way WD6 170 C8
Studlands Rise SG8 7 E6
Studlands Rise Fst Sch
SG8 7 E5
Studley Rd LU3 45 D1
Stump Cross SG8 15 C6
Sturgeon's Way SG4 22 B2
Sturla Cl SG14 113 B7
Sturlas Way EN8 162 D6
Sturmer Cl AL4 128 C2
Sturrock Way SG4 35 C6
Styles Cl LU2 46 C2
Such Cl SG6 23 B7
Sudbury Ct 2 AL1 127 E2
Sudbury Rd LU4 44 B6
Suffolk Cl
Borehamwood WD6 170 D4
London Colney AL2 142 C6
Luton LU4 44 A3
Suffolk Rd
Potters Bar EN6 158 E7
Royston SG8 7 E6
Sugar La HP1 123 B1
Sulgrave Cres HP23 100 C5
Sullivan Cres UB9 173 D1
Sullivan Way WD6 169 C3
Summercroft Pim Sch
CM23 77 C8
Summer Ct HP2 124 D5
Summer Dale AL8 89 D1
Summerfield AL10 130 A2
Summerfield Cl AL2 142 C5
Summerfield Rd
Luton LU1 62 F8
Watford WD25 154 A4
Summer Gr WD6 169 D3
Summer Hill WD6 170 A4
Summerhill Ct AL1 127 F4
Summerhouse La
Harefield UB9 173 A3
Radlett WD25 168 C8
Summerhouse Way
WD5 139 F1
Summerlands Rd AL4 128 C7
Summerleas Cl HP2 124 E3
Summer Pl WD18 166 F3
Summers Lo SG6 22 D6
Summers Rd LU2 46 C1
Summer St LU1 63 C1
Summers Way AL2 142 E4
Summerswood La EN6,
WD6 157 E4
Summerswood Prim Sch
WD6 170 B5
Summer Wlk AL3 83 E5
Summit Ct EN5 171 F6
Summit Rd EN6 144 E1
Sumpter Yd AL1 127 D3
Sunbury Ct
3 Barnet EN5 171 E5
St Albans AL1 128 B2
Sundale AL1 127 E4
Sunderland Ave AL1 128 A4
Sunderland Est WD4 139 B2
Sunderland Gr WD25 153 F5
Sundew Rd HP1 123 E2
Sundon Bsns Pk LU3 44 B8
SUNDON PARK 44 C7
Sundon Park Jun Sch
LU3 44 C8
Sundon Park Par LU3 44 C7
Sundon Park Rd LU3 44 C7
Sun Hill SG8 7 C5
Sun La AL5 86 A2
Sunmead Rd HP2 124 D5
Sunningdale
Bishop's Stortford
CM23 76 E6
Luton LU2 45 F3
Sunningdale Mews
AL7 89 F2
Sunnybank LU7 79 F7
Sunny Bank Prim Sch
EN6 159 A5
Sunnybank Rd EN6 159 A6

Sunnydell AL2 . . . . 141 B5
Sunnyfield AL9 . . . . 130 D8
Sunny Hill SG9 . . . . 40 F7
Sunnyhill Rd
  Hemel Hempstead
    HP1 . . . . 124 B3
  Maple Cross WD3 . . . . . . 172 D4
Sunnymead Orch SG7 . . . 5 A3
Sunnyside
  Lower Nazeing EN9 . . . . 135 F1
  Stansted Mountfitchet
    CM24 . . . . 59 E6
Sunnyside Cotts HP5 . . . 136 A5
Sunnyside Rd SG4 . . . . . . 35 A5
Sunridge Ave LU2 . . . . . . 45 E2
Sunnyview Cres HP3 . . . . 138 F8
Sunrise Ind Est LU2 . . . . . 46 A2
Sunset Dr LU2 . . . . 45 F3
Sunset View EN5 . . . . 171 E7
Sunshine House Sch
  HA6 . . . . 174 D4
Sun Sq 2 HP1 . . . . 124 D4
Sun St
  Baldock SG7 . . . . 23 E8
  Hitchin SG5 . . . . 34 E6
  Sawbridgeworth CM21 . . 97 F1
  Waltham Abbey EN9 . . . . 163 C6
Surrey Pl HP23 . . . . 100 A3
Surrey St LU1 . . . . 63 E6
Surrey Street Prim Sch
  LU1 . . . . 63 F6
Sursham Ct AL3 . . . . 83 E5
Sussex Cl EN11 . . . . 135 A7
Sussex Pl LU2 . . . . 46 D2
Sussex Rd WD24 . . . . 154 A1
Sutcliffe Cl
  Bushey WD23 . . . . 168 C5
  Stevenage SG1 . . . . 51 A8
Sutherland Ave EN6 . . . . 146 D3
Sutherland Cl EN5 . . . . . . 171 E5
Sutherland Ct
  Watford WD18 . . . . 166 C2
  Welwyn Garden City
    AL7 . . . . 110 F7
Sutherland Pl LU1 . . . . . . 63 D5
Sutherland Way EN6 . . . . 146 E3
Sutton Acres CM22 . . . . . 98 D7
Sutton Cl
  Hoddesdon EN10 . . . . . . 134 E4
  Tring HP23 . . . . 100 B6
Sutton Cres EN5 . . . . 171 D4
Sutton Ct SG12 . . . . 114 E8
Sutton Gdns
  Caddington LU1 . . . . 62 E3
  Luton LU3 . . . . 44 D6
Sutton Ho HP2 . . . . 124 E7
Sutton Path WD6 . . . . 170 A6
Sutton Rd
  St Albans AL1 . . . . 128 B3
  Watford WD17 . . . . 167 C6
Swale Cl SG1 . . . . 37 A3
Swallow Cl
  4 Bishop's Stortford
    CM23 . . . . 77 A4
  Enfield EN3 . . . . 162 C2
  Hertford SG14 . . . . 113 C6
  Welwyn Garden City
    AL7 . . . . 110 F6
Swallowdale La HP2 . . . . 125 B6
Swallow Dell Prim Sch
  AL7 . . . . 111 A5
Swallow End AL7 . . . . 110 F6
Swallowfields AL7 . . . . . . 110 F6
Swallow Gdns AL10 . . . . . 130 A3
Swallow La AL1 . . . . 142 B8
Swallow Oaks WD5 . . . . . 153 F7
Swallow Pk HP2 . . . . 125 B7
Swallows CM17 . . . . 118 C4
Swallows The AL7 . . . . . . 89 F2
Swallowtail Wlk HP4 . . . . 121 F7
Swan Cl WD3 . . . . 165 D2
Swan Ct
  2 Bishop's Stortford
    CM23 . . . . 76 F6
  Cheshunt EN8 . . . . 162 E5
  Chorleywood WD3 . . . . . 164 C5
Swanells Wood LU6 . . . . . 82 C4
Swan Field Ct AL6 . . . . . . 89 A4
Swan Field Ho 3
  WD3 . . . . 165 D2
Swanfield Rd EN8 . . . . . . 162 E6
Swangley's La SG3 . . . . . . 69 B4
Swanhill AL7 . . . . 90 A1
Swan La SG8 . . . . 1 F4
Swanland Rd
  South Mimms EN6 . . . . . 158 B5
  Welham Green AL9,
    EN6 . . . . 144 B3
SWANLEY BAR 145 B2
Swanley Bar La EN6 . . . . 145 B3
Swanley Cres EN6 . . . . . . 145 B2
Swanley Ct WD24 . . . . . . 154 C2
Swan Mead
  Hemel Hempstead
    HP3 . . . . 138 F6
  Luton LU4 . . . . 44 B4
Swan & Pike Rd EN3 . . . . 163 A1
Swan Rd EN8 . . . . 162 E5
Swans Cl AL4 . . . . 128 E2
Swan St SG7 . . . . 4 D4
Swanstand SG6 . . . . 23 D4

Swanston Grange LU4 . . . . 44 B2
Swanston Path 3
  WD19 . . . . 175 C7
Swan Way LU3 . . . . 116 A1
Swasedale Rd LU3 . . . . . . 45 A6
Sweet Briar
  Bishop's Stortford
    CM23 . . . . 76 B6
  Welwyn Garden City
    AL7 . . . . 111 A5
Sweetbriar Cl HP1 . . . . . . 124 A6
Sweyns Mead SG2 . . . . . . 51 C7
Swift Cl
  Letchworth Garden City
    SG6 . . . . 22 C1
  Royston SG8 . . . . 2 D1
  Stanstead Abbotts
    SG12 . . . . 115 C3
Swiftfields AL7 . . . . 111 A7
Swifts Green Cl LU2 . . . . 46 B5
Swifts Green Rd LU2 . . . . 46 B5
SWILLETT THE 164 B3
Swinburne Ave SG5 . . . . . 21 C1
Swinburne Cl SG8 . . . . . . 2 D1
Swingate SG1 . . . . 50 D5
Swing Gate Fst Sch
  HP4 . . . . 122 D3
Swing Gate La HP4 . . . . . 122 D2
Swinnell Cl SG8 . . . . 2 B5
Swiss Ave WD18 . . . . 166 E6
Swiss Cl WD18 . . . . 166 E6
Sword Cl EN10 . . . . 134 D3
Sworders Yd 3 CM23 . . . 76 D4
Sycamore App WD3 . . . . . 166 C4
Sycamore Ave AL10 . . . . . 130 A4
Sycamore Cl
  Hammond Street EN7 . . . 147 F4
  Hitchin SG4 . . . . 34 F3
  Watford, Garston
    WD25 . . . . 154 B4
  Watford WD3 . . . . 167 E7
Sycamore Dr
  Park Street AL2 . . . . 141 D4
  Tring HP23 . . . . 100 A4
Sycamore Ho HP2 . . . . . . 124 E4
Sycamore Rd WD3 . . . . . . 166 D4
Sycamore Rise HP22 . . . . 122 D3
Sycamores The
  Baldock SG7 . . . . 23 E8
  Bishop's Stortford CM23 . 77 B6
  Hemel Hempstead HP3 . . 137 F8
  Radlett WD7 . . . . 156 B5
  8 St Albans AL1 . . . . 127 D2
Sydney Chapman Way
  EN5 . . . . 171 F7
Sydney Rd WD18 . . . . 166 F4
Sylam Cl LU3 . . . . 44 E7
Sylvan Cl HP3 . . . . 125 A2
Sylvandale AL7 . . . . 111 C5
Sylvan Hts AL1 . . . . 128 A1
Sylvan Way AL7 . . . . 111 C5
Sylvia Ave HA5 . . . . 175 F4
Symonds Ct 8 EN8 . . . . . 148 D3
SYMONDS GREEN 50 A7
Symonds Green La
  SG1 . . . . 50 A6
Symonds Green Rd
  SG1 . . . . 50 A7
Symonds Rd SG5 . . . . 34 C4
Syon Ct 14 AL1 . . . . 128 A3

T

Tabbs Cl SG6 . . . . 23 B7
Tabor Cl SG6 . . . . 22 D7
Tacitus Cl 2 SG1 . . . . 51 C8
Tailors CM23 . . . . 76 B5
Takeley Cl EN9 . . . . 163 D6
Talbot Ave WD19 . . . . 167 E2
Talbot Ct HP3 . . . . 124 D1
Talbot Rd
  Harrow HA3 . . . . 176 F1
  Hatfield AL10 . . . . 130 A8
  Luton LU2 . . . . 45 A8
  Rickmansworth WD3 . . . 165 E1
Talbot St
  Hertford SG13 . . . . 113 C6
  St Albans AL3 . . . . 34 C8
Talbot Way SG6 . . . . 12 B1
Talisman St SG4 . . . . 35 C6
Tallack Cl HA3 . . . . 176 C3
Tallents Cres AL5 . . . . 86 D3
Tallis Way WD6 . . . . 169 E8
Tall Trees
  Hitchin SG4 . . . . 35 A4
  Royston SG8 . . . . 7 E6
Tamar Cl SG1 . . . . 37 A3
Tamar Gn HP2 . . . . 124 F8
Tamarisk Cl AL3 . . . . 127 D7
Tamarix Cres AL2 . . . . . . 142 A5
Tameton Cl LU2 . . . . 46 F2
Tamworth Rd SG13 . . . . . 113 F7
Tancred Rd LU2 . . . . 46 A4
Tanfield Cl EN7 . . . . 148 A4
Tanfield Cl LU2 . . . . 46 E1
Tanglewood
  Harpenden AL5 . . . . 85 F2
  Welwyn AL6 . . . . 90 A7
Tanglewood Cl HP4 . . . . . 176 E8
Tankerfield Pl AL3 . . . . . . 127 C3
Tanner Ho WD19 . . . . 167 B2
Tanners Cl AL3 . . . . 127 C4
Tanners Cres SG13 . . . . . 113 C4
Tanners Hill WD5 . . . . . . 154 A8
Tanners Way SG12 . . . . . . 116 D8
Tanners Wood Cl
  WD5 . . . . 153 E7

Tanners Wood Ct
  WD5 . . . . 153 E7
Tanners Wood Jun Mix Inf
  Sch WD5 . . . . 153 E7
Tanners Wood La
  WD5 . . . . 153 E7
Tannery Cl SG8 . . . . 7 C6
Tannery Drift SG8 . . . . . . 7 C6
Tannery Drift Sch SG8 . . . 7 C6
Tannery The SG9 . . . . 40 E7
Tannery Yd SG4 . . . . 66 F6
Tannsfield Dr 1 HP2 . . . . 124 F5
Tannsmore Cl 2 HP2 . . . . 124 F5
Tansycroft AL7 . . . . 111 B7
Tantivy Ct 5 WD17 . . . . . 167 C6
Tanworth Cl HA6 . . . . . . 174 C4
Tanworth Gdns HA5 . . . . 175 C1
Tanyard La AL6,SG4 . . . . 88 B8
Tanys Ct CM20 . . . . 117 F3
Tany's Dell CM20 . . . . . . 118 A3
Tany's Dell Com Prim Sch
  CM20 . . . . 118 A3
Tapster St EN5 . . . . 171 F6
Taransey HP3 . . . . 125 B1
Tarlings CM20 . . . . 117 F3
Tarpan Way EN10 . . . . . . 148 F6
Tarrant Ct SG1 . . . . 36 B1
Tarrant Dr AL5 . . . . 107 D7
Tassell Hall AL3 . . . . 105 F6
Tate Gdns WD23 . . . . 168 E2
Tates Way SG2 . . . . 36 B2
Tatlers La SG2 . . . . 51 E4
Tatsfield Ave EN9 . . . . . . 149 E8
Tatsford Villas EN9 . . . . . 135 C1
Tattershall Dr HP2 . . . . . . 105 B1
Tattle Hill SG14 . . . . 91 E2
Tattlers Hill HP22 . . . . . . 60 B3
Tatton St CM17 . . . . 118 C1
Tauber Cl WD6 . . . . 169 F5
Taunton Ave LU2 . . . . 46 B1
Taverners HP2 . . . . 124 E5
Taverners Way EN11 . . . . 135 A4
Tavistock Ave AL1 . . . . . . 141 D8
Tavistock Cl
  Potters Bar EN6 . . . . 159 D8
  St Albans AL1 . . . . 141 D8
Tavistock Cres LU1 . . . . . 63 E5
Tavistock Ct 3 LU1 . . . . . 63 E5
Tavistock Rd WD24 . . . . . 167 D8
Tavistock St LU1 . . . . 63 E6
Taylor Cl
  Harefield UB9 . . . . 173 C1
  St Albans AL4 . . . . 128 A8
Taylors Ave EN11 . . . . . . 135 A5
Taylor's Hill SG4 . . . . 34 F6
Taylors La HP23 . . . . 119 C3
Taylor's La EN5 . . . . 171 F8
Taylor's Rd SG5 . . . . 11 F8
Taylor St LU2 . . . . 63 E8
Taylor Trad Est SG13 . . . 114 B7
Taywood Cl SG2 . . . . 51 B2
TEA GREEN 88 A4
Teal Cl EN5 . . . . 162 C3
Teal Dr HA6 . . . . 174 C3
Teale Ho 5 EN11 . . . . 135 D8
Teal Ho WD5 . . . . 154 E3
Teal Way HP3 . . . . 138 F6
Teasdale Cl SG8 . . . . 2 D1
Teasel Cl SG8 . . . . 7 E5
Tebbutt Ct AL6 . . . . 90 C6
Tedder Ave SG16 . . . . 10 B5
Tedder Rd HP2 . . . . 125 A4
Tees Cl SG1 . . . . 36 F3
Teesdale
  Hemel Hempstead
    HP2 . . . . 124 F6
  Luton LU4 . . . . 44 C5
Tee Side SG13 . . . . 114 B7
Telford Ave SG2 . . . . 51 B6
Telford Cl WD25 . . . . 154 D4
Telford Ct
  Hatfield AL10 . . . . 129 F3
  St Albans AL1 . . . . 127 E2
Telford Rd AL2 . . . . 142 C4
Telford Way LU1 . . . . 63 D8
Telmere Ind Est 20
  LU1 . . . . 63 E6
Telscombe Way LU2 . . . . 46 C1
Temperance St AL3 . . . . . 127 C3
Tempest Ave EN6 . . . . . . 159 D7
Templar Ave SG7 . . . . 23 B6
Templar Ct HP3 . . . . 124 D1
Templars La SG4 . . . . 48 C5
Temple Bank CM20 . . . . . 118 B5
Temple Cl
  Cheshunt EN7 . . . . 162 A8
  Luton LU2 . . . . 45 E5
  Preston SG5 . . . . 34 B4
  Watford WD17 . . . . 166 F7
Temple Ct
  Hertford SG14 . . . . 92 D1
  Potters Bar EN6 . . . . 158 D8
TEMPLE DINSLEY 48 E6
TEMPLE FIELDS 118 A4
Temple Fields SG14 . . . . . 92 D1
Templefields Ent Ctr
  CM20 . . . . 118 A3
Temple Gdns
  Letchworth Garden City
    SG6 . . . . 23 C8
  Moor Park WD3 . . . . 174 B6
Temple Ho EN7 . . . . 162 A6
Temple La SG12 . . . . 92 F8
Temple Mead
  Hemel Hempstead
    HP2 . . . . 124 D5
  Roydon CM19 . . . . 116 B1

Templepan La WD3 . . . . . 152 E2
Templeton Ct
  18 Borehamwood
    WD6 . . . . 169 F8
  Enfield EN1 . . . . 162 C1
Temple View AL3 . . . . . . 127 C5
Templewood AL8 . . . . 89 D1
Templewood Prim Sch
  AL8 . . . . 110 D8
Tempsford AL7 . . . . 110 D5
Tempsford Ave WD6 . . . . 170 D5
Tensford Cl HA2 . . . . 176 C1
Tenby Dr LU4 . . . . 44 F3
Tenby Mews LU4 . . . . 44 E3
Tene The SG7 . . . . 23 F8
Tennand Cl EN7 . . . . 147 F5
Tennison Ave WD6 . . . . . 170 B4
Tennyson Ave
  Hitchin SG4 . . . . 35 C7
  Waltham Abbey EN9 . . . . 163 E5
Tennyson Cl SG8 . . . . 2 E1
Tennyson Ct SG8 . . . . 2 D1
Tennyson Ho 6 LU1 . . . . . 63 E5
Tennyson Rd
  Chiswell Green AL2 . . . . 141 B5
  Harpenden AL5 . . . . 86 A2
  Luton LU1 . . . . 63 E5
Tennyson Road Prim Sch
  LU1 . . . . 63 E5
Tenterfield Ho AL6 . . . . . 89 C4
Tenth Ave LU1 . . . . 44 C7
Tenzing Gr LU1 . . . . 63 C6
Tenzing Rd HP2 . . . . 125 A3
Teresa Gdns EN8 . . . . 162 D5
Terlings Pk CM20 . . . . . . 117 D4
Terminus St 8 CM20 . . . . 117 D1
Terrace The
  Essendon AL9 . . . . 131 E6
  Redbourn AL3 . . . . 106 A5
  Tring HP23 . . . . 100 A3
  Westmill SG9 . . . . 40 F2
Tethys Rd HP2 . . . . 124 F6
TEWIN 90 E2
Tewin Cl
  St Albans AL4 . . . . 128 C7
  Tewin AL6 . . . . 90 C5
Tewin Cowper CE Prim
  Sch AL6 . . . . 90 E2
Tewin Ct AL7 . . . . 110 F7
Tewin Hill AL6 . . . . 90 F5
Tewin Rd
  Hemel Hempstead
    HP2 . . . . 125 C3
  Welwyn Garden City
    AL7 . . . . 110 F7
Tewin Water Ho AL6 . . . . 90 B2
TEWIN WOOD 90 D5
Thackeray Cl SG8 . . . . . . 2 D1
Thames Ave HP2 . . . . 124 F8
Thames Cl LU3 . . . . 45 B3
Thamesdale AL2 . . . . 142 F4
Thanet Ho 1 WD18 . . . . . 166 F3
Thatched Cotts AL5 . . . . . 107 A7
Thatchers Croft HP2 . . . . 124 E7
Thatchers End SG4 . . . . . 35 C8
Thatchers The CM23 . . . . 76 C5
Thaxted Cl LU2 . . . . 46 F2
Thaxted Way EN9 . . . . . . 163 D6
Thaynesfield EN6 . . . . . . 159 D8
Thelby Cl LU3 . . . . 44 F6
Thele Ave SG12 . . . . 115 C4
Thele Est SG12 . . . . 115 E4
Thele Ho SG12 . . . . 115 C4
Theleway Cl EN11 . . . . . . 115 B1
Thellusson Way WD3 . . . 165 A2
Thelusson St WD7 . . . . . . 156 A3
Theobald
  Cheshunt EN8 . . . . 22 A3
Theobald Cres HA3 . . . . . 176 C2
Theobald Ct WD6 . . . . . . 170 A6
THEOBALDS 161 D8
Theobalds Cl EN6 . . . . . . 146 F1
Theobald's Grove Sta
  EN8 . . . . 162 D7
Theobald's La
  Cheshunt EN8 . . . . 162 B7
  Cheshunt EN8 . . . . 162 C7
Theobalds Park Camp Site
  EN7 . . . . 162 A7
Theobalds Park Rd
  EN2 . . . . 161 B3
Theobald's Rd EN6 . . . . . 146 F1
Theobald St
  Borehamwood WD6 . . . . 170 D2
  Radlett WD6,WD7 . . . . . 156 D2
Therfield CE Fst Sch
  SG8 . . . . 15 F7
Therfield Heath Nature
  Reserve* SG8 . . . . 7 A5
Therfield Rd AL3 . . . . 127 D6
Thetford Gdns LU2 . . . . . 45 E6
Thieves' La
  Hertford SG14 . . . . 112 F7
  Hertingfordbury SG14 . . . 112 F6
Third Ave
  Letchworth Garden City
    SG6 . . . . 23 C7
  Luton LU3 . . . . 44 D7
  Watford WD25 . . . . 154 D4
Thirlestane AL1 . . . . 127 F4
Thirlmere Rd LU4 . . . . . . 44 D1
Thirlmere SG1 . . . . 37 C2
Thirlmere Dr AL1 . . . . . . 128 B1
Thirlmere Gdns HA6 . . . . 174 C4
Thirsk Rd WD6 . . . . 157 A1
Thirston Path 1
  WD6 . . . . 170 A7

Thistle Cl HP1 . . . . 123 E2
Thistlecroft HP1 . . . . 124 B2
Thistle Dr AL10 . . . . 129 F8
Thistle Gr AL7 . . . . 111 C3
Thistle Rd LU1 . . . . 63 F7
Thistles The HP1 . . . . 124 B4
Thistley La SG4 . . . . 34 F1
Thomas Alleyne Sch The
  SG1 . . . . 50 C8
Thomas Bourne Ho 9
  HP4 . . . . 122 D4
Thomas Coram CE Mid
  Sch The HP4 . . . . 122 D2
Thomas Ct HP4 . . . . 121 F5
Thomas Gould Ho
  AL2 . . . . 122 A3
Thomas Heskin Ct 11
  CM23 . . . . 77 A7
Thomas Rochford Way
  EN8 . . . . 148 F4
Thomas Sparrow Ho
  AL4 . . . . 108 D8
Thomas Watson Cottage
  Homes EN5 . . . . 171 E4
Thomas Way SG8 . . . . . . 2 D1
Thompsons Cl
  Goff's Oak EN7 . . . . 147 F2
  1 Harpenden AL5 . . . . . . 86 A3
Thompsons Mdw SG8 . . . 1 F4
Thompson Way WD3 . . . . 165 A1
THORLEY 76 D2
Thorley Hall Stables
  CM23 . . . . 76 D2
Thorley High CM23 . . . . . 76 F2
Thorley Hill CM23 . . . . . . 76 F5
Thorley Hill Prim Sch
  CM23 . . . . 76 F4
THORLEY HOUSES 76 A5
Thorley La CM23 . . . . 76 F3
Thorley La E CM23 . . . . . 76 F3
Thorley La W CM23 . . . . 76 B4
Thorley Neighbourhood
  Ctr CM23 . . . . 76 D5
THORLEY PARK 76 D4
Thorley Park Rd CM23 . . 76 F4
THORLEY STREET 76 D2
Thornage Ct LU2 . . . . 45 D7
Thorn Ave WD23 . . . . 168 C3
Thornbera Cl CM23 . . . . . 76 F4
Thornbera Gdns CM23 . . 76 F4
Thornbera Rd CM23 . . . . 76 F4
Thornbury AL5 . . . . 86 D3
Thornbury Ct
  Hoddesdon EN11 . . . . . . 115 B2
  Stevenage SG2 . . . . 69 A8
Thornbury Gdns WD6 . . . 170 C5
Thorncroft HP3 . . . . 125 B1
Thorndyke Ct HA5 . . . . . . 175 F3
Thorne Cl 6 HP1 . . . . 124 B1
Thorne Rd HP22 . . . . 99 B4
Thorneycroft Ct LU3 . . . . 44 F4
Thorngrovth Dr EN3 . . . . 163 A2
Thornfield Rd CM23 . . . . 76 E8
Thorn Gr CM23 . . . . 77 B6
Thorn Grove Prim Sch
  CM23 . . . . 77 B6
Thornhill Rd
  Luton LU4 . . . . 44 F2
  Moor Park HA6 . . . . 174 C6
Thorndale 5 LU4 . . . . 44 C5
Thornton Gr HA5 . . . . . . 176 A4
Thornton Rd
  Barnet EN5 . . . . 171 E6
  Potters Bar EN6 . . . . 145 C1
Thornton St
  Hertford SG14 . . . . 113 D6
  St Albans AL3 . . . . 127 C4
Thorn Tree Dr HP23 . . . . 99 F4
Thorpe Cres WD19 . . . . . 167 C2
Thorpefield Cl AL4 . . . . . 128 D6
Thorpe Rd AL1 . . . . 127 D2
Thrales Cl LU3 . . . . 44 E7
THRALES END 85 E5
Thrales End La AL5 . . . . . 85 E5
Three Cherry Trees La
  HP2 . . . . 125 B7
Three Close La HP4 . . . . . 122 C4
Three Closes SG5 . . . . . . 20 C4
Three Corners HP3 . . . . . 125 A1
Three Houses La SG4 . . . 67 D5
Three Meadows Mews
  HA3 . . . . 176 F2
Three Rivers Mus of Local
  History* WD3 . . . . 165 E2
Three Star Cvn Pk
  SG6 . . . . 10 A3
Three Stiles SG8 . . . . 52 E4
Three Valleys Way
  WD23 . . . . 167 E4
Thremhall Ave CM23 . . . . 77 E8
Thresher Cl CM23 . . . . . . 76 C5
Thricknells Cl LU3 . . . . . . 44 E7
Thrift Farm La WD6 . . . . 170 C7
Thriftfield HP2 . . . . 124 D5
Thrimley La CM23 . . . . . . 58 C6
Thristers Cl SG6 . . . . 23 B3
THROCKING 26 F1
Throcking La SG9 . . . . . . 27 C3
Throcking Rd SG9 . . . . . . 39 D8
Thrums WD24 . . . . 154 B2
Thrush Ave AL10 . . . . 130 A3
Thrush Gn WD3 . . . . 165 C2
Thrush La EN6 . . . . 146 F3
Thrush Way LU4 . . . . 111 A3
Thumpers HP2 . . . . 124 E5
Thundercourt SG12 . . . . . 93 D2
Thunder Hall 1 SG12 . . . . 93 D2

THUNDRIDGE 93 E7
Thundridge Bsns Pk
SG12 . . . . .93 D7
Thundridge CE Prim Sch
SG12 . . . . .93 D7
Thundridge CE AL7 . . . . . .111 B5
Thurgood Rd EN11 . . . . . .135 A8
Thurlow CI SG1 . . . . .36 C2
Thurnall Ave SG8 . . . . .7 C5
Thurnall CI LU2 . . . . .45 E7
Tibbles CI WD25 . . . . .154 E4
Tibbs Hill Rd WD5 . . . . .6 C3
Tiberius Rd LU3 . . . . .44 F6
Tichborne WD3 . . . . .172 D5
Tiger Moth Way AL10 . . . .129 D6
Tilbury Ct 6 HA6 . . . . .175 D3
Tilecroft AL8 . . . . .89 D1
Tilehouse CI WD6 . . . . . . .169 F6
Tilehouse La WD3 . . . . . . .172 E2
Tilehouse St SG5 . . . . .34 E6
Tilekiln CI EN7 . . . . .147 F2
Tile Kiln CI HP3 . . . . .125 B2
Tile Kiln Cres HP3 . . . . . . .125 B2
Tile Kiln La HP3 . . . . .125 B2
Tilgate LU2 . . . . .46 D3
Tillers Link SG2 . . . . .51 A2
Tillotson Rd HA3 . . . . .176 B3
Tilsworth Wlk AL4 . . . . . . .128 C8
Timbercroft AL7 . . . . .89 F1
Timberidge WD3 . . . . .165 D5
Timber Orch SG4 . . . . .92 A2
Timbers CI AL5 . . . . .85 F2
Times CI SG5 . . . . .21 B2
Timplings Row HP1 . . . . . .124 B5
Timworth CI LU2 . . . . .46 D1
Tingeys CI AL3 . . . . .106 A5
Tinkers La HP23 . . . . .121 A6
Tinsley CI LU1 . . . . .63 B5
Tintagel CI
  Hemel Hempstead
  HP2. . . . . .124 D8
  Luton LU3 . . . . .45 B4
Tintern CI
  Harpenden AL5 . . . . .85 C4
  Stevenage SG2 . . . . .69 A7
Tinwell Mews WD4 . . . . . .170 D4
Tippendell La AL2 . . . . . . .141 C5
Tippet Ct SG1 . . . . .50 E6
Tiree CI HP3 . . . . .125 B1
Titan Ct LU4 . . . . .44 F1
Titan Rd HP2 . . . . .124 F6
Titchfield Rd EN3 . . . . .162 E2
Titchmarsh CI SG8 . . . . .7 D7
Tithe Barn CI AL1 . . . . . . .139 C2
Tithe Barn Ct WD5 . . . . . .139 F2
Tithe CI SG4 . . . . .67 F1
Titian Ave WD23 . . . . .168 C2
TITMORE GREEN 35 E2
Titmus SG1 . . . . .50 E6
Tittendell La SG4 . . . . .35 C2
Tiverton Ct AL5 . . . . .107 E6
Tiverton Rd EN6 . . . . .159 E8
Toddington Rd LU4 . . . . . . .44 C6
TODD'S GREEN 36 A2
Toland CI LU4 . . . . .44 C1
Tolcarne Dr HA5 . . . . .175 A1
Tollgate CI WD3 . . . . .164 F5
Tollgate Rd
  Colney Heath AL4,
  AL9 . . . . .143 E7
  Enfield EN3 . . . . .162 D4
  Welham Green AL9 . . . . . .144 A6
Tollhouse Point 7
  AL1 . . . . .127 E2
Tollpit End HP1 . . . . .124 A6
Tollsworth Way SG11 . . . . .55 D3
Tolmers Ave EN6 . . . . .146 E3
Tolmers Gdns EN6 . . . . . . .146 E3
Tolmers Mews WD3 . . . . . .146 E3
Tolmers Rd EN6 . . . . .146 E3
Tolpits CI WD18 . . . . .166 F4
Tolpits La WD18 . . . . .166 E2
Tomkins CI WD6 . . . . .169 E8
Tomlins SG8 . . . . .8 F1
Toms Croft HP2 . . . . .124 E2
Toms Field AL10 . . . . .129 E4
Toms Hill CI HP23 . . . . . . .101 D5
Toms Hill Rd HP23 . . . . . . .101 D5
Toms La WD4, WD5 . . . . . .139 D3
TONWELL 92 F7
Tonwell St Mary's CE Prim
  Sch SG12 . . . . .92 E7
Tooke CI HA5 . . . . .175 E2
Toorack Rd HA3 . . . . .176 F1
Tooveys Mill CI WD4 . . . . .139 A2
Topstreet Way AL5 . . . . . . .107 C8
Tormead HA6 . . . . .174 D4
Toronto Ho EN8 . . . . .162 D8
Torquay Cres SG1 . . . . .50 E7
Torquay Dr LU4 . . . . .44 D4
Torridge Wlk 2 HP2 . . . . .124 F8
Torrington Dr EN6 . . . . . . .159 D7
Torrington Rd HP4 . . . . . . .122 B4
Tortoiseshell Way
  HP4 . . . . .121 F6
Torwood CI HP4 . . . . .121 F4
Torworth Rd WD6 . . . . . . .157 A4
Tot La CM23, CM24 . . . . . .59 D4
TOTTERIDGE 171 C1
Totteridge Comm
  N20 . . . . .171 D1
Totteridge Ho N20 . . . . . . .171 C1
Totteridge Pk N20 . . . . . . .171 C1
Totteridge Rd EN3 . . . . . . .162 D2
Totteridge Village
  N20 . . . . .171 F1
Totton Mews AL3 . . . . .106 B5

Totts La SG2 . . . . .38 C1
Toulmin Dr AL3 . . . . .127 C7
Toulouse Ho 7
  WD18 . . . . .166 E5
Tovey CI EN11 . . . . .135 A8
Tovey CI
  London Colney AL2 . . . . . .142 D5
  Lower Nazeing EN9 . . . . . .149 E8
Tower CI
  Berkhamsted HP4 . . . . . .122 A3
  Hertford Heath SG13 . . . .114 C2
  Kneesworth SG8 . . . . .2 A5
  Little Wymondley SG4 . . . .35 F3
Tower Ctr 1 EN11 . . . . . . .135 A6
TOWER HILL 137 F2
Tower Hill
  Chipperfield WD4 . . . . . . .137 F1
  Much Hadham SG10 . . . . . .74 F2
Tower Hill La AL4 . . . . .108 F4
Tower Hts EN11 . . . . .135 A7
Tower Prim Sch SG12 . . . . .93 E3
Tower Rd
  Codicote SG4 . . . . .67 F2
  Luton LU2 . . . . .64 A8
  Ware SG12 . . . . .93 F2
Towers Rd
  Hemel Hempstead
  HP2. . . . . .124 E4
  Pinner HA5 . . . . .175 E2
  Stevenage SG1 . . . . .50 D4
Towers St SG14 . . . . .113 C8
Towers The SG1 . . . . .50 D4
Tower View
  Bushey WD23 . . . . .168 E2
  Hemel Hempstead HP1 . . .124 D4
  Whitwell SG4 . . . . .66 F5
Towne Way LU2 . . . . .64 A8
Towne Ctr AL10 . . . . .130 A6
Towne Rd SG8 . . . . .7 D5
Town Farm
  Cheddington LU7 . . . . . . .80 A7
  Wheathampstead AL4 . . . .108 D8
Town Farm CI SG8 . . . . .1 F4
Town Farm Cres SG11 . . . . .55 F2
Townfield WD3 . . . . .165 C2
Town Fields AL10 . . . . .32 A6
Town La SG2 . . . . .52 E4
Townley SG2 . . . . .23 D4
Town Mead Rd EN9 . . . . . .163 C5
Town Mill Mews 3
  SG14 . . . . .113 C6
TOWN PARK 117 E2
TOWNSEND 127 C6
Townsend HP2 . . . . .124 D5
Townsend Ave AL1 . . . . . . .127 E4
Townsend CE Sch
  AL3. . . . . .127 C8
Townsend CI
  Barkway SG8 . . . . .17 C3
  Harpenden AL5 . . . . .85 F1
  St Ippolyts SG4 . . . . .35 A3
Townsend Dr AL3 . . . . .127 D5
Townsend La AL5 . . . . .85 F1
Townsend Rd AL5 . . . . .86 A2
Townsend Way HA6 . . . . . .175 A3
Townshend St SG13 . . . . . .113 C6
Townsley CI LU1 . . . . .63 E6
Town Sq SG1 . . . . .50 D5
Tracey St 15 LU1 . . . . .63 E6
Trafalgar Ave EN10 . . . . . .134 F2
Trafford CI
  Shenley WD7 . . . . .156 A7
  Stevenage SG1 . . . . .36 E1
Traherne CI SG4 . . . . .34 F5
Trajan Gate SG2 . . . . .37 D1
Trapstyle Rd SG12 . . . . . . .93 A2
Travellers CI AL9 . . . . .144 C8
Travellers Encampment
  EN10 . . . . .148 D5
Travellers La
  Hatfield AL10 . . . . .130 B2
  Welham Green AL9 . . . . . .130 C1
Treacle La SG9 . . . . .25 F3
Treacy CI WD23 . . . . .176 C8
Trebellan Dr HP2 . . . . .124 F4
Treeby St EN3 . . . . .163 A2
Treehanger CI HP23 . . . . . .100 B4
Tretop CI LU2 . . . . .45 F1
Tretop Cres
  Luton LU2 . . . . .45 F1
  Oaklands AL6 . . . . .89 E7
Treetops CI HA6 . . . . .174 D5
Trefoil CI LU4 . . . . .44 A4
Trefusis Wlk WD17 . . . . . . .166 E8
Tregelles Rd EN11 . . . . . . .135 A8
Tremaine Gr HP2 . . . . .124 E7
Trent CI
  Shenley WD7 . . . . .156 A7
  Stevenage SG1 . . . . .50 E8
Trent Rd LU3 . . . . .45 B4
Tresco Rd HP4 . . . . .121 F5
Trescott CI LU2 . . . . .46 E2
Tresilian Sq HP2 . . . . .125 A8
Treslian Sq 1 HP2 . . . . . . .124 F8
Trevalga Way HP4 . . . . . . .124 F7
Trevellance Way
  WD25 . . . . .154 D6
Trevelyan Pl AL1 . . . . .127 C1
Trevelyan Way HP4 . . . . . .122 B6
Trevera Ct
  Cheshunt EN8 . . . . .162 B6
  Hoddesdon EN11 . . . . . . .135 A7
Trevor CI HA3 . . . . .176 F3
Trevor Rd SG4 . . . . .35 A8
Trevose Way WD19 . . . . . .175 C7
Trewenna Dr EN6 . . . . .159 D7
Triangle The SG4 . . . . .34 F6

Trident Ctr WD24 . . . . .167 C8
Trident Ind Est EN11 . . . . .135 C7
Trident Rd WD25 . . . . .153 F5
Triggs Way LU4 . . . . .46 E3
Trigg Terr SG1 . . . . .50 E6
Trimley CI LU4 . . . . .44 B5
TRIMS GREEN 97 C7
Trinder Rd EN5 . . . . .171 C4
TRING 100 B4
Tring Bsns Ctr HP23 . . . . . .99 E4
Tring Ford Rd HP23 . . . . . .100 A7
Tring Hill HP23 . . . . .99 C3
Tring Rd WD18 . . . . .166 E2
Tring Rd
  Berkhamsted HP4 . . . . . .121 D7
  Long Marston HP23 . . . . . .79 C3
  Wingrave HP22 . . . . .60 C1
Tring Sch HP23 . . . . .100 B4
Tring Sta HP23 . . . . .101 A5
TRING WHARF 100 B6
Trinity CI
  Bishop's Stortford
  CM23. . . . . .76 F6
  Northwood HA6 . . . . .174 E4
Trinity Ct
  Hertford SG14 . . . . .113 C8
  Watford WD17 . . . . .166 F8
Trinity Hall CI WD24 . . . . .167 C6
Trinity Ho
  2 Borehamwood
  WD6 . . . . .170 A5
  Cheshunt EN8 . . . . .162 E7
Trinity La EN8 . . . . .162 E7
Trinity Mews HP2 . . . . .125 D2
Trinity Pl SG1 . . . . .50 D6
Trinity Rd
  Hertford Heath SG13 . . . .114 C3
  Luton LU3 . . . . .45 A4
  Stevenage SG1 . . . . .50 C6
  Stotfold SG5 . . . . .11 F7
  Ware SG12 . . . . .93 E2
Trinity St CM23 . . . . .76 F4
Trinity Way CM23 . . . . .76 F6
Trinity Wlk Wlk
  Hemel Hempstead
  HP2. . . . . .125 D2
  Hertford Heath SG13 . . . .114 C3
Tristram Rd SG4 . . . . .22 B2
Triton Way HP2 . . . . .124 F5
Triumph Ct 12 LU1 . . . . . . .63 E6
Trojan Terr SG1 . . . . .97 E3
Troon Gdns LU2 . . . . .46 E7
Trooper Rd HP23 . . . . .101 C5
Trotters Bottom EN5 . . . . .158 B2
Trotter's Gap SG12 . . . . . .115 E4
Trotts Hill Prim Sch
  SG1 . . . . .36 F1
Trout Rise WD3 . . . . .165 B6
Troutstream Way
  WD3. . . . . .165 B5
Trouvere Pk HP1 . . . . .124 B5
Trowbridge Gdns LU2 . . . . .45 E3
TROWLEY BOTTOM 105 B8
Trowley Bottom AL3 . . . . . .105 B8
Trowley Hts AL3 . . . . .84 B2
Trowley Rise WD5 . . . . . . .153 F8
Truemans Rd SG5 . . . . .21 D2
Trumper Rd SG1 . . . . .36 F1
Trumpington Dr AL1 . . . . .141 D8
Truncalls LU1 . . . . .63 D5
Trundlers Way WD23 . . . . .168 E1
Truro Gdns LU3 . . . . .45 C5
Truro Ho 11 HA5 . . . . .175 F3
Trust Cotts HP4 . . . . .81 A1
Trust Ind Est SG4 . . . . .22 A2
Trust Rd EN8 . . . . .162 E5
Tubbs Croft AL7 . . . . .111 B5
Tucker's Row 4 CM23 . . . . .76 F6
Tucker St WD18 LU4 . . . . .167 C4
Tudor Ave
  Cheshunt EN7 . . . . .162 B8
  Watford WD24 . . . . .154 D2
Tudor CI
  Cheshunt EN7 . . . . .162 B8
  Hatfield AL10 . . . . .129 F2
  Hunsdonbury SG12 . . . . . .116 D8
  Stevenage SG1 . . . . .36 C1
Tudor Cres EN2 . . . . .161 C1
Tudor Ct
  Barnet EN5 . . . . .171 F5
  Borehamwood WD6 . . . . .169 E7
  Hitchin SG5 . . . . .34 D6
  Kneesworth SG8 . . . . .2 B4
  London Colney AL2 . . . . . .142 D5
  Rickmansworth WD3 . . . . .165 A1
  Sawbridgeworth CM21 . . . .97 E3
Tudor Dr WD24 . . . . .154 D2
Tudor Gdns HA3 . . . . .176 D1
Tudor Lo 3 HA6 . . . . .174 E3
Tudor Manor Gdns
  WD25 . . . . .154 D7
Tudor Par WD3 . . . . .165 A2
Tudor Prim Sch HP3 . . . . . .124 E1
Tudor Rd
  Harrow HA3 . . . . .176 D1
  Luton LU3 . . . . .45 B2
  Pinner HA5 . . . . .175 C1
  St Albans AL3 . . . . .127 E7
  Welwyn AL6 . . . . .89 B3
  Wheathampstead AL4 . . . .108 C8
Tudor Rise EN10 . . . . .134 E2
Tudor Sq 18 SG12 . . . . . . .93 D1
Tudor Way
  Hertford SG13 . . . . .113 A7
  Rickmansworth WD3 . . . . .165 A2
  Waltham Abbey EN9 . . . . .163 D6

Tudor Wlk
  17 Ware SG12 . . . . .93 D1
  Watford WD24 . . . . .154 D2
Tuffnells Way HA5 . . . . . . .85 D4
Tunfield Rd EN11 . . . . .115 B1
Tunnel Way LU7 . . . . .80 C3
Tunnel Wood CI
  WD17 . . . . .153 F2
Tunnel Wood Rd
  WD17 . . . . .153 F2
Turf La SG2 . . . . .36 B4
Turin Ho 16 WD18 . . . . . . .166 E5
Turkey St EN1, EN3 . . . . . .162 C2
Turkey Street Sta
  EN3 . . . . .162 C2
Turmore Dale AL8 . . . . . . .110 C5
Turnberry CI WD19 . . . . . .175 C7
Turnberry Dr AL2 . . . . .140 E1
Turner CI SG1 . . . . .36 C2
Turner Ct HP4 . . . . .122 A5
Turner Rd WD23 . . . . .168 C5
Turners CI
  Bramfield SG14 . . . . .91 C4
  Harpenden AL5 . . . . .86 A4
Turners Cres CM23 . . . . . . .76 C4
Turners Ct EN8 . . . . .162 D8
Turners Hill
  Cheshunt EN8 . . . . .148 D1
  Hemel Hempstead HP2 . . .124 E4
Turners Rd N LU2 . . . . .46 A2
Turners Rd S LU2 . . . . .46 A2
Turneys Orch WD3 . . . . . . .164 D4
Turnford Cotts 3
  EN10 . . . . .148 F5
Turnford Sch EN8 . . . . .148 E3
Turnford Villas EN8 . . . . . .148 F5
Turnpike Dr LU3 . . . . .31 C1
Turnpike Gn HP2 . . . . .124 F7
Turnpike La SG5 . . . . .21 E3
Turnstones The
  WD25 . . . . .154 E3
Turpin CI EN3 . . . . .163 A2
Turpins Chase AL6 . . . . .89 F7
Turpins Ride LU6 . . . . .112 F6
Turpins Ride SG6 . . . . .89 F7
Turpin's Ride SG8 . . . . .7 D5
Turpin's Rise SG2 . . . . .50 D8
Turpin's Way SG2 . . . . .51 D8
Tussauds CI WD3 . . . . .166 A4
Tuthill Ct SG8 . . . . .15 E7
Tuxford CI WD6 . . . . .156 E1
Tweed CI HP4 . . . . .122 B5
Twelve Acres AL7 . . . . .110 E4
Twelve Leys HP22 . . . . .60 B3
Twickenham Gdns
  HA3 . . . . .176 E3
Twigden Ct LU3 . . . . .44 E5
Twin Foxes SG3 . . . . .69 E3
Twin Oaks HA6 . . . . .174 B3
Twinwoods SG1 . . . . .50 F4
Twist The HP23 . . . . .100 D2
Twitchell The SG7 . . . . .23 F8
Two Acres AL7 . . . . .110 F3
Two Beeches HP2 . . . . .124 F8
Two Dells La HP5 . . . . .136 A4
Two Oaks Dr AL6 . . . . .90 C6
TWO WATERS 138 C8
Two Waters Prim Sch
  HP3 . . . . .138 D6
Two Waters Rd
  Hemel Hempstead
  HP3. . . . . .124 D1
  Hemel Hempstead HP3 . . .138 D8
Twyford Bsns Ctr The
  CM23 . . . . .77 A4
Twyford Bury La CM22,
  CM23 . . . . .77 A4
Twyford CI CM23 . . . . .77 A5
Twyford Dr LU2 . . . . .46 D1
Twyford Gdns CM23 . . . . . .76 F4
Twyford Ind Est CM23 . . . . .77 A5
Twyford Mews CM22 . . . . . .77 A3
Twyford Mill CM22 . . . . . . .77 A3
Twyford Rd
  Bishop's Stortford
  CM23. . . . . .77 A5
  St Albans AL4 . . . . .128 C7
  Welwyn Garden City AL7 . .111 C4
Tye End SG2 . . . . .69 B8
Tyfield CI EN8 . . . . .148 C1
Tylers AL5 . . . . .86 D1
TYLERS CAUSEWAY 132 D1
Tylers CI
  Buntingford SG9 . . . . .40 D7
  Kings Langley WD4 . . . . . .138 F3
  Tylers Cswy SG13 . . . . . . .132 C1
Tylersfield WD5 . . . . .154 A8
TYLER'S HILL 150 A8
Tylers Hill Rd HP5 . . . . . . .150 A8
Tylers Mead LU2 . . . . .45 E5
Tylers Way WD23,
  WD25 . . . . .168 E4
Tylers Wood AL6 . . . . .90 C6
Tynedale AL2 . . . . .142 F4
Tynemouth Dr EN1 . . . . . .162 A1
Typleden CI HP2 . . . . .124 D5
Tysoe Ave EN3 . . . . .163 A1
Tythe Rd LU4 . . . . .44 C6
Tyttenhanger Gn AL4 . . . .142 E8

Uckfield Rd EN3 . . . . .162 D2
Ufford CI HA3 . . . . .176 B3
Ufford Rd HA3 . . . . .176 B3
Ullswater CI SG1 . . . . .37 C2
Ullswater Rd HP3 . . . . .125 C1
Ulverston CI AL2 . . . . .127 F3
Underacres CI HP2 . . . . . . .125 A4
Underhill Inf Sch EN5 . . . .171 E4
Underhill Jun Sch
  EN5 . . . . .171 E4
Underwood Rd SG1 . . . . . . .36 C2
Union Chapel Ho 1
  LU1. . . . . .63 E6
Union Ct 10 HP4 . . . . .122 D4
Union Gn HP2 . . . . .124 D4
Union St
  Barnet EN5 . . . . .171 E6
  Luton LU1 . . . . .63 E6
Union Terr SG9 . . . . .40 E7
Units D1–D2 CM21 . . . . . . .97 F2
Unity Rd EN3 . . . . .162 D2
University CI WD23 . . . . . .168 A5
Univ of Bedfordshire
  LU1. . . . . .63 E7
Univ of Hertfordshire
  AL10. . . . . .129 F3
Unwin CI LU6 . . . . .22 E4
Unwin Pl SG2 . . . . .51 C3
Unwin Rd SG2 . . . . .51 C3
Updale CI EN6 . . . . .158 E6
Upland Dr AL9 . . . . .145 B6
Uplands
  Braughing SG11 . . . . .55 F6
  Croxley Green WD3 . . . . . .165 F3
  Luton LU3 . . . . .44 D8
  Stevenage SG2 . . . . .51 D7
  Ware SG12 . . . . .93 F2
  Welwyn Garden City AL8 . .89 C2
Uplands Ave SG4 . . . . .35 B6
Uplands Ct
  3 Bushey WD23 . . . . . . .168 D1
  Luton LU1 . . . . .63 E6
Uplands The
  Bricket Wood AL2 . . . . . . .140 E1
  Harpenden AL5 . . . . .107 A4
Upper Ashlyns Rd
  HP4 . . . . .122 B3
Upper Barn HP3 . . . . .138 F8
Upper Bourne End La
  HP1 . . . . .137 B8
Upper Clabdens SG12 . . . .93 F2
Upper Culver Rd AL1 . . . . .127 F5
Upper Dagnall St AL3 . . . .127 D3
UPPER DUNSLEY 100 C4
Upperfield Rd AL7 . . . . . . .110 F5
Upper George St LU1 . . . . .63 D7
Upper Gn
  Ickleford SG5 . . . . .21 E4
  Tewin AL6 . . . . .90 D3
Upper Green Rd AL6 . . . . . .90 E3
Upper Hall Pk HP4 . . . . . . .122 E2
Upper Heath Rd AL1 . . . . .127 F5
Upper Highway WD5 . . . . .153 D6
Upper Hill Rise WD3 . . . . .165 B3
Upper Icknield Way
  WD19 . . . . .167 E1
Upper Icknield Way
  Aldbury LU7 . . . . .80 E1
  Aston Clinton HP22 . . . . . .99 A3
  Tring HP23 . . . . .100 D8
Upper King St SG8 . . . . .7 D6
Upper Lattimore Rd
  AL1. . . . . .127 E3
Upper Marlborough Rd
  AL1. . . . . .127 E3
Upper Marsh La EN11 . . . .135 A5
Upper Maylins SG6 . . . . . . .23 C4
Upper Paddock Rd
  WD19 . . . . .167 E3
Upper Pk Rd N20 . . . . .117 B1
Upper Sales HP1 . . . . .123 F2
Upper Sean SG2 . . . . .51 A3
Upper Shot AL7 . . . . .111 A7
Upper Sword Terr 147 F5
Upper Station Rd
  WD7. . . . . .156 A4
Upperstone CI SG5 . . . . . . .11 F6
Upper Tail WD19 . . . . .175 E7
Upper Tilehouse St
  SG5 . . . . .34 E7
Upshire Rd EN9 . . . . .163 F7
Upton Ave AL3 . . . . .127 D4
Upton CI
  Luton LU2 . . . . .45 D6
  Park Street AL2 . . . . .141 D6
Upton Lodge CI
  WD23 . . . . .168 C2
Upton Rd WD18 . . . . .167 B6
Upwell Rd LU2 . . . . .46 B2
UPWICK GREEN 57 E5
Upwick Rd HP22 . . . . .99 A3
Urban Hive LU1 . . . . .44 C8
Urban Rd CM23 . . . . .77 B7
Uxbridge Rd WD3 . . . . . . .173 A8
Uxbridge Rd (Harrow
  Weald) HA3 . . . . .176 D3
Uxbridge Rd (Hatch End)
  HA5 . . . . .175 F3
Uxbridge Rd (Pinner)
  HA5 . . . . .175 D2
Uxbridge Rd (Stanmore)
  HA7 . . . . .176 F4

V

Vadis Cl LU3.................44 E7
Vale Ave WD6..............170 B4
Vale Cl AL5.................85 D4
Vale Cotts SG11...........54 D5
Vale Dr EN5................108 D7
Vale Dr EN5................171 F5
Vale Ind Pk WD18.........166 C1
Valence Dr EN7............148 A3
Valency Cl HA4.............174 F6
Valentine Ct WD6..........169 D3
Vale Rd WD23..............167 E4
Valerian Way SG2...........51 D8
Valerie Cl AL1.............128 B3
Valerie Ct WD23...........168 C2
Valeside SG14..............113 A5
Vallance Pl AL5............107 C7
Vallans Cl SG12.............93 D3
Vallansgate SG2............51 B1
Valley Cl
  Hertford SG13...........113 D5
  Pinner HA5..............175 B1
Valley Rd
  Studham LU6..............82 B4
  Waltham Abbey EN9.....163 C7
  Ware SG12................93 B2
  Whipsnade HU4...........81 E7
Valley Ct CM23.............76 E5
Valley Gn HP2..............105 B1
Valley Gn The AL8.........110 C7
Valley Ho EN8.............162 D8
Valley La AL3...............83 E1
Valley Rd
  Berkhamsted HP4........121 F6
  Codicote SG4.............67 F1
  Letchworth Garden City
    SG6....................22 D7
  Rickmansworth WD3.....165 B3
  St Albans AL3............127 F1
  Studham LU6..............82 B3
  Welwyn Garden City
    AL8...................110 B6
Valley Rise
  Lea Valley AL4............86 F2
  Royston SG8..............7 E6
Watford WD25..............154 B6
Valley Road S SG4...........88 F8
Valley Sch The SG2.........50 F2
Valleyside HP1.............123 F3
Valley The SG4..............66 E7
Valley View
  Barnet EN5...............171 E3
  Goff's Oak EN7...........147 C3
Valley Way SG2..............51 A3
Valley Wlk WD3............166 C4
Valpy Cl WD17..............153 F8
Vanburgh Ct EN5...........171 E5
Vancouver Rd EN10........148 E6
Vanda Cres AL1............127 F2
Vantage Ct EN5............171 F5
Vantage Mews HA6........174 D4
Vantorts Cl CM21...........97 F2
Vantorts Rd CM21..........97 E2
Vardon Rd SG1.............50 F8
Varna Cl LU3...............45 A3
Varney Cl
  Hammond Street EN7....148 A4
  Hemel Hempstead HP1...123 F3
Varney Rd HP1.............123 F3
Vaughan Mead AL3........106 A4
Vaughan Rd
  Harpenden AL5...........86 B1
  Stotfold SG5.............11 E7
Vauxhall Rd
  Hemel Hempstead
    HP2..................125 B3
  Luton LU1, LU2..........64 B5
Vauxhall Way LU2..........46 B1
Vega Cres HA6.............175 A5
Vega Rd WD23.............168 C2
Velizy Ave CM20...........117 D1
Venables Terr SG1..........50 D7
Venetia Rd LU2.............46 A4
Venice Ave WD18..........166 E5
Ventnor Gdns LU3...........45 A7
Ventura Pk AL2............141 F2
Venus Ct AL10.............129 E6
VENUS HILL................151 B8
Venus Hill HP3.............151 A8
Vera Ct WD19..............167 D2
Vera La AL6................90 B4
Verdana Cl WD18..........166 E4
Verdure Cl WD25..........154 E7
Veritys AL10...............130 A5
Verity Way SG1.............51 B8
Ver Mdw Cvn Site
  AL3....................106 C5
Verney Cl
  Berkhamsted HP4........121 F5
  Tring HP23...............100 C3
Vernon Ave EN3............162 E3
Vernon Cl CM23............76 E4
Vernon Dr UB9............173 C2
Vernon Rd
  Luton LU1................63 C8
  Watford WD17...........167 E4
Vernon's Cl AL1............127 C3
Veronica Ho AL7...........111 B4
Ver Rd
  Redbourn AL3...........106 C6
  St Albans AL3...........127 C3
Verulam Cl AL7............110 F6
Verulam Gdns LU3..........44 F6

Verulam Ind Est AL1.......127 F1
Verulamium Mus*
  AL3....................127 B3
Verulamium Roman
  Town* AL3.............127 A3
Verulam Rd
  Hitchin SG5..............34 F8
  St Albans AL3...........127 C4
Verulam Sch AL1..........128 A4
Verwood Rd HA2...........176 C1
Vespers Cl LU4............44 A2
Vesta Ave AL1.............141 C8
Vesta Rd HP2..............125 A6
Vestry Cl LU1..............63 D7
Veysey Cl **2** HP1.........124 B1
Viaduct Cotts LU1..........85 F8
Viaduct Rd SG12..........114 E8
Viaduct Way AL7............89 F2
Vian Ave EN3..............162 E4
Vicarage Cl
  Arlesey SG15.............11 A8
  Bishop's Stortford
    CM23..................76 F7
  Hemel Hempstead HP1...124 C2
  Northaw EN6.............145 F1
  Potters Bar EN6.........158 E7
  Shillington SG5...........19 F8
  Standon SG11.............55 E2
Vicarage Cswy SG13.......114 B4
Vicarage Gdns
  Flamstead AL3...........84 B1
  Marsworth HP23..........80 A2
  Potten End HP4..........123 B7
Vicarage Ho AL7...........110 F5
Vicarage La
  Bovingdon HP3..........137 B4
  Ivinghoe LU7..............80 F5
  Kings Langley WD4.......138 F2
  Stapleford SG14..........92 B2
Vicarage Rd
  Buntingford SG9..........40 E8
  Marsworth HP23..........80 A2
  Pitstone LU7.............80 D3
  Potten End HP4..........123 A7
  Ware SG12................93 E1
  Watford WD18............167 A4
  Wigginton HP23..........100 D1
Vicarage Road Prec
  WD18..................167 B5
Vicarage St LU1...........63 F7
Vicarage Wood CM20......118 A1
Vicerons Pl CM23...........76 D4
Victoria CE Fst Sch
  HPA....................122 C4
Victoria Cl
  Rickmansworth WD3.....165 D2
  Stevenage SG1...........50 D7
Victoria Cres SG8...........7 D7
Victoria Ct
  Harlow CM20.............117 E1
  2 Watford WD17.......167 C6
Victoria Dr SG5.............12 A5
Victoria La EN5............171 F5
Victoria Mews SG13.......113 A1
Victoria Pas WD18.........167 B5
Victoria Pl HP1............124 D3
Victoria Rd
  Berkhamsted HP4........122 C4
  Bushey WD23............168 B1
  7 Harpenden AL5......86 B1
  Hitchin SG5...............34 D8
  Waltham Abbey EN9......163 C5
  Watford WD24...........154 B1
Victoria Sq AL1............127 F2
Victoria St
  Luton LU1................63 E6
  St Albans AL1...........127 E3
Victoria Terr **9** SG5......34 D8
Victors Way EN5...........171 F6
Victory Ct
  Royston SG8...............7 E5
  St Albans AL1...........128 B3
Victory Rd HP4............122 A5
View Point SG1.............50 A5
Viewpoint Ct **8** HA5.....175 C1
Vigers Croft AL10..........129 F4
Villa Ct **3** LU2...........63 D8
Village Arc **8** AL1.......127 D3
Village Cl EN11............135 D8
Village Ct AL4.............128 D7
Village Mews HP3..........137 A4
Village St SG4.............49 F1
Village Way SG7...........5 A3
Villa Rd LU2................63 D8
Villiers Cl LU4..............46 A4
Villiers Cres AL4...........128 D6
Villiers Rd WD19..........167 E3
Villiers St SG13...........113 E6
Villiers-Sur-Marne Ave
  CM23..................76 D4
Vincent Cl EN8............148 E3
Vincent Ct
  Northwood HA6..........174 F2
  Stevenage SG1...........50 B8
Vincent Rd LU4.............44 D5
Vincenzo Cl AL9...........144 C8
Vine Cl AL8...............110 E8
Vine Ct **11** SG12.........93 D2
Vine Gr CM20.............117 E5
Vines The SG5.............11 E6
Vine Tree Cl WD3.........173 B8
Vineyards Hill EN6........146 B2
Vineyards Rd EN6.........146 A2

Vineyard The
  Hertford SG14...........113 D8
  Ware SG12...............94 A2
Vineyard Gate
  Shopping Centre
    AL8...................110 E8
Vintage Ct SG11...........55 C2
Vinters Ave SG1...........50 F5
Violet Ave EN2............161 D1
Violets La SG9.............43 B5
Violet Way WD3...........165 C5
Virgil Dr EN10.............148 F8
Virginia Cl LU2.............45 F3
Viscount Cl LU3............45 A5
Viscount Ct **14** LU2.....45 D1
Vivian Cl WD19............167 A1
Vivian Gdns WD19.........167 A1
Vixen Cl AL10.............130 B7
Vixen Dr SG13............114 A6
Vyse Cl EN5...............171 C5

W

Wacketts EN7.............148 A4
Waddesdon Cl LU2.........46 D2
Waddesdon Ct EN2........161 E1
Waddington Rd **3**
  AL3....................127 D3
Waddling La AL4...........87 D1
WADESMILL................93 D8
Wadesmill Rd
  Tonwell SG12, SG14......92 D3
  Ware SG12...............93 D2
Wades The AL10............130 A2
Wadham Rd WD5...........153 F8
Wadhurst Ave LU3.........45 C4
Wadley Cl **1** HP2........124 F2
Wadnall Way SG3..........68 F3
Waggoners Yd **4**
  SG12..................93 D2
Waggon Rd EN4............159 E2
Wagon Rd
  Ganwick Corner EN5.....159 A4
  Hadley Wood EN4........159 B2
Wagon Way WD3...........165 C6
Wagtail Cl AL10...........129 E7
Wain Cl EN6...............145 B2
Wainwright St CM23.......76 C5
Wakefields Wlk EN8........162 E8
Walace Ct EN3.............163 A2
Walcot Ave LU2............46 B1
Waldeck Rd LU3............63 C8
Waldegrave Pk AL5........86 D1
Walden End SG1...........50 E4
Walden Pl AL8.............110 D8
Walden Rd AL8............110 D8
Waleran Cl HA7...........176 F4
Waleys Cl LU3..............44 E8
Walfords Cl CM17.........118 C3
Walkden's SG7..............4 E4
Walker Gr AL10...........129 D6
Walker Prim Sch SG2......52 B8
Walkern Rd
  Benington SG2...........52 D5
  Stevenage SG1...........50 D8
  Watton at S SG14.........70 C6
Walkers Cl AL5............107 C7
Walkers Ct AL5............107 C7
Walkers' Ct SG7............23 F8
Walkers Rd AL5............107 B7
Walk The
  Hertford SG14...........113 A5
  Potters Bar EN6..........159 B7
Wallace Ct **10** SG5.......34 F8
Wallace Way SG4...........22 A2
Walled Garden The
  AL5....................92 A1
Walled Gdn The AL6........90 B2
Waller Ave LU4.............44 F3
Waller Dr HA6.............175 A2
Waller's Cl SG8.............9 F2
Waller Street Mall **3**
  LU1....................63 E7
Wallers Way EN11.........115 B1
Wall Hall Dr WD25.........155 B3
Wall Hall Man WD25.......155 B4
Wallingford Wlk AL1.......141 D8
WALLINGTON.............25 D8
Wallington Rd SG7.........13 D1
Wallis Ct EN9.............163 B4
Walnut Ave SG7............24 A7
Walnut Cl
  Chiswell Green AL2......141 B4
  Hitchin SG4.............35 A6
  Luton LU2..............46 B4
  Much Hadham SG10......37 A4
  Royston SG8...............7 D6
  Stotfold SG5.............11 F6
Walnut Cotts CM21.........97 E3
Walnut Ct
  Welwyn Garden City
    AL7...................110 E3
  Wheathampstead AL4....108 D8
Walnut Dr CM23............76 D3
Walnut Gr WD23...........167 F7
Walnut Gr
  Harlow CM20............117 B1
  Hemel Hempstead HP2...124 D3
  Welwyn Garden City
    AL7...................110 E3
Walnut Ho AL7.............110 E3
Walnut Tree Ave CM21.....97 E4
Walnut Tree Cl
  Aston SG2................51 D4
  Cheshunt EN8............162 D8
  Hoddesdon EN11.........135 A6

Walnut Tree Cres
  CM21..................97 E3
Walnut Tree Rd SG5........20 D3
Walnut Tree Wlk
  SG12..................114 E6
Walnut Way SG5............21 E4
Walpole Bldg **5** WD3....165 E1
Walpole Cl HA5...........176 A4
Walpole Ct SG2............69 C7
Walsam Cl SG2.............69 C7
Walsham Ct EN3...........162 C2
Walsh Cl SG5..............34 D7
Walshford Way WD6.......157 A1
Walsingham Cl
  Hatfield AL10...........129 F6
  Luton LU2...............45 D7
Walsingham Way AL2......142 C4
WALSWORTH...............22 A1
Walsworth Rd SG4.........35 A8
Walter Rothschild
  Zoological Mus The*
    HP23..................100 A3
Walters Cl HP2............124 A5
WALTHAM ABBEY.........163 D7
Waltham Abbey*
  EN9....................163 C6
WALTHAM CROSS.........162 F5
Waltham Cross Sta
  EN8....................162 F5
Waltham Ct LU2............46 C3
Waltham Gate EN8........148 F5
Waltham Gdns EN3.........162 C2
Waltham Holy Cross Inf
  Sch EN9................163 D6
Waltham Holy Cross Jun
  Sch EN9................163 D6
Waltham Rd
  Hoddesdon EN11.........135 C8
  Ware SG12...............114 D8
  Watford WD23............167 E5
Walton St LU1.............127 F5
Walverns Cl WD19.........167 C3
Wander Wharf WD4........139 B1
Wandon Cl LU2.............46 C4
WANDON END.............47 B1
Wannions Cl HP5..........136 A1
Wansbeck Cl SG1..........37 A3
Wansford Pk WD6.........170 E5
Warburton Cl HA3.........167 A8
Ward Cl
  Hammond Street EN7....148 A4
  Ware SG12...............93 C2
Ward Cres CM23...........76 E6
Warden Ct **5** LU2........63 E8
WARDEN HILL.............45 D7
Warden Hill Cl LU2.........45 C8
Warden Hill Gdns LU2......45 C8
Warden Hill Inf Sch
  LU3....................45 D7
Warden Hill Jun Sch
  LU3....................45 C7
Warden Hill Rd LU2.........45 C8
Ward Hatch CM20.........118 A3
Wardown Cres LU2.........45 E2
Wardown Ct LU3............45 D2
Wardown Park Mus*
  LU3....................45 D2
Wards Cotts WD6.........168 F7
Wards Dr WD3.............151 F3
WARE.....................93 F2
Wareham's La SG14.......113 C5
Ware Mus* SG12..........93 D2
Warenford Way WD6......170 A8
Ware Park Manor
  SG12..................92 E2
Ware Park Rd SG12,
  SG14..................113 E8
Ware Rd
  Hertford SG13...........113 E6
  Hoddesdon EN11.........115 A1
  Tonwell SG12............92 F6
  Watton at S SG14, SG12...71 C3
  Widford SG12............95 D4
WARESIDE..................94 A4
Wareside HP2.............105 A1
Wareside CE Prim Sch
  SG12..................94 E3
Wareside Ct AL7...........111 B5
Ware Sta SG12............114 E8
Warham Rd HA3...........176 F1
Warlow Cl EN3............163 A2
Warmark Rd HP1..........123 E5
Warminster Cl LU2.........46 F1
Warneford Pl WD19........167 E5
Warner Cl EN4............159 E2
Warner Rd LU4............114 D8
Warners Ave EN11........134 F4
Warners Cl SG2............51 C3
WARNERS END...........123 F4
Warners End Rd HP1......124 B4
Warren Cl
  Hatfield AL10...........130 B8
  Letchworth Garden City
    SG6....................22 D7
Warren Cotts SG8..........9 A1
Warren Ct
  Cheshunt EN8............148 E1
  Royston SG8...............7 D5
Warren Dale AL8...........89 D1
Warren Dell Prim Sch
  WD19..................175 C2
Warren Dr The LU1.........64 C1
Warrenfield Cl EN7.........162 A8

Warregate La EN6.........158 C8
Warrengate Rd AL9........144 C4
Warren Gn AL10...........130 B8
Warren Gr WD6............170 D5
Warren La
  Clothall SG7.............24 D7
  Cottered SG9............39 B6
  Stanmore HA7..........176 F8
Warren Park Rd
  SG14..................113 D7
Warren Pl **16** SG14......113 D6
Warren Rd
  Bushey WD23............168 D1
  Luton LU1...............62 F8
  St Albans AL1...........141 C7
WARREN'S GREEN.........37 D6
Warrensgreen La SG4.....37 D5
Warren Terr SG14.........113 D8
Warren The
  Harpenden AL5..........107 A6
  Kings Langley WD4......138 F2
  Radlett WD7............156 B6
  Royston SG8...............7 D5
Warren Way AL6............89 E4
Warren Wood Ind Est
  SG14..................91 F6
Warton Gn LU2.............46 E2
Warwick Ave EN6..........146 D4
Warwick Cl
  Bushey WD23............168 E2
  Cuffley EN6.............146 D4
  Hertford SG13...........113 C4
Warwick Ct
  Chorleywood WD3.......164 F6
  Luton LU4...............63 B8
Warwick Dr EN8...........148 D3
Warwick Ho **11** AL1.....127 D3
Warwick Mews WD3.......166 A3
Warwick Rd
  Bishop's Stortford
    CM23..................77 B6
  Borehamwood WD6......170 D4
  Enfield EN3............162 F2
  Pitstone LU7.............80 D3
  St Albans AL1...........127 F5
  Stevenage SG2...........51 C6
Warwick Rd E LU4..........63 B8
Warwick Rd W LU4.........63 B8
Warwick Way WD3........166 C5
WASHALL GREEN...........30 C1
Washington Ave HP2......124 E8
Wash La
  Dancers Hill EN6........158 C3
  South Mimms EN6.......158 C5
Wash The
  Furneux Pelham SG9......43 D5
  Hertford SG14...........113 D6
Watchlytes AL7............111 C6
Watchlytes Jun Mix Inf
  Sch AL7................111 C6
Watchmead AL7............111 A6
Waterbeach AL7...........111 D6
Watercress Cl SG2..........51 D5
Watercress Rd EN7........147 D5
WATERDALE...............140 C1
Waterdale SG13............113 C4
Waterdell La SG4............35 A2
Waterdell Pl WD3..........173 B8
WATER END
  Brookmans Park.........144 C5
  Hemel Hempstead........103 F1
Water End Rd WD6........169 F7
Waterend La
  Ayot St P AL4, AL6........88 E1
  Redbourn AL3............106 B5
Water End Rd HP4.........123 C7
Waterfall Cl EN11..........134 F7
Waterfield
  Chorleywood WD3.......164 C2
  Welwyn Garden City
    AL7...................111 B7
Waterfields Ret Pk
  WD17..................167 D5
Waterfields Way WD17,
  WD23..................167 D4
WATERFORD...............92 A2
Waterford Gn AL7..........111 B6
Waterfront The **22**
  SG14..................113 D6
Watergate The WD19.....175 D8
Waterhall Cotts SG13......132 D7
Water Hall Farm & Craft
  Ctr* SG4................66 F7
Waterhouse Gdns **7**
  LU1....................63 E5
Waterhouse La HP1........124 C3
Waterhouse The HP1......124 C3
Water La
  Abbots Langley WD4.....139 B2
  Berkhamsted HP4........122 C4
  Bishop's Stortford CM23..76 F8
  Bovingdon HP3..........137 B1
  Hertford SG14...........113 C5
  Hitchin SG5.............21 F1
  Stansted Mountfitchet
    CM24..................59 E6
  Watford WD17...........167 D5
Waterloo S **3** AL1.......128 B2
Waterloo La SG1...........21 A6
Waterlow Mews SG4.......35 E3
Waterman Ct WD19........167 B3
Watermark Way SG13.....113 F6
Water Mdws AL2...........141 E3
Watermill Ind Est SG9.....40 E6
Watermill La
  Hertford SG14...........113 D8

Watermill La continued
Stansted Mountfitchet
CM24 ....59 C6
Water Row 11 SG12 .....93 D1
Waters Dr 9 WD3 ....165 E1
Waters End SG5 ....11 E6
Waterside
Berkhamsted HP4 .....122 D4
Harpenden AL5 ....86 C3
Kings Langley WD4 ....139 A2
London Colney AL2 ....142 E4
Radlett WD7 ....156 B5
Stansted Mountfitchet
CM24 ....59 C6
Welwyn Garden City AL7 ..90 B1
Waterside Cotts AL9 ...130 E8
Waterside Ct
2 Hemel Hempstead
HP3 ....138 E7
Kings Langley WD4 ....139 B2
Waterside Ind Est
EN11 ....135 D5
Waterside Mews UB9 ..173 A4
Waterslade Gn SG3 .....45 B6
Watersplash Ct AL2 ...142 F4
Waterways Bsns Ctr 1
EN3 ....163 A1
Watery La
Flamstead AL3, AL5 ....84 E3
Hatfield AL10 ....129 E4
Marsworth HP23 ....79 F1
WATFORD 167 C3
Watford Arches Ret Pk
WD17 ....167 D4
Watford By-pass
WD6 ....169 C2
Watford Coll (annex)
WD23 ....167 D6
Watford County Ct
WD18 ....167 C5
Watford Ent Ctr
WD18 ....166 E3
Watford Field Rd
WD18 ....167 C4
Watford Football Gd &
Saracens RFC WD18 ..167 B4
Watford General Hospl
(Shrodells Wing)
WD18 ....167 B3
Watford Gram Sch for
Boys WD18 ....166 F5
Watford Gram Sch for
Girls WD18 ....167 B5
WATFORD HEATH 167 E2
Watford Heath WD19 ..167 D2
Watford Heath Farm
WD19 ....167 D2
Watford High Street Sta
WD17 ....167 C6
Watford Junction Sta
WD17 ....167 C7
Watford Mus★ WD17 ...167 C5
Watford North Sta
WD24 ....154 C2
Watford Sch of Music
WD17 ....154 A1
Watford Sta WD18 .....166 F6
Watkin Mews EN3 ......163 A2
Watkins Ct AL1 ....174 F2
Watkins Rise EN6 ......159 B7
Watling Cl 1 HP2 ......124 E6
Watling Ct WD3 ....169 D3
Watling Farm Ct HA7 ..169 E1
Watling Knoll WD7 ....155 F6
Watling Mans WD7 ....156 B3
Watling St
Elstree WD6 ....169 C6
Park Street AL2 ....141 D6
Radlett WD7 ....156 B3
St Albans AL1 ....141 C8
Watlington Rd CM17 ..141 C8
Watling View AL1 ......141 C8
Watling View Sch
AL1 ....141 D7
Watson Ave AL3 ....127 F6
Watson Rd SG1 ....50 C5
Watson's Wlk AL1 .....127 E2
Watsons Yd 8 SG12 ....76 F8
WATTON AT STONE 70 E4
Watton-at-Stone Prim
Sch SG14 ....70 D3
Watton at Stone Sta
SG14 ....70 F3
Watton Ho SG14 ....70 F3
Watton Rd
Knebworth SG3 ....69 A5
Ware SG12 ....93 C2
Watton at S SG3, SG14 ..70 B2
Watts Cl SG11 ....57 C2
Waulud Prim Sch LU3 ..44 E7
Waulds Bank Dr LU3 ..44 E7
Wavell Cl EN8 ....148 E4
Wavell Ho AL1 ....128 A2
Waveney HP2 ....124 F8
Waveney Rd AL5 ....86 A2
Waverley Cl SG2 ....69 A8
Waverley Gdns HA5 ...175 A2
Waverley Lodge AL5 ..127 D5
Waverley Rd AL3 ....127 D5

Waxhouse Gate AL1 ....127 D3
Waxwell Cl HA5 ....175 D1
Waxwell La HA5 ....175 D1
Wayfarers Pk HP4 ......121 F4
Wayletts Dr CM23 ....77 B7
Waynes Ct 9 LU1 ....63 E7
Wayre St CM17 ....118 C4
Wayre The CM17 ....118 C4
Waysbrook SG6 ....23 B5
Wayside
Chipperfield WD4 ......138 B1
Potters Bar EN6 ....159 D6
Shenley WD7 ....156 D6
Wayside Ave WD23 ....168 D3
Wayside Ct AL2 ....140 F1
Wayside The HP3 ......125 C2
Waysmeet SG6 ....23 B4
Waytemore Rd CM23 ...76 E6
Weald Fst Sch HA3 ....176 F2
Weald La HA3 ....176 F2
Weald Mid Sch HA3 ...176 F3
Weald Rise HA3 ....176 F2
Wealdwood Gdns
HA5 ....176 B4
Weall Gn WD25 ....154 B7
Weardale Ct EN5 ....171 C4
Weatherby Rd LU1 ......44 D2
Weavers Orch SG15 ....11 A4
Weavers Rd HP23 ....99 E4
Weaver St CM23 ....76 C4
Weavers Way SG7 ....24 A8
Webb Cl SG6 ....23 C5
Webber Cl WD6 ....169 D3
Webb Rise SG1 ....50 F7
Webley Ct 5 AL1 ....163 A2
Webster Ct 3 WD3 ....165 E1
Wedgewood Cl HA6 ...174 C4
Wedgewood Rd SG4 ....35 B7
Wedgwood Way SG1 ....37 B2
Wedgwood Gate Ind Est
SG1 ....37 B2
Wedmore Rd SG4 ....35 A6
Wedon Way SG7 ....13 C4
Weedon Ct LU6 ....10 C5
Weighton Rd HA3 ......176 D2
Welbeck Ct WD6 ....170 A6
Welbeck Rd 3 LU2 ......63 A8
Welbeck Rise HA5 .....107 D6
Welbury Ave LU3 ....45 C7
Welch Ho 2 EN3 ....162 D2
Welch Pl HA5 ....175 C2
Welclose St AL3 ....127 C3
Welcote Dr HA4 ....174 D4
Weldon Cl LU2 ....46 E1
Welham Cl
Borehamwood WD6 ...170 A8
Welham Green AL9 ....144 C7
Welham Ct AL9 ....144 C7
WELHAM GREEN 144 C7
Welham Green Sta
AL9 ....144 D8
Welham Manor AL9 ...144 C7
Welkin Gn HP2 ....125 C4
Wellands AL10 ....130 A7
Well App EN5 ....171 C4
Wellbrook Mews
HP23 ....100 B4
Wellbury Terr HP2 .....125 C3
Wellcroft LU7 ....80 F5
Well Croft HP1 ....124 B4
Wellcroft Cl AL7 ....111 A4
Wellcroft Rd AL7 ......111 A4
WELL END 157 C1
Well End Rd WD6 ......157 D1
Wellen Rise HP3 ....138 E8
Wellers Gr EN7 ....148 A3
Wellesley Ave HA6 ....175 C2
Wellesley Cres LU6 .....44 C8
Wellfield Ct AL10 ......130 A6
Wellfield Ct SG1 ....37 B1
Wellfield Rd AL10 ......130 A7
Well Garth AL7 ....110 E5
Wellgate Rd LU4 ....44 D2
Well Gn SG11 ....91 C4
Wellhouse Cl LU1 ....63 C4
Wellhouse La EN5 .....171 D5
Wellingham Ave SG5 ...21 D1
Wellington Ave HA5 ..175 F5
Wellington Ct WD19 ..175 F7
Wellington Cotts SG11 ..73 B7
Wellington Ho 3 LU1 ...63 D6
Wellington Dr AL7 ....111 C6
Wellington Ho 1
WD24 ....167 C7
Wellington Pl
Cheshunt EN10 ....148 C8
Kneesworth SG8 ....2 B5
Wellington Rd
London Colney AL2 ...142 D5
Pinner HA5 ....175 F2
St Albans AL1 ....128 B2
Stevenage SG2 ....51 C5
Watford WD17 ....167 B7
Wellington St
Hertford SG14 ....113 B7
Luton LU1 ....63 D7
Well La
Harlow CM19 ....117 A1
Mentmore LU7 ....61 B8
WELLPOND GREEN 56 D1
Well Rd
Barnet EN5 ....171 C4
Northaw EN6 ....145 E2
Well Row SG13 ....132 F6
Wells Cl
Hammond Street EN7 ..147 C6

Wells Cl continued
Harpenden AL5 ....85 E4
St Albans AL3 ....127 C4
Wellsfield WD23 ....167 E4
Wellside Cl EN5 ....171 C5
Wellstones WD18 ......167 B5
Wellswood Cl HP2 ....125 B4
Wells Yd
8 Ware SG12 ....93 D1
Watford WD17 ....167 B6
Welsummer Way EN8 ..148 D3
Weltmore Rd LU3 ....44 F6
WELWYN 89 B4
Welwyn By Pass Rd
AL6 ....89 C5
WELWYN GARDEN CITY
............................110 E7
Welwyn Garden City Sta
AL8 ....110 D6
Welwyn Hall Gdns AL6 ..89 C3
Welwyn North Sta AL6 ..89 F3
Welwyn Rd SG14 ......112 F7
Wendover Cl
Harpenden AL5 ....86 D1
St Albans AL4 ....128 C8
Wendover Ct AL6 ....89 C5
Wendover Dr AL6 ....89 C5
Wendover Ho WD18 ..166 E2
Wendover Way
Bushey WD23 ....168 C3
Luton LU2 ....45 F3
Wengeo La SG12 ....93 B2
Wenham Ct SG2 ....52 B8
Wenham Pl AL10 ....130 A6
Wenlock CE Jun Sch
LU2 ....64 B8
Wenlock St LU2 ....63 E8
Wensley Cl AL5 ....107 D6
Wensleydale
Hemel Hempstead
HP2 ....124 F6
Luton LU2 ....45 E1
Wensum Rd SG1 ....36 F3
Wensum Way WD3 ....165 D1
Wenta Bsns Ctr
WD24 ....154 D2
Wentbridge Path
WD6 ....157 A1
Wentworth Ave
Borehamwood WD6 ...169 F4
Luton LU4 ....44 C6
Wentworth Cl
Potters Bar EN6 ....159 A8
Watford WD17 ....153 F1
Wentworth Cotts
Dane End SG12 ....53 F2
Hoddesdon EN10 ......134 E1
Wentworth Ct EN5 ....171 E6
Wentworth Dr
Bishop's Stortford
CM23 ....76 D6
South Oxhey WD19 ...175 D5
Wentworth Rd
Barnet EN5 ....171 D5
Hertford SG13 ....113 C3
Wenwell Cl HP22 ....99 A3
Wesley Cl
Arlesey SG15 ....11 A4
Goff's Oak EN7 ....147 C3
Wesley Rd AL3 ....83 E5
Wessex Ct 7 EN5 ......171 D5
Wessex Dr HA5 ....175 E3
Westall Cl SG13 ....113 C5
West Alley SG5 ....34 E7
Westall Mews SG13 ...113 C5
West Ave
Baldock SG7 ....23 E8
Chiswell Green AL2 ...141 B6
Westbourne Mews
AL1 ....127 D3
Westbourne Mobile Home
Pk LU3 ....44 F5
Westbourne Rd LU4 ....45 B1
Westbrook Cl SG8 ....5 B8
Westbrook Ct SG4 ....37 A5
Westbrook Hay Prep Sch
HP1 ....137 D7
West Burrowfield
AL7 ....110 D4
Westbury EN8 ....148 D1
Westbury Ct SG5 ....34 D8
Westbury Farm Cl SG5 ..33 C3
Westbury Gdns LU2 ....45 E3
Westbury Pl SG6 ....22 E5
Westbury Prim Sch
SG6 ....22 E5
Westbury Rd
Moor Park HA6 ....174 E7
Watford WD18 ....167 B4
Westbush Cl EN11 .....114 F1
West Chantry HA3 ....176 B2
West Cl
Barnet EN5 ....171 B4
Hitchin SG4 ....22 B1
Hoddesdon EN11 ......135 A8
Stevenage SG1 ....50 F5
West Comm
Harpenden AL5 ....107 B6
Redbourn AL3 ....106 A4
West Common Cl AL5 ..107 B5
West Common Gr
AL5 ....107 B5
West Common Way
AL5 ....107 A5
Westcott AL7 ....111 D7
Westcroft HP23 ....100 A3
Westcroft Cl EN3 ......162 C1

Westcroft Ct EN10 .....135 A4
West Ct CM21 ....97 E3
West Dene HP2 ....104 A8
West Dr
Arlesey SG15 ....11 B4
Stanmore HA3 ....176 D4
Watford WD25 ....154 B3
West Drive Gdns HA3 ..176 D4
Westell Cl SG13 ....24 A8
WEST END 131 C5
West End SG7 ....4 C3
West End La
Barnet EN5 ....171 D5
Essendon AL9 ....131 C5
West End Rd EN7 ......147 F8
Westerdale
Hemel Hempstead
HP2 ....124 E6
Luton LU4 ....44 B5
Western Ave SG16 ......10 B3
Western Cl SG6 ....11 E1
Western House Hospl
SG12 ....93 E2
Western Rd
Lower Nazeing EN9 ...135 E1
Luton LU1 ....63 D6
Tring HP23 ....99 F3
Western Terr 1 EN11 ..115 B1
Western Way SG6 ....11 E1
Westfield
Welham Green AL9 ...144 F8
Welwyn Garden City
AL7 ....111 A7
Westfield Ave
Harpenden AL5 ....86 A3
Watford WD24 ....154 D1
Westfield Cl
Bishop's Stortford
CM23 ....76 B8
Cheshunt EN8 ....162 F8
Hitchin SG5 ....34 D7
Westfield Com Prim Sch
EN11 ....134 F7
Westfield Com Tech Coll
WD18 ....166 F3
Westfield Ct AL4 ....128 D6
Westfield Dr AL5 ....86 B4
Westfield Fst Sch
HP4 ....121 F5
Westfield La SG4 ....34 D7
Westfield Ph HA5 ......175 F3
Westfield Pl AL5 ....86 B4
Westfield Rd
Berkhamsted HP4 .....121 F5
Bishop's Stortford CM23 ..76 B8
Harpenden AL5 ....86 B4
Hertford SG14 ....113 C8
Hoddesdon EN11 ......134 F7
Pinner HA5 ....175 F3
Westfields AL3 ....141 A8
Westfield Wlk EN8 ....162 F8
Westgate SG1 ....50 D5
West Gate 1 CM20 ....117 C1
Westgate Ct EN3 ......162 D1
West Herts Bsns Ctr
WD6 ....170 B6
West Herts Coll Cassio
Campus WD17 ....154 A1
West Herts Coll (Dacorum
Campus) HP1 ....124 C4
West Herts Coll Leggatts
Campus WD24 ....154 A3
West Herts Coll Watford
Campus WD17 ....167 A6
West Hill Rd
Hoddesdon EN11 ......134 F8
Luton LU1 ....63 E5
Westholm SG6 ....22 F8
WEST HYDE 172 E3
West Hyde La SL9 .....172 A4
West La
Great Offley SG5 ....33 C2
Pirton SG5 ....20 C5
Westland Cl WD25 ....153 F5
Westland Dr AL9 ....144 E4
Westland Rd
Knebworth SG3 ....69 A5
Watford WD17 ....167 B7
West Lawn WD25 ......155 B3
Westlea Ave WD25 ....154 E2
Westlea Rd WD25 .....148 F8
Westlecote Gdns LU2 ..45 D4
WEST LEITH 99 E1
West Leith HP23 ....99 F1
West Lodge Cotts LU2 ..46 D5
Westly Wood AL7 ......111 A7
West Mead AL7 ....111 B3
Westmeade Ct EN7 ...148 B2
WESTMILL
Buntingford 40 F3
Hitchin 21 C1
Westmill La
Hitchin SG5 ....21 C2
Ickleford SG5 ....21 C2
Westmill Lawns SG5 ...21 D1
Westmill Rd
Hitchin SG5 ....21 D1
Thundridge SG12 ......93 A3
Westminster Ct
Cheshunt EN8 ....162 F6
St Albans AL1 ....127 C1
Westminster Ho 6
WD24 ....167 C7
Westmorland Ave LU3 ..44 F1

Westmount Apartments 5
WD18 ....166 F5
WESTON 24 C1
Weston Ave SG8 ....7 C7
Weston Cl EN6 ....158 F7
Westonia Ct EN3 ....162 E3
Weston Prim Sch SG4 ..24 C1
Weston Rd
Stevenage SG1 ....36 E1
Stevenage SG1 ....36 F2
Stevenage SG1 ....23 E7
West Pas HP23 ....100 A3
West Pl CM20 ....118 A3
Westray HP1 ....125 C1
West Rd
Berkhamsted HP4 .....122 A5
Bishop's Stortford CM23 ..76 E6
Harlow CM20 ....118 A3
Sawbridgeworth CM21 ..97 C3
Stansted Mountfitchet
CM24 ....59 C6
West Reach SG2 ....50 F2
Westridge Cl HP1 ......123 F3
West Riding
Bricket Wood AL2 .....140 F1
Burnham Green AL6 ...90 D5
Westron Gdns HP23 ..100 B4
West Side EN10 ....148 E6
West Sq 2 EN20 ....117 C1
West St
Hertford SG13 ....113 C5
Lilley LU2 ....32 D1
Ware SG12 ....93 D1
Watford WD17 ....167 B7
West Valley Rd HP3 ..138 D7
West View
Hatfield AL10 ....130 A7
Letchworth Garden City
SG6 ....22 C5
Standon SG11 ....73 A6
West View Ct WD6 ....169 D3
West View Gdns WD6 ..169 D3
West View Rd AL3 .....127 D4
Westview Rise HP2 ...124 D4
WEST WATFORD 167 A4
West Way
Harpenden AL5 ....86 C2
Luton LU2 ....46 C4
Rickmansworth WD3 ..165 B1
West Ways HA6 ....175 A1
Westwick Cl HP2 ......125 D2
Westwick Pl WD25 ...154 C5
WESTWICK ROW 125 E2
Westwick Row HP2 ...125 E2
Westwood Ave SG4 ....35 A6
Westwood Ct EN6 .....145 A1
Westwood St AL3 .....176 D8
Wetherall Mews 1
AL1 ....127 E2
Wetherby Cl SG1 ....51 C8
Wetherby Rd
Borehamwood WD6 ...169 E8
Enfield EN2 ....161 C1
Wetherfield CM24 ....59 D7
Wetherly Cl CM17 .....118 F4
Wethenne Link LU4 .....44 C5
Wexham Cl LU3 ....44 E8
Weybourne Cl AL5 ......86 D2
Weybourne Dr LU2 .....45 C7
Weymouth St HP3 ....138 D7
Weyver Ct 5 AL1 ......127 E4
Whaley Rd EN6 ....159 C6
Wharfdale
Hemel Hempstead
HP2 ....124 E6
8 Luton LU4 ....44 C5
Wharf La
Berkhamsted HP4 .....121 C8
Rickmansworth WD3 ..165 E1
Wharf Pl CM23 ....77 A6
Wharf Rd
1 Bishop's Stortford
CM23 ....76 B4
Hemel Hempstead HP1 ..124 B1
Hoddesdon EN10 ......148 B8
Wharf Row HP22 ....99 B4
Wharf Villas 5 HP1 ...124 B1
Wheatbarn AL7 ....111 B7
Wheat Cl AL4 ....128 A7
Wheatcotes SG3 ....69 C1
Wheatcroft EN7 ....148 B3
Wheat Croft CM23 .....76 C4
Wheatcroft Prim Sch
SG13 ....114 A7
Wheatfield
Hatfield AL10 ....130 B6
8 Hemel Hempstead HP2 ..124 D5
Wheatfield Ave AL5 ..107 A5
Wheatfield Cres SG8 ...7 E6
Wheatfield Rd AL5 ....107 A4
Wheatfields CM17 ....118 D6
Wheatfields Inf Sch
AL4 ....128 B2
Wheatfields Jun Mix Sch
AL4 ....128 B7
WHEATHAMPSTEAD
............................108 C2
Wheathampstead Rd
Harpenden AL5 ....107 E8
Wheathampstead AL5,
AL4 ....108 A8
Wheat Hill SG6 ....22 F8
Wheatlands SG2 ....51 C7
Wheatley Cl
Sawbridgeworth CM21 ..97 C3

Wheatley Cl continued
Welwyn Garden City
AL7 . . . . .111 A4
Wheatley Dr WD25 . . . . . .154 E1
Wheatley Rd AL7 . . . . . . .111 A4
Wheatleys AL4 . . . . .128 C5
Wheatlock Mead AL3 . .106 A5
Wheatsheaf Cotts
WD3 . . . . .152 A4
Wheatsheaf Dr SG12 . . . .93 B3
Wheatsheaf Rd SG12 . . . .95 D1
Wheelers Cl EN5 . . . . . . .135 F1
Wheelers La HP3 . . . . . . .124 E1
Wheelers Yd HP23 . . . . . .79 B4
Wheelright Cl WD23 . . . .168 B3
Wheelwrights SG4 . . . . . .66 C1
Wheelwrights Cl CM23 . .76 C4
WHELPLEY HILL 136 D5
Whelpley Hill Pk HP5 . .136 D5
WHEMPSTEAD 71 B7
Whempstead La SG12 . . .71 B6
Whempstead Rd SG12 . . .71 B7
Whernside Dr SG1 . . . . . .37 B4
Whetstone Cl AL6 . . . . . . .89 E8
Whetstone Cl AL6 . . . . . . .89 E8
Whinbush Gr **8** SG5 . . . .34 F8
Whinbush Rd SG5 . . . . . . .34 F8
WHIPPENDELL BOTTOM 138 C1
Whippendell Hill
WD4 . . . . .138 C1
Whippendell Rd
WD18 . . . . .166 F4
Whipperley Ct LU1 . . . . . .63 C5
Whipperley Inf Sch
LU1 . . . . .63 A6
Whipperley Ring LU1 . . . .63 A6
Whipperley Way LU1 . . . .63 A6
WHIPSNADE 82 A8
Whipsnade Wild Animal
Pk* LU6 . . . . .81 E7
Whisper Mews LU4 . . . . .44 D4
Whisper Wood WD3 . . . . .164 D4
Whisperwood Cl HA3 . . .176 E3
Whitby Rd LU3 . . . . .45 C1
Whitebarns SG9 . . . . .43 A5
Whitebarns La SG9 . . . . . .43 A6
Whitebeam Cl
4 Hammond Street
EN7 . . . . .147 E5
Shenley WD7 . . . . .156 F6
Whitebeams AL10 . . . . . .130 A2
White Beams AL2 . . . . . . .141 C3
White Bear CM24 . . . . . . .59 E8
Whitebroom Rd HP1 . . . .123 D4
Whitechurch Cl LU2 . . . . .46 D2
Whitechurch Gdns
SG6 . . . . .23 C3
White Craig Cl HA5 . . . . .176 A5
Whitecroft AL1 . . . . .142 B8
Whitecroft Rd LU2 . . . . . .64 A8
Whitecrofts SG5 . . . . .11 F6
Whitefield Ave LU3 . . . . . .44 C7
Whitefield Ho AL10 . . . . .130 C7
Whitefield Inf Sch LU3 . .44 E8
Whitefield Jun Sch
LU3 . . . . .44 E8
Whitefields Rd EN8 . . . . .148 C3
Whitefriars Ave HA3 . . . .176 F1
Whitefriars Dr HA3 . . . . .176 F1
Whitefriars Fst & Mid Sch
HA3 . . . . .176 E1
Whitefriars Trad Est
HA3 . . . . .176 D1
Whitegale Cl SG4 . . . . . . .35 A6
White Gate Gdns HA3 . . .176 F3
Whitegates SG7 . . . . .47 A6
Whitegates WD3 . . . . . . .166 A5
Whitehall Cl
Borehamwood WD6 . . . .170 A5
Lower Nazeing EN9 . . . . .135 E1
Whitehall Coll CM23 . . . .58 E1
Whitehall Cotts SG12 . . .116 D8
White Hall Farm SG14 . . .70 B8
Whitehall La
Bishop's Stortford
CM23 . . . . .58 E1
King's Walden SG4 . . . . .48 A4
Whitehands Cl EN11 . . . .134 F6
White Hart Cl SG4 . . . . . .40 E8
White Hart Dr HP2 . . . . . .125 A2
White Hart Rd HP2 . . . . . .125 A2
Whitehaven Cl EN7 . . . . . .147 E3
White Hedge Dr AL3 . . . .127 C5
Whitehicks SG6 . . . . .12 A1
Whitehill HP4 . . . . .122 D5
White Hill
Ashley Green HP3,
HP5. . . . . .136 C7
Flamstead AL3 . . . . .105 B8
Hemel Hempstead HP2 . .123 F2
Rickmansworth WD3 . . . .174 A4
Walkern SG2 . . . . .38 C2
Welwyn AL6 . . . . .89 A3
Whitehill Ave LU1 . . . . . . .63 D5
Whitehill Cl SG4 . . . . .35 A6
Whitehill Cotts AL6 . . . . . .89 A3
Whitehill Ct HP4 . . . . .122 D5

Whitehill Jun Sch SG4 . . .35 A5
Whitehill La LU7 . . . . .80 D3
Whitehill Rd SG4 . . . . .35 A6
Whitehorse La SG1 . . . . . .37 B3
White Horse La
Burnham Green AL6 . . . . .90 C7
London Colney AL2 . . . . .142 E5
Whitehorse St SG7 . . . . . .23 F8
Whitehorse Vale LU3 . . . .31 A1
White Ho The **6** EN8 . .148 D3
Whitehouse Ave WD6 . . .170 B5
White House Cl SG14 . . . .70 E3
White House Ct SG8 . . . . .17 D4
White House Ind Est
SG8 . . . . .159 A4
Whitehouse La WD5 . . . .140 C4
White House The SG6 . . .23 B5
Whitehurst Ave SG5 . . . . .21 F1
White La SG4 . . . . .49 C7
Whitelands Ave WD3 . . . .164 C5
Whiteleaf Rd HP3 . . . . . . .138 C8
White Lilac Cl SG12 . . . . .71 E7
Whiteley SG9 . . . . .27 C8
White Lion Ho **5**
AL10 . . . . .130 A6
White Lion St HP3 . . . . . .138 D7
White Orchards N20 . . . .171 F1
Whitepost Ct CM23 . . . . .77 A5
White Post Field CM21 . .97 D2
White Shack La WD3 . . . .152 F2
Whitesmead Rd SG1 . . . .50 E7
Whitestone Wlk HP1 . . . .124 A6
White Stubbs Farm
EN10 . . . . .134 A2
White Stubbs La EN10,
SG13 . . . . .133 C2
Whitethorn AL7 . . . . .111 B5
Whitethorn La SG6 . . . . . .23 A4
Whitethorn Way LU1 . . . .63 A6
Whitewaits CM20 . . . . . . .117 E1
Whiteway SG6 . . . . .23 C4
Whitewaybottom La LU2,
SG4 . . . . .66 A3
White Way The SG12 . . . .51 C7
Whitewebbs La EN2 . . . . .161 F4
Whitewebbs Mus of
Transport* EN2 . . . . . . .161 D4
Whitewebbs Pk*
EN2 . . . . .161 D4
Whitewebbs Rd EN2 . . . .161 C4
Whitewood Rd HP4 . . . . .122 A4
Whitfield Way WD3 . . . . .164 F1
Whit Hern Ct EN8 . . . . . .148 C1
Whitings Cl AL5 . . . . .86 C4
Whitings Hill Prim Sch
EN5 . . . . .171 C4
Whitings Rd EN5 . . . . . . .171 C4
Whitlars Dr WD4 . . . . . . .138 F3
Whitley Cl WD5 . . . . .154 A7
Whitley Ct EN11 . . . . .135 B8
Whitley Gn LU2 . . . . .46 D2
Whitley Rd EN11 . . . . . . .135 B8
Whitmores Wood
HP2 . . . . .125 B4
Whitney Dr SG1 . . . . .36 C1
Whittingham Cl LU2 . . . . .46 F1
Whittingstall Rd
EN11 . . . . .135 C8
Whittington La SG4 . . . . .50 E4
Whittington Way CM23 . .76 F3
Whittle Cl
Lower Stondon SG16 . . . .10 B4
Watford WD25 . . . . .153 F5
Whittlesea Cl HA3 . . . . . .176 C3
Whittlesea Path HA3 . . . .176 C2
Whittlesea Rd HA3 . . . . .176 C2
Whittle Way SG1 . . . . .50 D2
WHITWELL 66 E6
Whitwell Cl LU3 . . . . .45 B8
Whitwell Rd WD25 . . . . .154 D4
Whitworth Cres EN3 . . . .163 A2
Whitworth Jones Ave
SG16 . . . . .10 C5
Whitworth Rd SG1 . . . . . .37 B3
Whomerley Rd SG1 . . . . .50 E4
Whybrow Gdns HP4 . . . .122 C6
Whydale Rd SG8 . . . . .7 E5
Whytingham Rd HP23 . . .79 C1
Wick Ave AL4 . . . . .108 D8
Wicken Fields SG12 . . . . .93 C3
Wickets End WD7 . . . . . . .156 E6
Wickets The LU2 . . . . .45 E1
Wickfield SG4 . . . . .69 A2
Wickfield Cl SG3 . . . . .69 A2
Wickham Cl LU89 . . . . . . .173 D2
Wickham Rd HA3 . . . . . . .176 D1
Wickhams Wharf SG12 . .93 E1
Wickham Way SG11 . . . . .55 E3
Wick Hill LU6 . . . . .82 F8
Wicklands Rd SG12 . . . . .116 D8
Wickmere Cl SG3 . . . . . . .69 A2
Wickmere Cl LU2 . . . . . . .45 C7
Wick Rd HP23 . . . . .120 D8
Wickstead Ave LU4 . . . . .44 E4
Wick The
Hertford SG14 . . . . .92 C1
Kimpton SG4 . . . . .68 D1
Wickwood Ct AL1 . . . . . .128 B5
Widbury Gdns SG12 . . . . .93 F1
Widbury Hill SG12 . . . . . .93 F1
Widbury Ho SG12 . . . . . .94 A1
WIDFORD 95 E4
Widford Rd
Hunsdon SG12 . . . . .95 D2
Much Hadham SG10 . . . . .95 F7
Welwyn Garden City
AL7 . . . . .111 B6
Widford Sch SG12 . . . . . .95 D4
Widford Terr HP2 . . . . . . .105 A1

Widgeon Way WD25 . . . .154 E2
Widmer Dr HP2 . . . . .125 A5
Wieland Rd HA6 . . . . .175 A3
Wiggenhall Rd WD18 . . .167 C4
WIGGINGTON 100 D1
WIGGINTON BOTTOM
. . . . .120 D8
Wigginton Bottom
HP23 . . . . .120 D8
Wiggles La HP23 . . . . .99 F7
Wight Ho WD18 . . . . .166 F4
WIGMORE 46 E2
Wigmore Park Sh Ctr
LU2 . . . . .46 D2
Wigmore Pl LU2 . . . . .46 E1
Wigmore Prim Sch
LU2 . . . . .46 E2
Wigmores N AL8 . . . . . . .110 D7
Wigmores S AL8 . . . . .110 D6
Wigram Way SG2 . . . . . . .51 B3
Wilbraham's Almshouses
EN5 . . . . .171 F7
Wilbury Cl SG6 . . . . .22 C7
Wilbury Hills Rd SG6 . . . .22 C7
Wilbury Jun Sch SG6 . . . .22 D6
Wilbury Lo **8** EN5 . . . .171 D5
Wilbury Rd SG6 . . . . .22 E8
Wilbury Way AL3 . . . . . . .22 A3
Wilcon Way WD5 . . . . . . .154 D5
Wilcot Ave WD19 . . . . . . .167 E2
Wilcot Cl WD19 . . . . .167 E2
Wilcox Cl WD6 . . . . .170 C8
Wilcox Ct **8** SG1 . . . . . .50 E6
Wildacres HA6 . . . . .174 F7
Wild Cherry Dr LU1 . . . . .63 D5
Wilde Ct AL2 . . . . .142 B4
Wilderness The
3 Berkhamsted HP4 . .122 C4
Hertford SG14 . . . . .92 A1
Stapleford SG14 . . . . .91 F1
WILDHILL 131 D2
Wildhill Rd AL9 . . . . .131 B2
Wilding Ct **8** WD6. . . . .170 A5
Wildman Ct SG13 . . . . . . .114 A7
Wild Marsh Ct EN8 . . . . .162 E2
Wildoaks Cl HA6 . . . . . . .174 F4
Wildwood HA6 . . . . .174 D4
Wildwood Ave AL2 . . . . . .140 F1
Wildwood Cl WD3 . . . . . .166 F5
Wildwood La SG1 . . . . . . .50 E3
Wilford Cl HA6 . . . . .174 D3
Wilga Rd AL6 . . . . .89 B5
Wilkins Gr AL8 . . . . .110 D5
Wilkin's Green La
AL4 . . . . .129 C4
Wilkinsgreen Terr
AL4 . . . . .129 B3
Wilkinson Cl EN7 . . . . . . .147 C6
Willenhall Cl LU3 . . . . . . .45 A7
Willetts Mews EN11 . . . .135 A7
William Austin Inf Sch
LU3 . . . . .45 C4
William Austin Jun Sch
LU3 . . . . .45 C4
William Covell Cl EN2 . .160 F1
William Crook Ho
LU3 . . . . .123 F3
William Fiske Ho **13**
HP4 . . . . .122 C4
William Gray Ct AL10 . . .129 F4
William Pl SG2 . . . . .51 A3
William Ransom Prim Sch
SG4 . . . . .35 B7
William Ransom Way
SG4 . . . . .34 F7
Williams Ct LU7 . . . . .80 C2
Williamson St **1** LU1 . .63 E7
Williamson Way WD3 . . .165 A1
William St
18 Berkhamsted HP4 .122 D4
Luton LU1 . . . . .45 E1
Markyate AL3 . . . . .83 E5
William Sutton Ct LU2 . .46 B5
Williams Way WD7 . . . . .156 C4
WILLIAN 23 B2
Willian Church Rd SG6. . .23 A2
Willian Rd
Baldock SG7 . . . . .23 E6
Great Wymondley SG4,
SG6. . . . . .35 F7
Hitchin SG4, SG6 . . . . . . .22 E1
Willian Way
Baldock SG7 . . . . .23 E6
Letchworth Garden City
SG6 . . . . .23 A3
Willinghall Cl EN9 . . . . . .163 D7
Williton Rd LU2 . . . . .46 C2
Willoughby Cl EN10 . . . .134 E2
Willoughby Ct AL2 . . . . . .142 D5
Willoughby Rd AL5 . . . . .86 B4
Willoughby Way SG4 . . . .35 A6
Willoway LU1 EN5 . . . . . .171 D3
Willow Cl
Bishop's Stortford
CM23 . . . . .76 E8
Great Hormead SG9 . . . . .42 A8
Hammond Street EN7 . . .147 E5
Reed SG8 . . . . .16 D5
Willow Cnr SG13 . . . . . . .132 F5
Willow Cres AL1 . . . . .128 C3
Willow Ct
Harrow HA2 . . . . .176 C1
Harrow HA3 . . . . .176 F2
3 Hemel Hempstead
HP3 . . . . .138 E7

Willow Ct continued
Letchworth Garden City
SG6 . . . . .23 B2
Luton LU3 . . . . .44 E5
Willowdene EN8 . . . . .148 E4
Willow Dene
Bushey WD23 . . . . .168 E2
Pinner HA5 . . . . .175 D1
Willow Dr EN5 . . . . .171 E5
Willow Edge WD4 . . . . . .139 A2
Willow End HA6 . . . . .175 A4
Willowfield Lower Sch
LU1 . . . . .62 F4
Willowgate Trad Est
LU3 . . . . .44 B8
Willow Gn WD6 . . . . .170 D4
Willow Gr AL2 . . . . .89 D3
Willow La
Hitchin SG5 . . . . .34 D6
St Ippolyts SG4 . . . . .35 B2
Watford WD18 . . . . .167 A4
Willowmead SG14 . . . . . .113 B5
Willow Mead CM21 . . . . .97 E2
Willow Path EN9 . . . . . . .163 E5
Willows Cl HA5 . . . . .175 C1
Willowside AL2 . . . . .142 E4
Willowside Way SG8 . . . .7 C8
Willows Link AL10 . . . . . .129 F4
Willows La HP1 . . . . .103 F1
Willows Link SG2 . . . . . . .51 A1
Willows The
Buntingford SG9 . . . . . . .40 D8
Hemel Hempstead HP2 . .125 B5
Hitchin SG4 . . . . .35 A5
Rickmansworth WD3 . . .173 A8
St Albans AL1 . . . . .142 B7
Stevenage SG2 . . . . .51 A1
Watford WD19 . . . . .167 B2
Willowtree Lo
Moor Park HA6 . . . . .174 F5
1 Northwood HA6 . . . .174 F5
Willow Trees Cvn Site
SG16 . . . . .10 A4
Willow Tree Way SG5 . . . .21 F2
Willow Vale SG12 . . . . . . .114 E8
Willow Way
Chiswell Green AL2 . . . . .141 A4
Harpenden AL5 . . . . .86 C4
Hatfield AL10 . . . . .129 F2
Hemel Hempstead HP1 . .124 B5
Luton LU3 . . . . .44 E5
Potters Bar EN6 . . . . . . .159 B6
Radlett WD7 . . . . .155 E3
Willow Wlk AL4 . . . . .89 C8
Wilsden Ave LU1 . . . . . . .63 C6
Wilshere Ave AL1 . . . . . .127 C1
Wilshere Cres SG4 . . . . . .35 C8
Wilshere Ct **2** SG4 . . . .34 F6
Wilshere-Dacre Jun Sch
SG5 . . . . .34 E8
Wilshere Rd AL6 . . . . .89 A5
Wilsmere Dr HA3 . . . . . . .176 E3
Wilson Cl
Bishop's Stortford
CM23 . . . . .76 F5
Stevenage SG1 . . . . .36 D1
Wilsons La SG7 . . . . .4 C4
WILSTONE 79 D1
Wilstone Dr AL4 . . . . .128 C8
WILSTONE GREEN 99 D8
Wilstone Resr Nature
Reserve* HP23 . . . . .99 D7
Wilton Cl CM23 . . . . .77 B7
Wilton Cres LU3 . . . . .113 C4
Wilton Ct WD17 . . . . .167 C6
Wilton Rd SG5 . . . . .21 E1
Wilton Way SG13 . . . . . . .113 C4
Wiltshire Rd SG2 . . . . . . .51 A4
Wimborne Ct CM21 . . . . .97 D2
Wimborne Gr WD17 . . . .153 E2
Wimborne Rd AL3 . . . . . .63 C8
Wimple Rd LU2 . . . . .44 A2
Winch Cl SG4 . . . . .88 F8
Winchdells HP3 . . . . .139 A8
Winchester Cl
Bishop's Stortford
CM23 . . . . .76 D4
Stevenage SG1 . . . . .37 B2
Winchester Ct **4** EN5 . .171 F5
Winchester Ho AL3 . . . . .127 C2
Winchester Rd HA6 . . . . .174 F1
Winchester Way WD3 . . .166 B4
Winchfield LU1 . . . . .62 E4
Winchfield Way WD3 . . .165 C2
Winch St LU2 . . . . .45 F1
Windermere Ave AL1 . . .128 B1
Windermere Cl
Chorleywood WD3 . . . . . .164 D4
Hemel Hempstead HP3 . .125 C2
Stevenage SG1 . . . . .37 D2
Windermere Cres LU3 . . .44 F5
Windermere Ct **5**
WD17 . . . . .167 A7
Windermere Prim Sch
AL1 . . . . .128 B1
Windhill
Bishop's Stortford
CM23 . . . . .76 E7
Welwyn Garden City
AL7 . . . . .111 A7
Windhill Old Rd CM23 . .76 E7
Windhill Prim Sch
CM23 . . . . .76 E6
Winding Hill SG10 . . . . . .75 A4
Winding Shot HP1 . . . . . .124 A4
Winding Shott SG14 . . . . .91 C4
Windmill Ave AL4 . . . . . .128 C7

Windmill Cl
Barkway SG8 . . . . .17 C5
Ivinghoe LU7 . . . . .80 F5
Stansted Mountfitchet
CM24 . . . . .59 D6
Waltham Abbey EN9 . . . .163 E5
Windmill Cotts SG12 . . . .93 D6
Windmill Dr WD3 . . . . . . .165 F3
Windmill Field SG12 . . . .93 D6
Windmill Fields CM17 . . .118 F4
Windmill Hill
Buntingford SG9 . . . . . . .40 F6
Chipperfield WD4 . . . . . .151 F7
Hitchin SG4 . . . . .34 F7
Windmill La
Barnet EN5 . . . . .170 F3
Bushey WD23 . . . . .168 E1
Cheshunt EN8 . . . . .148 E1
Windmill Rd
Breachwood Green
SG4 . . . . .47 D2
Hemel Hempstead HP2 . .124 F2
Luton LU1 . . . . .63 F6
Markyate AL3, LU1 . . . . .84 B6
Windmills SG2 . . . . .71 E8
Windmill St WD23 . . . . . .168 E1
Windmill Trad Est LU1 . . .63 F7
Windmill Way
Much Hadham SG10 . . . .74 E1
Tring HP23 . . . . .99 F4
Windmore Ave EN6 . . . . .158 C8
Windmore Hall EN6 . . . . .158 C8
Windridge Cl AL3. . . . . . .127 A1
Windrush Cl SG1 . . . . .37 A3
Winds End Cl HP2 . . . . . .125 A5
Windsor Cl
Borehamwood WD6 . . . .170 A8
Bovingdon HP3 . . . . .137 A3
Cheshunt EN7 . . . . .148 A1
Hemel Hempstead HP3 . .124 D2
Northwood HA6 . . . . . . .175 A1
Stevenage SG2 . . . . .69 B7
Welwyn AL6 . . . . .89 B3
Windsor Ct
Borehamwood WD6 . . . .170 C7
Bushey WD23 . . . . .168 C2
Kings Langley WD4 . . . . .139 B2
8 Luton LU1 . . . . .63 D6
13 St Albans AL1 . . . . .128 A2
Windsor Dr SG14 . . . . . . .112 F7
Windsor Ind Est SG13 . . .114 B8
Windsor Gdns CM23 . . . .76 C7
Windsor Rd
Barnet EN5 . . . . .171 E3
Enfield EN3 . . . . .162 D3
Harrow HA3 . . . . .176 D2
Pitstone LU7 . . . . .80 D3
Royston SG8 . . . . .7 F6
Watford WD24 . . . . .154 C1
Welwyn AL6 . . . . .89 B3
Windsor St LU1 . . . . .63 D6
Windsor Wlk **8** LU1 . . .63 D6
Windsor Wood EN10 . . . .163 E6
Windward Cl EN3 . . . . . . .162 D4
Windy Rise SG12 . . . . .71 F7
Winfield Mobile Home Pk
WD25 . . . . .168 B8
Winford Dr EN10 . . . . . . .134 F1
Wingate Ct LU4 . . . . .44 F2
Wingate Gdns AL6 . . . . . .89 B5
Wingate Ho **8** AL1 . . . .128 A2
Wingate Rd LU4 . . . . .44 F2
Wingate Way LU4 . . . . . . .128 A2
WINGRAVE 60 C3
Wingrave CE Comb Sch
HP22 . . . . .60 A3
Wingrave Rd
Tring HP23 . . . . .100 B6
Wilstone HP23 . . . . .79 D1
Winifred Cl EN5 . . . . .170 F3
Winifred Rd HP3 . . . . . . .138 D7
Winkfield Cl LU4 . . . . .44 B1
Winnington Rd EN3 . . . . .162 C2
Winnipeg Way EN10 . . . .148 E6
Winsdon Ct **1** LU1 . . . .63 D6
WINSDON HILL 63 B7
Winsdon Rd LU1 . . . . .63 D6
Winslow Cl LU3 . . . . .45 C4
Winslow Rd HP22 . . . . . . .60 B3
Winston Churchill Way
EN8 . . . . .162 D6
Winston Cl
Harrow HA3 . . . . .176 F4
Hitchin SG5 . . . . .34 D7
Winston Ct HA3 . . . . .176 E3
Winston Way LU4 . . . . . . .129 A4
Winstre Rd WD6 . . . . . . .170 A8
Winterscroft Rd EN11 . . .134 F7
Winters La SG2 . . . . .38 C1
Winthorpe Gdns **7**
WD6. . . . . .169 F8
Winton App WD3 . . . . . . .166 C4
Winton Cl
Letchworth Garden City
SG6 . . . . .23 D8
Luton LU2 . . . . .45 D6
Winton Cres WD3 . . . . . . .166 B4
Winton Dr
Cheshunt EN8 . . . . .148 E2
Croxley Green WD3 . . . .166 C4
Winton Rd SG12 . . . . .93 F1
Winton Terr **5** AL1 . . . .127 E2
Wisden Rd SG1 . . . . .36 F1
Wisdom Dr SG13 . . . . . . .113 E6
Wiseman Cl LU2 . . . . .45 E7
Wisemans Gdns CM21 . .97 C1

Wistaria Dr AL2 . . . . .142 B5
Wistlea Cres AL4 . . . . .129 B1
Wistow Rd LU3 . . . . .45 A6
Witchford LU4 . . . . .44 B4
Withy Cl LU4 . . . . .44 B4
Withy Pl AL2 . . . . .141 C3
Witney Cl HA5 . . . . .175 F4
Witter Ave SG5 . . . . .21 E4
Witton Ho WD3 . . . . .164 D4
Wiveton Cl LU2 . . . . .45 D7
Woburn Ave CM23 . . . . .76 C7
Woburn Cl
  Bushey WD23 . . . . .168 C3
  Stevenage SG2 . . . . .69 C7
Woburn Ct LU4 . . . . .44 D5
Wodecroft Rd LU3 . . . . .45 B6
Wodson Park Sports & L
  Ctr SG12 . . . . .93 D4
Wolfsbane Ct 4 LU4 . . . . . .44 C5
Wolsey Ave EN7 . . . . .147 F2
Wolsey Bsns Pk
  WD18 . . . . .166 D2
Wolsey Mews HA6 . . . . . . .174 C7
Wolsey Rd
  Hemel Hempstead
    HP2 . . . . .124 D2
  Moor Park HA6 . . . . .174 D7
Wolston Cl LU1 . . . . .63 C7
Wolverley Ho SG7 . . . . .4 A4
Wolves Mere SG3 . . . . .69 A2
Wonnacott Pl EN3 . . . . . . .162 D3
Woodacre Dr AL6 . . . . .90 A8
Woodbank WD3 . . . . .165 C3
Woodbine Gr EN2 . . . . .161 D1
Woodbridge Cl LU4 . . . . . . .44 E4
Woodbrook Gdns
  EN9 . . . . .163 E6
Woodbury Hill LU2 . . . . .45 E2
Wood Cl AL10 . . . . .130 B5
WOODCOCK HILL 173 D6
Woodcock Hill
  Rickmansworth WD3 . . . . .173 E4
  Sandridge AL4 . . . . .108 E1
Woodcock Hill Barns
  WD3 . . . . .173 E4
Woodcock Lo SG13 . . . . . .132 C2
Woodcock Rd
  Luton LU1 . . . . .63 A7
  Royston SG8 . . . . .7 E8
  Stevenage SG2 . . . . .51 D2
Wood Comm AL10 . . . . . . .130 B8
Woodcote Cl EN8 . . . . .148 C1
Woodcote Ho 1 SG4 . . . . . .34 F7
Wood Cres HP3 . . . . .124 E1
Woodcroft SG5 . . . . .34 E6
Woodcroft Ave SG12 . . . . .115 E4
Woodcutter Pl AL2 . . . . . . .141 C4
Wood Dr SG2 . . . . .51 B2
WOOD END 53 D7
Wood End AL2 . . . . .141 C3
Wood End Cl HP2 . . . . .125 C4
Wood End Hill AL5 . . . . .85 D4
Wood End La AL3 . . . . .104 E8
Wood End Rd AL5 . . . . .85 D3
Wood End SG5 AL5 . . . . . . .85 D3
Woodfall Ave EN5 . . . . .171 F4
Wood Farm Rd HP2 . . . . . .124 E2
Woodfield Ave HA6 . . . . . . .174 E6
Woodfield Cl CM24 . . . . .59 E6
Woodfield Dr HP3 . . . . .125 D1
Woodfield Gdns HP3 . . . . . .125 D1
Woodfield La AL9 . . . . .145 E8
Woodfield Rd
  Radlett WD7 . . . . .156 A3
  Stevenage SG1 . . . . .36 C1
  Welwyn Garden City
    AL7 . . . . .110 F6
Woodfield Rise
  WD23 . . . . .168 D2
Woodfields
  Stansted Mountfitchet
    CM24 . . . . .59 E6
  2 Watford WD18 . . . . . . .167 C5
Woodfield Sch HP3 . . . . . . .125 C1
Woodfield Terr
  Harefield UB9 . . . . .173 B1
  Stansted Mountfitchet
    CM24 . . . . .59 E6
Woodfield Way AL4 . . . . . . .128 C6
Woodford Cres HA5 . . . . . .175 B1
Woodforde Cl SG7 . . . . .4 E4
Woodford Rd WD17 . . . . . .167 C7
Woodgate WD25 . . . . .154 B6
Woodgate Ave SG6 . . . . . . .160 B7
Woodgate Cres HA6 . . . . . .175 A4
Woodgate Mews
  WD17 . . . . .167 C8
Woodgrange Ct EN11 . . . . .135 A5
Wood Green Cl LU2 . . . . . . .46 B5
Wood Green Rd LU2 . . . . . . .46 C5
Wood Green Way
  EN8 . . . . .162 E8
WOODHALL 110 E4
Woodhall Ave HA5 . . . . . . .175 E2
Woodhall Cl LU3 . . . . .113 C8
Woodhall Dr HA5 . . . . .175 E2
Woodhall Gate HA5 . . . . . .175 D2
Woodhall Gr CM23 . . . . .76 D6
Woodhall Ho AL7 . . . . .110 F4
Woodhall La
  Hemel Hempstead
    HP2 . . . . .124 E4
  Shenley WD7 . . . . .156 F4
  South Oxhey WD19 . . . . . .175 E6
  Welwyn Garden City
    AL7 . . . . .110 E4

Woodhall Prim Sch
  WD19 . . . . .175 E6
Woodham Way SG12 . . . . .115 C4
Woodhill Ho AL9 . . . . .145 D8
Woodhouse Eaves
  HA6 . . . . .175 A5
Wood House La EN10 . . . . .134 A2
Woodhurst SG6 . . . . .22 F8
Woodhurst Ave
  WD25 . . . . .154 D4
Wood La
  Birchanger CM23 . . . . .59 E2
  Hemel Hempstead HP2 . . . .124 D2
  Meesden SG9 . . . . .30 A6
Woodland Ave
  Hemel Hempstead
    HP1 . . . . .124 B2
  Luton LU3 . . . . .45 B2
Woodland Cl
  Hemel Hempstead
    HP1 . . . . .124 B2
  Tring HP23 . . . . .99 F2
Woodland Ct LU2 . . . . .64 A7
Woodland Ct 1 AL3 . . . . . .127 F7
Woodland Dr
  St Albans AL4 . . . . .128 C4
  Watford WD17 . . . . .166 F8
Woodland Hts HA6 . . . . . . .174 B3
Woodland La WD3 . . . . . . .164 D6
Woodland Mount
  SG13 . . . . .113 F6
Woodland Pl
  Chorleywood WD3 . . . . . . .164 F5
  Hemel Hempstead HP1 . . . .124 B2
Woodland Rd
  Hertford Heath SG13 . . . . .114 C3
  Maple Cross WD3 . . . . . . .172 D5
Woodland Rise
  Studham LU6 . . . . .82 B7
  Welwyn Garden City
    AL8 . . . . .110 C8
Woodlands
  Bishop's Stortford
    CM23 . . . . .77 C8
  Brookmans Park AL9 . . . . .145 B4
  Caddington LU1 . . . . .62 E3
  Chiswell Green AL2 . . . . . .141 C4
  Harpenden AL5 . . . . .85 E2
  Radlett WD7 . . . . .156 A5
  Royston SG8 . . . . .7 E8
Woodlands Ave HP4 . . . . . .122 D3
Woodlands Cl
  Borehamwood WD6 . . . . . .170 B5
  Hoddesdon EN11 . . . . .135 A5
Woodlands Dr
  Bedmond WD5 . . . . .139 C3
  Harrow HA7 . . . . .176 F4
  Hoddesdon EN11 . . . . .135 A4
Woodlands Meade
  SG4 . . . . .37 B8
Woodlands Prim Sch
  WD6 . . . . .170 A4
Woodlands Rd
  Enfield EN2 . . . . .161 D1
  Hertford SG13 . . . . .113 F6
  Kings Langley HP3 . . . . . . .139 A4
  Thundridge SG12 . . . . .93 D6
  Thundridge SG12 . . . . .93 E7
  Watford WD23 . . . . .167 A4
Woodlands Sec Sch
  LU3 . . . . .44 F7
Woodland Terr SG13 . . . . . .114 B3
Woodland Way
  Baldock SG7 . . . . .23 F6
  Bedmond WD5 . . . . .139 F4
  Goff's Oak EN7 . . . . .147 B3
  Stevenage SG2 . . . . .51 A1
  Welwyn AL6 . . . . .90 A7
Wood Lane End HP2 . . . . . .125 B4
Woodlea AL2 . . . . .141 A6
Woodlea Gr HA6 . . . . .174 C4
Woodley Rd SG12 . . . . .93 F2
Woodleys CM20 . . . . .118 A1
Woodman Rd 8 HP3 . . . . . .124 E1
Woodmans Ho 7
  WD17 . . . . .167 C5
Woodmere Ave WD24 . . . . .154 E1
Woodmere LU3 . . . . .31 A1
Woodmill Mews EN11 . . . . .135 B8
Woodpecker Cl
  Bishop's Stortford
    CM23 . . . . .76 C6
  Bushey WD23 . . . . .168 C1
  Harrow HA3 . . . . .176 F2
  Hatfield AL10 . . . . .129 F2
Woodridge Way HA6 . . . . . .174 E4
Woodridings Ave HA5 . . . . .175 F2
Woodridings Cl HA5 . . . . . .175 F3
Woods Ave AL10 . . . . .130 B4
Woodshots Mdw
  WD18 . . . . .166 D4
Woodside
  Bishop's Stortford
    CM23 . . . . .77 D8
  Borehamwood WD6 . . . . . .169 F5
  Cheshunt EN7 . . . . .162 A8
  Hertford Heath SG13 . . . . .114 C2
WOODSIDE
  Slip End 63 A2
  Watford 154 B7
Woodside WD24 . . . . .154 A3
WOODSIDE 131 A2
Woodside Farm &
  Wildfowl Pk* LU1 . . . . . . .84 A8
Woodside Gdns AL4 . . . . . . .34 F7
WOODSIDE GREEN 77 F1
Woodside Ho AL8 . . . . .110 C7
Woodside Ind Pk SG6 . . . . . .23 B7

Woodside La AL9 . . . . .131 A1
Woodside Rd EN9 . . . . .63 B3
Woodside Prim Sch
  EN7 . . . . .147 B2
Woodside Rd
  Abbots Langley WD25 . . . .154 B8
  Bricket Wood AL2 . . . . . . .140 F2
  Welwyn AL6 . . . . .89 F3
  Woodside LU1 . . . . .63 B3
Woods Pl HP23 . . . . .100 A3
Wood St
  Barnet EN5 . . . . .171 D5
  Luton LU1 . . . . .63 F6
Woods The
  Radlett WD7 . . . . .156 B5
  South Oxhey HA6 . . . . . . .175 A5
Woodstock SG3 . . . . .68 F3
Woodstock Cl SG13 . . . . . .114 B4
Woodstock Rd
  Bushey WD23 . . . . .168 F2
  Hoddesdon EN10 . . . . .134 E4
Woodstock Rd N AL1 . . . . .128 B3
Woodstock Rd S AL1 . . . . .128 B3
Woodvale EN8 . . . . .162 C4
Wood Vale AL10 . . . . .130 B5
Woodvale Pk AL1 . . . . .128 B3
Wood View
  Cuffley EN6 . . . . .146 E4
  Hemel Hempstead HP1 . . . .124 B5
Woodville Court Mews
  AL7 . . . . .167 A7
Woodville Ct WD7 . . . . .167 A7
Woodville Pl SG14 . . . . . . .113 B8
Woodward Gdns HA7 . . . . .176 F3
Woodwaye WD19 . . . . .167 C2
Woodwicks WD3 . . . . .172 D5
Woolenmice Inf Sch
  SG1 . . . . .50 B6
Woolenwick Jun Sch
  SG1 . . . . .50 B6
Woolgrove Ct SG4 . . . . .22 B1
Woolgrove Rd SG4 . . . . .22 B1
Woolgrove Sch SG4 . . . . . . .23 D5
Woollam Cres AL3 . . . . .127 C7
Woollams AL3 . . . . .106 A4
Woollard St EN9 . . . . .163 C5
Woolmans CI EN10 . . . . . . .134 F1
Woolmer Cl WD6 . . . . .157 A1
Woolmerdine Ct
  WD23 . . . . .167 D6
Woolmer Dr HP2 . . . . .125 C3
WOOLMER GREEN 69 B2
Woolmers La SG14 . . . . . . .112 B2
Woolmer's Park Mews
  SG14 . . . . .112 B1
Woolners Way SG1 . . . . .50 C6
Woolpack Ho 1 EN3 . . . . . .162 D2
Woolston Ave SG6 . . . . .23 A4
Woolwich Ct 10 EN3 . . . . . .163 A1
Wootton Cl LU3 . . . . .45 B7
Wootton Dr HP2 . . . . .124 F8
Worboys Ct SG8 . . . . .1 F5
Worcester 12 AL1 . . . . . . .128 A2
Worcester Ho 12
  WD6 . . . . .170 A7
Worcester Rd AL10 . . . . . . .129 F6
Worcesters Ave LU4 . . . . . .162 A1
Worcesters Prim Sch
  EN1 . . . . .161 F1
Wordsworth Cl SG8 . . . . .2 D1
Wordsworth Ct AL10 . . . . .130 A6
Wordsworth Gdns
  WD6 . . . . .170 A4
Wordsworth Rd
  Harpenden AL5 . . . . .86 A3
  Luton LU4 . . . . .44 A2
Works Rd SG6 . . . . .23 C7
Worley Rd AL3 . . . . .127 D4
WORMLEY 148 E8
Wormleybury EN10 . . . . . . .148 D8
Wormley Ct EN10 . . . . .148 F7
Wormley Lodge Cl
  EN10 . . . . .148 F8
Wormley Prim Sch
  EN10 . . . . .148 E8
WORMLEY WEST END 147 F8
Wornham Ave SG1 . . . . .50 E6
Worsdell Way SG4 . . . . .35 B7
Worsted La SG9 . . . . .41 E7
Wortham Rd SG8 . . . . .7 C7
Wortham Way SG12 . . . . . . .51 B3
Wraglings The CM23 . . . . . . .77 B5
Wratten Cl SG5 . . . . .34 E6
Wratten Rd E SG5 . . . . .34 E6
Wratten Rd W SG5 . . . . .34 E6
Wrayfields SG5 . . . . .12 B8
Wraysbury Cl LU4 . . . . .44 D3
Wrenbrook Rd CM23 . . . . . . .76 F5
Wren Cl
  Kimpton SG4 . . . . .66 B1
  Luton LU2 . . . . .46 C6
  Stevenage SG2 . . . . .51 B6
Wren Cres WD23 . . . . .168 C1
Wrensfield HP1 . . . . .124 B3
Wren Wood AL7 . . . . .111 B7
Wrestlers Cl AL10 . . . . .130 C7
Wrexham Terr SG8 . . . . .7 D7
Wright Cl AL4 . . . . .108 E7
Wright's Bldgs WD17 . . . . .167 B7
WRIGHT'S GREEN 98 D7
Wright's Green La
  CM22 . . . . .98 D7
Wrights Mdw SG2 . . . . .52 B8
Wrights Orch SG2 . . . . .51 E2
Wrotham Bsns Pk
  EN5 . . . . .158 F2

Wrotham Pk* EN5 . . . . .158 F3
Wrotham Rd EN5 . . . . .171 E7
Wroxham Ave EN5 . . . . .171 F6 (check)
Wroxham Gdns
  Crews Hill EN2 . . . . .161 B4
  Potters Bar EN6 . . . . .158 D8
Wroxham Sch The
  EN6 . . . . .158 D8
Wroxham Way AL5 . . . . .86 C3
Wulfrath Way SG12 . . . . .93 C3
Wulstan Pk EN6 . . . . .159 D7
Wulwards Cl LU1 . . . . .63 B6
Wulwards Ct LU1 . . . . .63 B6
Wyatt Cl
  Bushey WD23 . . . . .168 E2
  Ickleford SG5 . . . . .21 D4
Wyatt's Cl WD3 . . . . .165 A6
Wyatt's Rd WD3 . . . . .165 A6
Wyburn Ave EN5 . . . . .171 F6
Wychdell SG2 . . . . .69 C8
Wych Elm CM20 . . . . .117 C1
Wych Elm La AL6, SG3 . . . . .68 F2
Wych Elms AL2 . . . . .141 B3
Wychford Dr CM21 . . . . .97 C1
Wychwood Ave LU2 . . . . . . .45 F3
Wychwood Way HA6 . . . . . .174 F3
Wycklond Cl SG5 . . . . .11 E6
Wycliffe Cl
  7 Cheshunt EN8 . . . . . . .148 D2
  Luton LU3 . . . . .45 C6
Wycliffe Ct WD5 . . . . .153 E7
Wycombe Pl AL4 . . . . .128 B6
Wycombe Way
  Luton LU3 . . . . .45 C6
  St Albans AL4 . . . . .128 B6
WYDDIAL 28 A3
Wyddial Gn AL7 . . . . .111 B6
Wyddial Rd SG9 . . . . .40 E8
Wyedale AL2 . . . . .142 F4
Wye The HP2 . . . . .125 A8
Wykeham Rise N20 . . . . . . .171 E1
Wyken Cl LU3 . . . . .45 A7
Wyldwood Cl CM17 . . . . . . .118 C6
Wyllyotts Cl EN6 . . . . .158 F7
Wyllyotts La EN6 . . . . .158 F7
Wyllyotts Pl EN6 . . . . .158 F7
Wylo Dr EN5 . . . . .171 A3
Wymondley Cl SG4 . . . . .35 A7
Wymondley Rd SG4 . . . . . . .35 B3
Wymondley Jun Mix Inf
  Sch SG4 . . . . .35 E4
Wymondley Rd
  Hitchin SG4 . . . . .35 B6
  Letchworth Garden City
    SG6 . . . . .23 A1
Wynches Farm Dr
  AL4 . . . . .128 D3
Wynchgate HA3 . . . . .176 E3
Wynchlands Cres
  AL4 . . . . .128 D3
Wyndham Rd LU4 . . . . .44 C2
Wyndhams End AL7 . . . . . .110 F2
Wynd The SG6 . . . . .22 F6
Wynlie Gdns HA5 . . . . .175 B1
Wynn Cl SG7 . . . . .13 A1
Wyrley Dell SG6 . . . . .23 A3
Wysells Ct SG6 . . . . .22 D7
Wyton AL7 . . . . .111 D6
Wyvern Cl LU4 . . . . .44 E3

Y

Yardley SG6 . . . . .23 C4
Yardley Ave LU7 . . . . .80 D4
Yardley Ct 14 AL5 . . . . .86 B1
Yarmouth Rd
  Stevenage SG1 . . . . .50 A7
  Watford WD24 . . . . .154 C1
Yarra Ho 6 AL1 . . . . .127 E3
Yately Cl LU2 . . . . .45 D7
Yavneh Coll WD6 . . . . .170 C5
Yearling Cl SG12 . . . . .114 F7
Yeatman Ho WD24 . . . . . . .154 B3
Yeats Cl SG8 . . . . .2 D1
Ye Cnr WD19 . . . . .167 E3
Yeomanry Dr SG7 . . . . .13 A1
Yeomans Ave AL5 . . . . .85 D3
Yeomans Ct CM23 . . . . .76 D6
Yeomans Ct HP2 . . . . .105 A1
Yeomans Dr SG2 . . . . .51 E2
Yeomans Keep WD3 . . . . . .164 F6
Yeomans Ride HP2 . . . . . . .105 A1
Yeovil Ct LU2 . . . . .46 B2
Yeovil Rd LU2 . . . . .46 B2
Yew Cl EN7 . . . . .147 E4
Yew Gr AL7 . . . . .111 C5
Yewlands
  Hoddesdon EN11 . . . . .135 A5
  Sawbridgeworth CM21 . . . . .97 E1
Yewlands Dr EN11 . . . . .135 A5
Yews Ave EN1 . . . . .162 B3
Yewstone Ct WD18 . . . . . . .167 A6
Yewtree Cl LU7 . . . . .80 E5
Yew Tree Cl HP5 . . . . .136 A3
Yew Tree Ct
  Elstree WD6 . . . . .169 D3
  Hemel Hempstead HP1 . . . .124 A1
Yew Tree Dr HP3 . . . . .137 B3
Yewtree End AL2 . . . . .141 B4
Yew Tree Pl CM23 . . . . .76 F8
Yew Wlk EN11 . . . . .135 A5
York Cl WD4 . . . . .139 A2
York Cres WD6 . . . . .170 D7
Yorke Gate WD17 . . . . .167 A4
Yorke Mead Prim Sch
  WD3 . . . . .166 A4
Yorke Rd WD3 . . . . .166 A3

Yorkes Mews 16 SG12 . . . .93 D1
York Ho
  15 Borehamwood
    WD6 . . . . .170 A7
  Hatfield AL9 . . . . .130 C7
  St Albans AL3 . . . . .127 C2
York House Sch WD3 . . . . .165 F7
York Rd
  Cheshunt EN8 . . . . .162 E6
  Hitchin SG5 . . . . .34 E8
  Northwood HA6 . . . . .175 A1
  St Albans AL1 . . . . .127 F4
  Stevenage SG1 . . . . .36 F1
  Watford WD18 . . . . .167 C4
York St LU2 . . . . .63 F8
York Terr EN2 . . . . .161 C1
York Way
  Hemel Hempstead
    HP2 . . . . .124 E2
  Watford WD25 . . . . .154 E3
  Welwyn AL6 . . . . .89 C3
Youngfield Rd HP1 . . . . . . .123 F4
Youngsbury La SG12 . . . . . . .93 E8
Youngs Mews SG14 . . . . . .113 C6
Youngs Rise AL8 . . . . .110 C6
Yukon Rd EN10 . . . . .148 E6
Yule Cl AL2 . . . . .140 F1

Z

Zambesi Rd CM23 . . . . .76 F5

Addresses

Name and Address	Telephone	Page	Grid reference

NG NH NJ NK

NM NN NO NP

NR NS NT NU

NX NY NZ

SC SD SE TA

SH SJ SK TF TG

SM SN SO SP TL TM

SR SS ST SU TQ TR

SW SX SY SZ TV

Any feature in this atlas can be given a unique reference to help you find the same feature on other Ordnance Survey maps of the area, or to help someone else locate you if they do not have a Street Atlas.

The grid squares in this atlas match the Ordnance Survey National Grid and are at 500 metre intervals. The small figures at the bottom and sides of every other grid line are the National Grid kilometre values (**00** to **99** km) and are repeated across the country every 100 km (see left).

To give a unique National Grid reference you need to locate where in the country you are. The country is divided into 100 km squares with each square given a unique two-letter reference. Use the administrative map to determine in which 100 km square a particular page of this atlas falls.

The bold letters and numbers between each grid line (**A** to **F**, **1** to **8**) are for use within a specific Street Atlas only, and when used with the page number, are a convenient way of referencing these grid squares.

Example *The railway bridge over DARLEY GREEN RD in grid square B1*

Step 1: Identify the two-letter reference, in this example the page is in **SP**

Step 2: Identify the 1 km square in which the railway bridge falls. Use the figures in the southwest corner of this square: Eastings **17**, Northings **74**. This gives a unique reference: **SP 17 74**, accurate to 1 km.

Step 3: To give a more precise reference accurate to 100 m you need to estimate how many tenths along and how many tenths up this 1 km square the feature is (to help with this the 1 km square is divided into four 500 m squares). This makes the bridge about **8** tenths along and about **1** tenth up from the southwest corner.

This gives a unique reference: **SP 178 741**, accurate to 100 m.

Eastings (read from left to right along the bottom) come before Northings (read from bottom to top). If you have trouble remembering say to yourself "Along the hall, THEN up the stairs"!

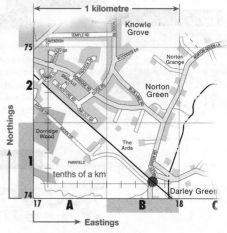

PHILIP'S MAPS
the Gold Standard for drivers

◆ **Philip's street atlases cover all of England, Wales, Northern Ireland and much of Scotland**

◆ Every named street is shown, including alleys, lanes and walkways

◆ Thousands of additional features marked: stations, public buildings, car parks, places of interest

◆ Route-planning maps to get you close to your destination

◆ Postcodes on the maps and in the index

◆ Widely used by the emergency services, transport companies and local authorities

For national mapping, choose **Philip's Navigator Britain** the most detailed road atlas available of England, Wales and Scotland. Hailed by Auto Express as 'the ultimate road atlas', Navigator shows every road and lane in Britain.

Street atlases currently available

England
Bedfordshire and Luton
Berkshire
Birmingham and West Midlands
Bristol and Bath
Buckinghamshire and Milton Keynes
Cambridgeshire and Peterborough
Cheshire
Cornwall
Cumbria
Derbyshire
Devon
Dorset
County Durham and Teesside
Essex
North Essex
South Essex
Gloucestershire and Bristol
Hampshire
North Hampshire
South Hampshire
Herefordshire Monmouthshire
Hertfordshire
Isle of Wight
Kent
East Kent
West Kent
Lancashire
Leicestershire and Rutland
Lincolnshire
Liverpool and Merseyside
London
Greater Manchester
Norfolk
Northamptonshire
Northumberland
Nottinghamshire
Oxfordshire
Shropshire
Somerset
Staffordshire
Suffolk

Surrey
East Sussex
West Sussex
Tyne and Wear
Warwickshire and Coventry
Wiltshire and Swindon
Worcestershire
East Yorkshire Northern Lincolnshire
North Yorkshire
South Yorkshire
West Yorkshire

Wales
Anglesey, Conwy and Gwynedd
Cardiff, Swansea and The Valleys
Carmarthenshire, Pembrokeshire and Swansea
Ceredigion and South Gwynedd
Denbighshire, Flintshire, Wrexham
Herefordshire Monmouthshire
Powys

Scotland
Aberdeenshire
Ayrshire
Dumfries and Galloway
Edinburgh and East Central Scotland
Fife and Tayside
Glasgow and West Central Scotland
Inverness and Moray
Lanarkshire
Scottish Borders

Northern Ireland
County Antrim and County Londonderry
County Armagh and County Down
Belfast
County Tyrone and County Fermanagh

Philip's maps and atlases are available from bookshops, motorway services and petrol stations.

For further details visit
www.philips-maps.co.uk